HISTORICAL ATLAS
OF LOUISIANA

by Charles Robert Goins
and John Michael Caldwell

University of Oklahoma Press : Norman and London

ST. JOHN THE BAPTIST PARISH LIBRARY
1334 WEST AIRLINE HIGHWAY
LaPLACE, LOUISIANA 70068

Also by Charles Robert Goins

Oklahoma Homes: Past and Present (with John Morris)
(Norman, 1980)

Historical Atlas of Oklahoma (with John Morris and
Edwin C. McReynolds) (Norman, 1965, 1976, 1986)

Library of Congress Cataloging-in-Publication Data

Goins, Charles Robert.
Historical atlas of Louisiana / by Charles Robert Goins
and John Michael Caldwell.
p.   cm.
Includes bibliographical references and index.
ISBN 0-8061-2589-6
1. Louisiana—Historical geography—Maps.
2. Louisiana—History.
I. Caldwell, John Michael, 1950-   . II. Title.
G1361.S1G6   1994   <G&M>
911'.763—dc20
ISBN: 0-8061-2589-6 (cloth)
ISBN: 0-8061-2682-5 (paperback)
94-6206
CIP
MAP

Made Possible Through a Grant from Louisiana Endowment
for the Humanities, State Affiliate of the National Endowment
for the Humanities.

Published with the assistance of the National Endowment for
the Humanities, a federal agency which supports the study of
such fields as history, philosophy, literature, and language.

The paper in this book meets the guidelines for perma-
nence and durability of the Committee on Production
Guidelines for Book Longevity of the Council on
Library Resources, Inc. ∞

Copyright © 1995 by the University of Oklahoma
Press, Norman, Publishing Division of the University.
All rights reserved. Manufactured in the U.S.A.

1 2 3 4 5 6 7 8 9 10

26.95

HISTORICAL ATLAS
OF LOUISIANA

CONTENTS

Preface
vii

Louisiana: An Overview of the Bayou State   ix

I. SITE AND SITUATION
1. Location within the Coterminous United States
2. Latitude and Longitude

II. PHYSICAL SETTING AND NATURAL RESOURCES
3. Natural Regions
4. Contour Map
5. Major Landforms
6. Rivers, Lakes, Waterways, and Floodways
7. Forest Types
8. Parks, Forests, and Wildlife Areas
9. Geologic Formations
10. Oil and Gas Production
11. Floodplain Deposits
12. Mississippi River Delta Systems
13. Hurricanes
14. Temperature Ranges in January and July
15. Frost Dates, Growing Season, and Precipitation

III. ABORIGINAL SETTING AND NATIVE AMERICAN TRIBES
16. Prehistoric Native American Cultures
17. Louisiana Indians in 1700
18. Indians of Southeastern Louisiana
19. Indians of Northeastern Louisiana
20. Indians of Northwestern Louisiana
21. Indians of Southern Louisiana
22. Immigrant Indians

IV. EUROPEAN CONTACT AND SETTLEMENT
23. Spanish Claims in the United States to 1763
24. Spanish Explorers in Louisiana
25. French Claims in the United States to 1763
26. French Explorers in Louisiana
27. Louisiana under French Rule, 1699–1763
28. Spanish and British Claims after 1763
29. Louisiana under Spanish Rule, 1763–1803
30. Louisiana in the American Revolution

V. POLITICAL DEVELOPMENT
31. The Louisiana Purchase and the Adams-Onís Treaty
32. American Explorers in Louisiana
33. Land Survey Systems
34. Township-and-Range System
35. The West Florida Rebellion
36. The War of 1812 and the Battle of New Orleans
37. Louisiana in 1861
38. The Civil War in Louisiana, 1861–1862
39. The Civil War in Louisiana, 1863
40. The Civil War in Louisiana, 1864–1865
41. Counties, 1805
42. Parishes and Parish Seats, 1812
43. Parishes and Parish Seats, 1861
44. Parishes and Parish Seats, 1886
45. Parishes and Parish Seats, 1990
46. U.S. House of Representatives Districts
47. Louisiana Supreme Court Districts
48. State House of Representatives Districts
49. State Senate Districts

VI. POPULATION AND URBANIZATION
50. Population of Territory of Orleans, 1810
51. Population of Louisiana, 1860
52. Population of Louisiana, 1900
53. Population of Louisiana, 1940
54. Population of Louisiana, 1990
55. African American Population, 1810 and 1860
56. African American Population, 1900 and 1940
57. African American Population, 1990
58. Cities of Northern Louisiana, 1990
59. Cities of Southwestern Louisiana, 1990
60. Cities of Southeastern Louisiana, 1990
61. La Nouvelle Orléans and Nueva Orleans: New Orleans in the Eighteenth Century
62. New Orleans, 1863
63. New Orleans and Environs, 1990
64. The French Quarter (Vieux Carre), 1990
65. Baton Rouge, ca. 1855
66. Baton Rouge and Environs, 1990
67. Shreveport, Bossier City, and Environs, 1990

VII. ECONOMIC GROWTH: TRANSPORTATION
68. Railroads to 1880
69. Railroads, 1915
70. Railroads, 1991
71. Modern Transportation Systems and Military Installations, 1990
72. Navigable Waterways, 1890
73. Selected Navigable Waterways, ca. 1990

VIII. ECONOMIC GROWTH: AGRICULTURE
74. Land in Farms, 1940 and 1987
75. Total Agricultural Production, 1985–1989
76. Total Animal Production, 1985–1989
77. Total Crop Production, 1985–1989
78. Sugar Production, 1850, 1910, 1985–1989
79. Rice Production, 1850, 1910, 1985–1989

80. Forest Production, 1985–1989
81. Cotton Production, 1850, 1910,
    1985–1989
82. Assorted Feed Grain and Soybean
    Production, 1985–1989
83. Marine and Freshwater Fisheries
    Production, 1985–1989
84. Cattle and Calves and Milk Production,
    1985–1989
85. Poultry and Horse Production, 1985–1989
86. Farm Tenancy, 1880, 1910, 1940, and
    1987

IX. ECONOMIC GROWTH: INDUSTRY AND
    COMMERCE
87. Manufacturing, 1985–1989
88. Wholesale and Retail Trade, 1985–1989
89. Service and Transportation Industries,
    1985–1989
90. Mining and Construction, 1985–1989
91. Finance, Insurance, Real Estate, and
    Public Administration, 1985–1989
92. Unemployment, 1986–1990
93. Per Capita Personal Income and
    Percentage of Population Sixty-five or
    Older

X. CULTURAL GROWTH
94. Selected Inactive Colleges and Academies
95. Active Colleges and Universities
96. Museums, Historic Sites, Libraries, and
    Archives
97. Folk and Culture Regions
98. Fairs, Festivals, and Other Events
99. Tourism

Gazetteer   xvi
References   xxvi
Index   xxxix

PREFACE

Medieval scholars writing on vellum often found that medium in short supply. Thus, they frequently erased a previous script and reused the "paper" for a new document. Such a document is called a palimpsest—a manuscript with the most recent words most plainly visible but with pale images of previous writers appearing as ghostly records of the past.

Any historical geography of humanity presents a similar image. The medium of the current physical and cultural landscape most clearly presents only the most recent efforts of human intervention. The present house, road, fence, field pattern, or church (in various states of life or decay) is accompanied by the abandoned railroad right-of-way, the effects of the long-lot survey system on village form, and the like. Some of these images can be shown in a printed format—an abstract rendering of the three-dimensional world into the two dimensions of the printed page. Other images cannot be so easily shown either because they do not lend themselves to the medium or because the information is so remote as to be indiscernible. Such information, however, be it real or myth or something in between, is written in the lives and memories of the millions of present and past Louisianians. It is said that the living memory of any one generation actually spans the length of five generations. We know our grandparents, who in turn knew their grandparents, thus bringing together the combined memories of all. The passing of generations blurs the record; that which was once seen face-to-face is now glimpsed only as in a mirror darkly. The authors of this volume hope that its contents can illuminate in map and in word both the seen and the unseen past.

This work could not have been accomplished without the record left by others. Some of that record was contemporaneous with events. Other parts are modern reflections winnowed from the mass of original, often conflicting information to create as true a picture as humans are capable of compiling. Maps, narratives, travelogues, monographs, articles, and other studies have been consulted to create our own rendering. To each past chronicler—listed in the references at the close of this work—we owe a debt of gratitude. Of course, any errors in this text should not be laid at their door but at our own.

Several individuals and groups have particularly assisted in the production of this work. No one involved deserves more of our thanks than James H. Anderson, cartographer extraordinaire, who painstakingly created most of the maps which are contained in this volume. Jim has assisted in previous atlases for the University of Oklahoma Press and is indeed a hero to authors who know him.

If the love of money is the root of all evil, the lack thereof is the bane of many a project. Dr. Kenneth Hoving, former Vice-Provost for Research Administration at the University of Oklahoma, and Ron D. Burton, Executive Director of the University of Oklahoma Foundation, provided early, crucial funding for this work. The Louisiana Endowment for the Humanities also provided funds at a later but no less critical time, for which we would like to thank the Endowment; its Executive Director, Dr. Michael Sartisky; Program Officer Kathryn Mettelka; and former board member Stan Tiner, who alerted us in the first place.

Various libraries and archives shared the assembled wealth of their holdings. Among these and their staffs are the University of Oklahoma Libraries (Cynthia Wolff, Government Documents, and John R. Lovett, Jr., Western History Collections); Louisiana Tech University Library (Stephen Henson, Barbara Crawford, Jackie Jenkins, and Ruth Ann Locke, Government Documents; and the late Jacqueline Vidrine, Special Collections); the Louisiana and Lower Mississippi Valley Collections, Louisiana State University (Faye Phillips, Lynn Roundtree, and the late Stone Miller); the Louisiana State Library (Grace Moore); the Historic New Orleans Collection; the Geography and Map Division, Library of Congress; and the Cartographic and Architectural Branch, National Archives and Records Administration. John W. Hall, Louisiana State University–Shreveport, shared his work on land surveys in Louisiana. Neil H. Suneson, Staff Geologist, Oklahoma Geological Survey, provided information on geologic time.

Agencies who were helpful include the Louisiana Office of State Climatology (John M. ["Jay"] Grymes, assisted by DeWitt H. Braud, Instructor, Department of Geography and Anthropology, Louisiana State University, and Farrell W. Jones, Systems Manager, CADGIS Research Laboratory, Louisiana State University); Louisiana Department of Transportation (Dot McConnell, Kay Henderson, and Ann Ladner); Office of the Clerk, Louisiana House of Representatives (Kathleen Randall); Office of the Secretary, Louisiana State Senate; Louisiana Association of Museums (Lori Gulick); Louisiana Cooperative Extension Service; Louisiana Department of Employment and Training, Louisiana Agricultural Statistics Service; Louisiana Department of Wildlife and Fisheries (Patsy Hernandez); Louisiana Department of State Parks (Linton Ardoin and David Floyd); the Planning Commissions of New Orleans, Baton Rouge, Shreveport, and Bossier City; the U.S.

Corps of Engineers; National Climatic Data Center; and National Marine Fisheries Service (Leryes J. Usie). Other agencies and staff members have slipped the memory of the authors; their assistance is acknowledged along with our apologies.

Richard L. Nostrand read the introductory essay and both tightened and otherwise improved its content. Christine Caldwell read the entire manuscript and saved us from various vague passages, inconsistent usages, and other errors.

David Davidson and Ellen King, University of Oklahoma Printing Services, provided able service in type orders. At the University of Oklahoma Press, John N. Drayton, Editor-in-Chief, has proved a friend and gentleman throughout the project. Patsy Willcox, Production Manager, was most helpful in the art and science of the work. We thank as well the various members of the Press who labor behind the scenes in the marketing, bookkeeping, and other work so necessary to a modern university press.

Lastly, we would pause to reflect upon the life and work of the late John Wesley Morris, who began the Press's informal series of atlases three decades ago. To his memory this work is fondly dedicated.

LOUISIANA: AN OVERVIEW OF THE BAYOU STATE

Mention Louisiana and several images come to mind: Mardi Gras, plantations, Cajuns, Huey Long, moss-laden live oaks, and water. Indeed, Louisiana has as its nickname "the Bayou State," and rightfully so. Water more than any other force has been involved in shaping the physical landscape of the state. Whether that force has come from the proverbial Mighty Mississippi or one of its smaller sister streams, or whether it has come from the violence of a hurricane, the actions of waves crashing upon the coastal wetlands, or the seemingly gentle showers which abound around the state, water in any of its guises carries out its complementary actions of erosion and deposition.

The Mississippi River annually carries three hundred million tons of sediments fed to it by dozens of tributaries draining the vastness of the North American interior. In times past, but much less frequently today, much of that sediment settled upon the river's massive floodplain each spring as floods spread over that region. Yet the majesty of the "Father of Waters" as we know it today represents but the modern manifestation of an ancient river whose Pleistocene ebb and flow carved out a massive valley over hundreds of thousands of years. That valley in turn became filled with sediments which formed the floodplain and its adjacent terraces. The various distributary deltas of this prehistoric Mississippi unfolded great fans of sedimentary deposits extending into the Gulf of Mexico, fans whose ragged edges are gradually disappearing under action by wave and tide.

Akin to the flooding of the Mississippi (and other streams) has been the introduction of various human cultures, races, and nationalities over the past twelve thousand years. As with the river's almost annual flood, so, too, did these invasions by humankind begin first as a trickle, slowly, almost silently, slipping over the bounds of what is today Louisiana and spreading into and over the land. At times the new human wave produced more local than regional effects. Often, however, this rising flow of humanity became a great flood, covering if not completely obscuring much of what came before, driving what could move fast enough to sanctuaries, drowning what could not move so swiftly to such havens, and laying down as with sediment a new layer of the cultural landscape.

Sometimes the intruders came in the regiments of tribal or foreign conquering expeditions, seeking to establish a hegemony in the name of tribe or nation or religion. On other occasions they came as individual immigrants or refugees seeking to start afresh. Sometimes change came announced with fireworks and cannon, hoopla and parades. Sometimes that change appeared in the quietude of a disease silently spreading among unsuspecting inhabitants. Sometimes a new landscape has been wrought by the determined action to create it. Sometimes only with the passing of one generation to the next has the change become apparent. At times the changes were distinctly political, at other times more economic, and in recent times more cultural.

As a new flood spreads over the land, it, too, is modified. A cross-current changes the flow in one area, eddies form, and movement slows. Nevertheless, each new flood modifies all or part of the landscape. Yet vestiges of that previous landscape often survive the new flood, remaining behind as relics, totems which remind us of what once was, even as adaptation is made to the new. The encounters, interactions, and mutual adaptation of humanity to land, and humankind with humankind, has left behind these relic landscapes, even as the oral, written, or material record assists in identifying, explaining, and understanding that past. The identification, mapping, and explanation of past and present landscapes and the process of change over time is the object of this volume.

The American continents had existed for eons without human inhabitants. During the Pleistocene epoch (approximately the last two million years of the earth's existence) great ice sheets formed at various intervals and spread over much of the higher latitudes. As the earth's water moved from liquid to solid form in the creation of these sheets and glaciers, worldwide ocean levels lowered, creating a land bridge across what is today the Bering Straits. Perhaps as long as fifty thousand years ago or even longer, Asiatic peoples crossed over that land bridge to a new continent since named North America. These Asiatic wanderers immigrated in several waves and would be only the first of many newcomers to this new (to humans) land. Over the subsequent millennia these peoples followed the supply of wild game, spreading to the south and east, adapting in various ways to the regions in which they found themselves. Woodland peoples differed from those on the plains, coastal dwellers from inland peoples.

Perhaps as long as twelve thousand years ago these peoples first reached the region now comprising the modern state of Louisiana. The land which they found was in many ways the same land which other newcomers millennia later would also encounter. These peoples would be called "Indians" by the Europeans who encountered them thousands of years later.

The earliest of Native American cultures known to have been within the bounds of present-day Louisiana lived a very basic life centered upon a hunting, fishing, and gathering economy. Because the waters of rivers, bayous, and the Gulf of Mexico represented the only alternative to foot transport, their banks and shores provided a natural habitat for these earliest people. The adjacent marshes, streams, and woodlands provided food supplies—both animal and plant—sufficient to their small numbers. These first immigrants lived a nomadic existence, following the supply of food, so little evidence of their presence remains except the occasional projectile point.

As domesticated plants such as corn and squash were introduced from Mexico, a more settled population developed. Small patches of land were cleared for agriculture, and villages appeared, again largely adjacent to stream courses. Trading networks developed among the various tribes whereby surplus commodities could be exchanged, often on a regional basis. At the same time, human impact upon the land became more evident. These new cultures created burial, effigy, temple, and perhaps other mounds, many of which are still evident today. The purpose of many of these mounds is known; others may be only speculated on. Larger settled populations also left the debris of their life behind in the form of middens, accumulations of refuse. The most elaborate culture of this prehistoric period flourished in the second millennium B.C. and was centered upon the Poverty Point site in modern West Carroll Parish. This culture extended its sway over much of the modern American Southeast through a widespread trading network.

At the time of French contact (and thereby the beginning of a continuous recorded history) at the turn of the eighteenth century, six linguistic groups, counting various tribes within each and totaling perhaps fifteen thousand people, inhabited that region of the lower Mississippi Valley known today as Louisiana. The linguistic gulf between the tribes was spanned by the use of the Mobilian jargon, which was known by someone in almost every locale. The tribes practiced the basic economic activities of agriculture, hunting, and fishing; trading was carried on both within and without the present state boundaries. Situated alongside streams and scattered across the land, these tribes interacted with each other and with other tribes while maintaining distinctive dress, housing, religion, and other traits. Pottery and basketry had evolved beyond mere utilitarian needs into expressions of artistry. Various schemes of tribal government united the members into organized communities.

American Indian cultures are believed by some to be more closely attuned to their environment than were their successors, yet no organized society exists without affecting the land. The relic mounds testify to the remolding of the landscape to satisfy the demands of Indian society and customs. The use of fire in the clearing of the land for agriculture and the introduction of nonnative species disrupted the natural vegetation patterns. The hunting of the ancient land mammals—the mammoth, the sloth, and the bison among them—led to their reduction or extinction. Still, in most cases the relatively small Indian population wrought correspondingly small disruptions. If the fertility of an area waned, the tribe moved on to new lands, leaving the "old fields" to be reclaimed by the primeval environment.

When Christopher Columbus encountered the "New World" on his trip to the East Indies, he was but the latest of a succession of visitors. Columbus, however, represented a new development in European history, the rise of the modern nation-state and the competition by those rival states for hegemony on the European continent and beyond. In many ways these developing European empires would be merely logical successors to their ancestors of the Mediterranean Basin and the Middle East. However, their newfound and potent economic power would catapult them into a greater, global prominence unknown to their predecessors.

Commerce was the means for amassing wealth for the new European states. Thus, safe passage over the oceans was crucial to their livelihoods. Control over colonies which would provide both raw materials and markets was also essential to the economic health of the imperial power. An expanding patchwork pattern of colonies emerged, colonies founded by a combination of private entrepreneurs combined with royal patronage or by the direct action of agents of the crown. Thus, the global exploring expeditions would often be followed by the conquest of an area, followed still later by the planning of settlements and the peopling of a colony by a citizenry loyal to whatever sovereign held sway.

The Spanish conquest of the advanced Aztec and Incan empires in Central and South America launched that kingdom into a preeminent role in the Americas. The wealth looted from those centers fueled still more expeditions led by conquistadors tantalized by the idea of other riches to be secured for themselves and their sovereign. A companion impulse was that of the church militant. The Roman Church, given imperial approval by Constantine, had seen religion coexistent with empire. The split of Christianity, the fall of the empire, and the expanding Moslem empire had ended that single unit. With the rise of the nation-state came also the urge by Western Christianity to reclaim the ever-expanding known world and its inhabitants and save them to the next. For the Spanish, that church militant was Roman Catholicism. After the Reformation and rise of Protestant churches, the rivalry of nations would be accompanied by that of their state religions, often with tragic results.

The sixteenth century saw the area of the present-day United States crossed by various Spanish parties in search of the Seven Cities of Cibola and other fabled treasure troves. These different expeditions added to the knowledge of the region and introduced the horse, pig, dog, and cattle to the continent. Also introduced were various European diseases—particularly smallpox—against which the first American peoples had no immunity. Over the course of a century and a half, populations were decimated, entire towns destroyed. From the Americas to Europe came corn, squash, and sugar and perhaps venereal disease.

Spain and her early rival Portugal were joined in the colonial quest in the Americas by France, England, the Netherlands, and Sweden. Various expeditions explored the bays, estuaries, and rivers of the Atlantic seaboard and planted small trading posts and agricultural settlements in the early seventeenth century. Eventually the race for New World colonial empire came to focus on the Spanish, British, and French. Trade with the eastern tribes took the French fur traders (coureurs de bois) further and further inland. In 1682, René-Robert Cavelier, Sieur de La Salle, and his party completed a journey aborted by Marquette and Joliet nine years previously and reached the mouth of the Mississippi River.

Claiming the entire drainage basin in the name of Louis XIV of France, La Salle thereby bestowed upon half the northern continent the name of that sovereign. La Louisiane would be further explored by the French (beset by Spanish protests) in the next decade, and in the closing years of the century colonizing efforts began.

These early efforts came to fruition under the brothers Le Moyne, especially Iberville and Bienville. A colony was begun at Biloxi, Mississippi, in 1699; a palisaded Fort de la Boulaye was established near the mouth of the Mississippi in 1700; and Natchitoches was founded in 1714 and New Orleans in 1718.

French colonizing efforts proved difficult at first, since the lure of easy riches continued to preoccupy the minds of many of those first to arrive. In time, however, a subsistence agriculture developed. In keeping with their tradition as traders with the Indians, the French also established posts in proximity to tribal allies, posts at which goods might be exchanged. Beyond the palisaded posts farms were established. The "old fields" of the Indians were used at first, then gradual clearing of other lands began. The Gulf coastal colonies were intended to be linked up with those in Canada to produce La Nouvelle France, a grand extension of the mother country. These colonies also represented rivals to both the English and the Spanish, but particularly the latter, with their adjacent colonies in both Florida and Texas.

As the threat of attack subsided and populations grew, settlements expanded upriver along the banks of the Mississippi and other streams. Water frontage being essential for transportation, grants of land were made with boundaries perpendicular to the banks; a system of "long lots" grew to parallel the watercourses. The natural levees of these streams provided the slight rise upon which a house and outbuildings might be erected.

The French were joined by other groups. During the 1720s Germans largely from the Rhine Valley migrated to the colony, eventually settling along the Mississippi in present-day St. Charles and St. John the Baptist parishes, an area still known as La Côte des Allemands (the German Coast), the "coast" in this case being the natural levees. These Germans proved industrious agriculturalists, which the colony desperately needed. Early farmers tried the traditional crops; not all of these thrived. In time they adapted to the Indian crops. Corn was used as animal feed, but rice served the French as a replacement for wheat whenever possible. Tobacco was another native crop grown, primarily for export; it was joined by indigo. The Louisiana colony passed through a series of regimes, ranging from private proprietorships to royal colony, in an attempt to derive some profit for the mother country; all failed in that objective.

Forcibly added to the mix of European and Indian cultures during the early years of the French regime was the institution of African slavery. Slavery was by no means a new idea, having been practiced by most civilizations of earlier times. Nor was it the first means attempted to solve the continuing shortage of agricultural labor. Both forced migration of the "lower classes" of French society and an attempt at enslaving the local Indian population had proved unsuccessful. The colonial government of the early eighteenth century then decided to emulate the system of black slavery already employed in various European colonies in the Caribbean.

Africa did not present a homogeneous front to the outside world. North Africa had been home to ancient civilizations since the Egyptians in the fifth millennium B.C. That civilization had been subsumed under the empire of Rome. After the collapse of the western empire, the southern shore of the Mediterranean divided into differing kingdoms, later to become part of the spreading Moslem Empire in the seventh and eighth centuries.

Sub-Saharan Africa was also home to several kingdoms from the early Christian era to the Middle Ages, including Ghana, Mali, and Songhay among them.

The sixteenth century witnessed the beginnings of the modern slave trade. The first African slaves to arrive in Louisiana came two centuries later. Over the course of the eighteenth century millions of enslaved Africans would be loaded into the holds of sailing vessels for the infamous "Middle Passage" to the Americas, a trip which a substantial fraction did not survive. Once in the Americas they would be sold as workers on plantations and elsewhere; this would be their fate in Louisiana.

Slavery began to be regulated in Louisiana in 1724 by the first Code Noir. This Black Code sought to bring some protection to the slaves themselves even while prescribing stringent measures in an attempt to prevent slave revolts. Over time this code would be revised by French and Spanish. The slave population in the colony numbered perhaps sixteen thousand in the 1780s, and twenty-eight thousand in 1803 at the time of the Louisiana Purchase.

After more than six decades of French rule, La Louisiane was ceded to Spain in the aftermath of yet another war among European powers. To save the colony from the British at the close of the French and Indian (Seven Years') War, France in 1763 deeded it over to her Iberian ally. At the close of the French regime, the settled area of the present state comprised the banks of the lower Mississippi and the Bayou Teche, with outliers about Natchitoches and present-day Monroe, Alexandria, and Marksville. A total population of perhaps seven thousand inhabited the region; half of those lived in or near the capital of New Orleans.

Under Spain's control La Luisiana entered into its heyday as a European colony. Although it remained a financial liability, it enjoyed an increased prosperity and settlement. Beyond a new sovereign with a foreign language there was, however, little impact upon the citizens who came with the territory. The old colonists largely continued in their traditional patterns of life. A short-lived rebellion in New Orleans was put down firmly but with little loss of life.

The Spanish used their much longer history as a colonial power to bring greater order and wealth to the colony. A more than sixfold increase in population occurred during the Spanish period. New settlers were recruited from Spanish lands to increase the economic strength and promote loyalty to the new owner. Among them was a group largely from the Canary Islands (the Isleños) who settled, among other areas, in present-day St. Bernard Parish.

These new settlers advanced upriver among the older French settlers, largely continuing the long-lot system. Regulations on the upgrading of levees were instituted to help prevent floods. Prescribed road maintenance along the levees improved land transportation. Land division maintained river frontage for each parcel and thereby created a linear settlement pattern lining the streams. In addition to the long lots, grants were also made for ranching purposes. These grants out on the western frontier of La Luisiana were usually square and contained up to a square league (forty-five hundred acres).

Besides Hispanic colonists other groups also arrived during the era of Spanish rule. Prime among them were the Acadians from former French Canada. These people had been forcibly evicted by the new British rulers and scattered among the British colonies along the Atlantic seaboard in an effort to dilute any concentration.

They gradually coalesced and moved into Louisiana during the 1760s. Finding much of the lower Mississippi lands taken, they struck out to the west, establishing settlements along the bayous skirting the southwestern Louisiana prairies, the frontier of the colony.

The same war that had seen Louisiana go to Spain in 1763 also saw Spanish Florida ceded to the British. That colony included within its bounds that part of modern Louisiana north of Lake Pontchartrain and the Bayou Manchac and east of the Mississippi—the area still known today as the Florida Parishes. For twenty years this area would remain in British hands.

The occupation of this region by Anglo-American and British settlers brought with it changes to that landscape. New names were given to old places. Land grants were made, but in the irregular system known as metes and bounds, not the long lots or square grants of the French and Spanish. Rather than the linear settlements along the river courses, such grants produced a more dispersed settlement pattern in the rural areas of this region. The Anglos also brought with them that frontier symbol, the log cabin, with its horizontal log construction. Early French builders, if they used logs, had placed them vertically then covered them with plaster. Later French houses were built of timbers interfilled with brick or clay, the whole covered with cypress siding or whitewashed.

After the close of the American Revolution and the Treaty of Paris (1783) Florida would revert to Spain, and the whole of the modern state of Louisiana would be united in fact for two decades. Then in 1803, France, having secretly retrieved Louisiana in 1800, sold the colony to the young United States of America. The new nation, seeking perhaps only the Isle of Orleans (those lands east of the Mississippi and south of the Bayou

Manchac) in order to secure free transit of the Mississippi River, gobbled up the entire domain and thus doubled the size of the new republic. All of present-day Louisiana except the Florida Parishes came with the purchase; the Florida Parishes would remain in Spanish hands for another decade.

At the time of the purchase, Louisiana had perhaps fifty thousand people. New Orleans, with a population of about ten thousand, accounted for a fifth of that total. Natchitoches, New Iberia, Vermilionville (modern Lafayette), Rapides (modern Pineville), Fort Miro (Monroe), Opelousas, and other small settlements lay scattered within the bounds of the present-day state. Agricultural settlers lined the Mississippi River from below New Orleans to upstream of Natchez. The settled area (within the present bounds of the state) also included much of the lands along the Red, Amite, Tangipahoa, Black, and Ouachita rivers and the Bayous Teche, Lafourche, and Manchac. Rude trails represented overland transport, and wind power reigned on water. The purchase was divided into the Territory of Orleans (all of the modern state of Louisiana with the exception of the Florida Parishes) and the Territory of Louisiana. In 1812 the Territory of Orleans, with the recently annexed Florida Parishes, entered the union as Louisiana, the eighteenth state.

The first six decades of the nineteenth century witnessed remarkable growth in Louisiana. It would accumulate such wealth as would not be seen again until the advent of the oil and gas industry at the turn of the next century. The motive force behind this wealth would be plantation agriculture and its twin currencies, cotton and sugar.

Technological advances in refining sugar and ginning cotton combined with national and world markets to bring wealth to the plantation owners. More numerous plantations cleared greater amounts of land and introduced still more slaves. (The foreign slave trade was halted in Louisiana in 1804, but the migration from other regions and natural increase continued to expand their numbers.) The plantation home so associated with the South was primarily the product of the mid-nineteenth century, with the more palatial homes to be found in the sugar country. Sugar may have been more profitable, but cotton did not suffer the same climatic restraints upon its growing region or labor requirements for its cultivation and thus spread over more of the state.

In addition to the thousands of plantation owners, tens of thousands of yeomen farmers moved into new lands in the state. Throughout the nineteenth century the majority of these immigrants would come from states further to the east, bringing with them an Upland South culture. By midcentury only the southwestern prairies, Atchafalaya Basin, and coastal areas represented large areas without settlements. The smaller streams whose banks were not yet occupied attracted these farmers to their neighborhoods. The uplands in the north were also more effectively occupied. The clearing of the Great Raft on the Red enhanced settlement along that river. The new American land survey system with its regular north-south, east-west grid of townships, ranges, and sections was platted upon the landscape and used in the division of the land. Slavery also existed among these yeomen, but not to as great a degree as in plantation agriculture. Still, slaveholding presented a status to which many aspired.

Another factor in the growth of Louisiana's antebellum prosperity was the steam engine, first made practical by the Scotsman James Watt in 1769. Steam would power the hundreds of river and ocean steamers which funneled the commerce of the Mississippi watershed through New Orleans. Steam also powered the few small manufacturing and processing plants that existed within the state. More importantly, steam fueled the looms elsewhere which consumed the cotton crop in the production of textiles.

At midcentury the state also began to be penetrated tentatively by yet another child of the steam age, the railroad. River steamers had brought about landscape change by opening up new areas to agriculture, by developing port cities, and by requiring early efforts at channel control. The railroad, however, would strike overland between river valleys, clearing a corridor as it went, a corridor which would widen as adjacent lands were settled, towns developed, and populations grew.

The new state of Louisiana, having survived an attempted British invasion in the War of 1812, would grow dramatically during the antebellum period. A population estimated at 50,000 at the time of the Louisiana Purchase would grow to 708,002 in 1860. New Orleans, with 168,675, was the largest city not only in the state but also anywhere in the South. Its port would rival New York in the flow of commerce. Shreveport, Baton Rouge (the capital), Monroe, Alexandria, and other cities paled in comparison to New Orleans but served their respective regions of the state.

The War between the States wrought havoc upon Louisiana, as with most of the defeated South. Private and public property was destroyed by invasion and counterattack. Expeditions along the Mississippi, Red, Teche and other streams devastated the cotton and sugar plantations, destroyed towns, and ruined transportation facilities. Thousands of lives—the cream of an entire generation—were lost to injury and death as Louisiana regiments fought both within the state and throughout the Confederacy. African Americans joined in on the federal side. The thirteenth amendment to the U.S. Constitution ended slavery and stripped owners of that combined human capital and labor supply.

Following the tumult of the war itself and the turmoil of Reconstruction, with its occupation by federal troops, Louisiana emerged changing in appearance. Many of its plantations saw their holdings divided. Most surviving plantations entered into a sharecropping system which parceled the land out primarily to the former slaves. The aptly termed "shacks" of the sharecroppers lined the fencerows of country lanes. The houses of the small farmer were not always much better. Much of yeoman agriculture, particularly in the less fertile areas, entered into a crop lien system akin to sharecropping. A type of economic servitude by both races replaced "that peculiar institution" of antebellum days.

The late nineteenth century witnessed still more immigration, and through that and natural increase the state's population grew from 708,002 in 1860 to 1,381,625 in 1900. Even then, there was still in the state a tremendous acreage in the public domain awaiting entry under the terms of the Homestead Act of 1862. By that act a quarter-section (160 acres) of the public domain entered upon, occupied, and improved over a five-year period could then obtained for a nominal fee. The growth of railroads blossomed as rails were laid across more and more of the state. Many of those lines duplicated then supplanted river routes to established cities. Still more opened up new areas to settlement and agriculture. Dozens of towns sprang into existence along with the new lines,

drawing in still more people.

The 1880s in particular witnessed another new culture entering the state. Midwestern farmers were recruited to settle the prairies of southwestern Louisiana, there to develop an agricultural economy based on rice. As with other distinct cultures, they brought with them their traditional ways. Some, like the I-frame house, would endure; others, such as their corn economy, changed.

In addition to their own literal modification of the landscape, the railroads entering the state in the late nineteenth century wrought other changes. Prime among these was the opening up of the vast timber reserves to exploitation and consumption. Although the forests had been harvested since prehistoric times, as with other commerce that work had been dependent upon river transport. The rails opened up the resources of the hill country to that harvest and also connected this new supply to the burgeoning markets in states whose own forests had already been felled. In the span of thirty years between 1890 and 1920 much of the vast pine forests were cut over and then largely abandoned.

Into part of that cutover acreage came still more people eking out a subsistence existence as farmers. For a few decades of the twentieth century such an enterprise could still prove successful. The Great Depression, the overproduction of almost every agricultural commodity, the entry of certain commodities from abroad, and the mechanization of agriculture particularly after World War II all combined to end such farming as a way of life. Much of the uplands would revert to forest, sometimes on an organized basis in the form of pine tree plantations and other times reclaimed naturally.

Even in those areas most suited for agriculture, changes occurred. Acreage allotment programs and price supports influenced levels of production

for those crops covered. New crops such as soybeans replaced traditional crops. The total amount of the state's land occupied by farms would drop; so, too, would the number of farms even as their average size increased.

The twentieth century has witnessed many other changes on the landscape. The rural-to-urban migration has seen not only the depopulation of the rural areas but also the growth of cities and the sprawl of their suburbs over the land. From a state that was only 26 percent urban in 1900, Louisiana in 1950 was 55 percent urban and neared 70 percent in 1990.

New Orleans would continue to be the largest city in the state. Yet the old New Orleans, coterminous with Orleans Parish, began to experience the urban problems of many another central city, decay and crime among them. By 1990 it had dropped below the half-million mark in population. On the other hand, its suburbs continued to expand. Baton Rouge as the capital enjoyed phenomenal growth as one recipient of the largesse of the oil boom as well as the growth of state government. Once the state's second city, Shreveport continued to serve as the metropolis in the northern part of the state.

Another population change was the emigration by many among the black population of the state. In part fueled by greater economic opportunity, in part by the mechanization of agriculture in the south, and in part by a means to escape the institutional segregation and racism in the state, this flight began early in the century but swelled after World War I. The portion of the state's population represented by African Americans dropped from almost half at the turn of the century to less than a third towards its close.

Another event of this century harkens back to an earlier period: the continuing infusion of new cultures into the state. New Orleans primarily represented a cosmopolitan city from colonial days. The immigrants of old European lands during the colonial period and nineteenth century have been complemented by Asian and Latin American groups. More recent have been increased numbers from eastern Asia and the Middle East, whose numbers are often found in the college towns of the state. While many cultures have been largely assimilated in the mainstream, a diversity of background is to be found in many towns throughout the state.

Sharing a lack of industry with much of the antebellum South, Louisiana entered into that economic sector late. Today, however, manufacturing plants of various sorts abound in the state, primarily in the metropolitan areas. Of particular significance in this century are the plants associated with the oil and gas industry. The Lower Mississippi Industrial Corridor stretching from just upriver of Baton Rouge downriver to New Orleans counts a string of plants occupying former plantations. Other manufacturing and refining complexes operate at Lake Charles, Shreveport, Lafayette, Monroe, Alexandria, and elsewhere.

The introduction of the personal automobile and resultant proliferation of parish, state, and federal highways has cast a web across the entire state. The interstate highway system, with its divided lanes unencumbered by a single traffic signal, has promoted high-speed transit across the nation. The personal automobile represents more than another shift in transportation systems or a symbol of the age of petroleum. The occupation of increased amounts of land by these ribbons of roadways pro-

vided means for further population shifts. Citizens were no longer dependent upon footsteps or mass transit for commuting. Suburbs developed on the flanks of cities; workers could live in one city and commute daily to and from their employment.

The discovery and exploitation of the oil and gas reserves of the state powered both the economy and state government from the 1920s through the 1980s. This growth also brought about its own landscape change, from the working or relic derricks or pumps, to the pipelines whose thousands of miles lie buried beneath the surface, to hundreds of manufacturing and processing plants. The pollution of the environment from spillage damaged ecosystems. The lure of work enticed tens of thousands of people to follow the oil boom from field to field. Offshore development drove a thirty-year court case to determine the actual coastline of Louisiana and thus divide that wealth between the state and the nation.

Thus has the physical and cultural Louisiana landscape come to exist in the form we know it today. Certainly the present rendering of that landscape would be alien to both Indian and French who came together at the beginning of the historic period three centuries ago. The successive waves of ethnic, religious, political, economic, technological, and other changes have wrought increasing modification of the land and its inhabitants. Few, if indeed any, areas remain untouched from the agents of such change. The interactions of culture and peoples, the tempo of modern life, the proximity to the symbolic "global village" bombards the

lives of Louisianians. So much has been wrought in only this century. A child of the Upland South moving with her parents from Alabama to Louisiana at the turn of the twentieth century could today bear witness to the evolution of the landscape in her own, single lifetime.

There are those who would place value judgments over these waves of change—judgments based upon a present-day set of values. Whereas previous generations might have used the terms "progress," "enlightenment," even "civilization" in characterizing the past, today one hears of "genocide" and "rape." Certainly there exists a greater (and needed) awareness of the impact of technology and sheer numbers upon society and landscape. This awareness which coalesced in the Progressive movement at the beginning of this century continues today in environmental movements of various shades and doctrine.

Change takes place only within the context of its own time and space; rarely is there in the agents of such change the thought, "Let us go and do some evil work today." In particular application to our own state, who knows how future generations will reflect upon the "Petroleum Century" (or two) and its effect on land and resources and people. The study of past landscapes and histories seeks first to identify and understand those pasts in their own time and space. Only when we achieve such understanding of what has been before are we better able to comprehend what is today and seek to improve what will be tomorrow. As Shakespeare says, "What is past is truly just but prologue."

Copyright © 1995 by the University of Oklahoma Press

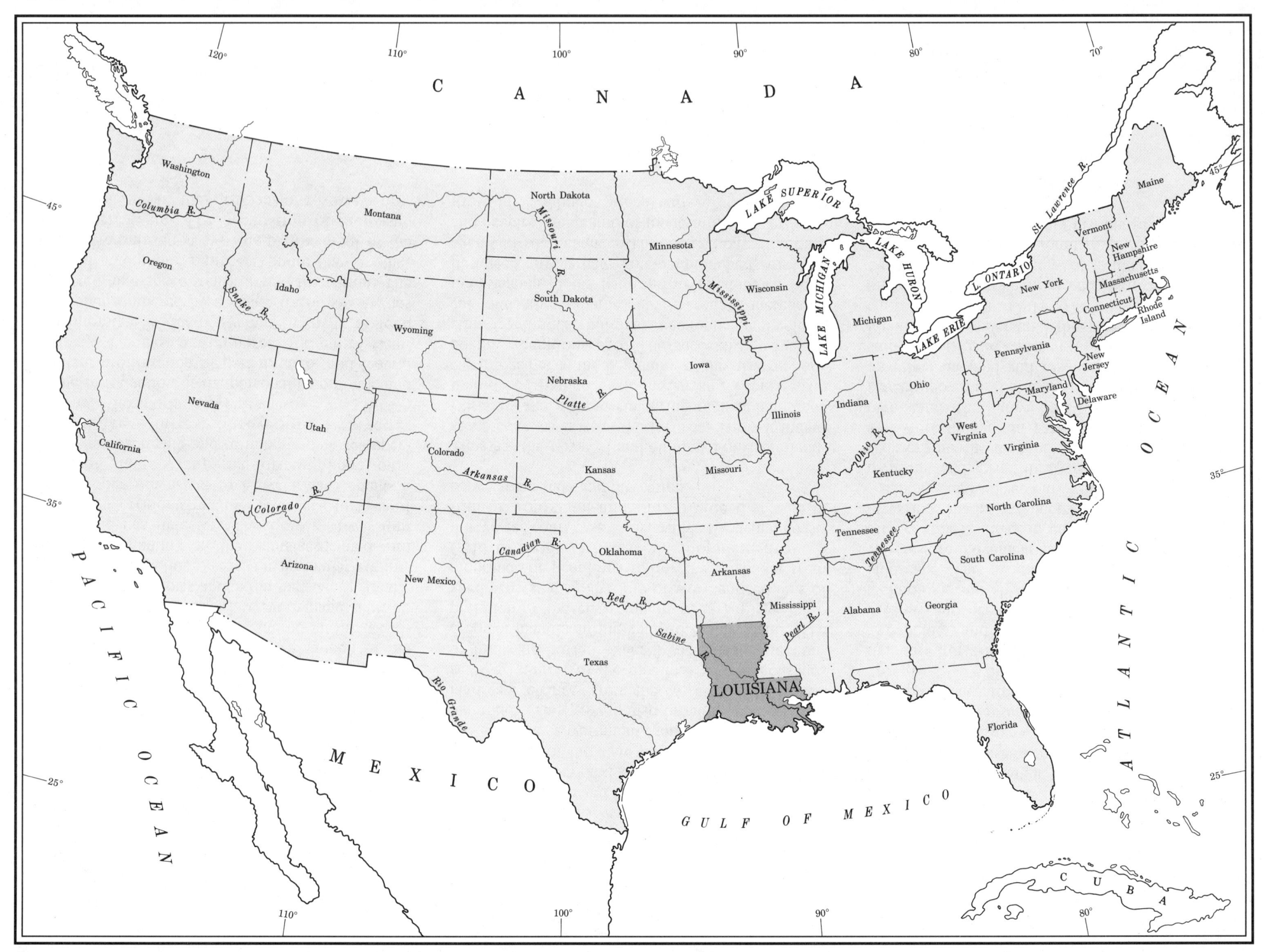

1. LOCATION WITHIN THE COTERMINOUS UNITED STATES

Louisiana lies along the southernmost tier of the coterminous forty-eight states, just east of a line drawn north to south through the center of those states. When the Louisiana Purchase was still new, the state was considered part of the Southwest. With the expansion of the nation westward to the Pacific, Louisiana became part of the South. Sometimes the state is referred to as part of the Deep South, a term used to denote those states bordering the Gulf of Mexico. In other, climatic and cultural terms Louisiana is located within the Sun Belt and is also a part of the Bible Belt.

Louisiana's shape approximates that of a boot with an eastern-pointing toe, its sole lapped by the waters of the Gulf. Its boundaries combine natural and artificial lines to provide that shape. On the south the Gulf of Mexico forms the boundary. On the west the line of 92° 3' west longitude forms the boundary from the northwest corner until intersecting the Sabine River; thereafter the boundary follows the center of the Sabine River to the Gulf. Louisiana's eastern boundary consists of the courses of two rivers—the Mississippi and the Pearl—and a line in the Gulf of Mexico. From approximately 33° north latitude south to 31° north latitude, the middle of the Mississippi River (actually a line following the course of that river in 1812 when Louisiana became a state) marks the boundary. South of 31° north latitude, the eastern boundary follows the Pearl River until that stream reaches the Gulf. Lastly, the northern boundary of the state consists of two separate east-west lines. The northernmost line lies just north of 33° north latitude; the northern boundary of that portion of the state known as the Florida Parishes generally follows 31° north latitude.

Three other states share borders with Louisiana. Texas looms to the west. Arkansas lies to the north. Because of Louisiana's shape, neighboring Mississippi lies to the north or to the east, depending upon where in Louisiana one is located.

Only Texas, Florida, and Hawaii extend further to the south than does Louisiana. Every state except Hawaii and Florida extends further north. Twenty-four states are in whole or in part east of Louisiana's easternmost boundary. Twenty-five states are in whole or in part west of Louisiana's westernmost boundary.

When one considers Louisiana's position on the globe, one sees that all of Europe lies north and all of South America lies east (as well as south) of the state. Louisiana has common latitude with much of North Africa, the Middle East, the Indian subcontinent, and China. Her longitude is shared by parts of Mexico, Honduras, and El Salvador and the Canadian provinces of Ontario, Manitoba, and the Northwest Territories.

Most of the present area of Louisiana came to the United States as part of the Louisiana Purchase. Part or all of fourteen states were carved out of the area encompassed in the purchase. Thus, that part of the present-day state of Louisiana which was included in the purchase comprises only a small fraction of the total territory bought from France in 1803.

Louisiana covers an area of 48,523 square miles; this ranks it thirty-first among the fifty states in size. It is smaller than any of the states with which it shares a boundary. Texas is more than five times Louisiana's size. Louisiana is only one-twelfth the size of the largest state (Alaska) but is forty-eight times the size of the smallest state (Rhode Island). It is but one-quarter the size of either France or Spain, the two European nations which controlled much of its past.

Of Louisiana's area, 3,593 square miles are water. This places the state sixth in overall water area, exceeded only by Alaska, Texas, Minnesota, Florida, and North Carolina. Louisiana also has an extensive coastal boundary, which places it in the top half-dozen states in this measurement.

Louisiana's location within the United States has affected its cultural and economic development. All or part of its current territory at one time lay within the colonial empires of France, Spain, and the United Kingdom (Great Britain). To its original mix of American Indian cultures, these imperial cultures and those of other nations and ethnic groups were added. The vast Mississippi River basin funneling its waters and commerce through the state still plays a major role in Louisiana's history. As a state on the boundary between land and sea, traversed by numerous streams, Louisiana contains contrasts in relief, soil, and vegetation. As a part of the old Confederacy, it experienced the results of defeat and occupation by a conquering force. All these factors and more have combined to produce the modern state of Louisiana.

Copyright © 1995 by the University of Oklahoma Press

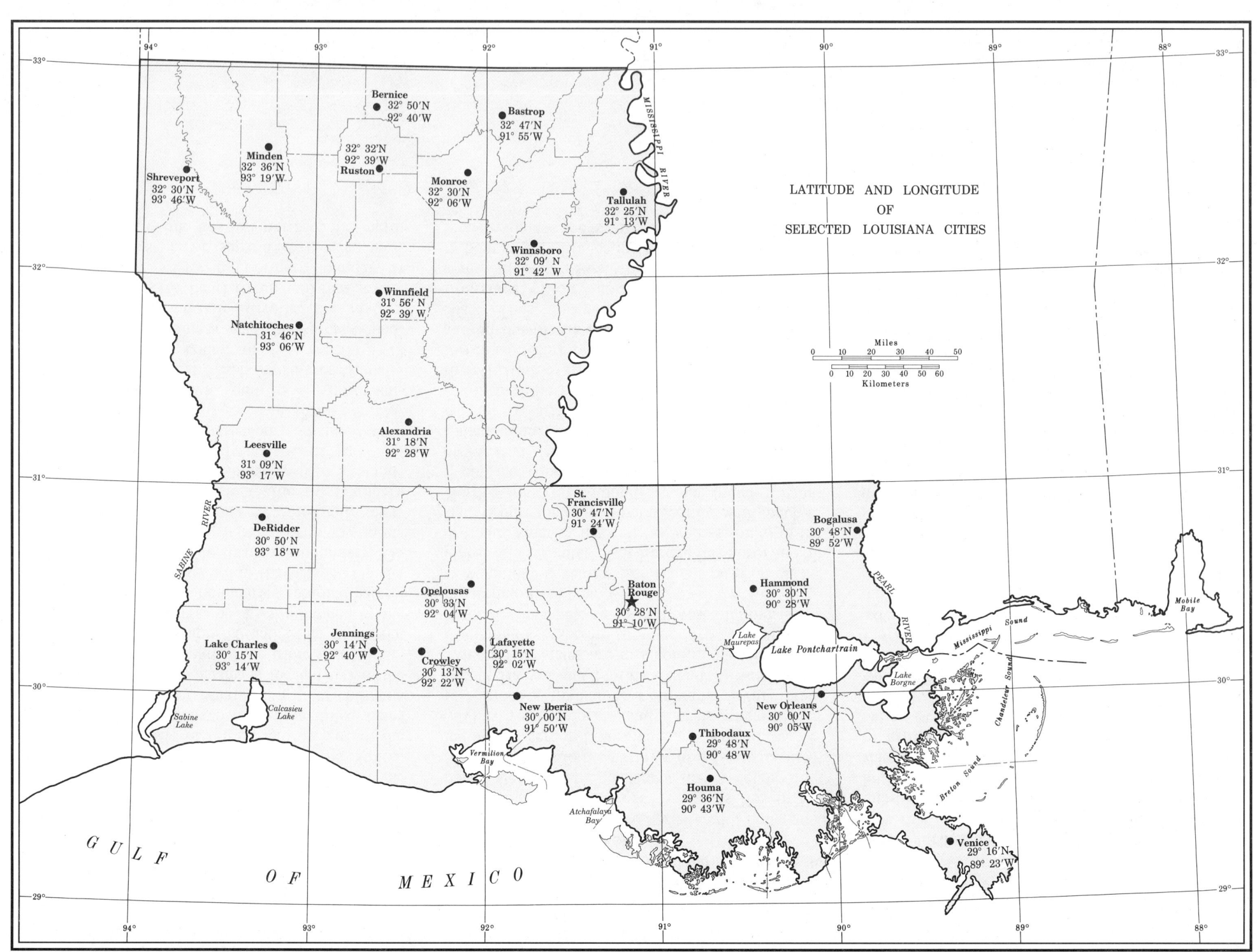

LATITUDE AND LONGITUDE
OF
SELECTED LOUISIANA CITIES

Bernice
32° 50′N
92° 40′W

Bastrop
32° 47′N
91° 55′W

Minden
32° 36′N
93° 19′W

32° 32′N
92° 39′W
Ruston

Shreveport
32° 30′N
93° 46′W

Monroe
32° 30′N
92° 06′W

Tallulah
32° 25′N
91° 13′W

Winnsboro
32° 09′ N
91° 42′ W

Winnfield
31° 56′ N
92° 39′ W

Natchitoches ●
31° 46′N
93° 06′W

Alexandria
31° 18′N
92° 28′W

Leesville
31° 09′N
93° 17′W

**St.
Francisville**
30° 47′N
91° 24′W

Bogalusa
30° 48′N
89° 52′W

DeRidder
30° 50′N
93° 18′W

Opelousas
30° 33′N
92° 04′W

**Baton
Rouge**
30° 28′N
91° 10′W

Hammond
30° 30′N
90° 28′W

Jennings
30° 14′N
92° 40′W

Lafayette
30° 15′N
92° 02′W

Lake Charles
30° 15′N
93° 14′W

Crowley
30° 13′N
92° 22′W

New Iberia
30° 00′N
91° 50′W

New Orleans
30° 00′N
90° 05′W

Thibodaux
29° 48′N
90° 48′W

Houma
29° 36′N
90° 43′W

Venice
29° 16′N
89° 23′W

MISSISSIPPI RIVER

SABINE RIVER

PEARL RIVER

*Sabine
Lake*

*Calcasieu
Lake*

*Vermilion
Bay*

*Atchafalaya
Bay*

*Lake
Maurepas*

Lake Pontchartrain

*Lake
Borgne*

Mississippi Sound

*Mobile
Bay*

Chandeleur Sound

Breton Sound

G U L F   O F   M E X I C O

Miles
0   10   20   30   40   50

0   10   20   30   40   50   60
Kilometers

2. LATITUDE AND LONGITUDE

Latitude and longitude represent an artificial but systematic means of locating places north and south of the equator (0° latitude) and east and west of the Prime (Greenwich) Meridian (0° longitude). Just as a circle has 360 degrees of arc in its circumference, a total of 360 degrees each of latitude and longitude encircle the globe. Each degree of latitude or longitude is divided into sixty minutes, and each minute into sixty seconds. Latitude is measured in degrees (then minutes and seconds) north or south of the Equator and ranges in value from 0° at the Equator to 90° at either the North or South Pole. Today east or west longitude ranges from 0° at the Prime Meridian (which passes through the Imperial Observatory at Greenwich outside London, England) to 180° at the opposite side of the globe. The International Date Line—the line at which each new day begins—follows 180° longitude for much of its path.

Louisiana's latitudinal bounds range from roughly 28° 55' to just north of 33° north. This spans the southernmost mouth of the Mississippi River delta to the Louisiana-Arkansas boundary. The longitudinal bounds lie between 88° 45' and 94° 3' west. These range from the eastern shores of the Chandeleur Islands in the Gulf of Mexico to the longitude which forms part of the western boundary of Louisiana with Texas.

Thus, the state extends through just over four degrees of latitude and slightly under four-and-one-half degrees of longitude. The length of a degree of latitude remains constant at approximately seventy miles; Louisiana's north-to-south distance is thus approximately 280 miles. The length of a degree of longitude does not remain constant but narrows as one moves from the equator toward either pole; the approximate distance for Louisiana's range of longitude totals 300 miles.

There are various ways to define the geographic center of an area. The U.S. Geological Survey has by one means determined that the geographic center of Louisiana lies in Avoyelles Parish, three miles southeast of Marksville. Another measure has placed that same center fifteen miles north of St. Francisville in West Feliciana Parish.

Lines of latitude (parallels) and longitude (meridians) help form a portion of the boundaries of Louisiana. The lines which form the two portions of the northern boundaries of Louisiana follow latitude lines closely. Between Louisiana and Arkansas the state line lies a varying distance north of 33° north latitude, closer to the parallel at the Mississippi River and increasingly north of the line as one moves west. The boundary between Louisiana and Mississippi in the Florida parishes closely follows 31° north latitude. A portion of the Louisiana-Texas boundary approximates 94° 3' west longitude. Boundaries may not follow either parallels or meridians exactly because of errors made when those lines were surveyed.

Longitudinal lines help define different time zones around the world. With 360 degrees of longitude and twenty-four hours in each day, each one-hour zone comprises 15 degrees of longitude. Not all time zone boundaries follow longitude precisely; other considerations such as state or national boundaries cause the time zone line to move east or west from precisely the same longitude. Louisiana lies in the Central Time Zone, one of four time zones which encompass the forty-eight coterminous states. The Central Time Zone roughly extends 7½ degrees of longitude east and west of 90° west longitude, approximately the same longitude as New Orleans.

Latitudinal location on the globe also affects Louisiana in several ways. The Tropic of Cancer (23½° north) and the Tropic of Capricorn (23½° south) mark the northern and southern limits on the globe where the sun's rays strike the earth's surface perpendicularly (at a 90° angle). Because Louisiana lies north of the Tropic of Cancer, the sun's rays never reach this perpendicular angle. This affects the climate of the state because there are noticeably different amounts of solar energy striking Louisiana and the surrounding region at different times of the year. Louisiana's latitudinal location also places it in a wind zone termed the "prevailing westerlies," where because of atmospheric pressure and the rotation of the earth, the winds generally blow from west to east. Finally, because of latitude Louisiana experiences greater difference in the length of daylight and darkness than do points closer to the equator but less difference than points closer to the poles.

Thus, latitude and longitude in their exact terms place Louisiana, its cities and people, in a specific part of the globe. By comparing the latitude and longitude of other sites and regions, one can determine an approximate direction and distance from any point in Louisiana. In addition, the latitude and longitude of the state, when compared with other portions of Earth, provide several relative locations on the globe, with important implications for weather, climate, and length and time of day.

Copyright © 1995 by the University of Oklahoma Press

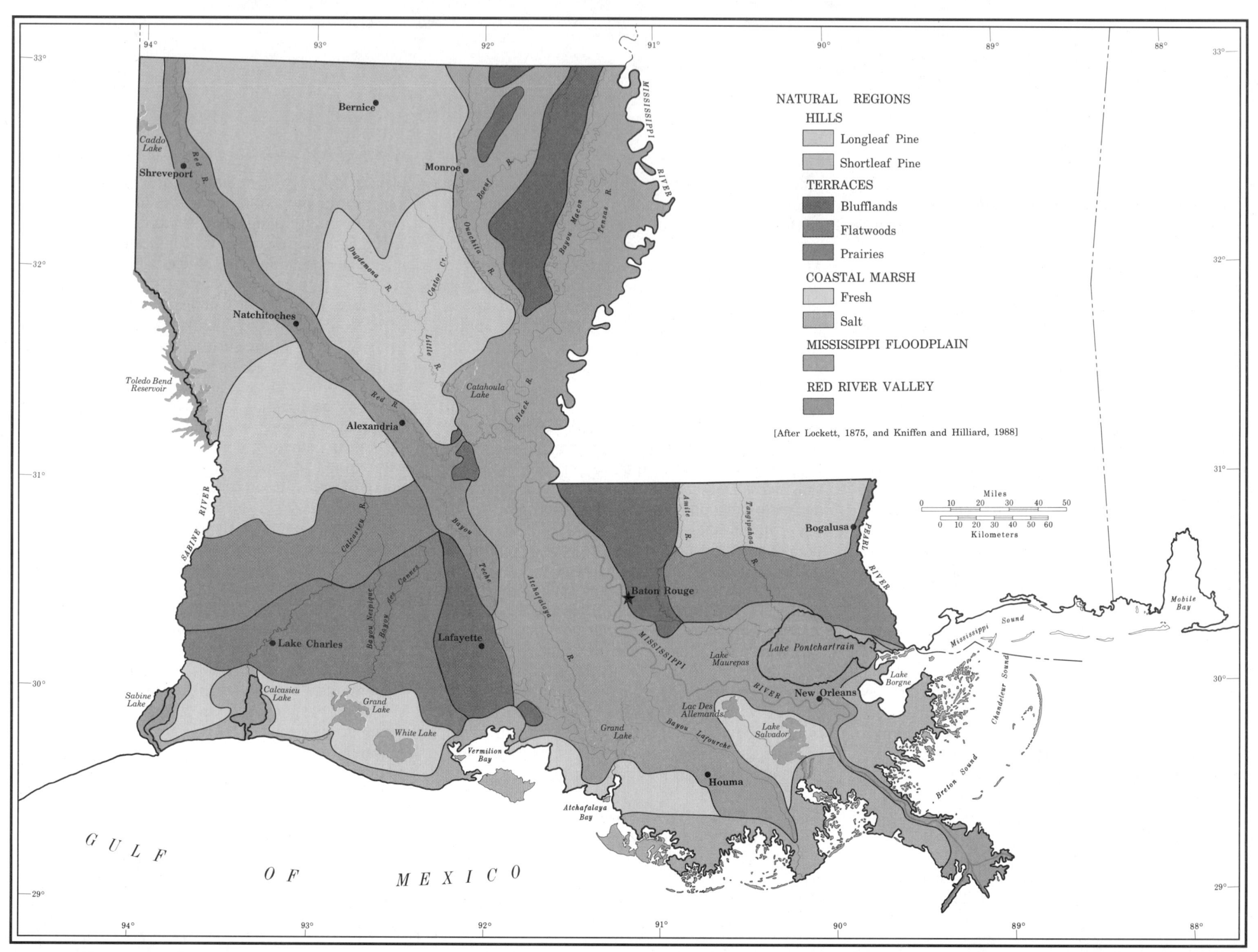

NATURAL REGIONS
HILLS
Longleaf Pine
Shortleaf Pine
TERRACES
Blufflands
Flatwoods
Prairies
COASTAL MARSH
Fresh
Salt
MISSISSIPPI FLOODPLAIN

RED RIVER VALLEY

[After Lockett, 1875, and Kniffen and Hilliard, 1988]

3. NATURAL REGIONS

Geographic regions can be defined on the basis of natural phenomena such as climate, soil, relief, and vegetation. These elements are of course interrelated. Some soils are more nutrient-rich than others, and thus support more lush vegetation; vegetation upon decay replenishes nutrients to the soil which nourished it. Relief influences drainage; freely drained soils are conducive to certain vegetation which cannot grow in poorly drained soils. The relative hardness of surface rock influences the paths of stream drainage. Climatic patterns also influence the natural vegetation of a region.

The delimitation of natural regions involves as much the geographer's art as science. From 1869 through 1874, Samuel H. Lockett of the Louisiana State Seminary (now Louisiana State University) traversed the state, compiled notes, and drafted a topographic map and manuscript dividing the state into several regions. A century later Lockett's regions and map were modified somewhat by Fred B. Kniffen of Louisiana State University's Department of Geography and Anthropology. The map shown is based largely on Lockett's work as modified by Kniffen. Lines separating the regions often represent zones of transition rather than sharply defined boundaries.

Five natural regions together comprise Louisiana. These regions are termed (1) coastal marshes, (2) the Mississippi floodplain, (3) the Red River valley, (4) terraces, and (5) hills. The first, fourth, and fifth terms denote topographic features which occur in many areas. The second and third are more specific and have exerted particular influences on the state.

The coastal marshes represent the transition zone between land and ocean. Both elevation and relief are low; rising above the low surfaces are cheniers and salt domes. The southern situation and marine influences produce the longest growing season in the state, as well as abundant rainfall, in the marshes; the coastal location also provides a gateway for hurricanes (Map 13). Both freshwater and saltwater marshes exist in these coastal wetlands, each with its typical vegetation. This region is important for its wildlife and fisheries resources; many refuges and preserves have been established (Map 8), and the fishing industry is an important economic asset (Map 83).

The Mississippi floodplain dominates the north-south axis of Louisiana. This region can be divided into (1) the passes, (2) natural levees, and (3) swamps. The passes represent the present delta, where both elevation and relief are low, where the river divides its flow into several distributary channels, and where lakes form between the natural levees of the channels. Specific features found here include mudlumps and bars. The natural levees represent those natural riverbanks built up over time by flood-deposited sediments; they stand somewhat above the surrounding floodplain and have in recent years been augmented by human endeavor. Natural levees follow along both the present and ancient courses of the Mississippi. Away from the levees occur swamps, occupying low-lying areas such as the Tensas Basin and the Atchafalaya Basin (Map 5). Soils vary with the relative size of the sediments composing their bulk.

The Red River valley represents on a smaller scale many of the features of the Mississippi floodplain focused on a single stream. A floodplain, natural levees, and low-lying areas occupied in former times by raft lakes (created by logjams on the river and now stabilized by human efforts)—all are contained within the valley. The red soils of the region carried by the river give that stream its name.

The terraces region comprises those ancient structures formed by the ice-age Mississippi, either along the flanks of the present floodplain or as "islands" surrounded by the more recent alluvial region. Three subregions comprise the terraces: (1) the blufflands, (2) the flatwoods, and (3) the prairies. The blufflands have the highest relief; the presence of loess (wind-deposited sediments) accounts for the more vertical slopes and higher relief. Both the flatwoods and the prairies have lower relief. They are distinguished from each other more vegetatively; the former's cover was a mixed longleaf pine forest, whereas the latter supported a grassland vegetation. All three terrace regions illustrate dendritic (tree-like branches) drainage patterns.

The hill country of western and north central Louisiana and the Florida Parishes represents the highest elevations in the state. Here are located the oldest rocks within Louisiana. Streams have dissected the raised uplands and ridges (cuestas, wolds), following strata of less resistant rock in a dendritic or a trellis pattern. Relief is also at its greatest and most varied, and the hills and valleys support a forest of mixed pine and hardwoods. Longleaf pine once dominated in the southern portions, and shortleaf pine in the northern.

Copyright © 1995 by the University of Oklahoma Press

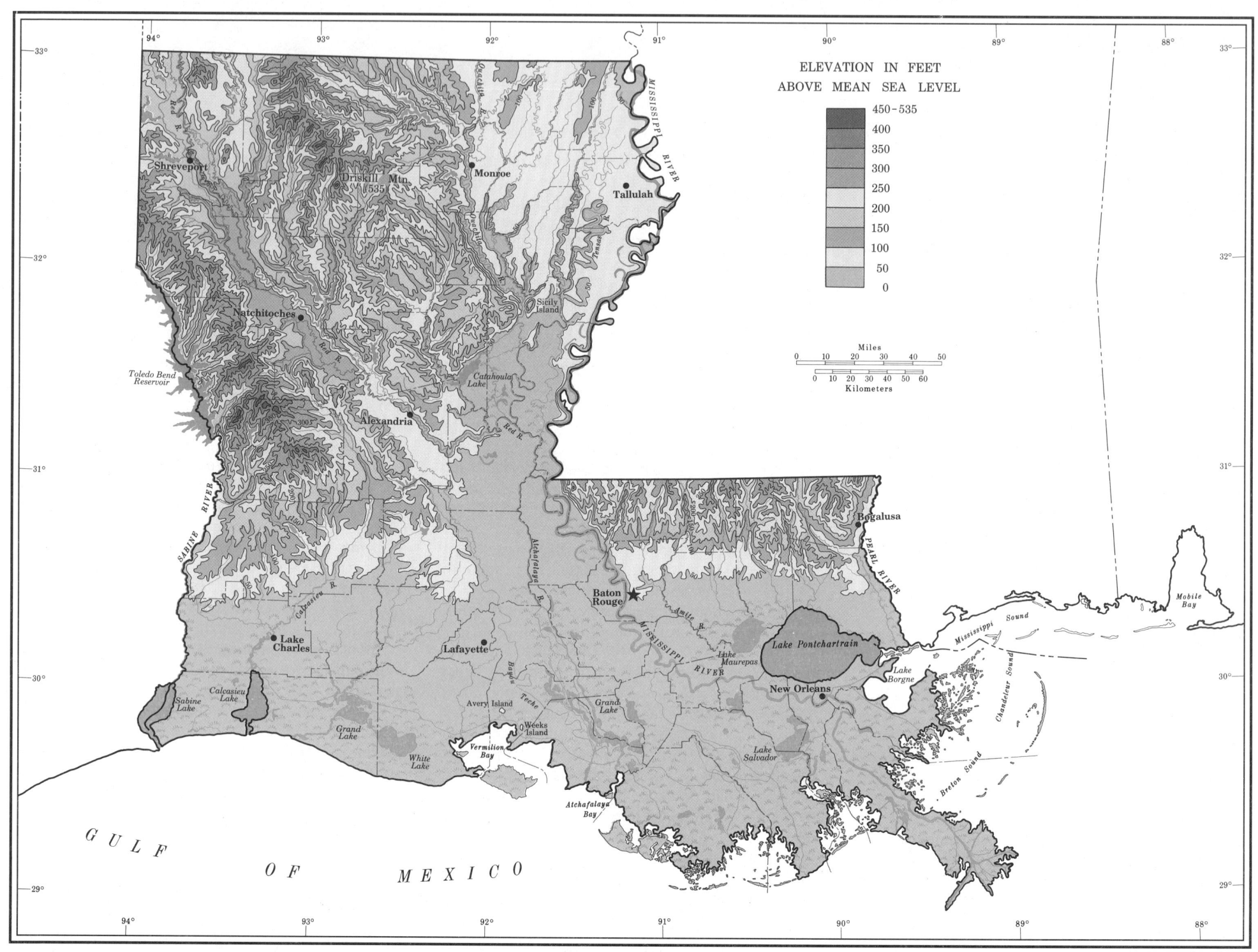

ELEVATION IN FEET
ABOVE MEAN SEA LEVEL

450 – 535
400
350
300
250
200
150
100
50
0

Miles
0 10 20 30 40 50

0 10 20 30 40 50 60
Kilometers

GULF   OF   MEXICO

4. CONTOUR MAP

Contours are lines which connect points of equal elevation, a measure of absolute height. Points along any given contour stand equally high above mean sea level. A contour map represents the reality of the earth's surface in two-dimensional cartography. The "contour interval" is the change in elevation between adjacent contours. Given the scale of the map and the speed of change in elevation, a contour interval might be as little as five feet but could range up into hundreds or thousands of feet.

Relief measures the difference between the highest and lowest elevations in a given area and is therefore a relative value. Areas of low relief have a more level terrain, and vice versa. Closely spaced contours denote high relief (steep slopes), while widely spaced contours denote low relief (more level slopes). Areas of high elevation may have low relief, just as areas of low elevation may have high relief. By considering both elevation and relief, one determines more of the topographic character of an area than either measure alone provides.

Louisiana's elevation ranges from 5 feet below mean sea level in part of New Orleans to 535 feet above sea level at the top of Mount Driskill in Bienville Parish. Thus, the total relief within the state as a whole measures only 540 feet. As a means of comparison, the Capitol at Baton Rouge stands 450 feet high; another nine stories on top would give it a height approximately equal to the state's total relief. As another comparison, we know that Baton Rouge lies along the fifty-foot contour. When that figure is added to the Capitol's

height, the top then stands five hundred feet above sea level. Mount Driskill stands only thirty-five feet higher.

Louisiana's geologic history is mirrored in the spacing of its contour lines. The Mississippi River alluvial floodplain and adjacent coastal plains largely shaped by the river in recent geologic time are reflected by both low elevations and low relief. All along the Gulf Coast one must travel several miles inland before reaching a point five feet or more above sea level. Much of the state lies below the fifty-foot contour; more than half is less than one hundred feet high. Throughout the floodplain proper of the Mississippi and along the southern and coastal regions of the state, relief is generally less than fifty feet. Exceptions do exist. The Five Islands (salt domes) reach much higher above the surrounding surface, to elevations up to 171 feet at Weeks Island.

Only when one reaches the upland areas does one find higher elevations and relief. Even there, however, neither the elevation nor the relief is great. A hilly surface exists, but the term "mount" when applied to Driskill and other summits should not be confused with mountains such as the Rockies or even the much lower Appalachians.

Three general areas of highlands exist in Louisiana: in the western and north central regions and along the northern portion of the Florida Parishes. In the Kisatchie Hills along the Natchitoches-Vernon parish border and in the region of Driskill Mountain in Bienville and Claiborne parishes, elevations rise above four hundred feet. These two upland areas are separated by

the valley cut by the Red River. The third upland region, in the Florida Parishes, has elevations approaching four hundred feet.

Local relief varies throughout the state, again greater in the hill country, where relief might equal three hundred feet within a few miles, as in the area around Mount Driskill. Contrasted with this are the prairies of southwest Louisiana, where relief is low except along stream valleys or terrace walls. The overall slope or inclination of the land in the prairies averages one foot per mile; in the coastal marshes the average slope is measured in inches per mile.

ELEVATIONS OF SELECTED CITIES
(in feet above sea level)

City	Elevation	City	Elevation
Alexandria	75	Mansfield	330
Arcadia	368	Marksville	87
Bastrop	130	Monroe	81
Baton Rouge	50	Morgan City	6
Bernice	226	Natchitoches	120
Bogalusa	100	New Iberia	20
Clinton	186	New Orleans	0
Columbia	61	Opelousas	70
Coushatta	132	Ruston	312
Gretna	5	St. Francisville	110
Hammond	44	Shreveport	204
Homer	281	Tallulah	91
Houma	14	Thibodaux	15
Lafayette	40	Vidalia	60
Lake Charles	22	Winnfield	118
Lake Providence	106	Winnsboro	72
Leesville	238		

Copyright © 1995 by the University of Oklahoma Press

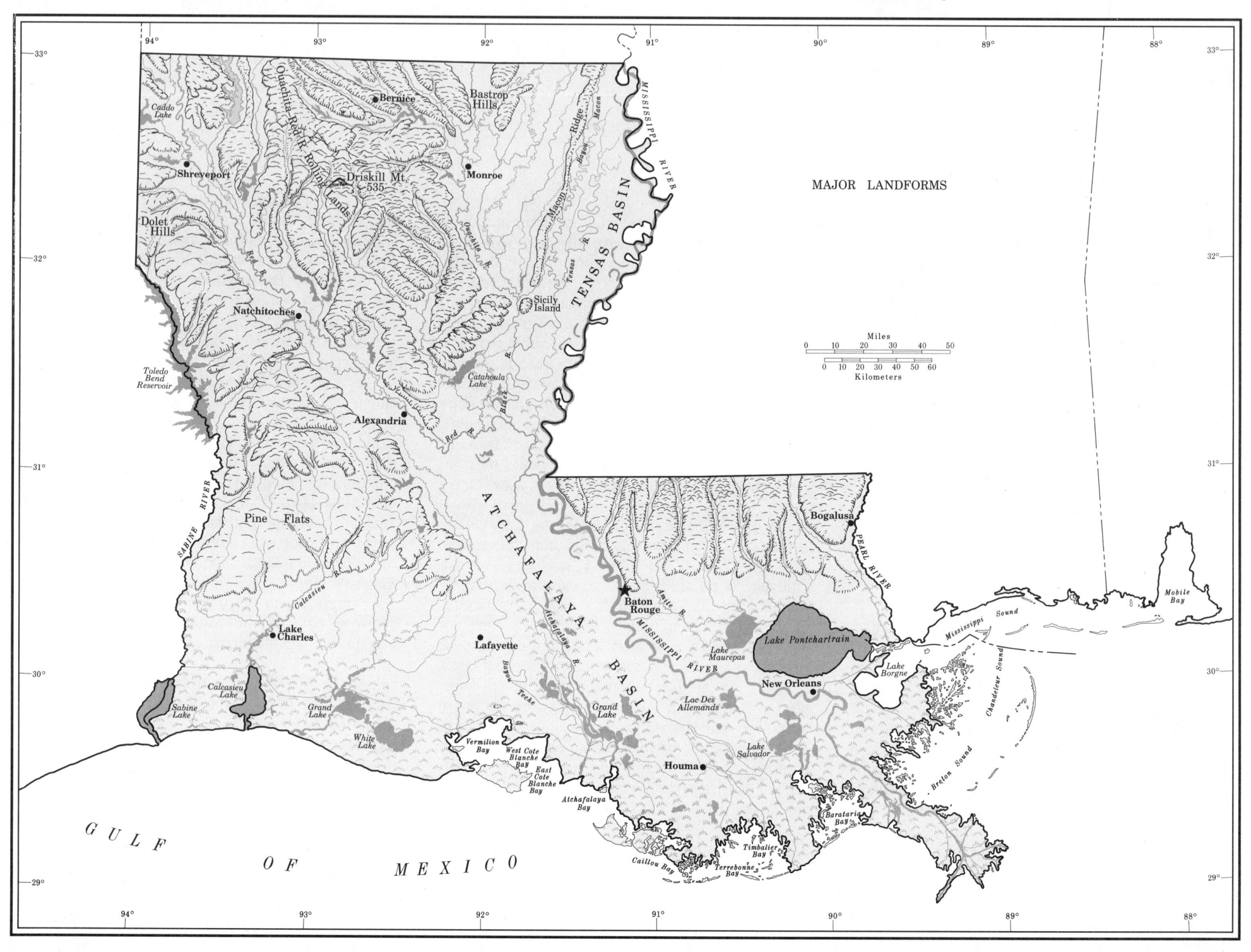

MAJOR LANDFORMS

Caddo
Lake

Bernice

Bastrop
Hills

Ouachita-Red R. Rolling Lands

Shreveport

Driskill Mt.
535

Monroe

Macon Ridge

Macon

Bayou

MISSISSIPPI RIVER

Dolet
Hills

Red R.

Ouachita R.

Tensas R.

TENSAS BASIN

Natchitoches

Sicily
Island

Black R.

Toledo
Bend
Reservoir

Catahoula
Lake

SABINE RIVER

Alexandria

Red R.

Pine   Flats

Bogalusa

ATCHAFALAYA   BASIN

PEARL RIVER

Calcasieu

Baton
Rouge

Amite R.

Lake
Charles

Lafayette

Atchafalaya R.

MISSISSIPPI RIVER

Lake
Maurepas

Lake Pontchartrain

Lake
Borgne

Mobile
Bay

Sabine
Lake

Calcasieu
Lake

Grand
Lake

Bayou Teche

Grand
Lake

New Orleans

Lac Des
Allemands

Mississippi

Sound

Chandeleur Sound

White
Lake

Vermilion
Bay

West Cote
Blanche
Bay

East
Cote
Blanche
Bay

Lake
Salvador

Breton Sound

Houma

Barataria
Bay

Atchafalaya
Bay

Timbalier
Bay

Caillou Bay

Terrebonne
Bay

G U L F   O F   M E X I C O

Miles
0 10 20 30 40 50

0 10 20 30 40 50 60
Kilometers

5. MAJOR LANDFORMS

A contour map (Map 4) provides us with an abstract view of the actual landscape, rendering the earth's surface in an exact yet artificial manner. Another means of portraying the surface features of a region is the physiographic diagram, a sort of sketch map. A physiographic diagram allows a somewhat three-dimensional view of landforms within only the two dimensions a flat map provides. Such a diagram also allows the addition of common names to the actual physical features.

All of Louisiana lies within the general region of the continent known as the Gulf Coastal Plain. Three subregions exist. The Florida Parishes are a part of the East Gulf Coastal Plain, and western Louisiana is a part of the West Gulf Coastal Plain. Separating them is the Mississippi Alluvial Plain.

A coastal plain contains low relief and overall low elevation, generally less than five hundred feet. The plain consists of sedimentary layers deposited by streams and by the ocean itself along its shifting coastline during the past seventy million years. Over time the interior of the state has become elevated, and because of continued erosion, older deposits have become exposed at the surface. At the same time, the eroded materials have been laid down along valleys and the shore. Thus, as one moves from shoreline inland, one generally moves from newer sediments to older, even as one moves into areas of higher elevation.

Several types of landforms are found within Louisiana. Hilly uplands are located in the western and north central parts of the state and in the Florida Parishes. These hills are associated with "domes," layers of rock which have been folded upward. As these domes wear away through erosion, layers of resistant rock form ridges (also called wolds or cuestas). One such dome is the Sabine Uplift in western Louisiana, centered in the area known as the Dolet Hills. The Nacogdoches and Kisatchie wolds are ridges which curve around the edges of the Sabine Uplift through the hills of western and north central Louisiana. The highest point in Louisiana—Driskill Mountain—is associated with the ridge pattern of the Nacogdoches Wold and stands some 535 feet above sea level in northern Bienville Parish. A second dome in north Louisiana is the Monroe Uplift.

In the Florida Parishes the hill country results from an upwarping (rock strata upwardly bending along a line) known as the Wiggins Anticline, whose features cross the Louisiana state line into Mississippi. The hill country in the western portion of the Florida Parishes is more rugged than its eastern area because of the presence of loess, generally thought to be wind-deposited sediments laid down during the ice ages. Vertical bluffs form in these silty deposits, creating a steeper terrain.

Several areas of ancient terraces are also found around the state. Terraces form over time when shifting global water levels cause rivers first to deposit, then to erode away alluvial material. If, at the same time, an uplifting of the entire area occurs, a terrace remains as a higher relic of a previous era. Although modern streams are also in the process of constructing terraces, many of the larger terrace features in Louisiana are remnants of the Pleistocene era, the period of the ice ages, when stream flow and sea level fluctuated widely and deposits were laid down over vast areas (Maps 9 and 11). The Pine Flats in central west Louisiana are part of these ancient terraces, as is an area skirting the Florida Parish hill country. Macon Ridge, Sicily Island, and the Bastrop Hills are also relic remnants of a previous Mississippi River terrace whose flanks have been eroded by the Ouachita, Tensas, and Mississippi rivers.

As the hills and terraces were uplifted over time, streams began to carve valleys through them. These valleys appear today in a variety of sizes, from the Mississippi and the Red through the Ouachita and Calcasieu to those of the smallest creeks and bayous. The floodplains of these watercourses provide a relatively level surface which contrasts to the uplands rising noticeably—sometimes steeply—along their flanks. Across these floodplains streams develop naturally into meandering paths which have shifted constantly through time until the advent of modern human efforts at restraining them. The Red River valley (the lower end of its overall basin), the Tensas Basin, and the Atchafalaya Basin are all examples of river basins.

The most recent physiographic area of Louisiana is located along the coast and interior south of the ancient terraces and Mississippi alluvial valley. This region of prairie, swamp, and marsh, largely flat with natural levees, cheniers, and salt domes punctuating its surface, represents the deposition of sediments by the Mississippi and other streams over the past six thousand years (Maps 11 and 12). Traversing the region are former distributary channels of the Mississippi as well as other bayous and rivers. Offshore are islands formed by the action of wind and water on deposits laid down over the millennia by the Mississippi River. The region of wetlands along Louisiana's coast is the most fragile of all the state's areas, subject to the ravages occasioned by both nature and humankind.

Copyright © 1995 by the University of Oklahoma Press

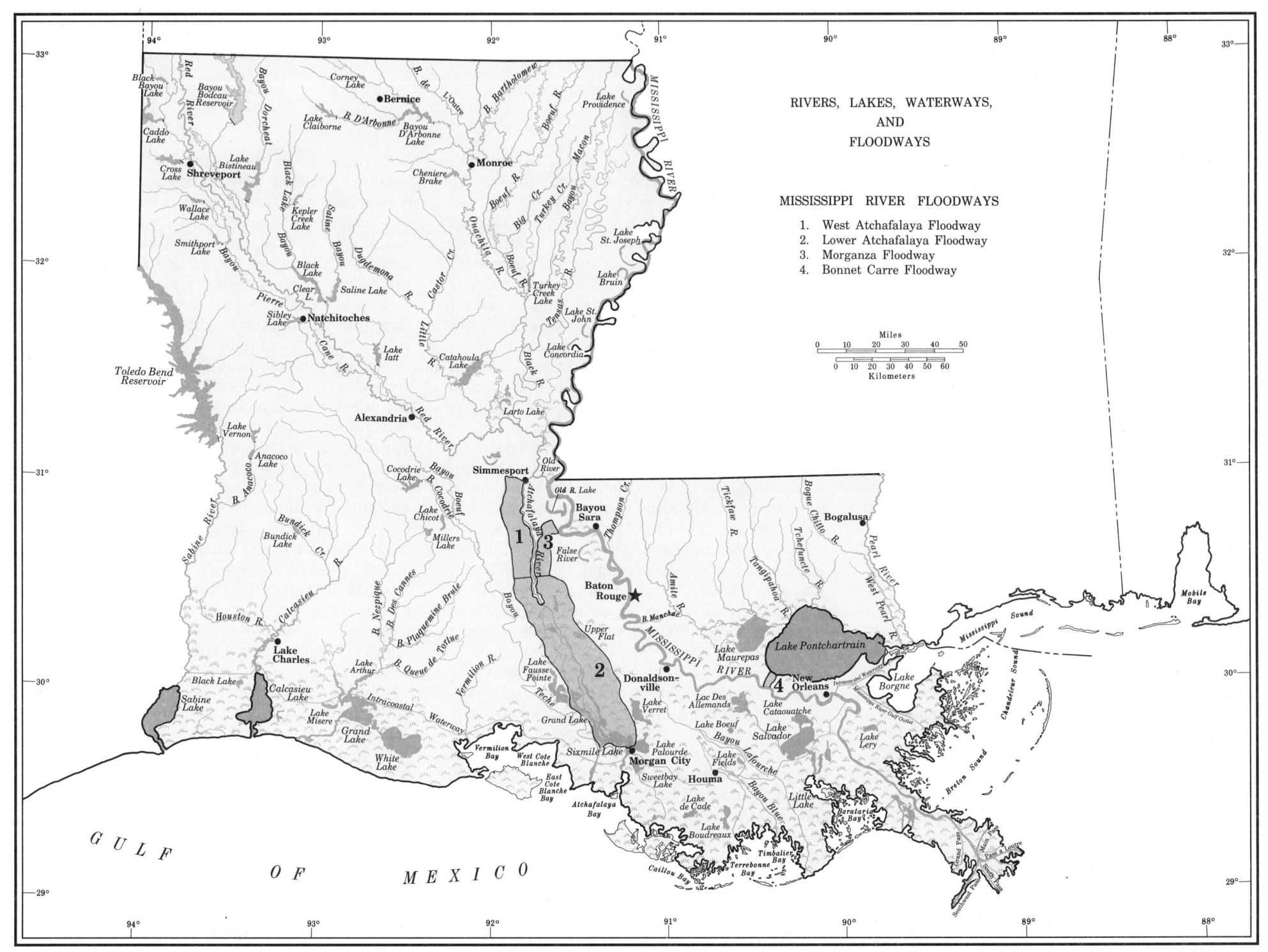

RIVERS, LAKES, WATERWAYS,
AND
FLOODWAYS

MISSISSIPPI RIVER FLOODWAYS

1. West Atchafalaya Floodway
2. Lower Atchafalaya Floodway
3. Morganza Floodway
4. Bonnet Carre Floodway

6. RIVERS, LAKES, WATERWAYS, AND FLOODWAYS

Louisiana is traversed by watercourses, from the Mighty Mississippi, the Father of Waters, to the smallest rivulet, intermittent with rainfall. At least twenty-nine streams are classed as navigable by the U.S. Army Corps of Engineers. Natural lakes also lie scattered about the state. Especially in the twentieth century, dams, levees, and other structures have been erected to create, "improve," or otherwise modify what nature provides.

The Mississippi River dominates not only the state but also the continent, with a drainage basin touching thirty-one states and two Canadian provinces and encompassing over 1,245,000 square miles. From the Arkansas boundary to the Gulf the river flows some 569 miles, but with an average gradient of only two and one-half inches per mile. The Mississippi this far downstream receives few tributaries but has over the eons fed several distributary streams (Map 12). Within Louisiana the river is widest in East Carroll Parish (7,600 feet) and narrowest at Irvine Light near Bayou Sara in West Feliciana Parish (1,700 feet). Since 1880 but especially following the disastrous 1927 flood, efforts have been made to stabilize the river in its present course by means of levees and artificial distributary "floodways" through which excess water is diverted.

Although pale in comparison with the Mississippi, other river systems drain various parts of the states. The second largest is the Red River, rising in New Mexico, entering Louisiana in the northwest corner, and moving southeastward to its confluence with the Atchafalaya and Mississippi at the "Old River" area. Tributaries to the Red include Bayou Pierre, Bayou Dorcheat, Saline Bayou, Black Lake Bayou, and Little River. In the northeast the Ouachita-Black flows southward

from Arkansas to the Red. In turn, the Ouachita-Black receives water from the Tensas River–Bayou Macon system, Boeuf River, Bayou D'Arbonne, Bayou de L'Outre, and Bayou Bartholomew.

Southwest Louisiana is drained by two main systems—the Sabine and the Calcasieu. Rising in north central Texas, the Sabine receives several small tributaries in Louisiana before falling into the Gulf. It forms the Louisiana-Texas border for almost three hundred miles. The Calcasieu, lying entirely within Louisiana, bends first to the east then back to the west before emptying into Calcasieu Lake, thence to the Gulf. Other major streams in this region are the Mermentau and Vermilion.

The major south Louisiana streams are the Teche, Atchafalaya, and Lafourche, all of whose courses lie totally within the state. All three are former courses of the Mississippi, the latter two more recently distributary streams. Bayou Teche winds its way from Port Barre, St. Landry Parish, to the Atchafalaya at Morgan City. The Atchafalaya emerges from the junction of the Red and Mississippi, thence flows southward to the Gulf. Recently the Mississippi has attempted to send more and more water down the Atchafalaya. Since 1954 the Old River Control Structure at Simmesport has been constructed and strengthened to prevent yet another change in the Mississippi's main channel. Further south, the Lafourche, once a natural distributary to the Mississippi, now feeds on water pumped over the levees at Donaldsonville on its route to the Gulf.

In the Florida Parishes several streams flow out from Mis sissippi generally southward to Lakes Maurepas, Pontchartrain, or Borgne. From west to east these streams include the Amite, Tickfaw,

Tangipahoa, Tchefuncte, Bogue Chitto, and Pearl. One tributary to the Amite, the Bayou Manchac, was once a distributary of the Mississippi used to help define the Isle of Orleans, so long the key to Louisiana.

The Intracoastal Waterway, a largely artificial watercourse, extends across Louisiana as part of a system that runs along the Atlantic and Gulf coasts. This 318-mile waterway affords an east-west route not provided by natural streams. Other watercourses created by the Corps of Engineers—Bonnet Carre, Morganza, and Atchafalaya floodways; Mississippi River–Gulf Outlet; and others—also assist navigation and flood control.

Various types of natural lakes exist. Cut-off or oxbow lakes (for example, False River, Bruin, Larto) form when a stream "cuts off" the neck of a meander (bend) to create a new course. Particularly along the valley of the Red, raft lakes (Caddo, Cross, Bistineau, Black, and others) were formed from waters dammed by the Great Raft, a tremendous logjam that clogged that river until it was finally removed in 1873. Lagoonal lakes (for example, White, Grand, Calcasieu) form along the coast when cheniers (beach ridges) act to slow the flow of rivers while also protecting the resulting lake from encroachment by the Gulf. Lakes Pontchartrain, Maurepas, and Catahoula exist in grabens, depressions in the earth bounded by faults. Other natural lakes are associated with the drainage in the vicinity of rivers, deltas, and salt domes. Of more recent vintage are reservoirs created by the damming of streams for flood control and recreational purposes. The largest of these is Toledo Bend; others include D'Arbonne, Claiborne, Sibley, and Cocodrie.

Copyright © 1995 by the University of Oklahoma Press

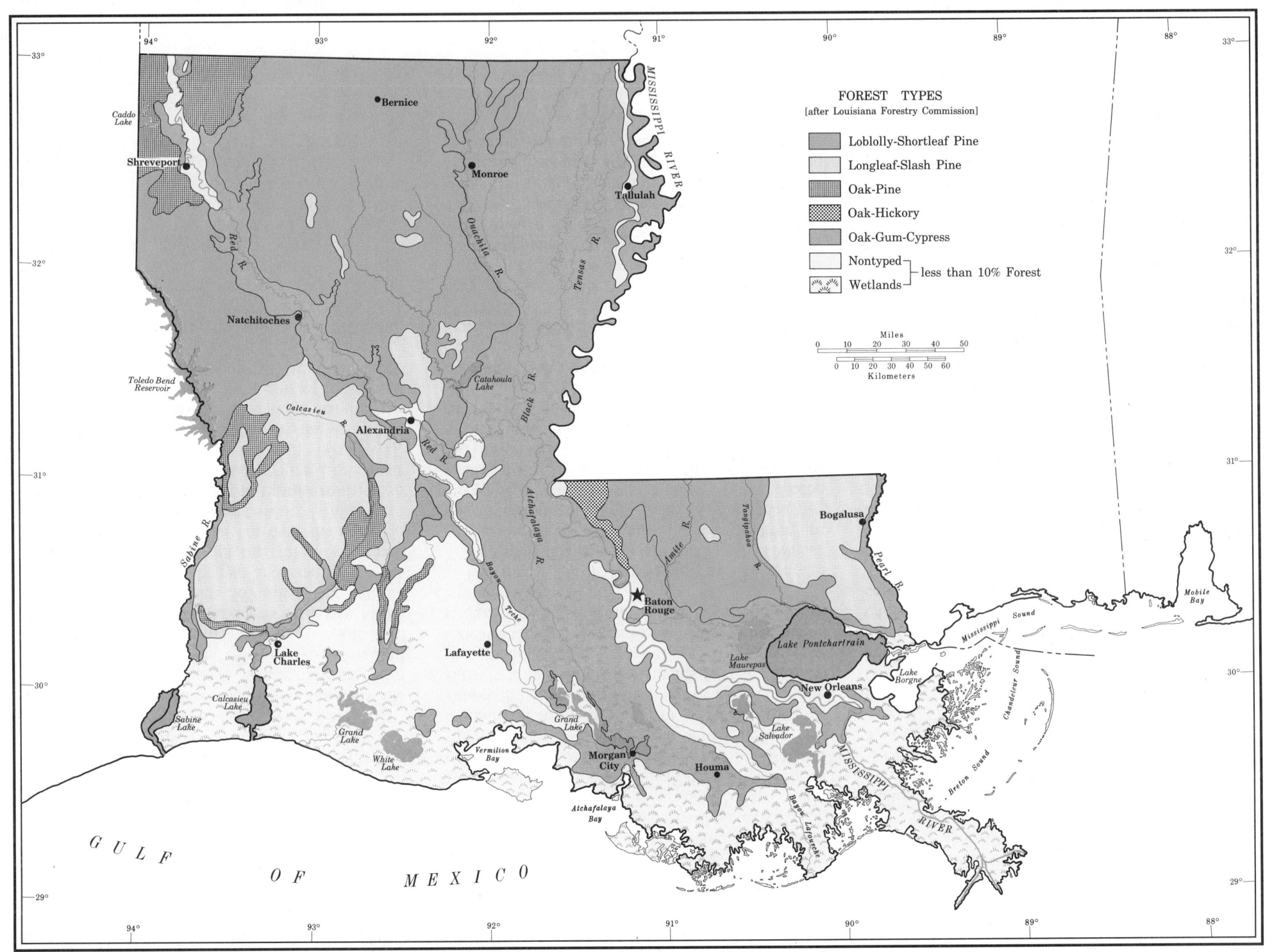

FOREST TYPES
[after Louisiana Forestry Commission]

Loblolly-Shortleaf Pine

Longleaf-Slash Pine

Oak-Pine

Oak-Hickory

Oak-Gum-Cypress

Nontyped ⎤
          ⎬— less than 10% Forest
Wetlands ⎦

Miles
0 10 20 30 40 50

0 10 20 30 40 50 60
Kilometers

Caddo Lake

Shreveport

•**Bernice**

•**Monroe**

•**Tallulah**

MISSISSIPPI RIVER

Red R.

Ouachita R.

Tensas R.

Natchitoches•

Catahoula Lake

Toledo Bend Reservoir

Calcasieu R.

Black R.

Alexandria•

Red R.

Atchafalaya R.

Sabine R.

Bogalusa

Amite R.

Tangipahoa R.

Pearl R.

★**Baton Rouge**

Lafayette•

Bayou Teche

Lake Maurepas

Lake Pontchartrain

Lake Borgne

Mississippi Sound

Mobile Bay

•**Lake Charles**

Calcasieu Lake

Sabine Lake

Grand Lake

White Lake

Vermilion Bay

Grand Lake

Morgan City

Houma•

Lake Salvador

New Orleans

Chandeleur Sound

Breton Sound

MISSISSIPPI RIVER

Bayou Lafourche

Atchafalaya Bay

G U L F   O F   M E X I C O

7. FOREST TYPES

Except for the coastal marshes and the southwestern prairies, the state's original, natural vegetation consisted of mixed forests of evergreen and deciduous trees. Travelers speak of towering forests and an almost parklike landscape in the hills and terraces; frequent fires plus the natural canopy of trees prevented extensive undergrowth. The alluvial valleys had produced equally magnificent stands of cypress, oak, magnolia and other hardwoods intermixed with canebrakes.

Louisiana's natural forests had developed over centuries. A complex pattern of oak, gum, magnolia, cottonwood, sycamore, cypress, tupelo, and other largely deciduous trees dominated in the alluvial, bluff, and terrace lands. Individual species varied largely with elevation and relief, hence susceptibility to flooding and ease of drainage. The uplands and part of the terraces were occupied by longleaf pine forests in some regions and in others by shortleaf or longleaf pine mixed to varying degrees with oak, hickory, and other hardwoods.

Human modification of the forest commenced with the earliest migration into the region. The forests provided food for both humans and the other animals on which they fed. Fire was another means by which these prehistoric inhabitants altered Louisiana's forests.

Historical development of the state's forest resources began in colonial times. However, the last decade of the nineteenth century and early decades of the twentieth witnessed the systematic cutting of the state's virgin forests. The major lumber companies, always in search of new supplies of timber, swooped down upon Louisiana from the north and east. Huge sawmills sprang up across the state, fed by the massive trees hauled in over logging railroads or dragged and skidded over the land or water by cable. Company towns developed around the major mills; other railroads sprang up in part to market the products of Louisiana's forests.

After the land was cut over, the major companies left the state for more western forests, following the old principle of "cut out and get out." Believing that decades or longer would be required for the forests to return, and seeking to escape a heavy tax burden, the companies let the land revert to the state for nonpayment of those taxes. Company towns disappeared, scrub forests took over, and small farmers bought much of the cut-over land. Erosion increased on the denuded landscape, and previously navigable streams silted.

Following World War II, much of the hill-country farm system proved uneconomical. Scrub forests occupied some land, but a new policy emerged of "sustained yield," of planting trees and treating the forest as a renewable resource. In addition to these new pine tree plantations, other former cut-over lands were turned into Kisatchie National Forest and state preserves. Today, 8 percent of Louisiana's forests are owned by various governments, 31 percent by wood-products companies, and 61 percent by individuals.

The present, generalized configuration of Louisiana's forests divides the state into five categories. About half of the total forest today is composed of hardwood species, and half of softwood species. Three-quarters of the softwood trees are loblolly pine and shortleaf pine.

A loblolly-shortleaf pine forest dominates north central Louisiana, an area west of the Red, and the middle of the Florida Parishes. A longleaf-slash pine forest is located largely in west central Louisiana and in the eastern third of the Florida Parishes. Both loblolly and slash pine have grown in predominance, even as the longleaf pine region has shrunk, because the former are well suited to growth on cut-over lands.

Oak-pine forests are situated in the northwest corner and on the border of the western longleaf-slash pine region. An oak-hickory forest grows on the bluffs along the western edge of the Florida Parishes. Finally, an oak-gum-cypress forest region occupies the Mississippi and Red River alluvial valleys and along the valleys of other watercourses.

Some regions have little if any forested areas today. The southwestern prairies and the coastal marshes are not naturally forested areas. Instead, they sustain natural grasses such as bluestem, broom sedge, water grass, and switchgrass, with trees following watercourses across the prairies or clumped on elevated portions of the marshes. Grazing occurs over much of the state. Urban areas occupy areas formerly forested. Other regions along the Red, Mississippi, and other alluvial areas are cultivated or industrialized. The state prison farm at Angola at the northwest corner of the Florida Parishes is another notable nonforested region.

Even the original "natural" forests of the region changed through time. Fires started by lightning favored those species that were better able to withstand the stress. Today's forest with its original as well as introduced species represents much more the direct and indirect human intervention of the past three centuries.

Copyright © 1995 by the University of Oklahoma Press

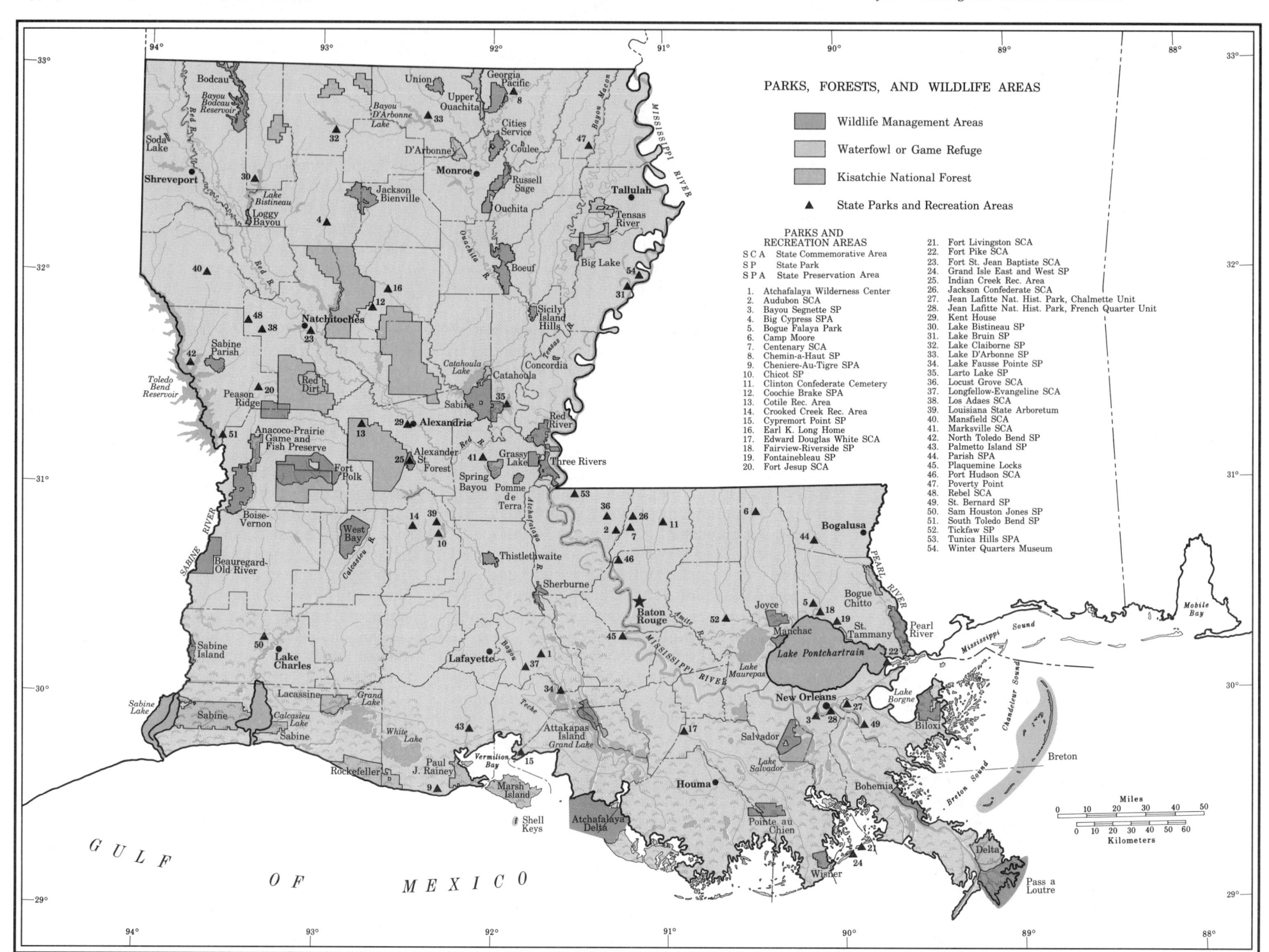

PARKS, FORESTS, AND WILDLIFE AREAS

- Wildlife Management Areas
- Waterfowl or Game Refuge
- Kisatchie National Forest
- ▲ State Parks and Recreation Areas

PARKS AND RECREATION AREAS

S C A State Commemorative Area
S P State Park
S P A State Preservation Area

1. Atchafalaya Wilderness Center
2. Audubon SCA
3. Bayou Segnette SP
4. Big Cypress SPA
5. Bogue Falaya Park
6. Camp Moore
7. Centenary SCA
8. Chemin-a-Haut SP
9. Cheniere-Au-Tigre SPA
10. Chicot SP
11. Clinton Confederate Cemetery
12. Coochie Brake SPA
13. Cotile Rec. Area
14. Crooked Creek Rec. Area
15. Cypremort Point SP
16. Earl K. Long Home
17. Edward Douglas White SCA
18. Fairview-Riverside SP
19. Fontainebleau SP
20. Fort Jesup SCA

21. Fort Livingston SCA
22. Fort Pike SCA
23. Fort St. Jean Baptiste SCA
24. Grand Isle East and West SP
25. Indian Creek Rec. Area
26. Jackson Confederate SCA
27. Jean Lafitte Nat. Hist. Park, Chalmette Unit
28. Jean Lafitte Nat. Hist. Park, French Quarter Unit
29. Kent House
30. Lake Bistineau SP
31. Lake Bruin SP
32. Lake Claiborne SP
33. Lake D'Arbonne SP
34. Lake Fausse Pointe SP
35. Larto Lake SP
36. Locust Grove SCA
37. Longfellow-Evangeline SCA
38. Los Adaes SCA
39. Louisiana State Arboretum
40. Mansfield SCA
41. Marksville SCA
42. North Toledo Bend SP
43. Palmetto Island SP
44. Parish SPA
45. Plaquemine Locks
46. Port Hudson SCA
47. Poverty Point
48. Rebel SCA
49. St. Bernard SP
50. Sam Houston Jones SP
51. South Toledo Bend SP
52. Tickfaw SP
53. Tunica Hills SPA
54. Winter Quarters Museum

The growth of parks, recreational areas, refuges, and the like, within Louisiana has paralleled similar national developments. The conservation movement of the late nineteenth and early twentieth centuries spurred the creation of national parks, forests, and wildlife refuges. Much of that effort centered in the western states, where public lands still predominated; older, more settled states had fewer such resources. State conservation efforts followed (and sometimes led) national programs, first to provide basic ecological protection and management and later to cater to increasing free time among citizens, to serve an important tourist industry, and also to preserve state cultural landmarks.

Louisiana is home to the Poverty Point National Historic Landmark (operated by the National Park Service), the Kisatchie National Forest (managed by the U.S. Forest Service), and the Jean Lafitte National Historical Park. The park combines areas within the Mississippi Delta to preserve the Chalmette Battlefield (site of the Battle of New Orleans); the Isleños Museum in St. Bernard Parish; a visitor center in the French Quarter in New Orleans; and 8,600 acres of wetlands with hiking trails south of the city. Poverty Point (also a State Commemorative Area) preserves a relic of an ancient Indian culture. Kisatchie National Forest comprises 598,000 acres in six separate units in central and northern Louisiana. The forest was created from cut-over acreage that resulted from the first wave of industrial lumbering at the beginning of the twentieth century. Today it combines a sustained-yield forest, a wilderness unit, and many recreational areas.

Although efforts began in 1924 to create a state parks commission in Louisiana, only in 1934 was such a department formed. Before that time, however, private and public efforts had resulted in the Fort Pike, Fort Macomb, and Longfellow-Evangeline state parks, together comprising 298 acres. The development of park areas has been slow; more than half the units and two-thirds of the areas have been acquired since 1970. Following the creation of a new master plan in the 1970s greater activity resulted, fueled by increased revenues from state bond issues. By 1986 there existed forty-two separate units operational or under development, stewarded by the Office of State Parks in the Department of Culture, Recreation, and Tourism. These units comprised almost 37,000 acres.

The Loisiana State Parks Plan classifies five types of areas under its control. State Preservation Areas are "areas of exceptional scenic value" unlikely to remain preserved if retained in private hands. State Preservation Sites are smaller equivalents of the first category—areas that contain a "unique natural feature of ecological or scientific interest." State Commemorative Areas comprise those areas "which, when evaluated on a statewide basis, possess historical, cultural, or memorial significance." State Parks contain natural areas which, "when evaluated on a statewide basis possess outstanding potential for recreational utilization." A State Experimental Site contains "a natural area to be developed for experimentation and the training of park personnel." The most common classification for state areas is the state park.

In addition to parks and forests there exist both state and federal wildlife refuges and wildlife management areas. These areas contain both privately and publicly owned lands operated as waterfowl and wild animal refuges. Areas such as the Marsh Island (Russell Sage) and Rockefeller refuges, combined with state efforts by the McIlhenny family, represent the earliest such refuges, set up by private money. Later public moneys would be added to these ecological preserves. Endangered species are protected in these areas even as hunting for more plentiful species is allowed under regulations.

The development of parks, refuges, and other, similar areas serves to preserve Louisiana's natural and cultural legacy, to provide areas of recreation for the state's residents, and to generate tourism income from both within and without the state's boundaries. As definitions vary, however, what constitutes appropriate preservation, recreation, or other use of such lands does not meet with universal agreement. Too, with the collapse of oil prices in the 1980s the pace of state support has slowed, as with most areas of state agency activity. As public awareness and public and private interest in the ecosystem expand and deepen, both the growth and use of national and state areas within Louisiana will accelerate.

Copyright © 1995 by the University of Oklahoma Press

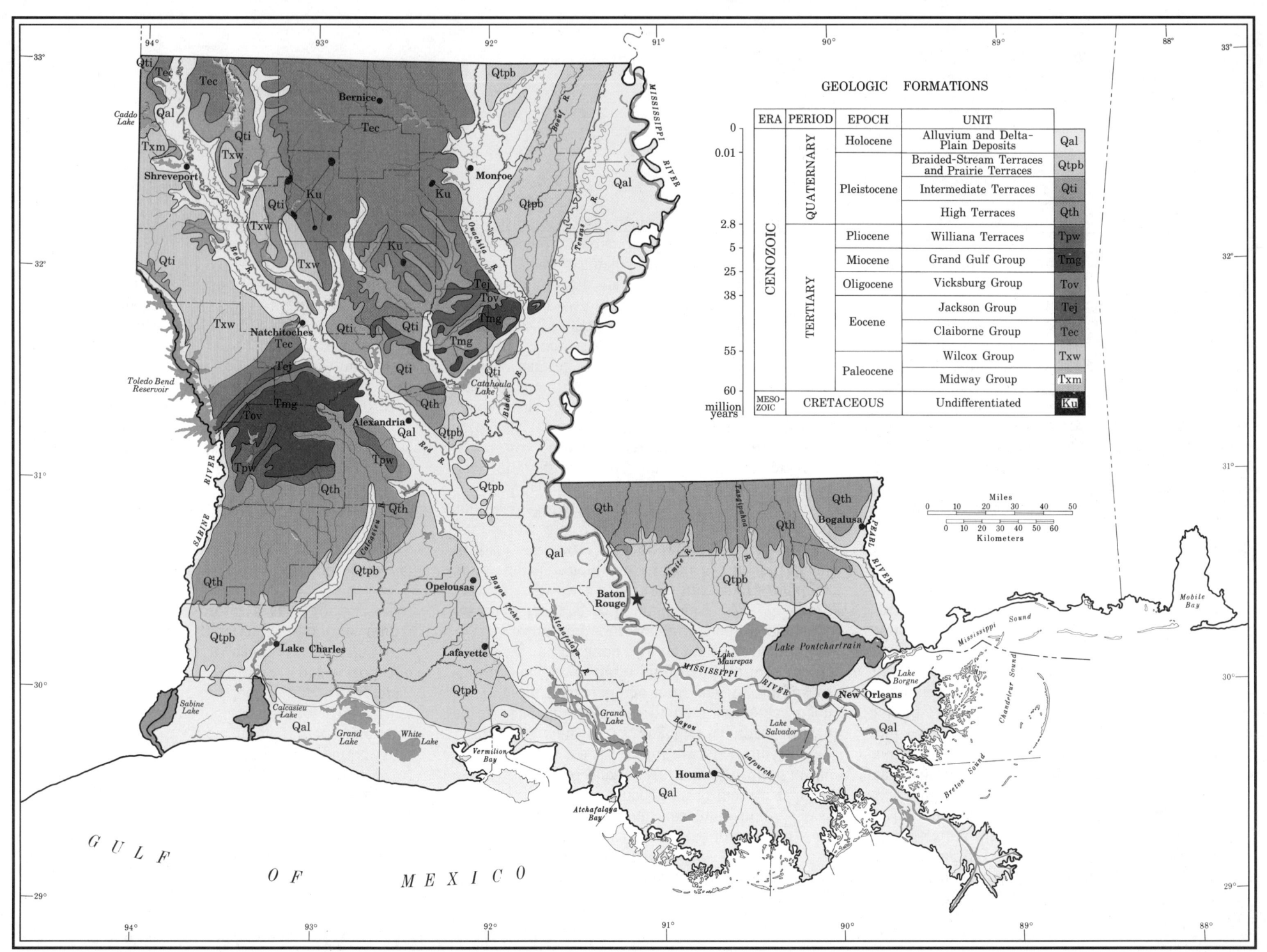

9. GEOLOGIC FORMATIONS

Geologists study the structure of the earth. In doing so they consider the physical forces at work as well as the history of particular formations. Across the millions of years of geologic history, various types of rock have been formed through the compression of sediments, the intrusion or extrusion of magma (molten rock from the earth's interior), or the heating and pressurization of existing rock. Through these methods are formed, respectively, sedimentary, igneous, or metamorphic rock.

Also occurring over these same eons have been shifts in the various plates which form the crust, the outer shell of the earth. Tectonic forces have caused the uplifting, downwarping, and fracturing of rock to produce often complex underground formations. The more recent period of the known ice ages has witnessed the rise and fall of sea level and the corresponding submergence or emergence of land surfaces. Erosion and deposition by wind, water, and ice have also shaped the land, wearing away at the surface while at the same time laying down elsewhere these sediments to form new deposits.

Geologic time is divided into five principal "eras": the Archeozoic (ancient life) and the Proterozoic (former life), dated to over 600 million years before the present (B.P.); the Paleozoic (old life), 600–225 million years B.P.; the Mesozoic (middle life), 225–70 million years B.P.; and the Cenozoic (new life), from 70 million years B.P. to the present. Practically all of Louisiana dates from the most recent era, the Cenozoic. Only in scattered areas of Bienville Parish and Ouachita Parish does one find older rock at or near the surface, older rock which has been pushed upward by interior salt domes as these features rose toward the surface.

The oldest widespread deposits in the state date from the Tertiary, one of the two (the other the Quaternary) "periods" into which the Cenozoic era is divided. These sedimentary rocks, called clays, shales, sandstones, limestones, conglomerates, and so on, based on the size of the original sediments which comprise them, were laid down in a broad expanse of water then covering much of the present state. As time progressed, the northern part of the present state was uplifted, and the Gulf receded. The various geologic "groups" of the five "epochs" which comprise the Tertiary period are found in the hill country of north central and western Louisiana.

During the Quaternary period, the most recent two million years of the earth's history, major changes occurred. The Pleistocene (most recent) epoch witnessed the advance and melting back of the great global ice sheets (although the ice never reached as far south as present-day Louisiana). During this ice age the Mississippi River was born, carrying with it the sediments scoured from the surface by the advancing ice. As the continental ice sheet formed, sea level dropped and the steeper gradient caused more erosion. Later, as the ice melted away and the sea level rose, the slighter gradient brought on more deposition than erosion. Thus, the cycle of erosion and deposition, combined with the gradual uplifting of the inland strata, produced a series of steplike surfaces from the prairies of southwest Louisiana to the various other terraces flanking the Mississippi floodplain.

Outliers such as Macon Ridge also date from the Pleistocene.

The Holocene (recent times) epoch, covering only the past ten thousand years, presents a seemingly more settled picture. The water level of the Gulf of Mexico has more or less stabilized, and the Mississippi and other streams are depositing new sediments on top of the older layers. The great floodplain of the Mississippi and the coastal plain seaward of the Quaternary terraces date from this most recent period. Various deltas built by the Mississippi have extended the coastline across south Louisiana from the Bayou Teche eastward to Lake Pontchartrain (Map 12). Until the middle of the twentieth century the Mississippi and other streams regularly flooded, laying down additional sediments on practically an annual basis. A meandering course across each floodplain added to the regional variation in deposits and alluvial erosion. With human efforts to control stream courses and prevent flooding (and with it the natural addition of sediments), much of the recently deposited coastal alluvium is being eroded away at a rate varying from 6 to 125 feet per year.

Thus, in geologic terms most of Louisiana at the surface is new. Generally the northern areas are older and more solid than the southern. However, even the passage of historic time illustrates the changes which the various geologic forces have brought to bear to form the structure of the state. Moreover, the story presented ever more clearly by the study of geology reveals the massive changes wrought in the earth over millions of years by processes whose causes are not yet fully understood and whose actions are still at work.

Copyright © 1995 by the University of Oklahoma Press

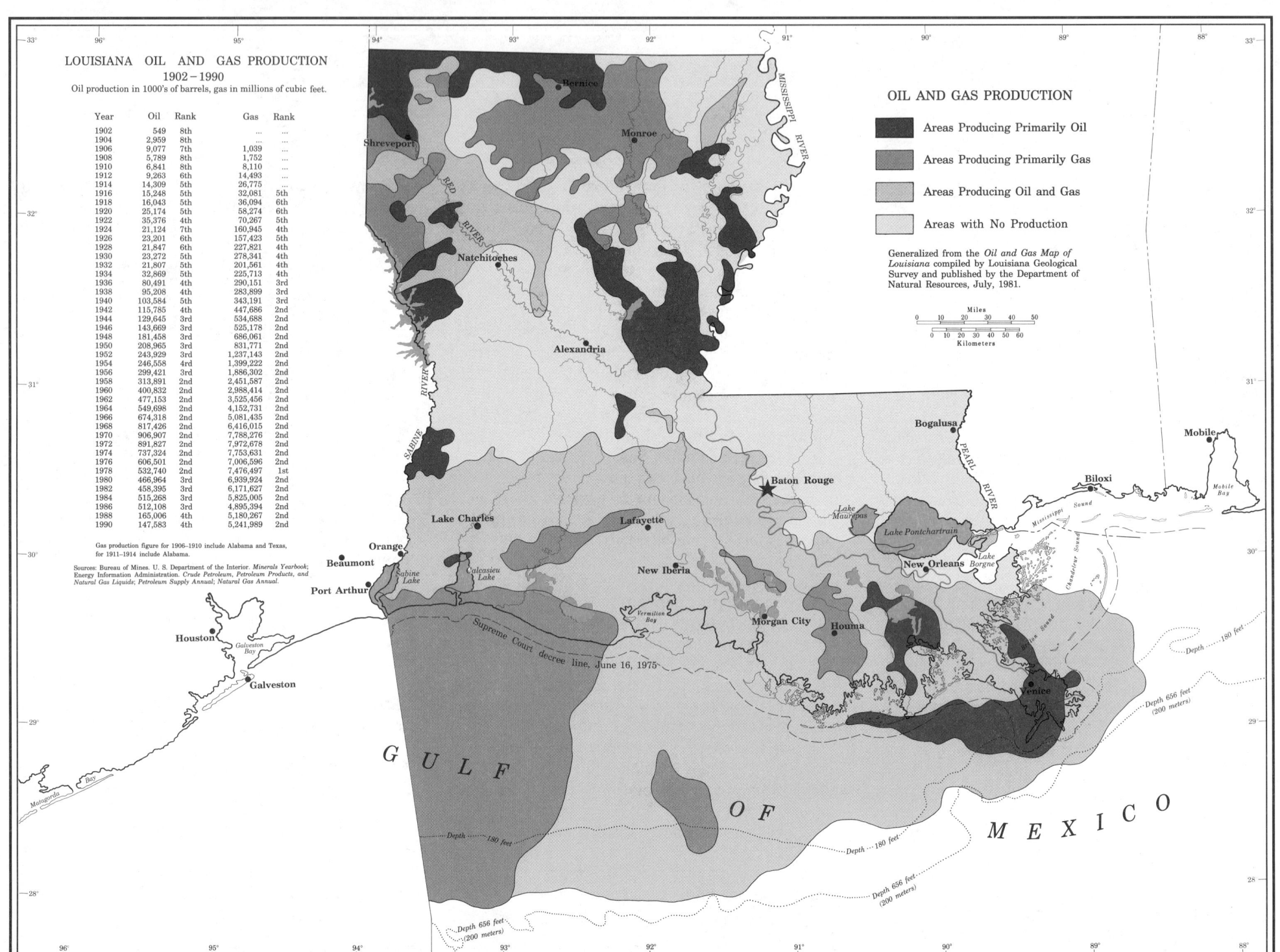

LOUISIANA OIL AND GAS PRODUCTION
1902–1990
Oil production in 1000's of barrels, gas in millions of cubic feet.

Year	Oil	Rank	Gas	Rank
1902	549	8th	...	...
1904	2,959	8th	...	...
1906	9,077	7th	1,039	...
1908	5,789	8th	1,752	...
1910	6,841	8th	8,110	...
1912	9,263	6th	14,493	...
1914	14,309	5th	26,775	...
1916	15,248	5th	32,081	5th
1918	16,043	5th	36,094	6th
1920	25,174	5th	58,274	6th
1922	35,376	4th	70,267	5th
1924	21,124	7th	160,945	4th
1926	23,201	6th	157,423	5th
1928	21,847	6th	227,821	4th
1930	23,272	5th	278,341	4th
1932	21,807	5th	201,561	4th
1934	32,869	5th	225,713	4th
1936	80,491	4th	290,151	3rd
1938	95,208	4th	283,899	3rd
1940	103,584	5th	343,191	3rd
1942	115,785	4th	447,686	2nd
1944	129,645	3rd	534,688	2nd
1946	143,669	3rd	525,178	2nd
1948	181,458	3rd	686,061	2nd
1950	208,965	3rd	831,771	2nd
1952	243,929	3rd	1,237,143	2nd
1954	246,558	4rd	1,399,222	2nd
1956	299,421	3rd	1,886,302	2nd
1958	313,891	2nd	2,451,587	2nd
1960	400,832	2nd	2,988,414	2nd
1962	477,153	2nd	3,525,456	2nd
1964	549,698	2nd	4,152,731	2nd
1966	674,318	2nd	5,081,435	2nd
1968	817,426	2nd	6,416,015	2nd
1970	906,907	2nd	7,788,276	2nd
1972	891,827	2nd	7,972,678	2nd
1974	737,324	2nd	7,753,631	2nd
1976	606,501	2nd	7,006,596	2nd
1978	532,740	2nd	7,476,497	1st
1980	466,964	3rd	6,939,924	2nd
1982	458,395	3rd	6,171,627	2nd
1984	515,268	3rd	5,825,005	2nd
1986	512,108	3rd	4,895,394	2nd
1988	165,006	4th	5,180,267	2nd
1990	147,583	4th	5,241,989	2nd

Gas production figure for 1906–1910 include Alabama and Texas,
for 1911–1914 include Alabama.

Sources: Bureau of Mines. U. S. Department of the Interior. *Minerals Yearbook*;
Energy Information Administration. *Crude Petroleum, Petroleum Products, and
Natural Gas Liquids; Petroleum Supply Annual; Natural Gas Annual.*

OIL AND GAS PRODUCTION

■ Areas Producing Primarily Oil

▨ Areas Producing Primarily Gas

▧ Areas Producing Oil and Gas

□ Areas with No Production

Generalized from the *Oil and Gas Map of
Louisiana* compiled by Louisiana Geological
Survey and published by the Department of
Natural Resources, July, 1981.

10. OIL AND GAS PRODUCTION

As an industry the extraction of Louisiana's oil and gas resources dates from the twentieth century. Existence of those resources had been known since earliest times, and petroleum seeping naturally to the surface had been used for medicinal and lubricating purposes. Edwin L. Drake's successful well in Titusville, Pennsylvania, in 1859 spurred brief interest in Louisiana during and after the Civil War. Indeed, the state's first petroleum company—the Louisiana Petroleum and Coal Oil Company—was organized in 1866. Both the lack of capital and a young technology caused this infant industry to be short-lived, however.

This situation changed in 1901 when the discovery of the Spindletop Field in adjacent Texas led to renewed drilling in southwest Louisiana. With only rudimentary geologic knowledge, drillers looked for similar physiographic features in this area of Louisiana, where natural seepage was known. On September 21, 1901, W. Scott Heywood brought in a well near Jennings; with the opening of the Jennings and nearby fields the oil boom had begun.

Production in north Louisiana commenced with a discovery in Caddo Parish in 1906. In time, production would spread across much of southern and northern Louisiana, with an absence of production across much of central Louisiana and the Florida Parishes. After the discovery of the Caddo Field (1906) came the Bull Bayou Field (1913), Monroe Gas Field (1916), Haynesville Gas Field (1921), Olla Field (1940), and Lake St. John Field (1942). Later in the century production moved offshore into the Gulf as well. These areas included the Main Pass Field (1948); the Eugene Island, Bay Marchand, and Vermilion Fields (1949); South Pass Field (1950); and West Cameron Field (1954).

As the century progressed, oil and gas production has been tied to an increasing knowledge of geology. Oil in south Louisiana is associated with (although not always present with) salt domes, those massive intrusions of solid salt which may lie totally beneath the surface alluvium or may protrude above that surface, as in the case of Avery Island and others. In the north supplies are located in structural domes, where the layers of rock themselves have been bent upward towards the surface.

Changing technologies and commercial operations have also characterized oil and gas production. Technological advances have allowed wells to be drilled over water, first on lakes (about 1910 on Caddo Lake) or offshore in the Gulf. On November 14, 1947, the first oil well drilled out of sight of land was brought in south of Morgan City. Rotary drills greatly increased the depth of wells, and angular drilling now allows shafts to be sunk into neighboring pools from the same rig station. Conservation practices, such as the control of gushers, commencing with the first state law in 1906, have allowed more of the resource to be saved.

An integration of production, transportation, and refining facilities has led to the emergence of corporations which dominate the oil industry. Since 1901 Louisiana has become crisscrossed by oil and gas pipelines transporting supplies. Refineries began to appear early in the century; the giant complex at Baton Rouge had its start in 1903. Today along the banks of the Mississippi River from Baton Rouge to New Orleans stand a variety of petrochemical facilities, and other, similar plants are located across the state.

From that initial well which opened the Jennings Field in 1901 the state's oil production burgeoned. The next year Louisiana stood eighth in the ranks of oil- producing states; in time it would move as high as second (behind Texas), and today it has slipped to third after Alaskan oil resources have become available. In natural gas production Louisiana has led the nation or boasted a close second, again to Texas.

Oil and gas production have dominated the state's economy in this century. The welfare state created by Governor Huey P. Long and perpetuated by his successors—political friend and foe alike—has been tied to taxes levied on this most important of the state's minerals. State services expanded beyond the ordinary tax base of other states. A setback to state coffers occurred in 1950 when the U.S. Supreme Court declared those offshore areas (tidelands) beyond the three-mile limit to be federal rather than state-owned. Further litigation resulted in a decree line in 1975 based on the report of a special master which located the Louisiana "coastline" and thereby the three-mile limit.

Revenues for the state from severance taxes peaked in 1982 at $971,677,140. The boom-and-bust nature of the industry, particularly the collapse of crude prices in the 1980s, led to difficult times even for the state's essential services. With the state's production of known reserves having peaked about 1970, oil and gas, though continuing to occupy a dominant role in extraction, refining, and manufacturing, will inevitably decline, causing the state to move to renewable resources and other enterprises as the basis for its economy.

Copyright © 1995 by the University of Oklahoma Press

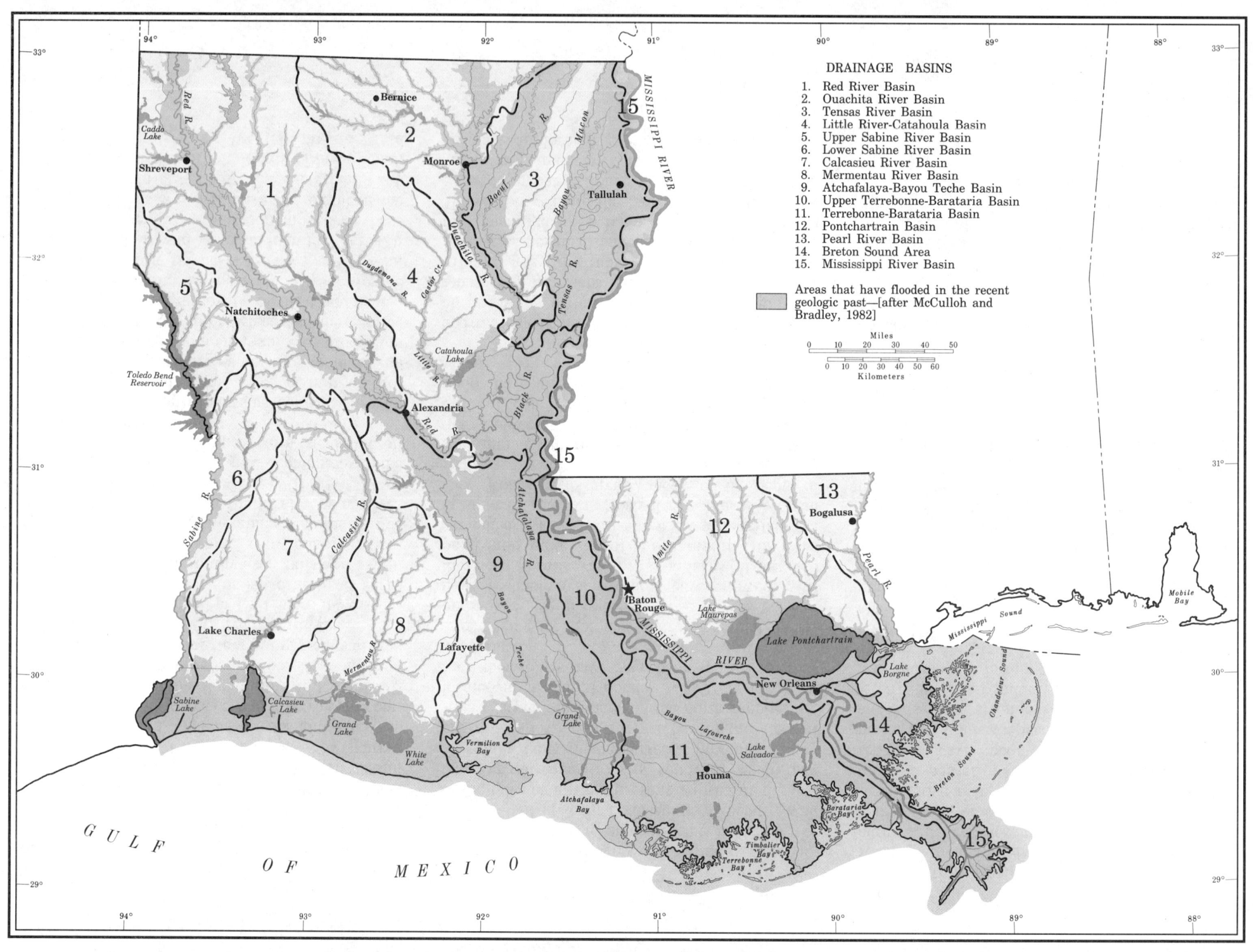

DRAINAGE BASINS

1. Red River Basin
2. Ouachita River Basin
3. Tensas River Basin
4. Little River-Catahoula Basin
5. Upper Sabine River Basin
6. Lower Sabine River Basin
7. Calcasieu River Basin
8. Mermentau River Basin
9. Atchafalaya-Bayou Teche Basin
10. Upper Terrebonne-Barataria Basin
11. Terrebonne-Barataria Basin
12. Pontchartrain Basin
13. Pearl River Basin
14. Breton Sound Area
15. Mississippi River Basin

Areas that have flooded in the recent geologic past—[after McCulloh and Bradley, 1982]

11. FLOODPLAIN DEPOSITS

Since the close of the Wisconsin Ice Age (the most recent of the known glacial periods) ten thousand years ago, the area of present-day Louisiana has witnessed widespread deposition of sediments by its myriad river systems. An estimated fifteen thousand square miles of land has been added by the Mississippi River alone. As the great global ice sheets melted, retreating toward higher elevations and the poles, the mean sea level rose, reducing the gradients of rivers. As these gradients lessened, the speed of the rivers' flow also decreased. In turn, sediments began to drop out as they became too heavy to remain suspended in the slowing water.

Erosion and deposition represent the two ends of the process by which water shapes the earth's surface. When erosion and deposition are carried out by water, the processes are termed alluvial, and the sediments deposited, alluvium. The faster water moves, the larger the size of sediments which are able to remain suspended in its flow. As the water slows, sediments drop to the bottom, from largest to smallest, producing layers which, when compacted, produce sedimentary rock.

Alluvial erosion produces valleys. Stream valleys are V shaped, widest at the top and tapering towards the bottom. The steeper the gradient (and thus the faster the flow) and the greater the volume of water of a stream, the wider and deeper the valley produced will be.

Over geologic time, as sea level receded, much deeper valleys were cut. When sea level rose again, these valleys were flooded and sediments were laid down in them, gradually filling in the base of the V. The original valley remained, though now partially filled. A flatter terrain developed, only part of which might be occupied by the modern stream. For example, during the Ice Ages the Mississippi River cut much more deeply into the earth on its way to a much farther "offshore" (in present terms) Gulf of Mexico. Today that "Grand Canyon of the Mississippi" is partially filled—at Baton Rouge three hundred feet deep—with sediments deposited over the past ten thousand years.

Such a resulting plain over which a river's natural course would wander is termed its floodplain. The size of the floodplain varies in proportion to the size of the river which formed it. As part of the natural cycle of events, streams fed by spring rains and the thaw of winter snow overflow their banks and spread that flow over their floodplains. These floods have spread new sediments over the land and have thus continued to build up the thickness of alluvium.

Along with floodplains, rivers also form deltas when they reach the sea. Over time these deltas reach farther and farther out into the sea as more and more deposits are laid down. Subdeltas form when a new distributary channel is created in a delta. New deltas are formed when rivers change their channel to the sea. The Mississippi River has over time had several deltas (Map 12) and thus has extended the coastal area seaward over much of Louisiana.

Finally, alluvial deposits are laid down in lakes. Lake water by wave action erodes the shore, carrying these sediments to the bottom. Also, many streams feed into lakes, thus adding to the alluvial deposits. Over time, lakes and artificial reservoirs can become more shallow as deposits build up which have no natural means of exit.

Floods, though natural, are destructive of many human endeavors—crops, houses, bridges, even lives—as well as of other forms of plant and animal life. Thus, particularly from the mid-twentieth century, attempts have been made to prevent flooding and stabilize major rivers in their current channels. Although damage from flooding now occurs less frequently, the natural replenishment of the land is also more rare.

Because Louisiana is traversed by many streams, floodplain deposits are widespread. Various river basins exist—those of the Mississippi, Red, Atchafalaya, Ouachita, Calcasieu, Pearl, and so on. Varying according to the size of the stream as well as the terrain over which they cross, floodplains vary from the wide expanse of the Mississippi valley to the more narrow plains of the hill country.

The cycle of erosion and deposition is a continuous, natural process, affected by but not contingent upon human endeavors. Each of the ancient deltas of the Mississippi, in turn deprived of additional sediments, has deteriorated by wind, wave, and stream action. Coastal wetlands, now without the regular feeding of sediments from floods, have also been encroached upon and obliterated by the equally natural erosive action of the Gulf. Any equilibrium, either natural or human-induced, remains transitory, lasting only until the next change in earth's history.

Copyright © 1995 by the University of Oklahoma Press

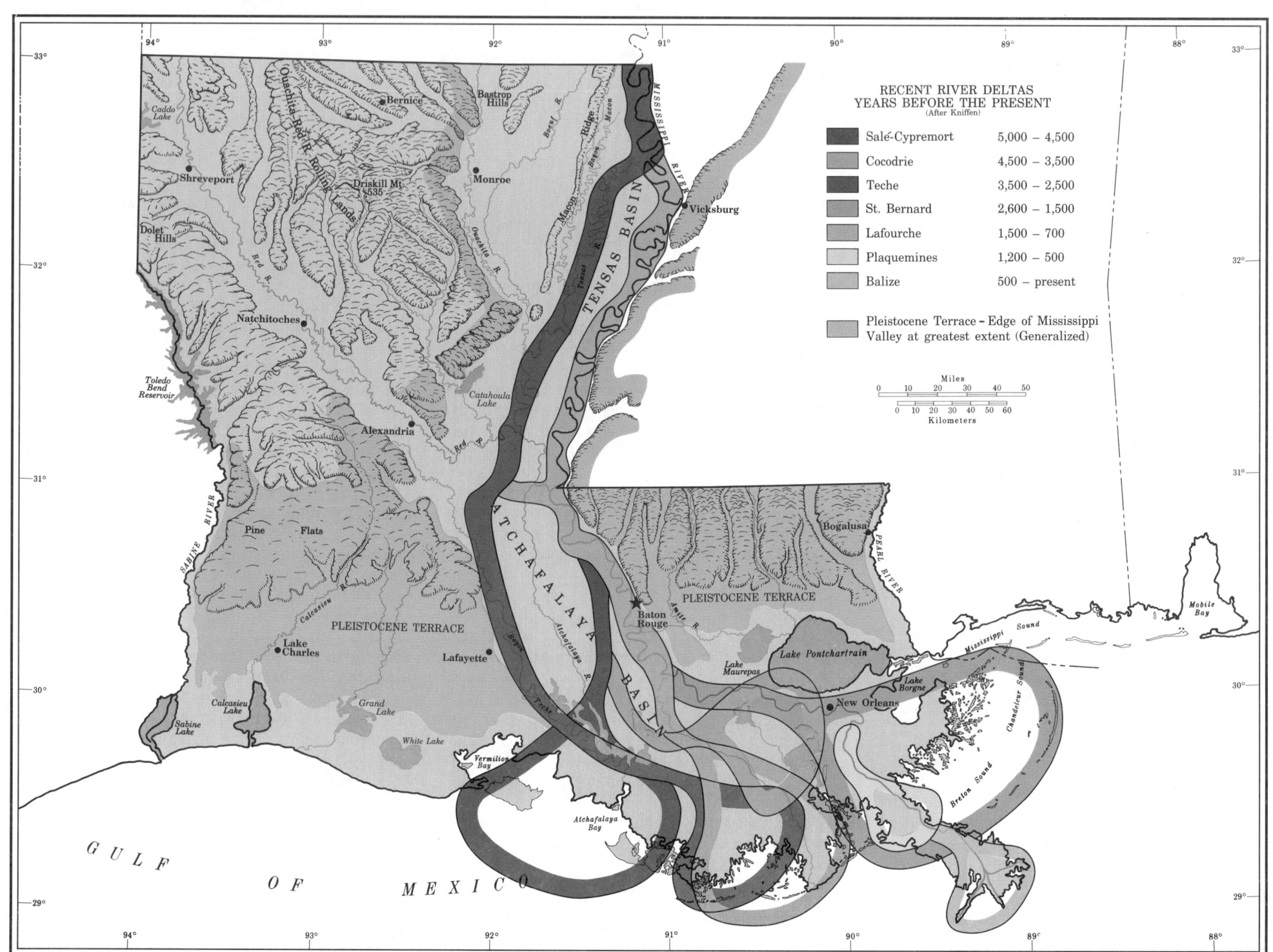

RECENT RIVER DELTAS
YEARS BEFORE THE PRESENT
(After Kniffen)

	Salé-Cypremort	5,000 – 4,500
	Cocodrie	4,500 – 3,500
	Teche	3,500 – 2,500
	St. Bernard	2,600 – 1,500
	Lafourche	1,500 – 700
	Plaquemines	1,200 – 500
	Balize	500 – present

Pleistocene Terrace – Edge of Mississippi
Valley at greatest extent (Generalized)

Miles
0   10   20   30   40   50

0   10 20 30 40 50 60
Kilometers

12. MISSISSIPPI RIVER DELTA SYSTEMS

The lower Mississippi River is created by the addition of the Missouri and Ohio rivers to the upper Mississippi. The present course of these two great tributaries approximates the southward limit of the great continental ice sheets during the most recent ice age. A much lower sea level increased the gradient (slope) of the Pleistocene Mississippi. That gradient, combined with the tremendous flow of water, cut a trench from ten to thirty miles wide and up to 440 feet deep in the earth's surface. As the ice sheet melted and the sea level rose, the gradient decreased and more deposition than erosion occurred. Sea water encroached upon formerly dry land. The great valley of the Mississippi began to fill with sediments (Map 11). A floodplain developed over which the modern river would wander until its present course became more or less stabilized in the twentieth century.

About six thousand years ago the great rise in sea level brought on by the melting of the ice sheets slowed, from perhaps five feet per century to less than one foot per century. About three thousand years ago the level of the Gulf more or less stabilized. Into the great embayment formed by the rising Gulf the Mississippi continued to empty its tremendous load of sediments.

Over the past five thousand years and more, with the shifting channel of the river, much of what is today south central and southeastern Louisiana was formed by the creation and abandonment of new deltas by the Mississippi. Seven generalized delta complexes have been postulated, although one study suggests a far more intricate system of sixteen delta lobes within five delta complexes. The seven generalized delta systems are named, in chronological order of years before present (B.P.): (1) Salé-Cypremort, 5000–4500 years B.P.; (2) Cocodrie, 4500–3500 years B.P.; (3) Teche 3500–2500 years B.P.; (4) St. Bernard, 2600–1500 years B.P.; (5) Lafourche, 1500–700 years B.P.; (6) Plaquemines, 1200–500 years B.P.; and (7) the present Balize, 500 years B.P. to the present.

The six earlier delta complexes followed various routes to the sea. For example, the Salé-Cypremort and Teche deltas formed at the respective mouths of those bayous. Each successive abandonment of an existing distributary channel and delta resulted from the Mississippi's selecting a shorter and more direct course to the sea. This remains true today, with the river's natural tendency to flow down the Atchafalaya River channel. These earlier delta complexes formed the classic triangular shape of the Greek letter *delta*, from which the present term is derived. They were also much larger than the current delta, in part because they were laid down in shallower water. The Teche Delta covered two thousand square miles, the Lafourche twenty-five hundred, and the St. Bernard three thousand.

As each successive delta was in turn abandoned, depriving it of new sediments, deterioration began. This resulted in part from wave erosion by the Gulf. The natural consolidation of sediments and tectonic forces also contributed, leading to the subsidence (sinking) of the entire deltaic plain. In turn, the sea encroached. Remnants of these ancient deltas remain. For example, the Chandeleur Islands are relics of the previous seaward extension of the St. Bernard complex.

The present Mississippi Delta has been built up over the past five hundred years. Its fifty-mile extension beyond the main shoreline attests to the great load of sediments with which the river battles the sea in forming new land. There are three main distributary channels in this Balize Delta: the Southwest Pass, the South Pass, and the Pass a Loutre. The present delta's shape is called "bird's foot," from the shape of its distributary channels. As cracks open in the natural levees formed by the channels, smaller distributary channels open and form new areas where sediments can be deposited and the delta enlarged. This newest delta is much smaller than earlier ones, occupying only about three hundred square miles of surface. Its above-water area is misleading, however; because of the depth of the Gulf, only about 18 percent of the delta lies above sea level.

Even as the major deposits were being laid down in the shifting deltas of the Mississippi, other sediments were being carried to the west by coastal currents. These sediments, combined with wave action and other, local deposits, resulted over time in the beach ridges known as cheniers. The region has been referred to as the Marginal Deltaic Plain. Thus, the Mississippi can be said to have formed in whole or in part the entire coastal region of Louisiana.

Copyright © 1995 by the University of Oklahoma Press

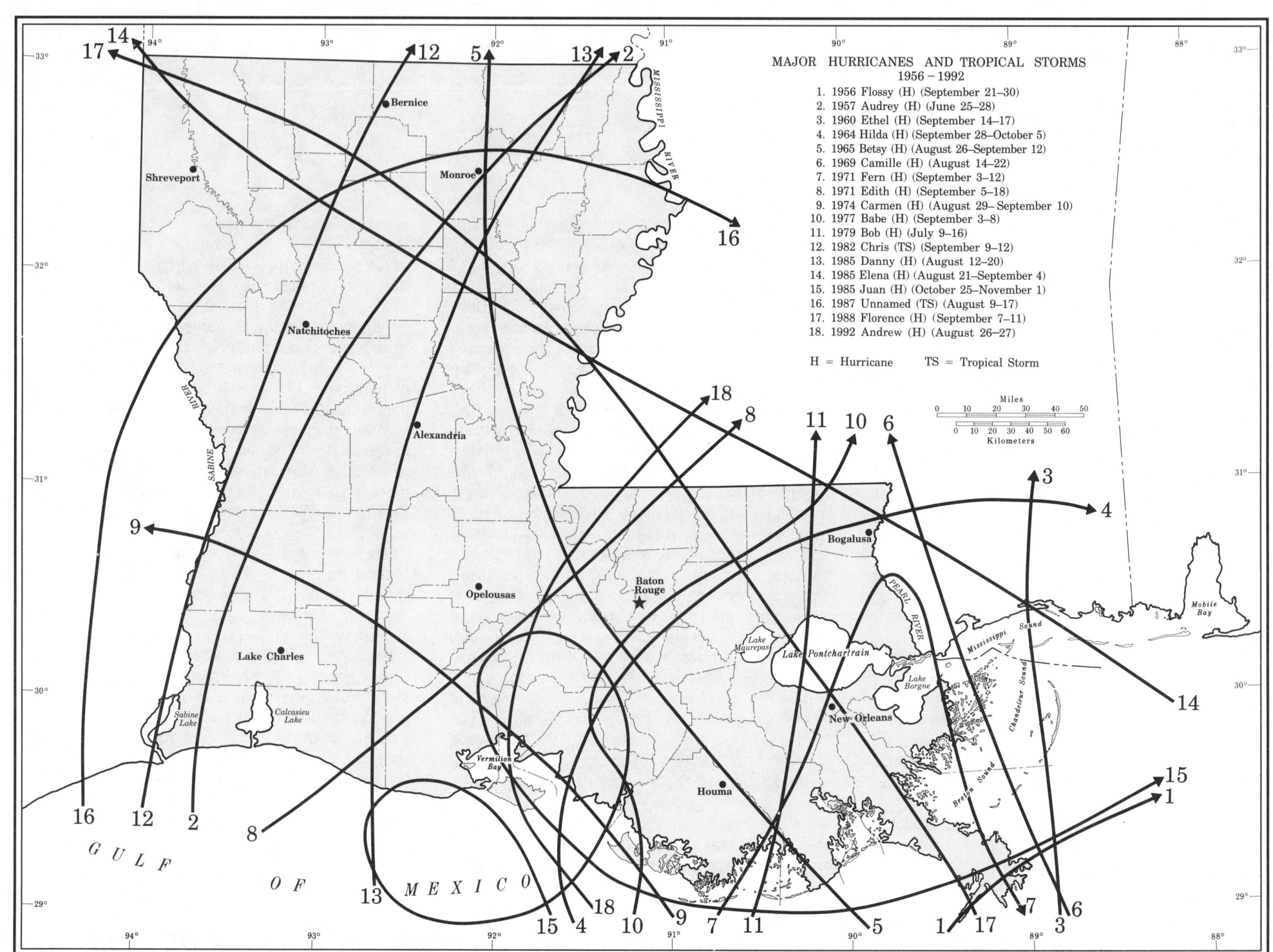

MAJOR HURRICANES AND TROPICAL STORMS
1956 – 1992

1. 1956 Flossy (H) (September 21–30)
2. 1957 Audrey (H) (June 25–28)
3. 1960 Ethel (H) (September 14–17)
4. 1964 Hilda (H) (September 28–October 5)
5. 1965 Betsy (H) (August 26–September 12)
6. 1969 Camille (H) (August 14–22)
7. 1971 Fern (H) (September 3–12)
8. 1971 Edith (H) (September 5–18)
9. 1974 Carmen (H) (August 29– September 10)
10. 1977 Babe (H) (September 3–8)
11. 1979 Bob (H) (July 9–16)
12. 1982 Chris (TS) (September 9–12)
13. 1985 Danny (H) (August 12–20)
14. 1985 Elena (H) (August 21–September 4)
15. 1985 Juan (H) (October 25–November 1)
16. 1987 Unnamed (TS) (August 9–17)
17. 1988 Florence (H) (September 7–11)
18. 1992 Andrew (H) (August 26–27)

H = Hurricane   TS = Tropical Storm

Miles
0   10   20   30   40   50

0   10   20   30   40   50   60
Kilometers

Hurricanes are large cyclonic storms which originate in the tropical latitudes as low-pressure areas. Fed by the heat released as water vapor condenses, these low-pressure areas (termed tropical disturbances) can intensify, progressing to form tropical depressions (with wind speeds of up to thirty-nine miles per hour), tropical storms (thirty-nine to seventy-three miles per hour), and hurricanes (seventy-four miles per hour and greater). As long as it remains over warm water, the storm can grow in size and intensity. However, once the storm encounters cooler waters or, especially, land, it begins to weaken and eventually disintegrates because it has been deprived of its fuel.

The structure of a hurricane consists of an inwardly spiraling movement of air at the surface. At intermediate altitudes this air moves rapidly upward. As the top of the storm is reached, this flow is again spiral, this time in an outward direction. An entire hurricane may extend thirty-five thousand to forty thousand feet into the atmosphere and reach one hundred to four hundred miles in diameter. At the center of a hurricane exists a calm region called the eye, where a downward flow of air produces an area without wind, cloud, or rain.

Hurricanes wreak destruction through several means. The straight winds accompanying the storm can cause damage, and the torrential rains associated with hurricanes can bring about local or areal flooding. A tidal surge of water generated by the storm can cause great destruction and loss of life when it reaches the coast, particularly in low-lying areas. Finally, hurricanes often spawn tornadoes, their more compact, faster-moving, and more dangerous cousins, with winds up to five hundred miles per hour and extreme low pressure at the core. Whether in association with hurricanes or not, Louisiana averaged about twenty-five tornadoes annually between 1961 and 1990. A record seventy-seven tornadoes were recorded in 1992 alone.

While the "average" hurricane extends over an area one hundred miles in diameter, gale force winds (forty miles per hour or greater) extend over an area four hundred miles in diameter. This representative storm contains heavy bands of clouds with torrential rains. The entire storm is an area of low barometric pressure. Deaths associated with the average hurricane result mainly from flooding caused by either the storm surge along the coast or the heavy rains farther inland.

The naming of hurricanes has had a varied history. From 1953 to 1979 the U.S. Weather Service assigned women's names to the storms in alphabetical order. Before that time, letters or phonetic names for letters were used, though not on a systematic national basis. Since 1979 men's names have been added to alternate with women's in each year's alphabetical sequence. Today there is a six-year cycle of names drawn up for use, with provision for retiring a name from the list for a particularly significant storm.

No season is truly free from hurricanes, but they occur more commonly in late summer and early fall. Hurricanes affect Louisiana more frequently in September than any other month. August is a close second, but the entire span of months from June through October can be termed the hurricane season.

During the past century (1890–1990) more than two dozen hurricanes have struck Louisiana, along with many tropical storms. Dozens more have brushed along the state's coast with slighter effect. On average a hurricane will hit the state once every four years. These storms will vary in strength and effect. By far the most deadly hurricane yet to strike Louisiana was Audrey, which on June 28, 1957, slammed into Cameron Parish with a ten-foot-plus storm surge that raced up to twenty miles inland on the low-lying coastal plain. Between four hundred and five hundred people died in the storm.

Other storms causing double-digit deaths were Betsy (September 1965) with fifty-eight, Hilda (October 1964) with thirty-seven, Juan (October 1985) and an unnamed 1947 storm with a dozen each, and Andrew (August 1992), with ten. Andrew wrought the greatest monetary damage on record, an estimated $2.4 billion in forty-three parishes. That single storm destroyed or damaged over 20,000 homes, demolished oil rigs, and damaged crops, fisheries, and timber as well as other public and private property.

With the advent of weather satellites, hurricanes can be traced from their formative stages through to disintegration. Because of their slow forward progress, these storms can thus can be avoided by alert citizens. Deaths usually occur from failure to appreciate the destructive powers of a hurricane. Those who witness the fury or aftermath of hurricanes rarely need be warned the next time one appears.

Copyright © 1995 by the University of Oklahoma Press

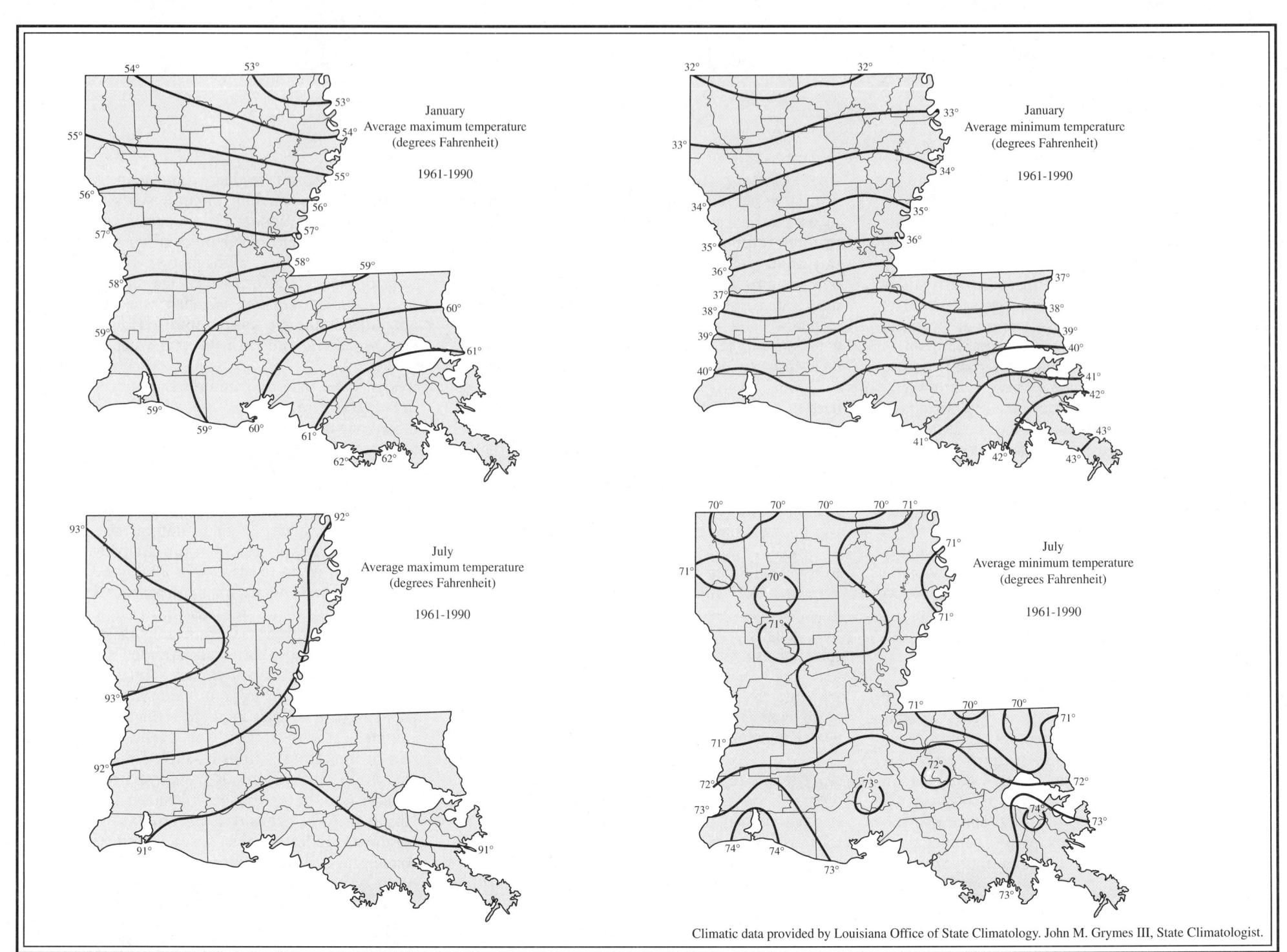

January
Average maximum temperature
(degrees Fahrenheit)

1961-1990

January
Average minimum temperature
(degrees Fahrenheit)

1961-1990

July
Average maximum temperature
(degrees Fahrenheit)

1961-1990

July
Average minimum temperature
(degrees Fahrenheit)

1961-1990

Climatic data provided by Louisiana Office of State Climatology. John M. Grymes III, State Climatologist.

Louisiana's weather is influenced by its latitudinal, continental, and coastal location. Its position in the subtropical latitudes places the state in the zone of prevailing westerly winds and also means that seasonal variations occur in the amount of solar energy received. Its continental position so situates the state that the prevailing winds cross land instead of water before reaching the state and thus are not modified by the relatively milder conditions of maritime air masses—those originating over water bodies. Too, the lack of any great elevation to the north allows continental (drier and more extreme in temperature) air masses—those originating over land areas—to penetrate the state more easily. Louisiana's Gulf region, with its coastal breezes, does experience some modification of temperatures and rainfall patterns because of its proximity to the sea, but not as much as would occur were that body located upwind of the state. Although one generally associates warmer temperatures with daylight and colder temperatures with darkness, the passage of fronts can produce just the opposite situation for a particular day.

Lines of equal temperature (isotherms) can be drawn on maps based on data from recording devices situated around the state. The most recent three decades of weather records—for this atlas 1961–1990—serve as the basis for calculating averages. Thus, precise records are important. Lines drawn are no more accurate than the devices and the people who maintain them.

JANUARY AVERAGE MAXIMUM AND AVERAGE MINIMUM TEMPERATURES

January experiences a wider range of temperatures than does July—a nine-degree range in the average maximum and an even wider eleven-degree range in the average minimum temperature. Absolute ranges for maximum temperature are from just below 53° F to just above 62° F. The equivalent minimums are from just below 32° F to just above 43° F.

The colder temperatures in north Louisiana result in part from that area's remoteness from the moderating influences of the Gulf of Mexico and coastal breezes therefrom. Too, north Louisiana is a much more frequent recipient of and longer host to visits from continental, even polar, air masses than is the southern part of the state. The frontal passages associated with the air masses produce cloud cover which reduces solar energy reaching the surface. The high-pressure zones moving in behind the front have the opposite result: clearing skies which allow heat to escape and thus lower the surface temperature.

JULY AVERAGE MAXIMUM AND AVERAGE MINIMUM TEMPERATURES

Ranges of temperature in July are approximately three degrees for the average maximum and four degrees for the average minimum, less than half the differentials for January. The average maximum ranges from just above 93° F in west central Louisiana to just below 91° F along the south. Average minimum temperatures range from just under 70° F in the north and northwest part of the state to just above 74° F in the southwest and a small area near New Orleans.

The relatively milder temperatures in the more southern latitudes result in part from the frequent showers along the coast during the summer months. Clouds producing this precipitation block solar energy from the earth's surface. In the north the continental high pressure allows more abundant sunshine, less humid air, and thus both warmer maximum and cooler minimum temperatures than south Louisiana experiences.

TEMPERATURE RECORDS IN LOUISIANA

The official temperature records for Louisiana as a whole occur in the months of August and February. The sites for these records lie within thirty miles of each other in adjoining parishes. Plain Dealing in Bossier Parish recorded 114° F on August 10, 1936; Minden in Webster Parish recorded minus 16° F on February 13, 1899. The record low in South Louisiana—0° F—occurred at Clinton on February 12, 1899, one day before the overall state record. The state's range of 130° in absolute temperature records obscures the more compact ranges already discussed.

Temperature ranges in Louisiana are thus affected by latitudinal, seasonal, and other factors. Within the state variations occur largely between the north and the south. These variations owe more to the moderating influence of the Gulf of Mexico than to any other influence. In general climatic terms, the north can be said to be more continental in nature, the south more maritime.

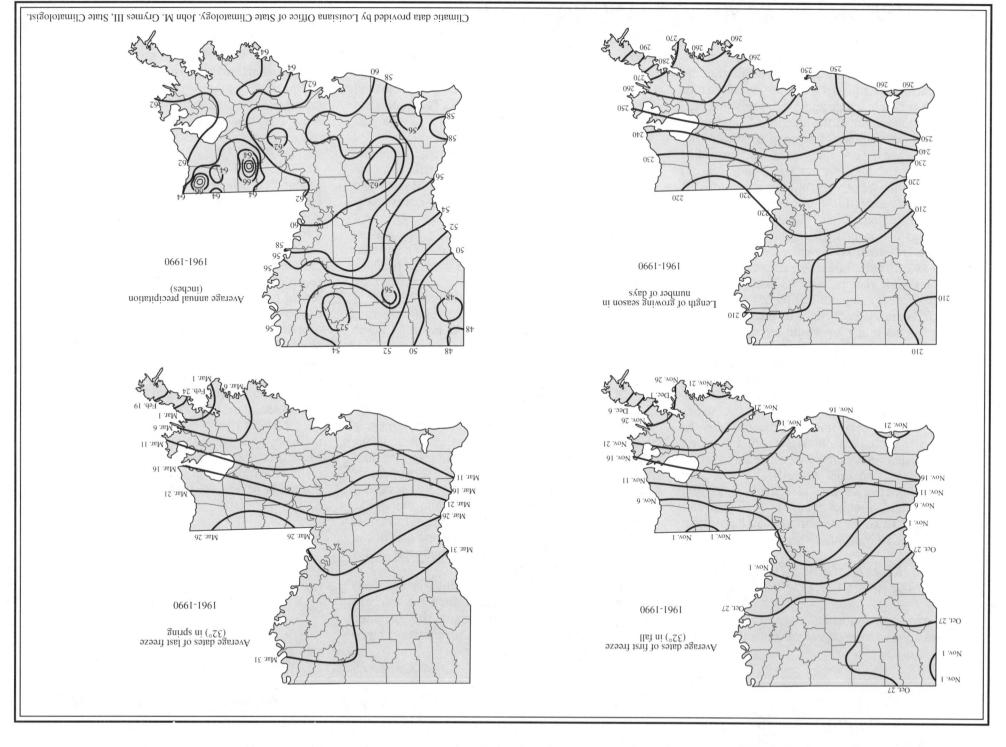

Average annual precipitation (inches)

1961-1990

Length of growing season in number of days

1961-1990

Average dates of last freeze (32°) in spring

1961-1990

Average dates of first freeze (32°) in fall

1961-1990

Climatic data provided by Louisiana Office of State Climatology, John M. Grymes III, State Climatologist.

Copyright © 1995 by the University of Oklahoma Press

15. FROST DATES, GROWING SEASON, AND PRECIPITATION

Louisiana's main climatic influences are her relative latitudinal position, her situation on the North American continent, and her location adjacent to the Gulf of Mexico (Map 14). Continental and maritime air masses vie for domination over the state; this battle seesaws during the year. Seasonal fluctuations in the relative strength of the air masses create varying temperature ranges and variations in the dates of average first and last freezes each year. As with general temperature and precipitation patterns, greater variation occurs as one moves inland from the Gulf.

Freezes occur in the fall, winter, and spring months when the state is invaded by a polar air mass. This cold air drops the atmospheric temperature somewhat, but actual freezes are more often assisted by other, accompanying factors. Polar air masses are associated with high pressure, thus fair skies; this absence of clouds allows heat to escape more easily into the atmosphere, thus lowering surface temperatures. Also, these air masses are relatively dry; the absence of water vapor deprives the atmosphere of a storage medium for residual heat. Cooler air, being heavier, sinks towards the surface. With a lack of wind to mix the air, by the second night of the arrival of the polar air mass, a freeze likely occurs, often just before sunrise.

The National Oceanic and Atmospheric Administration (NOAA) is the federal agency responsible for gathering weather data. From the official data turned in, NOAA or other agencies, such as the Southern Regional Climate Center or the Louisiana Office of State Climatology within the Department of Geography and Anthropology at Louisiana State University, can by computer or other means plot lines of equal occurrence of various weather phenomena. By converting tabular data to a map, one can view present thirty-year averages, the basis of climate. By comparing one set with those of a previous period, one can discern changes in climate.

AVERAGE DATE OF FIRST FREEZE IN THE FALL

The average first fall freeze occurs as early as late October in parts of north central and northeast Louisiana. Thereafter, the date becomes increasingly later as one moves west or south, then southeastward. At points within the Mississippi Delta the average first fall freeze occurs in early December. Freezes may occur in the north as early as mid-October and in the south as early as the first of December. However, parts of extreme south Louisiana do not experience a freeze every year.

AVERAGE DATE OF LAST FREEZE IN THE SPRING

The temporal pattern of spring freezes reverses that of autumn. As early as February 19 (on average) the lower Mississippi delta experiences its last freeze. Thereafter the date becomes later as one moves north, with the time of the average last freeze in north Louisiana being shortly after March 31.

GROWING SEASON

The span of days between the last killing freeze in the spring and the first killing freeze in the fall represents the growing season. This frost-free period in Louisiana on average varies from 210 days in north central Louisiana to more than 290 days within the Mississippi Delta. North Louisiana has a growing season ranging from 210 to 230 days. South Louisiana, with its proximity to the Gulf, has a growing season ranging from 230 to more than 290 days.

The growing season determines the successful cultivation of a variety of crops. For example, commercial production of sugar cane and citrus crops is relegated to the southern parts of the state.

Faster maturing crops can be grown in more widespread areas, and their commercial cultivation depends more upon topography, soil, and market than the length of the growing season.

PRECIPITATION

Average annual precipitation (the average of the past thirty years) within Louisiana increases from the northwest to the southeast. Caddo Parish precipitation averages about forty-eight inches per year. In the Florida Parishes, in St. Helena and Washington Parishes, islands of precipitation range upwards of seventy inches annually. Much of the south ranges from fifty-six to sixty-four inches. Individual sites within regions also vary in total precipitation.

Precipitation varies monthly as well. Peaks of over five inches in March, July, and December occur for the state as a whole. June and October mark low points for the entire state, with four and three inches respectively. Regional location modifies seasonal amounts, too. In the summer moist Gulf air produces almost daily showers along the coast, while the north, under the influence of high pressure, might remain dry. During the winter months cold fronts stalling in the north might produce sustained rains while the south would be the drier of the regions.

The great majority of Louisiana precipitation occurs in the form of rain. Thunderstorms are the common form of heavy rain, but tropical storms and hurricanes also bring heavy precipitation when they occur (Map 13). Snow occurs regularly in the north but only occasionally in the south; however, outbreaks of polar air pushing their way to the Gulf can produce heavy snows in the southern part of Louisiana. Sleet, hail, and freezing rain are less frequent forms of precipitation.

15. Frost Dates, Growing Season, and Precipitation

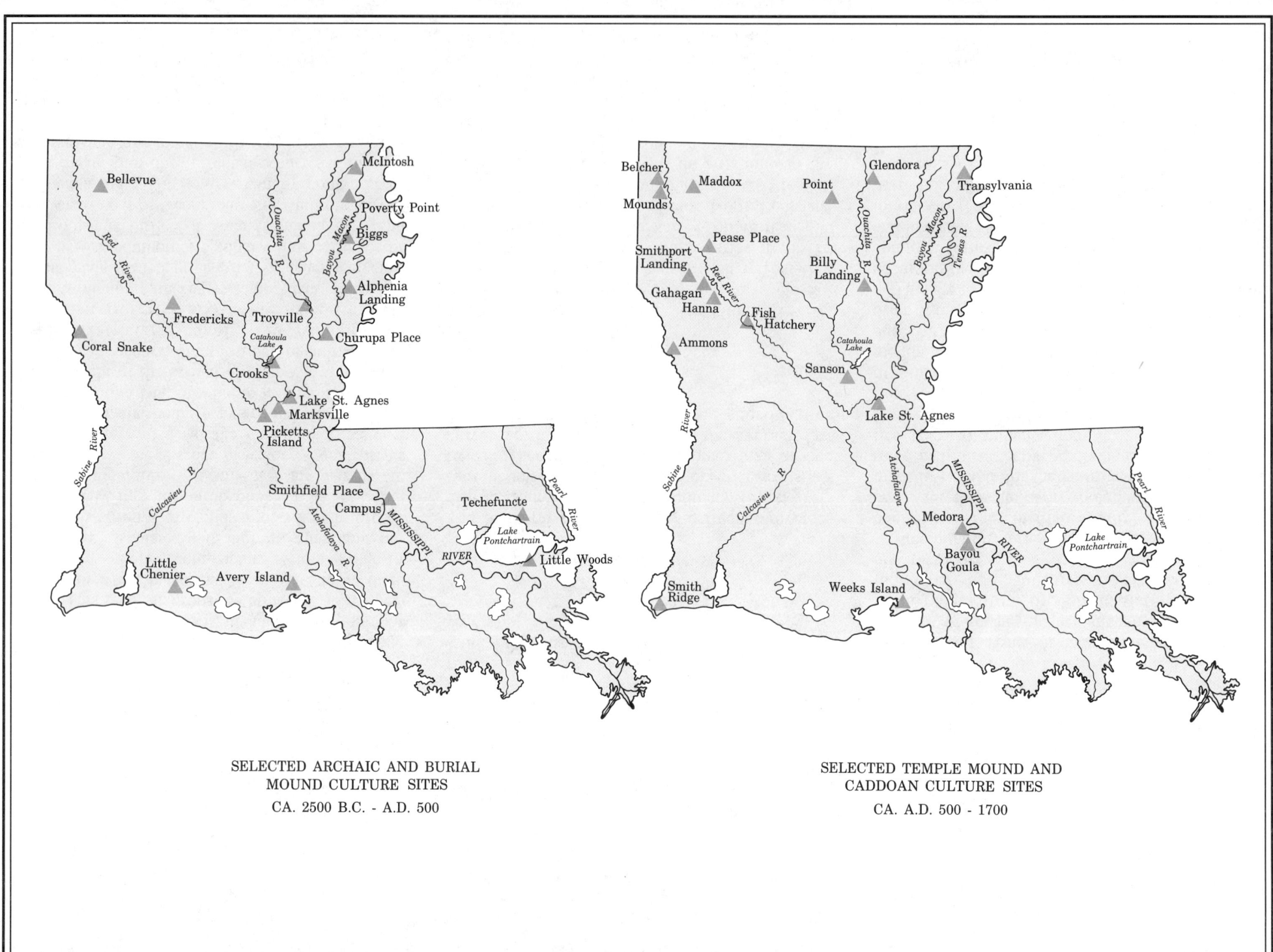

SELECTED ARCHAIC AND BURIAL
MOUND CULTURE SITES

CA. 2500 B.C. - A.D. 500

SELECTED TEMPLE MOUND AND
CADDOAN CULTURE SITES

CA. A.D. 500 - 1700

For our purposes, prehistoric in the sense of Native American cultures refers to the eras before European contact and especially before a permanent European presence and written history. The lack of that written history gives us the term *prehistoric*. Tribal history before the eighteenth century has been gathered for some tribes through oral tradition, deduced for others through the detective work of the archaeologist, and generalized for successive eras of time. Any presumed areal extent of culture often depends upon the degree of archaeological examination in any region; thus, each new discovery can literally rewrite the known story.

The area of modern Louisiana has been occupied by a succession of cultures from perhaps fifteen thousand years ago. Three generalized chronological eras have been devised: Paleo-Indian (from Greek *palai*, "ancient"; 15,000–6000 B.C.), Meso-Indian (from Greek *mesos*, "middle"; 6000–2000 B.C.) and Neo-Indian (from Greek *neos*, "new"; 2000 B.C. to the present). Archaeological evidence suggests several shifts in Louisiana's Native American cultures. A primary change occurred when an essentially nomadic society evolved into one of permanent village settlement. Tied to this, indeed a factor which assisted in this evolution, was the development of domesticated plants—the appearance of an agricultural system which increased the stability of a food supply hitherto based on hunting and gathering activities. Finally came a more complex material culture approximated by the appearance and development of pottery, tools, weapons, and so on.

The Paleo-Indians lived in hunting and gathering societies within an ecosystem of broad grasslands and large mammals such as long-horned bison, mammoths, and ground sloths, all now extinct. Wild plants supplemented animal food sources. Tribes migrated as food supplies diminished. The distribution of distinctive projectile (spear and arrow) points, with names such as Clovis, Pelican, Dalton, or San Patrice allows us to plot the distribution of these ancient societies.

Over time came the development of a more settled system in the Meso-Indian or Archaic Indian cultures. The somewhat nomadic existence of the previous era gradually moved toward a more settled pattern, although many villages were impermanent in nature. As the grassland vegetation changed to forests of pine and hardwood, giant mammals gave way to newer species. The white-tailed deer, bear, and waterfowl, for example, combined with an increased use of seafood and fish, provided a major food supply. This diet was augmented and supplemented by the gathering of hickory nuts and other plant species. The Indians also developed hand tools and rudimentary pottery. As they learned to use the environment more completely, including cultivating domesticated plants, population levels in turn increased.

In time more complex social structures rose. Among the most important of these was the Poverty Point Culture, centered about a town erected on concentric ridges thrown up over generations along the banks of Bayou Macon in present-day West Carroll Parish. This village site, with its adjacent effigy mound in the shape of a bird, as well as other burial mounds, was the second largest mound ever built in America's eastern woodlands. Present scholarship seems to reveal with increasing clarity a regional culture from Missouri to Florida centered on Poverty Point. Goods which could have come only through widespread trade have been excavated at the site.

Within the Neo-Indian period regional cultures appeared, with mounds serving as burial or temple sites. The Tchefuncte Culture (200 B.C.–A.D. 400) developed along coastal streams, along the sandy coastal ridges called cheniers, and around Lake Pontchartrain. Next came the Marksville Culture (A.D. 100–550), named for that town in Avoyelles Parish, occupying sites along the Red River and Bayou Teche as well as sites of the earlier Tchefuncte Culture. The Troyville Culture (A.D. 500–950) developed temple mounds. Deriving its name from a site at Jonesville in Catahoula Parish, it occupied areas along Bayou Lafourche, the Mississippi River, and elsewhere. This culture evolved into the more elaborate and widespread Coles Creek Culture (A.D. 950–1300). From A.D. 1300 (and in some instances earlier) a series of cultures termed Caddoan (along the upper Red River), Plaquemine (throughout the entire state), and Mississippian (along the Mississippi Valley) appeared.

Throughout the Neo-Indian period, pottery developed in specialized and more highly decorated forms and became more abundant. Domesticated maize, beans, squash, melons, sunflowers, tobacco, and gourds dominated the food supply, supplemented still by hunting, fishing, and gathering. Trade in salt and other raw and finished materials also flourished. Tribal organizations evolved, and population increased. This scene met the De Soto–Moscoso expedition and other early explorers. Some sources suggest that this Indian society was even then evolving. What that new stage might have been will remain unknown; Europeans and their own cultures had arrived in the New World.

Copyright © 1995 by the University of Oklahoma Press

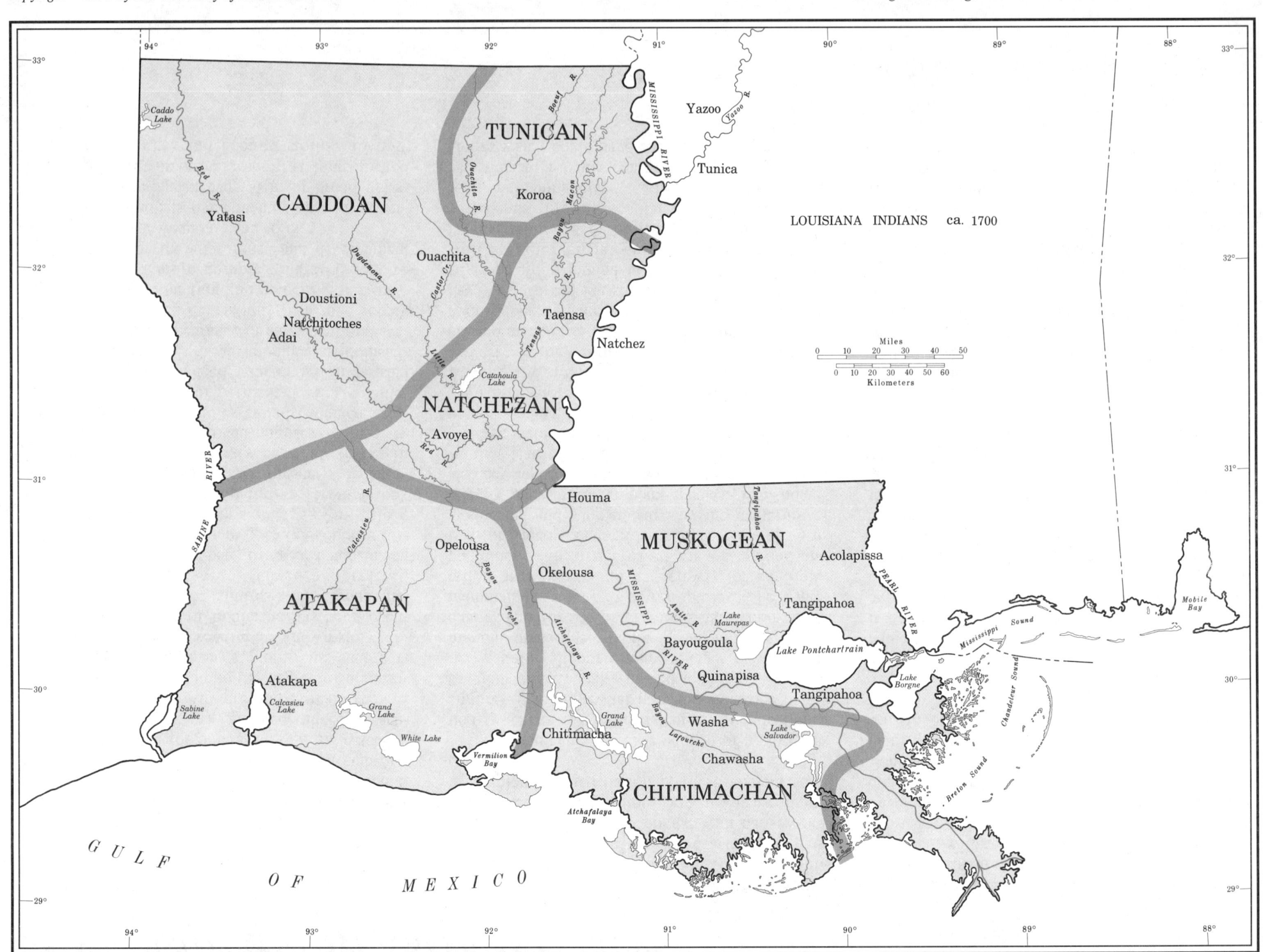

LOUISIANA INDIANS   ca. 1700

TUNICAN

CADDOAN

NATCHEZAN

ATAKAPAN

MUSKOGEAN

CHITIMACHAN

Yazoo

Tunica

Koroa

Yatasi

Ouachita

Doustioni

Natchitoches

Adai

Taensa

Natchez

Avoyel

Houma

Opelousa

Acolapissa

Okelousa

Tangipahoa

Bayougoula

Atakapa

Quinapisa

Tangipahoa

Washa

Chitimacha

Chawasha

Caddo Lake

Red R.

Dugdemona R.

Ouachita R.

Castor Cr.

Bueuf R.

Macon R.

Tensas R.

MISSISSIPPI RIVER

Bayou Macon

Yazoo R.

Little R.

Catahoula Lake

Red R.

SABINE RIVER

Calcasieu R.

Bayou Teche

Atchafalaya R.

MISSISSIPPI RIVER

Amite R.

Lake Maurepas

Tangipahoa R.

PEARL RIVER

Lake Pontchartrain

Lake Borgne

Mississippi Sound

Mobile Bay

Sabine Lake

Calcasieu Lake

Grand Lake

White Lake

Vermilion Bay

Grand Lake

Bayou Lafourche

Lake Salvador

Breton Sound

Chandeleur Sound

Atchafalaya Bay

Miles
0   10   20   30   40   50

0   10   20   30   40   50   60
Kilometers

G U L F   *O F*   *M E X I C O*

At the time of French exploration and settlement of present-day Louisiana, six Indian linguistic groups—the Caddoan, Tunican, Natchezan, Muskogean, Chitimachan, and Atakapan—were scattered throughout the territory. In the northwest lived the Caddoan tribes: the Adai, Doustioni, Natchitoches, Ouachita, and Yatasi. In the northeast the Koroa, Tunica, and Yazoo moved on both sides of the Mississippi River. Downriver from them lay the Natchezan linguistic group, the Natchez, Taensa, and Avoyel tribes. Along the fringes of the Florida Parishes and on the banks of the Mississippi south of the thirty-first parallel were scattered tribes of the Muskogean group: the Houma, Bayougoula, Acolapissa, Quinapisa (Mugulasha), Okelousa, and Tangipahoa. In the lower Atchafalaya River–Bayou Lafourche region lived the Chitimacha, Washa, and Chawasha tribes. Ranged across the southwest from Bayou Teche to and beyond the Sabine River were the Atakapa, with the Opelousa to their northeast.

Some generalizations may be made about the tribes living in or roaming through Louisiana in 1700. They resided in villages located in alluvial areas (along the banks of streams and lakes)—sites with more abundant food which also provided means of transportation and communication. Although some sites passed through the hands of successive tribes over a number of years, others more susceptible to flooding proved of shorter duration.

Villages ranged in size from a few dwellings to dozens or more. Each major settlement centered around the temple and the house of the chief. These structures faced each other across a plaza which may have been used for ceremonial or athletic events. Family dwellings were situated in proximity to fields and linked to the village nucleus by footpaths.

Tribal economies consisted of agriculture, hunting and fishing, gathering, and trade. Corn, beans, and squash represented the staple crops, each having originated in Mexico. The harvest usually did not last from one growing season to the next, so the gathering of wild plants provided an alternate source of foodstuffs. Among these supplements were hickory and other nuts, persimmons, wild sweet potatoes, plums, and wild rice. Hunting and fishing also contributed to the food supply. Hunting went on year-round, with periods of particular activity between planting and harvest and following the harvest. The white-tailed deer served as the favorite quarry, but bear, bison, raccoon, beaver, muskrat, turkey, and quail were also sought. Both freshwater and saltwater fish—oysters, clams, gar, shad, and buffalo fish—served as food sources.

Trade between tribes was widespread and included not only raw materials but also finished products, essential goods as well as "luxury" items such as certain shells, metals, and pearls. Communication between different linguistic groups was carried out in the Mobilian jargon, a pidgin (mixed) language derived principally from Choctaw. Trade activity employed native traders from each tribe as well as professional traders such as the Tunica and Avoyel. Products such as baskets or pottery might be exchanged for materials such as stone or hides directly, but media of exchange such as shells or pearls took their place in indirect exchange.

Indian religions viewed the world as but a single system, with no division between the sacred realm and that of the profane. The first humans were believed to have come from a chaotic underworld to a harmonious surface where the sun was the most sacred element. Life represented but one of a series of interconnected continuums. Humans were but one part of the whole of the natural world, one with animal or plant, living or dead. The supreme position of the sun resulted in several heliocentric (sun-centered) religions.

Tribal organization was based on kinship. Such kinships could be traced through the father (patrilineal) or through the mother (matrilineal). Some groups practiced marriage outside their own group (exogamy), while others married only within their same group (endogamy). The nuclear family provided the basis for some organizations; other used an extended family or a multiple family (clan) system. Power within the various tribes was a combination of these elements.

The year 1700 represents an historic change. From that point forward a continuous record of European-Indian relations exists. Europeans had already exerted influences on tribes, however; previous explorations had introduced the horse as well as European diseases into Indian society. Such influences would thereafter increase and pass in both directions. While the individual Louisiana tribes can be viewed each with its own history, one should remember that there existed a larger context not only within the bounds of the present state but also between all of the "New" World and the "Old."

17. Louisiana Indians in 1700

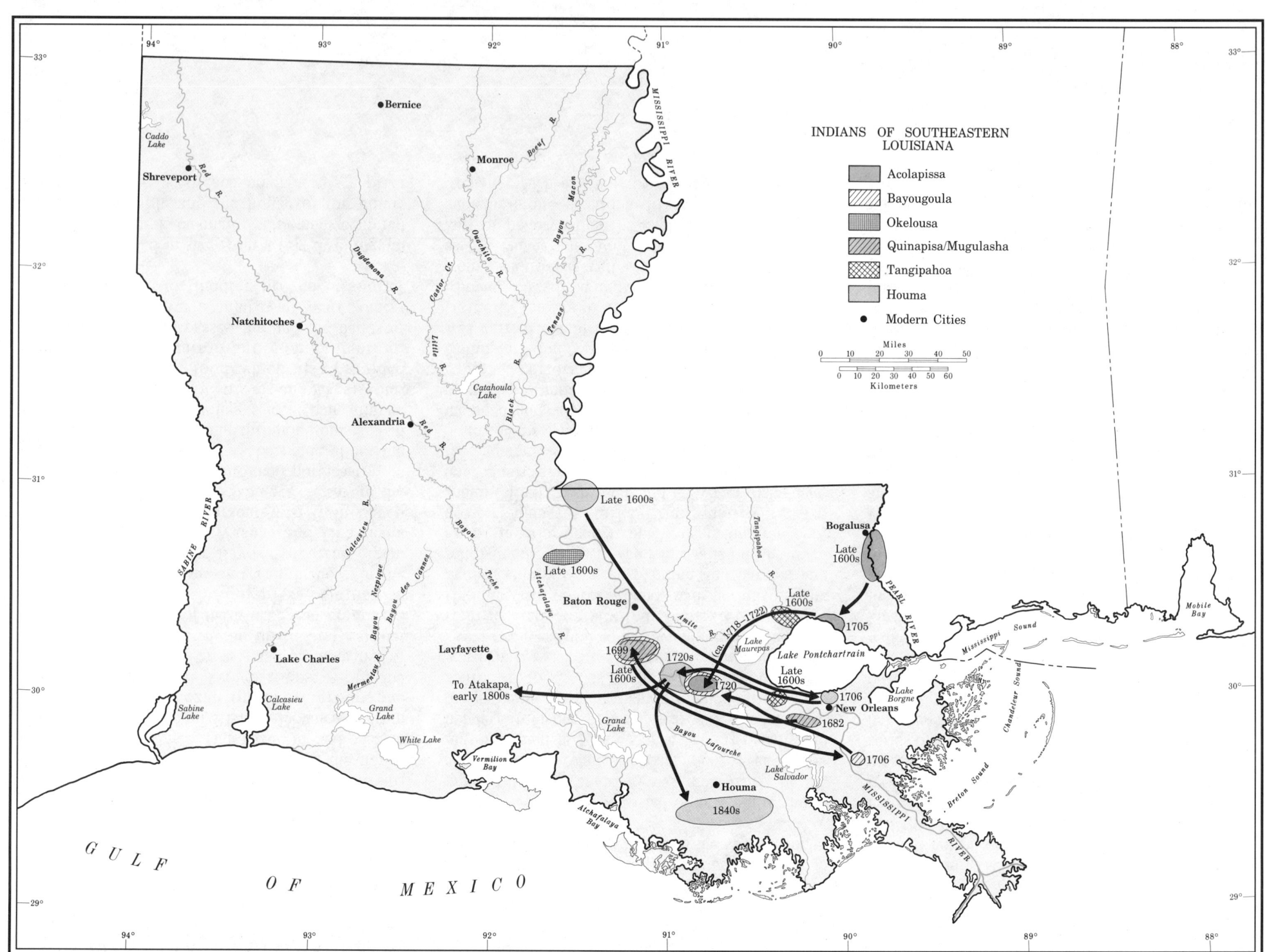

Copyright © 1995 by the University of Oklahoma Press

INDIANS OF SOUTHEASTERN
LOUISIANA

Acolapissa

Bayougoula

Okelousa

Quinapisa/Mugulasha

Tangipahoa

Houma

● Modern Cities

Miles
0   10   20   30   40   50

0 10 20 30 40 50 60
Kilometers

Late 1600s

Late 1600s

Late 1600s

Bogalusa

Late
1600s

Late
1600s

Baton Rouge

1705

1699

(ca. 1718–1722)

1720s

Late
1600s

1720

Amite R.

Lake
Maurepas

Lake Pontchartrain

Late
1600s

1706

Lake
Borgne

To Atakapa,
early 1800s

New Orleans

1682

1706

Houma

1840s

Lake
Salvador

Bayou Lafourche

Grand
Lake

Vermilion
Bay

Atchafalaya
Bay

Lake Charles

Layfayette

Sabine
Lake

Calcasieu
Lake

Grand
Lake

White Lake

Alexandria

Natchitoches

Shreveport

Caddo
Lake

Bernice

Monroe

Mississippi River

Tangipahoa R.

Pearl River

Mississippi Sound

Mobile
Bay

Chandeleur Sound

Breton Sound

Mississippi River

G U L F   O F   M E X I C O

SABINE RIVER

Red R.

Calcasieu R.

Mermentau R.

Bayou Nezpique

Bayou des Cannes

Teche

Atchafalaya R.

Dugdemona R.

Castor Ck.

Little R.

Ouachita R.

Black R.

Red R.

Catahoula
Lake

Tenasas R.

Bayou Macon

Boeuf R.

Arrayed about the margins of the Florida Parishes in 1700 were seven Muskogean tribes—the Acolapissa, Bayougoula, Houma, Quinapisa-Mugulasha, Okelousa, and Tangipahoa. Each of the seven spoke a Choctaw dialect, and their history is intertwined. Victims of intertribal hostilities, most moved frequently to escape oppression; too, like other tribes they were decimated by European diseases.

The La Salle expedition in 1682 sighted a Quinapisa ("Those Who See") village near present-day Hahnville. The tribe assaulted the French party during both their descent and ascent of the Mississippi. They also attempted to incite the Koroa and Natchez against the French. Four years later La Salle's lieutenant, Tonti, made peace with the tribe. When Iberville came up the Mississippi in 1699, he found no trace of the Quinapisa, but he later learned that they had merged with the Mugulasha ("People of the Other Side"); other sources suggest that the tribes were one and the same. At this time the Quinapisa-Mugulasha were living with the Bayougoula near the stream which bears the latter's name; together the tribes numbered four hundred to five hundred. In the spring of 1700 the Bayougoula attacked their fellow villagers, killing many and driving the rest away, ostensibly because of the Quinapisa's friendship with the Houma. The Quinapisa then became amalgamated within other tribes.

When first visited by the French in 1699, the Acolapissa ("Those Who See and Hear") lived in settlements stretching along the Pearl River. Their population at the time was variously estimated at between 150 and 300 warriors. By 1705 the Acolapissa had moved to Bayou Castine on the north shore of Lake Pontchartrain. The French set-tled the Natchitoches Indians among them soon after. The two tribes lived as neighbors until 1714, when a French effort to return the Natchitoches to the Spanish frontier prompted the Acolapissa to attack the Natchitoches, killing some and capturing or scattering the rest. Perhaps as early as 1718, but in any case by 1722, the Acolapissa had again moved, this time to the left bank of the Mississippi River above New Orleans. By that time they may have incorporated among them the Tangipahoa. At their new location the Acolapissa-Tangipahoa gradually became amalgamated first with the Bayougoula, then later with the Houma.

The Houma ("Red") greeted La Salle on his descent of the Mississippi in 1682. Living on the left side of the Mississippi opposite the mouth of the Red River, they early allied with the French. The Tunica, who had settled among them in 1700, rose up against their hosts soon after; the Houma survivors moved to Bayou St. John near New Orleans. They later moved upriver to present-day Ascension Parish, establishing two settlements. In 1739 the total Houma-Bayougoula-Acolapissa-Tangipahoa-Quinapisa-Mugulasha population was estimated at 270–300 adults. The tribes gradually sold most of their riverine landholdings to colonists. Some intermarried with the Atakapa and moved southwesterly; the remainder moved southward to the present-day parishes of Lafourche and Terrebonne. Today the Houma number eleven thousand—the state's largest surviving Indian group. The Houma today are recognized by the state, though not by the federal government, as a tribal group.

Iberville met the Bayougoula ("Bayou" or "River People") in 1699 at the site of the city which preserves their name, although this same tribe may have been the Pischenoa encountered by Tonti thirteen years earlier. At the time of the Iberville meeting, smallpox had devastated the tribe. In 1700 the Bayougoula (numbering perhaps a hundred families) attacked their neighbors, the Quinapisa-Mugulasha, killing or dispersing them. The Acolapissa and Tiou tribes were asked to take their place. Six years later the Taensa migrated from their Lake St. Joseph homeland to settle among the Bayougoula. They soon thereafter gave their new hosts the same treatment those hosts had accorded the Quinapisa-Mugulasha. The remaining Bayougoula fled downriver below New Orleans. Subsequently (by 1725) they moved upriver, forty-five miles above New Orleans. By 1739 they were living between the Acolapissa and the Houma and had practically fused with the latter tribe.

The Tangipahoa and Okelousa have a less-well-known history. The Tangipahoa ("Corn Gatherers" or "Corn-cob People") may have been a part of the Acolapissa along the Pearl River. By 1682, however, a Tangipahoa village had been built on the Mississippi downriver from the Quinapisa and destroyed by the Houma and their allies. Fleeing back to the Pearl in the first decade of the eighteenth century, the Tangipahoa moved to the river which today bears their name. Incorporation into another tribe seems to have been their fate. The Okelousa ("Black Water") have been described by some as a wandering people. Others suggest that they resided around two lakes to the west and upriver of Pointe Coupee. Allies in the 1682 Houma destruction of the Tangipahoa village, the Okelousa very likely were subsequently absorbed into a larger tribe.

Copyright © 1995 by the University of Oklahoma Press

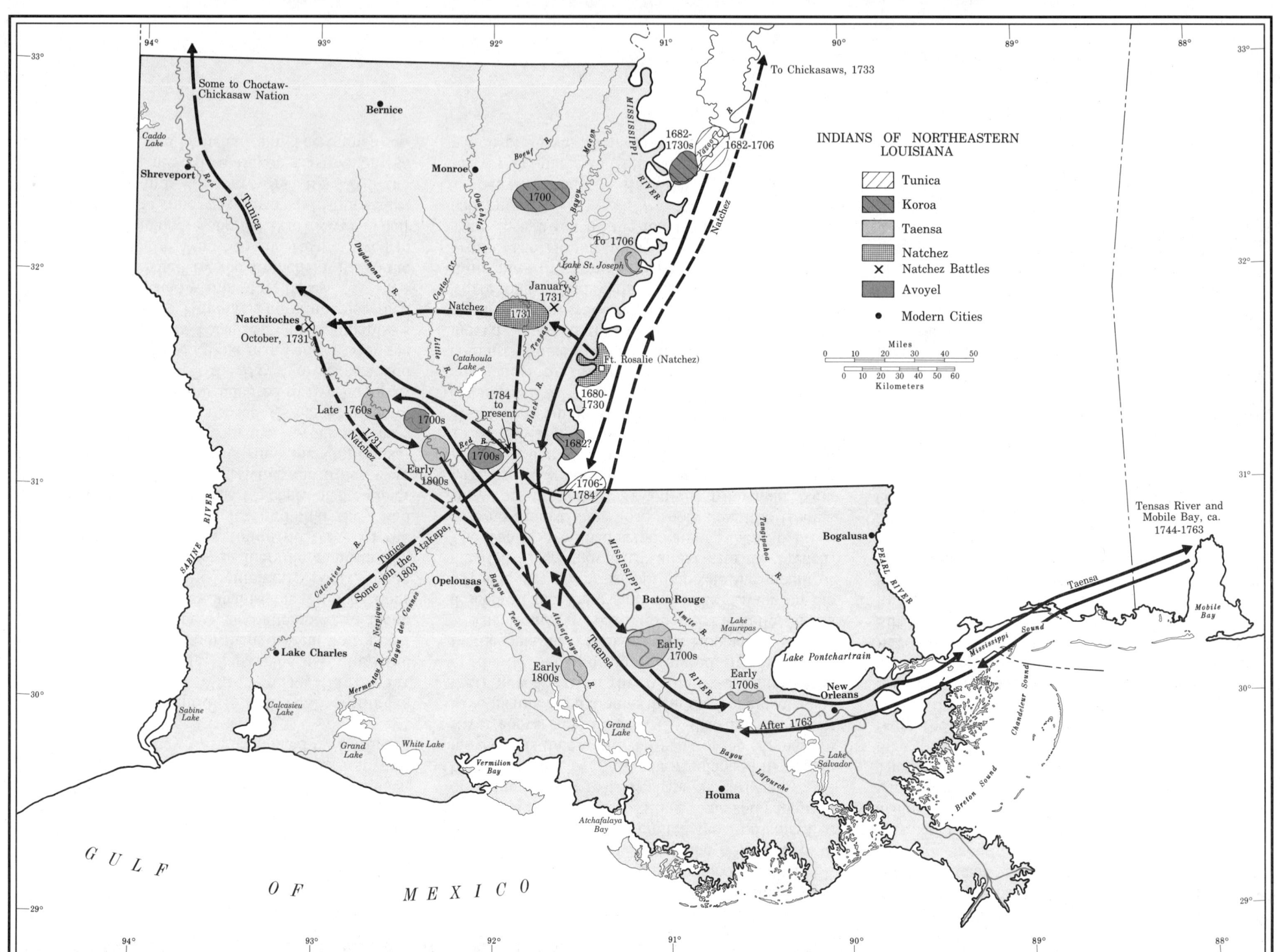

INDIANS OF NORTHEASTERN
LOUISIANA

Tunica
Koroa
Taensa
Natchez
✕ Natchez Battles
Avoyel

● Modern Cities

Miles
0 10 20 30 40 50

0 10 20 30 40 50 60
Kilometers

At the beginning of the eighteenth century, northeast Louisiana was occupied (and visited) by tribes of the Tunican (Tunica and Koroa) and Natchezan (Taensa, Natchez, and Avoyel) linguistic groups. The latter group outnumbered the former. The Natchez by their wars with the French exerted a far greater impact on Louisiana history.

The Taensa, first visited by La Salle and Tonti in 1682, represented the largest Natchezan tribe residing within Louisiana's present bounds. Living in several villages on Lake St. Joseph, they numbered approximately seven hundred in 1699. However, in 1706, because of the threat of the Yazoo and other tribes across the Mississippi, the Taensa moved downriver, settling among the Bayougoula. They soon rose up against their new hosts, however, killing some and scattering the remainder. In 1715 some Taensa moved to the left bank of the Mississippi at Bayou Manchac, while others established a village above New Orleans on the river's right bank.

After 1730 the Taensa migrated yet again, moving to settle along the Tensas River near Mobile Bay. They remained there until the British gained control of the region by the Treaty of Paris in 1763. The Taensa (with the Apalachee and Pacana totaling two hundred people) then returned to Louisiana, settling along the Red River near present-day Boyce. When the Taensa sold these lands to developers in 1803, some moved southwestward to the Bayou Boeuf. In 1812 they moved even further inland, settling along the Bayou Taensa, a tributary to Grand Lake. Gradually the Taensa were assimilated into other tribes, primarily the Chitimacha, although traces of Taensa culture continued into the twentieth century.

The Tunica ("People"), though largely living along the Yazoo River, also moved across northeastern Louisiana in the salt trade or in hunting and gathering parties. A Tunica village existed along the Ouachita as late as 1687. In 1706 the Tunica, fearful of tribes allied with the British, moved to the Houma village. Although initially well received, the Tunica shortly rose up against their hosts, killing over half and scattering the others. Between 1784 and 1803 the Tunica moved up the Red to Marksville Prairie, where many descendants remain. Some moved further west to join the Atakapa; still others moved to the Choctaw Nation in Indian Territory. Estimates of the Tunica population vary from La Harpe's 1719 total of 460 to the twenty-five warriors in Sibley's account of 1805. Today's Tunica-Biloxi, fewer than a hundred in number, form one of Louisiana's federally recognized tribes.

Like the Tunica, the Koroa lived along the Yazoo River, although some evidence suggests activity along and west of the Mississippi. By 1704, after encounters with the Quapaw and Illinois, the Koroa had probably returned to the Yazoo. They allied themselves with the Natchez in the ill-fated 1729 rebellion. In turn they were attacked by allies of the French, and still later by the Quapaw. After a 1731 joint attack with the Natchez against the Tunica, the Koroa moved among the Chickasaw and probably the Choctaw. The combined Koroa-Tunica-Yazoo population in 1699 has been estimated at two thousand; 300 families are estimated in 1702, and a Yazoo-Koroa-Ofo total of 250 families is given for 1722.

The Avoyel ("Stone People" or "Flint People"), unlike most tribes, migrated little; in fact they seem never to have left the region in which the French originally encountered them. Avoyel territory extended along the Red downriver from modern Alexandria to the confluence of the Red and Mississippi rivers. Villages are known to have existed near present-day Marksville and elsewhere along the Red. The Avoyel acted as middlemen for horses and cattle plundered by western tribes from the Spanish. Geographically stable, they suffered tremendous population loss during the eighteenth century. Sibley estimated their population as only a handful in 1805. Some descendants, however, remain in the Marksville area today.

Although occupying lands outside the present state, near the modern city of their name, the Natchez played an important role in Louisiana history. This tribe, though initially friendly to the French, turned against them in the early decades of the eighteenth century. This dissatisfaction resulted in part from the infiltration of British traders, who naturally stirred up resentment towards the French among the Natchez and other tribes. French encroachment on Natchez territory also caused hostility. The Natchez wars (of 1716, 1722, and primarily 1729–1731) resulted in several battles with the French and their Indian allies. The Natchez scattered across the state before regrouping and retreating into Chickasaw territory. Their warrior strength was estimated by Tonti as fifteen hundred in 1686; Iberville estimated fifteen hundred families in 1702; an estimate of seven hundred warriors was given in 1730.

Copyright © 1995 by the University of Oklahoma Press

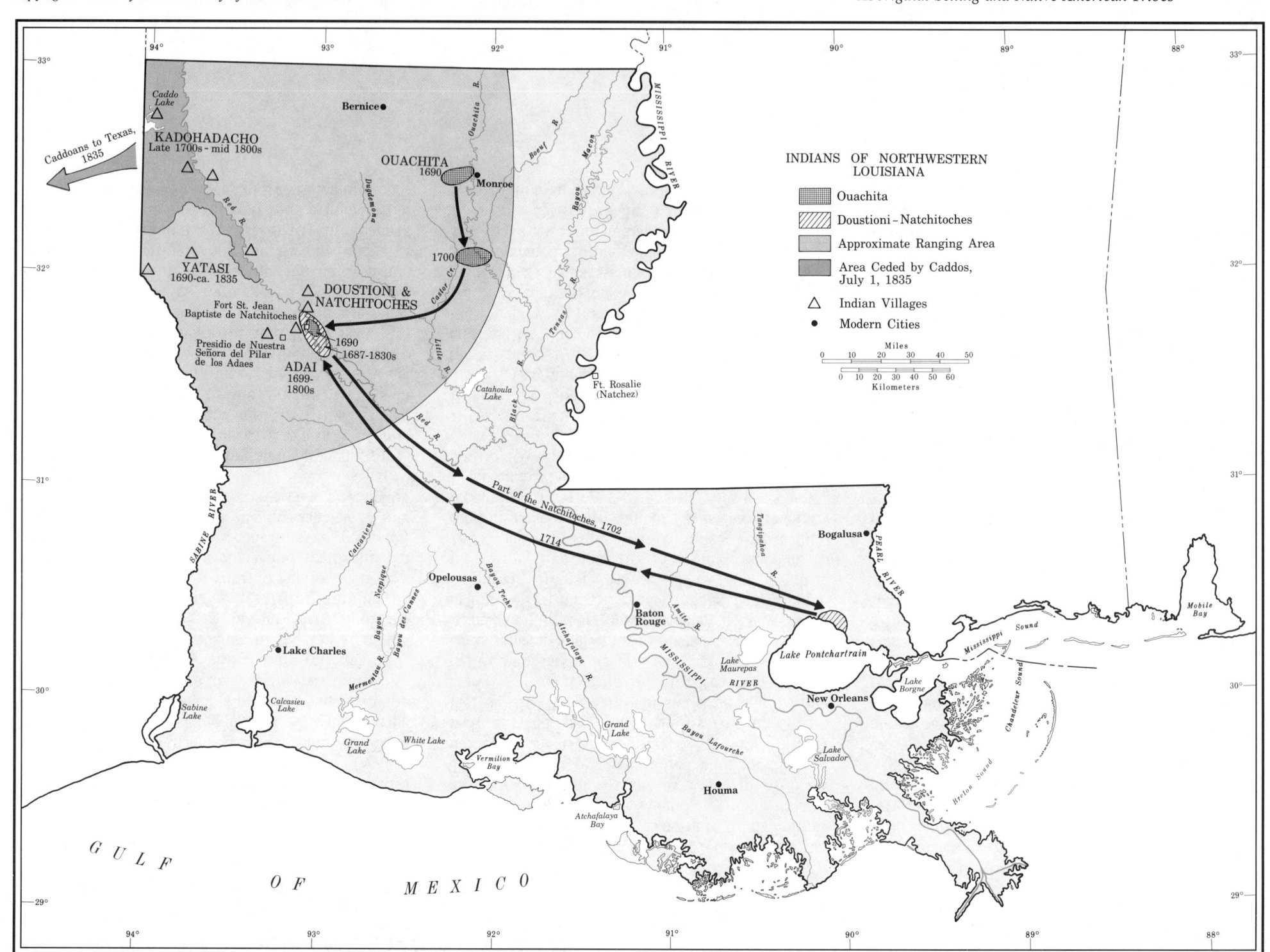

INDIANS OF NORTHWESTERN
LOUISIANA

Ouachita

Doustioni – Natchitoches

Approximate Ranging Area

Area Ceded by Caddos,
July 1, 1835

△ Indian Villages

● Modern Cities

Miles
0 10 20 30 40 50

0 10 20 30 40 50 60
Kilometers

Caddoans to Texas,
1835

KADOHADACHO
Late 1700s – mid 1800s

OUACHITA
1690

Bernice ●

Monroe ●

1700

YATASI
1690 – ca. 1835

DOUSTIONI &
NATCHITOCHES

Fort St. Jean
Baptiste de Natchitoches

Presidio de Nuestra
Señora del Pilar
de los Adaes

ADAI
1699 –
1800s

1690
1687 – 1830s

Caddo
Lake

Red R.

Dugdemona

Ouachita R.

Bœuf R.

Macon R.

Bayou

MISSISSIPPI RIVER

Castor Ck.

Little R.

Texas R.

Catahoula
Lake

Black R.

Ft. Rosalie
(Natchez)

Part of the Natchitoches, 1702

1714

Bogalusa ●

PEARL RIVER

Tangipahoa R.

SABINE RIVER

Calcasieu R.

Nezpique

Bayou des Cannes

Bayou Teche

Opelousas ●

Atchafalaya R.

Baton
Rouge ●

Amite R.

MISSISSIPPI
RIVER

Mobile
Bay

● Lake Charles

Mermentau R.

Sabine
Lake

Calcasieu
Lake

Grand
Lake

White Lake

Vermilion
Bay

Grand
Lake

Bayou Lafourche

Lake
Maurepas

Lake Pontchartrain

Lake
Borgne

New Orleans ●

Chandeleur Sound

Mississippi
Sound

Houma ●

Atchafalaya
Bay

Lake
Salvador

Breton Sound

G U L F   O F   M E X I C O

Northwestern Louisiana lay in the domain of the Caddo, confederations totaling perhaps two dozen tribes. A prehistoric Caddoan culture ranged across not only northwest Louisiana but also adjacent areas of Arkansas, Texas, and Oklahoma from the first millennium A.D. until the 1835 Caddo land cession. The Caddoans derived culturally from the Troyville–Coles Creek culture (Map 16) but with western plains influences.

In Louisiana the Caddo lived primarily along the Red River valley but ranged afield in search of food. The individual tribes were scattered across the region. Many frequently changed village sites, often because of the regular flooding of the rivers, which has obliterated much of the evidence of their presence. At the close of the seventeenth century the main Caddoan groups within the present-day bounds of Louisiana were the Ouachita, Yatasi, Doustioni, Natchitoches, and Adai.

The Ouachita ("Cow River People"), ranging as far east as the river which bears their name, had by 1700 largely returned to the area near present-day Natchitoches. Bienville met those still on the banks of the Ouachita; he estimated their number at seventy men. This group was scattered—some say destroyed—by invading tribes (the Taensa or perhaps the Chickasaw), with any remnant moving to the west along the Red River. There they joined with the Natchitoches or the Kadohadacho.

The Yatasi ("Those Other People") lived upstream along the Red northwest of Natchitoches, occupying several villages between present-day Coushatta and Logansport. After the French established their outpost at Natchitoches, some Yatasi moved there, while others migrated north among the Kadohadacho to escape the Chickasaw. Some later returned to their original homeland, settling near Logansport. Their number, when combined with the Doustioni and Natchitoches in 1718, was said to be eighty warriors; by 1825 the Yatasi had a total population of perhaps thirty-six.

The Doustioni ("Salt People") and Natchitoches ("Place of the Paw-paw") resided in the area of the present-day city of Natchitoches. They for the most part migrated less frequently than did other Caddoan tribes. However, in 1702, St. Denis moved a part of the Natchitoches tribe to the north shore of Lake Pontchartrain close to the Acolapissa. In 1714 the Natchitoches returned to their original home when St. Denis established Fort St. Jean Baptiste de Natchitoches, the oldest permanent settlement in the Louisiana Purchase. Before the Natchitoches left their Lake Pontchartrain home, an attack by their Acolapissa neighbors killed many and scattered the rest. The Natchitoches, Doustioni, and Yatasi together mustered eighty warriors in 1718. In 1805, John Sibley numbered thirty-two Natchitoches, which included the fused Doustioni.

The Adai ("Place along a Stream") lived to the southwest of the Natchitoches near present-day Robeline, adjacent to the disputed border of French Louisiana and Spanish Texas. A Spanish mission—San Miguel de Linares—was established there in 1717, destroyed by the French in 1719, and rebuilt by the Spanish in 1721 along with a fort, the Presidio de Nuestra Señora del Pilar de los Adaes. The Adai shared the fate of their Caddoan kinspeople, participating in the general Caddoan migration of the 1830s. Bienville estimated the Adai population as fifty warriors in 1700 and one hundred warriors in 1718. By 1805 some twenty men and even more women were noted by John Sibley.

The Kadohadacho ("Great Chiefs")—a main Caddoan confederation—lived at the close of the seventeenth century near the great bend of the Red River in southwestern Arkansas. They were visited by La Salle's companions in 1687 and his lieutenant Tonti in 1690. In the eighteenth century the Kadohadacho moved into the present bounds of Louisiana, settling first near Caddo Lake, then further downriver on the Red River.

The Caddoans acted as middlemen, trading with the French and other tribes. Their friendship with St. Denis and his descendants made the Caddoan region largely an oasis of peace and prosperity. They remained allied to the French and later the Spanish, objecting only in the late eighteenth century when the Choctaw, brought in by the Spanish, began to encroach upon Caddo territory.

After the Louisiana Purchase the Caddoan tribes, as other Indian groups, felt the pressure of encroaching white settlement. On July 1, 1835, a treaty with the United States was agreed upon, ceding approximately one million acres (including their lands in Louisiana) to the federal government. This treaty was the only Indian land cession with the United States signed within the bounds of Louisiana. After the cession the Caddo moved west, some to Texas, others to Mexico. In time they were expelled from their Texas lands, and in 1859, they moved up to the Indian Territory, present-day Oklahoma.

Copyright © 1995 by the University of Oklahoma Press

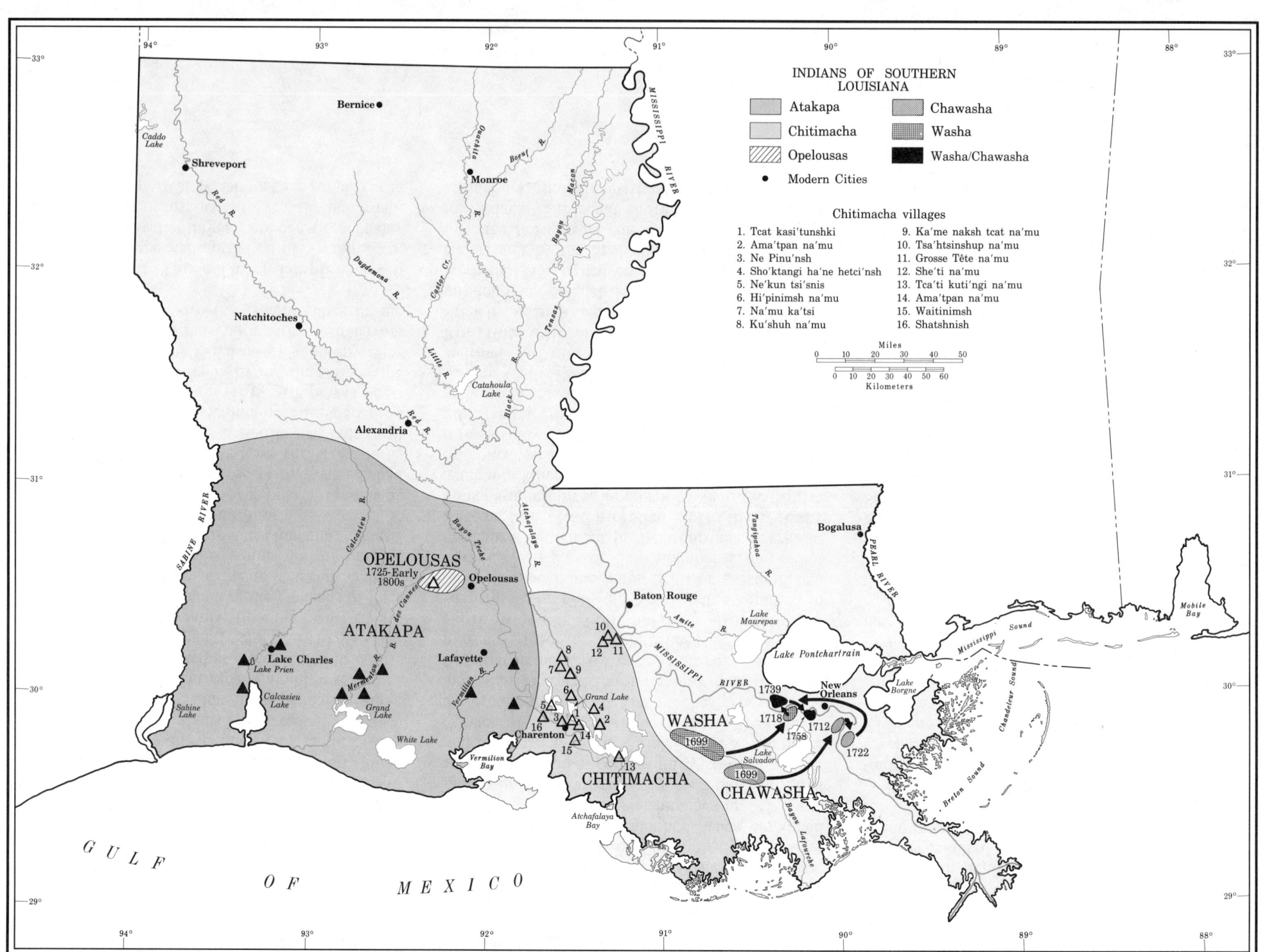

INDIANS OF SOUTHERN
LOUISIANA

Atakapa　　　Chawasha

Chitimacha　　Washa

Opelousas　　Washa/Chawasha

● Modern Cities

Chitimacha villages

1. Tcat kasi'tunshki
2. Ama'tpan na'mu
3. Ne Pinu'nsh
4. Sho'ktangi ha'ne hetci'nsh
5. Ne'kun tsi'snis
6. Hi'pinimsh na'mu
7. Na'mu ka'tsi
8. Ku'shuh na'mu
9. Ka'me naksh tcat na'mu
10. Tsa'htsinshup na'mu
11. Grosse Tête na'mu
12. She'ti na'mu
13. Tca'ti kuti'ngi na'mu
14. Ama'tpan na'mu
15. Waitinimsh
16. Shatshnish

The Atakapa occupied much of southwest Louisiana. They comprised a series of bands from Vermilion River on the east, stretching westward past the Mermentau River to the Calcasieu and lower Sabine rivers. Related bands lay beyond the Sabine in Texas, reaching to the Trinity River and Galveston Bay. The name Atakapa means "Man-eater" in Choctaw, but the tribe knew themselves as Ishak ("the People"). Initially isolated from the French occupants of Louisiana, the Atakapa traded with the French, though they otherwise remained largely untouched culturally by the Europeans. However, beginning with the 1760 sale to colonists of lands west of Bayou Teche, the occupation of Atakapan lands by Europeans pushed the tribe gradually westward. The last Eastern Atakapa village, on the Mermentau, was inhabited perhaps as late as the 1830s. Members of these bands joined the Western Atakapa; their last village, on Indian Lake (Lake Prien) was inhabited until the midnineteenth century. Other members of the tribe moved on into the Indian Territory. Swanton estimated the original Atakapan population at less than twenty-five hundred; Sibley numbered only fifty in 1805.

The Opelousas ("Black Haired" or "Black Headed"), kinspeople of the Atakapa, were first encountered by the French in 1725 on the prairies west of the present city of that name. In this region of the state they seem to have remained until they all disappeared, probably to join the Atakapa or the Bayou Chicot Choctaw. They originally numbered perhaps four hundred–five hundred; Sibley gave their population in 1805 as forty.

The Chitimacha ("Those Living on Grand River" or "Those Who Have Pots") homeland lay along Grand Lake and its environs and the upper reaches of Bayou Lafourche. Although they were one of the first allies of Iberville and the French, relations with them afterwards deteriorated. The Chitimacha in 1706 had been invited by the Taensa to share in the spoils remaining from the Taensa slaughter of the Bayougoula. Those Chitimacha who responded were themselves attacked and enslaved. A Chitimacha revenge effort failed later in 1706, but the disappointed war party killed a group of four Frenchmen, including the missionary St. Cosmé. The following year the French and their Indian allies in reprisal destroyed one of the Chitimacha villages. Thereafter the Chitimacha retreated into the more remote parts of their Atchafalaya Basin domain. Many were captured and sold as slaves, in return for which their kinspeople harassed French settlements along the Mississippi. Finally, peace between the tribe and the French was concluded in 1718. The next year a group of the tribe moved to the Mississippi, settling along a stretch of the river extending from Bayou Lafourche upriver as far as present-day Plaquemine. Gradually the Chitimacha lands were encroached upon and finally totally occupied. In 1699, La Harpe estimated seven hundred to eight hundred warriors among the tribe. Today about 250 Chitimacha live in the vicinity of Charenton and are a federally recognized group.

The Chawasha ("Raccoon Place") may have been those Indians who attacked the survivors of the De Soto-Moscoso expedition in 1543. When the French arrived in 1699, the Chawasha and Washa had villages along the Bayou Lafourche. Together the Chawasha, Washa, and Okelousas numbered two hundred warriors. Early allies of the French, the Chawasha joined in the French attack on the Chitimacha in 1707. The Chawasha themselves were attacked by a combined party of Natchez, Chickasaw, and Yazoo in 1715; many were killed, others enslaved. The French had moved the Chawasha to a new location on the Mississippi River in 1712, although sources differ about its exact location. After the Natchez War of 1729, the Chawasha were again attacked; some were killed by a group of slaves sent by the fearful citizenry of New Orleans. In 1739 the Chawasha and Washa were seen living on the left bank of the Mississippi near Les Allemands, and in 1758 they were in a village ten to fourteen miles upriver from New Orleans. By the early nineteenth century they had disappeared.

The Washa ("Hunting Place"), like the Chawasha, may have harassed the remnants of the De Soto-Moscoso expedition as it came down the Mississippi in 1543. At the time of French colonization in 1699, they lived in a village on the Bayou Lafourche, part of a total Washa-Chawasha-Okelousas group totaling seven hundred to eight hundred warriors. In 1718 the tribe moved to the right bank of the Mississippi about forty miles upriver from New Orleans. By 1739 they were in the same area as the Chawasha, on the left bank of the Mississippi near Les Allemands. Thereafter the Washa shared the same fate as the Chawasha, first moving downriver closer to New Orleans and then gradually fading from the pages of history.

Copyright © 1995 by the University of Oklahoma Press

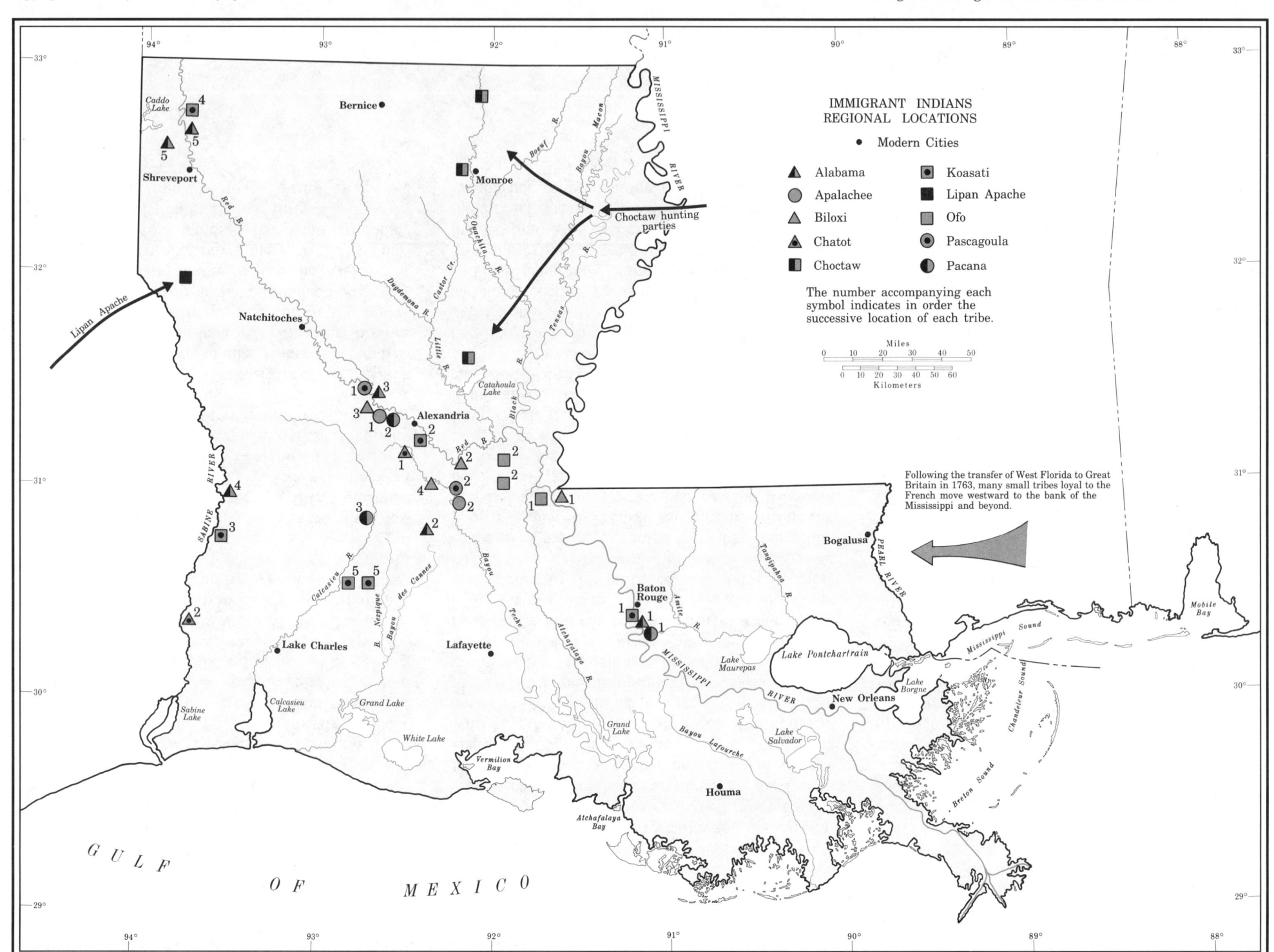

IMMIGRANT INDIANS
REGIONAL LOCATIONS

• Modern Cities

▲ Alabama   ◉ Koasati

⬤ Apalachee   ■ Lipan Apache

▲ Biloxi   ▣ Ofo

▲ Chatot   ◉ Pascagoula

◨ Choctaw   ◐ Pacana

The number accompanying each
symbol indicates in order the
successive location of each tribe.

Miles
0   10   20   30   40   50

0   10   20   30   40   50   60
Kilometers

Following the transfer of West Florida to Great
Britain in 1763, many small tribes loyal to the
French move westward to the bank of the
Mississippi and beyond.

Choctaw hunting
parties

Lipan Apache

GULF   OF   MEXICO

Various Indian tribes not resident in Louisiana at the time of French colonization later migrated to its territory, sometimes staying, but more often merely pausing for a short period before moving on. These migrations resulted from a combination of factors: (1) loyalty to one European empire over another; (2) escape from belligerent neighboring tribes; and (3) the systematic displacement of Indians by Europeans and their American descendants. Even as tribes migrated, total Indian population declined, the result of disease, war, and the disruption of tribal economies.

A major period of migration occurred following the Treaty of Paris (1763), in which France lost practically all its North American empire. That portion east of the Mississippi (exclusive of the Isle of Orleans), plus Canada went to Britain. Louisiana west of the Mississippi and the Isle of Orleans had been secretly ceded to Spain the previous year. Over a period of time, France had moved many diminishing tribes from Louisiana (and elsewhere in its empire) to the relative safety of the region around Mobile Bay. Many of these tribes declined to become subject to the British, choosing instead to move westward to the banks of the Mississippi and Red rivers. Thus the Apalachee, Chatot, Pascagoula, Mobile, Alabama, Koasati, and Pacana by 1765 had begun their own westward movement. The Lipan Apache, on the other hand, had moved east from Texas, first by force as slaves, then as residents of western Louisiana.

In addition to the disruption caused by their migration, many of the immigrant tribes endured further chaos in their lives during the late eighteenth century. The more dominant tribes such as the Choctaw took advantage of their smaller, more peaceful neighbors. The Choctaw, originally invited into Louisiana by the Spanish in an attempt to confound the British across the river, proved so troublesome that Spain attempted to contain them east of the Ouachita. Spanish authorities established Indian enclaves, such as that at Marksville Prairie in present-day Avoyelles Parish, and posted garrisons to protect them. Many tribes settled first along the Red River in central Louisiana; some remained there, while others moved on, primarily to the west and southwest.

Following the Louisiana Purchase of 1803, more tribal migrations occurred. Population pressures exerted by increased American migration prompted relocation. Even before the transfer of Louisiana from Spanish hands, first to Napoleonic France and thence to the United States, several tribes had sought and been granted lands along or beyond the Sabine River in Spanish Texas. In the early decades of the nineteenth century movement to these sites increased. Gradually the southeastern Indians, as well as those in Louisiana, succumbed to diplomatic and military pressures from the new national government. They ceded their homelands to the United States and joined a still larger movement to the "permanent" Indian Territory, present-day Oklahoma. Over time some tribes by and large vacated the new state of Louisiana, while others remained.

As the nineteenth century progressed, immigrant as well as "native" Louisiana tribes remaining in the state continued to lose population through hostilities and disease. Largely relegated to less fertile lands, these tribes also became more careful in their dealings with the dominant white culture. A mixed group of Indians, whites, and blacks developed in southwestern Louisiana, where they were given the pejorative "Red Bones." More Louisiana Indians eventually tried moving to the Indian Territory as the nineteenth century drew to a close, but of this group many gradually returned. Those remaining in Louisiana became more remote, both geographically and culturally, from the dominant Anglo culture. Many tribal identities became lost as tribes fused or died away.

The twentieth century has seen several changes in the life of Native Americans, Louisiana's tribes included. A permanent, exclusive homeland in the Indian Territory proved elusive as lands were allotted in severalty and tribal government diminished in authority. A consistent national policy has proved equally elusive; government attitudes have ranged from paternalism to emancipation. Tribes internally have often reflected an equally fractured nature.

Today several enclaves of tribes are scattered about the state, including primarily immigrant tribes. The federally recognized tribal groups are the Chitimacha (Map 21), Koasati, and Tunica-Biloxi (Map 19). Today several hundred Koasati reside in Allen Parish and retain more ethnic identity than most other Louisiana tribes. The Biloxi fused with the native Tunica, and today the total group numbers over one hundred. Five state-recognized groups are the native Houma (Map 18) and four bands of the Choctaw: the Jena Band in La Salle Parish (146 members); the Clifton Choctaw in Rapides Parish (about 200 members); the Louisiana Band in East Baton Rouge Parish (150 members); and the Choctaw-Apache of Ebarb, Sabine Parish (1,500 members).

Copyright © 1995 by the University of Oklahoma Press

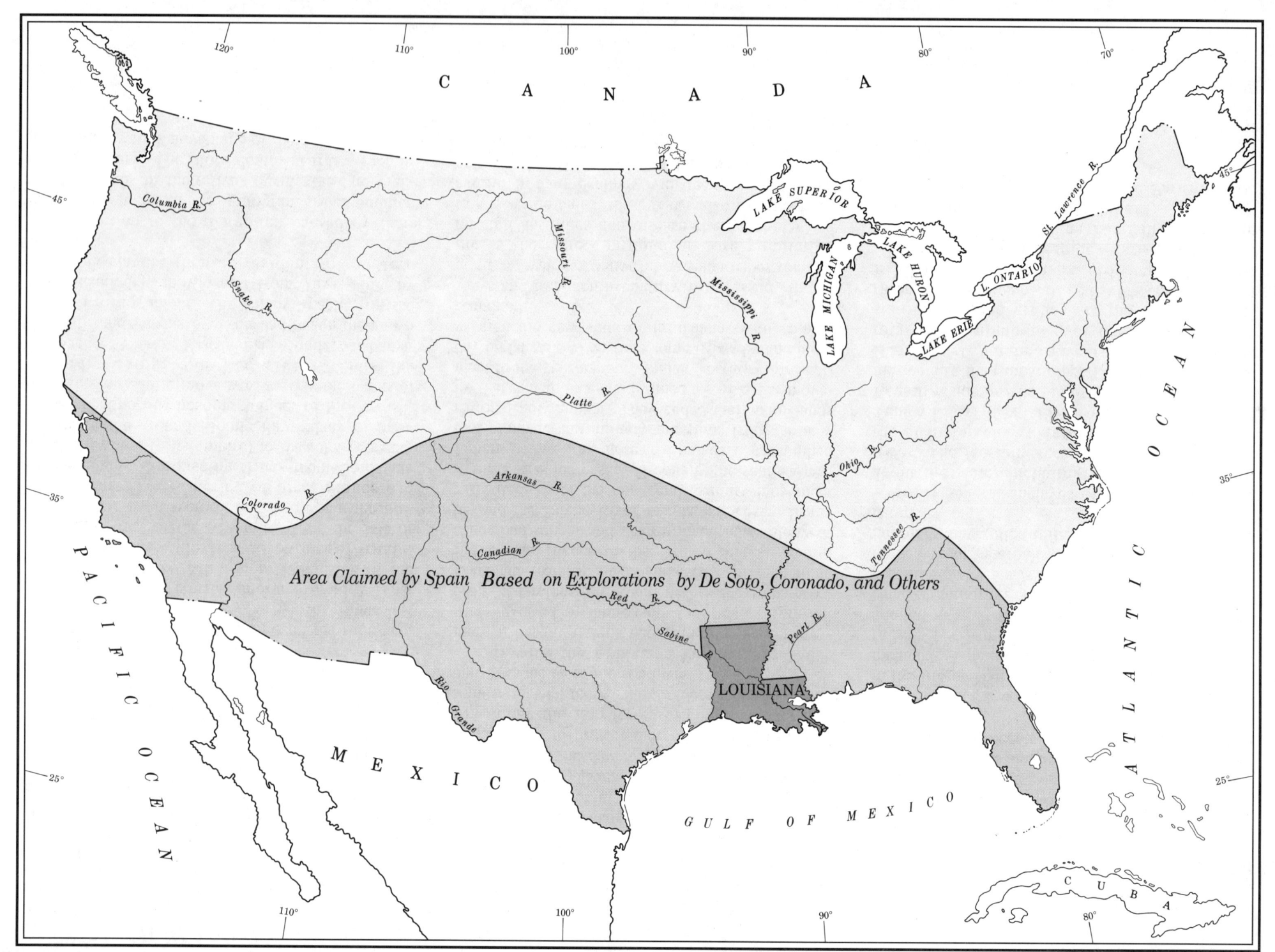

C A N A D A

PACIFIC OCEAN

ATLANTIC OCEAN

Columbia R.

Snake R.

Missouri R.

Mississippi R.

LAKE SUPERIOR

LAKE MICHIGAN

LAKE HURON

LAKE ERIE

L. ONTARIO

St. Lawrence R.

Platte R.

Ohio R.

Arkansas R.

Colorado R.

Canadian R.

Tennessee R.

Area Claimed by Spain Based on Explorations by De Soto, Coronado, and Others

Red R.

Sabine R.

Pearl R.

LOUISIANA

Rio Grande

M E X I C O

GULF OF MEXICO

C U B A

Spanish claims to the "New World" of North and South America arose out of the voyages of Christopher Columbus beginning in 1492. Although he sailed under the Spanish flag of Ferdinand and Isabella, Columbus himself was a native of Genoa in Italy and had connections with other European rivals of Spain. Thus the Spanish court early sought to legitimize its own claims to the exclusion of those rivals.

The source of this legitimacy was to be the pope. Although over the centuries the papacy had declined in actual temporal power, nations still used Rome as an arbiter in settling squabbles. Papal bulls (official documents sealed by the pope) had been issued since the twelfth century to confer or legitimize sovereignty. Thus, in 1493, Ferdinand and Isabella received such papal sovereignty over lands discovered and undiscovered in the Americas. Spain's only partner in the New World would be Portugal, to whom would go all lands east of a line drawn north to south through a point 100 leagues (approximately 350 miles) west of the Azores. To Spain would go all lands west of that line. This Line of Demarcation was then modified by the Treaty of Tordesillas, June 7, 1494, between Spain and Portugal. The meridian moved to the west, to a point 370 leagues (approximately 1,300 miles) west (47°–50° west longitude) of the Cape Verde Islands, intersecting South America near the mouth of the Amazon River.

For half a century other European powers, notably England and France, honored this treaty. However, with the rise of national feelings and power, England, France, and others began to contest Spanish claims. Spanish mistreatment of the Indians under the guise of Christianization aided these nations in their claim that the Treaty of Tordesillas no longer had force of law upon them.

During the sixteenth and seventeenth centuries, the decline of Spanish power vis-à-vis her major European rivals, France and England, became more and more apparent. Nevertheless Spain continued to insist on her exclusive claims to much of North America. The Gulf of Mexico was a "closed sea," she maintained, for the use of Spanish trade and commerce only. Official naval forces as well as pirates, whose plundering was winked at by the rivals' governments, however, contested those claims.

Spanish activity in the interior of North America did provide a basis for that nation's claims to ownership. From bases in the West Indies, Ponce de León, Lucas Vásquez de Alyllón, Pánfilo de Narváez, and Hernando de Soto traversed the coast and interior of the present-day southeastern United States as far west as Texas and as far north as Tennessee. In 1541, Francisco Vásquez de Coronado led an expedition over much of New Mexico, Texas, Oklahoma, and Kansas. Juan de Oñate in 1601 descended the Canadian River. These expeditions had as their primary goal the discovery of new sources of wealth, but none was discovered. Nevertheless they added to knowledge of the interior and to the legitimacy of Spanish claims to ownership.

French activity in the Gulf during the seventeenth century especially alarmed the Spanish. Particularly, news first of the descent of the Mississippi by La Salle, followed by his abortive attempts to establish a French fort near New Spain, led to efforts out of Mexico to locate the proposed colony and destroy it. Four Spanish naval expeditions set out between 1686 and 1688. Although the wreckage of one of La Salle's ships was spotted, no evidence of the fort was found. Then in 1689 the remnants of the fort were discovered. These French intrusions led to an expansion of Spanish missions in Texas, but these missions were abandoned in 1693.

Throughout the early eighteenth century, royal intermarriage brought the French and Spanish crowns closer in Europe. However, such family affiliation and regal intimacy did not extend to North America. Trading and other expeditionary forays from French Louisiana into Texas and New Mexico met with seizure of goods and imprisonment of personnel by the Spanish authorities. Even as late as the 1760s, when negotiations were underway to end the French and Indian (Seven Years') War, Spanish envoys objected to any cession of French territory to the British on the grounds that the French held such territory only by courtesy of the Spanish crown.

Copyright © 1995 by the University of Oklahoma Press

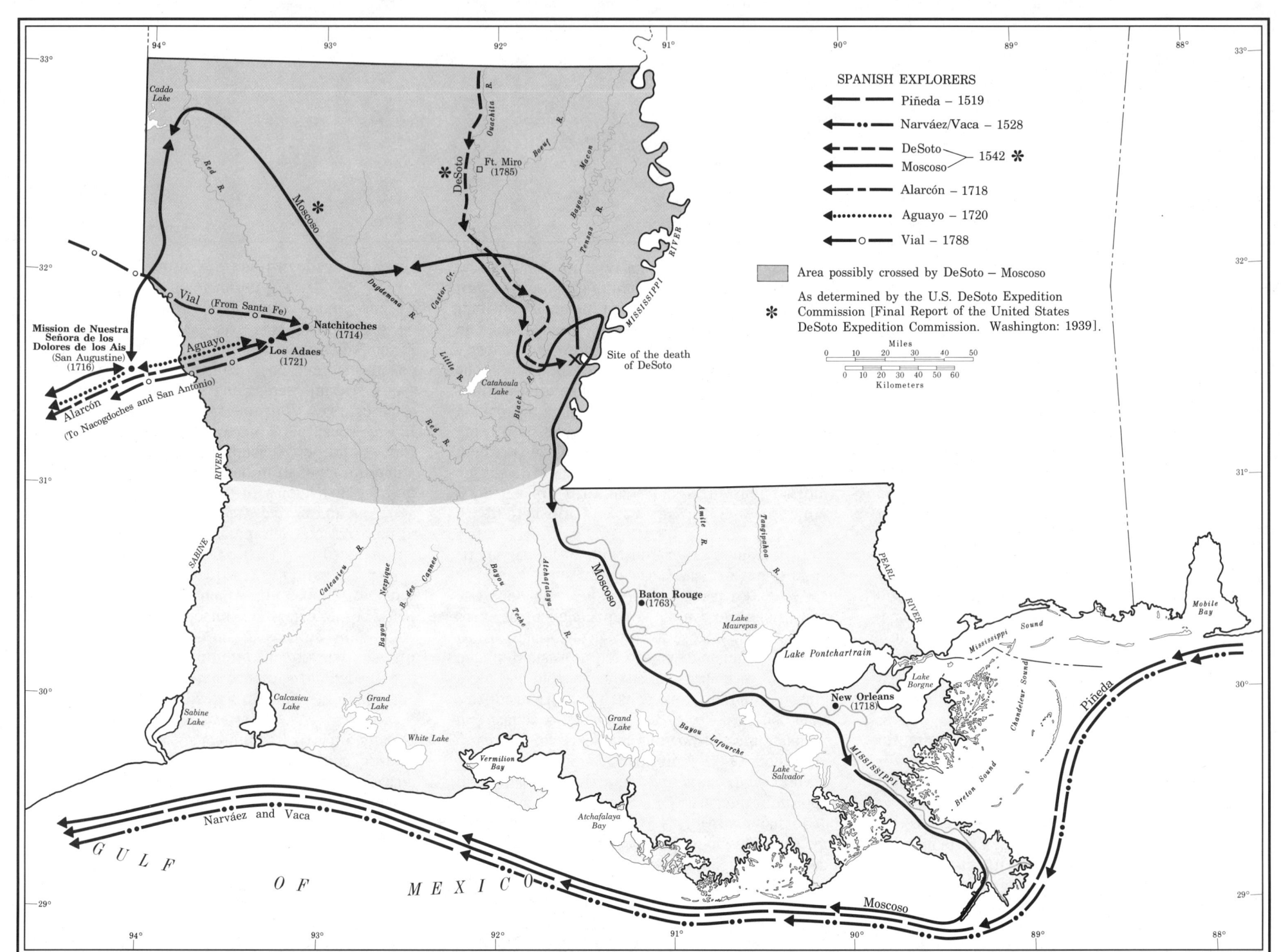

Spain pursued an aggressive exploration of the Western Hemisphere. Early colonies in the West Indies served as bases from which to penetrate both North and South America. During the first half of the sixteenth century, several expeditions added to the storehouse of knowledge about the coasts and interior of the Gulf and southeastern United States.

Alonso Alvarez de Piñeda in 1519 sailed along the northern Gulf Coast from Florida to Vera Cruz. He discovered the mouth of a great river, named by him the Río del Espiritu Santo ("River of the Holy Spirit"). This may have been the Mississippi River, but more likely it was the Mobile River.

In 1527, Pánfilo de Narváez organized an expedition of six hundred men to follow in the footsteps of Ponce de León. After losing two hundred men to desertion and storm, the expedition landed in Florida at Tampa Bay in April 1528. A march overland to St. Andrew Bay proved disastrous, so a fleet of small ships was built to sail along the Gulf Coast to Spanish settlements near the Panuco River in Mexico. After passing the mouth of the Mississippi, the fleet was wrecked by a storm. The survivors continued overland. A total of five, including the expedition's chronicler, Alvar Nuñez Cabeza de Vaca, finally reached Mexico in 1536.

In May 1539, Hernando de Soto—wealthy from his association with Francisco Pizarro in Peru—landed at Tampa Bay with 620 men in yet another foray to locate gold and silver in Florida. From 1539 to 1542 the expedition ranged over the southeast from modern-day Florida, Georgia, and the Carolinas westward through Alabama, Mississippi, and Arkansas. Some sources add Louisiana, Tennessee, Missouri, and even Oklahoma to the route. (Some scholars doubt that the expedition ever crossed into present-day Louisiana except in descending the Mississippi.)

In May 1541 the expedition became the first Europeans certain to have seen the Mississippi. De Soto died in May 1542 and was buried in that river. Luis de Moscoso de Alvarado took command. He led the men overland to Texas, then retraced his route to the Mississippi. Building seven barges, the remaining men floated downriver past hostile Indians to the Gulf. They sailed along the coast to Mexico, arriving with perhaps half of the original group. Although frustrated in their search for proverbial riches, the De Soto–Moscoso party did provide descriptions of an extensive area of the southern United States, including the earliest discussion of southern Indian cultures.

The new knowledge gained about the Gulf Coast and adjacent interior did not match the value of the wealth looted from the Inca and Aztec empires. Thus, Spanish interest in the interior waned. Spain established some bases in Florida principally to protect her shipping lanes, but no settlement was located within present-day Louisiana.

In the late seventeenth and early eighteenth centuries, Spain again exhibited interest in the region. Reconnaissance parties from Mexico probed the new French settlements along the lower Mississippi and Gulf Coast and carried out missionary work among the Indian population. However, they penetrated present-day Louisiana only as far as the French outpost at Natchitoches (established in 1714) and the Spanish presidio at Los Adaes (established in 1721).

Martín de Alarcón, governor of Coahuila y Tejas, crossed the Rio Grande in April 1718 to strengthen the Spanish hold on Texas. After founding a mission and laying out the present-day city of San Antonio in May, he pushed on into eastern Texas. Alarcón reached the mission San Miguel de los Adaes, fifteen miles from the French post at Natchitoches, on November 10, 1718, then returned to his capital.

In November 1721, the viceroy of Mexico sent Alarcón's successor, the Marqués de San Miguel de Aguayo, to again bolster the Spanish presence in Texas and push the French back into, if not out of, Louisiana. With five hundred dragoons and two companies of cavalry, Aguayo was met by offers of friendship and trade from both the French at Natchitoches and the Texas Indians. Still wary of French motives, he established the Presidio de Nuestra Señora del Pilar de los Adaes near the mission, leaving six cannon and one hundred soldiers behind to guard the international frontier against further French encroachment. Los Adaes served as the capital of Texas as long as France controlled Louisiana.

The Treaty of Paris in 1763 transferred Louisiana to Spain, ending a contentious time along the Louisiana-Texas border. Still, expeditions continued. Pedro Vial, in his efforts to determine a direct route from San Antonio to Santa Fe, descended the Red River on his return in 1788 to north Texas. There he struck out overland until reaching the Sabine, then followed that river before crossing overland to Natchitoches.

From De Soto to Vial, the foremost goal of Spanish exploration remained the search for wealth, be it fabled riches or the more modest if real returns from trade. The extension of Spanish control over the hemisphere formed a close second. Louisiana was never the focus of attention, but its proximity to Spanish territory and possession by a rival to Spanish authority did attract the latter's probes into the region.

Copyright © 1995 by the University of Oklahoma Press

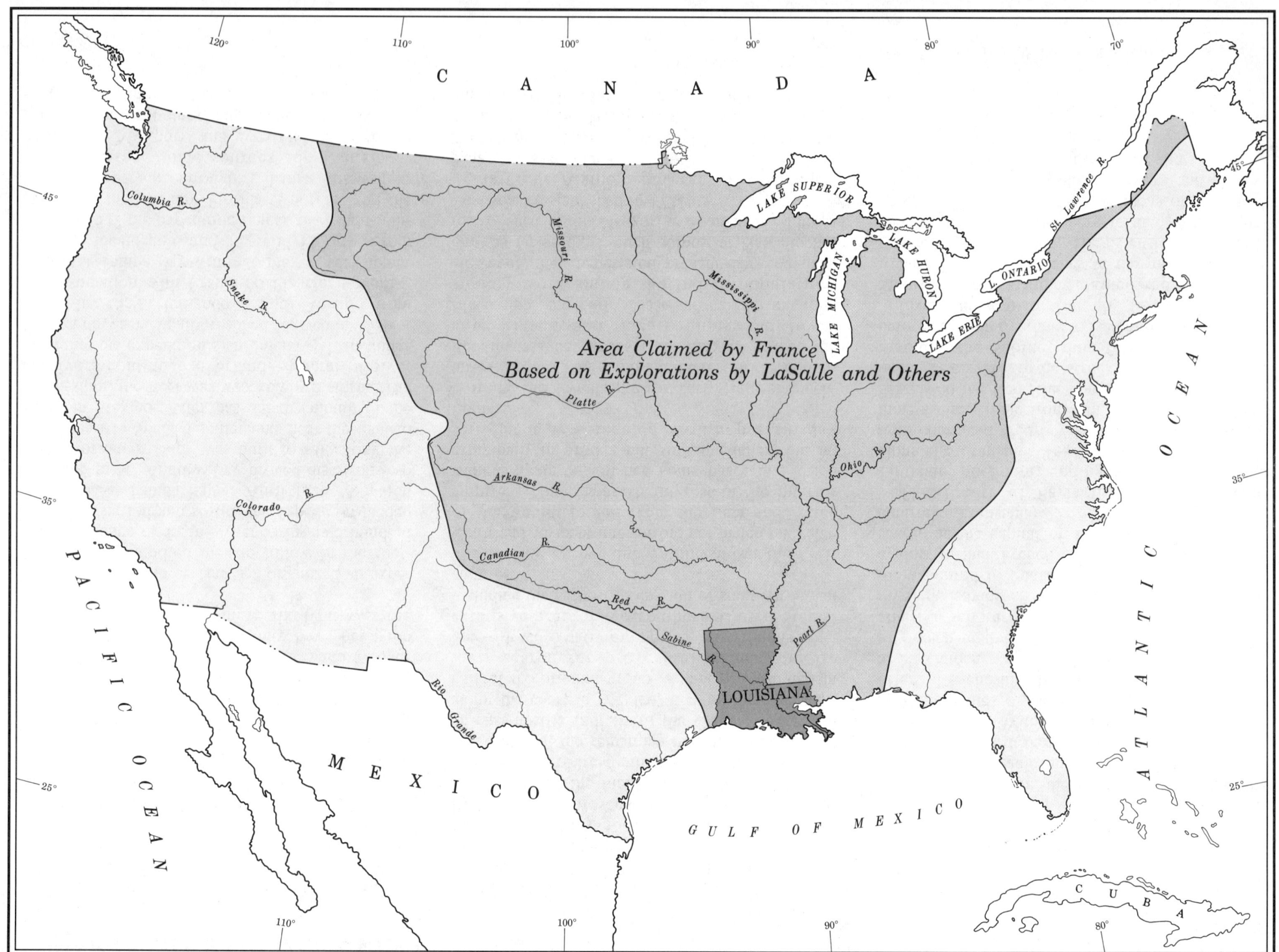

C A N A D A

Columbia R.

Snake R.

LAKE SUPERIOR

Missouri R.

Mississippi R.

LAKE MICHIGAN

LAKE HURON

LAKE ERIE

L. ONTARIO

St. Lawrence R.

Area Claimed by France
Based on Explorations by LaSalle and Others

Platte R.

Ohio R.

Arkansas R.

Colorado R.

Canadian R.

Red R.

Sabine R.

Pearl R.

LOUISIANA

Rio Grande

M E X I C O

G U L F   O F   M E X I C O

C U B A

P A C I F I C   O C E A N

A T L A N T I C   O C E A N

French claims to the Americas were based on early exploration and commercial fishing operations, particularly in the northwest Atlantic off Newfoundland and Labrador. By the first decade of the sixteenth century, perhaps as early as nine years after the Treaty of Tordesillas (1494), French fishing boats joined the vessels of other nations in the region. French ships also engaged in piracy against the Spanish and Portuguese treasure ships on the high seas and opened trade with Portuguese Brazil. However, only after the ascension of Francis I to the French throne in 1515 was the Treaty of Tordesillas deliberately violated.

In addition to the quest for empire, a continued search for the Northwest Passage to the Orient motivated French efforts. John de Verrazano was commissioned by France for a voyage of discovery in 1523–24 which revealed the barrier of the North American continent. Pope Clement VII in 1533 decided that the bull issued to Spain by his papal predecessor applied only to lands then known, not to those subsequently discovered. Thus, on July 24, 1534, Jacques Cartier, also acting on Francis's commission to search for the passage, explored the Gulf of St. Lawrence and claimed the region for France.

A second Cartier voyage in 1535 discovered the St. Lawrence River; he traveled upstream as far as the site of present-day Montreal. Erecting Fort St. Croix at the mouth of the St. Charles River, Cartier and his men passed a severe winter there before returning to France the following spring. Subsequent attempts by Cartier and others to establish a permanent French settlement in Canada

failed for the moment. Efforts to colonize further south also proved disastrous, with the Spanish massacre of hundreds of French Huguenot settlers in Florida in 1565. The two nations had tacitly agreed on a policy of maintaining peace in Europe even while pursuing a no-holds-barred policy in the New World.

The first decade of the seventeenth century saw new French activity in Canada. Samuel de Champlain and Pierre du Gast, Sieur de Monts, established Port Royal in Nova Scotia in 1604 and Quebec in 1608. The entire St. Lawrence Valley was in time settled by the French without objection from the Spanish. The English, however, proved a potent opponent of these French settlements. Anglo-French rivalry in the north mirrored that of Franco-Spanish rivalry in the south. This northern rivalry would continue until the demise of the French Empire in North America in 1763.

In the south, the Marquette-Joliet expedition of 1673 added to France's knowledge about the North American interior but did nothing to correct the mistaken notion that the prosperous provinces of New Spain lay but a short distance away. The exiled Spanish official Diego Dionisio de Peñalosa Briceño y Berdugo proposed several schemes to locate the fabled riches of the equally mythical kingdoms of Thegayo and Quivira as well as other plots for the French to conquer all or part of New Spain. Indeed, Robert Cavelier, Sieur de La Salle, couched his own later Louisiana explorations in terms more for the opportunity to gain proximity to Spanish riches than for the settlement of the region by the French.

La Salle descended the Mississippi in 1682, reaching its mouth in April. Perhaps in order to compete with Peñalosa he mapped the delta far to the west of its actual location so that it might gain proximity to the mines of Spanish Nueva Vizcaya. Thus might French claims to or plunder of these resources be pursued. However, when La Salle sailed again in 1684, Louis XIV of France had decided on a course of action which would not necessitate outright war with Spain. In any case, the expedition of 1684–87 proved a failure; La Salle himself was killed by his own men.

The French in Louisiana continually sought expansion into Spanish territory. From his Natchitoches outpost (founded in 1714) Louis Juchereau de St. Denis early penetrated Spanish Texas, prompting an increased Spanish presence in east Texas and west Louisiana. French traders to Santa Fe and among the Indians of Texas occasioned further Spanish activities and diplomatic exchanges which hinted at though never erupted into open warfare.

French claims came to an end in 1763 with the close of the French and Indian (Seven Years') War. France suffered disaster and defeat in both Europe and North America. Spain's entry as an ally had proved ineffectual. At the Treaty of Paris ending the war, France ceded Canada and Louisiana east of the Mississippi (exclusive of the Isle of Orleans) to Britain. By the Treaty of Fontainebleau a year earlier, Louisiana west of the Mississippi and the Isle of Orleans had been ceded to Spain. Thus ended the French Empire on mainland North America.

Copyright © 1995 by the University of Oklahoma Press

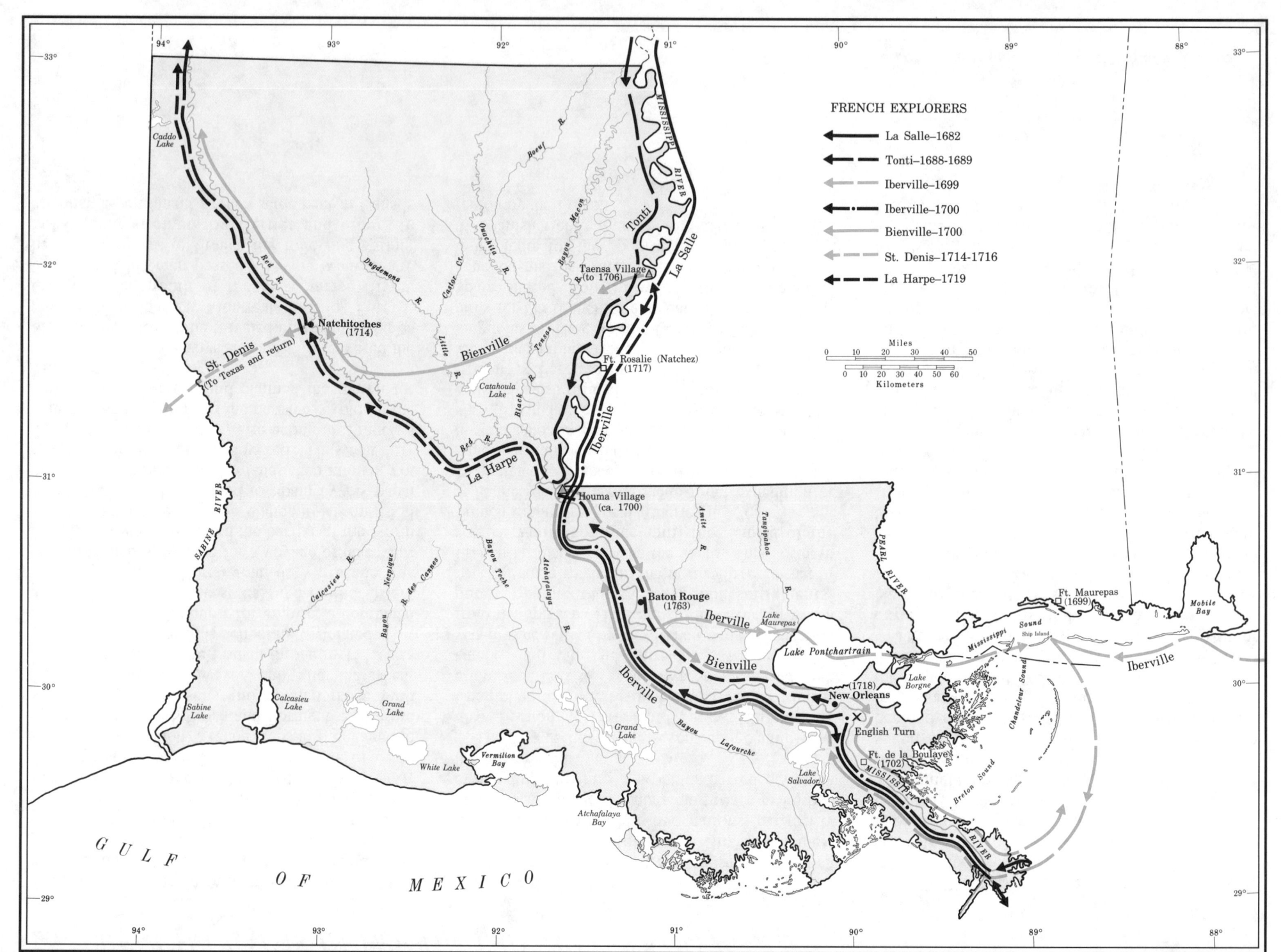

FRENCH EXPLORERS

La Salle–1682
Tonti–1688-1689
Iberville–1699
Iberville–1700
Bienville–1700
St. Denis–1714-1716
La Harpe–1719

Miles
0   10   20   30   40   50

0   10   20   30   40   50   60
Kilometers

French exploration in Louisiana grew out of its expanding Canadian fur trade. After eastern Canada was settled in the early seventeenth century, coureurs de bois and missionaries to the Indians moved westward. As these "runners in the wood" penetrated Indian territory, they acquired greater knowledge of the rivers, including the Mississippi.

In 1673, Louis, Comte de Frontenac, governor of New France, sent Father Jacques Marquette and fur trader Louis Joliet down the Mississippi. With five Frenchmen and several Mascouten Indians, they went downriver by canoe as far as the mouth of the Arkansas. Hesitating to venture farther for fear of meeting Spanish forces, the party returned to Canada.

René-Robert Cavelier, Sieur de La Salle, had enjoyed a successful trading career in the Great Lakes area. He now proposed to establish a French presence on the Gulf for both imperial and economic purposes. With a party of forty French and Indians, La Salle set out from Canada on February 6, 1682. After following the Illinois River, they reached the Mississippi on February 13, in March moved into what is now Louisiana, and on April 6 reached the delta. On April 9, La Salle took formal possession of the Mississippi Basin, naming it after King Louis XIV.

Returning to Canada, La Salle sailed on to France to organize a new expedition. On August 1, 1684, four ships with four hundred colonists sailed. The group, however, missed the Mississippi, some say purposefully, and landed at Matagorda Bay in Spanish-claimed Texas. The Texas colony proved disastrous; on March 18, 1687, La Salle and his nephew were assassinated by their own men after setting out overland for Canada.

Henri de Tonti, La Salle's lieutenant in 1682, returned south in 1686 and in 1688–89. The 1686 journey was made to join the second La Salle expedition. The latter trip, including a reconnoiter up the Red River, also attempted to locate his patron. Failing, Tonti left a note written on bark with an Indian chief, a message received a decade later by Iberville.

On October 24, 1698, a new Gulf effort sailed from France under Pierre Le Moyne, Sieur d'Iberville. The small fleet was met coolly by a newly established Spanish garrison at Pensacola. Sailing westward, the French paused at Mobile Bay before landing at Ship Island on February 10, 1699. On March 2, Iberville entered the North Pass of the Mississippi and moved upriver as far as the Houma village in modern West Feliciana Parish. On his return, Iberville led one group via Bayou Manchac and Lake Pontchartrain to the Gulf. His brother, Jean Baptiste Le Moyne, Sieur de Bienville, continued downriver, then back to Ship Island.

Establishing Fort Maurepas on Biloxi Bay, Iberville then returned to France for supplies and colonists. In his absence, Bienville reconnoitered the region. In September 1699 he met an English frigate moving up the Mississippi. Bienville convinced the ship's captain of France's claims; the vessel withdrew, and that bend ever after bore the name, the English Turn.

Iberville returned in 1700 and began further exploration of the Mississippi. Fort Boulaye was established upstream, and that spring Iberville, Bienville, and their companions journeyed upstream to the Taensa village on Lake St. Joseph. From there Bienville set off on March 22, 1700, to probe the frontier of New Spain. The French party, led by a Ouachita Indian guide, reached the

Yatasi Indians on April 20.

Louis Juchereau de St. Denis had accompanied Bienville on his 1700 cross-country journey. Returning to the Red River that fall, he began a friendship with the Natchitoches and other Caddoans which would last until his death. In 1713, St. Denis again ascended the Red to probe Spanish lands; he traded with the Asinai Indians in Texas in November. In July 1714, St. Denis led a party to the Presidio San Juan Bautista on the Rio Grande. Carried before the viceroy in Mexico City, St. Denis persuaded the official to hire him as a member of a Spanish party to reoccupy Texas in 1716, then returned to Louisiana.

Jean Baptiste Bénard de La Harpe departed New Orleans on December 17, 1718, to establish a trading post on the Red River among the Caddoan Nassonite. Reaching Natchitoches on February 20, 1719, he set out again on March 6 with seven French soldiers and thirteen Natchitoches Indians. On April 5 they reached the Nassonite village near modern Texarkana. Erecting a stockade to ward off a possible Spanish attack, La Harpe in late summer moved further upstream, reaching the Touacara or Tawakoni Indians in modern Oklahoma in September. After further travels in Oklahoma, he returned to his outpost on October 13. The outbreak of yet another war prevented La Harpe's further penetration of the interior in search of a route to Santa Fe.

The French explorers, like the Spanish, sought both wealth and empire. They learned from their predecessors, however, so trade, more than pillage, dominated their efforts. The contraband trade with Spanish Texas fueled many an effort along the frontier. Native tribes, again as with Spain, provided both a means and an end to French exploration.

Copyright © 1995 by the University of Oklahoma Press

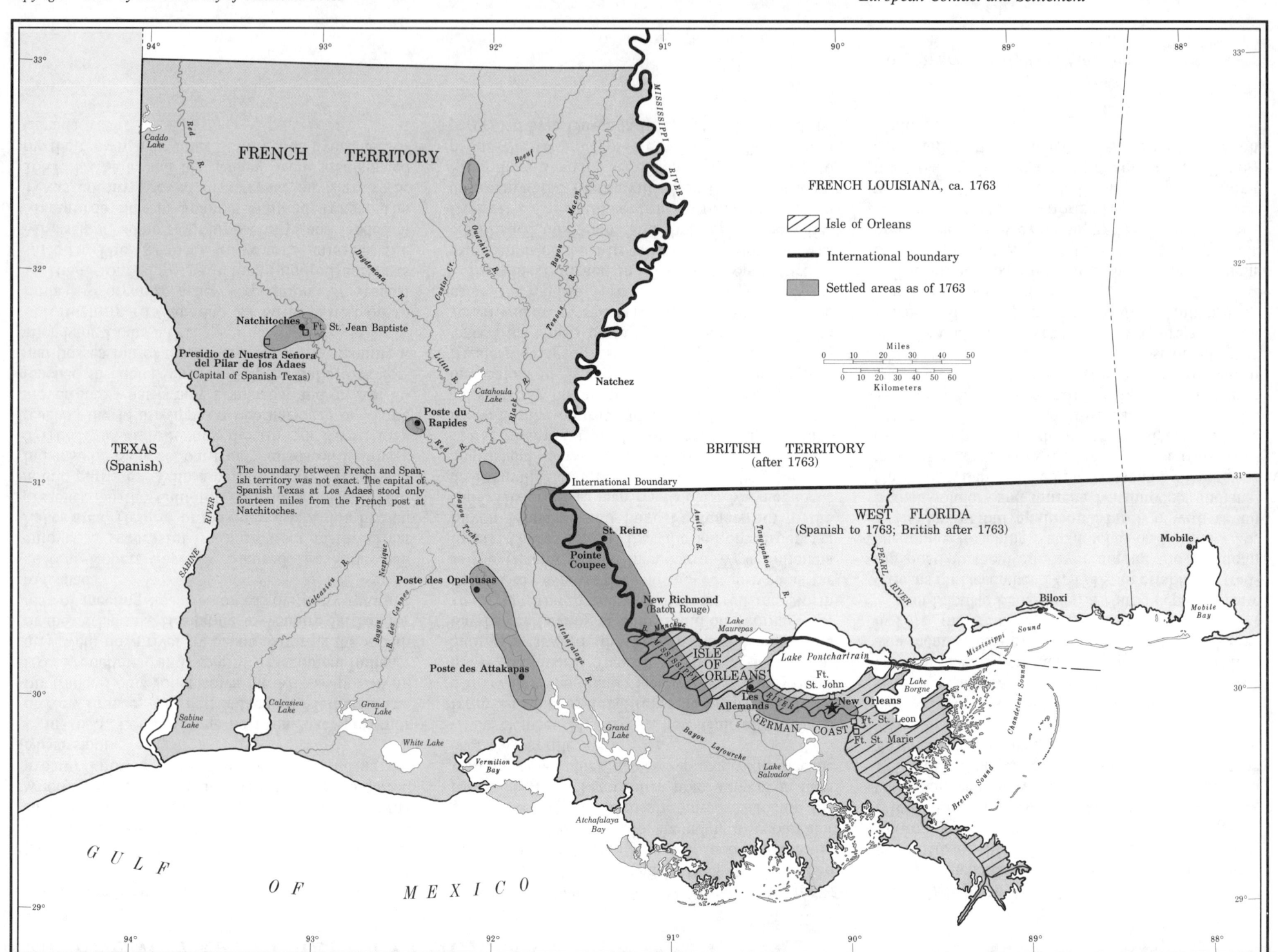

FRENCH LOUISIANA, ca. 1763

Isle of Orleans

International boundary

Settled areas as of 1763

Miles
0 10 20 30 40 50

0 10 20 30 40 50 60
Kilometers

FRENCH   TERRITORY

*Caddo
Lake*

Red   R.

Boeuf   R.

Ouachita R.

Dugdemona R.

Castor Cr.

Tensas R.

Bayou Macon

MISSISSIPPI   RIVER

Natchitoches ■ Ft. St. Jean Baptiste

**Presidio de Nuestra Señora
del Pilar de los Adaes**
(Capital of Spanish Texas)

Little R.

*Catahoula
Lake*

Black R.

Natchez

**Poste du
Rapides**

Red R.

TEXAS
(Spanish)

The boundary between French and Spanish territory was not exact. The capital of
Spanish Texas at Los Adaes stood only
fourteen miles from the French post at
Natchitoches.

SABINE RIVER

Bayou Teche

Bayou Nezpique

Bayou des Cannes

Calcasieu R.

Poste des Opelousas

Poste des Attakapas

Atchafalaya R.

International Boundary

BRITISH   TERRITORY
(after 1763)

Amite R.

Tangipahoa R.

PEARL RIVER

WEST   FLORIDA
(Spanish to 1763; British after 1763)

Mobile

St. Reine

**Pointe
Coupee**

New Richmond
(Baton Rouge)

B. Manchac

Lake Maurepas

*Lake
Pontchartrain*

Biloxi

*Mobile
Bay*

ISLE
OF
ORLEANS

Ft.
St. John

*Lake
Borgne*

Mississippi Sound

**Les
Allemands**

New Orleans ★
□ Ft. St. Leon

GERMAN COAST

RIVER

Chandeleur Sound

*Lake
Salvador*

Bayou Lafourche

□ Ft. St. Marie

Breton Sound

*Sabine
Lake*

*Calcasieu
Lake*

*Grand
Lake*

White Lake

*Vermilion
Bay*

*Grand
Lake*

*Atchafalaya
Bay*

G   U   L   F   O   F   M   E   X   I   C   O

From its founding in 1699 until 1762, Louisiana belonged to France. For those six decades the colony was variously the property of the crown (1699–1712, 1731–63), the personal business of financier Antoine Crozat (1712–17), or the enterprise of the Company of the Indies, a creation of the Scotsman turned French banker John Law (1718–31). Uniformly, Louisiana proved to all its owners a drain on their resources.

Louisiana's owners tried various means of populating the colony. Few free French citizens ventured to exchange Europe for the New France frontier. A brief policy of transporting vagrants, criminals, and the like proved disastrous. Colonists recruited elsewhere by the Company of the Indies, particularly from the German States, proved the most successful. African slaves may have been brought to the colony as workers as early as 1708; in 1716 several shiploads arrived for sale. The region did not treat any of its inhabitants lightly; the dangers of voyage, sultry climate, and indigenous diseases devastated every group without distinction.

Early settlements comprised outposts of the capital at Biloxi. Even when New Orleans became the capital in 1721, no great expansion occurred. Settlers generally ranged along south Louisiana watercourses, particularly the Mississippi River and Bayou Teche. In addition to New Orleans, settlements sprang up at Baton Rouge, Natchez, Rapides, Natchitoches, Pointe Coupee, and Les Allemands, largely the result of military or trading activity. Even at the close of French rule in 1762, New Orleans, largest of the "urban" centers, could boast of fewer than three thousand citizens out of a total colonial population of perhaps seven thousand.

When initial dreams of mineral wealth to rival that of Spanish colonies in Central and South America proved false, the French attempted to establish an economy based on agriculture and trade. Early agriculture began on sites of former Indian villages where the land was already cleared. Subsistence in nature, the crops barely met the needs of the local population. Only when the German colonists arrived in the 1720s did a more established agricultural system develop along the region astride the Mississippi which became known as the German Coast. Nevertheless, during the French period the colony's crops never proved adequate to its needs. Livestock supplies never reached self-sufficiency either, although cattle, hogs, horses, and sheep were raised.

Rice, sugar, tobacco, and indigo represented attempts at cash crops. Rice and tobacco proved most successful. Rice mills came into operation after 1740; tobacco was grown for export. Indigo's fortunes rose and fell with those of the rival East Indies; war often closed that supply and enhanced the Louisiana crop's value. Sugar had no real success, because a satisfactory refining process remained lacking. Cotton as yet proved poorly adapted to the area then settled.

Early manufacturing enterprises proved even less successful than agriculture. Products such as bricks, sawn lumber, barrels, pitch, and tar met local needs and provided some excess for overseas export. Along with the absence of production there also existed an absence of labor; apprenticeships provided the major supply.

The Mississippi River and other streams provided the principal transportation and trade routes. The sailing ships of the period moved among the French possessions and the mother country as well as up and down the Mississippi. Smaller vessels plied the various streams of the colony. Overland routes followed buffalo or Indian trails. New Orleans became the prime trading center, but every settlement carried on barter with English colonists upriver and Indian tribes throughout the region. Trade provided the colony's various proprietors with a rare means of gaining some profit. Agricultural products, minerals, and manufactured goods exchanged owners up and down the river.

Trade over the wider region proved even more difficult because of uncertainty over ship quality, corruption, and interimperial rivalries. Smuggling often replaced trade during periods of war. Exchange with the West Indies, overland to Texas and Mexico, and overseas to the mother country developed rather slowly during the period.

After 1719 a Superior Council governed the colony. The principal officials were the governor and the commissary-commissioner. Few men of true ability served in the posts; all suffered from the colony's political factionalism. The most important office holders in the period came from the extended Le Moyne family: Iberville, Bienville, and St. Denis. Bienville would serve as governor four times, a total tenure of more than three decades.

Each successive proprietor of Louisiana was relieved, even glad, to see it passed on to the next. The subsidies necessary to sustain the colony drained even the deepest pocketbook. As the French and Indian War drew to a close, France saw its New World empire threatened with loss to the British. It therefore engineered a transfer of Louisiana to Spain by means of the secret Treaty of Fontainebleau in 1762.

Copyright © 1995 by the University of Oklahoma Press

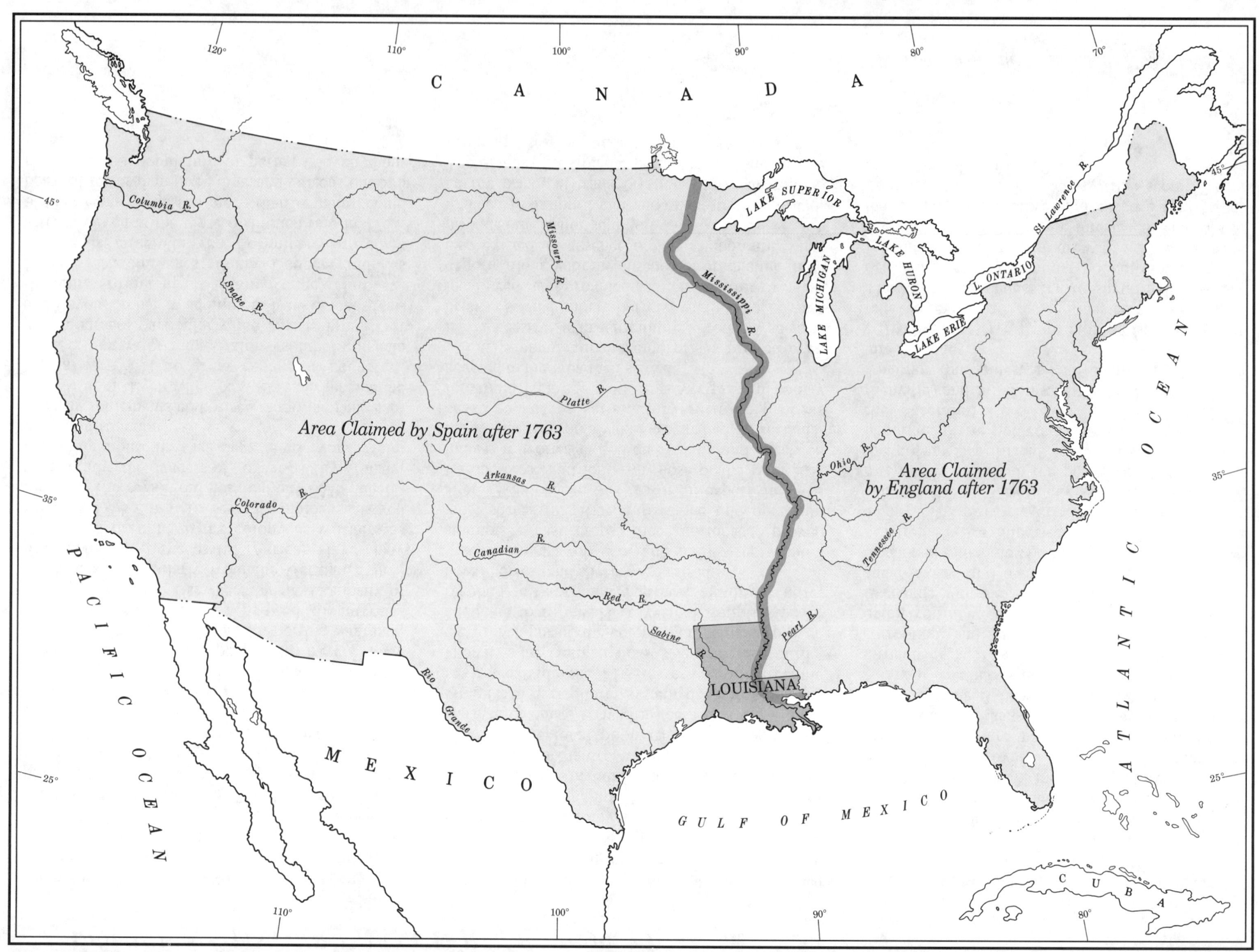

Area Claimed by Spain after 1763

Area Claimed by England after 1763

LOUISIANA

The New World empires of France, Spain, and Britain underwent dramatic changes following the conclusion of the Seven Years' (French and Indian) War. Although the war in North America had largely ended with the fall of Quebec and Montreal in 1760, the conflict in Europe lasted three more years. At its conclusion France lost practically all its possessions in North America; it retained only two small islands in St. Lawrence Bay. Both Britain and Spain enlarged their holdings on the continent, the latter even though it found itself on the losing side.

The Treaty of Paris (1763) ended the conflict. France ceded Canada and Louisiana east of the Mississippi (exclusive of the Isle of Orleans) to Britain. Spain signed over Florida to the British victors in exchange for regaining Cuba. To compensate Spain for its losses after entering the war in 1761 (and also to keep it out of British hands), France had ceded Louisiana west of the Mississippi, plus the Isle of Orleans, to Spain by the secret Treaty of Fontainebleau in 1762. (The Isle of Orleans comprised that portion of Louisiana east of the Mississippi River which lay south of the Iberville River [Bayou Manchac] and a line drawn across Lakes Maurepas and Pontchartrain to the Gulf.) The Treaty of Paris established Britain as the world's dominant colonial power. In North America, Britain and Spain found themselves eyeing each other across the length of the Mississippi River.

Spain, in assuming control of greater Louisiana, pumped money into its new possession. Fortifications were strengthened at key points along the frontier in an effort to prevent British encroachment. New colonists were recruited for settlement along the lower Mississippi River and neighboring stream courses. Louisiana entered into the era of its greatest colonial progress and prosperity.

The American Revolution altered once more the division of the North American continent. Three years after the Declaration of Independence was signed, Spain in 1779 entered the fray on the side of the American rebels and their French allies. Expeditions were launched against British Florida with great success (Map 30).

Yet another Treaty of Paris (1783) ended the Revolution and again redrew the national and imperial boundaries. The United States gained its independence and added to its territory the trans-Appalachian region east of the Mississippi and south from the Great Lakes to the northern boundary of Florida. That boundary followed the thirty-first parallel from the Mississippi east to the Chattahoochee River, down to its confluence with the Flint River, then east to St. Mary's river and downstream to the Atlantic. Spain regained Florida, disputing with the new United States that province's exact northern boundary between the Chattahoochee and Mississippi rivers until 1795. Britain retained control of Canada.

For the next two decades Spanish Louisiana faced the United States across the Mississippi River north of 31° north latitude. Spain, like France before it, distrusted British, now American, intentions. For the entire eighteenth century the excursions of traders west from the seaboard colonies, now states, had disrupted Louisiana, its imperial owners, and their Indian allies. Even with the retrocession of the colony to France and Louisiana Purchase of 1803, the zone of conflict merely shifted westward.

British policy also aimed at containing the newly independent United States. The British Empire looked askance at any expansion of its former colonies into regions it owned or coveted. As late as 1814, when Britain prepared to invade Louisiana during the War of 1812, Britain had not yet formally recognized U.S. ownership of the lands comprised in the Louisiana Purchase. Not until the Anglo-American Convention of 1818 did the United Kingdom formally accept U.S. boundaries in the north and west.

Further American settlement of the trans-Appalachian region had been restricted by the Royal Proclamation Line of 1763, by which the British government sought to separate the colonists along the Atlantic seaboard from the Indians in the interior. Even after redrawing the line, this policy against colonial western expansion and interaction (including hostilities) with the various Indian tribes did not prove successful. That western migration increased during and after the American Revolution. The region became ever more populous with settlers, whose voices swelled in a chorus demanding a commercial outlet for their products. Increasingly those demands centered on control of the Mississippi River.

Copyright © 1995 by the University of Oklahoma Press

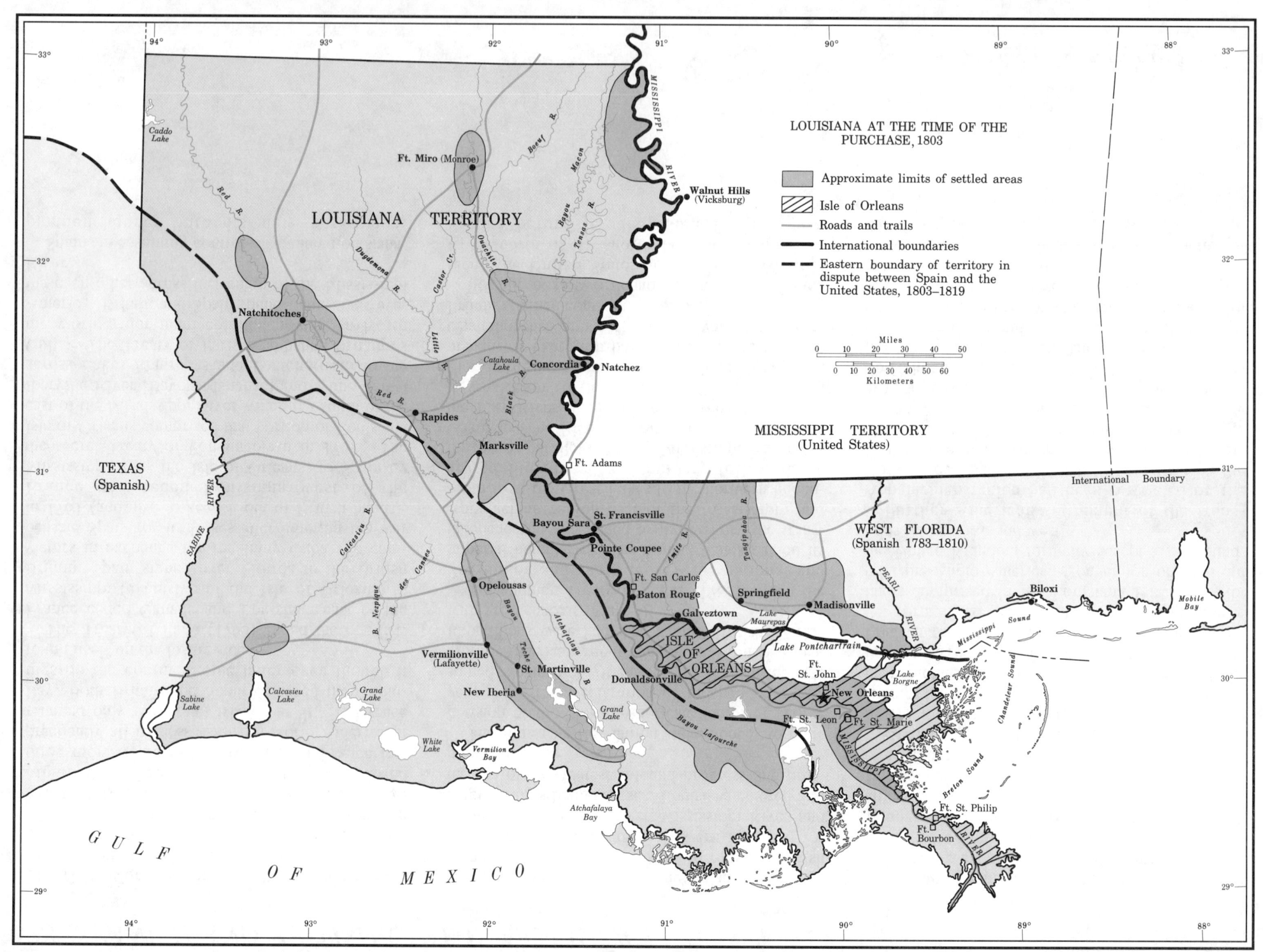

LOUISIANA AT THE TIME OF THE
PURCHASE, 1803

Approximate limits of settled areas

Isle of Orleans

Roads and trails

International boundaries

Eastern boundary of territory in
dispute between Spain and the
United States, 1803–1819

Miles
0   10   20   30   40   50

0 10 20 30 40 50 60
Kilometers

LOUISIANA   TERRITORY

Ft. Miro (Monroe)

Walnut Hills
(Vicksburg)

Caddo
Lake

Red R.

Dugdemona R.

Castor Cr.

Little R.

Ouachita R.

Boeuf R.

Bayou Macon

Tensas R.

MISSISSIPPI RIVER

Natchitoches

Catahoula
Lake

Concordia   • Natchez

Red R.

Black R.

Rapides

Marksville

Ft. Adams

MISSISSIPPI   TERRITORY
(United States)

TEXAS
(Spanish)

St. Francisville

Bayou Sara

Pointe Coupee

Amite R.

Tangipahoa R.

WEST FLORIDA
(Spanish 1783–1810)

International   Boundary

SABINE RIVER

Calcasieu R.

B. Nezpique

B. des Cannes

Opelousas

Ft. San Carlos
Baton Rouge

Springfield

Madisonville

Biloxi

PEARL RIVER

Bayou Teche

Atchafalaya R.

Galveztown

*Lake
Maurepas*

**ISLE
OF
ORLEANS**

Lake Pontchartrain

*Mississippi
Sound*

*Mobile
Bay*

Vermilionville
(Lafayette)

St. Martinville

New Iberia

Donaldsonville

*Grand
Lake*

Bayou Lafourche

Ft.
St. John

New Orleans

*Lake
Borgne*

Chandeleur Sound

*Sabine
Lake*

*Calcasieu
Lake*

*Grand
Lake*

*White
Lake*

*Vermilion
Bay*

*Atchafalaya
Bay*

Ft. St. Leon
Ft. St. Marie

Breton Sound

Ft. St. Philip

Ft.
Bourbon

MISSISSIPPI RIVER

G U L F   O F   M E X I C O

By the Treaty of Fontainebleau, signed November 3, 1762, France ceded to Spain the Isle of Orleans and that portion of Louisiana west of the Mississippi. France thus not only transferred a continuing financial drain to another empire, but also somewhat thwarted Britain's designs on France's American colonies. By the Treaty of Paris signed February 10, 1763, France lost much of its American empire to the British. Only the secret, earlier transfer of Louisiana to France's sometime ally Spain prevented further British domination in North America.

Spain did not immediately establish local control in Louisiana. Not until March 1766 did the first Spanish governor—Antonio de Ulloa—arrive. In October 1766 a revolt by some French citizens led to Ulloa's withdrawal to Cuba. The rebels could not believe that the mother country had deserted them. Three years later, in August 1769, the Spanish returned. Alejandro O'Reilly, at the head of twenty-four ships and two thousand men, reestablished control, punished the rebellion's ringleaders, and installed a new governor, Louis de Unzaga y Amezaga. Unzaga was in turn succeeded by Bernardo de Gálvez (1777–84); Estevan Miró (1784–91); Francisco Luis Hector, Baron de Carondelet (1791–97); Manuel Gayoso de Lemos (1797–99); Sebastián Calvo de la Puerta y O'Farril, Marquis de Casa Calvo (1799–1801); and Juan Manuel de Salcedo (1801–1803).

At the dawn of the Spanish period, Louisiana's population stood at between 6,000 and 7,500 scattered along the lower Mississippi and Bayou Teche, with outposts at Marksville, Rapides (Pineville), and Natchitoches. The first Spanish census (1769) counted more than 13,500, with much of the increase coming from the influx of Acadians cast out from former New France by their new British imperial landlords. Almost a quarter (3,190) of the 1769 total lived in New Orleans. At the close of the Spanish period the population had grown to nearly 50,000. This increase resulted largely from a generous immigration policy. Grants with a frontage of six to eight arpents (an arpent is a square area approximately 180 feet to the side) with a depth of forty arpents were given to those who would "occupy" the land. Other, larger grants were also made, for example, to Felipe Enrique Neri, Baron de Bastrop, over one million acres northeast of Fort Miro, and to Don Josef, Marquis de Maison Rouge, over two hundred thousand acres to the south. Many nationalities arrived: German, English, and French refugees from war, Canary Islanders, and a large number of Acadians.

Economically the colony continued to depend upon agriculture and trade. General agriculture—corn, wheat, barley, rice, vegetables, livestock, and poultry—prevailed, but specialty crops were also grown. These specialty crops included tobacco, indigo, and sugar. Improvements in sugar refining increased that crop's importance even as indigo production declined. Manufacturing for the most part consisted of processing the raw materials of farm and forest. Lumber mills became more numerous. Hide tanning, grain milling, candle making, syrup boiling, and brick making also took place. Most of the production was consumed locally.

Trade largely flowed along watercourses, those natural routes still most efficient for long-distance transport. Overland routes remained rude "traces," at best trails through the woods but more often than not "blazed" routes. Aside from local markets, trade centered on the river settlements, especially New Orleans. The colony's metropolis acted as way-station for American colonial and other foreign trade. Official Spanish policy aimed at controlling trade, even with other parts of its empire such as neighboring Texas. However, local officials often looked the other way so that the colony both imported necessities and exported any surpluses it had.

Spain established its own system of government in Louisiana. A *cabildo* (council) of ten members presided over by the governor ruled in the king's name. A commandant supervised each district in the colony and enforced official policy. Many French citizens were appointed to government posts. Although reconciliation of the French to Spanish rule occurred, more acculturation occurred in the opposite direction.

Spain retroceded Louisiana to Napoleonic France in 1800. However, a new French governor arrived only just before the Louisiana Purchase in 1803. As it had done with every rival who had previously held Louisiana, Spain would for years after the purchase feud with the United States over just where the boundaries between nation and empire lay.

Forty years of Spanish rule achieved far greater success than France had accomplished. The population increased fivefold, and the economic and cultural level advanced. New Orleans after the disastrous fire of 1788 was rebuilt in the Spanish style. Still, the colony remained a financial drain; Spanish subsidies and grants far exceeded those spent by Britain on its colonies. Spain left a relatively light imprint. Although the colony owed much more to its Iberian master, the historic and emotional ties to France have proved the greater attraction in the popular mind.

Copyright © 1995 by the University of Oklahoma Press

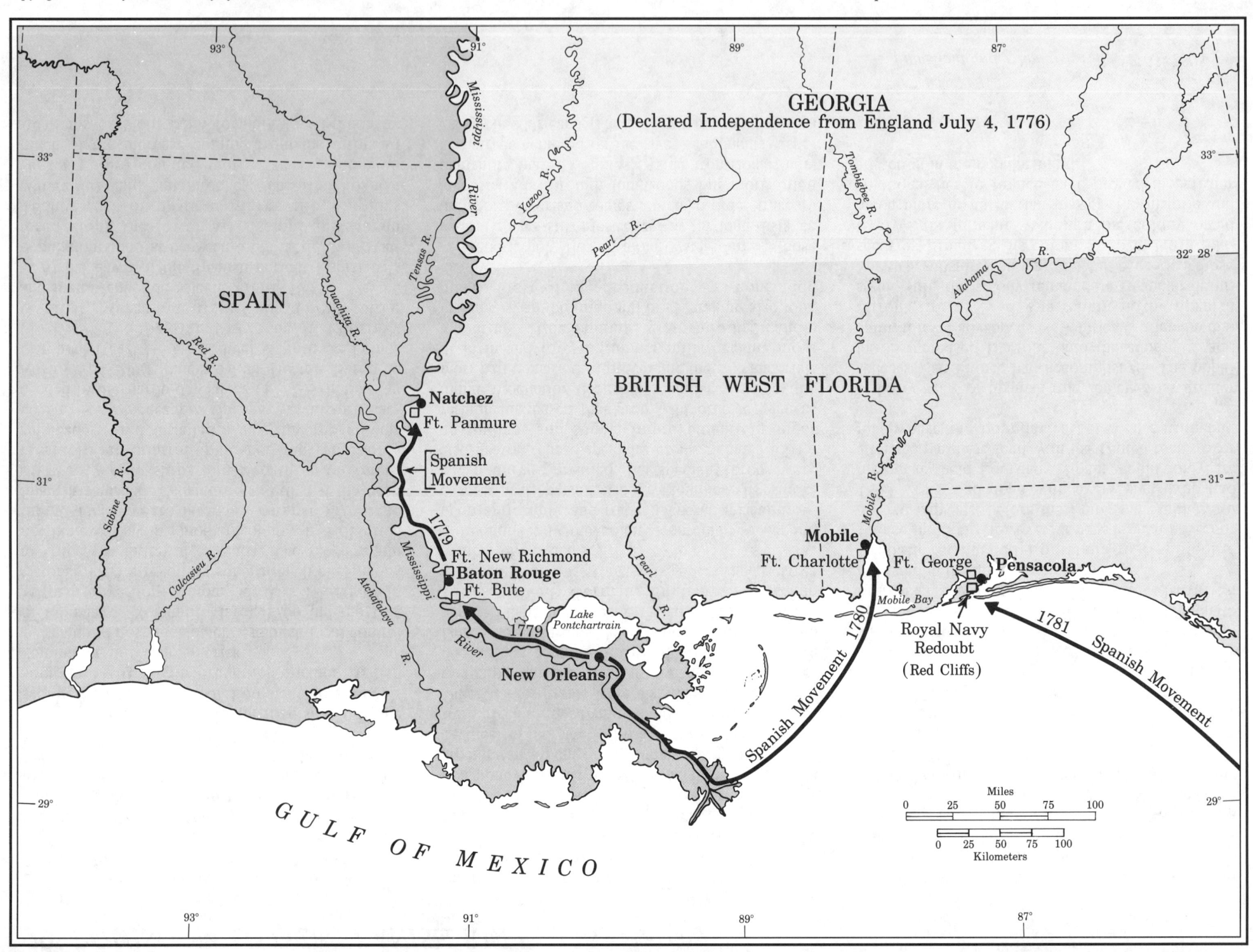

GEORGIA
(Declared Independence from England July 4, 1776)

SPAIN

BRITISH WEST FLORIDA

Mississippi River

Yazoo R.

Tensas R.

Ouachita R.

Red R.

Pearl R.

Tombigbee R.

Alabama R.

Natchez
Ft. Panmure

Spanish
Movement

1779

Mississippi River

Mobile
Ft. Charlotte

Mobile R.

Ft. George **Pensacola**

Ft. New Richmond
Baton Rouge
Ft. Bute

1779

Spanish Movement 1780

Mobile Bay

Royal Navy
Redoubt
(Red Cliffs)

*Lake
Pontchartrain*

Atchafalaya R.

Pearl R.

New Orleans

1781
Spanish Movement

Sabine R.

Calcasieu R.

G U L F   O F   M E X I C O

Miles
0   25   50   75   100

0   25   50   75   100
Kilometers

30. LOUISIANA IN THE AMERICAN REVOLUTION

The outbreak of the American Revolution did not immediately affect Louisiana. However, with British territory just across the Mississippi River and Bayou Manchac, with easy access to Spanish Louisiana by Rebel and Tory alike, and with increasing mutual distrust between Britain and Spain about each other's true motives, some preparation became necessary. Governor Luis de Unzaga had strengthened the militia before departing in 1777. His successor, Bernardo de Gálvez, maintained official Spanish neutrality while secretly assisting American agent Oliver Pollock obtain supplies for the revolutionary cause, particularly in the Ohio region. However, Gálvez also assisted British refugees from West Florida made homeless by renegade American James Willing. Willing had transformed his mission to secure West Florida's allegiance to the rebel cause into a pillaging raid on the region's plantations.

On May 8, 1779, Spain notified its empire that it would declare war against Britain in mid-June. Such a move did not imply Spanish support for a revolt by colonials so much as an opportunity to gain revenge upon an imperial rival. This change in official policy gave Galvez a legitimate opportunity to attack British territory. When a hurricane struck New Orleans and destroyed much of his supplies and equipment, Gálvez's initial efforts were delayed. Nevertheless, he succeeded in his plan to strike before the British forces in West Florida learned of war's declaration. On September 7, Gálvez easily captured Fort Bute on Bayou Manchac; the majority of its troops had already fallen back to the superior fortifications at Baton Rouge. Two weeks later, the Spanish forces attacked Fort New Richmond at Baton Rouge; its British commander surrendered on September 22, at the same time surrendering Fort Panmure at Natchez.

Although outnumbered in overall regional strength, Gálvez had succeeded by taking the offensive and concentrating his resources at strategic points. At the same time, other Spanish and American forces secured land and lake victories north and west of and along Lake Pontchartrain. Thus, the region west of the Pearl River quickly fell under Spanish control.

Gálvez's second offensive came in early 1780. Unable to convince the Spanish commander in Havana to launch a general Gulf Coast campaign, Gálvez with a smaller force plotted the capture of Mobile. In January the Spanish set sail, only to be tossed about by a storm on February 10. Landing near Fort Charlotte on Mobile Bay, the force regrouped, and, strengthened by some forces from Cuba, had surrounded the post by March 1. A lull occasioned by the exchange of diplomatic communications was broken by a Spanish attack. Launching an artillery barrage on March 10, Gálvez quickly brought about an agreement to surrender. The British prolonged negotiations for surrender, attempting to stall until a British relief expedition from Pensacola could arrive. On March 14, Gálvez took possession of the fort and Mobile even as British relief forces neared the fort, only to return to Pensacola when told of the post's surrender.

Spurred by success and the congratulations of the Spanish court, Gálvez in October 1780 readied his next campaign—an attack on Pensacola. He sailed from Havana early in the month with fifteen armed ships and almost four thousand men. For a third time, misfortune in the form of yet another storm scattered the fleet and ended the effort. By February 1781, however, Gálvez was again ready. He sailed from Havana the last day of the month and arrived off Pensacola on March 9. A feud between Gálvez and the more cautious Spanish naval commander José Calbo de Irazabal delayed moving closer. Finally Gálvez on March 18 took some Louisiana vessels he personally commanded and moved past the fire of British guns from the fort at Barrancas Coloradas ("Red Cliffs"). The next day the remainder of the fleet also successfully closed in. Thereafter the Spanish regrouped, and, enlarged by reenforcements from Mobile and New Orleans, laid siege to Fort George. A lucky shot on May 8 caused an explosion in a powder magazine. That explosion demolished a portion of the fort's walls, and the Spanish gained entrance thereby. After fierce fighting the opposing forces struck a truce; on May 10 the British surrendered, and Spain thus gained control of all of East Florida.

Gálvez returned to Louisiana to put down a rebellion begun at Natchez on April 22. His military successes there and in his previous campaigns solidified Spain's hold on the hearts and minds of its colonists. Spain's efforts on the winning side also added to Spanish territory. At the Treaty of Paris, 1783, which ended the American Revolution, Spain regained control of both East and West Florida as far north as the thirty-first parallel.

Copyright © 1995 by the University of Oklahoma Press

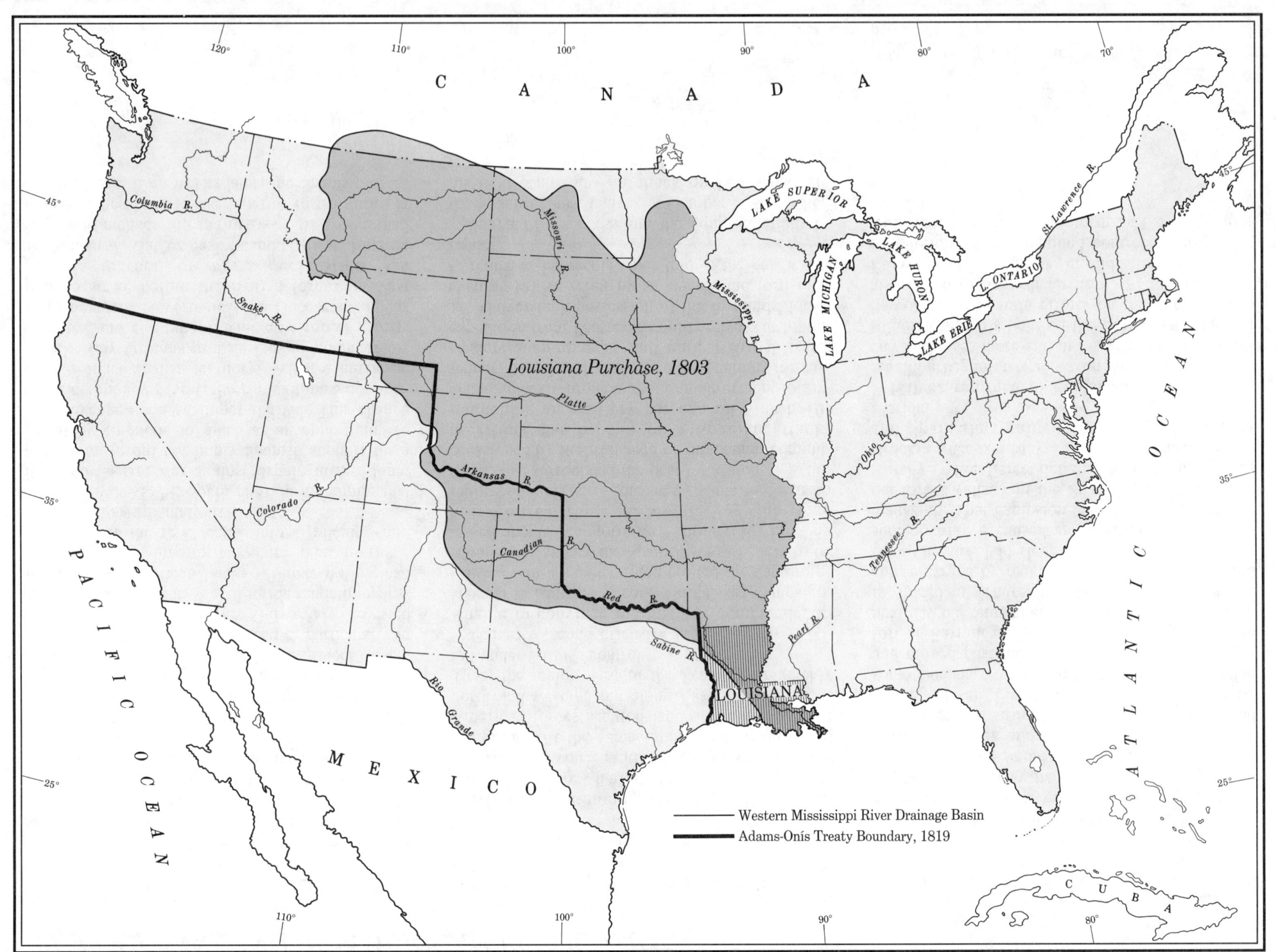

CANADA

LAKE SUPERIOR

Columbia R.

Snake R.

Missouri R.

Mississippi R.

LAKE MICHIGAN

LAKE HURON

LAKE ERIE

L. ONTARIO

St. Lawrence R.

Louisiana Purchase, 1803

Platte R.

Arkansas R.

Ohio R.

Colorado R.

Canadian R.

Tennessee R.

Red R.

Pearl R.

Sabine R.

LOUISIANA

Rio Grande

MEXICO

PACIFIC OCEAN

ATLANTIC OCEAN

CUBA

—— Western Mississippi River Drainage Basin
—— Adams-Onís Treaty Boundary, 1819

As the young United States continued settling the area west of the Appalachians, the importance of the Mississippi River to its commercial development became ever clearer. By the close of the eighteenth century more than one hundred thousand Americans lived in trans-Appalachia. The river provided a natural route for goods too bulky for overland transport. U.S. territory extended to the Mississippi as far south as 31° north latitude, but south of that line lay the Spanish Empire—Louisiana and Florida—and control of the river's mouth and its premier port, New Orleans.

Under the terms of the Treaty of San Lorenzo (1795) Spain granted U.S. citizens the right to navigate the river and deposit their goods at New Orleans. This action opened up not only international markets but also the numerous plantations along Louisiana's streams to American products. In 1802, however, these rights were withdrawn, adding fuel to a continuing debate centered more over how, rather than if, the United States should gain outright control of the Mississippi.

Further complicating the Mississippi River question were the geopolitics of late-eighteenth-century imperial Europe. Spain was in decline; Napoleonic France was in ascent and Louisiana's former owner. Spain became increasingly nervous about the boisterous American Republic and uneasy about the safety of its North and South American empire. After negotiations, France and Spain signed the secret Treaty of San Ildefonso in 1800, returning Louisiana and its inhabitants to France in exchange for guaranteeing the province of Tuscany in Italy to the Spanish Duke of Parma. France also agreed never to sell Louisiana to another power.

President Thomas Jefferson recognized the need for American control of the Mississippi River.

This dominion could be achieved by the U.S. purchase of the Isle of Orleans, plus all or part of Florida. Such an acquisition would give the new nation complete control of one bank of the river. After learning of the Treaty of San Ildefonso, Jefferson in 1802 instructed America's Ambassador to France Robert Livingston to begin negotiations for the needed territory. In 1803 the president named James Monroe special envoy to France and Spain to assist in the Louisiana question. In April 1803, informed of a British plan to invade Louisiana when war between England and France began anew, Napoleon decided to sell it all. Charles Maurice de Talleyrand-Périgord, his foreign minister, casually broached the idea to Livingston, but Minister of the Treasury François Barbé-Marbois negotiated the actual agreements.

In a series of documents signed in April and May 1803, Livingston and Monroe agreed on behalf of the United States to pay sixty million francs and assume American claims against France in the additional amount of twenty million francs in exchange for all of Louisiana. At the agreed-upon exchange rate of 5.3333 francs to the dollar, the sum approximated $15,000,000. The Congress agreed, and November 3, 1803, witnessed the official transfer. Bonds sold in England and the Netherlands financed the purchase; by 1823, when the last bonds and interest were paid off, the total spent had amounted to $23,313,567.73.

Years elapsed after the 1803 purchase before the exact boundaries would be determined. The documents specified no definite bounds, only that the colony came "with the full extent that it now has in the hands of Spain, and that it had when France possessed it." Spain and the United States each disputed the other's claims. Spain insisted

that the drainage divide of the Mississippi River was the western line (Map 29); the United States claimed La Salle's colony in Texas gave it rights to that territory. The result was a "No-Man's-Land" in the southwest portion of the present state—the "Free State of Sabine."

In 1810 a revolt in Spanish West Florida led to the U.S. annexation of the territory from the Mississippi to the Perdido (Map 35). Finally, in 1819, Secretary of State John Quincy Adams and Spanish Minister to Washington Luis de Onís negotiated the Florida Purchase Treaty, which brought the rest of Florida into U.S. hands and also set the western bounds of the purchase. That line ran from the Gulf up the right bank of the Sabine River to 32° north latitude, thence north to the Red River. The boundary then ran along the right bank of the Red to 100° west longitude and then north to the Arkansas River. Thence, the line ran along the right bank of the Arkansas to 42° north latitude, thence west to the Pacific. A year earlier the Anglo-American Convention of 1818 had fixed the United States' northern boundary at 49° north latitude from the Lake of the Woods to the continental divide of the Great Stony (Rocky) Mountains.

The 830,000 square miles included in the Louisiana Purchase immediately doubled the territory of the United States and thwarted British designs to confine the new nation to its 1783 boundaries. Not only did the purchase exceed the authority of Livingston and Monroe, but its bounds and resources also remained vague for decades. Louisiana forever altered the then-prevailing view of the role of the federal versus state governments and started the new nation on its trans-Mississippi march to the Pacific.

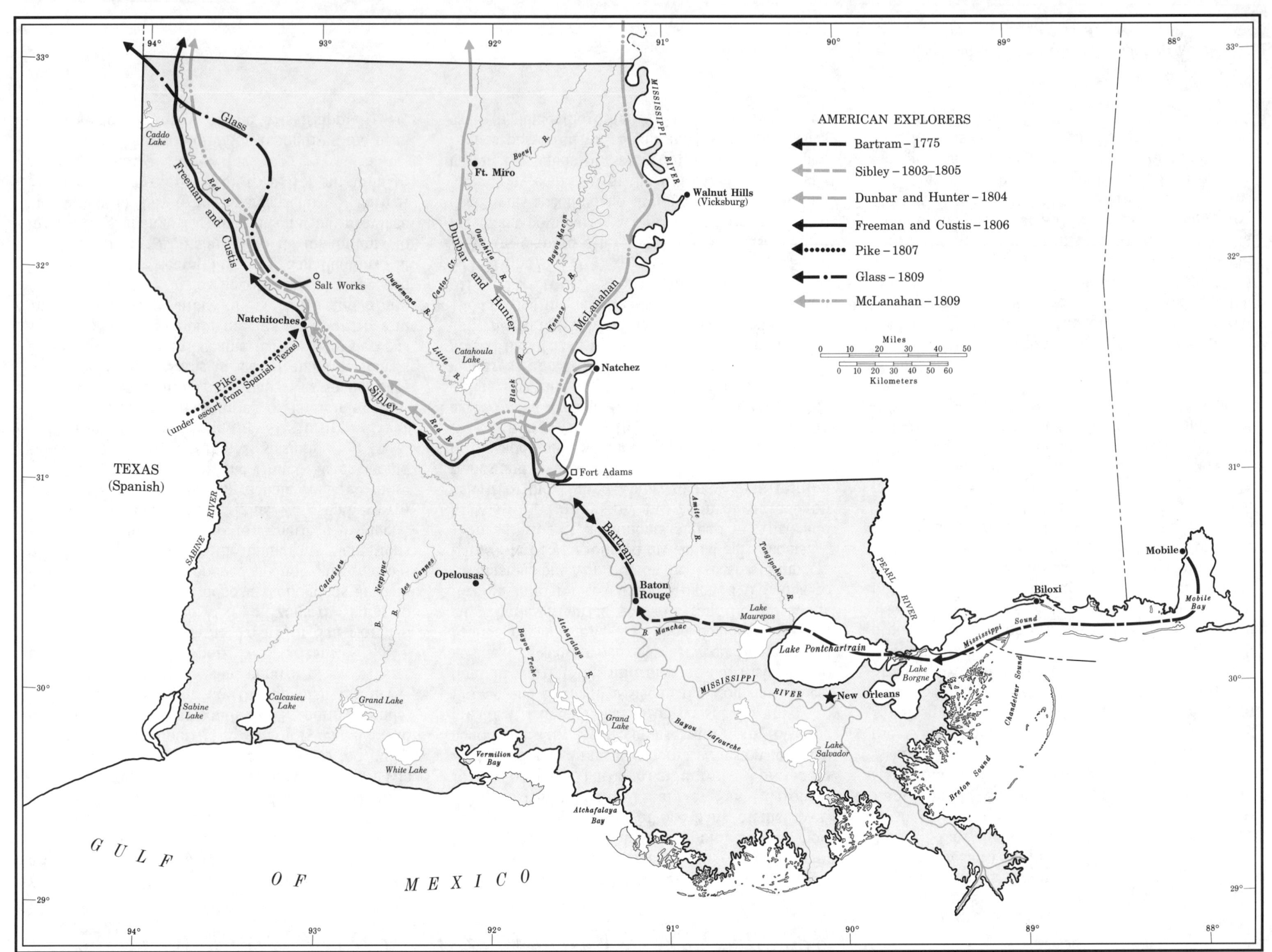

AMERICAN EXPLORERS

Bartram – 1775

Sibley – 1803–1805

Dunbar and Hunter – 1804

Freeman and Custis – 1806

Pike – 1807

Glass – 1809

McLanahan – 1809

Miles

Kilometers

TEXAS
(Spanish)

GULF   OF   MEXICO

Even before the American Revolution, the residents of British North America traveled to the trans-Appalachian West in trade and exploration. By far the most prominent was the celebrated Philadelphia naturalist, William Bartram, who in the course of an extended journey through the Carolinas, Georgia, and the Floridas visited present-day Louisiana in 1775. Between mid-October and mid-November, Bartram sailed west from Mobile through Lake Pontchartrain up the Bayou Manchac to the Mississippi River. Thence he went upriver with William Dunbar, visiting the area of Baton Rouge and Pointe Coupee before returning to Mobile by the same water route.

After the Louisiana Purchase, President Thomas Jefferson sought early exploration of the new territory. Even as Meriwether Lewis and William Clark journeyed overland in the north, Jefferson made new plans for the south, particularly the Red River of the South. The Spanish in Texas, uneasy over American intentions in the region and argumentative over the exact location of the boundary separating the two nation's territory (Maps 29 and 30), opposed these American efforts.

Dr. John Sibley, a physician, carried out his own exploration of the Red River beginning in 1803, a year after settling in Natchitoches. These excursions were not official in nature, nor were they accompanied by the scientific instruments desired by Jefferson. Nevertheless, Sibley provided a set of observations about the river itself and the various Indian inhabitants along its course.

In 1804, Sir William Dunbar of Natchez and Dr. George Hunter of Philadelphia—funded by a Congressional appropriation of three thousand dollars—led the first of the scientific expeditions envisioned by Jefferson. Leaving Natchez on October 15, the expedition had as its original route the Red River. The continued Spanish threat plus dissension among the Osage, with whom the leaders had intended to meet, caused the expedition to ascend instead the Ouachita River. Along the banks of that river the seventeen-man expedition found scattered settlements such as Fort Miro, site of present-day Monroe. These settlements consisted mainly of Canadian French but also of French and Spanish Creoles, with a few German, Irish, and American frontier folk. On December 6 the expedition reached the head of navigation on the Ouachita in Arkansas, then visited the nearby Hot Springs. The party began its return voyage on January 8, 1805, landing at Dunbar's plantation near Natchez on January 31. Although the expedition did not proceed as originally planned, it did provide technical data and experience for future efforts.

A second Congressionally funded expedition set out from Fort Adams on April 19, 1806. Headed by Thomas Freeman and Peter Custis, this group of thirty-seven men did follow the Red River. However, they had moved upriver only some 635 miles before they were intercepted by a Spanish force and ordered to return downriver. As with the first, this second American effort failed to cover any new territory, nor had the source of the Red River yet been identified.

The following year (1807) Zebulon Montgomery Pike returned to American territory at Natchitoches. In 1806 he had been sent out to explore the country between the Arkansas and Red rivers. Wandering by accident or design into Spanish territory on the upper Rio Grande, his party was met by Spanish troops and questioned in Santa Fe and Chihuahua before being released in east Texas.

In addition to the scientific expeditions commissioned by the federal government and the personal adventures of Sibley, additional knowledge about the western bounds of the newly purchased territory was garnered by the increasing number of American traders heading up for the profitable if illegal Santa Fe trade. A trio of Americans—J. McLanahan, Reuben Smith, and James Patterson—set out from St. Genevieve, Missouri, in December 1809. Led by a Spanish guide, the traders followed the Red River to its headwaters before the Spanish discovered and arrested them. They were taken first to Santa Fe, thence to Chihuahua, where they were imprisoned for two years.

Also in 1809, another American trader, Anthony Glass, returned to U.S. territory after a winter spent with the Pawnees and the Comanches. Upon their arrival in Natchitoches, Glass and his men told of their venturing as far west as the headwaters of the Colorado River in Texas, where Glass claimed to have been able to view the Rocky Mountains in the distance.

Accounts from traders of their journeys added more to the nation's storehouse of knowledge of Spanish territory than of the Territory of Orleans. Moreover, the interest generated by the traders' activities led to increased penetration of Spanish territory by U.S. citizens. This migration in turn led to the Texas Revolution of 1836 and the eventual annexation of western territory into the nation.

Copyright © 1995 by the University of Oklahoma Press

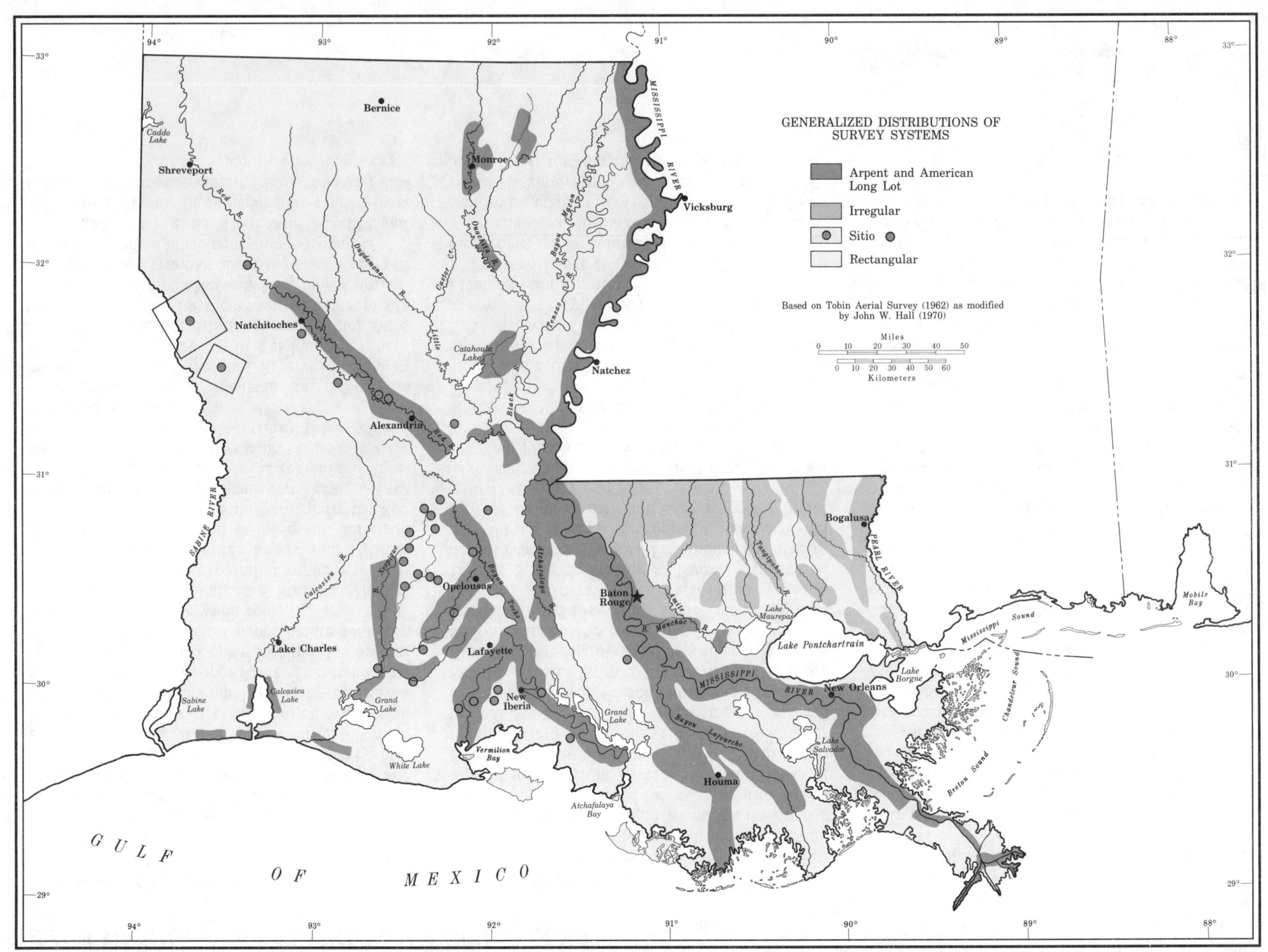

GENERALIZED DISTRIBUTIONS OF
SURVEY SYSTEMS

Arpent and American
Long Lot

Irregular

Sitio

Rectangular

Based on Tobin Aerial Survey (1962) as modified
by John W. Hall (1970)

Miles
0   10   20   30   40   50

0   10   20   30   40   50   60
Kilometers

As Europeans occupied the present area of Louisiana, they brought with them various methods of dividing the land into parcels for private ownership. Each successive European empire introduced a new or additional such "cadastral system." The entire land belonged to the crown, and grants were made to individuals as well as groups for settlement and occupation. To the French, Spanish, and English methods was added the American Rectangular Survey System. The present state's landownership patterns provide relic reminders of previous imperial owners coexisting within the more orderly framework of the rectangular system.

The French introduced the arpent or long-lot system of ownership. An arpent varied in length through time and represented an areal as well as a linear measure; in time the linear arpent became standardized at 192 feet. On average a distance of eight arpents (1,536 feet) was measured along a stream front. From the ends of this line, other lines were struck perpendicular to the river, back from the stream an average of forty arpents (7,680 feet). The resulting pattern represented quadrangles with the narrow sides parallel to the stream, that is, long lots. The arpent system is located primarily along navigable streams and especially the Mississippi, Atchafalaya, Ouachita, and Red rivers and Bayous Lafourche and Teche.

When Spain assumed ownership of much of Louisiana in 1763, it continued the long-lot system. Continued, too, were regulations on clearing and occupying the land, as well as levee maintenance and road building. Grants were made in a sequential manner, each new one adjacent to that most recently made so as to have a continuous road and levee system built along each stream. In addition to the long lots, Spain in the prairies and elsewhere in the region adjacent to Texas granted lands of one square league (about 4,428 acres) or more. These largely square-shaped grants were made for ranching purposes and were know as *sitios*. *Sitios* could be oriented in any direction and fronted on, or occupied both sides of, a stream.

In the Florida Parishes during the period of British ownership (1763–83), another cadastral system was employed. This irregular system, called metes and bounds, used lines running between natural features or artificial lines to determine boundaries for parcels of property. Grants ranged in size based on such factors as the number of family members and military rank. Irregularly shaped pieces of property resulted, sometimes with gaps between adjacent land claims. Many of these grants were located along the Amite River and Bayou Manchac and along the east bank of the Mississippi north of Bayou Manchac.

The Northwest Ordinance of 1785 launched the American Rectangular (township-and-range) Survey System. This method spread over most of trans-Appalachia. This system is discussed in detail in Map 34.

Survey systems influence other features of the cultural landscape. Fences often follow the bounds of each parcel to separate neighboring tracts, enclose fields, restrain livestock, and so on.

Canals and roads connect house to house, settlement to settlement. French and Spanish regulations on the long-lot system required houses to be erected on the front (stream) side of each parcel. Laws of inheritance meant that each original lot became divided into increasingly narrow lots, each with a house at the front. Thus, the roads, like the settlements, became linear in fashion, paralleling the stream, the original source of transportation.

Irregular surveys such as the metes and bounds produced equally irregular, dispersed settlement patterns, with farmsteads located in clearings surrounded by forest. Roads connected towns to farmsteads, converging at towns and at stream crossings and radiating out from each like a spiderweb. In the ranching *sitios,* the ranch house was located at the center, and roads followed the largely square sides of each. When the township-and-range system was employed, the roads delineating sections (and fractions thereof) formed the basic pattern. With the township-and-range system oriented in the cardinal directions (north, south, east, west), roads followed a similar path.

Today the basic framework of the township-and-range system overlays the entire territory of Louisiana, although there are some areas of the state which have never been completely surveyed. The older cadastral systems remain as irregular units within the more systematic township-and-range pattern. They remind us of the state's colonial past and the permanent imprint that past has placed on the landscape.

Copyright © 1995 by the University of Oklahoma Press

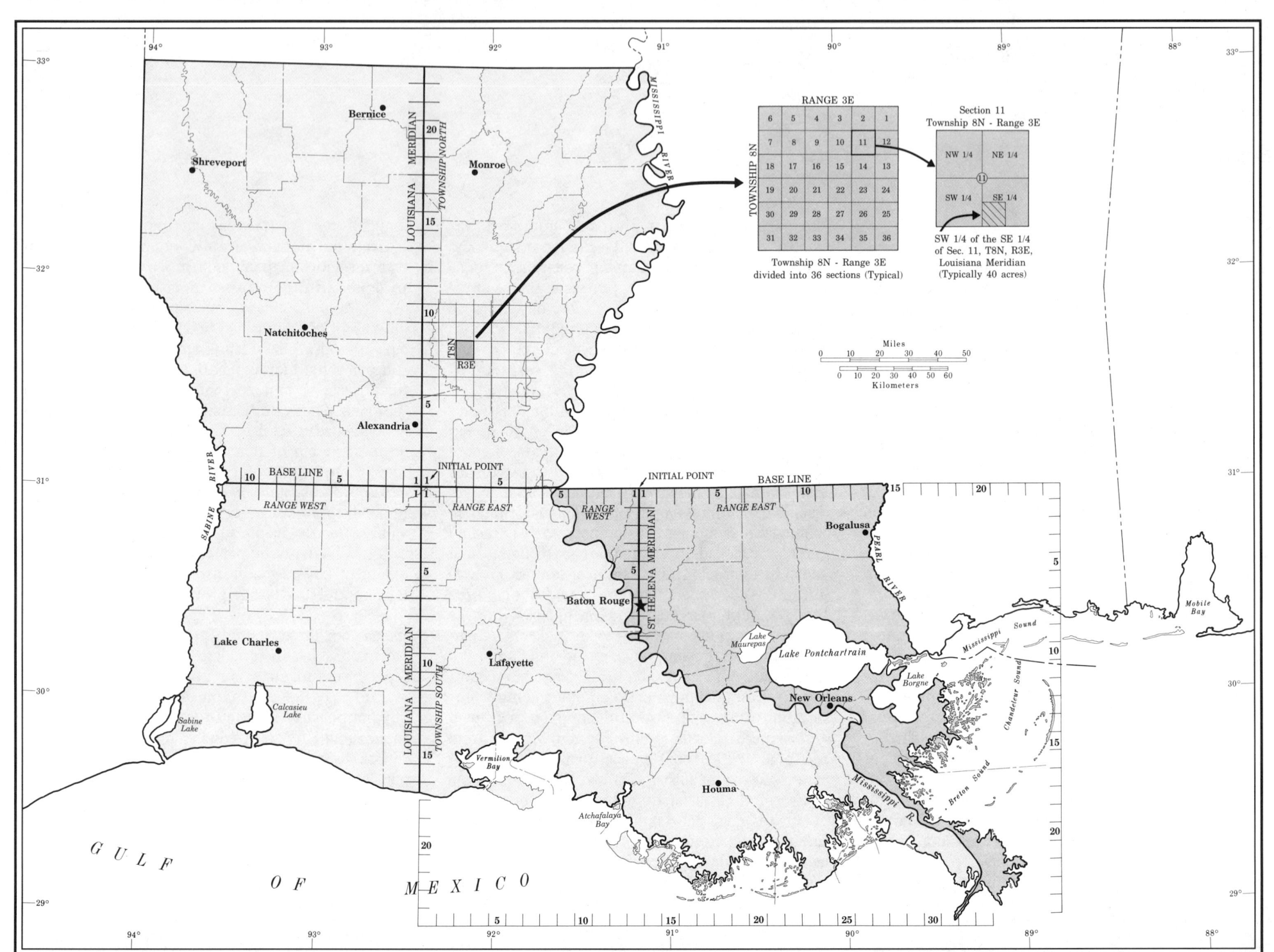

RANGE 3E

6	5	4	3	2	1
7	8	9	10	11	12
18	17	16	15	14	13
19	20	21	22	23	24
30	29	28	27	26	25
31	32	33	34	35	36

TOWNSHIP 8N

Township 8N - Range 3E
divided into 36 sections (Typical)

Section 11
Township 8N - Range 3E

| NW 1/4 | NE 1/4 |
| SW 1/4 | SE 1/4 |

SW 1/4 of the SE 1/4
of Sec. 11, T8N, R3E,
Louisiana Meridian
(Typically 40 acres)

Miles
0 10 20 30 40 50

Kilometers
0 10 20 30 40 50 60

The Northwest Ordinance of 1785 established a land survey system which extends over most of the United States with the exception of the original thirteen colonies. This survey system, commonly called the township-and-range system, employs squares of land. Each square measures six miles on each side and thus occupies thirty-six square miles of surface. These squares are called "townships," and they are arrayed in north-south rows called "ranges." Thence is the name "township-and-range" derived.

Because other survey systems already existed in Louisiana when it became part of the United States (Map 33), the township-and-range system overlays these older methods of describing land. At the time of the Louisiana Purchase in 1803, landowners already in place were assured that all valid claims would be preserved. That land not already settled—the public domain—was surveyed under the new American system. Thus, when one views a landownership map of Louisiana today, one can see a mixture of types of surveys and thereby generally determine what areas of the state were settled before Louisiana became a part of the United States.

Townships are located east or west of a principal meridian and north or south of a base line. Soon after the Louisiana Purchase, Congress passed "An Act for Ascertaining and Adjusting Land Titles and Claims to Land; Within the Territory of Orleans, and the District of Louisiana." Surveyors employed by the U.S. General Land Office established the Louisiana Meridian and the Base Line for the state. The Louisiana Meridian runs north to south at 92° 20' west of Greenwich, passing through the present towns of Farmerville, Eros, Pollock, Pineville, Turkey Creek, and Eunice. The Base Line runs east and west, lying slightly north of 31° north latitude, the line which then formed the northern boundary of Spanish West Florida (Map 35). The Louisiana Meridian and the Base Line meet in southeast Rapides Parish and form an "initial point" from which all of Louisiana west of the Mississippi River is surveyed.

The area east of the Mississippi River known as the Florida Parishes—the present parishes of West and East Feliciana, East Baton Rouge, St. Helena, Livingston, Tangipahoa, Washington, and St. Tammany—did not become a part of U.S. territory until after the West Florida Rebellion against Spanish rule in 1810. The township-and-range system for that region and the old Isle of Orleans employs the same Base Line but uses the St. Helena Meridian (91° 11' west of Greenwich) surveyed in 1822 as its principal meridian.

At six-mile increments north and south of the Base Line, a survey line marks the boundary between each succeeding "range." At equivalent intervals east and west of either principal meridian, a similar line marks the boundary between succeeding "townships." When the range lines and the township lines are overlaid one on the other, a grid of six mile squares—also called "townships"—forms for the entire state.

Each square township is divided into thirty-six "sections," each occupying one square mile (640 acres). These sections can also be divided, most often into quarter-sections (160 acres) on which settlement of the public domain most frequently occurred. Using standard abbreviations one can accurately describe the location of any parcel of land within the state which has as the basis for its survey the township-and-range system.

For that portion of the state surveyed along the Louisiana Meridian, the limits become sixteen ranges to the west, thirty-six ranges to the east, twenty-three townships to the north, and twenty-four townships to the south. Using the St. Helena Meridian, there are five ranges to the west and twenty-one ranges to the east. All townships in this district lie south of the Base Line and equal the twenty-four using the Louisiana Meridian.

Federal surveys in the state were completed in February 1861. However, not all of the state has ever been completely surveyed. Coastal and the more remote internal areas of the state have not yet been surveyed, nor have many of the offshore islands. Recent exploration for oil and gas have spurred the formal survey of many of these areas.

The use of the rectangular survey has affected the state's landscape. Section-line roads run largely in straight lines along those borders. Disposal of the public domain to individuals or corporations (as in railroad grants) occurred using entire sections or divisions thereof. The rural landscape of housing on quarter-sections produced a more scattered pattern than the linear settlements of the long lots but a more systematic distribution than in the irregular surveys. Such a landscape is most readily seen in the prairies of southwestern Louisiana, where the rectangular survey was most fully used.

Copyright © 1995 by the University of Oklahoma Press

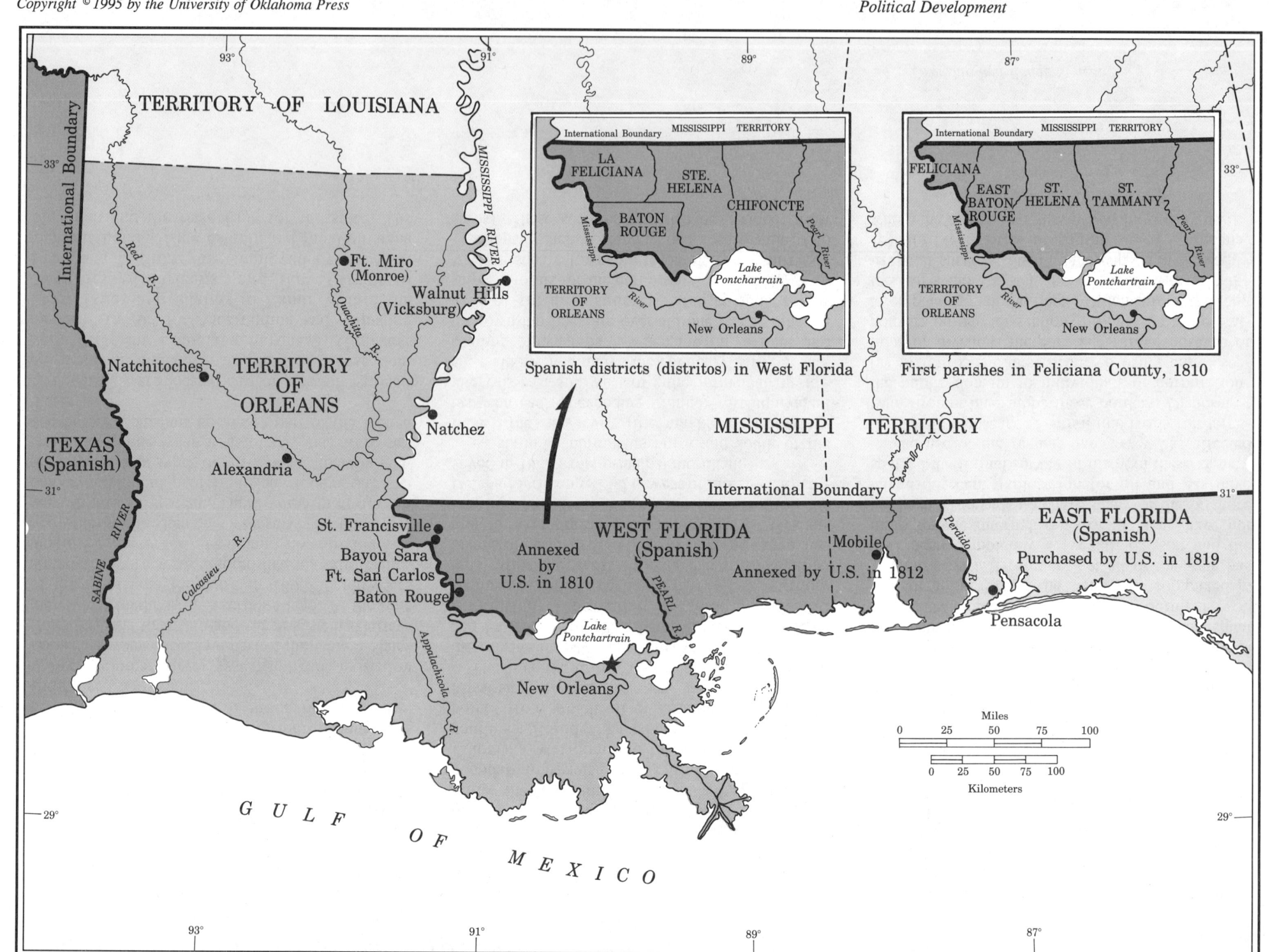

TERRITORY OF LOUISIANA

International Boundary

93°   91°   89°   87°

33°

Red R.

Ouachita R.

MISSISSIPPI RIVER

● Ft. Miro
(Monroe)

Walnut Hills ●
(Vicksburg)

**TERRITORY
OF
ORLEANS**

Natchitoches ●

● Natchez

TEXAS
(Spanish)

Alexandria ●

SABINE RIVER

Calcasieu R.

31°

MISSISSIPPI TERRITORY

International Boundary

St. Francisville ●

Bayou Sara
Ft. San Carlos □
Baton Rouge ●

Annexed
by
U.S. in 1810

WEST FLORIDA
(Spanish)

Mobile ●

Annexed by U.S. in 1812

PEARL R.

Appalachicoola R.

*Lake
Pontchartrain*

★ New Orleans

EAST FLORIDA
(Spanish)

Purchased by U.S. in 1819

Perdido R.

Pensacola ●

G U L F   O F   M E X I C O

29°

93°   91°   89°   87°

Inset 1:

International Boundary   MISSISSIPPI   TERRITORY

33°

LA
FELICIANA   STE.
HELENA   CHIFONCTE

BATON
ROUGE

Mississippi

River

TERRITORY
OF
ORLEANS

*Lake
Pontchartrain*

Pearl River

New Orleans ●

Spanish districts (distritos) in West Florida

Inset 2:

International Boundary   MISSISSIPPI   TERRITORY

FELICIANA

EAST
BATON
ROUGE   ST.
HELENA   ST.
TAMMANY

Mississippi

River

TERRITORY
OF
ORLEANS

*Lake
Pontchartrain*

Pearl River

New Orleans ●

First parishes in Feliciana County, 1810

Miles

0   25   50   75   100

0   25   50   75   100

Kilometers

35. THE WEST FLORIDA REBELLION

The Treaty of Paris (1783) which ended the American Revolution returned Florida to Spanish control. Before then, for twenty years the province had belonged to Great Britain, victor in the French and Indian War (1756–63). Between 1763 and 1783 (especially after 1770) Anglo-American settlers had begun to migrate to the region, since it lay outside the restrictive bounds of the Proclamation Line of 1763. By 1783 the region's population was estimated at over six thousand.

After the American Revolution this settlement by Americans intensified. At the time of the Louisiana Purchase in 1803 the region, particularly in the vicinity of Baton Rouge, was inhabited almost exclusively by emigrants from the United States. All the settlers had taken an oath of allegiance to Spain and were in no way oppressed by Spanish authorities. Nevertheless the population wanted to be a part of the United States.

The vague boundaries of the Louisiana Purchase led to confusion and counter-claims by the United States and Spain in the south and west. Parts of West Florida—from the Mississippi eastward to the Apalachicola River—had been claimed by the United States on the basis of old French occupation. Spain had claimed possession of a Florida north to 32° 28' north latitude. The Treaty of San Lorenzo (Pinckney's Treaty) of 1795 between U.S. envoy Thomas Pinckney and Spanish Minister of State Manuel de Godoy had settled the northern boundary of West Florida at 31° latitude. This accord opened up the Natchez country to undisputed U.S. possession and granted full passage of the Mississippi and right of deposit at New Orleans to American citizens.

That right of deposit was rescinded in 1802, leading to further unrest in West Florida. A brief insurrection in 1804 led by three brothers named Kemper proved unsuccessful. After the Kemper Insurrection little overt action was taken to establish the U.S. claim in fact as well as principle. This would all change in 1810.

In the summer of 1810 numerous West Florida citizens meeting at Bayou Sara brought forward a plan to establish a representative government which would still retain Spanish control. Local Spanish officials feigned agreement while secretly requesting reenforcements from the provincial capital at Pensacola to clamp down on the malcontents. The Americo-Floridians, learning of this request, decided to carry out military action.

In September, Philemon Thomas led a force of seventy-odd armed men south from St. Francisville to Baton Rouge. At 4:00 A.M. on September 23 the force gained entrance into Fort San Carlos and overwhelmed the smaller Spanish garrison there. The fort and the province fell into rebel hands.

At the same time as this military action, a convention was being held in St. Francisville which led on September 26 to a declaration of independence from Spain and the formation of the Republic of West Florida. A constitution and government patterned after that of the United States were put in place. At the same time, the Republic's leaders began to petition President James Madison for annexation into the United States.

On October 27, 1810, Madison (without mention of the Republic of West Florida) issued a proclamation ordering Governor William C. C. Claiborne of the Territory of Orleans to take possession of West Florida. With communications still in the frontier stage, this action did not take place until December. On December 10, 1810, Claiborne took symbolic possession of the region at Baton Rouge. On December 20 the area between the Mississippi and the Pearl rivers was constituted the County of Feliciana and divided into four parishes (Map 42). Later, the region between the Pearl and the Perdido rivers was annexed as the counties of Viloxi and Pascagoula. These would be added to the Mississippi Territory and later apportioned between the states of Mississippi and Alabama, which entered the Union in 1817 and 1819, respectively. The County of Feliciana and its four component parishes in the meantime were added to Louisiana at the time of statehood in April 1812.

Both Spain and Britain protested the annexation of West Florida by the United States. The Spanish cited the violation of the 1783 Treaty of Paris, to which the new United States was also a signatory. Britain still viewed the region as potential British territory and in any event did not favor U.S. expansion in any direction. British designs were largely dissipated by the War of 1812, and particularly the Gulf campaigns of 1813–14. Not until the Adams-Onís (Florida Purchase) Treaty of 1819 did Spain officially recognize the results of the West Florida Rebellion of 1810.

Copyright © 1995 by the University of Oklahoma Press

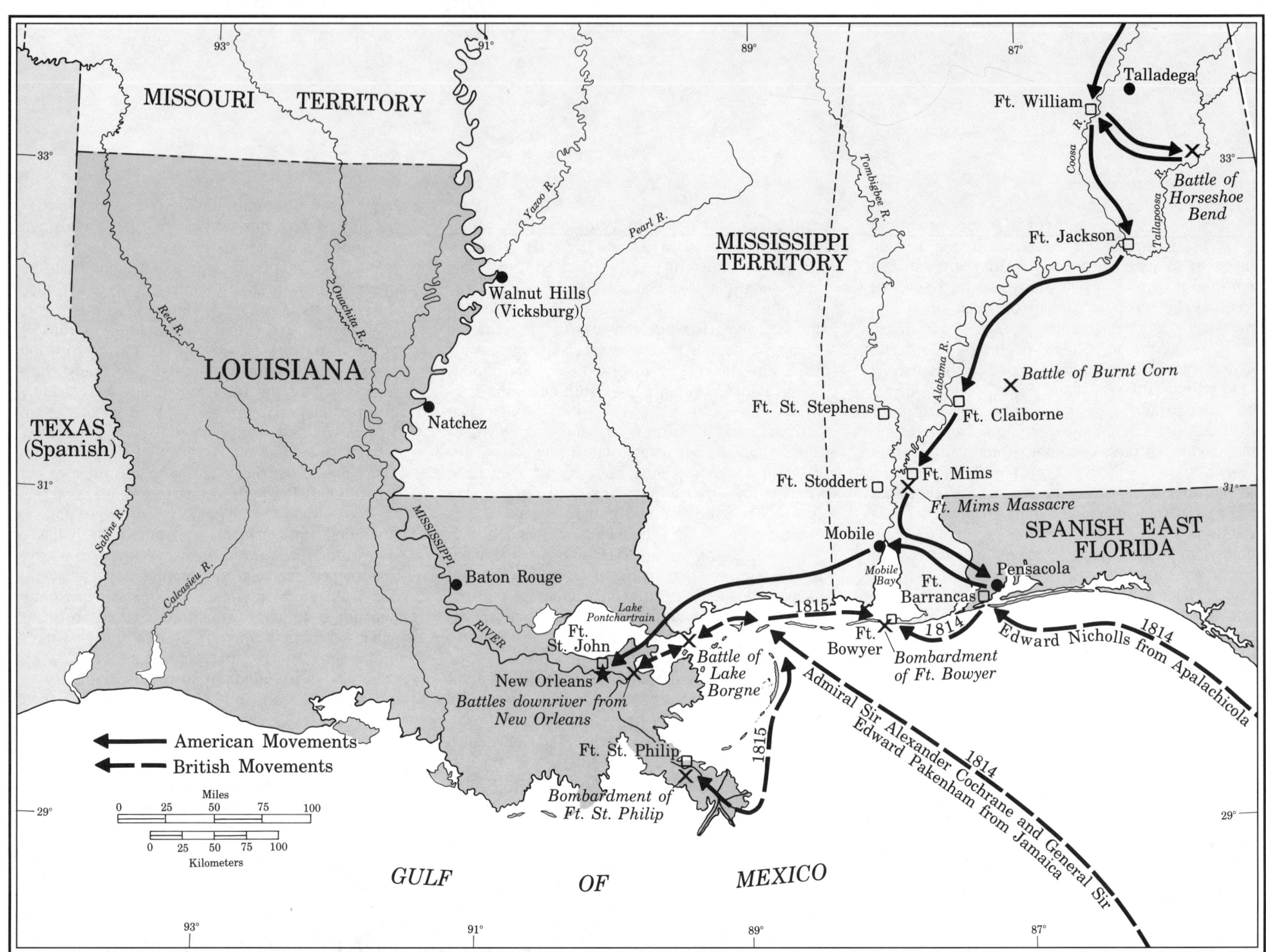

MISSOURI   TERRITORY

93°   91°   89°   87°

Talladega

Ft. William

33°   33°

Coosa R.

Yazoo R.   *Battle of*
Horseshoe
Bend

Pearl R.

MISSISSIPPI
TERRITORY

Ft. Jackson

Tallapoosa R.

Walnut Hills
(Vicksburg)

Red R.

Ouachita R.

LOUISIANA

Alabama R.   × *Battle of Burnt Corn*

Ft. St. Stephens   Ft. Claiborne

Natchez

TEXAS
(Spanish)

Sabine R.

Calcasieu R.

31°   Ft. Stoddert   × Ft. Mims   31°
Ft. Mims Massacre

SPANISH EAST
FLORIDA

Mobile

Baton Rouge   Pensacola
Mobile   Ft.
Bay   Barrancas

Lake
Pontchartrain   1815   1814
Ft.
St. John   Ft.   *Edward Nicholls from Apalachicola*   1814
RIVER   *Battle of*   Bowyer
New Orleans   *Lake*   *Bombardment*   1814
Battles downriver from   *Borgne*   *of Ft. Bowyer*
New Orleans

MISSISSIPPI

←——— American Movements
←- - - British Movements   1815

Miles
0   25   50   75   100

0   25   50   75   100
Kilometers

Ft. St. Philip

Bombardment of
Ft. St. Philip

Admiral Sir Alexander Cochrane and General Sir
Edward Pakenham from Jamaica

29°   29°

GULF   OF   MEXICO

93°   91°   89°   87°

The War of 1812 in the Old Southwest combined British intrigue with invasion in a strategy based on two beliefs. Great Britain did not accept the Louisiana Purchase as a legitimate transfer of territory to its former American colonies. Nor did the British consider the former citizens of France's Louisiana colony, so recently joined to the United States, to be truly loyal to their new national government.

Following war's declaration on June 18, 1812, the British stationed warships off the mouth of the Mississippi. This blockade disrupted commerce, bringing economic losses to New Orleans and its hinterland. In response, Governor William C. C. Claiborne of the new state of Louisiana reorganized the militia and also attempted to maintain morale.

During 1813, British agents among the Creeks incited that Indian nation to attack the Americans. On August 30 the Creeks captured Fort Mims, Mississippi Territory, and massacred half of the 550 people there. General Andrew Jackson led an American force south from Tennessee in a counteroffensive. A series of battles followed, culminating in a decisive American victory at Horseshoe Bend on March 27, 1814. The Treaty of Fort Jackson in August 1814 ended the Creek War, freeing Jackson to move against the British directly.

British forces had occupied Pensacola in Spanish Florida in July 1814. Another British army moved toward Mobile, but Jackson drove off that attacking army in September. In turn the Americans moved east, occupying Pensacola in November following a British withdrawal.

The close of 1814 saw a major British offensive against New Orleans and thus against U.S. control of the entire Lower Mississippi Valley. A fleet of fifty ships had gathered at Jamaica. The British naval expedition under Admiral Alexander Cochrane transported an army commanded by General Edward Pakenham. Sailing on November 26, the fleet moved north and west, reaching the entrance to Lake Borgne on December 10.

Jackson had moved with his troops from Mobile toward New Orleans. He arrived in that city on December 1 and immediately set to work strengthening the region's defenses and consolidating forces from north and east in the area around New Orleans. Although Jackson had learned that New Orleans would indeed be the target, he did not yet know which of several routes the British planned to use in their invasion.

The Battle of Lake Borgne opened the New Orleans campaign. On December 13 the British moved into the lake and were met the following day by six American gunboats. The small American force proved no match for the more numerous, better-armed British. However, the engagement did reveal more of the British strategy to Jackson.

Increased American activity followed the lake battle. Additional reenforcements, including Jean Lafitte's privateers at Barataria Bay, collected in the city. The British, too, had reorganized their forces, and on December 22 they set out from their Pea Island headquarters. Sailing across Lake Borgne, they landed the next morning (December 23) at Bayou Bienvenu. Jackson, alerted by residents along the bayou, marched seven miles downriver to the Chalmette Plantation. Setting up a line of defense in the afternoon, the Americans launched an attack on the nearby British camp that night. After an engagement lasting most of the night, the Americans withdrew behind their defensive positions.

Continuing to land troops, the British launched a first attack on December 28 but were repulsed by the Americans. On New Year's Day 1815, a British artillery barrage failed to open a breach in the American lines. The climactic battle of New Orleans took place on January 8. General Jackson with perhaps five thousand men faced General Pakenham with eight thousand soldiers. The foggy morning saw the British advance in solid ranks. First the American artillery, then the individual riflemen, opened fire on the British. Each successive British advance was repelled by the Americans. General Pakenham and other British commanders died during the final advance. The British had over two thousand killed, wounded, or missing, the Americans seventy-one.

Meanwhile the British fleet had sailed up the Mississippi to bombard Fort St. Philip on January 9–18, hoping to silence its guns and pass upriver. Failing, they returned to the coast and collected the remaining troops. In February the British captured Fort Bowyer at Mobile Bay as a prelude to further activity. Martial law remained in effect in Louisiana until March 13, when official notification arrived that the Treaty of Ghent had been signed on December 24, 1814, officially ending the war.

Thus the battles for New Orleans occurred after the war's official close. The struggle proved important to the United States not only in terms of its claim to the lands within the Louisiana Purchase but also by contributing to the Americanization of the former Franco-Spanish colony. The clash of cultures continued; slowly but surely, however, the unique territory became a full member of the United States.

Copyright © 1995 by the University of Oklahoma Press

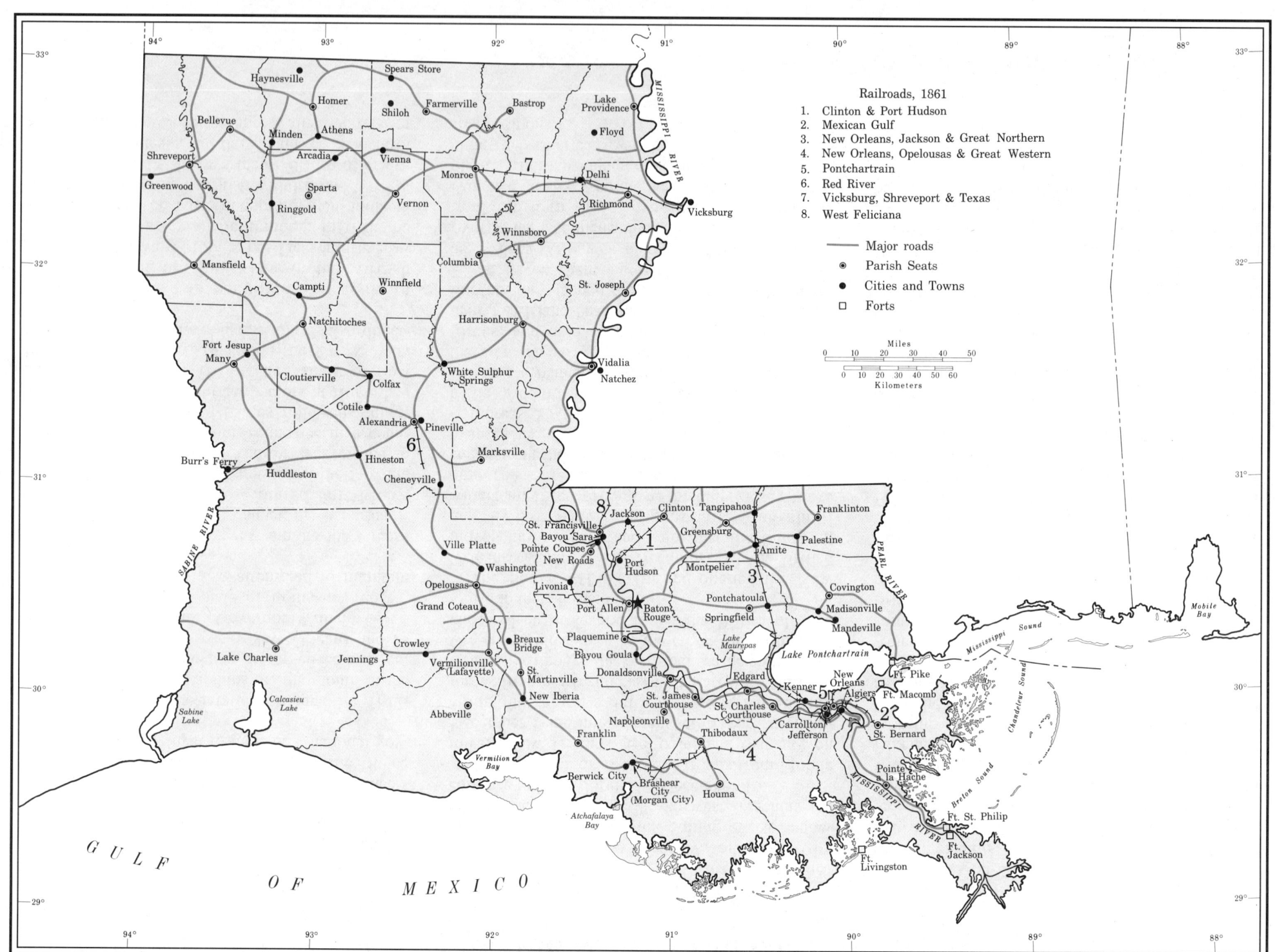

Railroads, 1861
1. Clinton & Port Hudson
2. Mexican Gulf
3. New Orleans, Jackson & Great Northern
4. New Orleans, Opelousas & Great Western
5. Pontchartrain
6. Red River
7. Vicksburg, Shreveport & Texas
8. West Feliciana

——— Major roads
⊙ Parish Seats
● Cities and Towns
□ Forts

Miles
0 10 20 30 40 50

Kilometers
0 10 20 30 40 50 60

In many respects Louisiana reached a watershed on the eve of the Civil War. New Orleans peaked as the South's preeminent trading center and metropolis even as railroads snaking across the nation presaged the rise of future rivals. The planter society which controlled the state's economic, political, and cultural life would soon, in Margaret Mitchell's words, be "gone with the wind," collapsing with the abolition of slavery. All this seemed beyond the state's comprehension as it debated its secession from the same union it had so eagerly sought to join at the century's dawn.

The Louisiana Purchase had brought 50,000 people and 830,000 square miles of territory into the new nation. The Territory of Orleans was the first to be carved from that domain and would be combined with part of Florida to form the eighteenth state in 1812. Gradually the former colonial population accepted its new status as citizens of the United States and combined with native and foreign-born immigrants to spread across the state. By 1860 the total population had leaped more than tenfold and stood at 708,002. New Orleans, with 168,675 citizens, was the largest city and port in the entire South (Map 62).

Economically the state expanded, with agricultural, commercial, and even manufacturing interests moving ahead. Agriculture was the key to the economic cycle of the state, even in such commercial centers as New Orleans. Scattered across the hill country lay small and large yeoman farmsteads, largely subsistence in nature but with cash crops, too. Large plantations were located in the valleys of the Red, the Mississippi, and associated streams. Plantations with fifty plus slaves numbered approximately sixteen hundred and account-ed for more than 43 percent of the state's arable land. Cotton in the north and sugar in the south were the major cash crops for the planters; the yeomen opted for the former because of the lower cash outlays required for its cultivation and processing. Corn represented the staple food for both humans and other animals, and a variety of garden crops also added to the land's production. Livestock were raised in association with most farms but were most important in the prairies of southwestern Louisiana.

Commercially, New Orleans boomed following the War of 1812. Flatboats were succeeded first by steamboats and then the railroad. European companies based in the Crescent City joined with native firms to handle much of the commerce of the entire Mississippi valley. Goods arriving in the city had to be transferred into ocean-going vessels for shipment through the Gulf to national or international markets. New Orleans docks and wharves hummed with the transshipment of both imports and exports. In 1860, $185 million in goods arrived in the city from upriver. Individuals called factors handled the business affairs of many planters who remained on the land. The factor received the crop, sold it as best he could, and received an average commission of 2.5 percent. He also bought supplies and extended credit on the same commission terms.

Manufacturing did not attract the same attention as other sectors of the economy—a situation blamed on a variety of causes ranging from the preeminence of agriculture (most aspired to the life of a planter) to an inertia on the part of Louisiana and other southerners. Lumber, flour, cotton, and iron millworks; brick and tile kilns; tanneries; dis-tilleries; and sugar refineries constituted the chief areas of manufacturing.

Transportation still centered on the state's myriad stream courses. Over the span of years from the purchase to the Civil War the old vessels of raft, flatboat, and keelboat were replaced by the steamboat. By the 1830s the railroad entered the picture but did not expand as quickly in the South as elsewhere in the nation. Other land transportation remained primitive, with but small improvements on the trails or vehicles of an earlier time.

Louisiana, as did the entire South, had a rigid social- political system. At the top of the pyramid stood the merchants and the planters, an oligarchy of wealth in land, slaves, or commerce. At the lowest level were the African American slaves, the fuel for the motor of the plantation system. Between stood the middle-class professionals, merchants, and yeoman farmers and the lower-class whites, both rural and urban. Just above the slaves were the free African Americans, whose numbers were in decline as the century progressed (Map 55).

Politically the state was run by the planter-merchants, though gradually greater access to the political process was obtained by white males in general. State political parties reflected the evolution of parties in the nation: Jeffersonian Democrats, National Republicans, Whigs, Democrats, Know-Nothings. As the debate over slavery grew ever more shrill, the standard political art of compromise weakened beyond repair. Before even the first shot was fired at Fort Sumter, South Carolina, on April 12, 1861, Louisiana had already severed its ties to the Union.

Copyright © 1995 by the University of Oklahoma Press

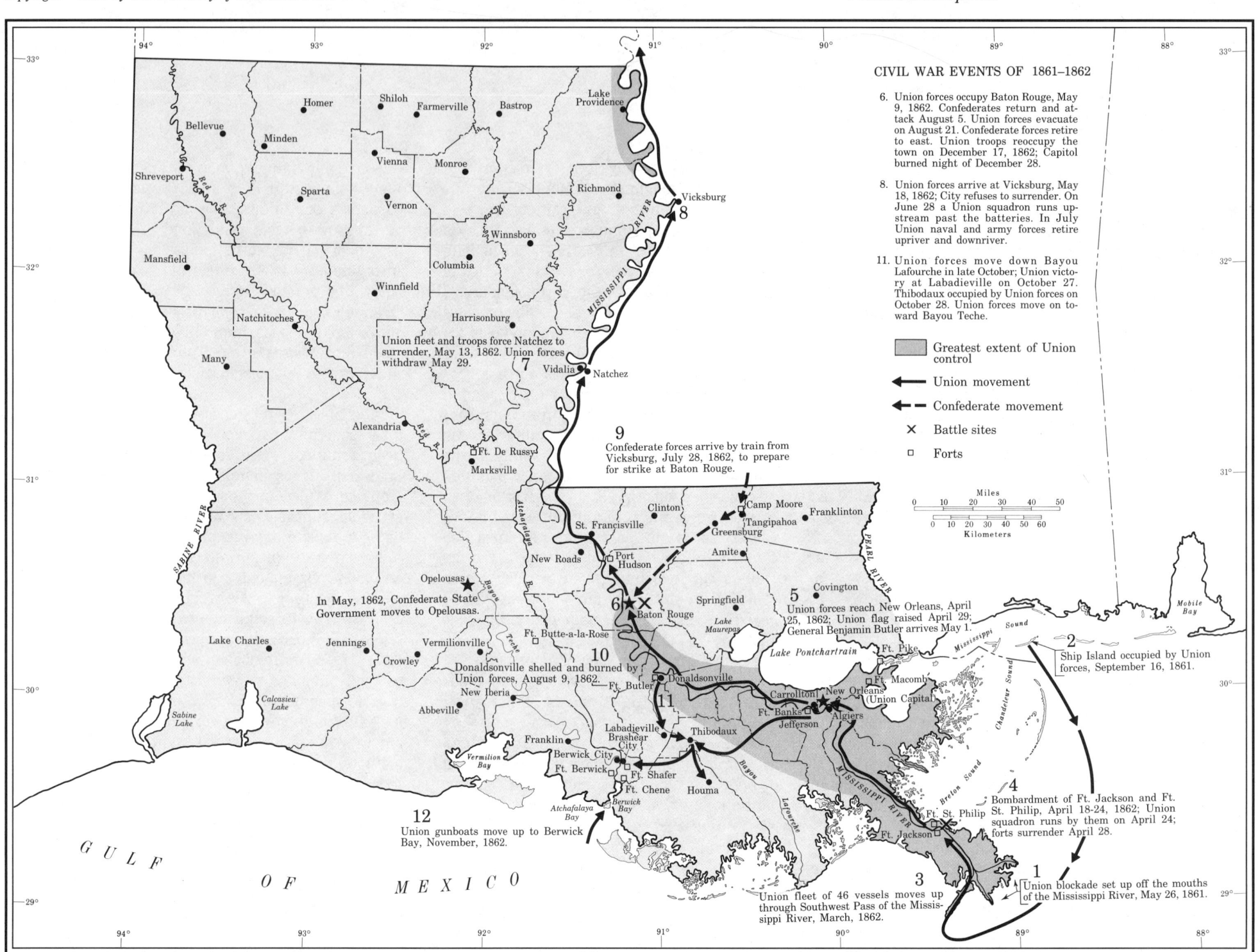

CIVIL WAR EVENTS OF 1861–1862

6. Union forces occupy Baton Rouge, May 9, 1862. Confederates return and attack August 5. Union forces evacuate on August 21. Confederate forces retire to east. Union troops reoccupy the town on December 17, 1862; Capitol burned night of December 28.

8. Union forces arrive at Vicksburg, May 18, 1862; City refuses to surrender. On June 28 a Union squadron runs upstream past the batteries. In July Union naval and army forces retire upriver and downriver.

11. Union forces move down Bayou Lafourche in late October; Union victory at Labadieville on October 27. Thibodaux occupied by Union forces on October 28. Union forces move on toward Bayou Teche.

Greatest extent of Union control

Union movement

Confederate movement

✕ Battle sites

▢ Forts

9 Confederate forces arrive by train from Vicksburg, July 28, 1862, to prepare for strike at Baton Rouge.

Union fleet and troops force Natchez to surrender, May 13, 1862. Union forces withdraw May 29.

7

In May, 1862, Confederate State Government moves to Opelousas.

5 Union forces reach New Orleans, April 25, 1862; Union flag raised April 29; General Benjamin Butler arrives May 1.

2 Ship Island occupied by Union forces, September 16, 1861.

10 Donaldsonville shelled and burned by Union forces, August 9, 1862.

4 Bombardment of Ft. Jackson and Ft. St. Philip, April 18-24, 1862; Union squadron runs by them on April 24; forts surrender April 28.

12 Union gunboats move up to Berwick Bay, November, 1862.

3 Union fleet of 46 vessels moves up through Southwest Pass of the Mississippi River, March, 1862.

1 Union blockade set up off the mouths of the Mississippi River, May 26, 1861.

GULF OF MEXICO

38. THE CIVIL WAR IN LOUISIANA, 1861–1862

Following Abraham Lincoln's election as president in November 1860 came a Southern call for secession. Louisiana's legislature followed the popular cry, calling for the election of a secession convention. On January 7, 1861, that vote gave an overwhelming majority to those favoring immediate secession. Whether this vote reflected a secessionist majority or merely a plurality combined with a silent majority fearful of speaking up, the result was secession. On January 26, 1861, Louisiana left the Union.

The remainder of 1861 saw preparation for war. Almost every parish organized a military unit, many of which had such colorful names as Alligator Rangers, Red River Sharpshooters, or Yankee Pelters. Although the state was open to naval attack via the Gulf and the Mississippi River, many early volunteers were shipped to the eastern theatre. State leaders, feeling more keenly the necessity of local defense, began to complain of this drain upon their militia. At the end of 1861, the Federals had established a naval blockade off the coast and engaged in a minor skirmish at the river's mouth, but only Ship Island had been occupied.

In 1862 the war came to Louisiana. Many of the dead or wounded from Shiloh, Antietam, and other out-of-state war zones were brought home for recuperation or burial. Moreover, the Union forces had decided that New Orleans was indeed the key to the Mississippi Valley and must be taken early.

In March, a Union fleet which had gathered earlier at Ship Island began ascending the Mississippi River. Forts St. Philip and Jackson represented the first line of Confederate defense; a chain had been stretched across the river to further delay enemy vessels. The Union fleet, commanded by David Farragut and David Porter, began bombarding the river forts on April 18. This shelling lasted continuously until April 24. Although structural damage, particularly to Fort Jackson, was substantial, little loss of Confederate guns or personnel occurred.

Deciding to run past the forts, the fleet advanced the night of April 23–24. The chain was cut, Confederate naval forces were overwhelmed when they chose to fight, and Farragut's squadron steamed on toward New Orleans, arriving April 25. As the Southern army evacuated the city with all the supplies it could carry, a standoff occurred between the civil authorities and the Federal navy. The downriver forts surrendered on April 28, and New Orleans itself was taken over on April 30.

A Union army commanded by Gen. Benjamin F. Butler arrived to occupy the city on May 1. Butler, more commonly known by his nickname "Beast," became the most hated individual in the state's history. He did, however, take effective control of New Orleans and remained in charge of Union forces until he was replaced later in the year by another political general, Nathaniel P. Banks.

The Union fleet, after capturing New Orleans, moved upriver to take Baton Rouge. On May 9, Union forces took control of the capital city; the legislators and governor had moved on to Opelousas. After taking Baton Rouge the fleet advanced to occupy Natchez, Mississippi, on May 13.

On August 5, Confederate troops under Gen. John C. Breckenridge, a former candidate for president, counterattacked the Union army at Baton Rouge. The fighting pushed the Union forces back to the banks of the Mississippi, where naval firepower halted the Confederate advance. The Southerners withdrew to the east, and the Union forces evacuated to New Orleans on August 21. Baton Rouge was heavily damaged by the fighting and sacked by soldiers, but it escaped a general burning at the last minute when Butler countermanded an earlier order.

Union gunboats then cruised up and down the Mississippi, inviting shelling from Confederate shore batteries. One such shelling came from the city of Donaldsonville, which fared worse than Baton Rouge. On August 9, Union forces bombarded, then set fire to, the city, rendering it a shell of its former self.

In October, Gen. Godfrey Weitzel led a Federal army down Bayou Lafourche, and on October 27 he defeated a Confederate force under Gen. Alfred Mouton at Labadieville. With other troops moving west from New Orleans along the railroad, Union forces then occupied Thibodaux on October 28 and moved on to take Houma and Brashear City by the end of the month. In December, Union forces again occupied Baton Rouge, and on the night of December 28 the capitol was burned. The war had begun in Louisiana; worse was yet to come.

Copyright © 1995 by the University of Oklahoma Press

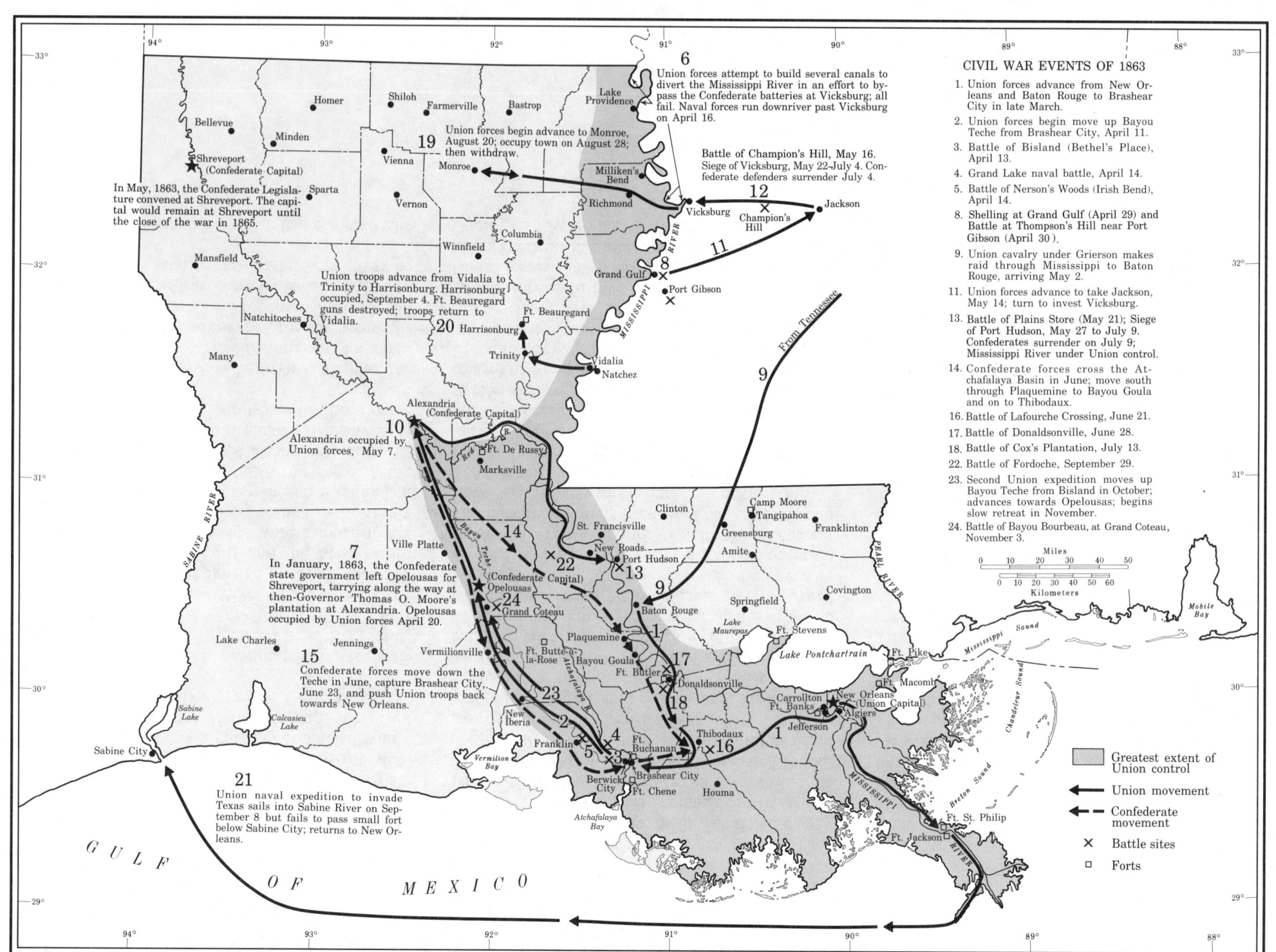

CIVIL WAR EVENTS OF 1863

1. Union forces advance from New Orleans and Baton Rouge to Brashear City in late March.

2. Union forces begin move up Bayou Teche from Brashear City, April 11.

3. Battle of Bisland (Bethel's Place), April 13.

4. Grand Lake naval battle, April 14.

5. Battle of Nerson's Woods (Irish Bend), April 14.

8. Shelling at Grand Gulf (April 29) and Battle at Thompson's Hill near Port Gibson (April 30).

9. Union cavalry under Grierson makes raid through Mississippi to Baton Rouge, arriving May 2.

11. Union forces advance to take Jackson, May 14; turn to invest Vicksburg.

13. Battle of Plains Store (May 21); Siege of Port Hudson, May 27 to July 9. Confederates surrender on July 9; Mississippi River under Union control.

14. Confederate forces cross the Atchafalaya Basin in June; move south through Plaquemine to Bayou Goula and on to Thibodaux.

16. Battle of Lafourche Crossing, June 21.

17. Battle of Donaldsonville, June 28.

18. Battle of Cox's Plantation, July 13.

22. Battle of Fordoche, September 29.

23. Second Union expedition moves up Bayou Teche from Bisland in October; advances towards Opelousas; begins slow retreat in November.

24. Battle of Bayou Bourbeau, at Grand Coteau, November 3.

6. Union forces attempt to build several canals to divert the Mississippi River in an effort to bypass the Confederate batteries at Vicksburg; all fail. Naval forces run downriver past Vicksburg on April 16.

Battle of Champion's Hill, May 16. Siege of Vicksburg, May 22-July 4. Confederate defenders surrender July 4.

Union forces begin advance to Monroe, August 20; occupy town on August 28; then withdraw.

In May, 1863, the Confederate Legislature convened at Shreveport. The capital would remain at Shreveport until the close of the war in 1865.

Union troops advance from Vidalia to Trinity to Harrisonburg. Harrisonburg occupied, September 4. Ft. Beauregard guns destroyed; troops return to Vidalia.

Alexandria occupied by Union forces, May 7.

In January, 1863, the Confederate state government left Opelousas for Shreveport, tarrying along the way at then-Governor Thomas O. Moore's plantation at Alexandria. Opelousas occupied by Union forces April 20.

Confederate forces move down the Teche in June, capture Brashear City, June 23, and push Union troops back towards New Orleans.

Union naval expedition to invade Texas sails into Sabine River on September 8 but fails to pass small fort below Sabine City; returns to New Orleans.

Greatest extent of Union control

Union movement

Confederate movement

× Battle sites

□ Forts

Miles
0 10 20 30 40 50

Kilometers
0 10 20 30 40 50 60

The war in 1863 focused on the Mississippi and the Bayou Teche–Atchafalaya River basin. Union forces from New Orleans and Baton Rouge under Gen. Nathaniel P. Banks assembled at Brashear City in March, then advanced on April 11. They fought the Confederates at Bisland (Bethel's Place) between Pattersonville and Centerville on April 13, then again on April 14 upstream at Nerson's Woods (Irish Bend) near Franklin. Also on April 14, Union naval forces triumphed on nearby Grand Lake. Skirmishing continually, the larger Union army pushed the Southerners back past New Iberia and Vermilionville. Taking Opelousas on April 20, Banks rested, then advanced and on May 7 reached Alexandria, occupied earlier that day by Adm. David Porter's fleet. The Confederates retreated toward Natchitoches, shifting their capital from Alexandria to Shreveport. Union forces dithered, then moved south to join in the Port Hudson campaign.

The Vicksburg and Port Hudson campaigns sought to gain control of the Mississippi and thus divide the Confederacy. Efforts to bypass Vicksburg by canals failed, so the fleet ran past the city's guns on April 16. Gen. Ulysses S. Grant shifted his command south from Milliken's Bend. On April 29, Union gunboats failed to silence Grand Gulf's batteries, but six miles downriver a Union army crossed into Mississippi and won an April 30 victory at Thompson's Hill near Port Gibson. Diversions by Gen. William T. Sherman and an earlier cavalry raid by Col. B. H. Grierson kept Confederate Gen. John C. Pemberton guessing at overall Union strategy. After defeating Pemberton at Champion's Hill on May 16, Grant began a siege of Vicksburg on May 22. Relief attempts from both Louisiana and Mississippi failed. The city was starved into surrender on July 4, one day after the Union victory at Gettysburg.

To the south, Union forces advanced on Port Hudson, the final Confederate fortress on the Mississippi, bombarding the citadel on May 8. After the Battle of Plains Store on May 21, the Confederates withdrew within the fortress. Augmented by veterans of the Teche campaign, Union besiegers in time outnumbered Confederate defenders by perhaps five to one. The entrenched Southerners repulsed major Union assaults on May 27, June 11, and June 14. A siege had begun on June 1. Both hunger and heat melted the defenders' morale and numbers. On July 9, two days after verifying the fall of Vicksburg, Port Hudson surrendered.

Failing to relieve either river fortress, Gen. Richard Taylor's Confederates launched two new thrusts. Col. J. P. Major's cavalry crossed the Atchafalaya to disrupt communications between Port Hudson and New Orleans. They surprised Union garrisons at Plaquemine (June 18) and Bayou Goula (June 19), then moved on Thibodaux. A clash at Lafourche Crossing south of that city, however, ended in a Union victory. Meanwhile, Gen. Alfred Mouton's Confederates had moved down the Teche. On June 23 they surprised the Union garrison at Brashear City, forcing its surrender. This success disheartened the Union army, which had just defeated Colonel Major. By June's end the Federals had withdrawn to New Orleans. The Southerners failed to take Fort Butler at Donaldsonville on June 28, but on July 13, they were victorious to the south at Cox's Plantation. They then gradually withdrew westward to Brashear City, then on to Franklin, followed just as gradually by a Union army.

The Federals then made several efforts to invade Texas. A naval force sailed into Sabine Bay on September 8, failed to pass a fort south of Sabine City, and retreated to New Orleans. An army advance across the upper Atchafalaya Basin was stalled by a Confederate victory at Fordoche on September 29. In October a third Union force moved up the Teche past Opelousas but was halted by low water levels. On November 3, Confederates attacked the slow Union retreat at Grand Coteau. Skirmishing continued until the Federals reached New Iberia on November 17.

Small engagements occurred elsewhere. Confederate thrusts from Lake Providence south to Vidalia proved largely ineffectual. After Vicksburg fell, Union forces followed the railroad to occupy Monroe briefly in late August before returning to Vicksburg. In September a Federal force from Vidalia destroyed Fort Beauregard after its defenders fled. After occupying Harrisonburg briefly, the Union forces withdrew.

Union efforts in 1863 suffered from disorganization, ineptitude, and miscommunication. On the other hand, the Confederates lacked the men and supplies to mount sustained campaigns. By year's end Federal power had expanded, and the Union navy patrolling the Mississippi effectively cut off Louisiana from the other Confederate states.

Civilians shared in the war's hardships. Both Union and Confederate armies often lived off the land. Raiding by soldiers and looting by newly freed slaves, combined with the burning of cotton to prevent its seizure by the enemy, derailed the economy. With defeat and privation came a loss of morale and disenchantment with conscription. Also, the appearance of "jayhawkers"—gangs of draft dodgers, deserters, and runaway slaves— added to civilian anxiety.

Copyright © 1995 by the University of Oklahoma Press

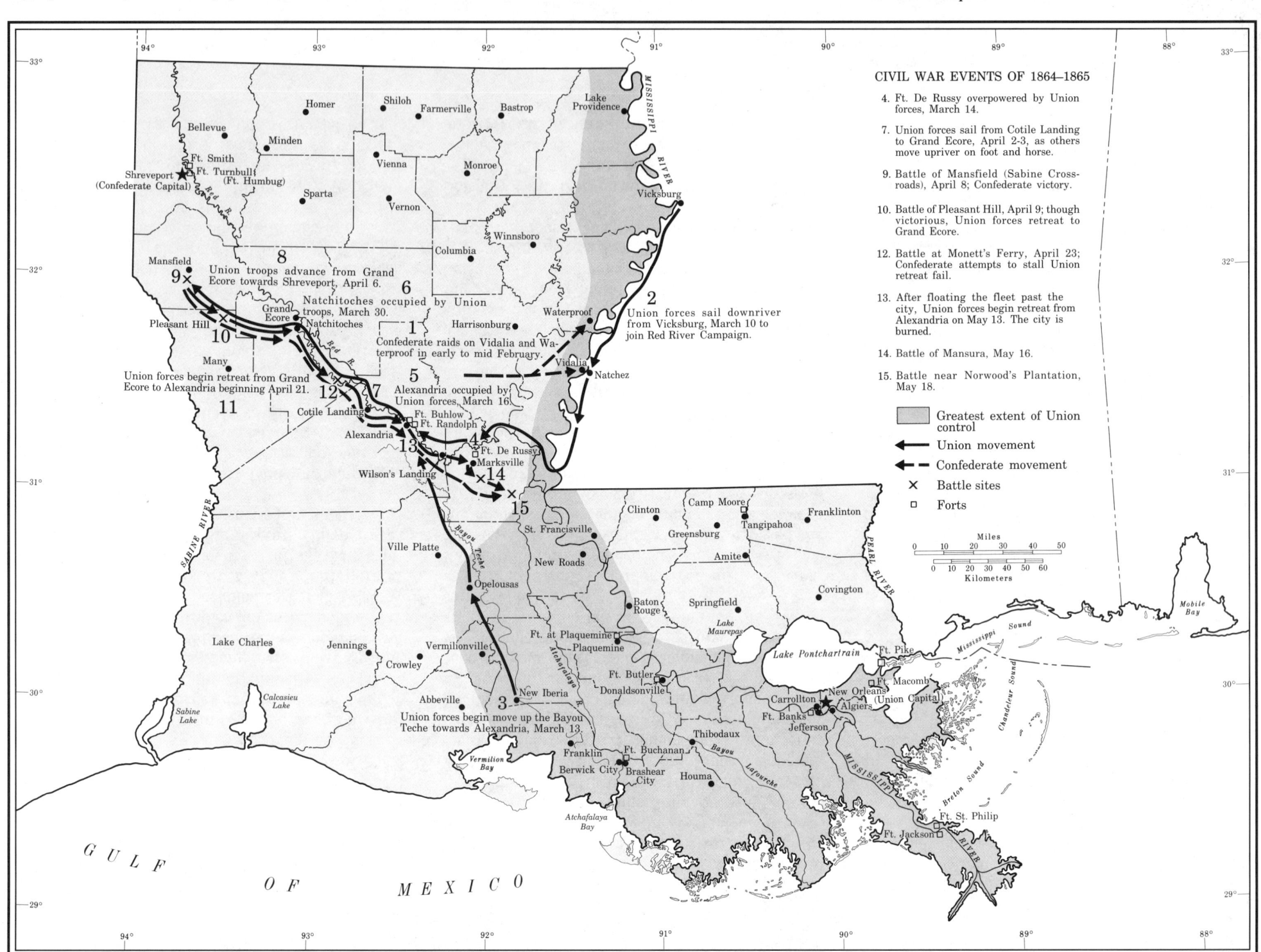

CIVIL WAR EVENTS OF 1864–1865

4. Ft. De Russy overpowered by Union forces, March 14.

7. Union forces sail from Cotile Landing to Grand Ecore, April 2-3, as others move upriver on foot and horse.

9. Battle of Mansfield (Sabine Cross-roads), April 8; Confederate victory.

10. Battle of Pleasant Hill, April 9; though victorious, Union forces retreat to Grand Ecore.

12. Battle at Monett's Ferry, April 23; Confederate attempts to stall Union retreat fail.

13. After floating the fleet past the city, Union forces begin retreat from Alexandria on May 13. The city is burned.

14. Battle of Mansura, May 16.

15. Battle near Norwood's Plantation, May 18.

Greatest extent of Union control

→ Union movement

⇢ Confederate movement

× Battle sites

□ Forts

Union troops advance from Grand Ecore towards Shreveport, April 6.

Natchitoches occupied by Union troops, March 30.

Confederate raids on Vidalia and Waterproof in early to mid February.

Union forces sail downriver from Vicksburg, March 10 to join Red River Campaign.

Union forces begin retreat from Grand Ecore to Alexandria beginning April 21.

Alexandria occupied by Union forces, March 16.

Union forces begin move up the Bayou Teche towards Alexandria, March 13.

Miles
0 10 20 30 40 50

Kilometers
0 10 20 30 40 50 60

40. THE CIVIL WAR IN LOUISIANA, 1864–1865

The spring of 1864 saw the last major Civil War campaign in the state—the Red River campaign. The Union plan, to overrun the remaining Confederate areas of Louisiana as well as to move into east Texas, was simple in design. The army and navy would move up the Red River to capture Shreveport (the Confederate capital and headquarters of Gen. Edmund Kirby Smith, commander of the Trans-Mississippi Department), then move on into Texas. Not only would the state come under complete Federal control, but the campaign would seize large quantities of cotton and other supplies from the Confederates.

In March, Union troops moved up the Teche and also downriver from Vicksburg, converging on Alexandria, which fell to the invaders on March 16. By early April the Red River had risen high enough to permit gunboats to accompany the troops, and the forces, under the overall command of Gen. Nathaniel P. Banks, moved upriver. Retreating before them, the Confederate forces under Gen. Richard Taylor declined to engage the Union army while it remained shielded by the gunboats.

After occupying Natchitoches, Banks decided to march overland via Pleasant Hill and Mansfield. This separation from the naval contingent gave Taylor his opportunity to attack. Following a skirmish three miles north of Pleasant Hill on April 7, the Confederates launched a concerted attack at Mansfield the following day. The Union army, hampered again by poor planning, retreated in haste to Pleasant Hill. On April 9, Taylor again attacked, but this engagement ended in a Union victory.

Throughout the campaign Banks enjoyed a strong advantage in men, but he did not follow up on his Pleasant Hill success. Citing shortages as well as uncertainty about true Confederate strength, he retreated on April 10 to Grand Ecore near Natchitoches. On April 21 the Union army decamped again and withdrew towards Alexandria. A small Confederate force attempted to slow the withdrawal at Monett's Ferry on April 23, but they were overwhelmed.

Reaching Alexandria on April 25, the Union force halted because the Red River was too low to allow the gunboats to pass over the rapids. Col. Joseph Bailey, an inventive army engineer, built dams which caused the water level to rise enough to allow the boats to pass. This success was followed by a boat bridge over the Atchafalaya which further hastened Banks's withdrawal toward New Orleans.

Upon leaving Alexandria on May 13, Union forces burned the city. The pursuing Confederates skirmished with the retreating Northern army at Wilson's Landing (May 14), Marksville (May 15), Mansura (May 16), and Norwood's Plantation (May 18). The overall advantage in the Red River campaign went to the Confederates, but the price in lives and destruction of property throughout the valley was high.

Although skirmishing in several areas of the state occurred during the remainder of 1864 and early 1865, the war was all but over. Confederate Gov. Henry Watkins Allen continued his efforts to keep the economy alive and improve morale. However, Gen. Robert E. Lee surrendered the Army of Northern Virginia to Gen. Ulysses S. Grant at Appomattox Courthouse on April 9, 1865. On May 18 General Smith left Shreveport for Houston. His lieutenant surrendered on May 26, and the general signed the documents on June 2.

Throughout the war Louisiana contributed fifty-six thousand men to the Confederacy and several thousand free blacks and freed slaves to Union forces. John D. Winters in his monumental *History of the Civil War in Louisiana* estimated that six hundred military engagements, primarily skirmishes, occurred in the state. He further estimated that one-fifth of the men enrolled in the Confederate armies (eleven thousand of the fifty-six thousand) had died in battle, as the result of wounds, or from disease. Many of the best and the brightest of the coming generation fell in the conflict. Fully half of the former wealth of the state—slaves, railroads, plantation and farm structures and livestock, mills, and so on—was swept away. Louisiana entered the period of political Reconstruction, from which grasp it would not finally be released until 1876. Moreover, the economic destruction caused the state to descend into a era of poverty that would last for generations.

Copyright © 1995 by the University of Oklahoma Press

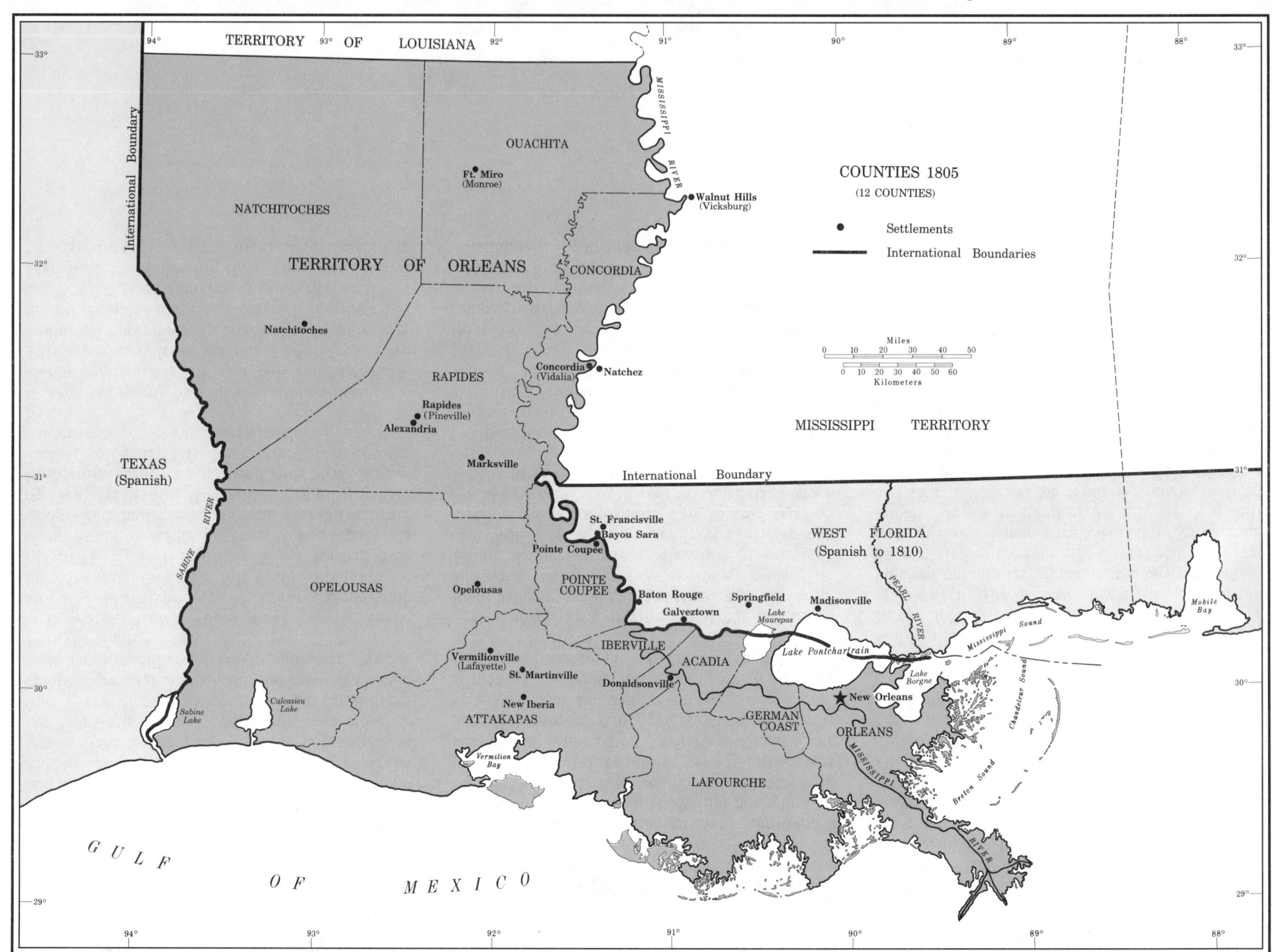

TERRITORY OF LOUISIANA

94° 93° 92° 91° 90° 89° 88°

33° 33°

International Boundary

MISSISSIPPI RIVER

OUACHITA

• Ft. Miro
(Monroe)

NATCHITOCHES

• Walnut Hills
(Vicksburg)

32° 32°

TERRITORY OF ORLEANS

CONCORDIA

COUNTIES 1805
(12 COUNTIES)

• Settlements

───── International Boundaries

Natchitoches •

RAPIDES

Concordia
(Vidalia) • • Natchez

Miles
0 10 20 30 40 50

0 10 20 30 40 50 60
Kilometers

MISSISSIPPI TERRITORY

TEXAS
(Spanish)

Rapides •
(Pineville)
Alexandria •

SABINE RIVER

31° • Marksville

International Boundary 31°

St. Francisville •
• Bayou Sara

WEST FLORIDA
(Spanish to 1810)

PEARL RIVER

Pointe Coupee •

*Mobile
Bay*

OPELOUSAS

POINTE
COUPEE

Opelousas •

• Baton Rouge

• Springfield
• Madisonville

Galveztown •

*Lake
Maurepas*

Mississippi Sound

IBERVILLE

Lake Pontchartrain

30° Vermilionville •
(Lafayette)
• St. Martinville

ACADIA

*Lake
Borgne*

Chandeleur Sound

30°

Donaldsonville •

*Sabine
Lake*

*Calcasieu
Lake*

• New Iberia

ATTAKAPAS

GERMAN
COAST

★ New Orleans

ORLEANS

*Vermilion
Bay*

LAFOURCHE

Breton Sound

MISSISSIPPI RIVER

G U L F

O F   M E X I C O

29° 29°

94° 93° 92° 91° 90° 89° 88°

Although Louisiana's civil divisions are today called parishes—a unique name in the United States—this was not always so. The earliest divisions of the territory, once it became a part of the United States, were termed counties. The name parish soon replaced county for such civil divisions, but the former divisions continued to be used for certain electoral and taxation purposes. In 1843 the county was abolished as an electoral unit, and in the 1845 and subsequent constitutions of the state the term is omitted.

In 1805, two years after the Louisiana Purchase, Louisiana was known as the Territory of Orleans. It consisted of the area west of the Mississippi River plus the Isle of Orleans—that portion east of the Mississippi and south of the Bayou Manchac. The remainder of the present state east of the Mississippi River—the Florida Parishes—had not been universally accepted as being included in the Purchase. They remained a part of Spanish West Florida.

The governing body of the Territory of Orleans in 1805 was called the Legislative Council. In that year the council divided the territory into twelve counties: Acadia, Attacapas (Attakapas), Concordia, German Coast, Iberville, La Fourche (Lafourche), Natchitoches, Opelousas, Orleans, Ouachitta (Ouachita), Pointe-Coupée, and Rapides. The act creating the counties defines them as follows:

The county of Orleans shall comprehend all that portion of the country lying on both sides of the river Mississippi from the Balize to the beginning of the parish of Saint Charles, including the parishes of Saint Bernard and Saint Louis; the county of German Coast shall comprehend the parishes of Saint Charles and Saint John the Baptist, commonly called the first and second German Coasts; the county of Acadia shall comprehend the parishes of Saint James, and the Ascension, commonly called the first and second Acadian Coasts; the county of La Fourche shall comprehend the parish of Assumption; the County of Iberville shall comprehend the parish of Saint Gabriel, and so much of the parish of Saint Bernard as lies within the territory of Orleans; the county of Pointe-Coupée shall comprehend the parish of Saint Francis; the County of Concordia shall comprehend all that portion of country lying within the following boundaries, to wit: Beginning at the mouth of Red River, and ascending the same to Black river; then along Black river to the Tensa river, and along the same to the Tensa Lake; then by a right line, easterly to the Mississippi, and down the same to the point of beginning; the county of Ouachitta shall comprehend all that country commonly called and known by the name of the Ouachita settlements; the county of Rapides shall comprehend the settlements of Rapides, Avoyelles, Catahoula, Bayou Boeuf, Bayou Robert, and all other settlements which now are or may be made in the vicinity thereof, and which may in the opinion of the superior court lie nearer or more conveniently to the court house or seat of justice of the said county of Rapides than to the court house, or seat of justice of any other county; the county of Natchitoches shall comprehend the parish of St. Francis; the county of Opelousas shall comprehend the parish of Saint Landry, commonly called the parish of Opelousas; and the county of Attacapas shall comprehend the parish of Saint Martin, commonly called the parish of Attacapas. The county court of each county respectively shall fix and determine the seat of justice thereof, in such a manner as may be most convenient for the inhabitants at large.

The parishes referred to in these definitions are not parishes in the sense of civil divisions but in terms of ecclesiastical units. These ecclesiastical parishes represented an easy method of defining regions in terms that the inhabitants at the time could recognize. However, the ecclesiastical parishes themselves had never been exactly bounded, nor did such parishes exist everywhere in the state. Therefore, physical features and zones separating islands of settled areas are used to bound the new counties in these sparsely settled regions. In many instances lines drawn to illustrate the county boundaries might better be thought of as transition zones from one to the next. Given the scattered distribution of the population in much of the territory, imprecise lines did not yet present a problem.

Copyright © 1995 by the University of Oklahoma Press

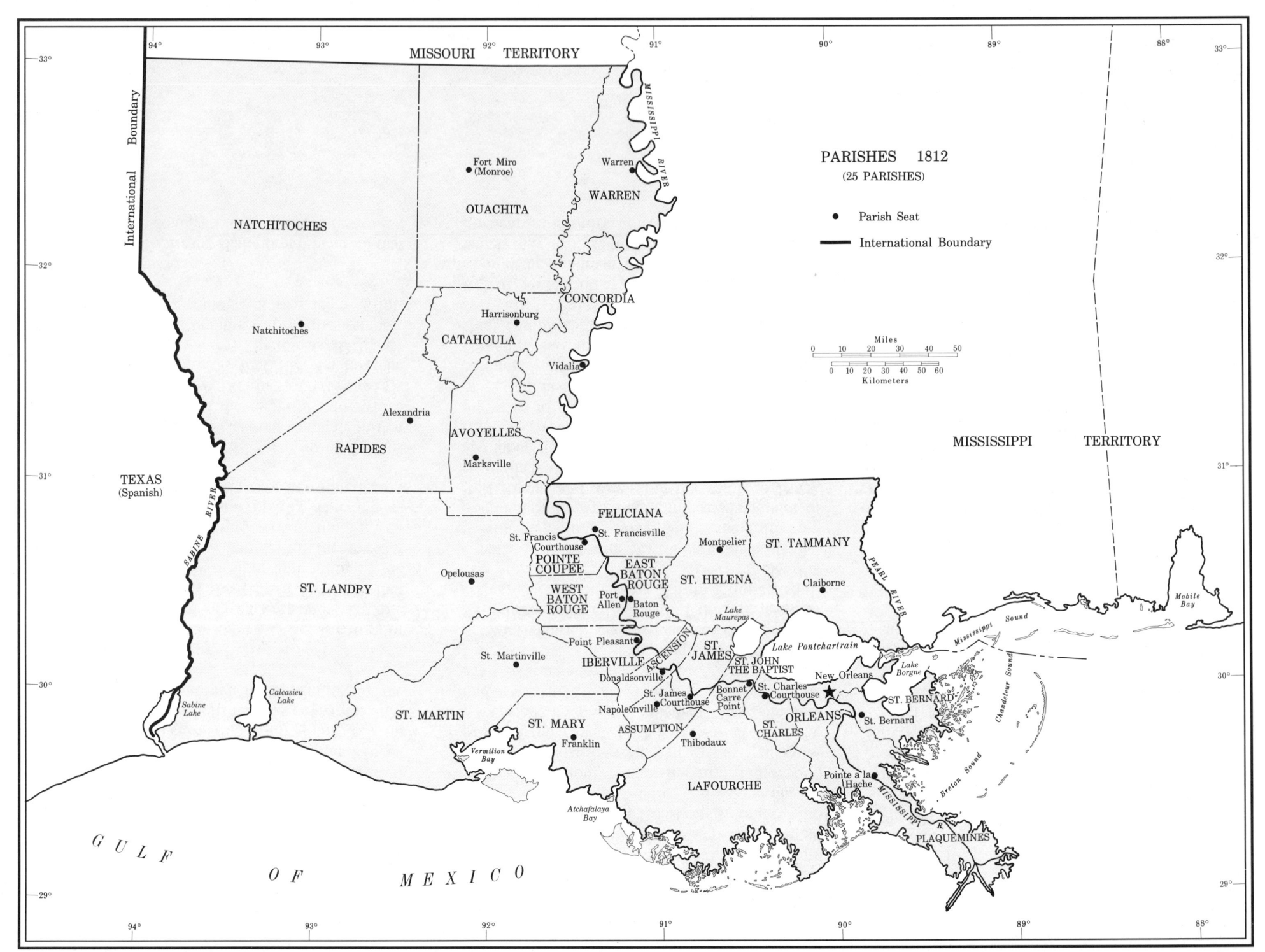

MISSOURI TERRITORY

MISSISSIPPI RIVER

Fort Miro (Monroe)

Warren

WARREN

OUACHITA

NATCHITOCHES

CONCORDIA

Harrisonburg

CATAHOULA

Natchitoches

Vidalia

TEXAS (Spanish)

SABINE RIVER

Alexandria

RAPIDES

AVOYELLES

Marksville

MISSISSIPPI TERRITORY

FELICIANA

St. Francis Courthouse

St. Francisville

Montpelier

ST. TAMMANY

POINTE COUPEE

EAST BATON ROUGE

ST. HELENA

Claiborne

PEARL RIVER

Mobile Bay

ST. LANDRY

Opelousas

WEST BATON ROUGE

Port Allen

Baton Rouge

Point Pleasant

St. Martinville

IBERVILLE

ASCENSION

ST. JAMES

Lake Maurepas

Lake Pontchartrain

Lake Borgne

Mississippi Sound

ST. JOHN THE BAPTIST

New Orleans

Chandeleur Sound

Donaldsonville

St. James Courthouse

Bonnet Carre Point

St. Charles Courthouse

ST. BERNARD

St. Bernard

ST. MARTIN

Calcasieu Lake

Sabine Lake

Napoleonville

ST. MARY

Franklin

ASSUMPTION

ST. CHARLES

ORLEANS

Thibodaux

Vermilion Bay

LAFOURCHE

Pointe a la Hache

Breton Sound

MISSISSIPPI R.

Atchafalaya Bay

PLAQUEMINES

G U L F   O F   M E X I C O

PARISHES 1812
(25 PARISHES)

• Parish Seat

—— International Boundary

Miles
0 10 20 30 40 50

0 10 20 30 40 50 60
Kilometers

International Boundary

In 1807, two years after the Legislative Council of the Territory of Orleans had carved its domain into twelve counties (Map 41), the first territorial legislature redivided that same territory into nineteen parishes. The boundaries of these initial parishes were based largely on ecclesiastical boundaries dating from the period of Spanish control (1763–1800), as had the original twelve counties. Nine of the new parishes were designated only by name, usually the name of the old ecclesiastical district; for example, "The Parish of St. Charles shall form the fourth parish." Five other new parishes are based on the areas of population, as in "The settlements of Ouachita shall form the fourteenth" parish. Four others contain some reference to definite points, such as "The City of New Orleans with its precincts as they formerly stood." Only one, Concordia, possessed definite boundaries, because it came with the same definite boundaries by which Concordia County had earlier been designated.

By reusing the old ecclesiastical units, the new parishes, as had the old counties, employed terms familiar to the citizenry. However, the same state of imprecision associated with the original counties remained. Maps contemporary to the period, as well as those of more recent vintage, often disagree on the lining out of the parishes. The legislature empowered the governor to draw more exact lines in cases of disputes and report the same to the next legislative session. This state of cartographic confusion would continue for much of the early nineteenth century.

Between 1807 and 1812, when Louisiana entered the Union as the eighteenth state, seven additional parishes came into being. Four of these were created out of that portion of Spanish West Florida added to Louisiana following the rebellion against Spanish rule in 1810 (Map 35). The region east of the Mississippi River to the Perdido River was denominated the County of Feliciana on December 7, 1810. That portion of the County of Feliciana west of the Pearl River was divided into four parishes on December 22, 1810—Feliciana, East Baton Rouge, St. Helena, and St. Tammany. These four were added to Louisiana; the remainder of West Florida was attached to the Mississippi Territory and later split between the states of Mississippi and Alabama.

Three other parishes were created before 1812 by the division of existing parishes. In 1808, Catahoula Parish was carved out of Rapides Parish. Warren Parish came into existence in 1811, comprising the former northern portion of Concordia Parish. Finally, in 1811, St. Mary Parish was formed from part of Attakapas Parish, the remainder being renamed St. Martin Parish.

In addition to their bounds, these earliest parishes obtained their names largely from previous ecclesiastical units. As such, various saints of the Roman Catholic Church—Bernard, Charles, Helena, James, John the Baptist, Landry, Martin, and Mary—lent their names to the list. One was named for the non-Catholic "saint" Delaware Indian Chief Tammany. Festivals in the Catholic tradition—Ascension and Assumption—also supplied names, as did Indian names and terms: Avoyelles, Catahoula, Natchitoches, Ouachita, and Plaquemines. French and Spanish individuals and terms were another source, contributing Baton Rouge, Concordia, Iberville, Lafourche, Orleans, Pointe Coupee, Rapides, and Feliciana. Only Warren derived from an Anglo-Saxon name, and its history was a short one.

The government of each parish was located in a parish seat. These were at times courthouses standing alone, situated in some convenient location either near the geographic center of fairly evenly settled parishes or equally distant from existing population centers in more randomly populated parishes. In other parishes the courthouse was sited in an existing village that became the seat. Areas of settlement, particularly in the less-populated western and northern portions of the territory, formed the nuclei about which the original parishes were centered and new ones created. Some isolated courthouses standing alone later became towns in their own right; others burned (a common fate for such edifices), and the seat moved to another site.

Copyright © 1995 by the University of Oklahoma Press

PARISHES 1861
(48 PARISHES)

● Parish Seat

33°

94° 93° 92° 91° 90° 89° 88°

CLAIBORNE
Homer

UNION
Farmerville

MOREHOUSE
Bastrop

Lake
Providence

CARROLL

MISSISSIPPI RIVER

Bellevue

CADDO
BOSSIER

Shreveport

Monroe

Richmond

MADISON

Sparta
BIENVILLE

Vernon
JACKSON

OUACHITA

FRANKLIN

32°

DE SOTO

Mansfield

Winnfield

CALDWELL
Columbia

Winnsboro

TENSAS

St. Joseph

Natchitoches

WINN

Harrisonburg

Many

NATCHITOCHES

CATAHOULA

Vidalia

SABINE

SABINE RIVER

Alexandria

CONCORDIA

31°

RAPIDES

Marksville

AVOYELLES

WEST
FELICIANA

EAST
FELICIANA

ST.
HELENA

WASHINGTON
Franklinton

St.
Francisville

Clinton

Greensburg

ST. LANDRY

New Roads

EAST
BATON
ROUGE

ST. TAMMANY

PEARL RIVER

POINTE
COUPEE

WEST
BATON
ROUGE

LIVINGSTON

Covington

Mobile
Bay

Opelousas

Port Allen

★ Baton
Rouge

Springfield

Lake
Maurepas

Lake Pontchartrain

Mississippi Sound

CALCASIEU

Vermilionville
(Lafayette)

Plaquemine

ASCENSION

ST. JOHN
THE BAPTIST

Edgard

ORLEANS

Lake
Borgne

Lake Charles

LAFAYETTE

St. Martinville

IBERVILLE

Donaldson-
ville

St. Charles
C.H.

New Orleans

ST. BERNARD

Chandeleur Sound

Abbeville

ST. MARTIN

Napoleonville

St. James
Courthouse

ST. JAMES

ST.
CHARLES

JEFFERSON

Carrollton

St. Bernard

Sabine
Lake

Calcasieu
Lake

VERMILION

Franklin

ASSUMPTION

Thibodaux

LAFOURCHE

Pointe a la
Hache

Breton Sound

Vermilion
Bay

ST. MARY

Houma

TERREBONNE

PLAQUEMINES

Atchafalaya Bay

G U L F   O F   M E X I C O

Miles
0 10 20 30 40 50

0 10 20 30 40 50 60
Kilometers

29°

Between 1812, the year that Louisiana entered the Union, and 1861, the eve of its secession and the outbreak of the Civil War, the number of parishes in the state almost doubled. Whereas the number of parishes stood at twenty-six in 1812, in 1861 (in fact, since 1852) there were forty-eight. In addition, one of those in existence in 1812—Warren Parish in northeast Louisiana—had been dissolved in 1814 and the name dropped off the list of civil divisions.

The proliferation of parishes during the five decades following statehood occurred largely in the hill country of northern and northwestern Louisiana and in the Florida Parishes. Most of those sections' increases, however (thirteen of the fifteen new parishes created), took place in the last half of the period. The clearing of the Great Raft on the Red River upstream to Shreveport by the 1840s opened up that stream to greater commerce and attracted new settlers. The increase in settlement in the regions brought with it the need for additional civil divisions.

The enormous Natchitoches Parish gave birth to seven complete parishes and parts of two others. Claiborne (1828) and Caddo (1838) were spawned first. Bossier, De Soto, and Sabine were all created in a single year, 1843. Bienville came into existence in 1848. Parts of the old district went into Jackson and Winn parishes. Natchitoches Parish itself remained—one of the original nineteen—but in much reduced size.

Another of the great northern parishes, Ouachita, divided into four complete units and contributed to a fifth. Union (1839), Morehouse (1844), and Jackson (1845) joined the original Ouachita. Part of the original Ouachita district became a portion of Carroll Parish (1832). Carroll and Madison (1838) parishes comprised much of what had been Warren Parish (1811–1814) before that territory was returned to the bounds of Concordia Parish.

The two other north Louisiana parishes of Catahoula and Concordia also divided. Caldwell (1838), Franklin (1843), and Winn (1852) had once been entirely or largely within the bounds of Catahoula. The 1812 parish of Concordia, enlarged by the dissolution of Warren Parish in 1814, split to form a second parish (Tensas) in 1843.

In the south, six of the eight new parishes created came into existence in the first half of this period. In the Florida Parishes, Feliciana divided (1824) into eastern and western parishes of the same name. St. Helena lost its southern section when Livingston Parish was created in 1832. St. Tammany Parish was divided in 1819; the northern portion of its old territory was christened Washington Parish. In southeastern Louisiana, Lafourche Parish divided into Lafourche and Terrebonne parishes in 1822. Three years later, in 1825, Jefferson Parish was created from part of Orleans.

Three parishes were formed on south Louisiana's western frontier. St. Martin Parish was divided, with its western half becoming Lafayette Parish in 1823. Over half of the old St. Landry Parish became Calcasieu Parish, located in the state's southwestern corner, in 1840. Lafayette Parish itself was further divided; its southern portion was lopped off in 1844 to form Vermilion Parish.

Also taking place during this time was the increased precision with which the parishes were bounded. Parish rivalries produced legislative alterations favoring first one party, then another. Various other acts of the state legislature aimed at clearing up the less fractious vagueness of the lines. In 1818 the offices of state surveyor and parish surveyors were created to assist in this process. Then in 1835 the various police juries of adjoining parishes were empowered to more accurately define parish lines when agreement between both groups could be reached. The Constitution of 1845 put limits on the legislative ability to create new parishes. As the century progressed, greater stability of the state among its civil units came into being.

Individuals provided the major source of new parish names for this period. Exclusive of the east-west split of Feliciana, fifteen of the remaining twenty-two parishes originating during this time were named for individuals. Most prominent were U.S. presidents (Washington, Jefferson, Madison, and Jackson) and other national statesmen (Carroll and Franklin). State and local individuals provided another six names (Claiborne, Livingston, Caldwell, Bossier, Morehouse, and Winn), France two (Lafayette and Bienville), and Spain one (De Soto). Providing three names each were French terms (Terrebonne, Sabine, and Vermilion) and Indian names or terms (Caddo, Calcasieu, and Tensas). The final name, Union, symbolized the increasing national concern of the period.

Copyright © 1995 by the University of Oklahoma Press

PARISHES 1886
(59 PARISHES)

● Parish Seat

From the opening of the Civil War through the course of that conflict and Reconstruction to the restoration of "Bourbon" (the dominant white oligarchy) rule, the number of Louisiana parishes grew from forty-six to fifty-eight. No new parishes had been created in the 1852–1868 period. In the succeeding eighteen years twelve parishes were formed, eleven in the first nine years and one at the close of the second nine.

The Reconstruction Era (1865–1876) saw ten new parishes come into being in both northern and southern parts of the state. In 1868, Richland Parish in the northeast and Iberia Parish in the south were formed. Richland was composed of parts of Carroll, Ouachita, and Franklin parishes. Iberia came from parts of St. Martin and St. Mary parishes. In a noticeable curiosity, Iberia Parish actually separated the two parts of St. Martin Parish from each other.

The following year, 1869, another pair of parishes was created. Grant took land from Rapides and Winn parishes in central Louisiana. Tangipahoa Parish in the Florida Parishes received land from St. Helena, Livingston, Washington, and St. Tammany parishes. Tangipahoa was the first new civil subdivision created in the Florida Parishes since Livingston Parish in 1832.

Only one new parish, Cameron, was established in 1870, its territory coming from the Gulf coastal area of Calcasieu Parish. However, in 1871, three parishes were formed—Webster, Red River, and Vernon—all in the north and west. Parts of Claiborne and Bienville parishes were carved out to form Webster. More of Bienville plus the northwest portion of Natchitoches Parish were taken to create Red River Parish. Southern portions of Natchitoches and Sabine, with the western section of Rapides, joined to form Vernon Parish.

After a one-year lull in 1872, Lincoln Parish was created in 1873, formed from adjoining areas of Union, Claiborne, Jackson, and Bienville parishes. Four years later, in 1877, Carroll Parish divided into East and West Carroll parishes. The creation of Acadia from southwestern St. Landry Parish in 1886 closes the period for new parishes. However, additional changes in the boundaries of existing parishes also occurred. Some of these realignments were, as in previous decades, picayunish in nature, limited in scope, and often obscure as to reason.

Since 1845 succeeding state constitutions sought to bring more order to parish creation. They addressed such concerns as minimum area and population both for proposed parishes and any which would suffer reduction by the creation of new parishes. The Constitution of 1879 reached the ultimate in these considerations, marking perhaps the sense of the delegates that enough civil divisions had come into being. Beginning with that constitution, provisions were inserted permitting voters to dissolve parishes, although no such event has yet occurred.

An effort to create Troy Parish in 1890 failed because a new unit would push the number of representatives beyond the constitutional limit. The years 1908–1912 saw the final five parishes spring into existence. La Salle was created from the western half of Catahoula Parish in 1908. Evangeline Parish came from the western portion of St. Landry Parish in 1910. Allen, Beauregard, and Jefferson Davis parishes all came into being in 1912, formed by the quartering of the old Calcasieu Parish. With the creation of these final three, all the state's sixty-four parishes were in place (Map 45).

Of the eleven parishes originating in the 1861–1886 period, four were named for individuals: two Republican presidents (Grant and Lincoln), a noted statesman (Webster), and a former Confederate leader (Cameron). Indian names provided Acadia and Tangipahoa; Spain provided Iberia; and English, Richland. Two parish names, Red River and Vernon, came from the river and George Washington's home. The east-west split of Carroll contributed the final names.

La Salle, the first European to descend the Mississippi to its mouth and the basis for French claims to the Mississippi Valley, provided the name for the first of the final five parishes created. The Acadian heroine of Longfellow fame, Evangeline, was also honored. Finally, Confederate leaders Allen, Beauregard, and Jefferson Davis gave their names to the most recent parishes.

PARISHES 1990
(64 PARISHES)

● Parish Seat

CADDO BOSSIER CLAIBORNE UNION MOREHOUSE

Oak Grove

Lake Providence

WEST CARROLL

EAST CARROLL

Benton

Homer LINCOLN Farmerville Bastrop

Minden

Ruston

WEBSTER Arcadia Monroe Rayville RICHLAND Tallulah

Shreveport JACKSON OUACHITA

BIENVILLE MADISON

RED RIVER Jonesboro TENSAS

WINN Columbia Winnsboro

Mansfield Coushatta FRANKLIN

CALDWELL St. Joseph

Winnfield LA SALLE

DE SOTO

SABINE Natchitoches GRANT Harrisonburg

NATCHITOCHES Colfax Jena

Many

CATAHOULA

Vidalia

VERNON CONCORDIA

Alexandria

Leesville Marksville

WEST FELICIANA EAST FELICIANA ST. HELENA WASHINGTON

RAPIDES

AVOYELLES

ST. LANDRY Saint Francisville Clinton Greensburg Franklinton

DeRidder ALLEN EVANGELINE Amite

Oberlin Ville Platte New Roads EAST BATON ROUGE Livingston TANGIPAHOA Covington

BEAUREGARD Opelousas POINTE COUPEE

WEST BATON ROUGE Baton Rouge LIVINGSTON ST. TAMMANY

JEFFERSON DAVIS ACADIA Port Allen

Lake Charles ST. MARTIN Plaquemine Lake Maurepas

Lafayette ASCENSION Lake Pontchartrain

Jennings Crowley LAFAYETTE ST. Martinville IBERVILLE Donaldsonville ST. JOHN THE BAPTIST New Orleans ORLEANS Lake Borgne

CALCASIEU Abbeville ST. JAMES Edgard Chalmette

CAMERON New Iberia ASSUMPTION Convent Hahnville Gretna ST. BERNARD

Napoleonville ST. CHARLES JEFFERSON

Cameron VERMILION IBERIA Franklin ST. MARTIN Thibodaux

Pointe a la Hache

Sabine Lake Calcasieu Lake

Vermilion Bay

ST. MARY Houma LAFOURCHE

Atchafalaya Bay TERREBONNE

PLAQUEMINES

MISSISSIPPI RIVER

SABINE RIVER

PEARL RIVER

Mobile Bay

Mississippi Sound

Chandeleur Sound

Breton Sound

G U L F   O F   M E X I C O

Miles
0 10 20 30 40 50

0 10 20 30 40 50 60
Kilometers

33°   32°   31°   30°   29°

94°   93°   92°   91°   90°   89°   88°

Louisiana is unique among the states of the Union in that its civil divisions are called parishes. This practice dates to a period even before statehood. The first governing body of the Territory of Orleans (that part of the Louisiana Purchase included in the present state), the Legislative Council, in 1805 divided the territory into twelve counties (Map 41). In 1807 the territory (now including all the present state) was redivided into nineteen parishes, largely along the old Spanish ecclesiastical (church) boundaries. The Constitution of 1812, which brought the state into the Union, continued using *parish* and *county,* although the latter term gradually faded from use and was omitted from subsequent constitutions of the state.

Today Louisiana has sixty-four parishes. This number has remained constant since 1912, when Allen, Jefferson Davis, and Beauregard parishes were created. The parishes vary in area from Cameron (1,417 square miles) to West Baton Rouge (194 square miles). In population Orleans Parish holds the first position (496,938), with Jefferson Parish (448,306) in second place. Tensas Parish has the smallest population (7,103).

Most of Louisiana's sixty-four parishes are governed by a "police jury." This group also derived from the early nineteenth century, when the county government was headed by a county judge and justices of the peace. In 1807 the judge and justices were joined by a selected "jury of twelve inhabitants" to meet at least once a year. In 1811 the term "police jury" was first used. In time justices of the peace and the judges, too, ceased to control the groups. Today even the number of members which comprise a police jury varies. Election to the police jury has been by ward instead of a parish-wide basis since 1816. The police jury shares with several elected officials—for example, sheriff, assessor, clerk of court, and others—the authority for governing the parish.

Exceptions to the police jury rule operate under a commission or council form of government. Some of these are of long standing. Orleans Parish and the City of Orleans are coextensive, and both parish and city governments are consolidated under a council-mayor system. East Baton Rouge Parish government partially coincides with that of the city of Baton Rouge in a council-mayor-president plan in which the members of the Baton Rouge City Council join others elected from outside the city limits on a parish council presided over by the mayor of Baton Rouge. Jefferson Parish uses a council-president system, in which the elected council exercises legislative powers and the elected president the administrative authority. In 1960 the legislature amended the state constitution to allow any parish the "home-rule" option of setting up alternate forms of government. The Constitution of 1974 expanded that privilege. Plaquemines, Lafourche, and St. Charles have all taken advantage of these provisions.

Louisiana parishes derive their names from various sources. Perhaps the most common are those parishes named after persons. French (Bienville, Iberville, La Salle, Lafayette, Evangeline, Orleans) and Spanish (De Soto) proper names are found, but far more numerous are American names. These include presidents (Washington, Jefferson, Madison, Jackson, Lincoln, and Grant), other statesmen (Carroll, Livingston, Franklin, and Webster), Louisiana governors (Claiborne and Allen), Confederate figures (Beauregard, Cameron, and Jefferson Davis), and others (Bossier, Morehouse, Winn, and Caldwell).

Catholic church parishes (in the ecclesiastical sense) and saints provide the names of Ascension, Assumption, St. Bernard, St. Charles, St. Helena, St. James, St. John the Baptist, St. Landry, St. Martin, and St. Mary. One saintly name not Catholic in derivation is St. Tammany, a Delaware Indian chief. Other Indian names include Caddo, Natchitoches, Avoyelles, Calcasieu, Plaquemines, Catahoula, Ouachita, Tangipahoa, and Tensas.

Other parish names come from the languages of Spain and France as well as the United States. Spanish contributed Iberia, Feliciana, and Concordia. French gave the state Acadia, Lafourche, Baton Rouge, Terrebonne, Pointe Coupee, Rapides, Sabine, and Vermilion. English contributed Red River, Richland, Union, and Vernon.

Copyright © 1995 by the University of Oklahoma Press

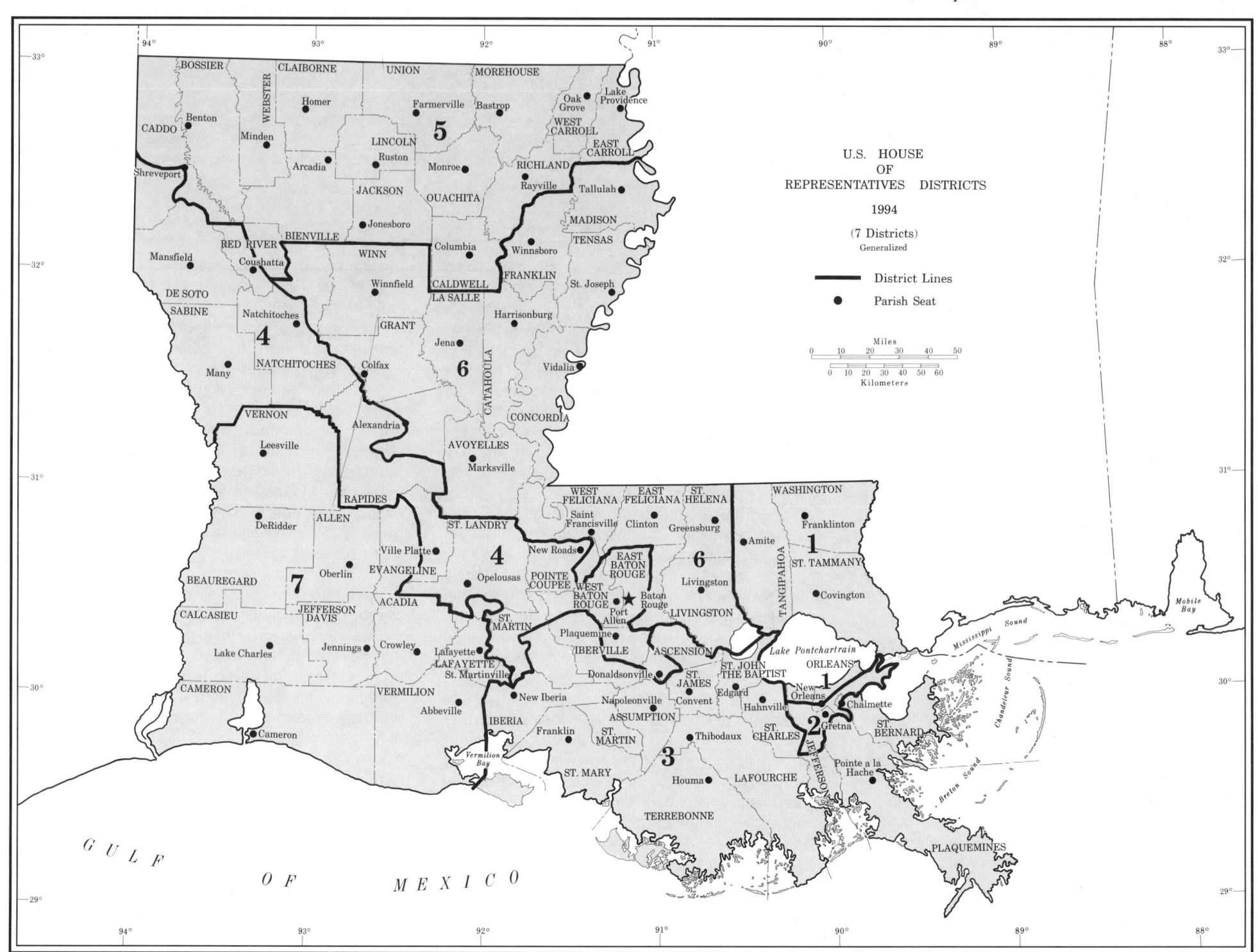

U.S. HOUSE
OF
REPRESENTATIVES DISTRICTS

1994

(7 Districts)
Generalized

—— District Lines

● Parish Seat

Miles
0 10 20 30 40 50

0 10 20 30 40 50 60
Kilometers

The Constitution of the United States (1789) established a government based upon the twin principles of separation of powers and checks and balances. Power would be divided among three branches, the executive, the legislative, and the judicial. However, no single branch would hold supreme power; each branch would be held in check by powers granted to the others. The Congress of the United States comprises the legislative branch. Often termed "the first branch," the powers and duties of the Congress are discussed in Article I of the Constitution.

The Congress is itself divided into two chambers—the Senate and the House of Representatives. Delegates to the Constitutional Convention debated over whether legislative representation should be equal for the various states or whether they should be based on population. The Congress represents the compromise reached by the delegates. The Senate would be composed of the same number of members from each state, while the House would be apportioned on the basis of population.

From the first Congress to the present, each state has been empowered to send two senators to Washington, D.C., regardless of the population of the state. Each senator must be at least thirty years old. Each must also have been a U.S. citizen for at least nine years and a resident of the state which he or she represents. The total number of senators through time has thus equaled double the number of states in the Union. Louisiana joined the Union as the eighteenth state in 1812; therefore, with its senators added, the Senate totaled thirty-six members. Today, with fifty states, the total number of senators is one hundred. Before the passage of the Seventeenth Amendment to the Constitution in 1913, each state's senators were elected by that state's legislature. Thereafter, the senators have been elected by direct vote of the eligible electorate on a statewide basis.

The House of Representatives, on the other hand, has its membership apportioned among the states on the basis of population, with members elected from particular districts of the states. Each representative must be at least twenty-five years old, a U.S. citizen for seven years, and a resident of the state from which she or he is elected. The total number of representatives has increased through time from the original sixty-five. It finally stabilized (except for a brief period after Hawaii and Alaska joined the Union in 1959) in 1913 at 435 members. Thus, as the population has increased since that time, the number of citizens represented by each member of the House has also increased.

Although each member of the House is elected from a particular district of the state, custom rather than law dictates that he or she must actually reside in that district. The drawing of the boundaries for these various districts falls to the state legislature. Over time some states on occasion have drawn such lines for partisan or other advantages, producing oddly shaped districts. This practice is called gerrymandering.

From 1842 until 1911, Congress required the legislatures to draw district boundaries to include roughly equivalent populations in each district. For fifty years thereafter this equally apportioned provision was dropped. During this same period, rural to urban migration occurred. The end result was a set of districts with widely varying populations. In 1962 the Supreme Court of the United States, in the case *Baker* vs. *Carr,* ruled that such practices were unconstitutional; this decision required extensive redrawing of the state's districts for three successive Congresses, beginning with the ninety-first in 1969. After each census, the number of seats in the House is divided among the states, and the legislature must draw new boundaries on the basis of the Court's "one person, one vote" ruling.

When Louisiana joined the Union in 1812, it was entitled to one representative (among the total of 181) for its seventy-seven thousand citizens. Over time the total number of representatives Louisiana sent to the House increased as the state's population grew, to three (1820), four (1840), five (1860), six (1870), and seven (1900), until it reached eight in 1910, where it remained until 1992, when it fell back to seven. The scant increase in Louisiana's population during the 1980s, combined with the increasing national population, caused its allotted number of seats to decline for the first time.

In the decades before the Civil War, Louisiana enjoyed a lively political mix, especially when the Whigs and the Jacksonian Democrats presented roughly equal party strengths. During Reconstruction, Republicans enjoyed ascendancy in the areas under federal control. However, after the restoration of autonomy the Democratic party assumed dominance and retained that almost absolute control until late in the twentieth century. Like most of the Old South, Louisiana Democrats were noted for lengthy tenure in office, the importance of party factions instead of inter-party rivalries, and the disfranchisement of minorities, particularly African Americans. With the passage of various civil rights legislation, the modest resurgence of the Republican party, and a general change in attitude and culture, the political landscape has become much more diverse.

As this atlas goes to press, three different sets of district lines have been drawn in little over a year, driven by judicial proceedings regarding racial gerrymandering. The U.S. Supreme Court has ruled that the districts shown above will be used for the 1994 elections. However, another set may replace them by 1996.

Copyright © 1995 by the University of Oklahoma Press

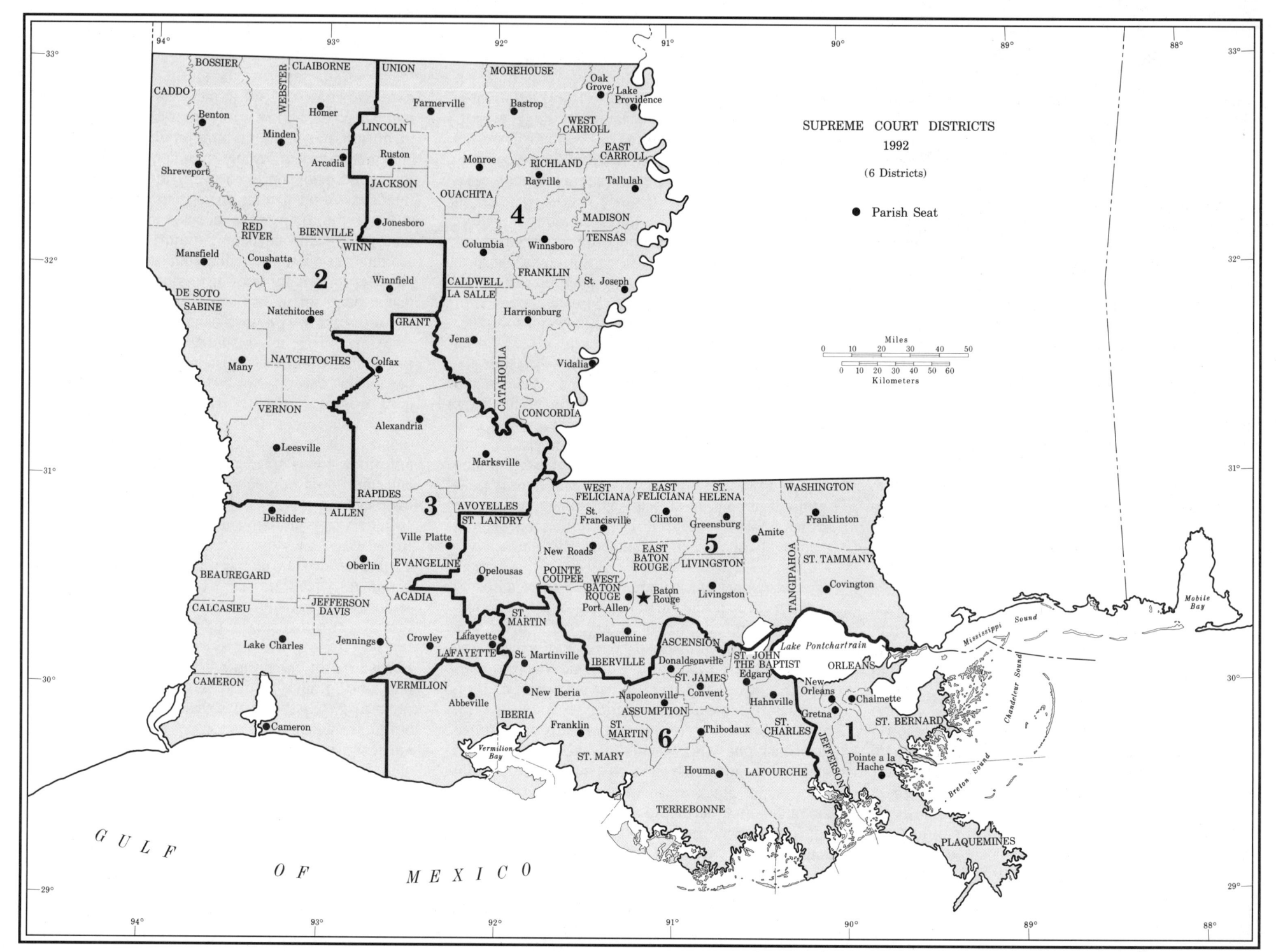

SUPREME COURT DISTRICTS
1992

(6 Districts)

● Parish Seat

The Supreme Court of Louisiana sits atop a judicial pyramid composed of almost four hundred justices of the peace, three hundred mayor's courts, fifty city courts, two parish courts, four family and juvenile courts, forty district courts, and five courts of appeal. As with the judicial branch of the federal government, the Louisiana judiciary shares in the powers of government with the executive (the governor) and the legislative branches. The district courts, courts of appeal, and supreme court form the most important levels in the judicial pyramid. Beneath them are the courts of limited (traditionally called inferior) jurisdiction, those whose authority to hear cases is circumscribed in some way.

Unlike any other state in the Union, Louisiana law has for its basis French civil law instead of English common law. Civil law is a code law; that is, although written by various entities, it is adopted by legislative bodies. Common law, on the other hand, is unwritten or case law based upon prior judicial interpretations. Louisiana's most recent civil code is today more than a century old (adopted in 1870). Although in the nineteenth century distinctions between civil law and common law as practiced in the state were real, today these distinctions are less prominent.

Originally all judges at every level were appointed by the governor with the advice and consent of the state senate, much as federal judgeships are still filled. However, after the 1840s appointive versus elective means of filling judgeships jockeyed for prominence with successive constitutions. Since 1904 the justices of the state supreme court have been elected. The length of term has also varied; today each justice serves a ten- year term.

All judges above the rank of justice of the peace must have been admitted to the practice of law in the state for a minimum of five years before their election. Also, each candidate must have been a resident within the jurisdiction of that court for which he or she is a candidate for at least two years. Judges in the parish and district courts and above are prohibited from practicing law. However, they are relatively well paid when compared to their counterparts in other states and the relative income of the Louisiana citizenry. Since the Constitution of 1974 there has been no age requirement for judges.

The supreme court consists of seven justices. From each of Districts Two through Six one justice is elected; from District One—centered in New Orleans—two justices are selected. The chief justice position is filled by that justice senior in terms of service on the court. Justices of the supreme court can be defeated for reelection or removed by impeachment. Historically, former state legislators have made up about one-third of the supreme court's members.

Under the state's constitution the supreme court holds "general supervisory jurisdiction over all other courts." As such, the court not only functions as the court of last appeal at the state level, but it also establishes a code of regulation for the entire judicial system. The dual powers thus conferred on the court add to its workload. With the increasing number of cases to be considered, the supervisory powers of the court have not been fully utilized.

The supreme court's jurisdiction varies. In its original jurisdiction, the court handles only disciplinary actions against attorneys. In its capacity as an appellate court, it hears those cases which can be appealed directly to it from a trial court as well as those which must first go through one of the courts of appeal. The Constitution of 1974 specifies four types of cases which are appealed directly to the supreme court: (1) lower court decisions declaring a law or ordinance unconstitutional, (2) felony convictions, (3) other criminal convictions with a fine in excess of five hundred dollars or a prison term in excess of six months, and (4) district court decisions reviewing a ruling of the Public Service Commission. Amendments passed in the past decade have granted the courts of appeal the power to hear criminal cases.

Judicial reform remains a major emphasis both within and without the system. Structural reform aimed at expediting the process garners support. Access to legal services by persons of any socioeconomic position is another reform, and the distribution of judicial districts about the state has also recently come under review.

Copyright © 1995 by the University of Oklahoma Press

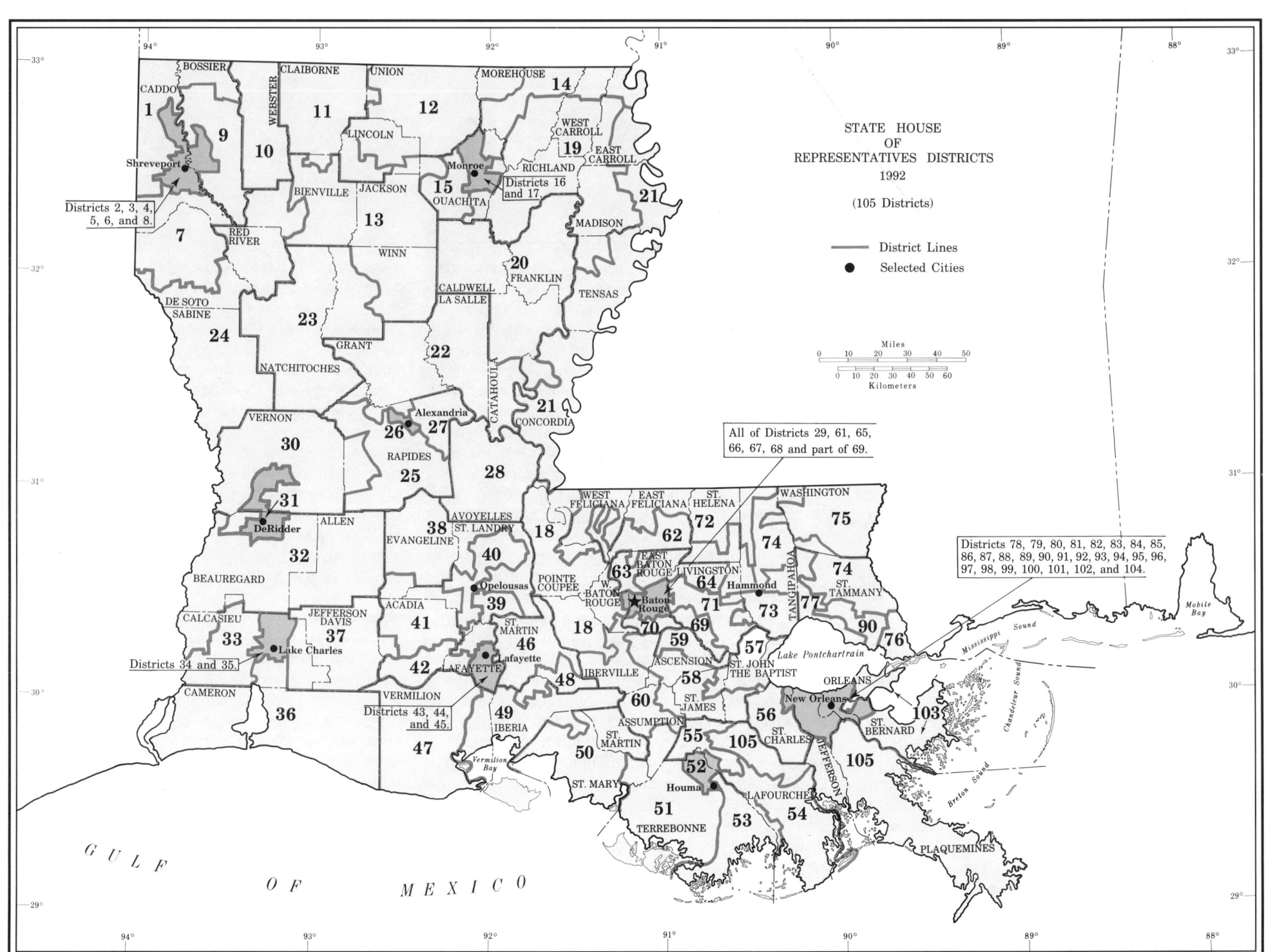

STATE HOUSE
OF
REPRESENTATIVES DISTRICTS
1992

(105 Districts)

——— District Lines

● Selected Cities

Districts 2, 3, 4, 5, 6, and 8.

Districts 16 and 17.

All of Districts 29, 61, 65, 66, 67, 68 and part of 69.

Districts 78, 79, 80, 81, 82, 83, 84, 85, 86, 87, 88, 89, 90, 91, 92, 93, 94, 95, 96, 97, 98, 99, 100, 101, 102, and 104.

Districts 34 and 35.

Districts 43, 44, and 45.

Miles
0 10 20 30 40 50

0 10 20 30 40 50 60
Kilometers

48. STATE HOUSE OF REPRESENTATIVES DISTRICTS

Since statehood Louisiana has used a bicameral (two-chamber) legislative body. From 1812 to 1921 this body was called the general assembly; the Constitution of 1921 changed the name to legislature. This legislature is composed of a senate and a house of representatives. Also since statehood members of both bodies have been directly elected by the electorate of the state. That electorate has changed over the decades from white, property owning males to universal manhood to women's suffrage. Attempts to restrict minority voting, particularly voting by African Americans, have met with judicial and statutory defeat. The age of voting has also declined to a minimum of eighteen years.

Louisiana has had eleven constitutions, the earliest in 1812, the latest 1974. Other constitutions date from 1845, 1852, 1861, 1864, 1868, 1879, 1898, 1913, and 1921. The state constitution sets the requirements for both the house and the senate. Members of the house today serve a four-year term; before the Constitution of 1879 made that period the term of office, representatives served two-year terms, as did (and still do) the members of the U.S. House of Representatives.

Today, members of the house must be at least eighteen years of age before their election. Also each must have been a Louisiana citizen for at least two years. Unlike U.S. representatives, state representatives by law must be residents (at least one year prior to election) of the district they represent.

The Louisiana House of Representatives has a membership of 105. Thus, the state is divided into 105 house districts; the use of multimember districts is no longer practiced. As expected, areas of dense population (urban areas) have much smaller districts than do the more rural portions of the state.

The legislature after every census must redraw the boundaries of the state house districts. Following its 1962 *Baker* vs. *Carr* decision regarding the U.S. House's "one person, one vote" apportionment, the U.S. Supreme Court in 1963 also extended that principle to state legislative districts. Further, the Court decreed that this standard would apply to both chambers in bicameral legislatures.

After the Constitution of 1921, which apportionment would not have fit the Court's regulations, the Louisiana Legislature ignored the requirement that it reapportion itself after each census. Successive reapportionments—often the result of lawsuits from the underrepresented—following the Court's ruling moved the state closer into compliance with the law. Thus, in the tremendous upheaval brought on by the Court's ruling, rural Louisiana's legislative strength—a holdover from a previous era of a more even population distribution—was reduced to its current portion of the total population. The urbanized areas, particularly suburbs, gained in representational strength. Also, Republican and African American candidates enjoyed more success in getting elected. Thus, interparty and interracial competition joined the existing factional competition within the dominant Democratic party.

The legislature meets annually. A general session begins in odd-numbered years on the last Monday in March and is limited to sixty legislative days (a day on which either or both chambers are meeting) within an eighty-five-day period. A 1993 constitutional amendment limits sessions in even-numbered years to fiscal matters, beginning the last Monday in April and lasting for up to thirty legislative days within a forty-five-day period. Placing the session within the longer calendar period allows legislators to consult with constituents as well as to study the issues more carefully. The legislature may also be called into special session by the governor. Legislative staff activity goes on year-round, whether the legislature is in session or out of session.

The house is presided over by a speaker, who possesses broad powers of appointment. The speaker appoints the chair, vice-chair, and member of each of the fifteen standing committees except the Committee on Appropriations. That committee is composed of seven members appointed by the speaker and eight elected by the house itself. The speaker also appoints the house members of conference committees, which meet to settle differences between house- and senate-passed versions of the same legislation. In the past the speaker has more often been closely tied to, usually allied with, the incumbent governor in the pursuit of a gubernatorial program. The state's more powerful executive branch has proposed its own candidates for legislative leadership posts. More recently the legislature has shown a greater degree of independence.

Copyright © 1995 by the University of Oklahoma Press

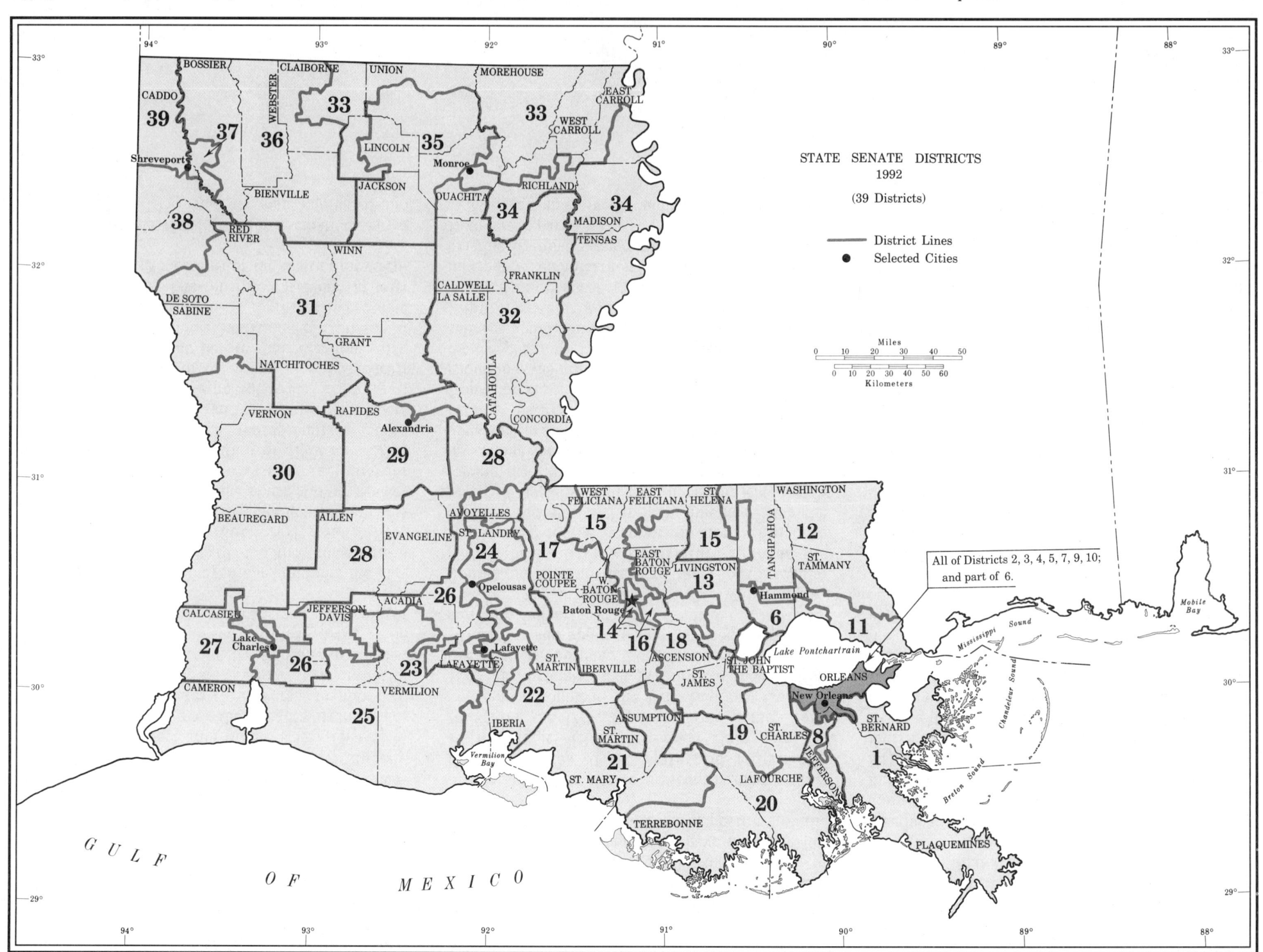

STATE SENATE DISTRICTS
1992

(39 Districts)

——— District Lines

● Selected Cities

All of Districts 2, 3, 4, 5, 7, 9, 10;
and part of 6.

The Senate of Louisiana, like the state house of representatives (Map 48), dates from statehood. It was first part of a general assembly, the name of which the Constitution of 1921 changed to legislature. Since 1812 the state senate, unlike the U.S. Senate (Map 46), has always been elected by direct vote of the electorate, however broadly or narrowly that base has varied. Like the state house of representatives, the state senate is created by the state constitution. Over the eleven state constitutions dating between 1812 and 1974, the senate has varied in its makeup. So, too, have the qualifications for senate membership varied.

From 1812 to 1879 the legislature met annually, with the exception of the period 1845 to 1852, when it convened every other year. From 1879 to 1954 the legislature met in biennial sessions lasting up to sixty calendar days. Since 1954 the sessions have been annual and are today limited to sixty legislative days within an eighty-five-day period beginning the third Monday in April.

Senators serve four-year terms, unlike their federal counterparts, who have six-year terms. Until the Constitution of 1879, these terms overlapped so that the possibility of a complete turnover of the membership did not exist. Since the Constitution of 1879, all the senators have been elected at the same time; thus, their term of office runs concurrently with that of the governor and the house of representatives. In an essentially one-party state,

this had led to the appearance of factions within the Democratic party. This factionalism, combined with the powers of the governor, has led to great influence in the legislature by that incumbent executive.

As with state representatives, state senators must be at least eighteen years of age, must have been a citizen of the state for at least two years, and must reside in their district for at least one year before election. The state is divided into thirty-nine senate districts on the basis of population. In another difference with the U.S. Senate, the state senate, indeed all state legislative bodies, must be apportioned on the basis of population and may not be evenly divided among political subdivisions.

Senate districts are recarved following each census, which occurs every ten years. The legislature reapportions itself on the basis of statute as well as judicial decision. Voters may file to challenge the resulting boundaries. Previous suits have brought state legislatures under the "one person, one vote" rule. Other suits challenge boundaries on the basis of diluting the voting strength of certain (usually ethnic) population groups. By virtue of population density, urban districts are much smaller than their rural counterparts.

The senate is presided over by a president elected from the membership. This was a change in the Constitution of 1974; previously the lieutenant

governor had presided. The president of the senate possesses broad powers of appointment equal to those of the speaker of the house and historically has often been allied with the incumbent governor.

The senate maintains fifteen standing committees, including three separate judiciary committees designated by the letters A, B, and C. Committee chairs are chosen by the president of the senate; often they are affiliated with the current governor. Although selections based solely on length of tenure do not occur, the more senior members of the senate tend to hold a great proportion of the chairs. There is rotation among the chairs, as well as among the memberships held by the various senators. Standing committees have the power to meet outside the regular sessions of the legislature, but all law-making must occur when the body is in official session.

The legislature operates within a political culture dominated by a north-south division in the state. A generally Protestant north and a generally Catholic south have over the past decades swapped positions in relative economic and political power. As the south Louisiana population increased, so, too, did its economy with the expansion of the oil and gas industry. At the same time, the northern area lost population or did not grow as rapidly as did the south, and its economy did not enjoy the same gains as did its rival region.

Copyright © 1995 by the University of Oklahoma Press

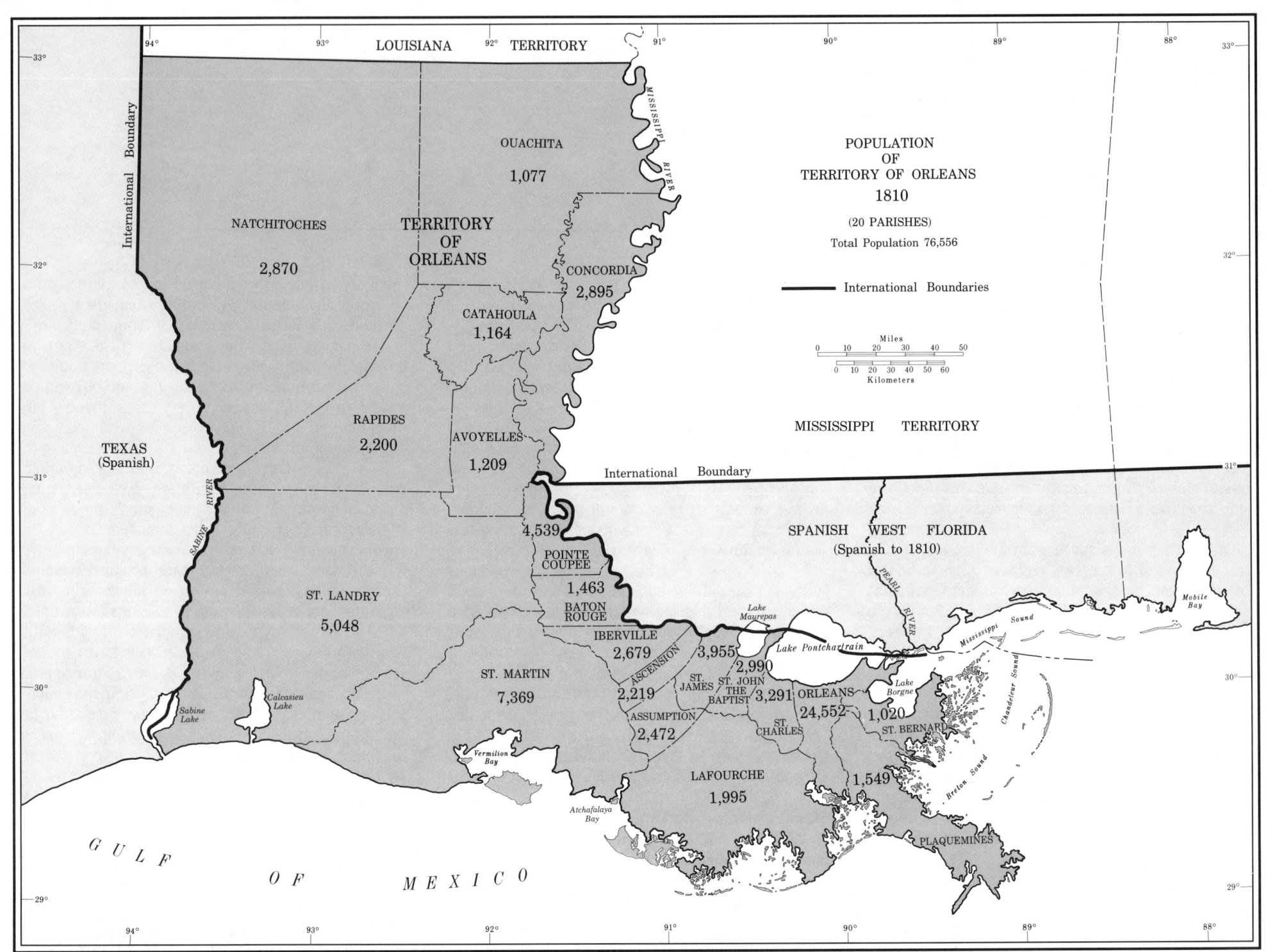

LOUISIANA TERRITORY

OUACHITA
1,077

NATCHITOCHES
2,870

**TERRITORY
OF
ORLEANS**

CONCORDIA
2,895

CATAHOULA
1,164

POPULATION
OF
TERRITORY OF ORLEANS
1810

(20 PARISHES)

Total Population 76,556

International Boundaries

Miles
0 10 20 30 40 50

0 10 20 30 40 50 60
Kilometers

RAPIDES
2,200

AVOYELLES
1,209

MISSISSIPPI TERRITORY

TEXAS
(Spanish)

SABINE RIVER

International Boundary

4,539

POINTE
COUPEE
1,463

SPANISH WEST FLORIDA
(Spanish to 1810)

ST. LANDRY
5,048

BATON
ROUGE

IBERVILLE
2,679

3,955

PEARL RIVER

Lake
Maurepas

Lake Pontchartrain

Mississippi Sound

Mobile
Bay

ASCENSION
2,219

2,990

Lake
Borgne

Calcasieu
Lake

ST. MARTIN
7,369

ST.
JAMES

ST. JOHN
THE
BAPTIST

3,291

ORLEANS
24,552

1,020

ST. BERNARD

Chandeleur Sound

Sabine
Lake

ASSUMPTION
2,472

ST.
CHARLES

Vermilion
Bay

LAFOURCHE
1,995

1,549

Breton Sound

Atchafalaya
Bay

PLAQUEMINES

G U L F   O F   M E X I C O

Seven years after the Louisiana Purchase, Louisiana participated in its first census. The U.S. Constitution mandates a census every ten years so that the national House of Representatives will have the information needed to be apportioned correctly. In more recent years the distribution of population among the several states and their subdivisions has been the basis for allocation of various funds appropriated by the Congress for specific purposes.

At the time of the 1810 census modern Louisiana had not yet joined the Union as a state. It remained a territory—the Territory of Orleans. (The Territory of Louisiana at that time referred to the remainder of the expanse of the Louisiana Purchase.) Nor did the Territory of Orleans yet encompass the entire bounds of the present state. The area of the Florida Parishes remained within the possession of Spain. Later in that census year a rebellion in West Florida (Map 35) would lead to the addition of part of that region to the Territory of Orleans, all of which would enter the Union as the State of Louisiana in 1812.

Nearly fifty thousand people came with Louisiana at the time of the purchase in 1803. By far the largest groups within that population were French and Spanish colonials and African American slaves. Other immigrant groups included those from the German states, Canary Islanders, and Acadians. Newly independent Americans migrated after the American Revolution, joining a smaller number of British North Americans who had come before the revolution. The flow of American immigrants into the new territory would increase dramatically after its transfer to the United States.

The total population of the Territory of Orleans in 1810 stood at 76,556. This group largely resided along the navigable streams of southern Louisiana, with some scattered outposts along streams in the north (Map 29). The agricultural nature of much of the population and the dependence upon watercourses as the primary means of transport of both people and goods produced elongated settlements along the natural levees of the myriad streams and in the upcountry adjoining these streams.

By far the most populous of the twenty then-present parishes was Orleans, with 24,552 (32 percent of the total). The city and suburbs of New Orleans alone accounted for 17,242 (22 percent). New Orleans had long been the colossus of Louisiana settlements, a status which would endure. Second to Orleans Parish was St. Martin Parish (called Attakapas in the census listings), with a population of 7,369. This parish included the long settled areas along the Bayou Teche. St. Landry Parish (termed Opelousas in the census), with 5,048, came next, followed by a string of parishes along the Mississippi River. The least populous parish was St. Bernard, with 1,020 citizens. Second lowest was Ouachita, one of the largest parishes by area but with a population of only 1,077.

Of the total count, more than half of Louisiana's population (55 percent) was African American, the vast majority slaves (Map 55). Only the white population was counted by gender, with males outnumbering females 18,940 (55 percent) to 15,371 (45 percent). Only 17,242 (those within the city and suburbs of New Orleans) lived in what could be termed urban areas by any definition; the other three-quarters of the population resided in the rural regions of the territory, in small towns, large and small plantations, and individual farmsteads.

Louisiana (the Territory of Orleans), with its 76,556 citizens, represented just over 1 percent of the total U.S. population of 7,239,881. The territory had fewer citizens than Rhode Island and only four thousand more than Delaware. The average density of 1.7 persons per square mile compared with a national average of 4.3 persons per square mile. (The national figure represented a substantial drop since 1800 because of the extraordinary increase in area brought about by the Louisiana Purchase.)

The territory's average density belied the extraordinary differences between the concentrated population of New Orleans and the settled areas along the Mississippi and other rivers. Averages of less than one person per square mile occurred in the hill and prairie parishes of the north and west. Only in terms of its immediate neighbors did Orleans Territory's population seem large. The Mississippi Territory had a population numbering 40,352; census enumerators noted widely scattered settlements over what is now Arkansas; Texas remained in Spanish hands.

Copyright © 1995 by the University of Oklahoma Press

POPULATION OF LOUISIANA
1860
(48 PARISHES)
Total Population 708,002

DECENNIAL POPULATION – 1810 TO 1860

Year	Total Population	Number Increase	Percent Increase
1810	76,556		
1820	153,407	76,851	100.4
1830	215,739	62,332	40.6
1840	352,411	136,672	63.4
1850	517,762	165,351	46.9
1860	708,002	190,240	36.7

Miles
0 10 20 30 40 50

0 10 20 30 40 50 60
Kilometers

BOSSIER

CLAIBORNE
16,848

UNION
10,389

MOREHOUSE
10,357

CARROLL
18,052

CADDO
11,348

12,140

BIENVILLE
11,000

JACKSON
9,465

4,727
OUACHITA

MADISON

FRANKLIN
14,133

6,162

13,298

DE SOTO

WINN
6,876

4,833
CALDWELL

TENSAS
16,078

SABINE
16,699

NATCHITOCHES

CATAHOULA
11,651

5,828

CONCORDIA

13,805

25,360

RAPIDES

13,167

AVOYELLES

WEST FELICIANA

EAST FELICIANA

ST. HELENA
7,130

WASHINGTON
4,708

ST. LANDRY

POINTE COUPEE
11,671

14,697

23,104

17,718

EAST BATON ROUGE

LIVINGSTON

ST. TAMMANY
5,406

CALCASIEU

7,312
WEST BATON ROUGE

16,046

4,431

5,928

9,003

12,674

14,661
IBERVILLE

11,484
ASCENSION

ST. JOHN THE BAPTIST

ORLEANS
174,491

LAFAYETTE

11,499

VERMILION

ST. MARTIN

15,379
ASSUMPTION

ST. JAMES
7,930

ST. CHARLES

JEFFERSON

4,076

4,324

16,816

14,044

5,297

15,372

ST. BERNARD

TERREBONNE

8,494

12,091

LAFOURCHE

PLAQUEMINES

MISSISSIPPI RIVER

SABINE RIVER

PEARL RIVER

Lake Maurepas

Lake Pontchartrain

Lake Borgne

Mississippi Sound

Mobile Bay

Chandeleur Sound

Breton Sound

Sabine Lake

Calcasieu Lake

Vermilion Bay

Atchafalaya Bay

G U L F   O F   M E X I C O

Over the span of its first half-century of statehood, the population of Louisiana would increase by 825 percent, from 76,556 to 708,002. Other demographic changes also occurred. The state was becoming less rural but only slightly so. Whites outnumbered blacks within the state. Males (369,994) still outnumbered females (338,008), though by a smaller margin (52 percent to 48 percent) than in 1810.

Overall, the density of population stood at 15.6 per square mile, compared with a national figure of 10.6; the 1810 figures had been 1.7 and 4.3 per square mile, respectively. Yet this density was not evenly applied to the entire state. The original core along the lower Mississippi and the bayous of southern Louisiana still existed. This core had now expanded upriver past the 1810 nestling around Natchez practically as far north as the Arkansas boundary. The clearing of the Great Raft on the Red River by the 1840s opened up that territory to greater population. (For a series of decennial maps, see Hilliard, *Atlas of Antebellum Southern Agriculture* [1984], 22–26.)

The growth in population from 1810 was more than just the natural increase of a resident population. Migration brought thousands more, from the eastern and northern states of the Union as well as from trans- Atlantic nations. In 1860, 21.5 percent of the total population was foreign-born. Ireland (34.8 percent) and Germany (30.4 percent) accounted for most of these residents; France was a distant third. The foreign-born were a distinctly urban group; New Orleans accounted for 82 percent of the state's total. Mississippi, Alabama, and Georgia were the big three in states of birth for intranational migrants; New York was the surprise in fourth place. Many other people passed through on their way elsewhere in the Mississippi Valley. Slaves and free African Americans also grew in number during the overall period, even as their percentage of the total population declined (Map 55).

Of its cities and towns (Map 37), New Orleans (Map 62) remained the state's colossus, with a population of 168,675 (23.8 percent of the total). Algiers (5,816) and Jefferson (5,107), neighboring semisuburbs to New Orleans, stood second and fourth in the state. Louisiana's third city was the capital, Baton Rouge (Map 65), with the modest population of 5,428. Less than half the capital's population was to be found in the state's next-largest city, Shreveport (2,190). Other towns in excess of 1,000 population were Plaquemine (1,663), Donaldsonville (1,475), Alexandria (1,461), Homer (1,451), Thibodaux (1,380), and Minden (1,146).

By far the majority of the state's population lived in rural areas. The largest plantations were themselves small communities, with owners, overseers, other managers, slaves and their families congregated in a rural nucleus. Smaller plantations with fewer slaves coexisted with the larger units, usually in the "delta" region of the state. Yeoman farmers dominated the upland areas, though slavery penetrated every region of Louisiana.

Even though the state's population remained overwhelmingly rural (73.9 percent) it was less rural than had been the case a half-century earlier. The rural-urban balance shifted throughout the period, however. For all practical purposes the rural-urban rise and fall illustrates the varying rates of increase for New Orleans as compared to the rest of the state.

Orleans Parish again loomed as the most populous civil division, with almost a quarter of the total population. Second stood Rapides (25,360), with but one-seventh the population of its sister parish. Rapides combined with the nine next-largest parishes contained the second quarter of the population. The least-populated twenty-three parishes contained another quarter of the total. St. Bernard again had the lowest population (4,076), a mere 0.6 percent of the total; Vermilion (4,324) and Livingston (4,431) parishes were scarcely more populous.

Compared with the United States as a whole, Louisiana's population grew much faster (825 percent) than did the national population (334 percent) for the period. Whereas the state represented 1.1 percent of the total national population in 1810, it had 2.2 percent of that total in 1860. Less populous than all but one of the seventeen states (but the largest territory) in 1810, by 1860 it ranked seventeenth of thirty-three. Compared to its neighboring states, Louisiana had more than Arkansas (435,450) or Texas (604,215) but fewer than Mississippi (791,305).

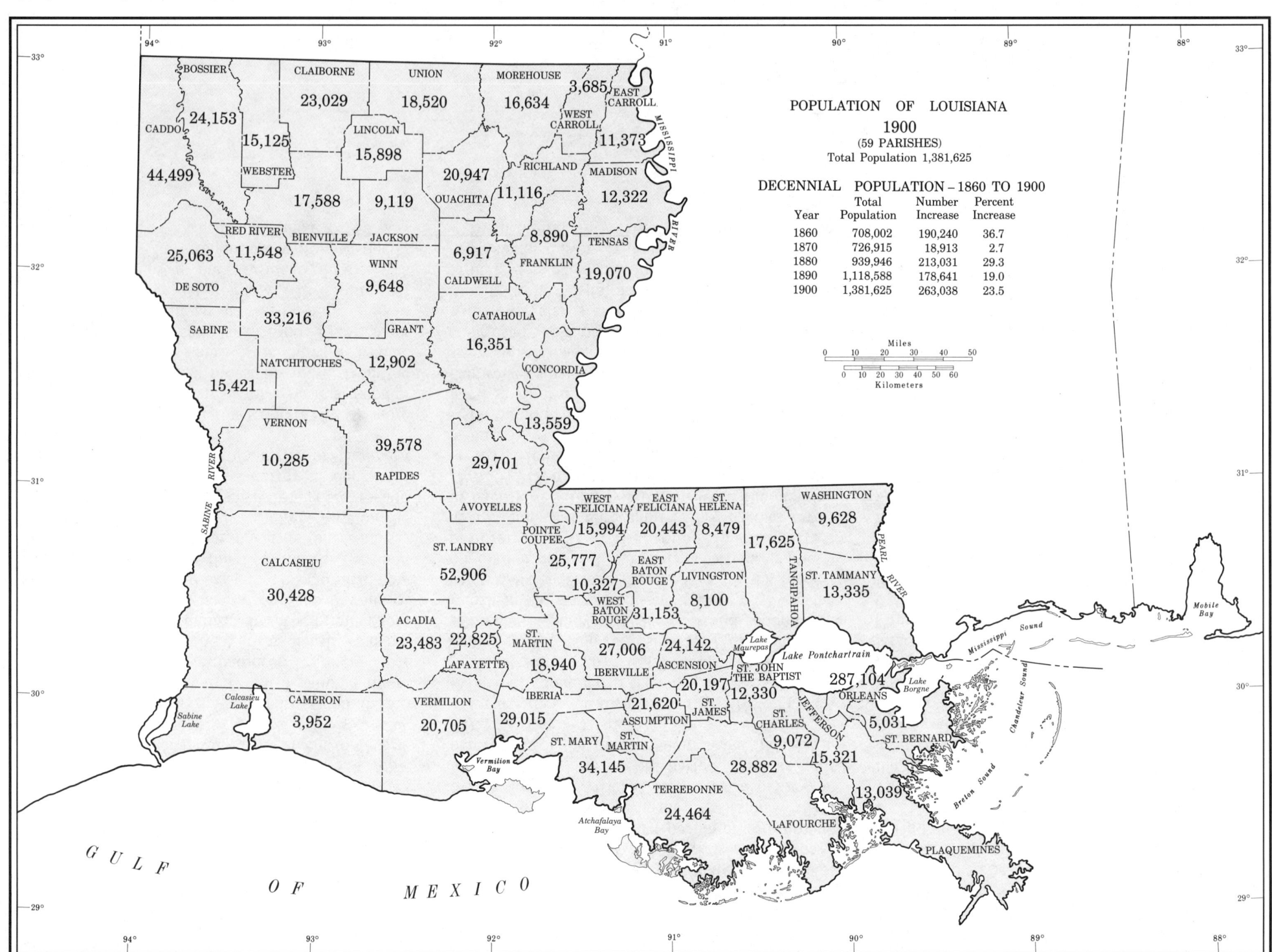

POPULATION OF LOUISIANA

1900

(59 PARISHES)

Total Population 1,381,625

DECENNIAL POPULATION – 1860 TO 1900

Year	Total Population	Number Increase	Percent Increase
1860	708,002	190,240	36.7
1870	726,915	18,913	2.7
1880	939,946	213,031	29.3
1890	1,118,588	178,641	19.0
1900	1,381,625	263,038	23.5

BOSSIER 24,153
CLAIBORNE 23,029
UNION 18,520
MOREHOUSE 16,634
EAST CARROLL 3,685
CADDO 44,499
15,125
WEBSTER 17,588
LINCOLN 15,898
WEST CARROLL 11,373
RICHLAND 11,116
MADISON 12,322
OUACHITA 20,947
JACKSON 9,119
TENSAS 8,890
RED RIVER 11,548
BIENVILLE
WINN 9,648
CALDWELL 6,917
FRANKLIN 19,070
DE SOTO 25,063
SABINE 33,216
GRANT 12,902
NATCHITOCHES
CATAHOULA 16,351
CONCORDIA 13,559
VERNON 15,421
10,285
RAPIDES 39,578
29,701
AVOYELLES
WEST FELICIANA 15,994
EAST FELICIANA 20,443
ST. HELENA 8,479
17,625
WASHINGTON 9,628
PEARL RIVER
POINTE COUPEE 25,777
ST. LANDRY 52,906
EAST BATON ROUGE 10,327
LIVINGSTON 8,100
TANGIPAHOA
ST. TAMMANY 13,335
CALCASIEU 30,428
WEST BATON ROUGE 31,153
ACADIA 23,483
22,825
ST. MARTIN 18,940
IBERVILLE 27,006
ASCENSION 24,142
LAFAYETTE
ST. JOHN THE BAPTIST 20,197
ORLEANS 287,104
LAKE BORGNE
CAMERON 3,952
VERMILION 20,705
IBERIA 29,015
21,620
ASSUMPTION
ST. JAMES 12,330
ST. CHARLES 9,072
JEFFERSON 15,321
ST. BERNARD 5,031
13,039
ST. MARY 34,145
ST. MARTIN
TERREBONNE 24,464
LAFOURCHE 28,882
PLAQUEMINES

GULF   OF   MEXICO

Calcasieu Lake
Sabine Lake
Vermilion Bay
Atchafalaya Bay
Lake Maurepas
Lake Pontchartrain
Mobile Bay
Mississippi Sound
Chandeleur Sound
Breton Sound
SABINE RIVER
MISSISSIPPI RIVER

From the eve of the Civil War to the turn of the century, Louisiana's population grew from 708,002 to 1,381,625. This increase amounted to 673,623 persons, or 95.1 percent. Even as the state was becoming more populous, it was also becoming slightly less rural. The percentage racial mix indicated a continuing increase in the white portion of the total. African Americans now amounted to only 47 percent of the total (Map 56). By sex, males slightly outnumbered females, 694,733 (50.3 percent) to 686,892 (49.7 percent). Among the states Louisiana ranked twenty-third of forty-five; by comparison it was seventeenth of thirty-three in 1860.

The overall density of the state stood at 30.4 per square mile. Almost double the 1860 figure, this compared to a national population density of 25.6. By this time practically all the state had been settled to some extent, with the exception of those areas not hospitable to human habitation. Still, the relative density varied widely between urban and rural areas and within each of these two classes because of city size and the intensity of agricultural use of the land.

Areas of particular growth were in the northern and western parishes. Railroad transportation (Maps 68–70) allowed lower-cost, speedier, and more dependable shipment of goods and people than did the still primitive roads. The expansion of these lines opened up for settlement new areas away from the navigable streams. Railroads also made possible the cutting of the state's primeval forests, leaving the cutover land in part to new agriculturalists. The increase of population in these regions was reflected in the creation of new parishes (Map 44).

Orleans Parish remained the most populous of all the civil divisions, with 287,104 persons, 20.8 percent of the total. St. Landry was second among the fifty-nine parishes with 52,906 (3.8 percent), followed by Caddo's 44,499 (3.2 percent). No other parish contained even 3 percent of the state's residents. At the other end of the list stood West Carroll Parish, with 3,685 (0.3 percent). Other parishes with less than 0.5 percent of the total were Cameron (3,952; 0.3 percent) and St. Bernard (5,031; 0.4 percent). In all, twenty-two of the state's sixty-four parishes had individual populations under 13,816 or 1 percent of the state's total.

The growth of towns and cities continued. New Orleans (with its "suburbs") and Baton Rouge—the only cities of greater than 2,500 persons in 1860—had been joined by thirteen more this year. These were Shreveport (now the second-largest city [16,013], with Baton Rouge [11,269] dropping to third), New Iberia, Lake Charles, Alexandria, Monroe, Crowley, Donaldsonville, Plaquemine, Lafayette, Thibodaux, Houma, Opelousas, and Franklin. Still, New Orleans (287,104) overshadowed all other urban areas in the state. It represented 20.8 percent of the state's population and was still the largest city in the entire South.

Despite the increasingly larger numbers of urban dwellers, Louisiana remained considerably rural in character. Its 73.5 percent rural population represented practically the same percentage of the total as in 1860 (73.9 percent). Of these the majority lived on farmsteads, not in smaller towns and villages of less than the twenty-five hundred "urban" figure. Compared with the nation, Louisiana was more rural, 73.5 percent to 61.3 percent. Among Southern states, however, its percentage was lower than the region's 84.8 percent; indeed, it was the most urban Southern state at the turn of the century, thanks to New Orleans.

The foreign-born segment of Louisiana's population numbered 52,903, 3.8 percent of the total. The absolute number, down from a total of 81,029 in 1860, represented an even smaller percentage than that of forty years earlier, given the increase in total population. The South as a region attracted few foreign-born residents; residents of each of the states were largely born within the state, almost certainly within the region.

Louisiana's share of the national population decreased to 1.8 percent from its 1860 share of 2.2 percent. Compared with its three neighboring states it was the most urban, second in density, and third in overall population. Texas with its 3,048,710 citizens ranked first in numbers; those citizens, however, represented an overall density of 11.6 per square mile, and only 14.9 percent were urban. Mississippi's 1,551,270 residents represented the greatest density, 33.5 per square mile, but only 5.3 percent of the total was urban. Arkansas ranked fourth in population (1,311,564), third in percentage urban (6.9 percent), and third in density (24.7 per square mile).

Copyright © 1995 by the University of Oklahoma Press

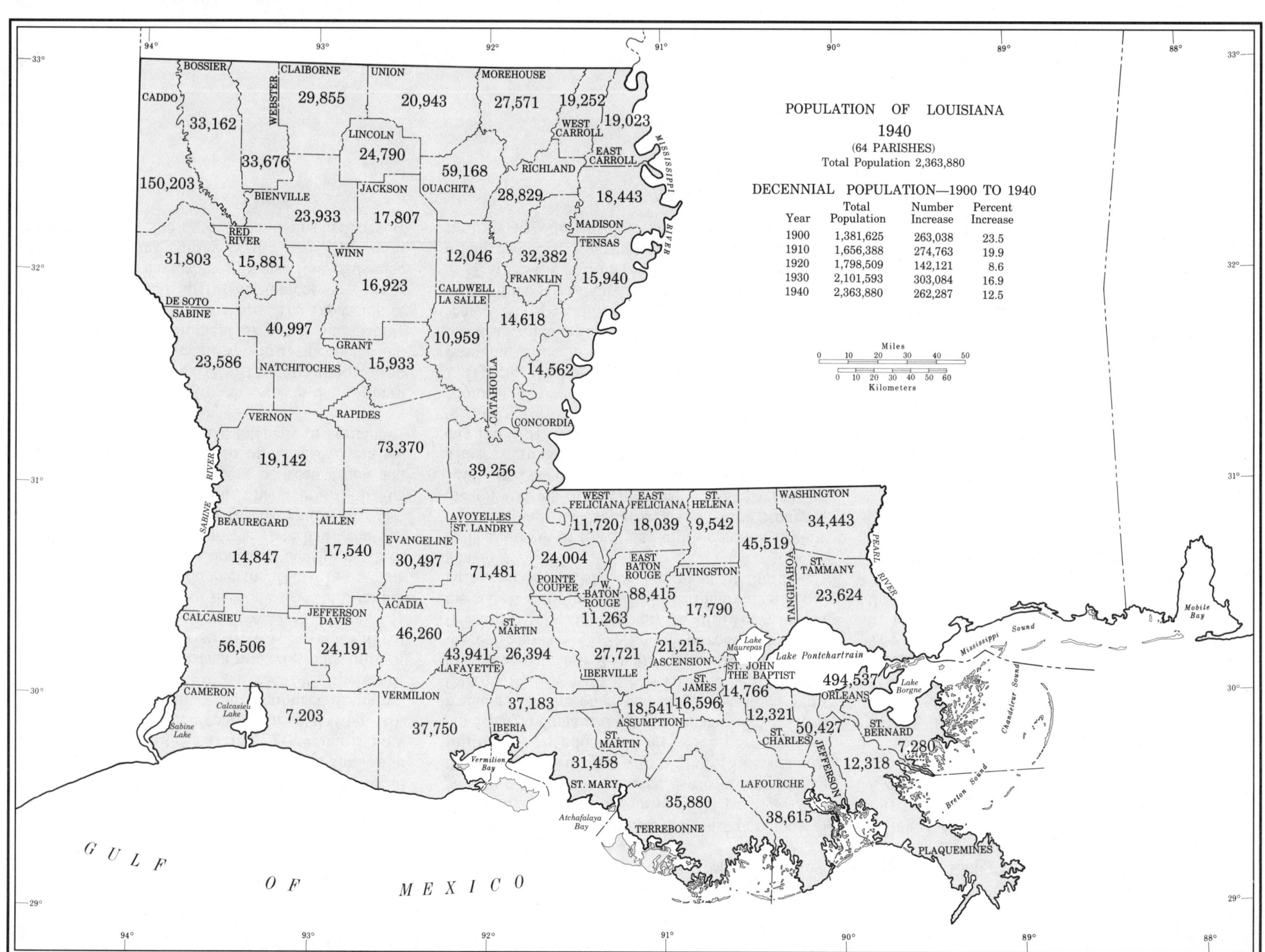

POPULATION OF LOUISIANA

1940

(64 PARISHES)
Total Population 2,363,880

DECENNIAL POPULATION—1900 TO 1940

Year	Total Population	Number Increase	Percent Increase
1900	1,381,625	263,038	23.5
1910	1,656,388	274,763	19.9
1920	1,798,509	142,121	8.6
1930	2,101,593	303,084	16.9
1940	2,363,880	262,287	12.5

53. POPULATION OF LOUISIANA, 1940

The first four decades of the twentieth century saw changes in Louisiana's population, changes which in most cases would strengthen as the remainder of the century progressed. The rural-to-urban shift began to accelerate. The racial composition of the state also changed as the percentage of the total represented by African Americans declined.

In 1940 the total state population numbered 2,363,880, not quite double the 1900 figure of 1,381,625. Overall, the increase of this forty-year period was a total of 982,255 or 71.1 percent. Each decade showed an increase over the preceding period, ranging from a 19.9 percent jump in the 1900–1910 period downward to only 8.6 percent in the 1910–1920 decade. The scant increase in the 1910–1920 period reflected a decline in the total black population in the state (Map 56). The density of population in 1940 stood at 52.3 per square mile; this compared with a national average of 44.2.

The rural-to-urban population shift lessened the difference between these standings. From almost three-quarters (73.5 percent) of the population in 1900, the rural sector declined to just under three-fifths (58.5 percent) in 1940. Indeed, 1940 would be the last census in which more than half of the state remained rural in nature. The 1940 urban figure (41.5 percent) remained below the national average of 56.5 percent. Moreover, no longer was Louisiana the most urban state in the South; Florida (55.1 percent) and Texas (45.4 percent) had both outstripped the state in this measure.

Whereas when the century dawned there were fifteen "urban" places in Louisiana, in 1940 there were now fifty-four. Still, twenty-three of the sixty-four parishes had no urban area, no central place of greater than twenty-five hundred population. These rural parishes often contained more population than did their urban kin.

New Orleans remained the premier city in Louisiana and the South, although this proved to be the last census in which it would hold its regional ranking. Four other cities in the state exceeded 25,000: Shreveport (98,167), Baton Rouge (34,719), Monroe (28,309), and Alexandria (27,066). Five cities had populations ranging from 10,000 to 22,000: Lake Charles (21,207), Lafayette (19,210), Bogalusa (14,604), New Iberia (13,747), and Gretna (10,879). Another eighteen cities ranged between 5,000 and 10,000 in population, and twenty-six more exceeded the minimum 2,500 but fell below 5,000.

Many of the cities, towns, and villages were a century old or older. Others came into being with the extension of railroads and the cutting of the state's ancient forests beginning in the late nineteenth century. Government programs beginning with the Great Depression also tended to attract population to the parish seats and other centers where the government programs were administered.

As before, Orleans remained first in the ranks of the parishes, with 494,537 (20.9 percent). Second came Caddo with 150,203 (6.4 percent), then East Baton Rouge, 88,415 (3.7 percent), Rapides, 73,370 (3.1 percent), and St. Landry, 71,481 (3.0 percent). Four of the five highest-ranked parishes in population had one of the top five cities in the state; only Ouachita with Monroe did not make the group. At the low end in population were two parishes, each with 0.3 percent of the total: Cameron (7,203) and St. Bernard (7,280). Four other parishes each contained less than 0.5 percent of the total: St. Helena (9,542), La Salle (10,959), West Baton Rouge (11,263), and West Feliciana (11,720).

The foreign-born population within Louisiana continued to decline. Only 27,973 of the residents (1.2 percent) were born outside the United States or its possessions. This contrasted to 52,903 (3.8 percent of the total) only forty years earlier. Indeed, some 86.9 percent of the state's population in 1940 had been born within the state's bounds, down slightly from the 88.0 percent of the 1900 census.

Overall, the gender balance within the state had shifted to a slight female majority, 50.4 percent to 49.6 percent. Among whites, males still constituted a scant majority at 50.1 percent of the total. Black females made up the majority of that race, with 51.3 percent. Compared with her neighboring states, Louisiana was the most densely settled, and second in both total and urban population. Texas with 6,414,824 held close to three times Louisiana's population. Texas's urban population accounted for 45.4 percent of the total, and its overall density was only 24.3 persons per square mile. Mississippi remained third in population, with 2,843,796. Its density was 46.1 per square mile and its portion urban was 19.8 percent. Arkansas's total was 1,949,387, with a density of 37.0 per square mile and a 22.2 percent urban population.

Copyright © 1995 by the University of Oklahoma Press

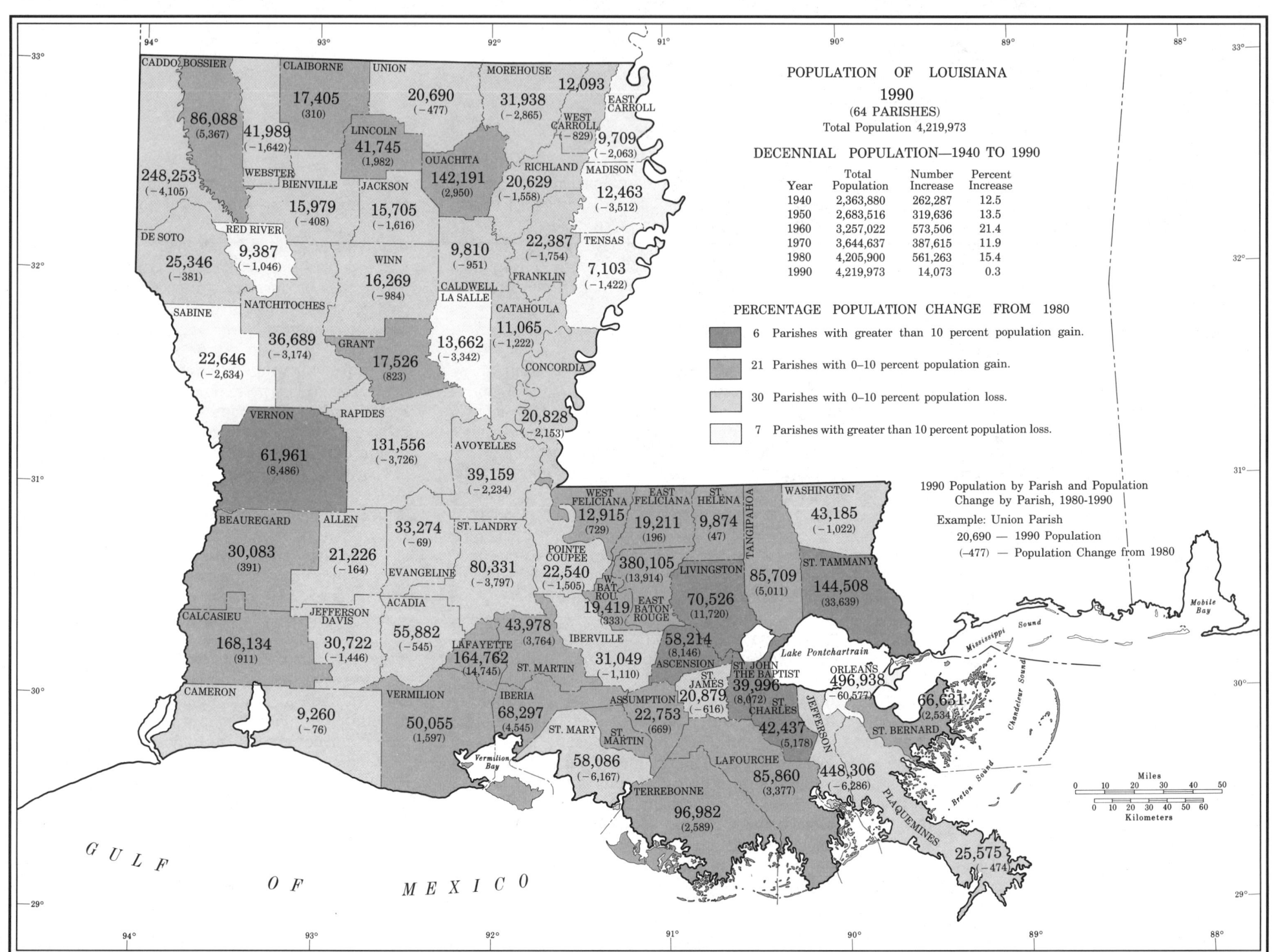

POPULATION OF LOUISIANA
1990
(64 PARISHES)
Total Population 4,219,973

DECENNIAL POPULATION—1940 TO 1990

Year	Total Population	Number Increase	Percent Increase
1940	2,363,880	262,287	12.5
1950	2,683,516	319,636	13.5
1960	3,257,022	573,506	21.4
1970	3,644,637	387,615	11.9
1980	4,205,900	561,263	15.4
1990	4,219,973	14,073	0.3

PERCENTAGE POPULATION CHANGE FROM 1980

6 Parishes with greater than 10 percent population gain.

21 Parishes with 0–10 percent population gain.

30 Parishes with 0–10 percent population loss.

7 Parishes with greater than 10 percent population loss.

1990 Population by Parish and Population Change by Parish, 1980-1990

Example: Union Parish

20,690 — 1990 Population

(−477) — Population Change from 1980

From 1940 to 1990, Louisiana's population increased both in number and in its urban nature. However, the 1990 census witnessed reversals of two historic trends. That total recorded only a minute growth from the previous count. Also the decline in the percentage of blacks among the total population reversed, if again only slightly (Map 57).

In 1990 the state population numbered 4,219,973, a growth of almost 80 percent above the 1940 total of 2,363,880. Each succeeding census had recorded growth. The decennial increases for the period peaked in a 21.4 percent jump during the baby-boom decade, 1950–1960. A historic trough occurred during the economically troubled 1980–1990 decade, with a minuscule increase of 0.3 percent. The state's population density grew from 52.3 per square mile in 1940 to 94.8 per square mile in 1990.

This last half-century has also witnessed increasing urbanization. The 1940 census represented the last count in which the rural population outnumbered the urban—58.5 percent to 41.5 percent. In 1950 the urban areas accounted for 54.8 percent, a percentage that would rise to near 70 percent by 1990. In 1940 the state had 54 urban places (incorporated or census-designated); in 1990 there were 166 such places. Only eight of sixty-four parishes remained entirely rural, that is, lacking a central place of 2,500 or more. Although fewer than the twenty-three in 1940, this number is remarkable for a state of 4 million persons with an overall density of nearly 100 per square mile.

New Orleans (496,938) remained the state's first city, but its population declined through much of the period as its suburbs expanded. Baton Rouge (219,531) succeeded Shreveport (198,525) as the second-largest city beginning with the 1980 census. Six other places exceeded 50,000 people in 1990: Metairie (149,428), Lafayette (94,440), Kenner (72,033), Lake Charles (70,580), Monroe (54,909), and Bossier City (52,721). Of this half-dozen only Monroe had exceeded 25,000 a half-century before, when Bossier City had boasted only 5,786 and Kenner fell below the urban definition with only 2,375. Moreover, four of these six urban centers lay in south Louisiana. Five other cities totalled 25,000–50,000 each; of this group Alexandria was the northernmost city. Of thirty-one cities between 10,000 and 25,000, fewer than a quarter lay in north Louisiana. Clearly a regional shift was accompanying the rural-to-urban movement.

Orleans Parish, despite a declining total, retained its premiere position with 496,938, but its share of the total population had fallen from 20.9 percent in 1940 to 11.8 percent in 1990. It was now challenged by its suburban neighbor Jefferson Parish, with 448,306 (10.6 percent). East Baton Rouge Parish, with 380,105 (9.0 percent) had also increased its share. Caddo, with 248,253 (5.9 percent), and Calcasieu, with 168,134 (3.4 percent), rounded out the five most populous parishes. Tensas Parish occupied the least populous rung with 7,103, or 0.2 percent of the total. Whereas in 1940 only six parishes each represented less than 0.5 percent of the state total, in 1990 twenty-two parishes were in that group.

The 1980–1990 period witnessed large-scale economic distress for the state and a near halt in its population growth. Thirty-seven of sixty-four parishes posted population declines. Madison Parish lost 22 percent of its population; six others—La Salle, East Carroll, Tensas, Orleans, Sabine, and Red River—also posted double-digit declines. Twenty-seven parishes showed increases, six in double digits: St. Tammany (30.3 percent), St. John the Baptist (25.3 percent), Livingston (19.9 percent), Ascension (16.3 percent), Vernon (15.7 percent), and St. Charles (13.9 percent).

For much of Louisiana the 1980–1990 decline merely continued trends for the previous half-century. Its citizenry was moving from farm to town and from north to south. East Carroll, West Carroll, and Tensas parishes showed consistently declining totals from 1940 to 1990. Another seven northern parishes posted declines in four of the five censuses. Eighteen parishes at least doubled their 1940 population by 1990, led by St. Bernard (815 percent), Jefferson (789 percent), and St. Tammany (512 percent). Of these growing parishes, only Bossier and Ouachita lay in the north. Of the nine parishes losing 25 percent or more of their 1940 total by 1990, none lay south of Alexandria.

Louisiana remains the most densely populated state and the second most populous among its neighbors. Texas, with 16,986,510, holds four times Louisiana's population, yet Texas's 64.9 persons per square mile is second to Louisiana's 94.8. Mississippi and Arkansas ranked third and fourth, respectively, in both categories. In population Mississippi numbered 2,573,216 and Arkansas, 2,350,725. In density, Mississippi's 54.8 per square mile exceeded Arkansas's 45.1.

Copyright © 1995 by the University of Oklahoma Press

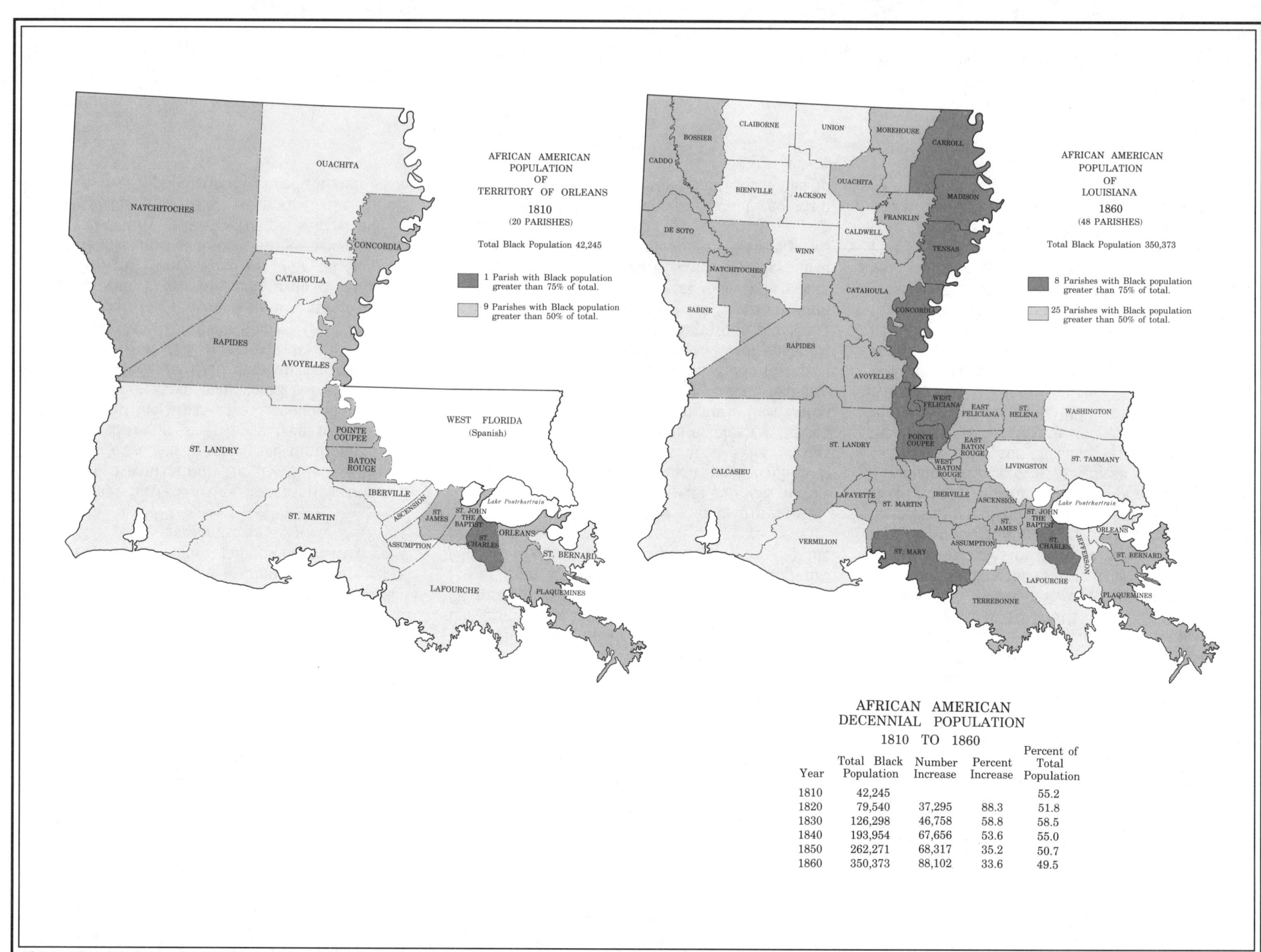

AFRICAN AMERICAN
POPULATION
OF
TERRITORY OF ORLEANS
1810
(20 PARISHES)

Total Black Population 42,245

1 Parish with Black population greater than 75% of total.

9 Parishes with Black population greater than 50% of total.

AFRICAN AMERICAN
POPULATION
OF
LOUISIANA
1860
(48 PARISHES)

Total Black Population 350,373

8 Parishes with Black population greater than 75% of total.

25 Parishes with Black population greater than 50% of total.

AFRICAN AMERICAN
DECENNIAL POPULATION
1810 TO 1860

Year	Total Black Population	Number Increase	Percent Increase	Percent of Total Population
1810	42,245			55.2
1820	79,540	37,295	88.3	51.8
1830	126,298	46,758	58.8	58.5
1840	193,954	67,656	53.6	55.0
1850	262,271	68,317	35.2	50.7
1860	350,373	88,102	33.6	49.5

55. AFRICAN AMERICAN POPULATION, 1810 AND 1860

From the early eighteenth century to the Emancipation Proclamation of 1863 (and its effective application through the defeat of the South in the Civil War) the black population of Louisiana largely constituted slaves. African American slavery began after other sources of agricultural labor failed. As early as 1708, Bienville may have imported two black slaves from the West Indies, where slavery had long been practiced. In 1712 the practice of slavery was officially sanctioned. From a very small beginning the African American population (both free and slave) swelled as a percentage of the total population, peaking at 58.5 percent in 1830 and declining slowly thereafter.

The purchase of slaves rose and fell with the fortunes of the agricultural economy. Slaves represented both property and labor in the cotton and sugar plantation systems of Louisiana, as well as in other farming operations. Though foreign slave trading was officially prohibited in the United States after 1807, smuggling still occurred, and the domestic trade remained legal. Too, planters moved westward to new lands, taking slaves with them. The natural increase of the slave population also contributed to the total. S. B. Hilliard provides maps of slave populations for the entire South from 1810 to 1860 in his *Atlas of Antebellum Southern Agriculture* (1984).

Small numbers of free blacks coexisted at a social status between that of slaves and the majority white population. These free blacks grew in number throughout the colonial and most of the antebellum period, with the largest percentage of them living in New Orleans. In cities and towns this group constituted for the most part tradesmen, carpenters, and workers in the mechanical trades.

In the rural areas they were farmers, a small number of them planters with slaves of their own. By and large the descendants of slaves themselves, free African Americans were required to carry proof of their freedom. As the slavery debate grew, and more restrictive laws regarding black freedoms came into being, a less hospitable atmosphere toward the free blacks developed. Many of them emigrated from Louisiana during the 1840s and 1850s.

Although slavery was closely tied to the agricultural economy, not all slaves worked as field hands. Blacks served in the home as domestics, others learned such trades as carpentry and blacksmithing, and some even served to oversee their fellow slaves. Black members of the militia participated in the colonial wars and the War of 1812.

African Americans in Louisiana were governed by particular rules called the Code Noir, or Black Code. Bienville as governor promulgated the first such code in 1724. This code was modified during the Spanish period. An 1806 code was largely concerned with the prevention of uprisings. A revolt in 1811 in St. Charles Parish proved to be the largest slave revolt ever in the nation but also the last ever to occur in Louisiana. Other revisions of the code followed in 1846 and 1855, though the latter revision was declared unconstitutional by the state supreme court. The code regulated not only the rights of slaves and other blacks but also the prerogatives of the slaveholder. Although slaves were relegated to an inferior position, the opportunity for judicial protection was extended to them. More than one observer has stated that the best protection the slave had was his or her value as property and the loss the owner would sustain

through the slave's injury or death.

In 1810 ten of the territory's twenty parishes had populations greater than 50 percent black. These ranged from St. James Parish (50.3 percent) to St. Charles Parish (75.1 percent). Almost all this population outside of New Orleans represented slaves. Among free blacks, Orleans Parish contained 5,727 of the 7,585 total, or 75.5 percent.

Fifty years later, even though blacks represented only 49.5 percent of the total population, their distribution within the state largely followed the plantation culture. Thirty-three of the state's forty-eight parishes held majority black population; eight of these were more than three-quarters African American. Concordia Parish ranked highest, with blacks representing 91.0 percent of the total; Tensas Parish came a close second at 90.8 percent. At the opposite end stood Orleans Parish, with a quarter of the state's population but only 14.5 percent African American. On the other hand, Orleans contained almost 60 percent of all free blacks within the state, 10,939 of the 18,647 total.

Other than generally condemning slavery as an institution, writers have not always agreed on its application. Regional attitudes and political agendas have produced varying portrayals of slave life from a paternalistic, rustic simplicity with occasional aberrant evil slaveholders to the opposite extreme. The most unfortunate legacy of slavery was a continuing white attitude towards blacks as essentially inferior beings. This attitude would lead to a racially based, institutionalized relegation of blacks as a group to the lowest rung of the social, economic, and political ladder.

Copyright © 1995 by the University of Oklahoma Press

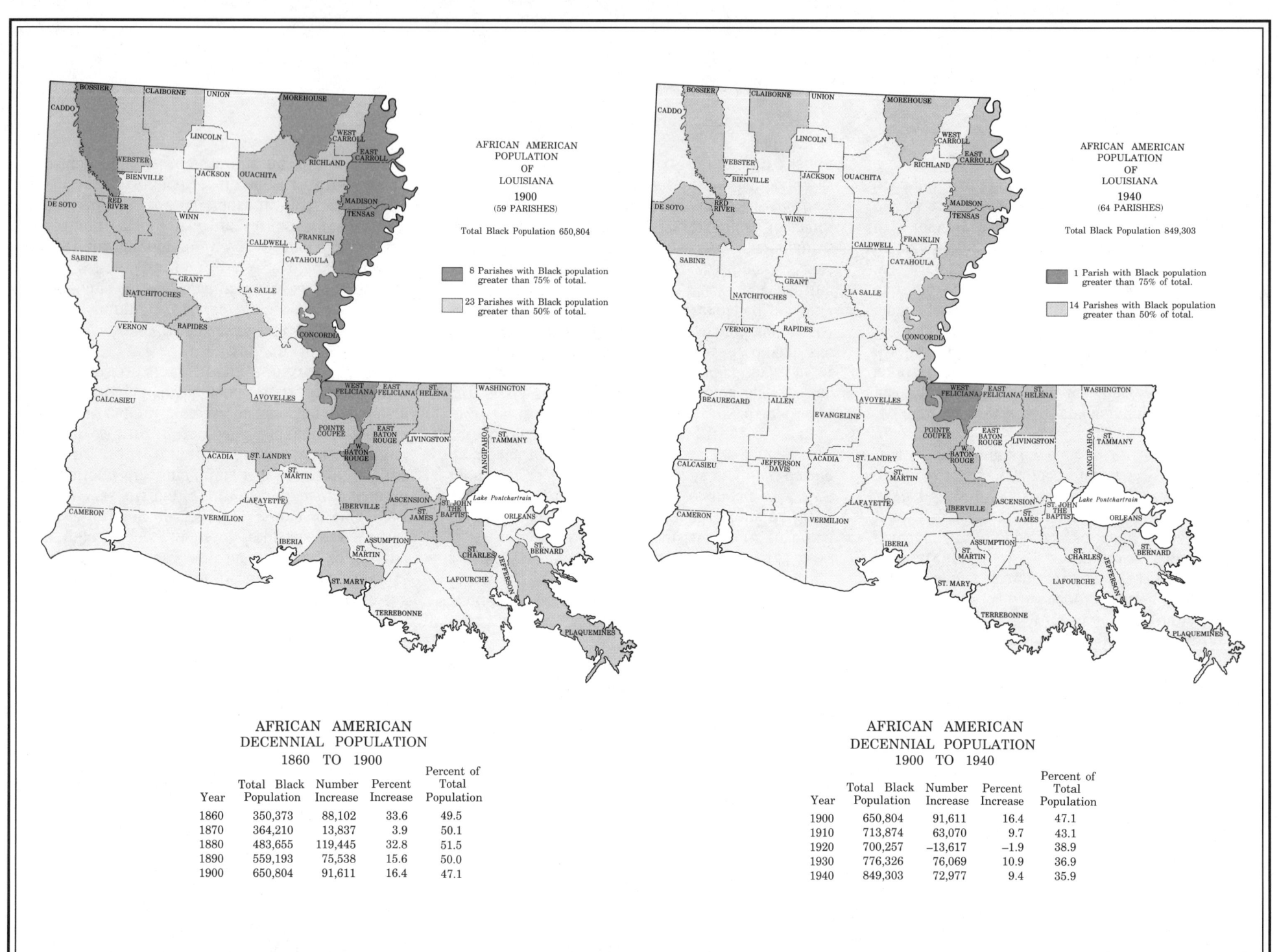

AFRICAN AMERICAN
POPULATION
OF
LOUISIANA
1900
(59 PARISHES)

Total Black Population 650,804

8 Parishes with Black population
greater than 75% of total.

23 Parishes with Black population
greater than 50% of total.

AFRICAN AMERICAN
POPULATION
OF
LOUISIANA
1940
(64 PARISHES)

Total Black Population 849,303

1 Parish with Black population
greater than 75% of total.

14 Parishes with Black population
greater than 50% of total.

AFRICAN AMERICAN
DECENNIAL POPULATION
1860 TO 1900

Year	Total Black Population	Number Increase	Percent Increase	Percent of Total Population
1860	350,373	88,102	33.6	49.5
1870	364,210	13,837	3.9	50.1
1880	483,655	119,445	32.8	51.5
1890	559,193	75,538	15.6	50.0
1900	650,804	91,611	16.4	47.1

AFRICAN AMERICAN
DECENNIAL POPULATION
1900 TO 1940

Year	Total Black Population	Number Increase	Percent Increase	Percent of Total Population
1900	650,804	91,611	16.4	47.1
1910	713,874	63,070	9.7	43.1
1920	700,257	−13,617	−1.9	38.9
1930	776,326	76,069	10.9	36.9
1940	849,303	72,977	9.4	35.9

On the eve of the Civil War, African Americans represented 49.5 percent of Louisiana's population. The thirteenth through fifteenth amendments to the Constitution, as well as laws passed during Reconstruction, in theory provided full political and social participation, but these laws were not always enforced. Still, between 1868 and 1896, 133 blacks served in the state's legislature. Louisiana also had three black lieutenant governors during that period.

After the restoration of state rule in 1877, the Bourbons (Redeemers), through first intimidation and then statute, scaled back these rights. Although the process was motivated by old attitudes toward race, economic and political factors also spurred it on. Blacks now constituted economic competition in agriculture and the trades. Moreover, African Americans, by voting Republican, the party of emancipation, threatened the Bourbon Democrats' hold on power. The poll tax, literacy test, and property requirement discouraged poor whites as well as blacks from voting. However, the Grandfather Clause of the state's Constitution of 1898 presented a loophole from the literacy and property requirements, exempting those who could prove their father or grandfather had been entitled to vote before Radical Reconstruction (1867). This and similar clauses elsewhere in the old Confederacy would be declared unconstitutional in 1915. In the interim they had the desired effect; from 130,344 registered black voters in 1896, the number fell to 5,320 only four years later. Not until the 1960s would these constitutional and statutory biases towards blacks be swept away.

Until the twentieth century, the African American population remained largely tied to the land. For the most part, however, the land they tilled did not belong to them. They, along with many whites, were part of the larger tenant-farmer and sharecropping systems of Southern agriculture. In particular, the cotton economy was based on such systems. In their simplest terms, sharecropping and tenancy meant that the landowner and the landtiller divided the proceeds of the crop more or less equally. From their share the tenant sharecroppers paid for all their family's necessities for the year. Many considered sharecropping and tenant farming to be forms of yet another type of slavery—this time economic—for anyone of any race caught within it.

Several distinct migration trends among blacks took place in the decades following the Civil War. Internally there was a movement, particularly among young blacks, to cities, where economic opportunity was greater and where racial bias was less open than in rural areas. The hope of economic and social enhancement also prompted emigration. In the 1870s and 1880s many blacks migrated to the west, particularly to Kansas. These "Exodusters" were prompted by the promise of free land and greater personal freedom, but the reality of the new situation did not match their initial hope.

Of greater importance was the northern migration of African Americans from throughout the South. This movement began in the early twentieth century but swelled after World War I. The decline of the cotton kingdom, the increasing mechanization of agriculture, the booming indus-trialization of the North, and the attraction of urban areas all contributed to the attractive nature of the North. In 1900, 85.2 percent of the nation's black population lived in the South; by 1940 that figure had dropped to 72.0 percent.

Louisiana in 1900 showed subtle changes in the distribution of its black population. The percentage of population represented by African Americans had slipped from 49.5 percent in 1860 to 47.1 percent in 1900. The concentrations which had been reflected in the 1860 distribution had largely continued. Thirty-one of the state's fifty-nine parishes had majority black populations, ranging up to 93.5 percent in Tensas Parish.

Forty years later the effects of emigration on Louisiana's population showed up dramatically in both the number and distribution of African Americans within the state. During the 1910–1920 period there had occurred an absolute drop in the number of blacks in Louisiana; in each of the other three decennial periods the increase in the black population occurred at a smaller rate than in the state's population as a whole. The percentage of the total population represented by African Americans dropped to 35.9 percent in 1940; that number still represented a higher figure than for the South as a whole. Only fourteen of the sixty-four parishes contained a majority black population. Only one parish, West Feliciana with 76.4 percent, showed a black population greater than three-quarters of the total, down from eight such parishes forty years earlier. Only ten parishes registered an increase in the percentage of blacks in their populations. This out-migration would continue for four more decades before reversing.

Copyright © 1995 by the University of Oklahoma Press

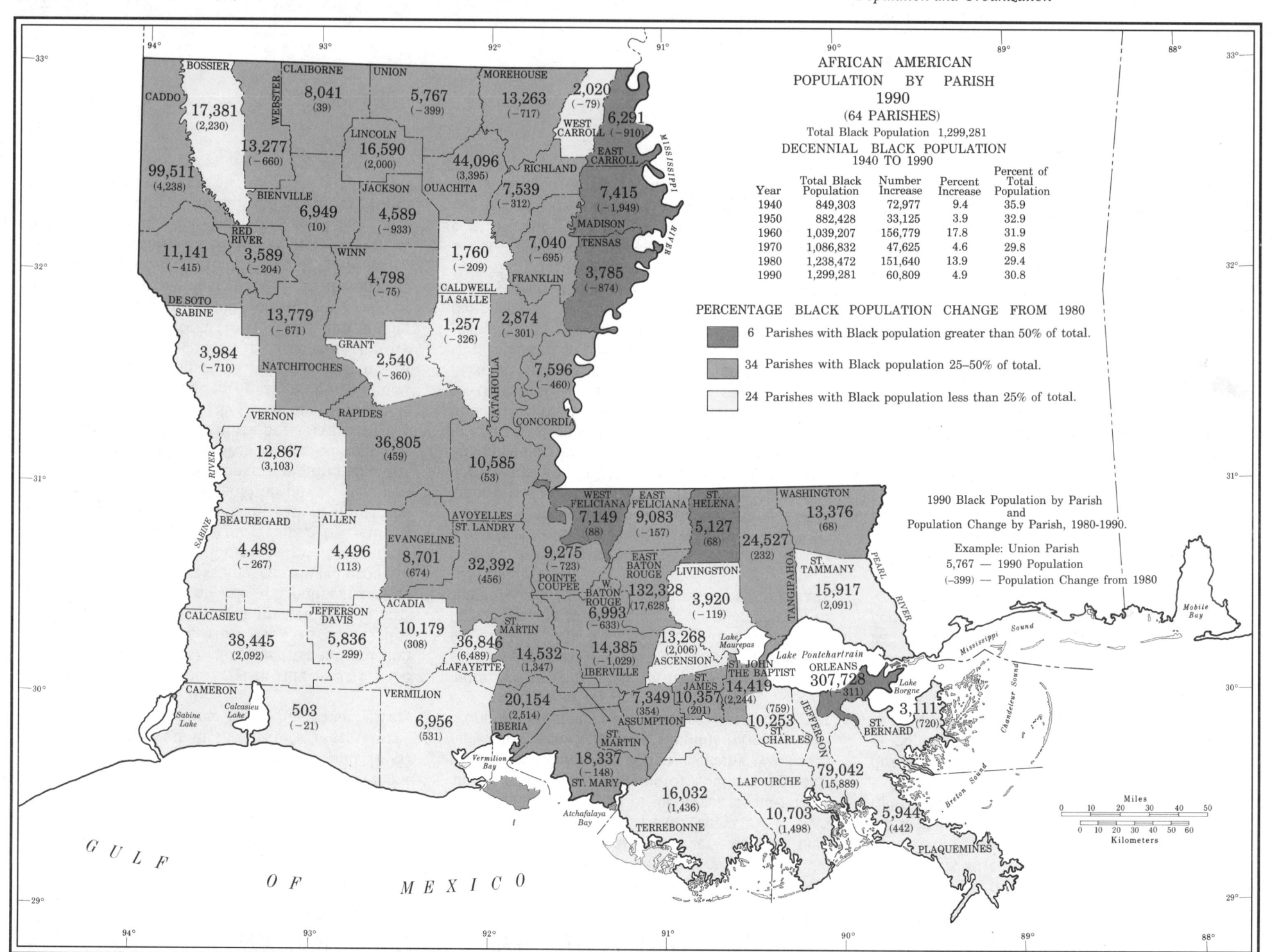

AFRICAN AMERICAN
POPULATION BY PARISH
1990
(64 PARISHES)
Total Black Population 1,299,281
DECENNIAL BLACK POPULATION
1940 TO 1990

Year	Total Black Population	Number Increase	Percent Increase	Percent of Total Population
1940	849,303	72,977	9.4	35.9
1950	882,428	33,125	3.9	32.9
1960	1,039,207	156,779	17.8	31.9
1970	1,086,832	47,625	4.6	29.8
1980	1,238,472	151,640	13.9	29.4
1990	1,299,281	60,809	4.9	30.8

PERCENTAGE BLACK POPULATION CHANGE FROM 1980

6 Parishes with Black population greater than 50% of total.

34 Parishes with Black population 25–50% of total.

24 Parishes with Black population less than 25% of total.

1990 Black Population by Parish
and
Population Change by Parish, 1980-1990.

Example: Union Parish
5,767 — 1990 Population
(−399) — Population Change from 1980

In the 1940 census blacks represented slightly more than one-third of Louisiana's total population. This figure represented a continuing decline from the beginning of the century, when blacks accounted for slightly less than one-half the total. The decline caused by the emigration of African Americans, particularly following World War I, would continue as the century progressed towards its close.

The emigration of blacks to the North represented yearnings for new opportunities, both economic and social. With the mechanization of agriculture came a decline in tenancy, as larger and larger acreages came to be cultivated by tractor and harvested by picker. The virtual peonage that tenant farming in large part represented had held the farmers to the land. As they were released—or forced—from the system, they found in the manufacturing plants of the metropolitan North an opportunity to escape tenancy, the rural land, and the rigidly segregated society of the South.

From 1940 to 1980 the percentage of Louisiana's population comprised of African Americans continued gradually to decline. Standing at 35.9 percent in 1940, the percentage fell to 29.4 percent in 1980, then rebounded slightly to 30.8 percent in 1990. Only in the 1980–1990 decennial period did the percentage growth in black population outstrip the growth of the total population.

The evolving civil rights movement which came to the fore in the late 1950s and early 1960s swept away much of the de jure segregation of the South. State by state, the 1954 *Brown* vs. *Board of Education* ruling outlawing separate but equal schools was enforced, leading to the integration of public schools and colleges. The Voting Rights Act of 1965 eliminated the contrivances used to prevent blacks (and others) from exercising the privilege of the ballot. Housing, manpower training, preschool education, and other programs arising from the Great Society presidency of Lyndon B. Johnson improved the lot of blacks and of poor individuals everywhere.

With this often reluctant metamorphosis of Southern society the lot of individual African Americans improved, and relations between blacks and whites entered a new era. Blacks were elected to office at every level of government and became a potent force at election time. Open appeals to racial fears by the white political structure faded by degrees if they did not completely disappear. In that way the political "establishment" learned the lessons taught by the Long family, particularly Earl K. Long, who as governor moved to integrate segments of Louisiana before the force of judicial decisions intervened. White political figures openly courted black voters, even as blacks themselves were elected to the mayorship of New Orleans, to the Congress and the legislature, and to lesser positions around the state.

More recently a return migration of blacks to the South has been noted. Some of those returning are retirees, leaving the northern factory towns for the warmer climate and lower cost of living of the South. Others speak of a more open accommodation between black and white in this the newest South, particularly in urban areas and among the professions and technical trades.

The growth in black population between 1980 and 1990 may represent such a trend, or the slight increase in black numbers may indicate only the state's economic distress at the time. For whatever reason, African American numbers increased even as those of white and other groups within the population declined. The percentage of blacks within the population increased for the first census since 1830.

In 1990 only six parishes in the state had majority black populations, a decline from the total of fourteen such parishes in 1940. Orleans Parish alone accounted for a quarter of the state's total blacks. At 61.9 percent African American, Orleans was second only to East Carroll Parish with its 64.8 percent black total. Other majority-black parishes were Madison (59.5 percent), West Feliciana (55.4 percent), Tensas (53.3 percent), and St. Helena (51.9 percent).

Between 1980 and 1990 forty of the state's sixty-four parishes showed an increase in the percentage of their population represented by African Americans. Blacks generally represent a greater portion of the population in the river parishes and in the three largest metropolitan parishes—Orleans, East Baton Rouge, and Caddo—but are less prominent in southwestern Louisiana and its cities. The North-to-South migration among blacks nationally may be a cause of this increase in black numbers. What effect this trend—particularly should it continue or increase—will have on the South as a region and Louisiana in particular in the next century is unclear.

Copyright © 1995 by the University of Oklahoma Press

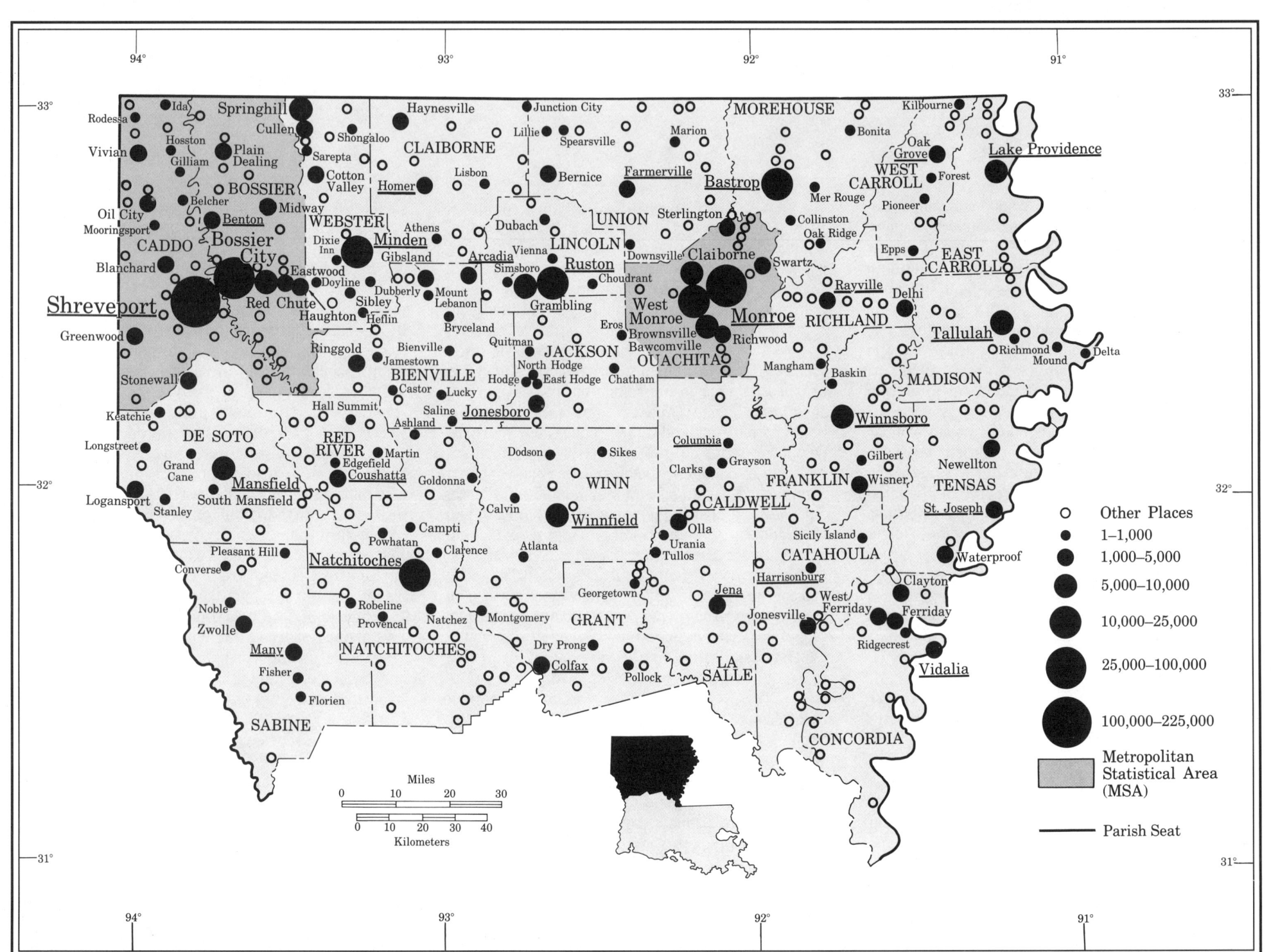

"Places" as settlements come in a myriad of sizes and shapes. People may speak of the "old home place"—a site perhaps now without a structure of any sort. Other "places" develop around crossroads, country schools, stores, and churches; rural areas abound with such nodes absent from almost any map but known to the local population. A place then can be thought of as an area about which there is some central focus. One may also call these "central places" or "agglomerated settlements."

In terms of larger communities—towns or cities—these places can be categorized according to size (Map 59) as well as function (Map 60). One most often thinks of such places as being incorporated, with legal boundaries of a specific nature. But there are other such places with up to tens of thousands of inhabitants within an unincorporated area whose bounds have been assigned by the Bureau of the Census.

Before the earliest written record, north Louisiana abounded with agglomerated settlements of Native Americans. The Poverty Point site in West Carroll Parish may have counted a population of several thousands and represented a regional trading focus not unlike modern metropolitan areas in the first and second millennia B.C. Less sizeable and more transitory settlement sites lie scattered about the northern parishes, some marked by relic mounds and others as yet undiscovered or lost, destroyed by the meandering rivers along which they were situated.

During the Franco-Hispanic colonial period, agglomerated clusters developed primarily along river and bayou courses. Natchitoches (1714) represents the oldest settlement within the bounds of the Louisiana Purchase. These sites often were adjacent to Indian villages. Others came into being at sites where river courses changed as a result of rapids, blockages such as the Great Raft of the Red River, or some high point less susceptible to flooding than neighboring lands.

Forts became surrounded by homes. Farmers settled along the more fertile valleys, then slowly into the more remote uplands. The European introduction of the wheel led to greater overland transport, which later increased as railroads (in the nineteenth century) and modern highways (in the twentieth) snaked across the land. The mesopotamic areas in turn produced settlements of various sizes distant from the nearest navigable stream. The clearing of the forests, the development of the region's gas and oil resources, the appearance of new commercial and business enterprises, and the rise and decline of subsistence farming also helped to bring about the birth, expansion, or decline of towns.

The 1990 Census of Population counted 148 cities, towns, and census-designated places in twenty-six northern parishes. Only 36 such places had 1990 populations greater than they had in 1980. The regional metropolis Shreveport was the only northern Louisiana city with more than 100,000 people; its 1990 total numbered 198,525. Shreveport alone exceeded the combined population (191,899) of all 140 places in northern Louisiana with populations under 10,000. Monroe (54,909) and Shreveport's sister city, Bossier City (52,721), account for the other cities in excess of 50,000. Two metropolitan statistical areas, Shreveport and Monroe, are found in this region.

At the opposite end of the population spectrum, eighty-nine places counted fewer than one thousand residents each. Another twenty-six had populations in excess of one thousand but less than twenty-five hundred, the lower limit for a census urban designation. Five parishes—Caldwell, Grant, Tensas, Red River, and West Carroll—had no single place classified as urban.

The 1990 population of these twenty-six parishes totaled 929,595—22 percent of the state's total. This figure represented a slight decline from 1980, when the population stood at 956,301, or 23 percent of the state's total of 4,205,900. Twenty-one of the twenty-six parishes showed population losses instead of gains for the period. The share accounted for by the region's cities, towns, hamlets, and so on, remained the same in 1990 as in 1980: 62 percent. The northern parishes account for far more than their proportional share of places of under one thousand, with 61 percent of the total.

The relative population decline in these northern parishes can be ascribed to various reasons. Less abundant natural resources, whether the depletion of the region's oil and gas or the decline of an agricultural system based on people instead of machines, represent one cause. A less well connected and varied transportation system is another. The modern migration to metropolitan areas, whether for greater work opportunities or the more abundant amenities attractive to various segments of the population, combined with fewer such regional urban magnets, is still another. Yet the northern parishes retain a charm and way of life attractive to many; their future population will remain dependent upon employment opportunities and the publicizing of qualities which will attract or retain population in the smaller cities and towns of the region.

58. Cities of Northern Louisiana, 1990

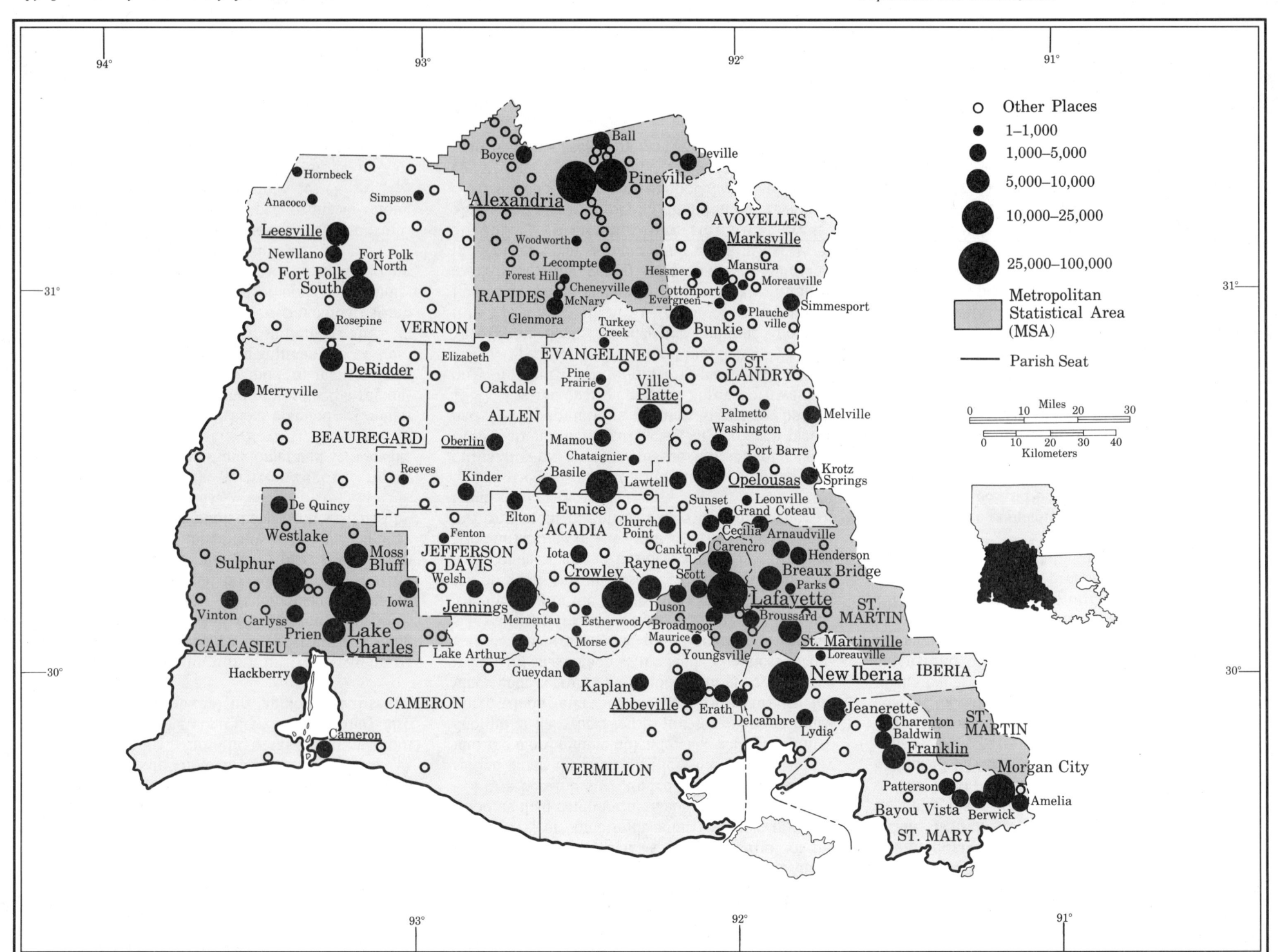

Other Places ○
1–1,000
1,000–5,000
5,000–10,000
10,000–25,000
25,000–100,000

Metropolitan Statistical Area (MSA)

—— Parish Seat

Hornbeck
Boyce
Ball
Deville
Anacoco
Simpson
Alexandria
AVOYELLES
Leesville
Woodworth
Marksville
Newllano
Fort Polk North
Lecompte
Mansura
Moreauville
Fort Polk South
Forest Hill
Hessmer
Cottonport
RAPIDES
Cheneyville
Evergreen
Plauche ville
Simmesport
McNary
Rosepine
Glenmora
Bunkie
VERNON
Turkey Creek
ST. LANDRY
Elizabeth
EVANGELINE
DeRidder
Pine Prairie
Ville Platte
Melville
Merryville
Oakdale
Palmetto
Washington
ALLEN
Mamou
Port Barre
BEAUREGARD
Oberlin
Chataignier
Krotz Springs
Reeves
Kinder
Basile
Lawtell
Opelousas
De Quincy
Eunice
Sunset
Leonville
Grand Coteau
Westlake
Fenton
Church Point
Cankton
Cecilia
Arnaudville
Sulphur
Moss Bluff
JEFFERSON DAVIS
Iota
Carencro
Henderson
Welsh
Crowley
Rayne
Scott
Breaux Bridge
Vinton
Carlyss
Iowa
Jennings
Parks
Prien
Lake Charles
Mermentau
Duson
Lafayette
ST. MARTIN
CALCASIEU
Lake Arthur
Estherwood
Broadmoor
Broussard
Hackberry
Gueydan
Morse
Maurice
St. Martinville
Loreauville
Youngsville
CAMERON
Kaplan
New Iberia
IBERIA
Abbeville
Erath
Jeanerette
ST. MARTIN
Delcambre
Charenton
Cameron
Lydia
Baldwin
VERMILION
Franklin
Morgan City
Patterson
Amelia
Bayou Vista
Berwick
ST. MARY

Miles
0   10   20   30

0   10   20   30   40
Kilometers

Agglomerated settlements come in a variety of sizes. Terms for increasing size—hamlets, villages, towns, and cities—are fuzzy about when the essentially rural hamlet moves on to become a village before metamorphosing into a town. Cities are recognized as larger places, and the term metropolis is used both to denote in absolute terms a very large city as well as to mean, in relative terms, the largest city of a parish, region, or the state.

Hamlets can be thought of as groups of houses—with or without a central focus such as a church or a store—which form what would be essentially a small rural community. The functions of "urban" life begin to appear, but the character remains rural. Crossroads or rural church clusters come readily to mind as hamlets.

As more nonresidential structures and functions appear, these clusters gain greater focus as nonrural communities. The Bureau of the Census offers a typology of sizes based upon population. A village has a population ranging from 150 to 1,000. A town numbers from 1,000 to 5,000. Any place in excess of 5,000 inhabitants is designated a city. Although the lower limit for an "urban" place has been set at 2,500 for those places outside wider urban areas, the life of the village or smaller town is different from that of the hamlet and rural areas.

As cities have grown the Bureau of the Census has devised several other terms of a statistical nature. These terms identify unincorporated population clusters and create in a spatial sense the hinterland of metropolitan areas. A census designated place is any "closely settled population center without corporate limits." The minimum population for such places is five thousand within urbanized areas and one thousand outside such areas. A metropolitan area is any "large population nucleus, together with adjacent communities which have a high degree of economic and social integration with that nucleus." A metropolitan statistical area (MSA) includes one or more central parishes containing the area's main population concentration and an urbanized area with at least fifty thousand inhabitants. The MSA may also include outlying parishes which have close economic and social relationships with the central parishes. These relationships must have a specific level of commuting to the central parishes and must also meet certain standards regarding metropolitan character such as population density, urban population, and population growth. Although such entities are creations of the census, they represent real concentrations of urban life and provide useful measures of the magnetic forces exerted by major urban centers.

Much of southwestern Louisiana developed cities at a later date than did other parts of the state. The colonial riverine outposts and settlements—Opelousas, St. Martinville, New Iberia, and others—sprang up, sometimes alongside the existing Indian villages. However, the prairies and pine forests and swamps remained largely the preserve of the rancher and trapper. As transportation improved and new technologies opened the prairie to rice cultivation and the forest to lumbering, these areas came alive with small towns. Some towns grew into urban centers; others withered with the passing of natural resources. Modern centers grew with the development of oil and gas as well as the military at Camp, then Fort Polk.

In 1990 a total of 106 central places were located in sixteen southwestern Louisiana parishes. Of this total more than half (55) had 1990 populations greater than they had in 1980, this during a decade in which the state's total population grew but slightly. No one city numbered more than 100,000, although Lafayette at 94,440 edged toward that number. Lake Charles (70,580), Alexandria (49,188), and New Iberia (31,838) were the only other cities in excess of 25,000. Alexandria, Lafayette, and Lake Charles represent the three MSAs in this area of the state; Alexandria may lose that designation after the closing of nearby England Air Force Base in 1992.

Only twenty-six places had fewer than 1,000 population, and thirty-four numbered between 1,000 and 2,500. These sixty places accounted for 57 percent of all such places in the region but only 11 percent (67,730) of the total population of the places. However, only one parish—Cameron—lacked a single urban place as defined by the Bureau of the Census.

These sixteen parishes had a total 1990 population of 1,046,766—25 percent of the state's total (4,219,973). This represented the same proportion as the 1980 population figures for region and state—1,030,551 and 4,205,900, respectively. Seven of the sixteen parishes had gained population between 1980 and 1990, placing this region between the mostly declining in numbers of the northern parishes and the mostly gaining parishes of the southeast.

Copyright © 1995 by the University of Oklahoma Press

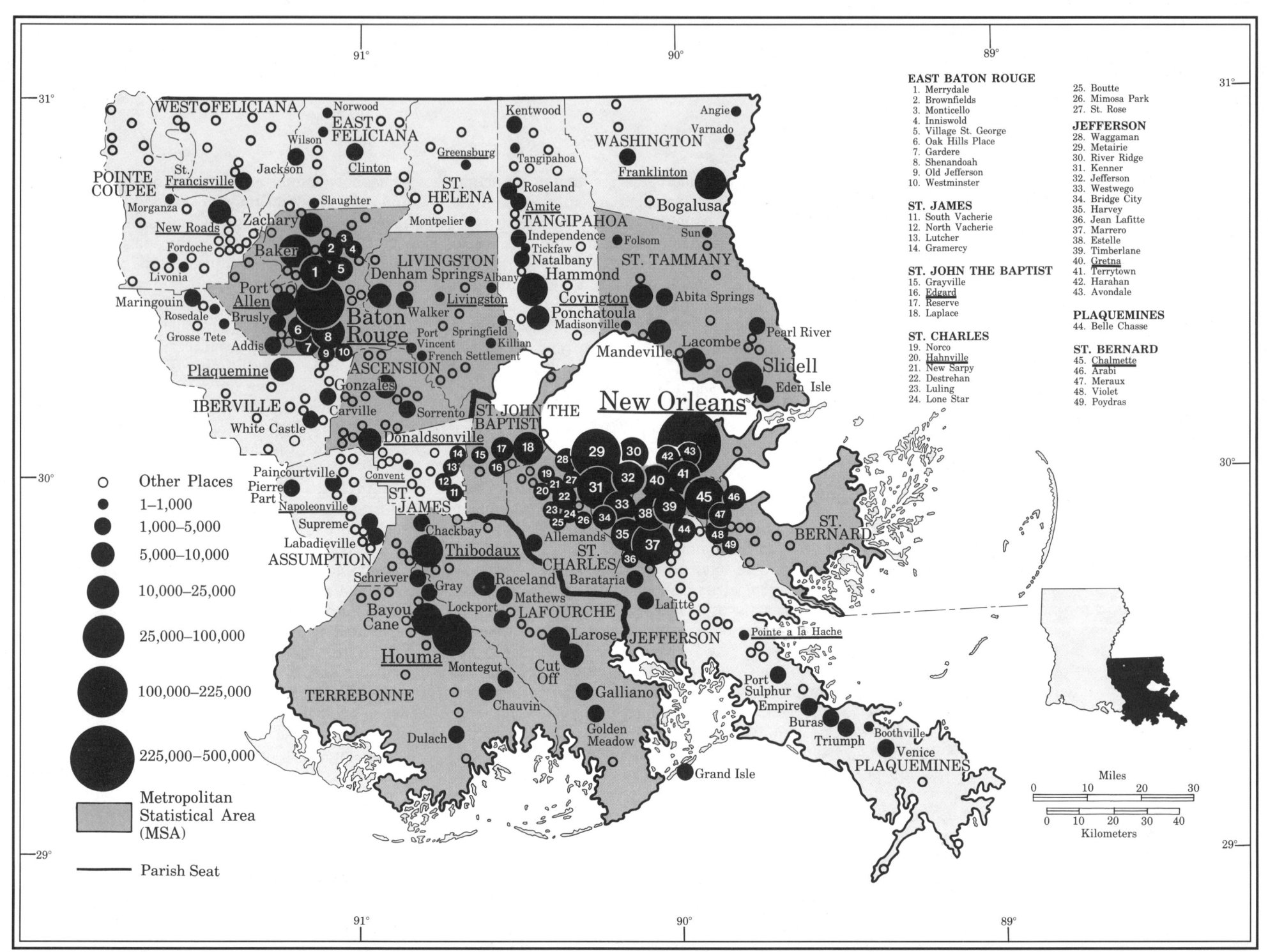

EAST BATON ROUGE
1. Merrydale
2. Brownfields
3. Monticello
4. Inniswold
5. Village St. George
6. Oak Hills Place
7. Gardere
8. Shenandoah
9. Old Jefferson
10. Westminster

ST. JAMES
11. South Vacherie
12. North Vacherie
13. Lutcher
14. Gramercy

ST. JOHN THE BAPTIST
15. Grayville
16. Edgard
17. Reserve
18. Laplace

ST. CHARLES
19. Norco
20. Hahnville
21. New Sarpy
22. Destrehan
23. Luling
24. Lone Star

25. Boutte
26. Mimosa Park
27. St. Rose

JEFFERSON
28. Waggaman
29. Metairie
30. River Ridge
31. Kenner
32. Jefferson
33. Westwego
34. Bridge City
35. Harvey
36. Jean Lafitte
37. Marrero
38. Estelle
39. Timberlane
40. Gretna
41. Terrytown
42. Harahan
43. Avondale

PLAQUEMINES
44. Belle Chasse

ST. BERNARD
45. Chalmette
46. Arabi
47. Meraux
48. Violet
49. Poydras

Other Places

○ 1–1,000

● 1,000–5,000

● 5,000–10,000

● 10,000–25,000

● 25,000–100,000

● 100,000–225,000

● 225,000–500,000

Metropolitan
Statistical Area
(MSA)

—— Parish Seat

Miles

Kilometers

Cities and towns serve various functions. Some functions represent the reason for the city's founding. Other functions may be added, while the original falls away. Many places have several functions, others only one.

In addition to their common focus as an economic center, five general categories of town functions may be used to classify Louisiana's central places: (1) transportation nodes; (2) dormitory or bedroom communities; (3) adjuncts to military bases; (4) civil government centers; and (5) physical and cultural resource centers.

Transportation nodes exist at the intersection of various transportation routes. Such sites may be at the connection of a hinterland to a water (or rail) route. Other centers may exist at the intersection of railroad lines or of highways. At any point where passengers or goods may need to "turn" from one route to another, transportation centers result.

Dormitory or bedroom communities have resulted from the suburbanization of society. As a result of the ease of commuting afforded by first interurban rail lines, then buses and automobiles, populations have shifted outward, creating places of residence distant from places of work.

Military towns exist to serve the various units of the armed forces situated about the state. Air bases, army camps or forts, and naval bases are today the modern descendants of frontier posts with small garrisons. The middle of the twentieth century witnessed a burgeoning of these posts, and the closing decades of the century have seen the beginning of closures with accompanying economic disruption.

Civil government centers exist at any level. The expansion of federal agencies and services beginning with the New Deal in the 1930s has brought federal work to many regional centers. State government itself began greatly to expand beginning with the governorship of Huey P. Long; this expansion has grown still more since World War II. Parish and local governments have increased as well. The most easily identifiable of such centers are the state capital and the parish seats, but the increase in services has affected more than just these places.

Physical and cultural resource centers have over time grown up to exploit the natural resources of an area. Lumber towns, oil and gas centers, salt and sulphur extractive centers, and so on, represent the majority of these centers. Others, however, exploit the natural setting or cultural resources to cater to the tourist trade; older spa areas have been supplanted by modern purveyors of services for the increased free time among the state's (and nation's) population (Map 98).

In 22 southeastern Louisiana parishes, the 1990 census located some 137 places. Of these, some 69 (half) were census-designated places, by far the largest number in any of the three sections. Three cities had populations in excess of 100,000: the state's first, second, and fourth cities, New Orleans (496,938), Baton Rouge (219,531), and Metairie (149,428). Four other cities ranged between 25,000 and 100,000: Kenner (72,033), Marrero (36,671), Chalmette (31,860), and Houma (30,495). Of these seven cities, Metairie, Marrero, and Chalmette were census-designated. Three metropolitan statistical areas (MSAs) are to be found in this section: New Orleans, Baton Rouge, and Houma-Thibodaux.

At the lower end of the spectrum, this section counted only thirty-one places of fewer than one thousand residents each. A further twenty-seven had more than one thousand but fewer than the census urban cut-off of twenty-five hundred. Only two parishes—St. Helena and West Feliciana—lacked a single population center of over twenty-five hundred.

These twenty-two parishes accounted for 2,243,612 people in 1990, 53 percent of the state's total of 4,219,973. Fifteen of the twenty-two parishes experienced a population gain from 1980 to 1990, representing more than half of the civil subdivisions gaining in population. However, the proportional share of the state's total did not change from 1980, when 2,219,048 of 4,205,900 citizens of the state lived in this section.

These parishes are among the earliest settled in the state. The rivers and bayous of southern Louisiana offered not only fertile soils for cultivation but also the only swift means of early commerce. Both town and plantation society represented agglomerated settlements, the larger plantations themselves small villages, each with its central economic focus. In time the river cities, as well as others, attracted railroads, then highways, to reach out into the hinterlands to draw more commerce their way. The exploitation of land and water added to the economic livelihood of city and town, whether that exploited resource be fish, lumber, oil, tourism, or something else. The presence of the capital in this section for practically the entire history of the state has led to growth resulting from the civil functions of that government.

Copyright © 1995 by the University of Oklahoma Press

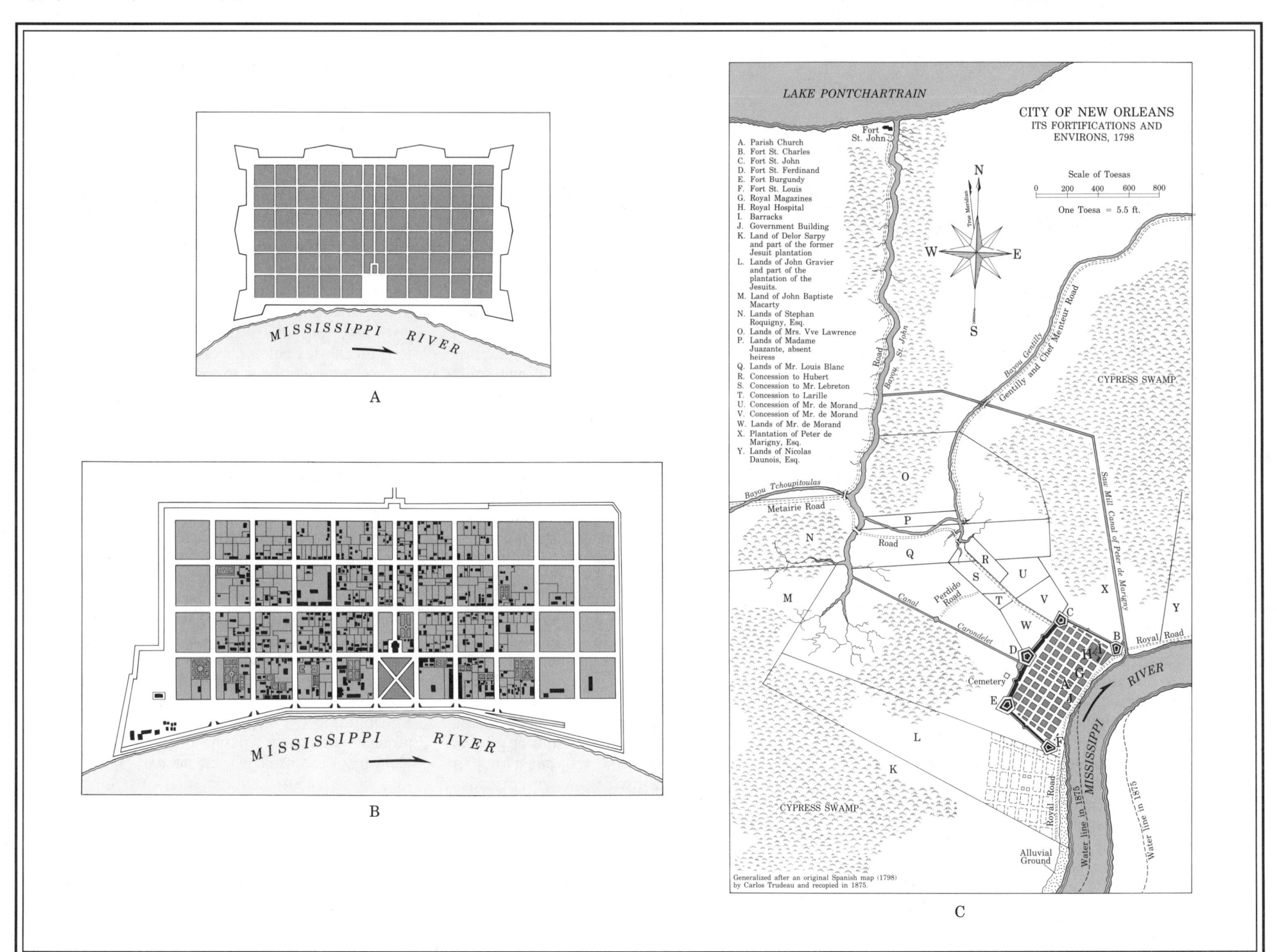

A

B

CITY OF NEW ORLEANS
ITS FORTIFICATIONS AND
ENVIRONS, 1798

A. Parish Church
B. Fort St. Charles
C. Fort St. John
D. Fort St. Ferdinand
E. Fort Burgundy
F. Fort St. Louis
G. Royal Magazines
H. Royal Hospital
I. Barracks
J. Government Building
K. Land of Delor Sarpy and part of the former Jesuit plantation
L. Lands of John Gravier and part of the plantation of the Jesuits.
M. Land of John Baptiste Macarty
N. Lands of Stephan Roquigny, Esq.
O. Lands of Mrs. Vve Lawrence
P. Lands of Madame Juazante, absent heiress
Q. Lands of Mr. Louis Blanc
R. Concession to Hubert
S. Concession to Mr. Lebreton
T. Concession to Larille
U. Concession of Mr. de Morand
V. Concession of Mr. de Morand
W. Lands of Mr. de Morand
X. Plantation of Peter de Marigny, Esq.
Y. Lands of Nicolas Daunois, Esq.

Scale of Toesas

0   200   400   600   800

One Toesa = 5.5 ft.

LAKE PONTCHARTRAIN

CYPRESS SWAMP

CYPRESS SWAMP

MISSISSIPPI RIVER

Generalized after an original Spanish map (1798) by Carlos Trudeau and recopied in 1875.

C

61. LA NOUVELLE ORLEANS AND NUEVA ORLEANS
New Orleans in the Eighteenth Century

New Orleans's beginnings as Louisiana's premier city seemed inauspicious. The French proprietors recognized the necessity of a permanent presence on the Mississippi River. Jean Baptiste Le Moyne, Sieur de Bienville, had bluffed the British into withdrawing at the English Turn in 1699, but France's rival's designs on the river and its hinterland remained undisguised. Thus, in 1717, the Company of the West (predecessor of the Company of the Indies) authorized the founding of a new settlement. This planned city would be named after the Duke of Orleans, regent and, more importantly, protector of the company's founder, the financier extraordinaire John Law.

Equally inauspicious was the site selected for the new city. A high ground would have been preferable, but no flood-free location existed along the Mississippi south of present-day Baton Rouge. The lower delta consisted of canebrakes and cypress swamps punctuated by higher natural levees along existing and abandoned stream courses. In addition to a high-ground site, access to a "backdoor" route to the Gulf less treacherous than navigating the mouths of the Mississippi also was necessary.

In 1717, Bienville chose a location near the head of Bayou St. Jean (John), a short stream feeding into Lake Pontchartrain but with headwaters less than two miles from the Mississippi. This site had long been a portage for the Indians. The surrounding region had begun to emerge above sea level only a few thousand year earlier, when the St. Bernard delta complex was laid down by the Mississippi. In the subsequent centuries, natural levees had formed to provide some higher terrain on which to plant the city. Still, much of the region lay below actual sea level. In the spring of 1718, initial clearing of the site began.

A design following the convention of the period was laid down in March 1721 by the colony's engineer, Pierre Le Blond de la Tour; Map A shows an augmented plan drawn up by his assistant, Adrien de Pauger, in 1724. A gridiron which would eventually measure eleven blocks wide and six blocks deep was platted on the cane- and cypress-covered landscape next to the river. Each block stood three hundred feet to the side, with lots in each square facing streets both parallel and perpendicular to the river. A central square to be used for ceremonial occasions—the Place d'Armes (now Jackson Square)—stood in the center of the first row of squares. Around this square the church and major civil and military government buildings were planned.

Only gradually was the gridiron filled in by actual citizenry and buildings. At the close of 1721 the city's population stood at just over 370. Still, in 1722, New Orleans became the capital of Louisiana and would remain so until 1813. Hurricanes wrecked the early palmetto-thatched huts which had been erected; in each case the city was rebuilt, but only gradually were these rude structures replaced by wooden and later still by brick ones. Warehouses were erected along the river's levees, themselves augmented to lessen the danger of floods, although floods still came. By the middle of the seventeenth century (Map B) the front two-thirds of the tiers had largely been settled.

A major fire in 1788 destroyed most of the city, and two other fires damaged it in 1792 and 1794. A new construction code thereafter required structures of more than one story to be manufactured of brick or adobe and topped with tile roofs. By this time the colony had passed into Spanish hands. The city which arose from the fire-ravaged landscape resembled Spain moreso than France.

Water remained the easiest means of transport until the railroads and improved "highways" of the nineteenth century. Thus, in the 1790s Governor Carondelet had a canal built which connected Bayou St. John with a turning basin for small ships at the city's back door, the latter surviving today in the name of Basin Street. Embryonic roads stretched out along the natural levees both up and down the Mississippi, connecting the city to its plantation region. As Louisiana prepared for yet another transfer via the Louisiana Purchase of 1803, the population of New Orleans proper stood at about ten thousand. Of this total most were of French or Spanish extraction, but English, Irish, and American backgrounds were also to be found. One-third of the total consisted of free African Americans or slaves. More citizens resided on the plantations surrounding the city. The original La Tour–Pauger plan—the present Vieux Carre—was already poised for expansion into planned but as yet unfilled suburbs (Map C). Despite a seemingly impossible site—nestled along the Mississippi—this outpost on the river had become the capital and largest city in the colony.

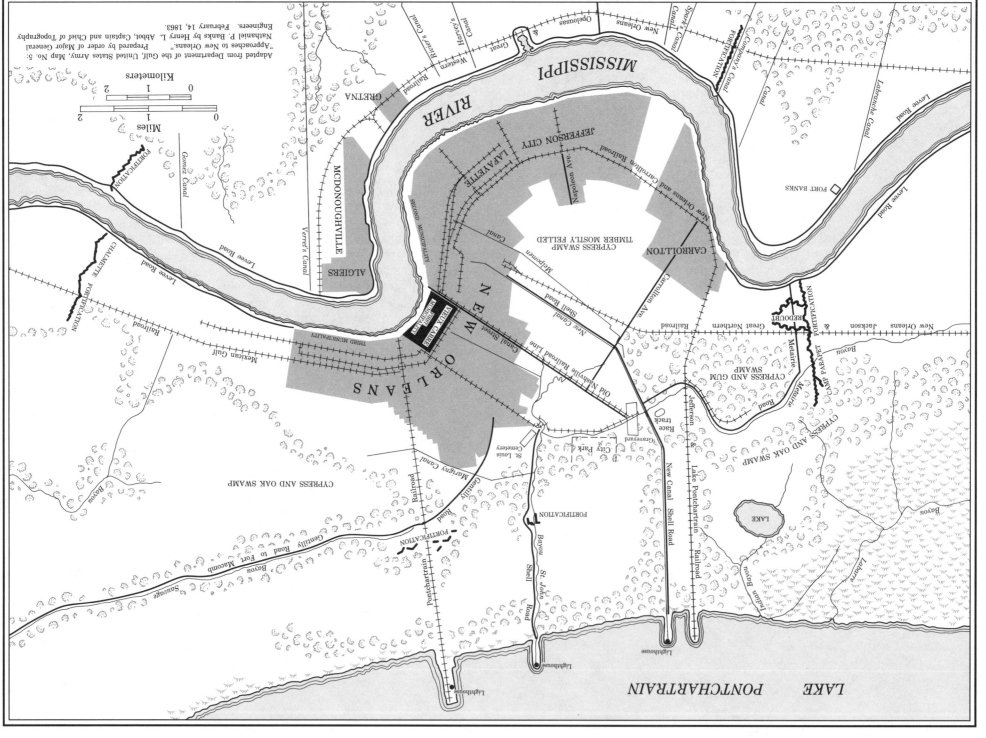

Population and Urbanization

Copyright © 1995 by the University of Oklahoma Press

Adapted from Department of the Gulf, United States Army, Map No. 5: "Approaches to New Orleans." Prepared by order of Major General Nathaniel P. Banks by Henry L. Abbot, Captain and Chief of Topography Engineers. February 14, 1863.

Miles

Kilometers

LAKE PONTCHARTRAIN

MISSISSIPPI RIVER

NEW ORLEANS

GRETNA

MCDONOUGHVILLE

ALGIERS

CHALMETTE

JEFFERSON CITY

LAFAYETTE

CARROLTON

CYPRESS SWAMP TIMBER MOSTLY FELLED

CYPRESS AND GUM SWAMP

CYPRESS AND OAK SWAMP

VIEUX CARRE FIRST MUNICIPALITY

SECOND MUNICIPALITY

THIRD MUNICIPALITY

FORT BANKS

REDOUBT

CAMP PARAPET

FORTIFICATION

Lighthouse

LAKE

62. NEW ORLEANS, 1863

The first half of the nineteenth century witnessed the development of New Orleans into the premier urban center of not only Louisiana but also the entire South. By the outbreak of the Civil War, however, the city's zenith in the nation's economic and population history had been reached. This growth and beginning eclipse resulted in large measure from a single factor—the Mississippi River as the highway of American commerce.

At the time of the Louisiana Purchase the city's population was estimated to be 10,000. Seven years later the first U.S. census for the new territory showed that population to have risen by over 72 percent, to 17,242; this made New Orleans the largest city west of the Appalachians and fifth largest in the entire nation. Over the next three decades the city's population continued to increase dramatically—by 58 percent, to 27,176, in 1820; by 70 percent, to 46,082, in 1830; and by 122 percent, to 102,193, in 1840, almost a 500 percent increase over the 1810 figure. By 1840, New Orleans was the nation's third city but practically in a tie for second with Baltimore (102,313). The 1840s witnessed a pause in its prolific growth rate—only a 14 percent increase, to 116,375, in 1850—but the following decade saw a 45 percent increase, to 168,675 in 1860.

Over the course of the century the city's old walls had been razed, as had the forts, and the moats had been filled in. The Vieux Carre was now bounded by boulevards: Esplanade, Rampart, and Canal. Plantations both upriver and downriver were developed into new suburbs (originally called faubourgs and named for the former plantations from whence they came). Americans settled upriv-er, while Creole spillover from the old town and newer immigrants settled downriver. The resulting street pattern for each new addition to the city limits reflected the old arpent landownership system, with major streets running perpendicular to the river—following the land boundaries—and cross-streets tending to parallel its course.

From 1836 to 1852 the city was divided into three self-governing "municipalities." The French Quarter constituted the First Municipality. Upriver, the new "American" city formed the Second Municipality, while its opposite number downriver—the spillover of the Vieux Carre and new European immigrants—constituted the Third. Adjacent to the Second Municipality was the city of Lafayette, while still further upriver were the cities of Jefferson and Carrollton, connected by commerce and transportation to the urban center.

In 1852 the municipalities were united and renamed districts—the Second Municipality, the First District; the First Municipality, the Second District; and the Third Municipality, the Third District. Lafayette became the Fourth District. The old municipality terms continued on maps, however, as did even the old faubourgs.

New Orleans's growth to its commercial zenith was tied to the river. The Mississippi and its tributaries provided the only low-cost method of transporting the commodities of the entire Midwest to market. New Orleans was the preeminent port—the gateway to the river—in the eighteenth and early nineteenth centuries. Indeed, a desire to control the river had led to the Louisiana Purchase (Map 31). The invention of the steamboat allowed transportation of goods in bulk upstream, whereas before only downstream, current-driven commerce was possible for such goods. As long as the Mississippi remained the highway of commerce, New Orleans's fortunes waxed.

The economic transformation which would bring the rapid expansion of New Orleans to a close and contribute to the rise of its urban, commercial rivals was the development of alternate methods of low-cost transportation: canals and the railroad. The Erie Canal in 1825 provided an east-west route between the Old Northwest and the East Coast ports much shorter than the downriver and coastal trade. Railroad fever began in the late 1820s and accelerated thereafter. However, the iron horse did not immediately engender the same enthusiasm in New Orleans as elsewhere. The Crescent City, which before 1850 saw a wide variety of midwestern goods arrive for export, by 1860 was more concentrated on cotton and sugar and the lower valley trade.

The Civil War with its economic disruptions affected New Orleans but less drastically than much of the rest of the South. Occupied in April 1862 without physical destruction, the city remained occupied until the end of Reconstruction in 1877. In 1863, Gen. Nathaniel P. Banks, commander of the Union forces, directed the creation of a map which formed the basis for that shown above. For all practical purposes the city remained tied to the natural levee system. New canals and railroads connected the various parts of the city and environs to Lake Pontchartrain and beyond. Surrounding the urbanized area were the remaining swamps and other rural areas.

Copyright © 1995 by the University of Oklahoma Press

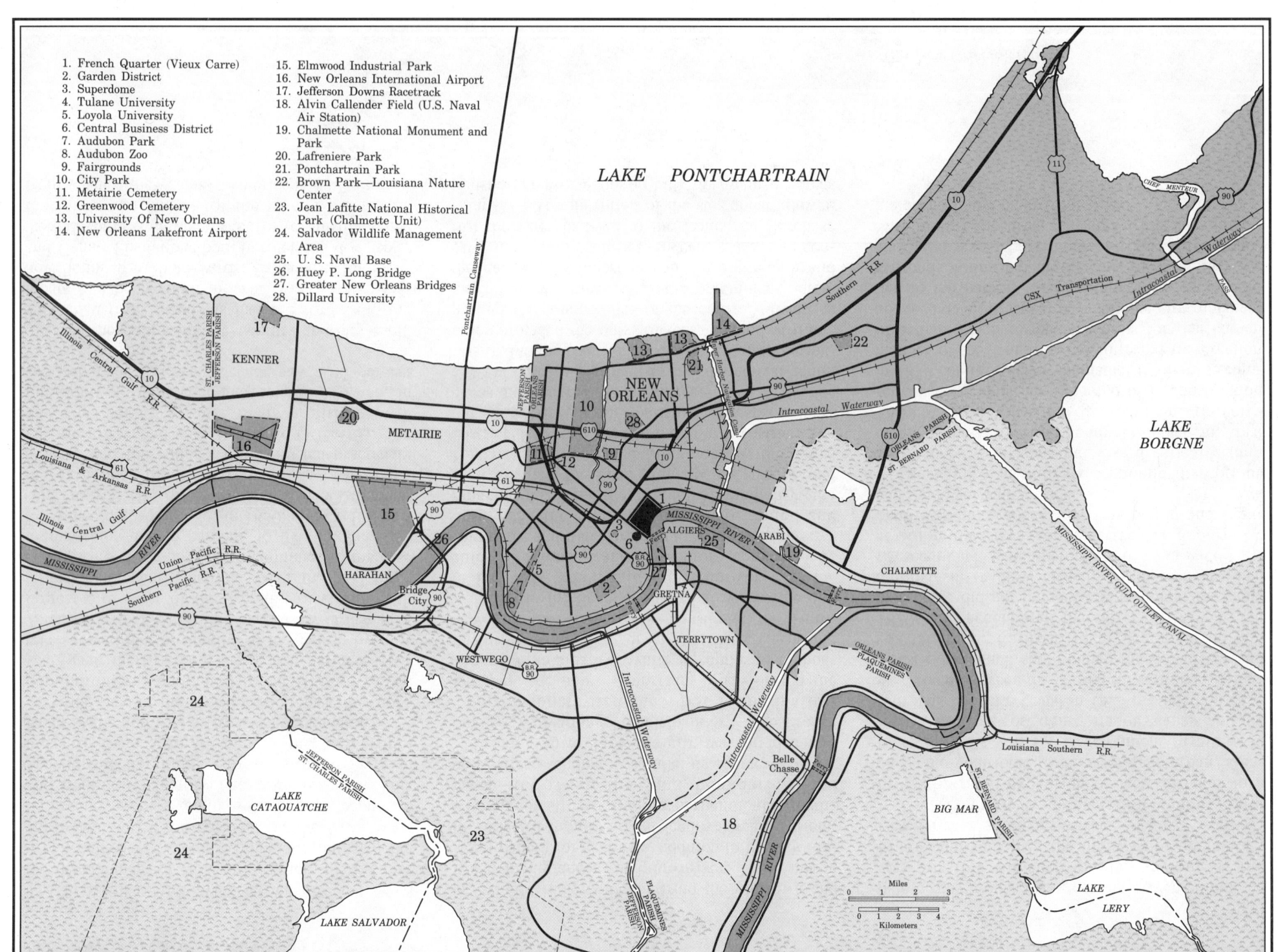

1. French Quarter (Vieux Carre)
2. Garden District
3. Superdome
4. Tulane University
5. Loyola University
6. Central Business District
7. Audubon Park
8. Audubon Zoo
9. Fairgrounds
10. City Park
11. Metairie Cemetery
12. Greenwood Cemetery
13. University Of New Orleans
14. New Orleans Lakefront Airport
15. Elmwood Industrial Park
16. New Orleans International Airport
17. Jefferson Downs Racetrack
18. Alvin Callender Field (U.S. Naval Air Station)
19. Chalmette National Monument and Park
20. Lafreniere Park
21. Pontchartrain Park
22. Brown Park—Louisiana Nature Center
23. Jean Lafitte National Historical Park (Chalmette Unit)
24. Salvador Wildlife Management Area
25. U. S. Naval Base
26. Huey P. Long Bridge
27. Greater New Orleans Bridges
28. Dillard University

Following the Civil War, New Orleans transformed itself, restructuring its trade, reaching out with new railroad linkages, and reestablishing its role as a regional, if not national, commercial center. In the 125 years following the close of the war, New Orleans expanded to encompass within its metropolitan area, if not its corporate boundaries, portions of six parishes. The New Orleans Metropolitan Statistical Area in 1990 included Jefferson, Orleans, St. Bernard, St. Charles, St. John the Baptist, and St. Tammany parishes and held a population of 1,238,816. New Orleans alone had declined from a 1960 peak of 627,525 to a 1990 figure of 496,938, still enough to mark it the largest city in the state.

The Mississippi River continued as a highway of commerce, but the barge came to replace the steamboat as the common carrier of those goods that did not require speedy delivery. Railroads first reached out as the mode for more rapid transport; the Illinois Central, Southern Pacific, Kansas City Southern, Texas and Pacific, Southern, and Louisville and Nashville systems all focused on New Orleans (Maps 68–70). By the mid-twentieth century, however, the truck and the private automobile had replaced the freight and passenger trains as highways—state, federal, then interstate—snaked across the landscape. The railroad systems largely combined or closed, their past glory reflected in the ballad about the Illinois Central train, "The City of New Orleans."

The port of New Orleans continued its importance. A major period of rebuilding occurred at the turn of the century. The Eads jetties at South Pass built in 1879 symbolized continuing efforts to keep ocean-going vessels moving upriver. A second rebuilding and relocating phase began in the 1960s as the older wharves downtown were removed, replaced in turn by newer facilities to the east. Oil and its products in large measure determine the relative health of the lower Mississippi River ports, including New Orleans.

The great surge in population in the early to mid-nineteenth century was replaced by more modest growth rates thereafter. From 1860 to 1960 the population grew modestly, averaging just over 14 percent per decade. Beginning in 1970, successive censuses have indicated a decline in population within the city limits even as its suburbs expanded. New Orleans has been surpassed as the major Southern urban center, falling behind Atlanta, Dallas–Fort Worth, Houston, and Miami in population.

For much of its history New Orleans had been confined to the higher ground of the natural levees, the lower-lying areas being too easily or permanently flooded. The development of the Wood pump in the city in the late nineteenth century, however, provided the means for high-volume vertical drainage to expel the excess waters into Lake Borgne. In the twentieth century lands were drained and levees extended; development towards Lake Pontchartrain increased. In the 1920s the Lakefront Project actually extended the shoreline three thousand feet offshore by the construction of a seawall and filling in of the enclosure. An additional two thousand acres were thereby created.

Following World War II the suburban boom hit metropolitan New Orleans, extending the urbanized areas into neighboring parishes. A new landscape was created, often homogeneous, particularly since much of it came into being within a relatively short time. The completion of the Lake Pontchartrain Causeway in 1956 and the later interstate highway system opened up the area north and east of the lake, extending the city's "bedroom-community" reach even across the state line into Mississippi.

Today New Orleans is a city caught up in the usual problems of urban America. The central business district has not emptied to so great an extent as elsewhere, thanks to the proximity of the Vieux Carre as well as more modern tourist attractions such as the Superdome and Rivergate complex. Yet these same developments have not met with universal praise or always equitable economic outcomes. The lack of centralized planning outside the Dock Board and the Levee Board has created a patchwork of contrasting wealth and poverty as well as racial and ethnic segregation.

The long-term conservative approach to government, largely the product of generations of old New Orleans families, has in turn been modified by the city's changing racial mixture. The concentrations of blacks in the central city, combined with the civil rights movement, has led to a greater participation by minorities in city government. Meanwhile, the longstanding cultural institutions and attractions of New Orleans—the French Quarter, Bourbon Street, Tulane University, Mardi Gras, and others—have made it a mecca for tourists from the state and elsewhere. New Orleans, unlike any other city in the state and indeed the region, is sui generis—an amalgam of its colonial past and riverine location.

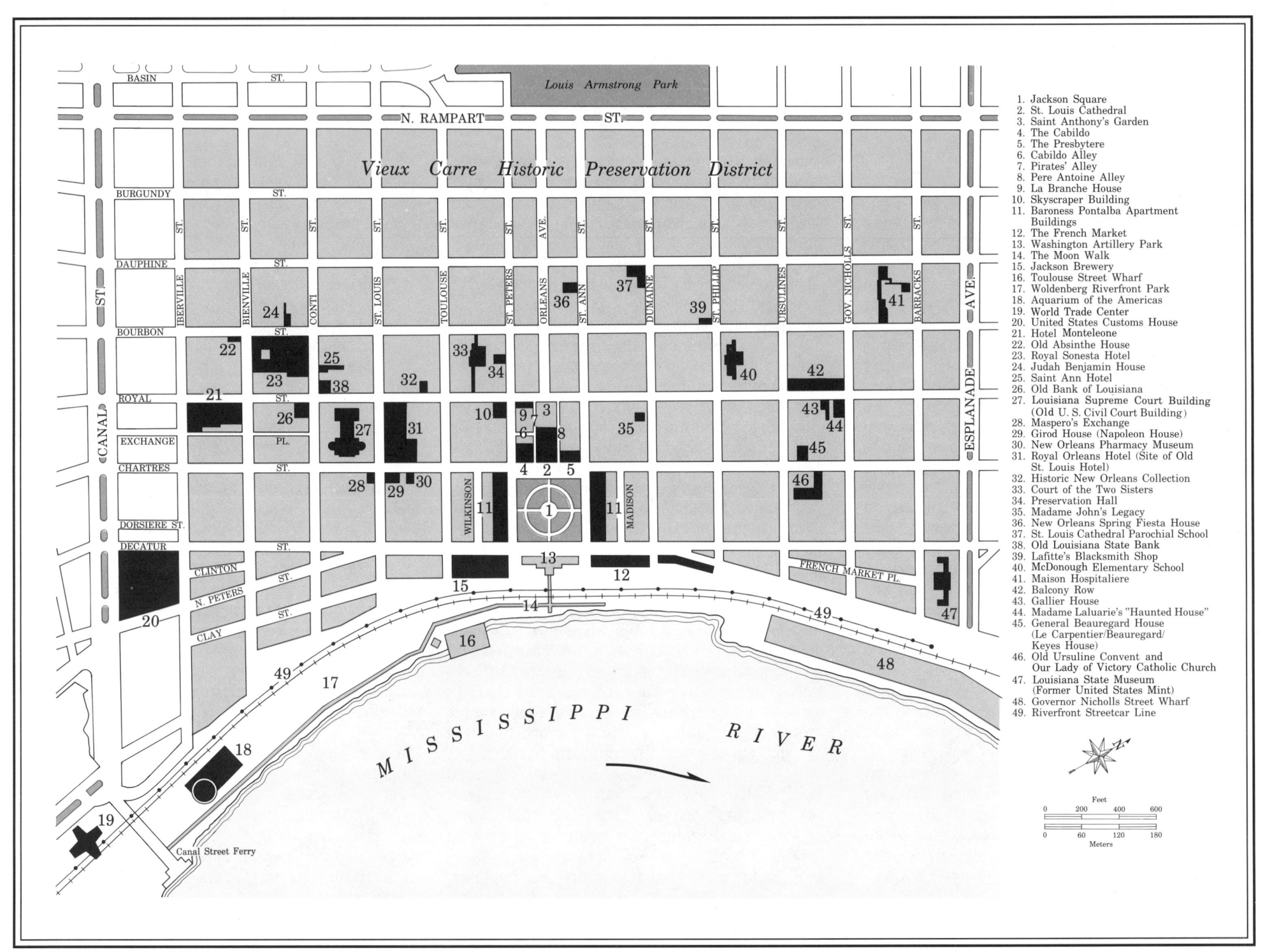

Vieux Carre Historic Preservation District

MISSISSIPPI RIVER

Canal Street Ferry

1. Jackson Square
2. St. Louis Cathedral
3. Saint Anthony's Garden
4. The Cabildo
5. The Presbytere
6. Cabildo Alley
7. Pirates' Alley
8. Pere Antoine Alley
9. La Branche House
10. Skyscraper Building
11. Baroness Pontalba Apartment Buildings
12. The French Market
13. Washington Artillery Park
14. The Moon Walk
15. Jackson Brewery
16. Toulouse Street Wharf
17. Woldenberg Riverfront Park
18. Aquarium of the Americas
19. World Trade Center
20. United States Customs House
21. Hotel Monteleone
22. Old Absinthe House
23. Royal Sonesta Hotel
24. Judah Benjamin House
25. Saint Ann Hotel
26. Old Bank of Louisiana
27. Louisiana Supreme Court Building (Old U. S. Civil Court Building)
28. Maspero's Exchange
29. Girod House (Napoleon House)
30. New Orleans Pharmacy Museum
31. Royal Orleans Hotel (Site of Old St. Louis Hotel)
32. Historic New Orleans Collection
33. Court of the Two Sisters
34. Preservation Hall
35. Madame John's Legacy
36. New Orleans Spring Fiesta House
37. St. Louis Cathedral Parochial School
38. Old Louisiana State Bank
39. Lafitte's Blacksmith Shop
40. McDonough Elementary School
41. Maison Hospitaliere
42. Balcony Row
43. Gallier House
44. Madame Laluarie's "Haunted House"
45. General Beauregard House (Le Carpentier/Beauregard/ Keyes House)
46. Old Ursuline Convent and Our Lady of Victory Catholic Church
47. Louisiana State Museum (Former United States Mint)
48. Governor Nicholls Street Wharf
49. Riverfront Streetcar Line

Feet
0   200   400   600

0   60   120   180
Meters

64. THE FRENCH QUARTER (VIEUX CARRE), 1990

The French Quarter remains the symbol of New Orleans, the image which most readily comes to the public mind when the city's name is mentioned. No less important, the Quarter—the Vieux Carre—anchors the city to its past. The original and most longlasting of the city's neighborhoods, it has survived more often through luck or neglect rather than plan to the present day.

The Quarter is bounded by the river and three boulevards—Esplanade, Rampart, and Canal—which replaced the old city's eighteenth-century walls. Its colonial architecture is largely Spanish rather than French, the city having been rebuilt following the several disastrous fires of the late eighteenth century. Scattered throughout, however, are buildings of newer eras, symbols of what might have happened had the Quarter followed the fate of so many other American cities and kept architecturally current.

The survival of the French Quarter in so much of its original form into the early twentieth century was accidental rather than purposeful. Americans were too busy developing the newer district upriver of the Quarter. Meanwhile, the old Creole families remaining in the district diminished through time by generational emigration. Commercial encroachment by the city's business district combined with the general lack of interest to produce an increasing general decrepitude about the Quarter.

This attitude of benign neglect changed in the 1930s through a combination of influences. Ultimately a 1936 amendment to the state constitution led to the creation on March 3, 1937, of the Vieux Carre Commission to regulate the architectural integrity of the Quarter. A previous ordinance passed by the city in 1924 had never been enforced. Rehabilitation of existing structures by the WPA had helped create new interest in the area. The commission's authority was frequently challenged, with cases being carried up to the state supreme court. A particular complaint resounded that the group's power went beyond the preservation of individual historic structures to the survival of the ambiance of an entire historic district—the *tout ensemble* concept. In each case, however, the authority of the commission was upheld.

The Quarter today contains a variety of juxtaposed architectural styles. The old Ursuline Convent on Chartres remains the sole French Colonial structure in the district. The Cabildo and the Presbytere on Jackson Square are the most important surviving structures of the Spanish period; other buildings from the period were later "modernized" to fit the prevailing custom. The Greek Revival and other antebellum structures include the Pontalba Buildings and the rebuilt St. Louis Cathedral, also facing Jackson Square. Cast iron galleries became a prominent feature of the period. The post–Civil War period saw little activity outside commercial buildings and "shotgun" rental houses.

The twentieth century early on saw the destruction of entire blocks, as when the original buildings were razed to erect the Civil Courts Building, now being renovated for the State Supreme Court. Fires also destroyed other older buildings, which in turn were replaced by newer styles of architecture. Following the creation of the Vieux Carre Commission, new structures were to be in the traditional style of the French Quarter, which policy allowed for a wide variety of interpretations.

The second half of the century has seen a major battle over and defeat of the proposed "Riverfront Expressway," which would have cut off the Quarter from the river even more so than the commercial waterfront had previously done. The removal of many of the old wharves and the defeat of the expressway has enabled the Quarter, particularly the prime tourist area around Jackson Square, to once again become open from the river. The rehabilitation of existing buildings—even newer ones like the old Jax Brewery—has also attracted more visitors while maintaining the integrity of the facade, though not always without debate. Recently the proposal for a general development of the Mississippi waterfront—a grand design titled Riverfront 2000—has engendered still further discussion. The newly completed Aquarium of the Americas plus other planned convention and museum facilities will fill the site between Canal Street and Elysian Fields. For a historic district which the National Trust for Historic Preservation has placed on its most endangered list for historic sites, because of earlier development, such proposals can only add fuel to an already lengthy debate.

In one sense the French Quarter has come full circle. Its site on the Mississippi was dismissed early on by many in the French colony as unworkable. The persistence of the entire city has in large part been a result of human battles against nature, particularly the flooding Mississippi and its delta landscape. The Vieux Carre, as the longest-surviving portion of a city three decades away from its tricentennial, once again is in the midst of a debate over survival.

Copyright © 1995 by the University of Oklahoma Press

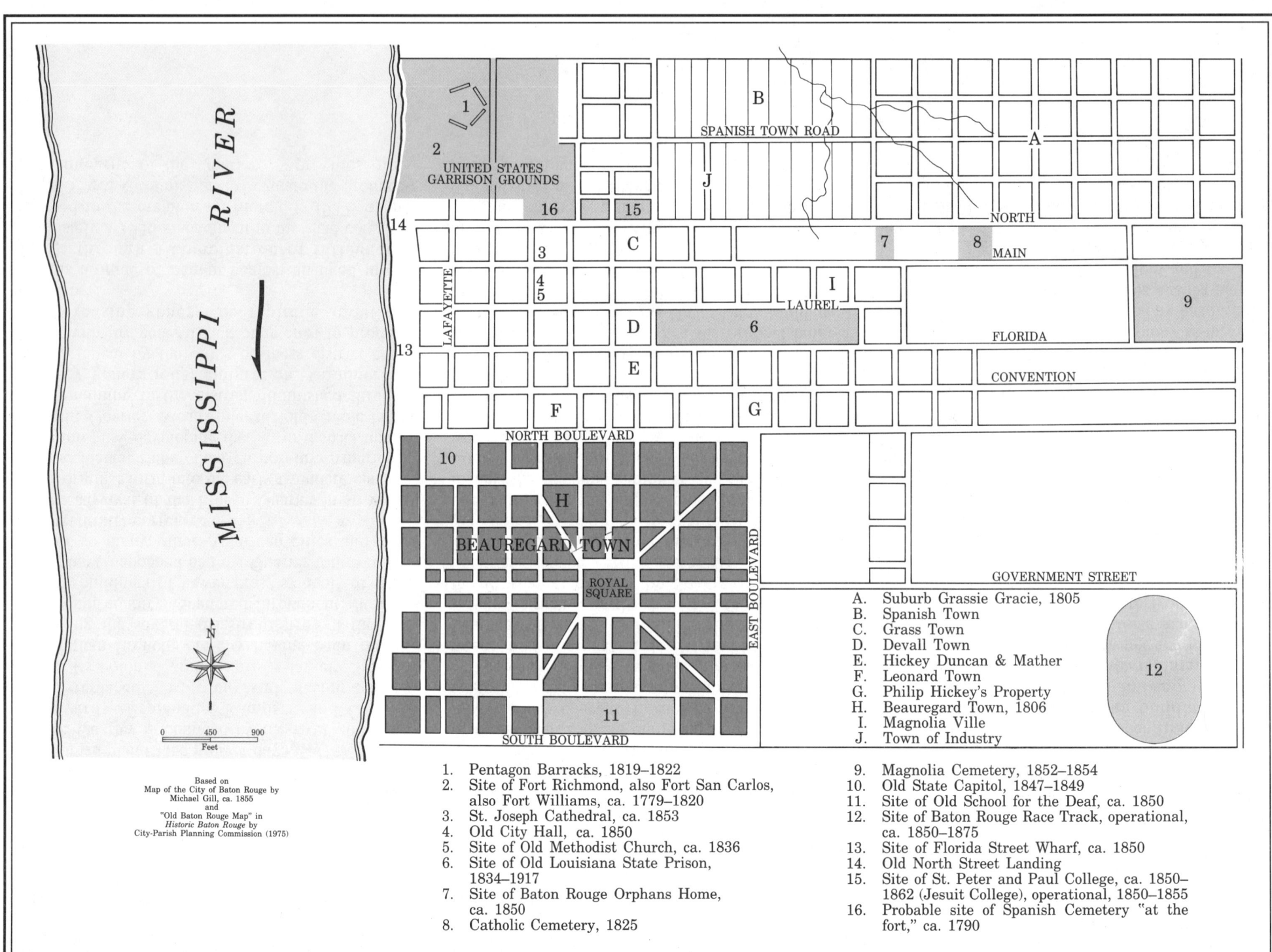

1. Pentagon Barracks, 1819–1822
2. Site of Fort Richmond, also Fort San Carlos, also Fort Williams, ca. 1779–1820
3. St. Joseph Cathedral, ca. 1853
4. Old City Hall, ca. 1850
5. Site of Old Methodist Church, ca. 1836
6. Site of Old Louisiana State Prison, 1834–1917
7. Site of Baton Rouge Orphans Home, ca. 1850
8. Catholic Cemetery, 1825
9. Magnolia Cemetery, 1852–1854
10. Old State Capitol, 1847–1849
11. Site of Old School for the Deaf, ca. 1850
12. Site of Baton Rouge Race Track, operational, ca. 1850–1875
13. Site of Florida Street Wharf, ca. 1850
14. Old North Street Landing
15. Site of St. Peter and Paul College, ca. 1850–1862 (Jesuit College), operational, 1850–1855
16. Probable site of Spanish Cemetery "at the fort," ca. 1790

A. Suburb Grassie Gracie, 1805
B. Spanish Town
C. Grass Town
D. Devall Town
E. Hickey Duncan & Mather
F. Leonard Town
G. Philip Hickey's Property
H. Beauregard Town, 1806
I. Magnolia Ville
J. Town of Industry

Based on
Map of the City of Baton Rouge by
Michael Gill, ca. 1855
and
"Old Baton Rouge Map" in
Historic Baton Rouge by
City-Parish Planning Commission (1975)

65. BATON ROUGE, ca. 1855

The city of Baton Rouge originated as a concession granted by the crown to the D'Artaguette family and located on the east bank of the Mississippi five leagues (seventeen miles) upriver of Bayou Manchac. Within that parcel of land stood a bluff on which Iberville and the members of his party on March 17, 1699, spotted a post bloodied from fish and bear heads hung there. In the Choctaw language that post was termed *istrouma*, which in English was translated as "reddened post," which in turn in French was *baton rouge*. The bluffs on which *le baton rouge* was located represent the first flood-free landscape as one moves upriver on the Mississippi.

The settlement at the D'Artaguette concession faded from history in the 1720s, for reasons which remain unknown. Not until 1763 was another settlement known to be there, but this second founding would be permanent. Following the close of the French and Indian War in 1763, the British gained control of the Florida Parishes (Maps 27 and 28) and thus the site of *le baton rouge,* then near the southwest corner of British North America, facing the Spanish empire beyond the Mississippi and the Bayou Manchac.

The British established Fort Bute on Bayou Manchac and Fort New Richmond north of present-day Baton Rouge. Plantations were granted to British citizens in the vicinity of the forts, as well as elsewhere in West Florida. No town per se existed at the forts, but an agricultural and trading economy centered on these plantations flourished throughout the two decades of British ownership, interrupted by the Spanish invasion during the American Revolution (Map 30) and the transfer to Spanish authority following its conclusion.

The Spanish gave New Richmond the name Fort San Carlos, and official Spanish policy, though moderated by knowledgeable local officials, still differed markedly from British. Still, most of the British as well as newly American landholders remained on their grants, having pledged allegiance to a new imperial master. By the 1780s Baton Rouge had begun to develop, with its earliest forms, Spanish Town and Beauregard Town, laid out by about 1805–1806. As with New Orleans, these divisions largely followed the grants made on the arpent surveys. However, since the Mississippi here flowed generally north-to-south, the resulting street patterns differed from those of New Orleans, except where the dreams of the drafters offered other embellishments.

The United States acquired Louisiana from Napoleonic France in 1803, and Spanish Florida was thus separated from the rest of the Spanish empire by the new American nation. In 1810 the West Florida Rebellion occurred (Map 35), and Baton Rouge was captured by the rebels. West Florida passed into a brief independence and then was annexed to the United States, with that portion west of the Pearl River added to the Territory of Orleans and entering the Union as the new state of Louisiana in 1812. At the time, Baton Rouge consisted of the fort, a dozen frame houses, and several dozen cabins.

In 1810, Baton Rouge had again become the name of the site; seven years later the town was incorporated. Spanish Town and Beauregard Town grew gradually, although the latter—splendidly drawn up by its founder—did not achieve the shape of his vision until after the Civil War. Other, smaller villages within the overall settled area of the "town" were Grass Town, Devall Town, Hickey, Duncan, Mather, and Leonard Town.

As with New Orleans, the economic life of early Baton Rouge was tied to the Mississippi River. River commerce and the steamboat led to economic growth, tied closely with the health of the surrounding agricultural enterprises. With Louisiana's strategic position in the Old Southwest, Baton Rouge became a military post as well; from 1819 to 1822 the Pentagon Barracks were built near the site of the old fort.

In 1846, Baton Rouge became the capital of Louisiana and remained so until the state was occupied by Union troops in the Civil War. It attained its position as capital from the anti–New Orleans feelings of Protestant Louisiana. When a new site had to be chosen, Baton Rouge presented the opportunity to place the capital near, if not actually in, the Crescent City. A capitol was built by 1850 in the form of a medieval castle; this burned to the walls during the Union occupation in 1862, then was rebuilt and survives to the present. Other state projects also were built in the new capital.

By the 1840s the city's population had begun to grow. Its 1840 total of 2,269 more than doubled to 5,429 in 1860. (The respective New Orleans figures were 102,193 and 168,675.) French, British, and Spanish descendants of the colonial settlers combined with slaves and free African Americans as well as newer American and European migrants. Baton Rouge was the largest city outside the New Orleans environs.

Copyright © 1995 by the University of Oklahoma Press

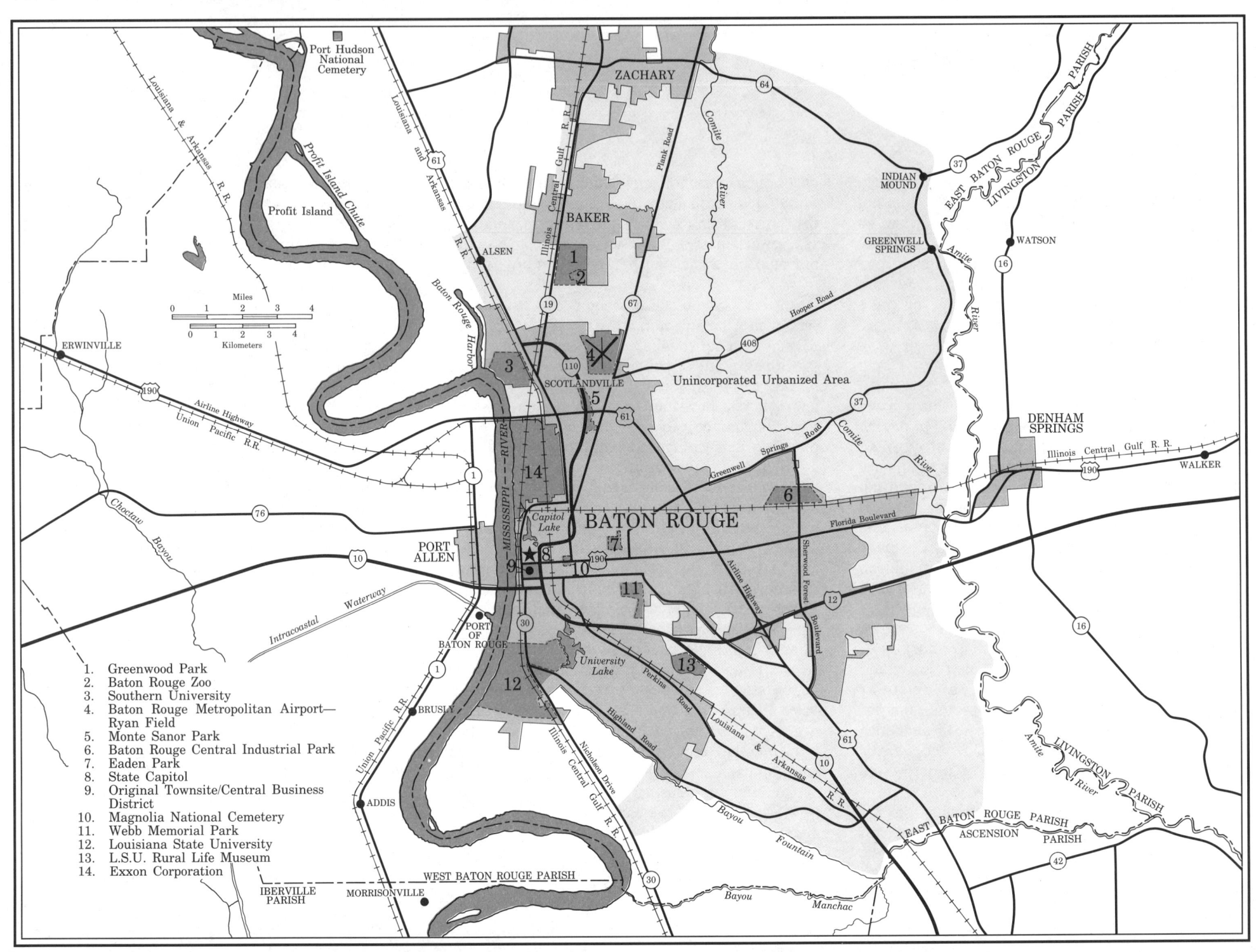

1. Greenwood Park
2. Baton Rouge Zoo
3. Southern University
4. Baton Rouge Metropolitan Airport—
   Ryan Field
5. Monte Sanor Park
6. Baton Rouge Central Industrial Park
7. Eaden Park
8. State Capitol
9. Original Townsite/Central Business
   District
10. Magnolia National Cemetery
11. Webb Memorial Park
12. Louisiana State University
13. L.S.U. Rural Life Museum
14. Exxon Corporation

From 1862 to 1877, the end of Reconstruction, Baton Rouge was an occupied city. During the course of the Civil War the Confederate capital had departed to Opelousas, thence Alexandria, and finally Shreveport; New Orleans remained the Federal capital during the war and for years thereafter. Naval and land engagements, particularly the battle on August 5, 1862, had devastated much of Baton Rouge. This devastation, coupled with the aftereffects of the war itself, affected not only property but also spirit and investment. Even the reinstatement of the capital in the city—postponed until 1882—deprived the city of that modest infusion of activity into a rather moribund community.

The return of the capital coincided with the arrival of another boon to the community: direct railroad connections. Before this time only the Baton Rouge, Grosse Tete, and Opelousas Railroad was in operation, offering limited rail service to the west, provided that one ferried across the Mississippi to Port Allen. Following the 1883 arrival of the New Orleans and Mississippi Valley Railroad (later part of the Illinois Central), Baton Rouge eventually secured other connections by way of the Louisiana and Arkansas (Kansas City Southern) Railroad and via Port Allen with the Missouri Pacific and Texas Pacific lines.

At the turn of the century Baton Rouge—although the state's third largest city after New Orleans (287,104) and Shreveport (16,013)—had a population of only 11,269. The city began a series of improvements aimed at enhancing its image and building on its economic base as the regional trade center and state capital. The Louisiana State Seminary of Learning had relocated to the city in 1869 and was renamed Louisiana State University a year later. Other state agencies also provided work, but civic leaders sought different sources of employment.

In 1909, Baton Rouge launched into a new era when the Standard Oil Company announced that the city would be the site for a new oil refinery. Located north of the city proper at that time, the refinery sustained the city's economy for decades. In the early years of World War II the plant was producing three-quarters of the aviation fuel in the nation. Standard Oil, in addition to supplying petroleum products, also supplied a target for Huey P. Long in his rise to power in the state in the 1920s and 1930s, first as governor, then later as U.S. senator. For Baton Rouge, however, the refinery and other petrochemical plants located in the region from the 1930s on provided one of the three pillars of the economy. By 1940 fully a third of the city's population was supported by the refinery. Today the refinery anchors a string of plants located along the Mississippi River between the capital and New Orleans.

A second economic base remains the Port of Baton Rouge. The city lies 230 miles upriver of the Gulf of Mexico and represents the farthest inland deepwater port in the country. Second in tonnage only to New Orleans among state ports, Baton Rouge lies at the head of a channel five hundred feet wide and forty feet deep maintained in the Mississippi River. This channel, coupled with the natural resources of the region, helps maintain the industrial corridor located along the lower valley.

The city's third economic base is state government. Especially since the reign of Huey P. Long, state expenditures and the apparatus to manage them have risen. Southern University joined LSU in Baton Rouge. Other agencies sprang up during and after the Depression. Since the 1930s the state has expanded government services largely based on revenue derived from severance and other taxes on the petrochemical industry, leaving the citizens of Louisiana to enjoy the benefits of those services without the necessity until recently of having to pay for them.

As the economy expanded and the rural-to-urban migration of the twentieth century continued, the city limits of Baton Rouge expanded to north, south, and east. Northward, the presence of Standard, then Esso, now Exxon refinery produced a series of suburbs along its eastern bounds. To the south a new, enlarged campus for Louisiana State University fueled an expansion in that area along the Mississippi. This campus relocation provided room for a new state capitol, completed in 1932. The general eastward trend of the old city followed existing and new transportation routes, particularly highways. The first bridge across the Mississippi at Baton Rouge was completed in 1940, and the Interstate 10 bridge was built downriver in 1968. Today the city is one of suburban neighborhoods. The old central business district has largely declined, replaced by newer shopping malls in various sizes and shapes.

In 1947 the city and East Baton Rouge Parish governments merged, forming a single government with a mayor-president system. Today Baton Rouge is the second largest city in the state. At its various definitions the population stands at 219,531 (city), 380,105 (parish), and 528,264 (metropolitan statistical area, including East Baton Rouge, West Baton Rouge, Livingston, and Ascension parishes).

66. Baton Rouge and Environs, 1990

Copyright © 1995 by the University of Oklahoma Press

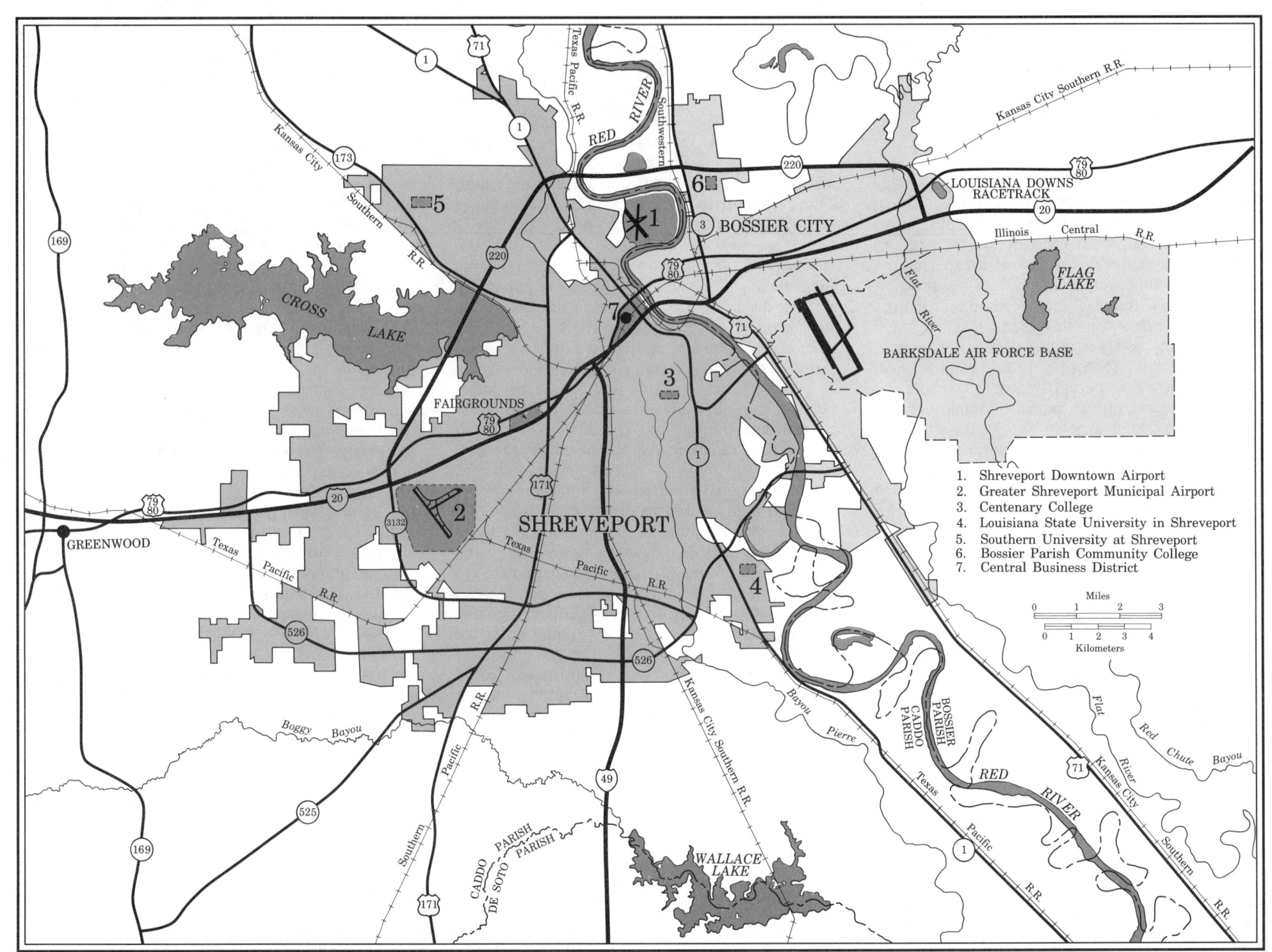

1. Shreveport Downtown Airport
2. Greater Shreveport Municipal Airport
3. Centenary College
4. Louisiana State University in Shreveport
5. Southern University at Shreveport
6. Bossier Parish Community College
7. Central Business District

Shreveport owes its beginnings to the cession of the Caddo Indian lands in 1835 and the first clearing of the Great Raft—a tremendous logjam—on the Red River. The former event opened up the land to non-Indian settlement and development. The latter opened up the Red and thus the region to waterborne commerce, the most practicable in an era of rude traces and trails in the piney woods. Incidentally, it would be the Superintendent of Western Waters Improvement Henry Miller Shreve whose name became attached to the new town, though he never established a residence there.

Incorporated by the state legislature in 1839, Shreveport became the seat of Caddo Parish, which had been created the year earlier. From its vantage on the Red, the city attracted the agricultural trade of the surrounding area, particularly since the re-forming of the raft upstream caused it to be the head of navigation on the river. King Cotton reigned during this era, and the baled produce of that crop from the surrounding parishes and over into Texas flowed through the city. Shreveport's importance increased during the Civil War as its role of entrepôt for goods shipped overland from Texas and even Mexico expanded. Eventually, as the Mississippi fell under Federal control, Shreveport furthered its economic role at the same time as its military and political role increased. The state capital moved there in May 1863 to escape the advancing Federal troops. Maj. Gen. Edmund Kirby Smith, chief of the Confederate's Trans-Mississippi Department,

established his command headquarters there in 1864. As the Confederacy collapsed, the city was occupied in June 1865, remaining under Federal control through the end of Reconstruction in 1877.

Rail transportation in the region dates from 1858, when a rail line opened from Marshall to a terminus just west of the Texas-Louisiana border. A connection to Dallas (the Texas and Pacific Railroad) opened in 1873, to New Orleans (again the Texas and Pacific) in 1882, and eastward via the Vicksburg, Shreveport and Pacific in 1884. The Kansas City Southern and other lines later made Shreveport a regional rail hub. Commerce on the Red River, finally and permanently cleared of its logjam in 1873, peaked in 1883–1884 but declined thereafter. However, by the mid-1990s the river was once again scheduled to be open to barge traffic as far upstream as Shreveport.

An attitude of civic improvement, the beginning of rural-to-urban migration, and the discovery of oil in northern Caddo Parish in 1905 led to a period of population growth and areal expansion for the city. Various manufacturers in glass, lumber, and automobile, telephone, and other products located in the city and its environs. The oil and gas as well as forest resources of the region contributed to the city's growth as a regional center. The 1933 dedication of Barksdale Air Force Base across the Red River in Bossier City also bolstered both the urban and the regional economy.

As a governmental and economic center the city acted as a magnet for population, following in the general urbanization and then suburbanization pat-

terns of the nation. The existing traffic flow concentrations of river and railroad have been strengthened by highway and air patterns. Today Shreveport acts as the nucleus of one of the seven metropolitan statistical areas of the state, encompassing Caddo and Bossier parishes.

Shreveport for the century between the censuses of 1880 and 1980 ranked second in population among the state's cities. For the first half of the twentieth century it numbered twice the population of Baton Rouge, the state's third city. After 1940, however, with the expansion of government, the industrialization along the lower Mississippi, the superior transportation resources of the Mississippi itself, and a general regional population shift from north to south Louisiana, Louisiana's capital began to gain on, then surpass, Shreveport in size.

Today Shreveport, at 198,525, has a population larger than any of the parishes in its Louisiana hinterland, indeed larger than all but three parishes (besides Caddo) in the entire state. Shreveport's economic influence has spread beyond the state's bounds into both eastern Texas and southern Arkansas. The completion of Interstate 49 will provide north-south connections equal to the east-west route along Interstate 20. Its educational institutions, both private and public, assist its other parish, state, and federal governmental installations in providing one economic base, even as the changing private sector at the close of the age of petroleum expands and contracts.

Copyright © 1995 by the University of Oklahoma Press

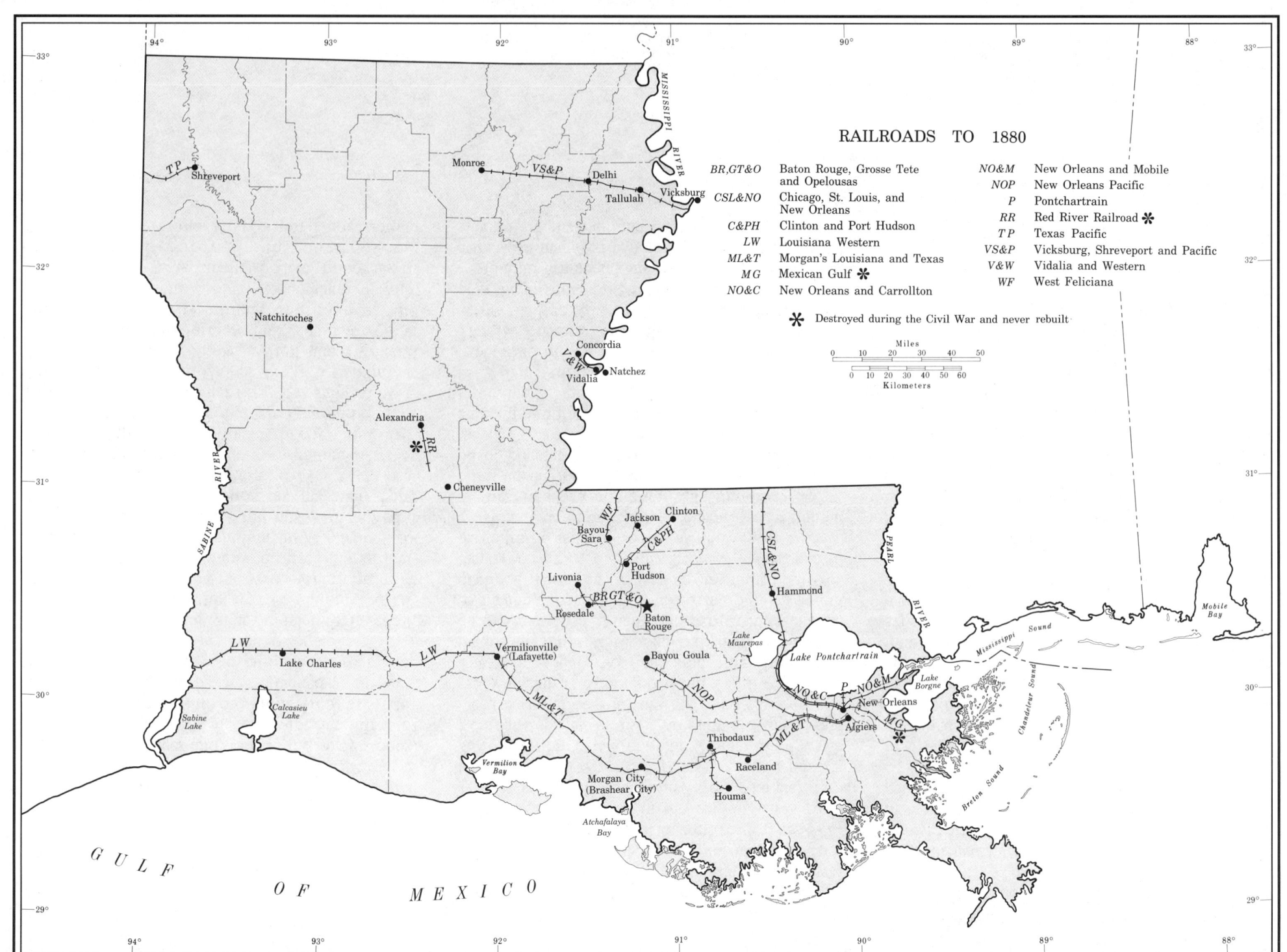

RAILROADS TO 1880

BR,GT&O	Baton Rouge, Grosse Tete and Opelousas	*NO&M*	New Orleans and Mobile
CSL&NO	Chicago, St. Louis, and New Orleans	*NOP*	New Orleans Pacific
C&PH	Clinton and Port Hudson	*P*	Pontchartrain
LW	Louisiana Western	*RR*	Red River Railroad ✳
ML&T	Morgan's Louisiana and Texas	*TP*	Texas Pacific
MG	Mexican Gulf ✳	*VS&P*	Vicksburg, Shreveport and Pacific
NO&C	New Orleans and Carrollton	*V&W*	Vidalia and Western
		WF	West Feliciana

✳ Destroyed during the Civil War and never rebuilt

Louisiana's railroad development represented but the local symptoms of a national fever. Many railroad charters were granted, some for lines never built; such ventures represented more a raid on the public treasury by means of state purchase of the company's stocks and/or bonds. From the 1830s the state's railroads slowly expanded until the Civil War brought general destruction to the system. Following that conflict came a period of renewed construction. From 40 miles of track in 1835 the state's system expanded to 652 miles in 1880.

Most railroads built in the antebellum period were short lines within cities or connecting them with their economic hinterland. The six-mile Pontchartrain Railroad opened in 1831 between New Orleans and Lake Pontchartrain. The West Feliciana Railroad, chartered in 1831 and completed in 1842, ran twenty-seven miles from Bayou Sara on the Mississippi through St. Francisville to Woodville in southern Mississippi. The Clinton and Port Hudson Railroad, incorporated in 1833, spanned the twenty-five miles between those two cities, with a five-mile spur to Jackson.

The New Orleans and Carrollton Railroad, chartered in 1840, ran between those cities, with various branches to the Mississippi. It operated a union depot at Carrollton with the Jefferson and Lake Pontchartrain Railroad, running from that city to the lake. Both lines together totaled only fourteen miles. In central Louisiana the Alexandria and Cheneyville, chartered in 1833 and reincorporated in 1835 as the Red River Railroad Company, ran sixteen miles from Alexandria to the Bayou Boeuf.

In 1835 the New Orleans and Nashville Railroad was incorporated to connect those cities but laid only thirty-one miles of track, from New Orleans to just beyond Bayou Labranche. The Mexican Gulf Railroad Company, chartered in 1837 to build a line from New Orleans to the Gulf of Mexico (with a branch to Lake Borgne), also ran into financial difficulties and was sold, having completed the branch to Proctorville but not the main Gulf line. Last, the Grosse Tete and Baton Rouge Plank Road Company (1852) reincorporated (1854) as the Baton Rouge, Grosse Tete, and Opelousas Railroad. Starting from the Mississippi bank opposite Baton Rouge, the line reached Bayou Grosse Tete in 1857, then laid twelve additional miles of track beyond the bayou by 1862.

Three major railroad corporations were chartered during the 1850s. The New Orleans, Jackson, and Great Northern, incorporated in 1852, surveyed a line northward from New Orleans to the Mississippi boundary. Service opened in August 1854 to Osyka on the state line, a distance of eighty-eight miles. Four years later this line was completed to Canton, Mississippi, where it connected with the Mississippi Central Railroad.

The New Orleans, Opelousas, and Great Western Railroad was also incorporated in 1852, to connect New Orleans with Texas, thence perhaps to the Pacific. The line opened in stages from late 1854 to early 1857, when it ran for a total of eighty miles from Algiers to Brashear (later Morgan) City on Berwick's Bay. (A branch ran to Raceland.) Steamers ferried people and goods from that point to Texas.

The Vicksburg, Shreveport and Texas Railroad was created in 1852 to run from the Mississippi opposite Vicksburg through Monroe to Shreveport and the Texas state line. The line reached Tallulah (September 1857), then Delhi (fall 1859), and finally Monroe (January 1861), a total of just over seventy-four miles. At the time of the Civil War, grading work had begun on the line west from Shreveport. This segment was later subcontracted to the Southern Pacific and opened in 1866 as part of the Texas and Pacific Railway Company.

During the Civil War, Louisiana railroads suffered both neglect and destruction. Federal and Confederate troops alike sought to prevent the opponent's use of the lines. Dismantling of tracks, destruction of bridges, and confiscation or destruction of rolling stock left short-line and main-line roads largely in ruins by war's end.

Reconstruction witnessed more schemes to raid the public treasury but little new mileage. The major antebellum lines were rebuilt or refurbished. A financial panic in 1873 halted most construction, but new building began later in the decade. The North Louisiana and Texas, then the Vicksburg, Shreveport, and Pacific—successors to the Vicksburg, Shreveport and Texas—rebuilt the line to Monroe and started on toward Shreveport. The Vidalia and Western opened in 1873 from Vidalia to Concordia. In 1880 the Louisiana Western opened from Vermilionville (Lafayette) to Orange, Texas, connecting with the old New Orleans, Opelousas, and Great Western (now Morgan's Louisiana and Texas), which had built westward from Brashear City to Vermilionville. The New Orleans and Mobile Railroad connected its namesakes. By 1880 the New Orleans Pacific had extended from New Orleans to Bayou Goula, later to push on to Shreveport

Copyright © 1995 by the University of Oklahoma Press

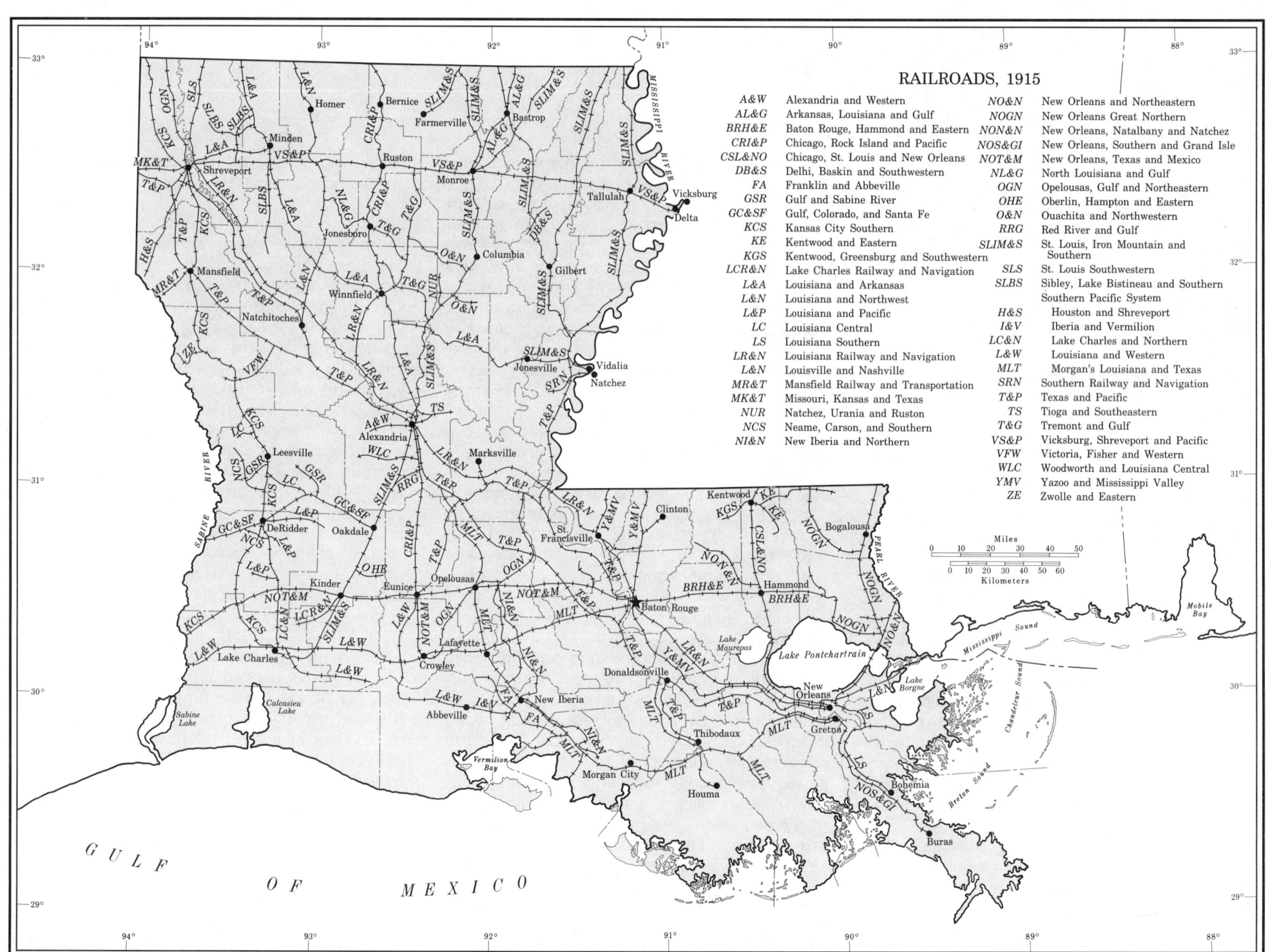

RAILROADS, 1915

A&W	Alexandria and Western	NO&N	New Orleans and Northeastern
AL&G	Arkansas, Louisiana and Gulf	NOGN	New Orleans Great Northern
BRH&E	Baton Rouge, Hammond and Eastern	NON&N	New Orleans, Natalbany and Natchez
CRI&P	Chicago, Rock Island and Pacific	NOS&GI	New Orleans, Southern and Grand Isle
CSL&NO	Chicago, St. Louis and New Orleans	NOT&M	New Orleans, Texas and Mexico
DB&S	Delhi, Baskin and Southwestern	NL&G	North Louisiana and Gulf
FA	Franklin and Abbeville	OGN	Opelousas, Gulf and Northeastern
GSR	Gulf and Sabine River	OHE	Oberlin, Hampton and Eastern
GC&SF	Gulf, Colorado, and Santa Fe	O&N	Ouachita and Northwestern
KCS	Kansas City Southern	RRG	Red River and Gulf
KE	Kentwood and Eastern	SLIM&S	St. Louis, Iron Mountain and Southern
KGS	Kentwood, Greensburg and Southwestern		
LCR&N	Lake Charles Railway and Navigation	SLS	St. Louis Southwestern
L&A	Louisiana and Arkansas	SLBS	Sibley, Lake Bistineau and Southern
L&N	Louisiana and Northwest		Southern Pacific System
L&P	Louisiana and Pacific	H&S	Houston and Shreveport
LC	Louisiana Central	I&V	Iberia and Vermilion
LS	Louisiana Southern	LC&N	Lake Charles and Northern
LR&N	Louisiana Railway and Navigation	L&W	Louisiana and Western
L&N	Louisville and Nashville	MLT	Morgan's Louisiana and Texas
MR&T	Mansfield Railway and Transportation	SRN	Southern Railway and Navigation
MK&T	Missouri, Kansas and Texas	T&P	Texas and Pacific
NUR	Natchez, Urania and Ruston	TS	Tioga and Southeastern
NCS	Neame, Carson, and Southern	T&G	Tremont and Gulf
NI&N	New Iberia and Northern	VS&P	Vicksburg, Shreveport and Pacific
		VFW	Victoria, Fisher and Western
		WLC	Woodworth and Louisiana Central
		YMV	Yazoo and Mississippi Valley
		ZE	Zwolle and Eastern

The three decades following 1880 represent the most active period of railroad construction in Louisiana. Total rail mileage in the state increased ninefold, from 652 in 1880 to 5,728 in 1915. That latter figure would represent the peak mileage for Louisiana. Railroads had now supplanted river transport as the chief means of ferrying both goods and people.

The late nineteenth and early twentieth centuries saw the expansion of existing rail lines and the construction of new ones. Cities competed for attracting the rails, and towns often grew or declined depending on their success in those endeavors. Several lines were built as logging roads, initially feeding raw timber to the giant sawmills which sprang up as the state's virgin forests were cut over but surviving as general railroads thereafter. Smaller logging roads diverging from the main line did not usually survive, nor were they meant to.

Unlike the first lines built in Louisiana, these new railroads did not serve merely as feeders to river cities, transporting goods only the short distances necessary to make connection with river- or ocean-going vessels. That short-line role did continue for those goods destined for transit overseas or to river cities not yet part of the rail network. For domestic shipment, however, the goods (and people) remained on the rails. Indeed, there came to be direct competition between rail and water as some lines were laid down parallel to river courses in the state. Other lines struck out across the country, tracing direct routes between rail hubs.

With the proliferation of rail lines not only in Louisiana but also throughout the South and the nation at large, two types of consolidation occurred. Holding companies bought up individual lines, creating regional and national networks criss-crossing the landscape, carrying raw materials or finished goods from city to city, region to region. The Southern Pacific system, for example, in 1915 included as constituent lines within the state the Houston and Shreveport, Louisiana and Western, and Morgan's Louisiana and Texas, all connected via the southwest to California and the northern Pacific coast. The Chicago, Rock Island, and Pacific system, expanding west and south from Chicago, had incorporated the Arkansas Southern, running from north to south through central Louisiana. The Illinois Central; St. Louis, Iron Mountain and Southern; and Missouri Pacific represented other rail networks in the state.

Along with the consolidation of individual lines into national systems came the development of rail centers. Towns located at the junction of two lines fared better than those along a single line. Even more importantly, those cities situated on even more lines developed still greater economic strength. Often these towns represented the old river ports, now made stronger with rail connections. New Orleans, Shreveport, Baton Rouge, and Alexandria were served by six or more lines. Other towns new and old developed as smaller rail hubs.

In a larger context the railroad influenced statewide the entire system of towns and villages. The location of such routes led to the creation of entirely new towns in previously uninhabited areas, the growth of existing towns where they fell along the chosen route, and the fading away of previously existing cities. Shiloh, home to Concord Institute and birthplace to two governors of Louisiana (William Wright Heard and Ruffin G. Pleasant), failed to attract the Arkansas Southern as it was constructed south through Union Parish in the 1890s. Businesses left for the new railroad town of Bernice; a fire in 1899 destroyed much of old Shiloh; and today the site is a mere rural crossroads with no hint of former glory. This story would be repeated across the state.

Railroad financing led to local, state, and national inducements to determine the route as well as the construction of new lines. Towns often traded municipal bonds for railroad bonds in hopes of attracting lines. Outright land grants became impossible, and resentment grew against companies that had them. Some lines forfeited previous concessions because of failure to comply with the terms of their grant. With increased concentration of railroad properties and the general rise of populism came resentment of the larger rail combines and their economic monopoly.

Through the connecting of towns, the settlement of granted (and adjacent) lands via colonization schemes, and the transport of people and goods, railroads brought Louisiana and the United States into greater unity. Goods and people moved more swiftly across the state and nation. The rails also opened up more of the state to the transportation services previously enjoyed only by river ports, at the same time creating new markets for goods and services. The original commercial hub of New Orleans saw its influence diluted and now shared by regional centers in the state and beyond the borders. The era of the steamboat had passed, and railroads were in their heyday.

Copyright © 1995 by the University of Oklahoma Press

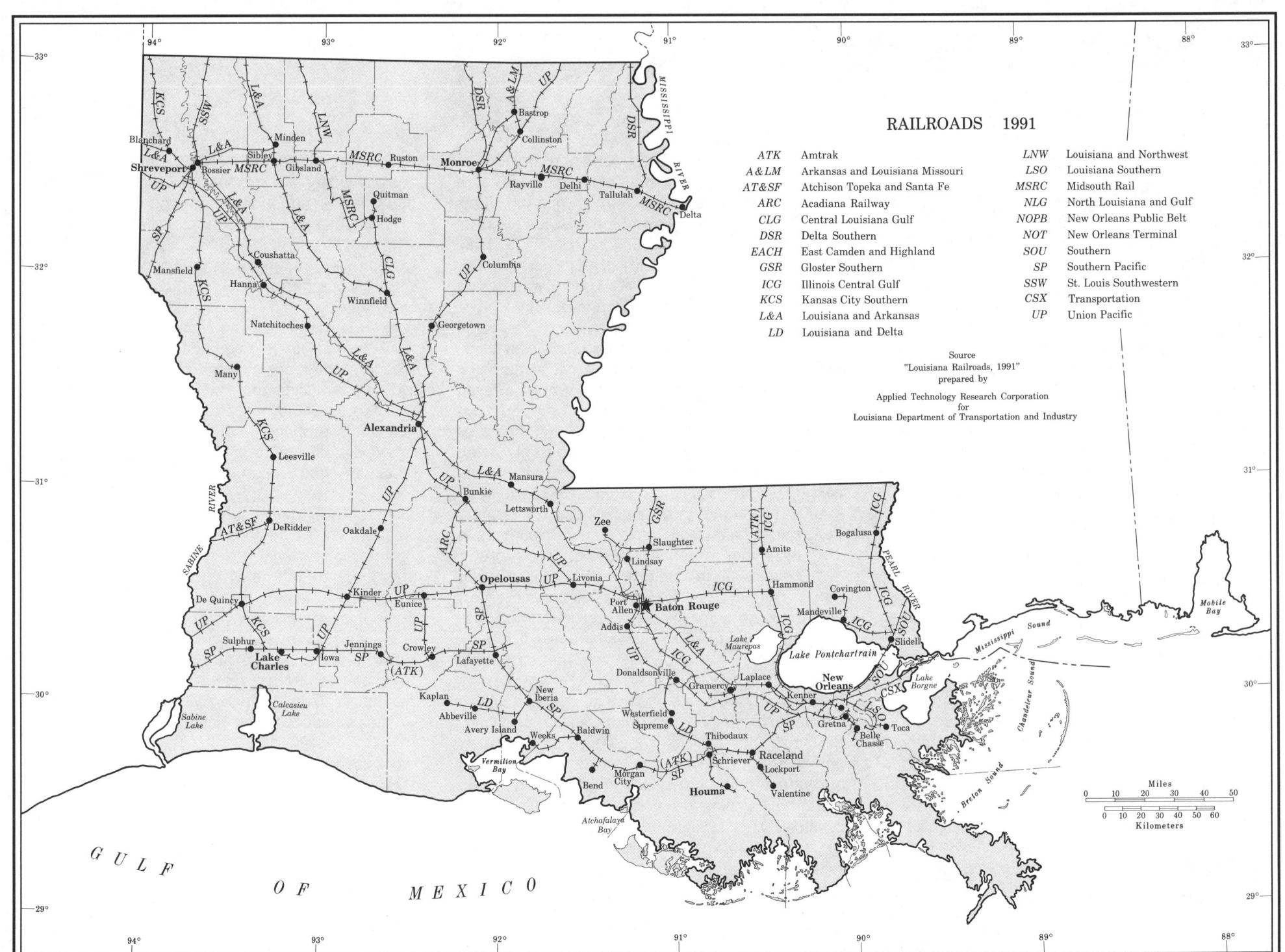

RAILROADS 1991

ATK	Amtrak	LNW	Louisiana and Northwest
A&LM	Arkansas and Louisiana Missouri	LSO	Louisiana Southern
AT&SF	Atchison Topeka and Santa Fe	MSRC	Midsouth Rail
ARC	Acadiana Railway	NLG	North Louisiana and Gulf
CLG	Central Louisiana Gulf	NOPB	New Orleans Public Belt
DSR	Delta Southern	NOT	New Orleans Terminal
EACH	East Camden and Highland	SOU	Southern
GSR	Gloster Southern	SP	Southern Pacific
ICG	Illinois Central Gulf	SSW	St. Louis Southwestern
KCS	Kansas City Southern	CSX	Transportation
L&A	Louisiana and Arkansas	UP	Union Pacific
LD	Louisiana and Delta		

Source
"Louisiana Railroads, 1991"
prepared by

Applied Technology Research Corporation
for
Louisiana Department of Transportation and Industry

After reaching a peak in mileage in 1915, Louisiana's railroads entered into a period of prolonged decline in both extent and importance. Buffeted by increasing costs of technological change, by periods of government operation during the first and second world wars, and by the growth of the automobile and trucking industries as movers of people and goods, the railroads retrenched. Parallel lines were no longer an option. The growth of lines which had come into being primarily as a means of harvesting the stands of virgin timber ended when those stands were cut over. Later in the period the fortunes of national railroad companies often led to the shift of segments back into local hands or, barring location of a buyer, of abandonment and even the taking up of track. In 1986 the total number of miles stood at 3,347, less than 60 percent of the 5,728-mile peak in 1915.

Louisiana's railroads in 1915 reflected their premier role as movers of the nation's passengers and freight. Moreover, for Louisiana many lines and hundreds of miles of track owed their existence squarely to the continuing exploitation of the state's timber resources. That exploitation also peaked in 1915, when the state contributed almost 12 percent of the nation's lumber production. Also important to the system was the transport of the state and region's petroleum resources, whether crude or refined.

Railroads gradually lost their passenger traffic to a new invention, the automobile. This loss was not greatly mourned, however, since after 1920 passenger service was largely not self-sustaining. For areas served by the rails, the shift to automobiles (and buses) occurred only as highways improved from the muck and mire of the 1910s and 1920s to the increasing number of hard-surfaced routes thereafter. The automobile and bus duplicated or superseded the railroad in route and schedule. A more modern rival to both is the airplane, particularly jet service, with its ability to whisk passengers swiftly across region, nation, and ocean far faster than either railroad or automobile.

Freight traffic was also siphoned off from the railroad. Trucking firms again duplicated or went beyond the service areas of the railroad and were able to provide dock-to-door service for merchants on a more flexible schedule. Moreover, their routes were subsidized by the state. The construction of the interstate highway system only enhanced cross-country trucking firms. Pipelines also represented a rival to the railroads in the transfer of petrochemical resources. A rebirth of barge traffic on the rivers also provided an alternate system for bulk transport.

Moreover, the rise of government regulatory agencies affected the economic health of railroads. Decisions affecting rate schedules often worked against railroad interests and in favor of those of the railroads' rivals. The prolonged reluctance of agencies to allow rail systems to reduce or eliminate passenger service or abandon branch lines also contributed to the economic decline of many lines.

Louisiana's rail system was also affected by the overall health of the national systems that operated lines in the state. In addition to the effects of government agencies, labor costs also increased and unions imposed the retention of operating personnel on each train long after their usefulness had ended. The movement of manufacturing plants away from the north to the south also affected the health of many national companies. Mismanagement of lines also led to troubles for the system.

The result of all these factors has been a decline in rail mileage for the state along with the disappearance of many long familiar names. Many systems in existence at the turn of the century remain in the state today, but many branch lines have now been eliminated. Some systems such as the Illinois Central have shrunk in size, their lines in the state taken over by regional companies such as Mid-South Rail. Still others, such as the Chicago, Rock Island, and Pacific, have disappeared entirely from state and nation. The Rock Island, whose proposed merger with the Union Pacific never received approval from the Interstate Commerce Commission, finally ceased to exist. Much of its tracks in the state have now been taken up, the old right-of-way slowly disappearing into brush and forest.

Those cities which retain rail linkages today are served by leaner companies whose traffic is entirely freight. The Amtrak passenger system does serve New Orleans, yet the landscape is dotted by dozens of other towns whose very beginnings were tied to the rail lines built a century ago. A line connecting those dots traces the route of rails that once were but are no more. In the space of a single lifetime the railroad has lost its central role in the cultural and economic life of the nation and state and must now compete with rival forms of transport.

Copyright © 1995 by the University of Oklahoma Press

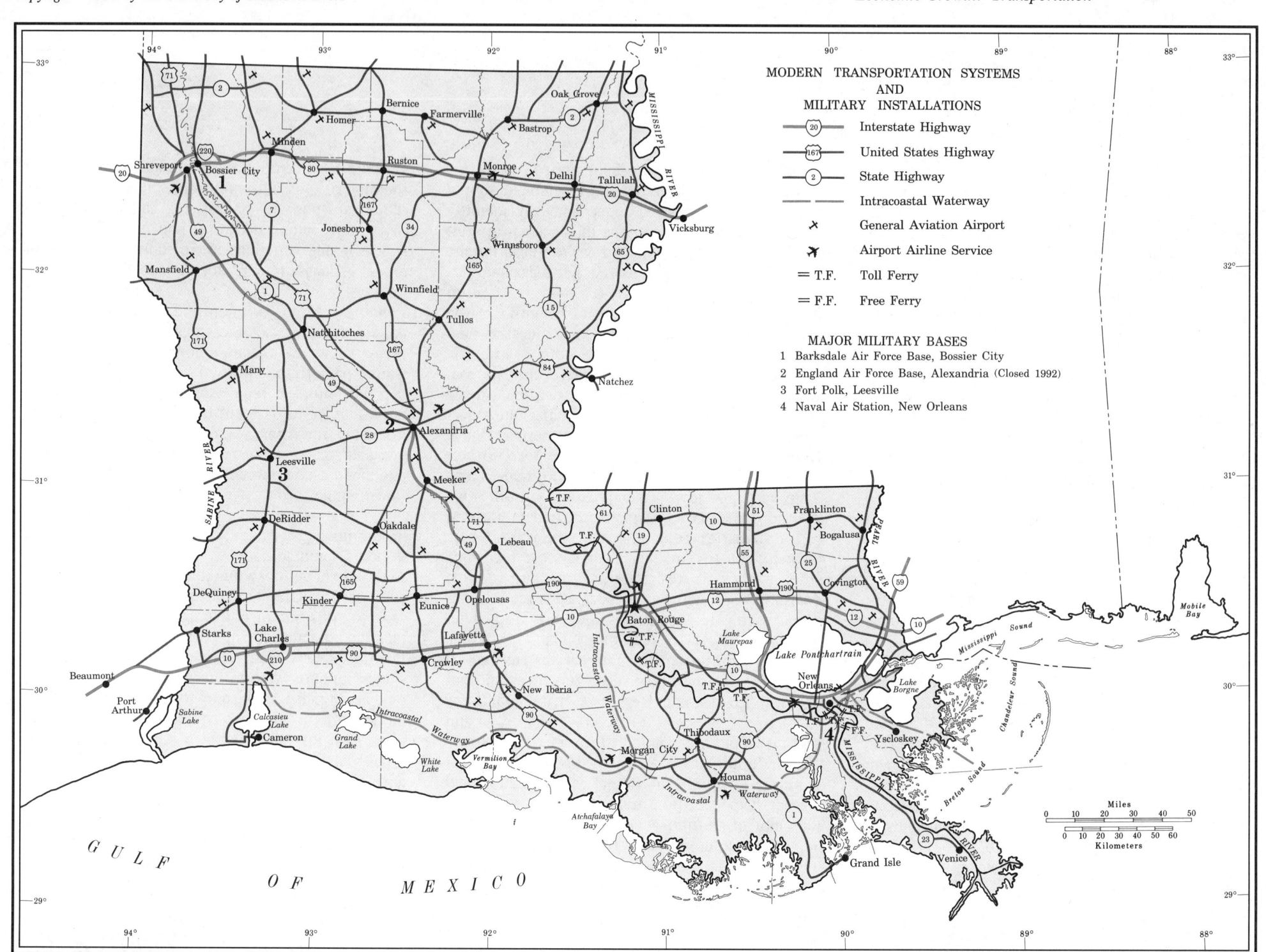

MODERN TRANSPORTATION SYSTEMS
AND
MILITARY INSTALLATIONS

══20══	Interstate Highway
─167─	United States Highway
─2─	State Highway
─ ─ ─	Intracoastal Waterway
✕	General Aviation Airport
✈	Airport Airline Service
═ T.F.	Toll Ferry
═ F.F.	Free Ferry

MAJOR MILITARY BASES
1 Barksdale Air Force Base, Bossier City
2 England Air Force Base, Alexandria (Closed 1992)
3 Fort Polk, Leesville
4 Naval Air Station, New Orleans

Overland transportation in Louisiana remained primitive for some time. The extensive watercourses provided an alternative means of transport; moreover, these same streams at times presented considerable obstacles to cross-country travel. The Mississippi River would not be bridged in Louisiana until spanned at New Orleans in 1935 and at Baton Rouge in 1940. Even today, the expense of construction means that ferries outnumber bridges across the Father of Waters.

The earliest land routes were mere pathways through the woods and canebrakes and across the prairies, paths first established by the buffalo and later followed by earliest immigrants to the continent—the Indians. These paths often paralleled streams; others struck out across country. European migration first followed these ancient routes, then enhanced them. Natural levees along various streams were improved by regulations requiring colonists to maintain these shoreline ridges in an attempt to control flooding. The levees produced a higher roadbed along these streams. Other routes were established for military or trade purposes.

The legislature in 1818 made public those roads located on lands fronting along any river or bayou. Before the advent of road taxes, citizens were required to contribute a term of road service annually. Other roads originated as toll roads operated under charter by private owners for a number of years before reversion to public ownership.

Speed improved as human footsteps were replaced by equine hoofsteps, then by horse- or ox- or mule-drawn vehicles. Widened to accommodate these new vehicles, routes remained subject to muck and mire brought about by the state's frequent rains. One early advancement came in 1874 when the Shed Road was constructed from near Bossier City nine miles into the hill country. This covered toll road proved profitable until the railroad appeared in 1887. Planks, cobblestones, or bricks provided an alternative street surface in many cities into the twentieth century, a convenience lacking in rural areas. Some relics of these early-day streets have been preserved to the present.

Overland rail transportation would be displaced in the twentieth century by the arrival of the internal combustion engine and its use in commercial trucking and private automobiles. The state began the first construction of modern roads in 1911. In 1916, Congress passed the first Federal Aid Road Act to provide a federal-state funding partnership. The 1921 state constitution created a State Highway Commission to coordinate the ongoing work.

Extensive highway paving efforts commenced under the administrations of Huey P. Long and Oscar K. Allen (1928–1936). Today a system of hard-surfaced roadways covers the state, a network complemented by dirt or gravel roads in the more rural areas. From parish routes to national highways, this system connects the smallest hamlet to state, regional, and national centers. The most recent addition to this network is the Interstate Highway System, initiated as a means of assisting the national defense by connecting major urban hubs. Cities have expanded to embrace the system, thus defeating the designers' intent that the system should exist independent of the cities its connected. Today two major east-west arteries (I-10 and I-20) cross the state. Two north-south highways (I-55 and I-59) converge on New Orleans. I-49 is being built as a north-south route to connect Lafayette with Shreveport in the west. The proposed I-69 has generated jockeying among cities desirous of being included along its eventual route.

Air represents the swiftest means of long-distance travel. In earlier days any level surface could accommodate aircraft. Many towns today have airports which can handle smaller, usually propeller-driven, planes. Modern long-distance air travel is by jets, which need longer runways, limiting the cities served. Commercial service is today primarily centered on New Orleans and Baton Rouge, with secondary centers at Alexandria, Lafayette, Lake Charles, Monroe, and Shreveport.

The Intracoastal Waterway stretches across southern Louisiana. This waterway is part of a 2,455-mile system reaching from New Jersey to Texas, and maintained by the U.S. Army Corps of Engineers. Although not meant for ocean-going vessels, the waterway provides a coastal passage protected from the normal conditions of the Atlantic Ocean and Gulf of Mexico. In Louisiana it provides an east-west route not offered by the general north-south trend of the state's rivers.

Since the French established Fort Boulaye in 1700, numerous military installations have been located within the state's bounds. Colonial and early statehood forts stood as sentinels on the frontier or facing a rival power. In modern times they have been a component of the national defense network. With the seeming end of the Cold War and a reshuffling of national resources, several bases are scheduled to close, with sharp economic impact on the communities dependent upon them.

71. *Modern Transportation Systems and Military Installations, 1990*

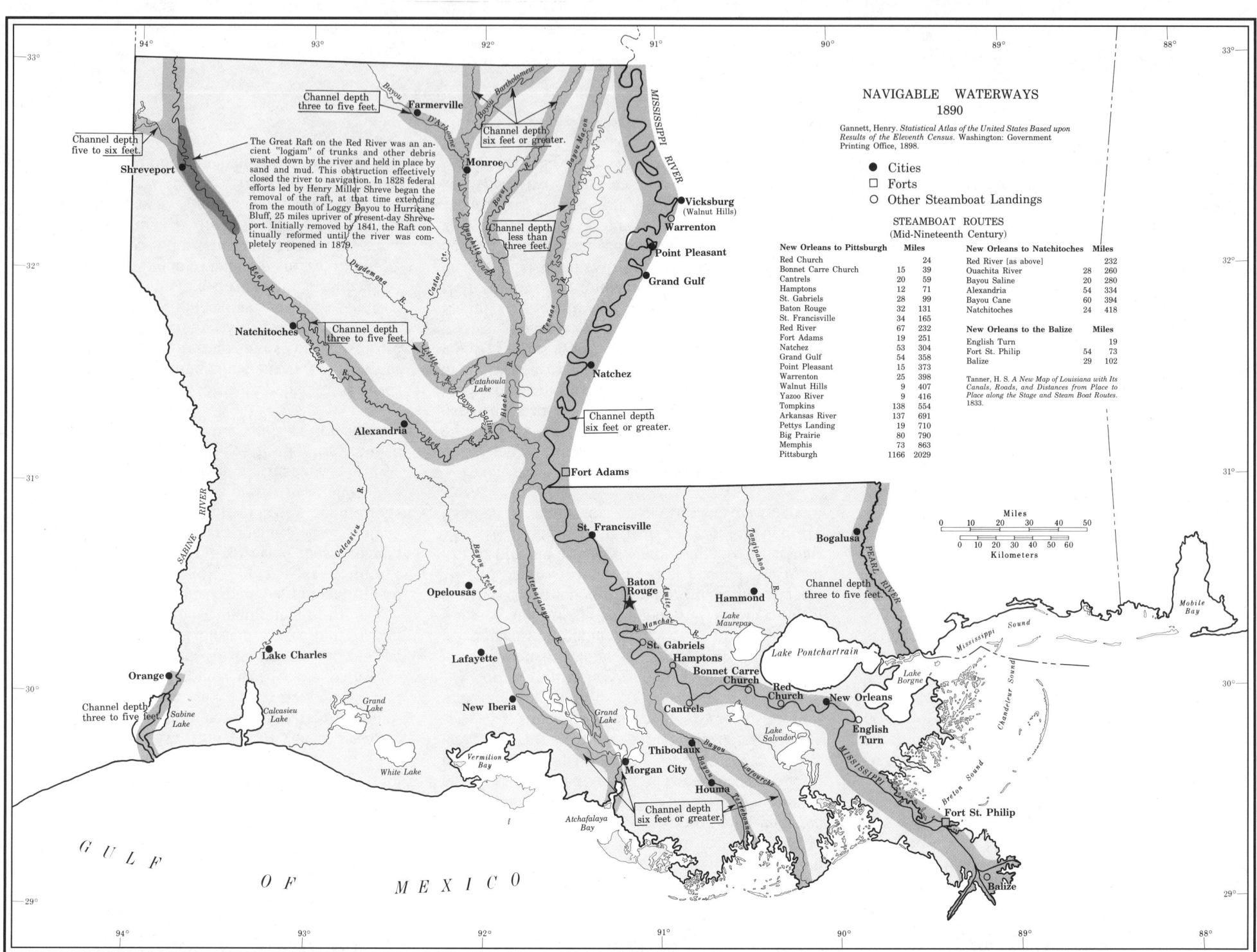

NAVIGABLE WATERWAYS
1890

Gannett, Henry. *Statistical Atlas of the United States Based upon Results of the Eleventh Census.* Washington: Government Printing Office, 1898.

● Cities
□ Forts
○ Other Steamboat Landings

STEAMBOAT ROUTES
(Mid-Nineteenth Century)

New Orleans to Pittsburgh		Miles
Red Church		24
Bonnet Carre Church	15	39
Cantrels	20	59
Hamptons	12	71
St. Gabriels	28	99
Baton Rouge	32	131
St. Francisville	34	165
Red River	67	232
Fort Adams	19	251
Natchez	53	304
Grand Gulf	54	358
Point Pleasant	15	373
Warrenton	25	398
Walnut Hills	9	407
Yazoo River	9	416
Tompkins	138	554
Arkansas River	137	691
Pettys Landing	19	710
Big Prairie	80	790
Memphis	73	863
Pittsburgh	1166	2029

New Orleans to Natchitoches		Miles
Red River [as above]		232
Ouachita River	28	260
Bayou Saline	20	280
Alexandria	54	334
Bayou Cane	60	394
Natchitoches	24	418

New Orleans to the Balize		Miles
English Turn		19
Fort St. Philip	54	73
Balize	29	102

Tanner, H. S. *A New Map of Louisiana with Its Canals, Roads, and Distances from Place to Place along the Stage and Steam Boat Routes.* 1833.

Channel depth three to five feet.

Channel depth five to six feet.

Channel depth six feet or greater.

The Great Raft on the Red River was an ancient "logjam" of trunks and other debris washed down by the river and held in place by sand and mud. This obstruction effectively closed the river to navigation. In 1828 federal efforts led by Henry Miller Shreve began the removal of the raft, at that time extending from the mouth of Loggy Bayou to Hurricane Bluff, 25 miles upriver of present-day Shreveport. Initially removed by 1841, the Raft continually reformed until the river was completely reopened in 1879.

Channel depth less than three feet.

Channel depth three to five feet.

Channel depth six feet or greater.

Channel depth three to five feet.

Channel depth three to five feet.

Channel depth six feet or greater.

Louisiana's rivers have provided arteries of commerce since the appearance of the state's first inhabitants. Indeed, the network of stream courses dictated the location of settlements for centuries, since they provided a readily available alternative to foot traffic. Archaeological work has revealed the existence of an extensive trading network among the region's prehistoric dwellers reaching across most of the present-day southeastern United States. In the case of the Poverty Point culture, that network extended into the upper Middle West as well. Illinois slate, Appalachian soapstone, Arkansas quartz, and even Great Lakes copper have been found within present-day Louisiana. These nonnative materials were exchanged for shells, sandstone, animal skins, salt, and other items in abundance within the Lower Mississippi Valley yet scarce elsewhere.

From the time of dugout canoes and skin boats, then the pirogues of the early French colonial period, rivers provided swift transport as long as the direction traveled followed the river's flow. Moving upstream against strong current was often difficult, if not impossible, even with the advent of wind-powered vessels. With the settlement of the Middle West came an even greater flow of commerce, carried by flatboat, bateaux, and keelboat. The flatboat was essentially a large barge, up to sixty feet long, which upon arrival was broken up and sold for lumber or firewood. A bateaux was also a flat-bottom boat but also sharp-ended and thus more easily towed upstream by a crew toiling along the shore or poled along the shallows near the shore. The keelboat had a shallower draft and thus even less resistance to the current. These last vessels, up to seventy-five feet in length, were a vast improvement on earlier modes.

The development of the steamboat in the early nineteenth century revolutionized river transport. In 1811 the *New Orleans*—first of the Mississippi steamboats—set sail from Pittsburgh for her namesake city. These pioneer steamboats lacked the power to move all the way upriver against the Mississippi's flow, so their days were spent in the lower reaches of the stream. In early years they represented only a modest change in traffic. New Orleans in 1814 received twenty-one river steamboats; that same year 598 flatboats and 324 barges also arrived.

Central to the success of the river steamboat was Henry Miller Shreve, who developed a flat-bottomed boat that presented less drag than had earlier incarnations of the vessel. Shreve also developed a new engine—with horizontal instead of vertical cylinders—which provided greater power. Within a decade thereafter, hundreds of steamboats of various sizes were plying their trade throughout Louisiana and upstream along the Mississippi and its tributaries. The most magnificent steamboats—floating palaces upon the river—measured almost three hundred feet in length and carried more than six hundred passengers. They could also be of the more serviceable type, smaller, less elegant, plying the smaller bayous or rivers. Of whatever variety, steamboats represented in their time the means of choice insofar as transportation was concerned. The heyday of the river steamer occurred before 1860, even though they continued to ply the rivers for decades afterward. Antebellum commerce of the entire Mississippi Valley was largely funneled through New Orleans. The Crescent City vied with New York as the nation's leading port.

Although the Civil War interrupted commerce

and wreaked havoc on vessels, traffic resumed soon afterward. But the heyday of the river steamboat had already passed. Its rival the railroad had reached across the Appalachian barrier and was on its way to stretching from Atlantic to Pacific. The railroad did not suffer the same reliance on nature as did the steamboat, which could be halted by low water on the rivers or at the mouths of the Mississippi. Midwestern canals also rerouted traffic to the east which had earlier flowed through the port of New Orleans. Railroads in particular offered swifter, more reliable, more widely available passenger transportation. Spectacular accidents, primarily boiler explosions, did not increase any sense of security among steamboat passengers.

River traffic, however, did not cease. The emergence of towboats and barges beginning in the 1840s took much of the freight traffic. These vessels were much cheaper to build and operate; barges could be added or deposited at various ports. Too, they could reach even shallower drafts than the river steamer.

Federal efforts at internal improvements on Louisiana rivers began in the 1820s when Henry Miller Shreve was hired to remove the Great Raft on the Red River. By 1890 more than $20,000,000 had been spent on the Lower Mississippi River, its tributaries, and other Louisiana streams. The Lower Mississippi alone had received $17,978,450 in federal moneys. The Red River system came in second with $1,733,265 spent since 1828. Third was the Ouachita-Black system, with $414,000 spent over the preceding two decades. The Teche, Terrebonne, Lafourche, and D'Arbonne were among other bayous receiving federal appropriations.

Copyright © 1995 by the University of Oklahoma Press

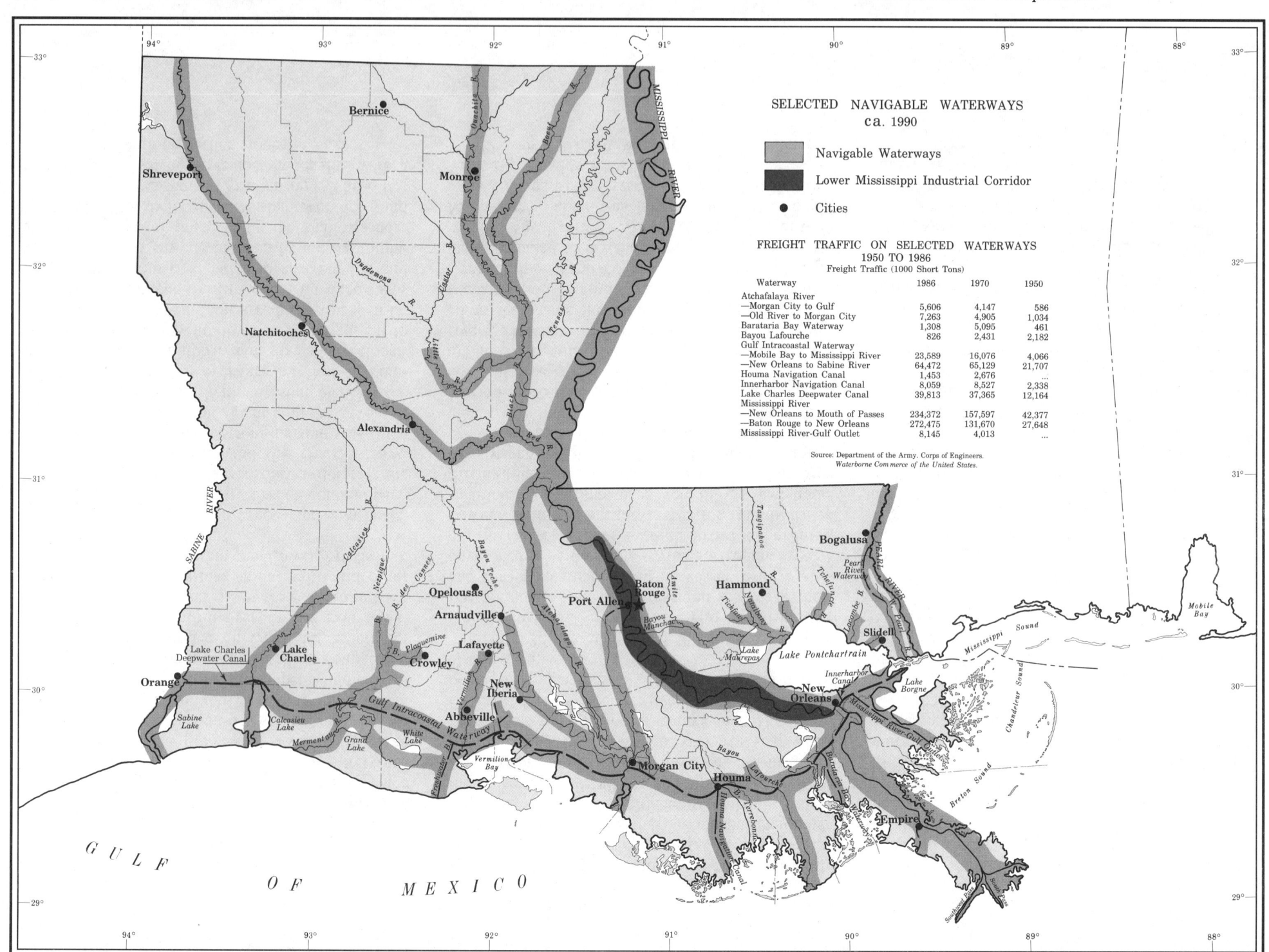

SELECTED NAVIGABLE WATERWAYS
ca. 1990

Navigable Waterways

Lower Mississippi Industrial Corridor

● Cities

FREIGHT TRAFFIC ON SELECTED WATERWAYS
1950 TO 1986
Freight Traffic (1000 Short Tons)

Waterway	1986	1970	1950
Atchafalaya River			
—Morgan City to Gulf	5,606	4,147	586
—Old River to Morgan City	7,263	4,905	1,034
Barataria Bay Waterway	1,308	5,095	461
Bayou Lafourche	826	2,431	2,182
Gulf Intracoastal Waterway			
—Mobile Bay to Mississippi River	23,589	16,076	4,066
—New Orleans to Sabine River	64,472	65,129	21,707
Houma Navigation Canal	1,453	2,676	...
Innerharbor Navigation Canal	8,059	8,527	2,338
Lake Charles Deepwater Canal	39,813	37,365	12,164
Mississippi River			
—New Orleans to Mouth of Passes	234,372	157,597	42,377
—Baton Rouge to New Orleans	272,475	131,670	27,648
Mississippi River-Gulf Outlet	8,145	4,013	...

Source: Department of the Army. Corps of Engineers.
Waterborne Commerce of the United States.

Twentieth-century river commerce has centered upon the barge, towed or pushed up and down navigable streams. The river steamboat is today merely a relic, operated as a tourist attraction locally or, as in the case of the *Delta Queen* and others, for longer excursions. Federal outlays on navigation and flood control projects designed and constructed by the U.S. Army Corps of Engineers have increased exponentially. Yet streams which were navigable a century ago by the steamboat are today closed to commerce. The rivers' nineteenth-century rival, the railroad, has been joined by the trucking industry, the personal automobile, and the pipeline in the quest for cargo and passengers.

River traffic early in this century was greatly reduced because of the rival modes of transport and the changing products being carried. In 1918 the creation of the Federal Barge Line, to be operated by the U.S. Railroad Administration, was authorized by the Congress. Six years later the Inland Waterways Corporation was formed to take charge of this work; the corporation would remain operated by the government until privatized in 1953. Federal entry into barge operations was joined by greater activity among private operators as well.

By far the greatest federal influence on river transport in this century, however, has been the channelization of existing streams and the construction of canals connecting natural stream courses and the Gulf. This work has fallen to the U.S. Army Corps of Engineers, which is charged with maintaining minimum depths for oceangoing vessels as well as for barge traffic on the many streams of the state and nation. Much of this work has been on streams formerly navigable but which in this century have become clogged because of erosion following the cutting over of the state's forests and the increased level of cultivation.

With their many flood-control and navigation projects, the corps has redrawn the waterways map of the state. This work has not gone without challenge, however, and local opposition, combined with more stringent requirements for economic feasibility, has led to fewer new projects as well as curtailment of projects previously authorized. Commercial interests, flood-control interests, environmentalists, and ordinary citizens have combined in shifting alliances to foster or hinder this work.

River commerce is contested directly and indirectly by its rivals in the railroad, trucking, and pipeline industries. These other carriers may contest the development of projects and the setting of rates as well as provide alternative transportation. In particular, the pipeline industry is the largest rival in the movement of the rivers' major cargo, oil and gas, from areas of production to areas of processing and consumption. This network of underground carriers is the product of this century.

River commerce today is largely to be found on the Mississippi River and the Gulf Intracoastal Waterway. The traffic is almost exclusively cargo, not passengers. Crude and refined petroleum products constitute the bulk of the cargo. Oceangoing vessels may sail up the Mississippi as far as Baton Rouge, and the stretch of river between the capital and New Orleans is flanked with industrial plants occupying former plantations. Lake Charles also receives oceangoing vessels through the Calcasieu River and Pass. These deepwater ports, however, are artificially maintained and are a testimony to the corps' talents and the congressional delegation's ability to bring federal outlays to the state.

International trade passes through the three deepwater ports. Such trade in 1986 accounted for 37 percent of the total tonnage at New Orleans, 31 percent at Baton Rouge, and 59 percent at Lake Charles. Crude petroleum is the major import at each port, accounting for 36 percent at New Orleans, 18 percent at Baton Rouge, and 93 percent at Lake Charles. Such imports fuel the petrochemical industries at those locations. The Port of New Orleans also imports a substantial amount of basic chemicals and chemical products. Second and third on the list of Port of Baton Rouge imports are iron ore and nitrogenous chemical fertilizers. Major exports by tonnage from the Port of New Orleans are corn (25 percent), soybeans (22 percent), coal and lignite (15 percent), and animal feed (6 percent). Port of Baton Rouge exports include coal and lignite (24 percent), animal feed (17 percent), and grain mill products (11 percent). Over half the exports from the Port of Lake Charles is coke petroleum.

The larger tonnage is devoted to domestic shipping up and down the rivers or across the Intracoastal Waterway. Raw materials, processed materials, and manufactured products all move along the courses. Crude petroleum, marine shells, sulphur, iron and steel alloys and products, other minerals, chemical products, gasoline, fuel oil, and agricultural products such as corn and soybeans are the most frequent items found. Along many of the shorter routes to the Gulf in south Louisiana, crude petroleum or petroleum products make up the bulk of such shipments.

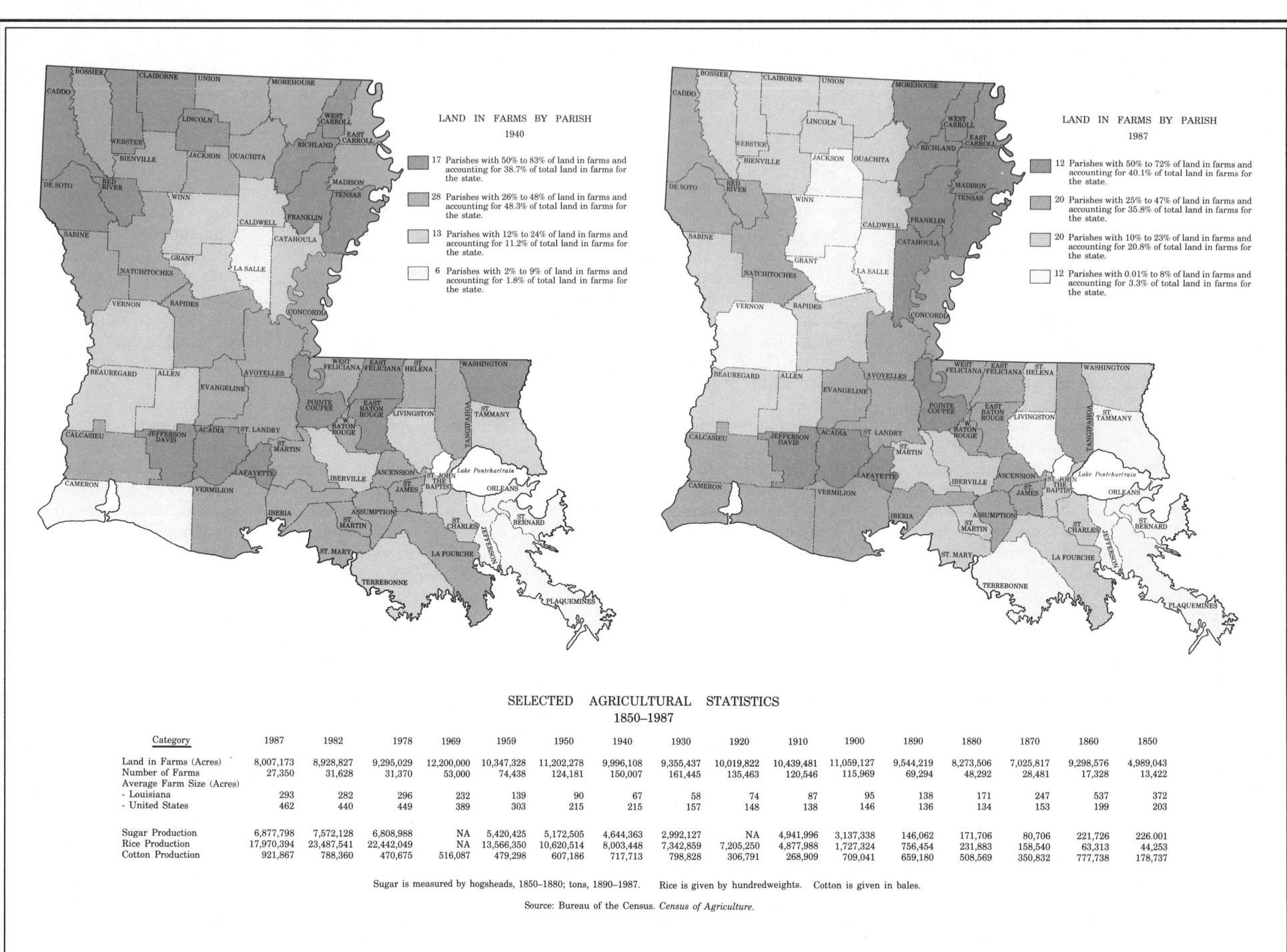

**LAND IN FARMS BY PARISH
1940**

17   Parishes with 50% to 83% of land in farms and accounting for 38.7% of total land in farms for the state.

28   Parishes with 26% to 48% of land in farms and accounting for 48.3% of total land in farms for the state.

13   Parishes with 12% to 24% of land in farms and accounting for 11.2% of total land in farms for the state.

6   Parishes with 2% to 9% of land in farms and accounting for 1.8% of total land in farms for the state.

**LAND IN FARMS BY PARISH
1987**

12   Parishes with 50% to 72% of land in farms and accounting for 40.1% of total land in farms for the state.

20   Parishes with 25% to 47% of land in farms and accounting for 35.8% of total land in farms for the state.

20   Parishes with 10% to 23% of land in farms and accounting for 20.8% of total land in farms for the state.

12   Parishes with 0.01% to 8% of land in farms and accounting for 3.3% of total land in farms for the state.

SELECTED AGRICULTURAL STATISTICS
1850–1987

Category	1987	1982	1978	1969	1959	1950	1940	1930	1920	1910	1900	1890	1880	1870	1860	1850
Land in Farms (Acres)	8,007,173	8,928,827	9,295,029	12,200,000	10,347,328	11,202,278	9,996,108	9,355,437	10,019,822	10,439,481	11,059,127	9,544,219	8,273,506	7,025,817	9,298,576	4,989,043
Number of Farms	27,350	31,628	31,370	53,000	74,438	124,181	150,007	161,445	135,463	120,546	115,969	69,294	48,292	28,481	17,328	13,422
Average Farm Size (Acres)																
- Louisiana	293	282	296	232	139	90	67	58	74	87	95	138	171	247	537	372
- United States	462	440	449	389	303	215	215	157	148	138	146	136	134	153	199	203
Sugar Production	6,877,798	7,572,128	6,808,988	NA	5,420,425	5,172,505	4,644,363	2,992,127	NA	4,941,996	3,137,338	146,062	171,706	80,706	221,726	226.001
Rice Production	17,970,394	23,487,541	22,442,049	NA	13,566,350	10,620,514	8,003,448	7,342,859	7,205,250	4,877,988	1,727,324	756,454	231,883	158,540	63,313	44,253
Cotton Production	921,867	788,360	470,675	516,087	479,298	607,186	717,713	798,828	306,791	268,909	709,041	659,180	508,569	350,832	777,738	178,737

Sugar is measured by hogsheads, 1850–1880; tons, 1890–1987.   Rice is given by hundredweights.   Cotton is given in bales.

Source: Bureau of the Census. *Census of Agriculture.*

Agriculture appeared in Louisiana perhaps two thousand years ago when the Indian inhabitants moved beyond merely gathering the natural bounty of the land to the domestication of plants. Maize (corn), squash, and beans formed the grand triumvirate of this early farming. All three had been earlier domesticated in Mexico and later introduced into Louisiana. Native plants, including the sunflower, which had enjoyed a place in this early farming, were reduced to a secondary role.

Early agriculture was indeed primitive by modern standards. The ground was broken up with rudimentary hoes; sharp sticks were used to puncture the ground for planting. Different plants might inhabit adjacent hills or rows in the field or be placed in separate fields altogether. Care of the fields was continual, as much to protect the growing crops from animals as to rid the fields of weeds. To the European farmers the Indian fields presented a jumble of plants rather than the orderly rows to which they were accustomed.

This early agriculture was a primary activity in the floodplains along the several rivers—site of most of the population—or in natural clearings elsewhere. Native Americans also cleared land in forests, but there was as yet not so large a population that extensive clearing was necessary. Besides, the flooding of the rivers continually introduced a fresh supply of nutrients to the soil.

Although agriculture had not been among the reasons for the early exploration and settlement of the land by Europeans, it was a practical necessity. By and large Europeans adapted the New World's crops to their own use and customs of farming. Indian "old fields" were taken over, and new lands were cleared along the rivers for the raising of food crops as well as cash crops of indigo, rice, tobacco, and later, sugar and cotton.

As the colony/territory/state's population grew, new areas were opened to agriculture. New immigrants from Europe were joined by the westward movement of owners whose lands to the east had been exhausted; a ready supply of cheap land encouraged this migration. Plantations focused on cash crops and fueled by slavery predominated in the south and along the Mississippi and Red rivers. They were neighbors, however, to the more numerous subsistence yeoman farmers. When the Civil War and Reconstruction swept away slavery, plantations fell into a tenant farming or crop lien system (Map 86). Tenants readily fell victim to virtual peonage to the owner even as small farmers shared the same fate with the local merchant. At the same time, the railroads opened up more of the hill country. As the virgin forests were felled, farmers entered into those regions, again practicing largely subsistence agriculture.

With the clearing of new lands, the infusion of new settlers, and the evolution of the plantation system came a dramatic increase in the number of farms in the state. Part of this increase was artificial, since each tenant was counted as a separate farm even though he did not own the land itself. Still, the number of farms grew steadily until 1930, after which a decline set in to the present day. The number of farms in 1987 stood at 27,350, only 17 percent of the 1930 figure of 161,445.

Improvements in seed and fertilizer and the mechanization of agriculture spelled the doom of subsistence farming as a way of life. Yields per acre rose even as labor requirements dropped. Particularly in the last fifty years, traditional agriculture has vacated the hill country, which has turned to pine tree plantations as an alternate "farm." Corporate and family acreages along the floodplains and on the prairies produce foodstuffs for local, national, and international trade and consumption. Still, the kitchen garden or even just a few tomato plants dot the yards of city and rural dweller alike. Another change has been in the growth of livestock as an alternative to crops. Increasing prosperity among Americans led to a similar increase in the consumption of meat; Louisiana would share in this trend.

One measure of agriculture is the amount of land in farms. Such a measure counts all of the acres classified as belonging to a farm, whether that land be under cultivation, in pasture or forest, or some other form. By that measure, about 18 percent of Louisiana's land was in farms at the first Census of Agriculture in 1850. By the turn of the century, that figure had advanced to between 35 and 40 percent, where it has largely remained. However, in 1987 the figure dropped to only 28 percent.

Another modern trend has been an increase in the average size of farms. A major factor in this trend has been the rural exodus from marginal farming areas. Another factor has been an increase in the average size of farm necessary to support a family. Still a third reason has been the ability of a family through investment in machinery to manage larger and larger tracts of land.

74. Land in Farms, 1940 and 1987

Copyright © 1995 by the University of Oklahoma Press

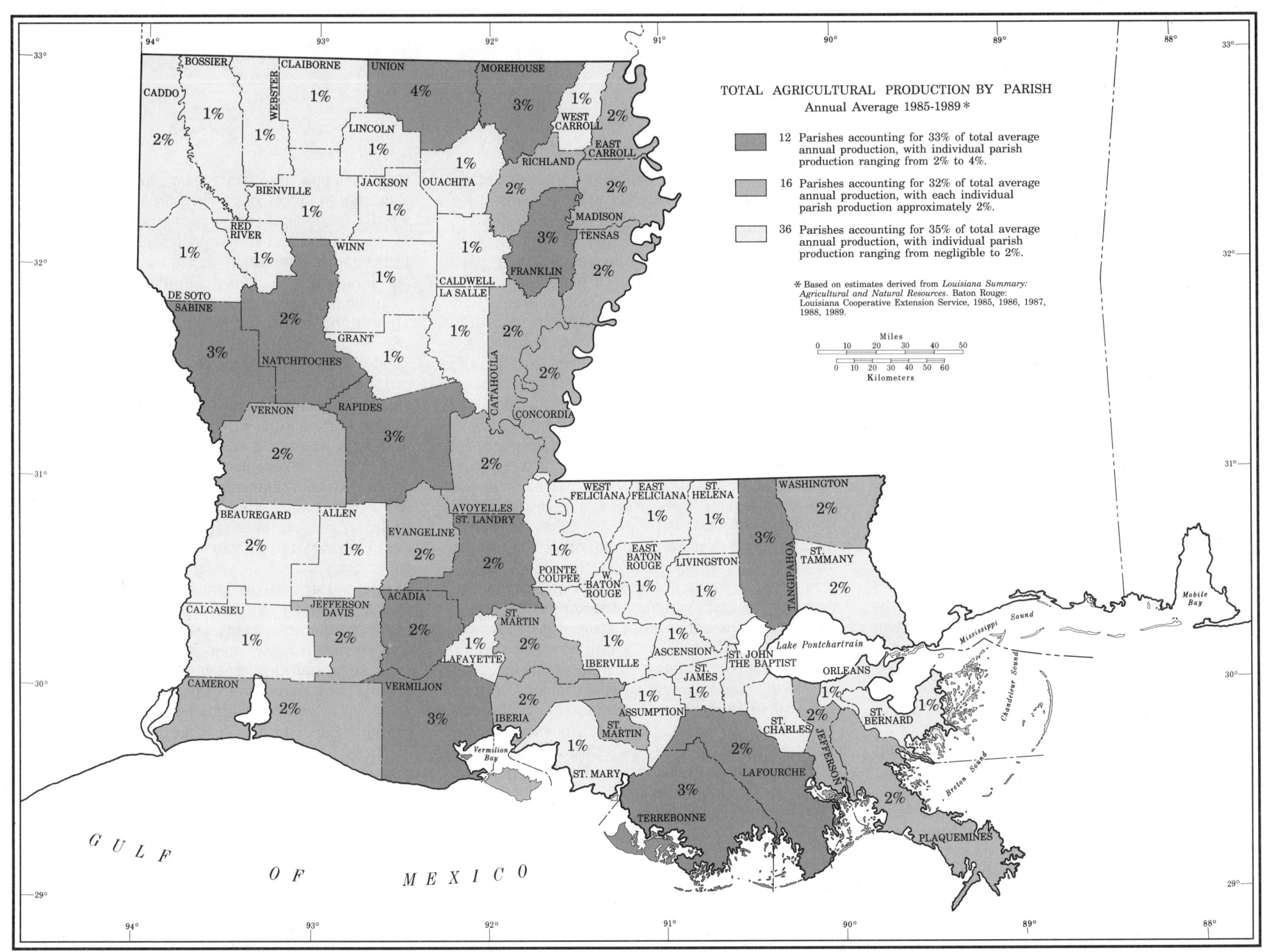

TOTAL AGRICULTURAL PRODUCTION BY PARISH
Annual Average 1985-1989 ✱

12 Parishes accounting for 33% of total average annual production, with individual parish production ranging from 2% to 4%.

16 Parishes accounting for 32% of total average annual production, with each individual parish production approximately 2%.

36 Parishes accounting for 35% of total average annual production, with individual parish production ranging from negligible to 2%.

✱ Based on estimates derived from *Louisiana Summary: Agricultural and Natural Resources*. Baton Rouge: Louisiana Cooperative Extension Service, 1985, 1986, 1987, 1988, 1989.

Louisiana's agricultural history reflects both national and regional themes. Early subsistence farming came to share the colony/state with a developing parallel slave-based plantation system fueled almost exclusively by blacks. Following the Civil War a sharecropping system succeeded slavery; then came the radical changes brought about by the mechanization of agriculture.

Total farm population has declined; moreover, in the 1987 Census of Agriculture more farm operators than not had a principal occupation separate from farming. Individual or family-operated farms declined in number; among the various ownership categories only the corporation-owned farm increased in number. Over the past fifty years farms in the state have dropped from 150,000 to 27,350; part of this decline is accounted for by a change in definition, yet by any definition it is significant.

The average size of farms grew from 67 acres fifty years ago to 293 acres in 1987. This compares with a national average of 462 acres. On average, Louisiana farms in 1987 produced only 75 percent of the national average market value of goods per farm: $49,000 as compared with $65,165 nationally. In 1987 the average Louisiana farmer had $37,400 in expenses; nationally the average was $51,797.

One can define agriculture and "agricultural products" in any of numerous ways. The Louisiana Cooperative Extension Service employs one such method in estimating gross agricultural production. The various components are divided into animal (Map 76) and crop (Map 77) categories. Using the parish-level data available, one can compute the average share of total production (and of each crop) which each parish contributes to the whole.

Of the state's estimated total agricultural production according to these extension service categories, crop production accounted on average for 65 percent and animal production for 35 percent of the total over the five years 1985–1989. This is a division for the gross value. When the value added by processing these raw agricultural products is factored in, crops now comprise 78 percent and animals 22 percent of the total estimated value. Of the value-added total, forestry alone accounts for a large majority of that sum.

Louisiana, with the alluvial origins of its soils and abundant rainfall, supports a wide variety of agricultural pursuits. Over the state's history few areas have been exempt from crop cultivation of some sort. Even those areas which do not lend themselves to cultivation usually possess varieties of wildlife which contribute to Louisiana's renewable products. Thus, given the expanse of arable land and the wide variety of products encompassed in our definition of agriculture, no major concentration of production exists to the total exclusion of any part of the state. The Mississippi and other floodplains exist as areas of concentrated crop production. Areas of concentration also appear for many of the various component parts of agriculture.

Every parish contributes to the total, and the range of contribution among most parishes is slight. Were agricultural production evenly divided among the state's sixty-four parishes, each parish would account for approximately 1.6 percent of the total. Reasons for variation from that equality of contribution include the area of each parish, the type of land (slope, fertility, texture, and so on), the annual variations in temperature and rainfall, and the amount and value of commodities produced. When the parishes are measured against the hypothetical mean, twenty-nine parishes exceed it and thirty-five parishes fall below. The variation in per-parish contribution to the total ranges from 4 percent to 0.2 percent. Union Parish averages the largest total contribution, St. John the Baptist the smallest.

Fully a third of the state's total agricultural production comes from twelve parishes scattered throughout the state. Union Parish in the top spot contributes primarily to animal (poultry) but also to crop (forestry) production. Tangipahoa (milk, forestry, and commercial vegetables) and Sabine (poultry and forestry) illustrate a common theme among most (but not all) agricultural parishes—a combination of one or more strong contributions in both animal and crop categories. Among this top group only Terrebonne (89 percent animal) and Morehouse (96 percent crop) parishes show an overwhelming preponderance in one category.

Another third of the state's agricultural production comes from sixteen parishes, each of which averages approximately 2 percent of the state's total. The final third is produced by the thirty-six (more than half of the state) remaining parishes. As with the top third, these two categories show no overall regionalization but instead are scattered throughout the state.

Copyright © 1995 by the University of Oklahoma Press

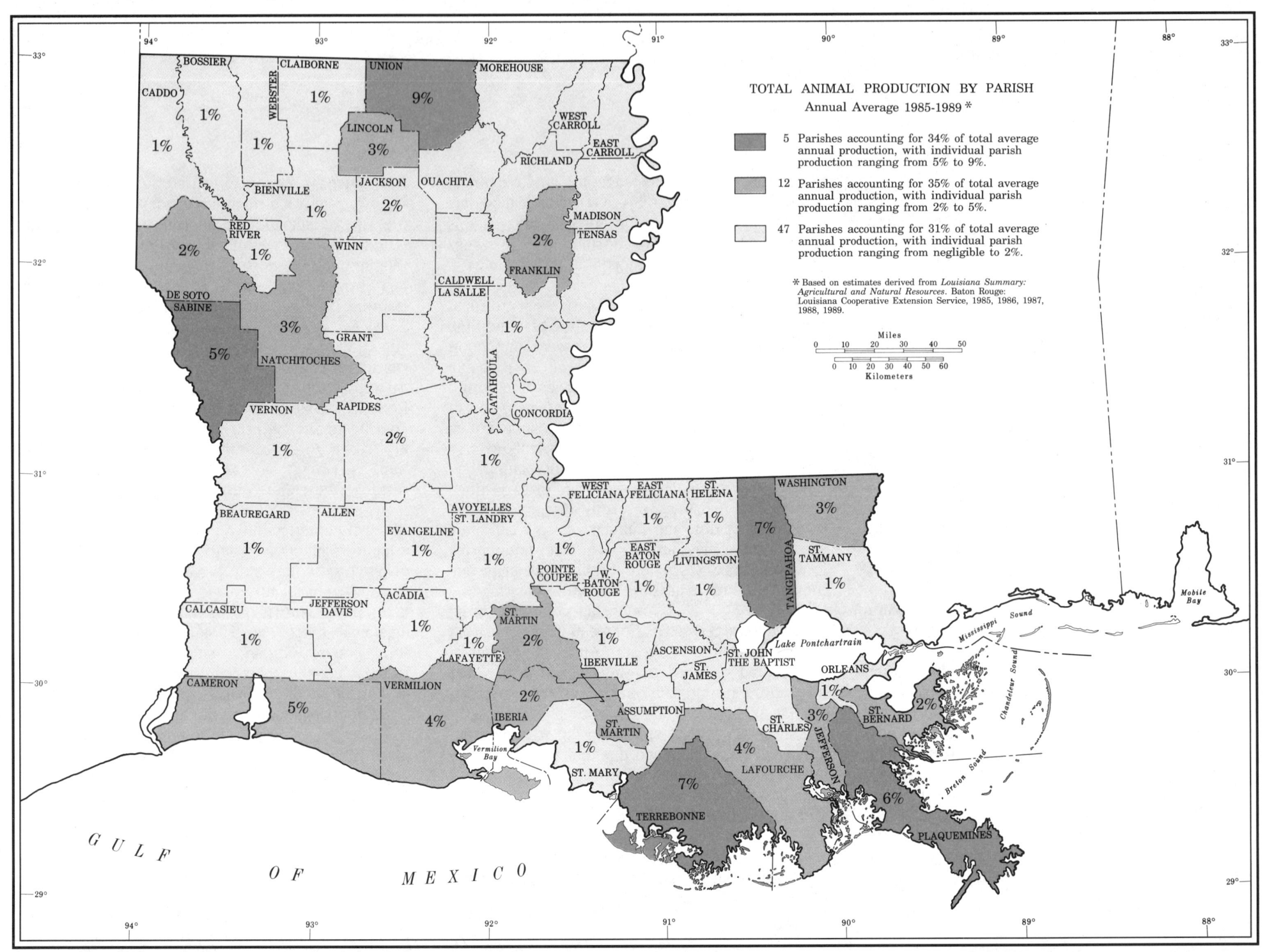

TOTAL ANIMAL PRODUCTION BY PARISH
Annual Average 1985-1989 *

5 Parishes accounting for 34% of total average
annual production, with individual parish
production ranging from 5% to 9%.

12 Parishes accounting for 35% of total average
annual production, with individual parish
production ranging from 2% to 5%.

47 Parishes accounting for 31% of total average
annual production, with individual parish
production ranging from negligible to 2%.

* Based on estimates derived from *Louisiana Summary:
Agricultural and Natural Resources*. Baton Rouge:
Louisiana Cooperative Extension Service, 1985, 1986, 1987,
1988, 1989.

Miles
0   10   20   30   40   50

0   10   20   30   40   50   60
Kilometers

Animal production within the state includes both wild and domesticated species. Over time the catch of "natural" products has become supplemented by the propagation of fur, fish, fowl, and other products. The various species of animals are grown, caught, or slaughtered not only for food but also for skins and other products. The 1987 Census of Agriculture calculated a total market value of $77,117,431,000 for all livestock and livestock products from all U.S. farms. Louisiana's contribution was $410,304,000 or 0.5 percent of that national census.

The Louisiana Cooperative Extension Service includes ten types of animal products in its annual survey of agricultural and natural resources. These types in order of estimated economic gross value are (1) marine fish, 32 percent of the total; (2) poultry, 22 percent; (3) cattle and calves, 21 percent; (4) milk, 13 percent; (5) freshwater fish, 6 percent; (6) horses, 4 percent; (7) swine, 1 percent; (8) alligators, 0.5 percent; (9) furs, 0.4 percent; and (10) sheep, 0.1 percent. The first six categories will be discussed individually (Maps 83–85); the remaining four can be treated in some detail here.

The swine industry has paralleled the cattle industry in that from colonial times two alternate systems developed. The Spanish system of husbanding animals under strict regulations produced better-quality, more fit animals. The Anglo-Saxon open-range system was a lackadaisical alternative, in which attention to the animals was seasonal, and quality suffered as a result. Over the twentieth century the swine industry has declined in overall production. From a peak in the 1930s and 1940s the production has dropped to perhaps one-tenth of what it was at its height. Much of this decline

reflects changing dietary patterns in the United States, as first beef, then chicken, replaced pork as first in per capita consumption. Another important factor has been changes in the scale of production, with large swine operators in the Midwest dominating the market.

Alligators and fur production again represent a continuation of historical production. The French fur trappers—coureurs de bois—developed trading networks among the various Indian tribes throughout much of North America, and Louisiana would be no different. Alligator hunting is a later development which in this century brought that animal in danger of extinction within the state. In turn, state regulations were brought into effect to protect the species. Both alligator and fur production in recent years have witnessed the development of "farms" which have supplanted the "wild" harvest in importance.

Sheep production, as with swine, has seen a precipitous decline during the twentieth century. From a peak production of 5,322,000 pounds in 1933 the production and number of sheep on Louisiana farms has decreased to the low to mid-300,000s pound range by the late 1980s. Likewise, wool production, after reaching a peak of 826,000 pounds in 1941, has declined to approximately 100,000 pounds annually today.

When the production value of each of the ten categories of animal production is combined and an annual average calculated for the 1985–1989 period, one can rank the state's parishes in their overall contribution to this type of production. Many parishes may specialize in one type of production—poultry, cattle, and so on. Others, however, may combine several areas of animal husbandry to account for their spot on the list. Some

parishes have only a small contribution to make to the overall animal production of the state. The distribution of animal production within the state is regional, reflecting proximity to supply, proximity to markets, and competing land uses, as well as other factors.

The percentage contribution by parish ranges from 9 percent of the total for Union Parish downward to 0.03 percent in St. John the Baptist Parish. Union Parish is particularly strong in the poultry category, which accounts for 89 percent of its overall animal production. St. John the Baptist Parish has only a small cattle and calf production and some areas of crawfish production.

Five parishes alone account for a third of the state's animal production. In addition to Union these are Terrebonne (7 percent, with a strong marine fishery component), Tangipahoa (7 percent, dairying), Plaquemines (6 percent, marine fisheries), and Sabine (5 percent, poultry) parishes. Twelve parishes produce another one-third of the average annual total. These are Cameron (5 percent, marine fisheries), Lafourche (4 percent, marine fisheries), Vermilion (4 percent, marine fisheries and calves), Washington (4 percent, milk), Jefferson (3 percent, marine fisheries), Lincoln (3 percent, poultry), Natchitoches (2 percent, poultry), Iberia (2 percent, marine fisheries), St. Martin (2 percent, freshwater fisheries), De Soto (2 percent, milk), St. Bernard (2 percent, marine fisheries), and Franklin (2 percent, freshwater fisheries) parishes. The final third of production comes from 47 parishes ranging from Rapides (less than 2 percent of the total) to St. John the Baptist Parish.

Copyright © 1995 by the University of Oklahoma Press

TOTAL CROP PRODUCTION BY PARISH

Annual Average 1985-1989 *

11 Parishes accounting for 34% of total average annual production, with individual parish production ranging from 2% to 4%.

17 Parishes accounting for 34% of total average annual production, with each individual parish production approximately 2%.

36 Parishes accounting for 32% of total average annual production, with individual parish production ranging from negligible to 1%.

* Based on estimates derived from *Louisiana Summary: Agricultural and Natural Resources.* Baton Rouge: Louisiana Cooperative Extension Service, 1985, 1986, 1987, 1988, 1989.

Miles
0 10 20 30 40 50

0 10 20 30 40 50 60
Kilometers

Crops produced in Louisiana include those varieties grown for direct or processed consumption as human food, those which are grown as animal feed, and those which provide other products for humankind. Some crops may serve more than one purpose. Today some crops—pine trees, for example—are cultivated which previously were harvested only from natural growth. More of Louisiana's plant life is being treated as not only renewable but also cultivatable.

The Census of Agriculture in 1987 calculated a total marketed value of $58,931,085,000 for all crops and crop products from U.S. farms. The total marketed value of crops was 43 percent of the combined total represented by all crop and all livestock products. Louisiana contributed $929,858,000 to the crop total, a 1.6 percent share.

Seventeen classes of crops are listed by the Louisiana Cooperative Extension Service in its annual survey of agricultural production. In order by estimated gross farm value these are (1) forests, 29 percent; (2) soybeans, 15 percent; (3) cotton, 15 percent; (4) sugarcane, 10 percent; (5) rice, 9 percent; (6) home gardens, 8 percent; (7) feed grains, 6 percent; (8) nursery stocks and ornamentals, 2 percent; (9) commercial vegetables, 2 percent; (10) sweet potatoes, 1.5 percent; (11) hay sold off the farm, 1 percent; (12) fruit crops, 0.5 percent; (13) sod production, 0.4 percent; (14) pecans, 0.3 percent; (15) Christmas trees, 0.2 percent; (16) peanuts, 0.02 percent; and (17) tobacco, 0.003 percent. Numbers one through five and seven will be discussed on individual maps; home gardens need not be discussed here. A few lines may suffice for each of the other products, which together account for only six percent of the estimated total value.

Nursery stock and ornamentals are economy-driven, subject to the health of the overall economy in Louisiana and the neighboring states of Mississippi and Texas, which act as market for the state's products. Commercial vegetables refer to a variety of products, including cucumbers, squash, broccoli, cabbage, onions, collards, eggplant, okra, sweet corn, tomatoes, snap beans, and tabasco and other peppers. Many if not all of these crops are also grown in home gardens for consumption. The commercial production of these vegetables depends not only on the natural conditions necessary for growth. Of equal importance to their success is the processing and marketing apparatus necessary to move the produce from the field to the store and the relative value of more traditional agricultural crops.

Sweet potatoes represent a sizable single commercial vegetable. New varieties have fueled increased production in the state. Competition, especially with North Carolina, affects the value of the crop and thus the relative acreage planted each year.

Hay sold for off-the-farm use includes alfalfa and other grasses. Alfalfa is a more valuable product per ton, whereas the other grasses in this category occupy the larger acreage. Hay sold off the farm represents less than one-half the total estimated production of that class of products, the majority being fed on farm.

Fruit crops in Louisiana include strawberries, citrus crops, peaches, blueberries, and others. The citrus and peach production is susceptible to freezes, and in recent years the Louisiana citrus industry has been wiped out on several occasions. Strawberries occupy a smaller acreage but are valuable to the state's economy as well. In freeze years they represent the majority of the value in this class of product.

Sod production, pecans, peanuts, and tobacco together comprise less than 1 percent of the estimated gross value of crop production. Sod is a growing industry. Pecans are harvested both from planted and wild trees, with planted orchards accounting for only 25 percent of the trees. Peanuts are a crop where, in exchange for federal price supports, farmers in turn agree to an allotted number of acres. Morehouse Parish contains most of the quotas for this crop. Tobacco production in the state, though steady, remains a negligible part of overall tobacco production.

With the wide variety of crops included in the state's production, particularly the widespread forest resources, the distribution of crop production by parish does not show the same wide range as in animal production. Morehouse Parish leads the state in the percentage of the overall crop production, with 4 percent of the total. At the opposite end is St. Charles Parish, which contributes only 0.2 percent of the total.

The regional distributions shown in several of the major components of the state's production fade when the overall production is plotted. With crop production, eleven parishes—contributing from 4 percent down to 2 percent—are needed to comprise the first third of production. In addition to Morehouse these are Rapides, Franklin, Tensas, St. Landry, Richland, Acadia, East Carroll, Madison, Evangeline, and Vermilion parishes. A second set of seventeen parishes—contributing approximately 2 percent each—make up a second third of the state's total. Louisiana's remaining thirty-six parishes together contribute the final third in the state's crop production.

Copyright © 1995 by the University of Oklahoma Press

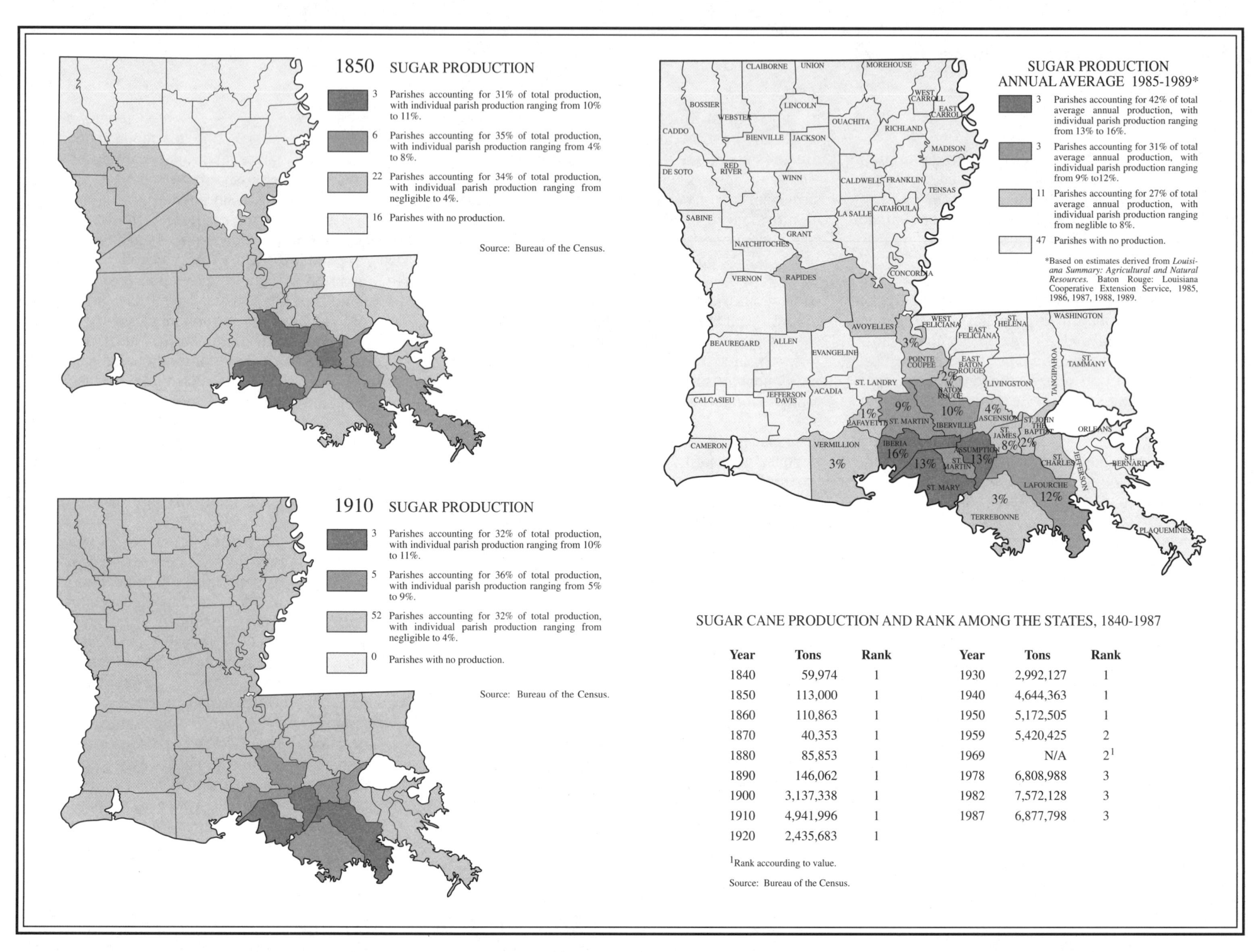

1850 SUGAR PRODUCTION

3 Parishes accounting for 31% of total production, with individual parish production ranging from 10% to 11%.

6 Parishes accounting for 35% of total production, with individual parish production ranging from 4% to 8%.

22 Parishes accounting for 34% of total production, with individual parish production ranging from negligible to 4%.

16 Parishes with no production.

Source: Bureau of the Census.

1910 SUGAR PRODUCTION

3 Parishes accounting for 32% of total production, with individual parish production ranging from 10% to 11%.

5 Parishes accounting for 36% of total production, with individual parish production ranging from 5% to 9%.

52 Parishes accounting for 32% of total production, with individual parish production ranging from negligible to 4%.

0 Parishes with no production.

Source: Bureau of the Census.

SUGAR PRODUCTION ANNUAL AVERAGE 1985-1989*

3 Parishes accounting for 42% of total average annual production, with individual parish production ranging from 13% to 16%.

3 Parishes accounting for 31% of total average annual production, with individual parish production ranging from 9% to 12%.

11 Parishes accounting for 27% of total average annual production, with individual parish production ranging from neglible to 8%.

47 Parishes with no production.

*Based on estimates derived from *Louisiana Summary: Agricultural and Natural Resources*. Baton Rouge: Louisiana Cooperative Extension Service, 1985, 1986, 1987, 1988, 1989.

SUGAR CANE PRODUCTION AND RANK AMONG THE STATES, 1840-1987

Year	Tons	Rank	Year	Tons	Rank
1840	59,974	1	1930	2,992,127	1
1850	113,000	1	1940	4,644,363	1
1860	110,863	1	1950	5,172,505	1
1870	40,353	1	1959	5,420,425	2
1880	85,853	1	1969	N/A	2[1]
1890	146,062	1	1978	6,808,988	3
1900	3,137,338	1	1982	7,572,128	3
1910	4,941,996	1	1987	6,877,798	3
1920	2,435,683	1			

[1]Rank accourding to value.

Source: Bureau of the Census.

Sugar represented one of the two major plantation crops in antebellum Louisiana. Yet, as with its sister crop, cotton, sugar played only a minor role in the colonial agricultural economy. Technological change would propel it to the preeminent role in the decades just preceding the Civil War, a glory to which it would never return.

The introduction of sugar into Louisiana occurred in the early French period of the eighteenth century. Bienville mentions the crop in his report of 1733. This early sugar suffered from the lack of a successful refining process, the only product was a sodden mass that leaked from the barrels in which it was shipped. Then, in 1795, Etienne de Bore, a planter near New Orleans, purchased a new variety of sugar cane seed, hired Antoine Morin, a West Indian sugar maker, and achieved success. In less than a decade seventy-five plantations were growing sugar cane, and over a dozen refineries were in operation.

Sugar cane actually requires fifteen to twenty-two months for optimum growth, so in Louisiana it is grown only as long as freezes can be avoided. Today a 250-day growing season is regarded as the minimum. Planting usually occurs from September through early October. Growth begins the following spring and advances rapidly in hot, rainy summer months. Harvesting takes place from October through December (or even early January) of the following year.

Over time the sugar crop expanded from southern Louisiana bayous up the Mississippi and Red River valleys as far inland as the Natchitoches area. Greater protection from frosts becomes a necessity as one moves north. Today the thirty-first parallel approximates the northern limit

of sugar production in the state, and the sugar region extends from Plaquemines Parish westward to Bayou Vermilion.

The earliest refining process for sugar was the open-kettle method. After the time of grinding (harvest) the cane would be pressed between rollers to extract the juice. This juice would then be boiled through several stages until it crystallized. About 1832, Norbert Rillieux, a free black, adapted the vacuum-pan method in sugar production in the state. A partial vacuum in the pan led to a more economical means of sugar refining.

An antebellum sugar plantation required about twice the capital as did a cotton plantation. The restricted area of the state in which sugar could be grown, plus the returns from sugar production, led to intensive cultivation of the crop. Sugar yielded a 10 percent return on capital invested in those days, however, and many of the grander plantation homes surviving today belonged to the sugar planters and were built in the crop's heyday just before the Civil War.

Following the war, sugar production changed to a contract-wage system. Many planters had been ruined, and their lands were bought out by Northern capitalists and others who had migrated to the state after the conflict. In time, corporations came to dominate the production and refining of the sugar crop. Blacks still provided the labor. Louisiana's first attempts to organize agricultural labor came in the 1880s when the Knights of Labor attempted to unionize the sugar workers. This proved unsuccessful when imported gunmen and local people broke the strike in the Thibodaux Massacre of 1887, in which at least thirty blacks were killed.

Over time sugar enjoyed the same advances in mechanization, improved fertilizers, and more productive species as did other Louisiana crops. The industry also had the advantage of tariff protection for most of the period. Sugar is widely grown in many tropical areas outside the United States, areas with much lower costs of production. Declining early in the twentieth century, sugar acreage tended upwards after protective measures were enacted by Congress in the 1930s. This rise continued through the 1960s and early 1970s, then reversed after the Sugar Act of the 1930s was not renewed. Diseases began to attack the prevailing species, and a low was set in 1927 when only 89,000 acres were harvested. Newer varieties were introduced in the late 1920s; twentieth-century peaks came in 1964 (345,000 acres harvested) and in 1973 (341,000 acres).

Sugars, syrups, and molasses are the first manufactured products derived from sugar. By-products include the final molasses (usually called "blackstrap") used in ethyl alcohol production, cattle feeds, and cooking. Cane fiber from the stalk is used widely in the production of building board, with some also going into cattle feed.

Only seventeen of Louisiana's sixty-four parishes grow sugar. Iberia alone accounts for 16 percent of the estimated total production over the 1985-1989 period. Both St. Mary and Assumption parishes produced approximately 13 percent and Lafourche Parish almost 12 percent. These four parishes represent over half the state's sugar production. No other parish produces 10 percent of the total, and the three smallest sugar-producing parishes—St. Charles, Avoyelles, and Rapides—together account for less than 1 percent.

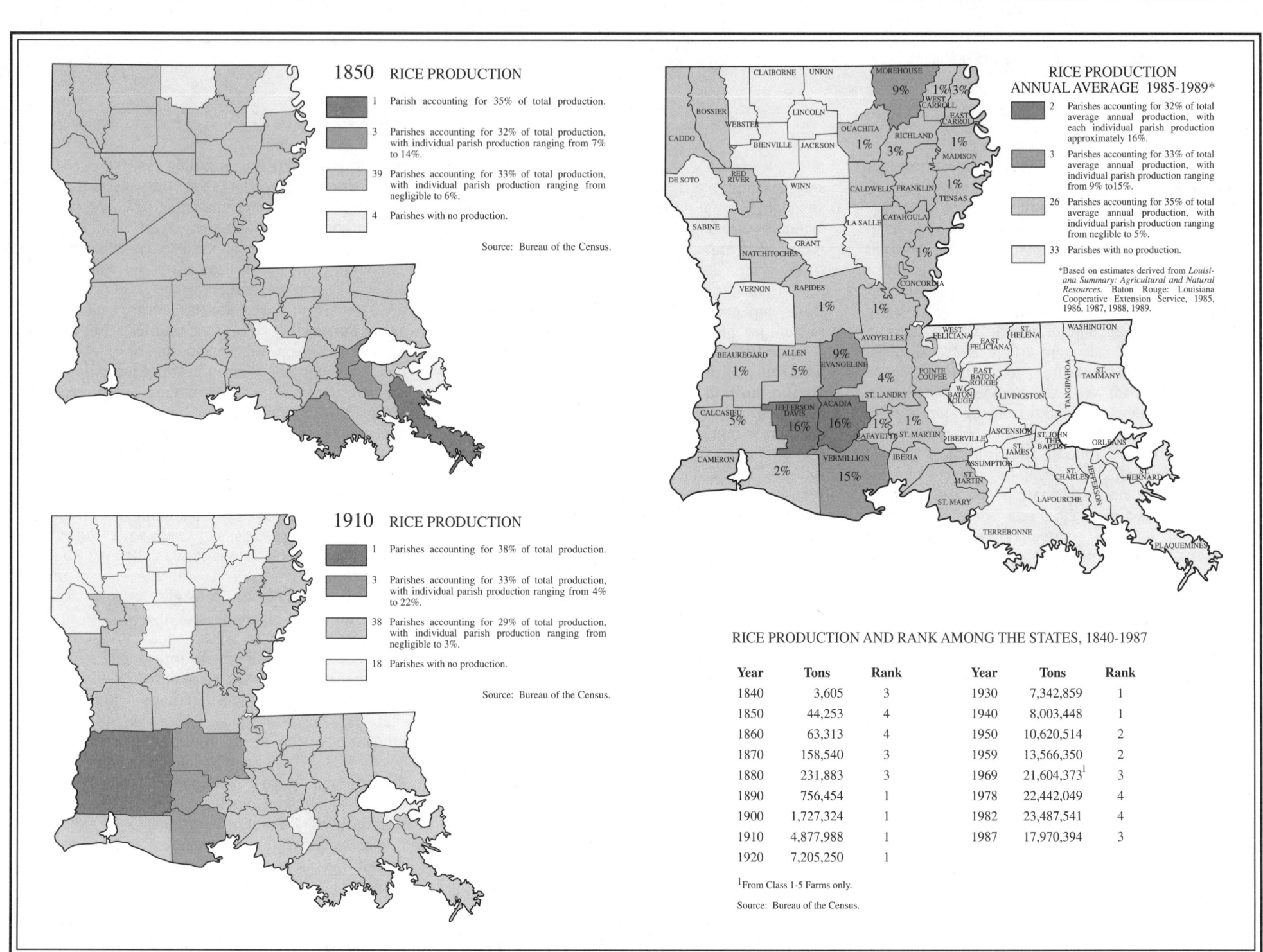

1850 RICE PRODUCTION

1   Parish accounting for 35% of total production.

3   Parishes accounting for 32% of total production, with individual parish production ranging from 7% to 14%.

39   Parishes accounting for 33% of total production, with individual parish production ranging from negligible to 6%.

4   Parishes with no production.

Source: Bureau of the Census.

1910 RICE PRODUCTION

1   Parishes accounting for 38% of total production.

3   Parishes accounting for 33% of total production, with individual parish production ranging from 4% to 22%.

38   Parishes accounting for 29% of total production, with individual parish production ranging from negligible to 3%.

18   Parishes with no production.

Source: Bureau of the Census.

RICE PRODUCTION ANNUAL AVERAGE 1985-1989*

2   Parishes accounting for 32% of total average annual production, with each individual parish production approximately 16%.

3   Parishes accounting for 33% of total average annual production, with individual parish production ranging from 9% to 15%.

26   Parishes accounting for 35% of total average annual production, with individual parish production ranging from neglible to 5%.

33   Parishes with no production.

*Based on estimates derived from *Louisiana Summary: Agricultural and Natural Resources.* Baton Rouge: Louisiana Cooperative Extension Service, 1985, 1986, 1987, 1988, 1989.

RICE PRODUCTION AND RANK AMONG THE STATES, 1840-1987

Year	Tons	Rank	Year	Tons	Rank
1840	3,605	3	1930	7,342,859	1
1850	44,253	4	1940	8,003,448	1
1860	63,313	4	1950	10,620,514	2
1870	158,540	3	1959	13,566,350	2
1880	231,883	3	1969	21,604,373[1]	3
1890	756,454	1	1978	22,442,049	4
1900	1,727,324	1	1982	23,487,541	4
1910	4,877,988	1	1987	17,970,394	3
1920	7,205,250	1			

[1]From Class 1-5 Farms only.

Source: Bureau of the Census.

Rice has been among Louisiana's agricultural products since colonial times. Over the years, however, it has expanded from a product for home consumption to a product for export and a staple of the state's economy. This increased importance came about especially after the crop expanded into the prairies of southwestern Louisiana.

Rice requires about the same growing season as does cotton, approximately two hundred days. Unlike cotton, rice requires irrigation to grow properly, but this irrigation serves primarily to control weeds and keep a clean harvest, not to water the crop. In early colonial days rice patches were small and output was termed "providential," that is, whatever product resulted came from the natural allocation of water and soil. Rice cultivation expanded as more experience was gained and new varieties were introduced. Although slave labor was sometimes involved, rice cultivation was often carried out by small farmers. Rice before the Civil War in no way rivaled cotton or sugar as a plantation crop.

After the end of the Civil War, with sugar suffering from diseased stock, rice made inroads along the Mississippi River where water could be pumped over the levees to irrigate the fields. New Orleans developed into a commercial rice center, with milling and distribution facilities. Sugar, however, made a comeback with new varieties and additional capital. Rice production in turn migrated into southwest Louisiana, hitherto a region of cattle production and sparse population.

In the 1880s the prairies of southwestern Louisiana had gained new transportation access with the completion of the Louisiana and Western and Morgan's Louisiana and Texas (later part of the Southern Pacific) railroads. Vast tracts of the prairies were bought up by land companies such as J. B. Watkins's North American Land and Timber Company. Such companies in turn sold this land to immigrant farmers, largely from the Middle West. The Southern Pacific and others also actively promoted the area for agricultural settlement. The immigrant farmers in time substituted rice for the corn and hog economy they had left. Dr. Seaman A. Knapp of the Iowa Agricultural College had been brought in and recommended rice as a staple. Knapp's search for new rice species abroad and the work of S. L. Wright in developing new varieties of rice locally led to a major rice-producing area.

The prairies were suited for rice culture not only because of their topography and fertility but also because of the existence of a clay "hardpan"—an impervious layer of soil—beneath the surface. This hardpan produced a barrier which retained the irrigation water in the rice fields above. The regional streams and impoundment of natural rainfall early on provided sufficient water supplies, and a system of canals brought this supply to the fields. Shallow wells into the groundwater provided an alternate source. In recent years rice farmers have had concerns about retaining an adequate supply of high-quality water.

Rice also represents a crop in which mechanization and better varieties of seed have led to increased production. Early machinery was modified from its application for wheat production; in time, equipment specifically made for rice arrived directly from the factory. Binding, threshing, and milling machines all take their turn in the harvest and refining of rice. As with many other agricultural products, rice has its own festival, at Crowley in October.

During the twentieth century the acreage planted in rice has fluctuated widely, ranging from 390,000 acres in 1983 down from a high of 682,000 acres in 1954. Particularly since World War II the productivity per acre has increased tremendously, more than doubling from the early decades to the most recent. Total production has varied with the number of acres planted even as the increasingly productive species have created a general upward trend. On average the recent crops have produced in excess of two billion pounds of rice annually. Modern production is usually given in terms of hundredweight.

Rice today is no longer grown continuously but in rotation with grass pasturage and soybeans. Federal regulations also limit the acreage to be planted in return for price supports. Rice is planted from March to June. Once the green shoots reach a height of three to four inches, the fields are flooded with water two to six inches deep and are kept submerged for approximately three months or until the rice has headed. At harvesting the fields are drained and allowed to dry in order for the machinery to do its work. The harvested rice is then milled and marketed in various forms, largely as white (polished) or brown (unpolished) rice. Some residue is sold as cattle feed.

Thirty-one of the state's sixty-four parishes have grown rice in at least one of the years 1985–1989, but more recently that number has dropped to twenty-nine. Rice is grown not only in the southwestern prairies but also in the alluvial areas of the Mississippi and Red rivers. Almost a third of the rice over the 1985–1989 crop years came from Jefferson Davis and Acadia parishes. The second third was grown in Vermilion, Evangeline, and Morehouse parishes, the next three largest producers. The other twenty-six producing parishes accounted for from 5 percent to less than 1 percent each and together accounted for yet another third of the state's total production.

Copyright © 1995 by the University of Oklahoma Press

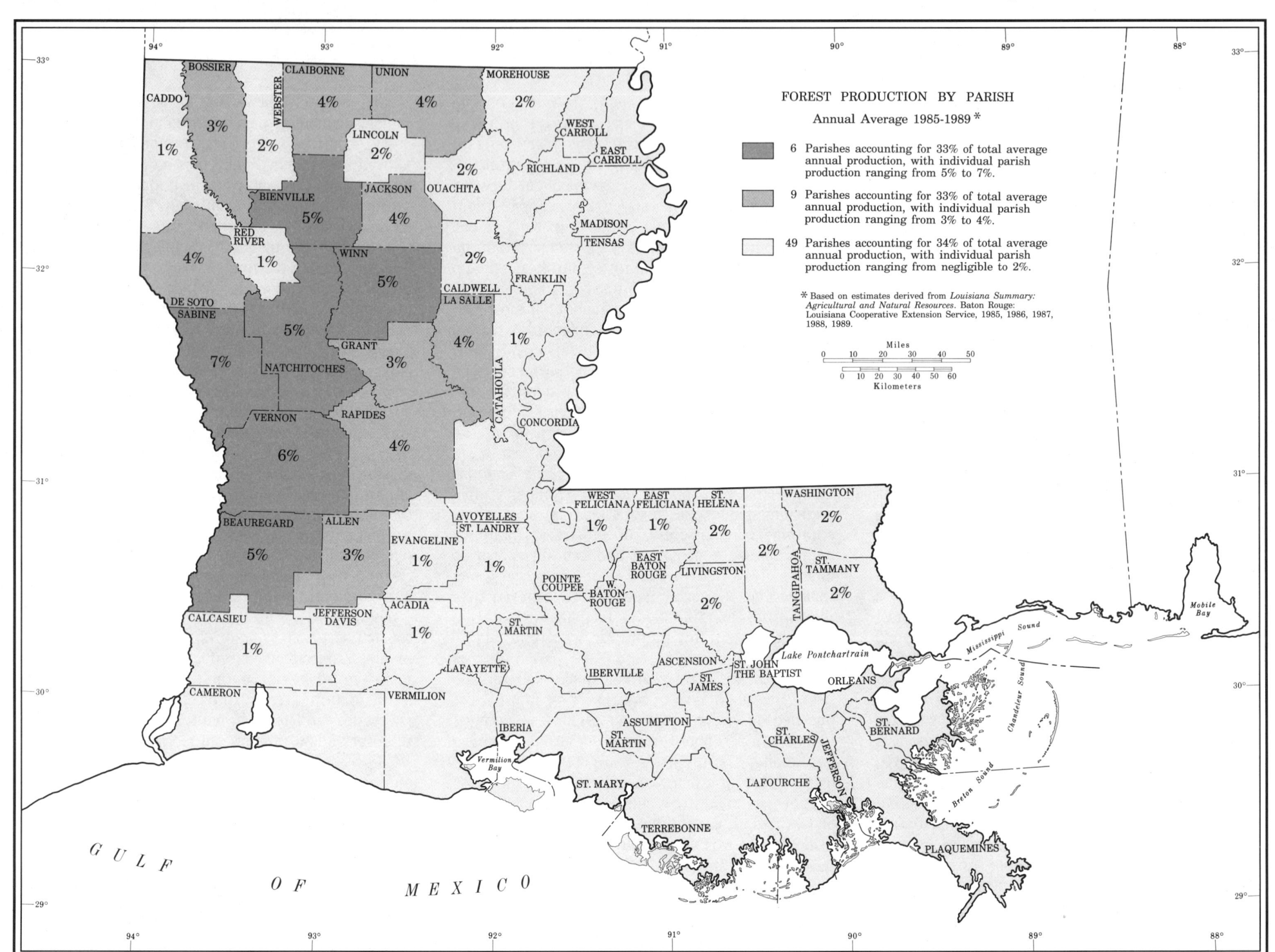

FOREST PRODUCTION BY PARISH

Annual Average 1985-1989 *

6 Parishes accounting for 33% of total average annual production, with individual parish production ranging from 5% to 7%.

9 Parishes accounting for 33% of total average annual production, with individual parish production ranging from 3% to 4%.

49 Parishes accounting for 34% of total average annual production, with individual parish production ranging from negligible to 2%.

* Based on estimates derived from *Louisiana Summary: Agricultural and Natural Resources*. Baton Rouge: Louisiana Cooperative Extension Service, 1985, 1986, 1987, 1988, 1989.

Miles
0 10 20 30 40 50

0 10 20 30 40 50 60
Kilometers

The usage of Louisiana's forests dates from the earliest inhabitants. The woods provided fuel and other supplies to the Indian tribes. European colonization increased that use. Lumber as well as naval stores (tar, pitch, and turpentine) were needed in the colony and elsewhere. At the turn of the twentieth century, however, came the full-scale cutting over of the state's virgin forests, largely in the space of the 1890–1920 period. Since the 1920s trees have been treated as a renewable resource, and new species have come to dominate the state's forests.

The colonial lumber industry used waterways for transportation. Thus, before the advent of a railroad system, the industry grew along the various streams of the state, with logs cut and floated downstream to mills along the banks. Processing of the logs took place in small mills powered by human or other animal labor, then later by water and steam. Cypress was of greatest importance for local use and trade, although some pine and oak were also exported.

Between 1876 and 1888 public lands in the South could be acquired through cash purchase. This temporarily superseded the Homestead Act of 1862, which had limited acquisition to 160 acres per homesteader. During this period, particularly 1881–1883, over one million acres of the public domain in Louisiana passed into the hands of largely Northern speculators.

As the nation's northern and midwestern forests became depleted, operators from those states began to migrate to Louisiana and other southern states. Although much land had passed from the public domain into private hands earlier, about 1905 the competitive purchase of these lands for lumber harvest began. Railroads had already begun to penetrate the forested areas of the states, particularly the pine forests. Some of these rail lines served primarily as logging roads, feeding felled timber to massive sawmills. Smaller logging roads extended back from practically every mill head to bring in saw fodder. Technological advances in sawmilling dramatically increased the capacity of these mills.

Both pine and hardwood varieties were harvested, largely for market to the north and east. Entire towns sprang up at the junction of mill site and rail line; other established towns experienced rapid growth in association with timber exploitation. For much of the first two decades of the twentieth century Louisiana ranked in the top three lumber producing states in the nation, competing with Washington and Michigan for the top spot. In 1915 the state produced almost 12 percent of the nation's lumber; from 1913 through 1918 its share exceeded 10 percent annually. Production crested in 1913 at 4,161,560,000 board feet, and the proportion of the nation's total in 1915 at 11.75 percent.

As the forest resources began to play out after 1920, the large operators began to move on to the Pacific Northwest for those resources. Left behind were large areas of cutover land which reverted to the state for nonpayment of taxes. Conventional wisdom that the forests would take centuries to recover proved wrong. The growth of different species, conservation work pioneered in Louisiana by Henry Hardtner, and the appearance of new wood products retained the industry in the state in a different form.

Today Louisiana's forest industry operates on the basis of sustained yield. The harvest recurs over a period of decades. For example, in stands younger than twelve years, some thinning may be made for fence posts. Trees for pulpwood are thinned out at intervals beginning at twelve to fifteen years and recurring over the next fifteen to twenty years. At thirty years and over, timber for saw logs and other products may be harvested. A new plantation economy based upon pine trees rather than cotton or sugar has thus come into existence. Louisiana's forests—both pine and hardwood—feed a variety of industries, including paper and allied products, lumber and wood products, and wood furniture.

Each of Louisiana's sixty-four parishes contributed some amount, however small, to the average estimated annual production for 1985–1989. Individual parish contributions ranged from 7 percent of the total downward to production that makes the term "negligible" seem an exaggeration. Six parishes in the north and west sections account for a third of the production: Sabine, Vernon, Winn, Beauregard, Bienville, and Natchitoches. A second third comes from eight parishes in the same region. About 92 percent of the value of production comes from pine, the remainder from hardwood species. Of the pine production some three-quarters is used as pulpwood.

Copyright © 1995 by the University of Oklahoma Press

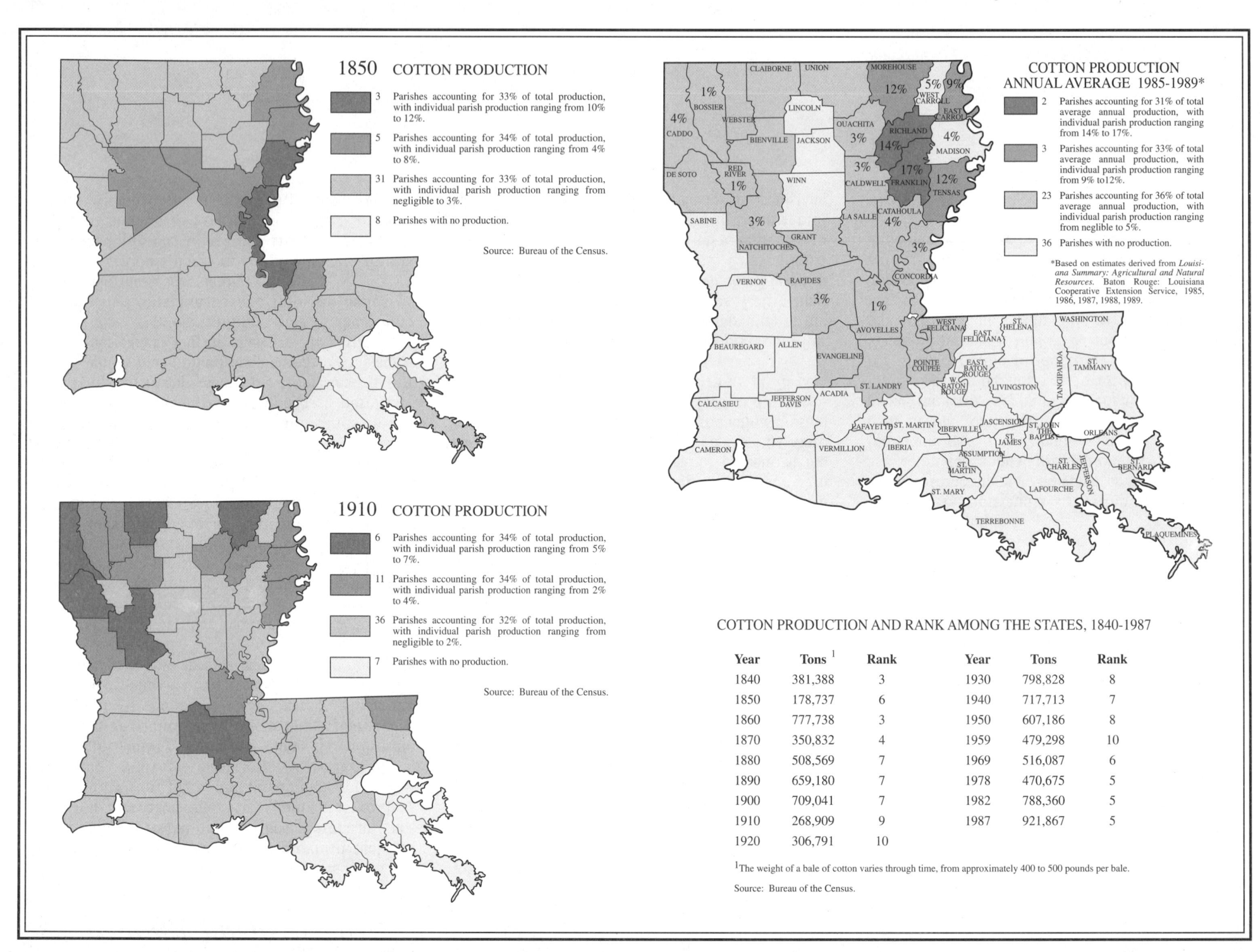

1850 COTTON PRODUCTION

3 Parishes accounting for 33% of total production, with individual parish production ranging from 10% to 12%.

5 Parishes accounting for 34% of total production, with individual parish production ranging from 4% to 8%.

31 Parishes accounting for 33% of total production, with individual parish production ranging from negligible to 3%.

8 Parishes with no production.

Source: Bureau of the Census.

COTTON PRODUCTION ANNUAL AVERAGE 1985-1989*

2 Parishes accounting for 31% of total average annual production, with individual parish production ranging from 14% to 17%.

3 Parishes accounting for 33% of total average annual production, with individual parish production ranging from 9% to 12%.

23 Parishes accounting for 36% of total average annual production, with individual parish production ranging from negligible to 5%.

36 Parishes with no production.

*Based on estimates derived from *Louisiana Summary: Agricultural and Natural Resources.* Baton Rouge: Louisiana Cooperative Extension Service, 1985, 1986, 1987, 1988, 1989.

1910 COTTON PRODUCTION

6 Parishes accounting for 34% of total production, with individual parish production ranging from 5% to 7%.

11 Parishes accounting for 34% of total production, with individual parish production ranging from 2% to 4%.

36 Parishes accounting for 32% of total production, with individual parish production ranging from negligible to 2%.

7 Parishes with no production.

Source: Bureau of the Census.

COTTON PRODUCTION AND RANK AMONG THE STATES, 1840-1987

Year	Tons [1]	Rank	Year	Tons	Rank
1840	381,388	3	1930	798,828	8
1850	178,737	6	1940	717,713	7
1860	777,738	3	1950	607,186	8
1870	350,832	4	1959	479,298	10
1880	508,569	7	1969	516,087	6
1890	659,180	7	1978	470,675	5
1900	709,041	7	1982	788,360	5
1910	268,909	9	1987	921,867	5
1920	306,791	10			

[1] The weight of a bale of cotton varies through time, from approximately 400 to 500 pounds per bale.

Source: Bureau of the Census.

One of the major agricultural crops for almost two centuries, cotton was early introduced into French colonial Louisiana. Its expansion as a staple crop resulted from a technological innovation, the cotton gin, in 1793. Paired with sugar as the major plantation crops in antebellum Louisiana, cotton more readily survived the abolition of slavery, only to find its kingly reign ended by lower prices, the arrival of the boll weevil, alternative textiles, and competing crops in the twentieth century.

Cotton came to Louisiana with Iberville at the turn of the eighteenth century, but almost a century would elapse before it came to importance. Agriculture itself was low in the minds of early colonists, with their search for riches without work. Indigo and tobacco, even sugar, competed with cotton for the attention of agriculturalists. Early-settled areas did not provide the best soils for cotton because of the less than necessary drainage and frequent flooding, nor was there yet any easy means of separating lint from seed in the plucked bolls.

The invention of the cotton gin by Eli Whitney—along with the development of power looms—provided the technology to more cheaply produce cotton textiles. A growing urban population provided a ready market for these textiles at home and abroad. As Louisiana's population increased, more and more lands opened up to yeoman farmer and planter alike. River bottomland and bluff land along the ancient terraces provided the best areas for cotton production. Although cotton will grow in a variety of soil types, a well-drained, deep loam represents the best natural environment. Rainfall should be regular but tapering off as the bolls mature in order to provide a dry picking season, whether by hand or mechanical picker.

Cotton vied with sugar in antebellum Louisiana's plantation economy. The former could grow in more northern areas of the state and did not require as great a capital investment as did the latter. Sugar, however, produced the greater return on investment of labor, whereas cotton was more land-intensive. Each was tied to areas into which river transportation extended, land transit being still in a frontier stage.

Following the disruption and destruction brought on by the Civil War, cotton entered into a share-cropping and crop-lien system. Under these systems tenant farmers provided the labor to the landowners to produce the crop. They then shared in the return earned by the cotton. Originally developed as a more economical alternative to a wage-based system, the share-cropping and crop-lien systems would plague the state and region until the next century. Black and white farmers alike suffered under this system. Still, cotton remained a popular crop because of the cash earned from the sale of the baled product; no other crop provided such a cash return over such a large portion of the state (Map 86).

The appearance of the boll weevil in the early twentieth century increased the risks of cotton production. Price fluctuations during and after World War I added to the economic uncertainty of the crop. Beginning with the Agricultural Adjustment Act of 1933 and extending through subsequent legislation, a system of acreage allotments with guaranteed base prices has improved the general lot of producers even as it has driven marginal producers from the fields.

An end to farm tenancy came with the mechanization of agriculture. The tractor took over the work previously powered by the mule. Mechanical pickers, which developed into a mass-producible form in 1944, not only lessened the time necessary to harvest the crop but also harvested it more cheaply than hand labor could. Increased fertilization and better seed products enhanced the productivity of the crop. Insecticides and herbicides battled the boll weevil and other animal and weed pests. The twentieth century has seen larger, more efficient cotton farms even as a generation of farmers has left the land. Over the past century, acreage in cotton has fluctuated downward from a peak of 1,953,000 harvested acres in 1930 to an average of 600,000 in the 1980s. At the same time, yield per acre has increased. More bales were produced in 1987 than in 1930, and on one-third the acreage. Total production does show wide ranges from year to year.

Twenty-eight of Louisiana's sixty-four parishes grew cotton during the years 1985–1989—a distribution of production which has remained fairly constant. Today's cotton parishes are located in the northern areas of the state, largely in the alluvial valleys of the Mississippi and Red rivers. The two largest cotton-producing parishes—Franklin and Richland—have accounted for almost a third of the cotton grown over the past five years. A second third came from the adjacent parishes of Tensas, Morehouse, and East Carroll. Production in the twenty-three parishes in the lowest third ranged from almost 5 percent of the total down to a negligible amount. Twelve of the parishes each had less than 1 percent of the total produced.

Copyright © 1995 by the University of Oklahoma Press

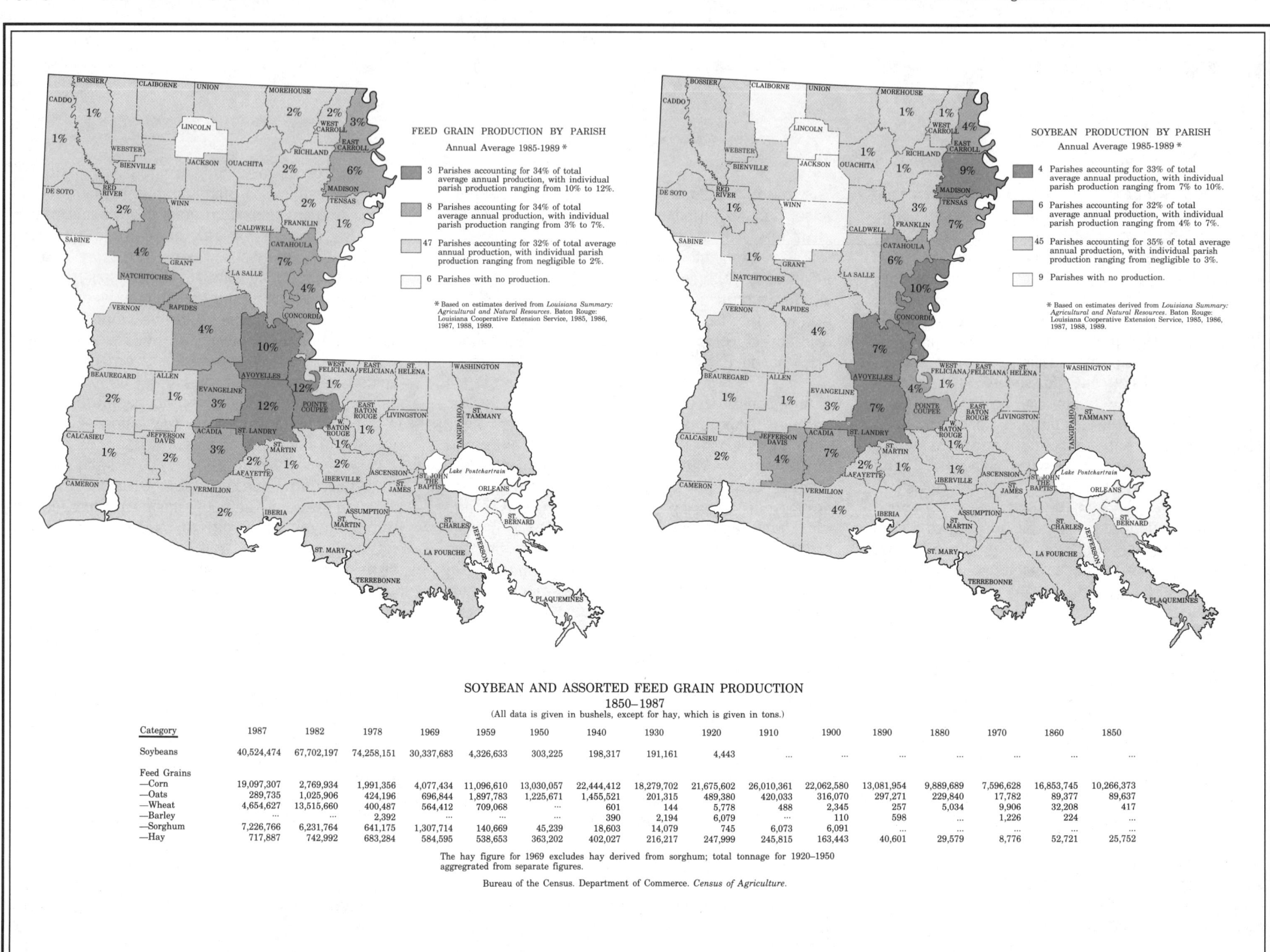

FEED GRAIN PRODUCTION BY PARISH

Annual Average 1985-1989 *

3 Parishes accounting for 34% of total average annual production, with individual parish production ranging from 10% to 12%.

8 Parishes accounting for 34% of total average annual production, with individual parish production ranging from 3% to 7%.

47 Parishes accounting for 32% of total average annual production, with individual parish production ranging from negligible to 2%.

6 Parishes with no production.

* Based on estimates derived from *Louisiana Summary: Agricultural and Natural Resources.* Baton Rouge: Louisiana Cooperative Extension Service, 1985, 1986, 1987, 1988, 1989.

SOYBEAN PRODUCTION BY PARISH

Annual Average 1985-1989 *

4 Parishes accounting for 33% of total average annual production, with individual parish production ranging from 7% to 10%.

6 Parishes accounting for 32% of total average annual production, with individual parish production ranging from 4% to 7%.

45 Parishes accounting for 35% of total average annual production, with individual parish production ranging from negligible to 3%.

9 Parishes with no production.

* Based on estimates derived from *Louisiana Summary: Agricultural and Natural Resources.* Baton Rouge: Louisiana Cooperative Extension Service, 1985, 1986, 1987, 1988, 1989.

SOYBEAN AND ASSORTED FEED GRAIN PRODUCTION
1850–1987
(All data is given in bushels, except for hay, which is given in tons.)

Category	1987	1982	1978	1969	1959	1950	1940	1930	1920	1910	1900	1890	1880	1970	1860	1850
Soybeans	40,524,474	67,702,197	74,258,151	30,337,683	4,326,633	303,225	198,317	191,161	4,443	...	...	...	...	...	...	...
Feed Grains																
—Corn	19,097,307	2,769,934	1,991,356	4,077,434	11,096,610	13,030,057	22,444,412	18,279,702	21,675,602	26,010,361	22,062,580	13,081,954	9,889,689	7,596,628	16,853,745	10,266,373
—Oats	289,735	1,025,906	424,196	696,844	1,897,783	1,225,671	1,455,521	201,315	489,380	420,033	316,070	297,271	229,840	17,782	89,377	89,637
—Wheat	4,654,627	13,515,660	400,487	564,412	709,068	...	601	144	5,778	488	2,345	257	5,034	9,906	32,208	417
—Barley	...	...	2,392	...	...	...	390	2,194	6,079	...	110	598	...	1,226	224	...
—Sorghum	7,226,766	6,231,764	641,175	1,307,714	140,669	45,239	18,603	745	6,073	6,073	6,091	...	...	...	...	...
—Hay	717,887	742,992	683,284	584,595	538,653	363,202	402,027	216,217	247,999	245,815	163,443	40,601	29,579	8,776	52,721	25,752

The hay figure for 1969 excludes hay derived from sorghum; total tonnage for 1920–1950 aggregated from separate figures.

Bureau of the Census. Department of Commerce. *Census of Agriculture.*

Feed grains—corn, wheat, oats, and grain sorghum—have long been a staple of Louisiana agriculture. Indians had grown corn for centuries. European settlers adopted it for their own use when their familiar wheat did not prosper so well in the first French-settled areas. Grains—particularly corn—represented food both for the farmer and the farmer's family and for the animal stock.

As with other aspects of colonial Louisiana, the cultivation of feed grains was part of a subsistence system, producing enough for the grower's consumption with little if any left for sale. In time, as more and better agriculturalists migrated to the colony, farmers became more productive through adaptation to the local conditions and through sheer labor. Grains grew on both plantation and farm in antebellum Louisiana. Corn represented the most important of the grain crops. Grown alongside the commercial crops of cotton and sugar, corn provided nutrition for both human and animal consumption. Feed grain cultivation continued with little change through the share-cropping system and was easily adapted to mechanized agriculture.

Feed-grain acreage, particularly corn, began a decline after the introduction and expansion of soybeans beginning in the 1930s, however. From over a million acres planted in the 1920s and 1930s, corn acreage dropped to under one hundred thousand acres for most of the 1970s and 1980s. Some rebounding above the hundred-thousand-acre level has occurred as growers switch crops on the basis of anticipated return. Despite yields per acre six to seven times those of the 1920s and 1930s, total corn production has also declined.

Today corn is grown in more parishes (fifty-six) than any other feed grain. Wheat is grown in fifty-two parishes, grain sorghum in fifty, oats in only thirty-seven. Corn accounts for 44 percent of feed grain production by value, grain sorghum 29 percent, wheat 25 percent, oats a mere 2 percent.

Feed grains over the 1985–1989 period were grown in all but six of the state's sixty-four parishes. Pointe Coupee, St. Landry, and Avoyelles parishes produced in double digits and accounted for a third of the total crop. Eight other parishes—Catahoula, Madison, Concordia, Natchitoches, Rapides, East Carroll, Evangeline, and Acadia—produced another third, with percentages ranging from 7 percent down to 3 percent.

When corn, wheat, oats, and grain sorghum are considered individually, only Avoyelles and Madison parishes rank in the top ten producing parishes for each. St. Landry Parish appears for all but oats. St. Landry, Pointe Coupee, and Avoyelles grow half of all the corn. Catahoula accounts for close to a quarter of the grain sorghum, and West Carroll and Madison for a quarter of the oats. Pointe Coupee at 11 percent represents the sole double-digit wheat-producing parish.

A more recent addition to Louisiana's agriculture is the soybean. The introduction of soybeans arose from a number of factors. In the 1930s these included a reduction in cotton acreage and efforts by the Soil Conservation Service to improve soil quality. Later, improved markets and realization of their potential uses spurred cultivation. Native to Asia, soybeans, which come in a variety of sizes and colors, have since World War II taken over a considerable acreage. They have replaced corn, cotton, and also previously forested lands. Soybeans can be used for a variety of products—oil, flour, and meal. Today they represent in monetary return the state's most important crop.

Soybean acreage first appeared in the 1920 Census of Agriculture and reached a modern peak in 1980 at 3,450,000 acres. Actual peak production occurred a year before in 1979 with 93,800,000 bushels. As with agriculture in general, yields have tended upwards through the twentieth century. Soybeans are easily cultivated using mechanized agriculture and thus are especially popular in the more level terrains of the state to which such agriculture is most applicable.

Averages for estimated soybean production during the 1985–1989 period show Concordia and Madison parishes as the two largest producers of soybeans, at 10 percent and 9 percent, respectively, of the estimated total. With St. Landry and Avoyelles parishes they account for a third of the state's production. A second third came from six parishes—Tensas, Acadia, Catahoula, East Carroll, Pointe Coupee, and Jefferson Davis—with individual parish contributions ranging from 7 percent to 4 percent. Another forty-five parishes produced the final third, thirty-five of these accounting for less than 1 percent each. In all, fifty-five of the state's sixty-four parishes produced soybeans during the 1985–1989 period.

82. Assorted Feed Grain and Soybean Production, 1985–1989

Copyright © 1995 by the University of Oklahoma Press

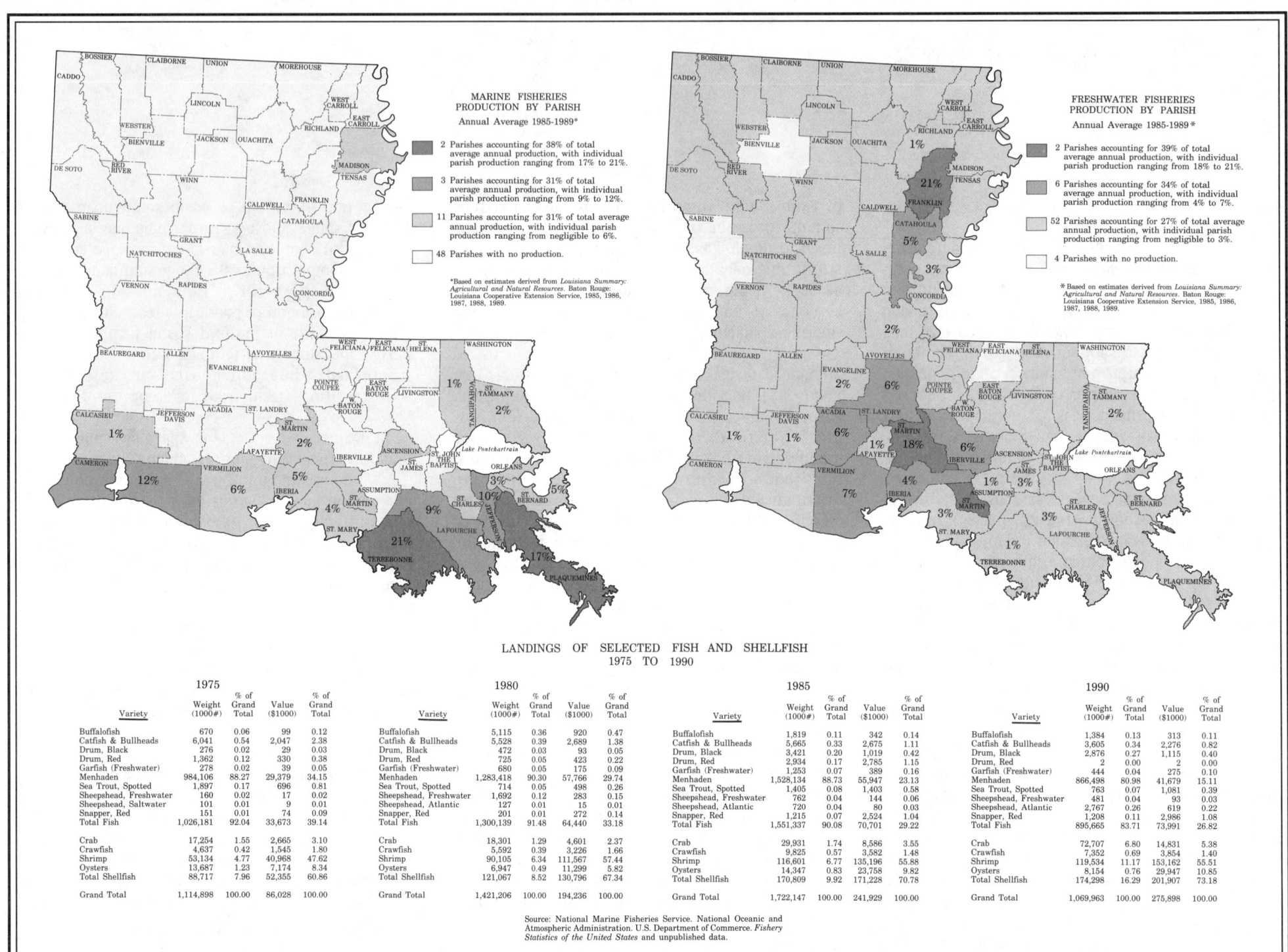

MARINE FISHERIES
PRODUCTION BY PARISH
Annual Average 1985–1989*

2 Parishes accounting for 38% of total average annual production, with individual parish production ranging from 17% to 21%.

3 Parishes accounting for 31% of total average annual production, with individual parish production ranging from 9% to 12%.

11 Parishes accounting for 31% of total average annual production, with individual parish production ranging from negligible to 6%.

48 Parishes with no production.

*Based on estimates derived from *Louisiana Summary: Agricultural and Natural Resources.* Baton Rouge: Louisiana Cooperative Extension Service, 1985, 1986, 1987, 1988, 1989.

FRESHWATER FISHERIES
PRODUCTION BY PARISH
Annual Average 1985–1989*

2 Parishes accounting for 39% of total average annual production, with individual parish production ranging from 18% to 21%.

6 Parishes accounting for 34% of total average annual production, with individual parish production ranging from 4% to 7%.

52 Parishes accounting for 27% of total average annual production, with individual parish production ranging from negligible to 3%.

4 Parishes with no production.

*Based on estimates derived from *Louisiana Summary: Agricultural and Natural Resources.* Baton Rouge: Louisiana Cooperative Extension Service, 1985, 1986, 1987, 1988, 1989.

LANDINGS OF SELECTED FISH AND SHELLFISH
1975 TO 1990

1975

Variety	Weight (1000#)	% of Grand Total	Value ($1000)	% of Grand Total
Buffalofish	670	0.06	99	0.12
Catfish & Bullheads	6,041	0.54	2,047	2.38
Drum, Black	276	0.02	29	0.03
Drum, Red	1,362	0.12	330	0.38
Garfish (Freshwater)	278	0.02	39	0.05
Menhaden	984,106	88.27	29,379	34.15
Sea Trout, Spotted	1,897	0.17	696	0.81
Sheepshead, Freshwater	160	0.02	17	0.02
Sheepshead, Saltwater	101	0.01	9	0.01
Snapper, Red	151	0.01	74	0.09
Total Fish	1,026,181	92.04	33,673	39.14
Crab	17,254	1.55	2,665	3.10
Crawfish	4,637	0.42	1,545	1.80
Shrimp	53,134	4.77	40,968	47.62
Oysters	13,687	1.23	7,174	8.34
Total Shellfish	88,717	7.96	52,355	60.86
Grand Total	1,114,898	100.00	86,028	100.00

1980

Variety	Weight (1000#)	% of Grand Total	Value ($1000)	% of Grand Total
Buffalofish	5,115	0.36	920	0.47
Catfish & Bullheads	5,528	0.39	2,689	1.38
Drum, Black	472	0.03	93	0.05
Drum, Red	725	0.05	423	0.22
Garfish (Freshwater)	680	0.05	175	0.09
Menhaden	1,283,418	90.30	57,766	29.74
Sea Trout, Spotted	714	0.05	498	0.26
Sheepshead, Freshwater	1,692	0.12	283	0.15
Sheepshead, Atlantic	127	0.01	15	0.01
Snapper, Red	201	0.01	272	0.14
Total Fish	1,300,139	91.48	64,440	33.18
Crab	18,301	1.29	4,601	2.37
Crawfish	5,592	0.39	3,226	1.66
Shrimp	90,105	6.34	111,567	57.44
Oysters	6,947	0.49	11,299	5.82
Total Shellfish	121,067	8.52	130,796	67.34
Grand Total	1,421,206	100.00	194,236	100.00

1985

Variety	Weight (1000#)	% of Grand Total	Value ($1000)	% of Grand Total
Buffalofish	1,819	0.11	342	0.14
Catfish & Bullheads	5,665	0.33	2,675	1.11
Drum, Black	3,421	0.20	1,019	0.42
Drum, Red	2,934	0.17	2,785	1.15
Garfish (Freshwater)	1,253	0.07	389	0.16
Menhaden	1,528,134	88.73	55,947	23.13
Sea Trout, Spotted	1,405	0.08	1,403	0.58
Sheepshead, Freshwater	762	0.04	144	0.06
Sheepshead, Atlantic	720	0.04	80	0.03
Snapper, Red	1,215	0.07	2,524	1.04
Total Fish	1,551,337	90.08	70,701	29.22
Crab	29,931	1.74	8,586	3.55
Crawfish	9,825	0.57	3,582	1.48
Shrimp	116,601	6.77	135,196	55.88
Oysters	14,347	0.83	23,758	9.82
Total Shellfish	170,809	9.92	171,228	70.78
Grand Total	1,722,147	100.00	241,929	100.00

1990

Variety	Weight (1000#)	% of Grand Total	Value ($1000)	% of Grand Total
Buffalofish	1,384	0.13	313	0.11
Catfish & Bullheads	3,605	0.34	2,276	0.82
Drum, Black	2,876	0.27	1,115	0.40
Drum, Red	2	0.00	2	0.00
Garfish (Freshwater)	444	0.04	275	0.10
Menhaden	866,498	80.98	41,679	15.11
Sea Trout, Spotted	763	0.07	1,081	0.39
Sheepshead, Freshwater	481	0.04	93	0.03
Sheepshead, Atlantic	2,767	0.26	619	0.22
Snapper, Red	1,208	0.11	2,986	1.08
Total Fish	895,665	83.71	73,991	26.82
Crab	72,707	6.80	14,831	5.38
Crawfish	7,352	0.69	3,854	1.40
Shrimp	119,534	11.17	153,162	55.51
Oysters	8,154	0.76	29,947	10.85
Total Shellfish	174,298	16.29	201,907	73.18
Grand Total	1,069,963	100.00	275,898	100.00

Source: National Marine Fisheries Service. National Oceanic and Atmospheric Administration. U.S. Department of Commerce. *Fishery Statistics of the United States* and unpublished data.

The fishing industry within Louisiana represents a major source of income. Together both marine (saltwater) and freshwater species account for almost two-fifths by value of the state's estimated gross animal production. Of that total, marine species by value are worth almost four times the freshwater varieties. Both marine and freshwater species are harvested from the wild. Aquaculture—the "farming" of fish—has also become important in recent years. New means of faster transport to more distant markets and changes in diet have increased demand for Louisiana's product. In some cases the demand for certain species, such as redfish, has led to protection of the species in order to sustain its survival. Demand has also increased the value of the product even as the total volume of production has stabilized.

Before 1917 marine fisheries accounted for less of the total than did freshwater fisheries. In that year, however, the shrimp trawl was introduced, and the marine industry expanded. Other technological improvements that added to its value included refrigeration and faster methods of transporting the catch to distant markets before it could spoil.

Shellfish account for the bulk of the value of the Louisiana catch. The state leads the nation in shrimp production, and this product alone accounts for more than half the value of the state's marine total. When the trawl replaced the beach seine as the primary means of harvest in 1917, the total shrimp catch mushroomed. Later, larger vessels and more equipment were developed to harvest the offshore shrimp. The advent of quick-freezing in 1934 led to the nationwide distribution of the Louisiana product.

Both oysters and crabs are also important in the marine fish industry; together they account for about 15 percent of the total. Oysters must compete with both marine predators and human encroachment into their production areas. The crab harvest is an increasing share of the total marine production.

Several varieties of finfish are included in the Louisiana catch, making up about 10 percent (excluding menhaden) of the total marine product. Snapper, flounder, trout, pompano, drum, sheepshead, and others are caught. Redfish became a best-seller when Cajun cuisine caught on nationwide; more recently limits have been placed on its catch. The most successful finfish by value has been the menhaden, also called the pogy or the American sardine. Alone, menhaden averages about 15 percent of the total. The seined menhaden catch is converted into fish oil, fish meal (used as animal food), and fertilizer.

As would be expected, marine fisheries production is centered in parishes with access to coastal and Gulf waters. Only sixteen of the state's sixty-four parishes contribute to this production. Terrebonne and Plaquemines lead the list, accounting for 38 percent of the total. Cameron, Jefferson, and Lafource parishes account for a second third of the total, with the final third coming from the remaining eleven parishes in the group.

Although it is not of the same monetary value as marine fisheries, the freshwater catch is also important to the state's economy. However, the wild catch is being increasingly supplemented by farming even as the former declines because of environmental problems such as increased pollution. Both catfish and crawfish are now farmed, a trend that is increasing. In addition to these two mainstays of freshwater fish, other species of importance include buffalofish, garfish, and choupique. Fishbait is also a component part of the overall measure of freshwater fish production.

The distribution of parishes producing freshwater fish reflects both natural sources as well as farming areas. Sixty parishes harvest some freshwater products, but eight parishes account for over 70 percent of the total. Franklin and St. Martin parishes together produced 39 percent, the former almost entirely catfish and the latter a similar preponderance of crawfish. Six parishes produce another 34 percent. Fifty parishes contribute the remaining product, with shares of the total ranging from 3 percent down to only token production.

83. *Marine and Freshwater Fisheries Production,*
1985–1989

Copyright © 1995 by the University of Oklahoma Press

CATTLE AND CALVES PRODUCTION BY PARISH
Annual Average 1985-1989*

8 Parishes accounting for 34% of total average annual production, with individual parish production ranging from 3% to 6%.

13 Parishes accounting for 30% of total average annual production, with individual parish production ranging from 2% to 3%.

42 Parishes accounting for 36% of total average annual production, with individual parish production ranging from negligible to 2%.

1 Parish with no production.

*Based on estimates derived from *Louisiana Summary: Agricultural and Natural Resources*. Baton Rouge: Louisiana Cooperative Extension Service, 1985, 1986, 1987, 1988, 1989.

MILK PRODUCTION BY PARISH
Annual Average 1985-1989*

1 Parish accounting for 36% of total average annual production.

3 Parishes accounting for 39% of total average annual production, with individual parish production ranging from 9% to 21%.

38 Parishes accounting for 25% of total average annual production, with individual parish production ranging from negligible to 3%.

22 Parishes with no production.

*Based on estimates derived from *Louisiana Summary: Agricultural and Natural Resources*. Baton Rouge: Louisiana Cooperative Extension Service, 1985, 1986, 1987, 1988, 1989.

CATTLE AND MILK PRODUCTION
1850–1987

Category	1987	1982	1978	1969	1959	1950	1940	1930	1920	1910	1900	1890	1880	1870	1860	1850
Cattle/Calves (Total)	813,295	1,003,833	1,052,216	1,417,300	1,655,869	1,284,616	1,051,901	729,690	804,241	804,795	699,631	581,103	470,601	335,261	516,807	575,342
Milk Cows	83,381	100,159	112,316	138,333	205,433	275,810	329,894	223,429	176,936	279,097	214,151	167,223	146,454	102,076	129,662	105,576
Working Oxen	...	...	...	...	...	...	...	...	...	...	...	41,975	41,729	32,596	60,358	54,968
Milk Sold (gallons)	102,441,860	109,302,326	119,186,047	116,279,070	64,155,447	39,544,508	22,796,995	14,735,718	5,334,031	4,501,119	39,251,413	12,881,927	256,241	833,928	...	...

Bureau of the Census. Department of Commerce. *Census of Agriculture*. Department of Agricultural Economics and Agribusiness, Louisiana Agricultural Experiment Station, Louisiana State University. *Agricultural Statistics and Prices for Louisiana, 1909–1985* [for milk production, 1969–1982]. National Agricultural Statistics Service [for milk production, 1987].

French colonists introduced cattle into Louisiana. The Spanish period saw the expansion of ranching operations onto the prairies of southwest Louisiana. There, royal land grants of up to a square league (about forty-four hundred acres) were made by the Spanish governor to those willing to establish ranching operations. Thus, Louisiana came to represent the easternmost expansion of the Spanish cattle complex which existed over western North America and South America.

The Spanish system was a well-regulated operation, with rules on branding and supervised herding. These regulations assisted in maintaining and improving the quality of the stock. An alternate system existed in the pineywoods and other areas settled by Anglo-Saxon immigrants. There, an open-range system of almost wild livestock (swine as well as cattle) developed. Once a year the cattle were rounded up for branding; most of the year they largely fended for themselves on the natural bounty of the land.

Today, supported by scientific and economic improvements in stock and in processing, both meat and dairy production have increased in value and in volume if not always in sheer number of animals. Together they account for approximately one-third of the total estimated animal production in the state—cattle and calves for 21 percent, dairy products for 13 percent. As in other agricultural pursuits, the trend in both beef and dairy production is towards a smaller number of producers with larger operations. Dietary changes among Americans have seen beef challenged by chicken as a dietary mainstay even as beef succeeded pork early in the twentieth century as first in per capita meat consumption in the nation. Worries over cholesterol and fat have also affected the dairy industry, resulting in new products but overall lower per capita consumption of those products. Louisiana itself has also seen competition from domestic and foreign sources which have affected prices, hence production.

Over much of the twentieth century the total number of cattle and calves tended upwards, reached a plateau during the 1950s to the 1970s, then declined. Production and marketing have followed the same trend. From a high of 547 million pounds produced in 1972, the total had declined to the range of 300–350 million pounds in the 1980s. Over the 1985–1989 period cattle and calf production was to be found in every parish except Orleans. Only Vermilion Parish (at 6 percent) accounted for more than 5 percent of the estimated gross production. Three parishes contributed approximately 4 percent; five parishes, 3 percent; and the remainder from 2 percent down to only negligible production.

A third of the estimated average 1985–1989 cattle/calf production came from eight parishes: Vermilion, Cameron, Rapides, Red River, Caddo, Calcasieu, Lafourche, and Evangeline. The thirteen next largest producing parishes contributed another third of the total. The remaining forty-two parishes with production accounted for the remainder of the estimated total.

As did beef production, for centuries dairy production formed a part of every homestead that could afford a milk cow; this was true in the city as well as on the farm. In time dairy herds came into existence, and commercial operations formed to supply the state's needs. From the 1920s to 1954 the number of dairy cattle increased to reach a total of more than three hundred thousand head. From that point there began a steady decline in numbers, to the present total of fewer than ninety thousand head. Even as the number of animals declined, however, the average milk production per cow more than quadrupled, from approximately 2,200 pounds annually to 9,500 pounds. Just as beef peaked in 1972, so did total dairy production at 1,132 million pounds. Since that time the total has declined to average in the 900-million-pound range in recent years.

In the 1985–1989 period, dairy production occurred in forty-two of the state's sixty-four parishes. Tangipahoa Parish—milk shed for the state's southern urban centers—alone accounted for more than a third of the average estimated total. Washington, De Soto, and St. Helena parishes accounted for more than a second third. The remaining thirty-eight producing parishes accounted for the remainder, just over one-quarter of the total sum.

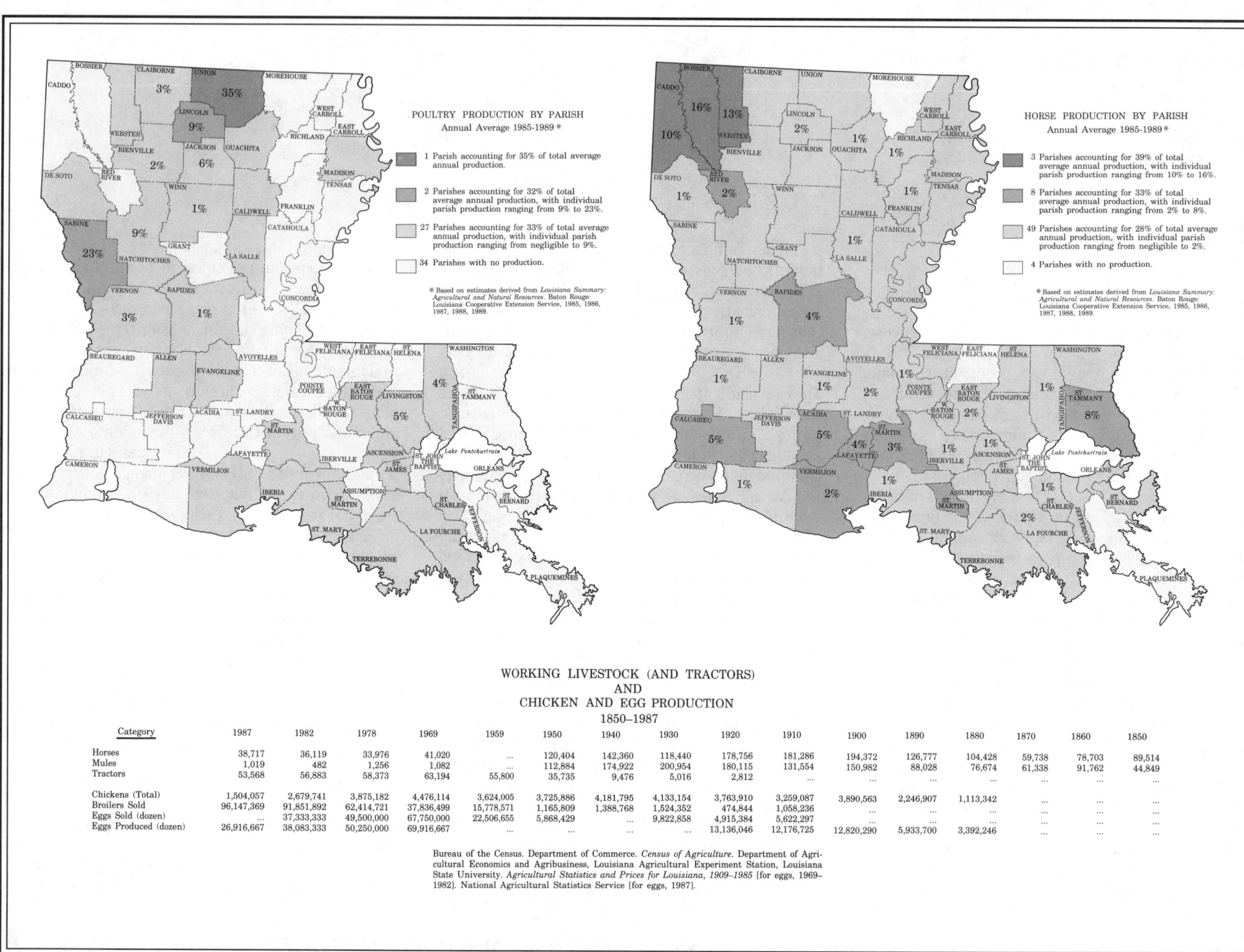

POULTRY PRODUCTION BY PARISH
Annual Average 1985-1989 *

1 Parish accounting for 35% of total average annual production.

2 Parishes accounting for 32% of total average annual production, with individual parish production ranging from 9% to 23%.

27 Parishes accounting for 33% of total average annual production, with individual parish production ranging from negligible to 9%.

34 Parishes with no production.

* Based on estimates derived from *Louisiana Summary: Agricultural and Natural Resources*. Baton Rouge: Louisiana Cooperative Extension Service, 1985, 1986, 1987, 1988, 1989.

HORSE PRODUCTION BY PARISH
Annual Average 1985-1989 *

3 Parishes accounting for 39% of total average annual production, with individual parish production ranging from 10% to 16%.

8 Parishes accounting for 33% of total average annual production, with individual parish production ranging from 2% to 8%.

49 Parishes accounting for 28% of total average annual production, with individual parish production ranging from negligible to 2%.

4 Parishes with no production.

* Based on estimates derived from *Louisiana Summary: Agricultural and Natural Resources*. Baton Rouge: Louisiana Cooperative Extension Service, 1985, 1986, 1987, 1988, 1989.

WORKING LIVESTOCK (AND TRACTORS) AND CHICKEN AND EGG PRODUCTION 1850–1987

Category	1987	1982	1978	1969	1959	1950	1940	1930	1920	1910	1900	1890	1880	1870	1860	1850
Horses	38,717	36,119	33,976	41,020	...	120,404	142,360	118,440	178,756	181,286	194,372	126,777	104,428	59,738	78,703	89,514
Mules	1,019	482	1,256	1,082	...	112,884	174,922	200,954	180,115	131,554	150,982	88,028	76,674	61,338	91,762	44,849
Tractors	53,568	56,883	58,373	63,194	55,800	35,735	9,476	5,016	2,812	...	...	...	...	...	...	...
Chickens (Total)	1,504,057	2,679,741	3,875,182	4,476,114	3,624,005	3,725,886	4,181,795	4,133,154	3,763,910	3,259,087	3,890,563	2,246,907	1,113,342	...	...	...
Broilers Sold	96,147,369	91,851,892	62,414,721	37,836,499	15,778,571	1,165,809	1,388,768	1,524,352	474,844	1,058,236	...	...	...	...	...	...
Eggs Sold (dozen)	...	37,333,333	49,500,000	67,750,000	22,506,655	5,868,429	...	9,822,858	4,915,384	5,622,297	...	...	...	...	...	...
Eggs Produced (dozen)	26,916,667	38,083,333	50,250,000	69,916,667	...	...	...	...	13,136,046	12,176,725	12,820,290	5,933,700	3,392,246	...	...	...

Bureau of the Census. Department of Commerce. *Census of Agriculture*. Department of Agricultural Economics and Agribusiness, Louisiana Agricultural Experiment Station, Louisiana State University. *Agricultural Statistics and Prices for Louisiana, 1909–1985* [for eggs, 1969–1982]. National Agricultural Statistics Service [for eggs, 1987].

The commercial production of poultry products—largely broilers and eggs—has increased tremendously over the past fifty years in Louisiana. Chickens and eggs for home consumption, plus a little extra for barter or sale, had been produced since colonial days for both basic sustenance and cash, the proverbial "egg money." Beginning in the 1930s, however, poultry farming began to move South from the Middle Atlantic and Midwestern states. This change was spurred by moves to diversify farming, supplement other crops, or furnish a practical alternative to the small operator whose allotments did not provide sufficient cash income. Prime movers behind this expansion were feed dealers who saw such operations as new outlets for their product. A more recent incentive has been the changing dietary patterns of Americans, with chicken replacing beef in many households. Louisiana would share in this growth.

Poultry products in the years 1985–1989 were the second highest contributor of value to overall animal production in the state, second to marine fisheries but more valuable than cattle. This industry is tied to commercial production of both broilers and eggs. Over the twentieth century total egg production first advanced, then declined even as output per laying hen has increased. Egg production peaked about 1969 with rival figures ranging between 713 million and 839 million, then declined to 300 million in 1989. From 13 percent of the estimated total value of poultry production in 1985, edible eggs fell to 3 percent of the estimate in 1989.

Broiler production is marked by close ties between producer and processor, reflecting the original impetus given by feed dealers. A vertical integration of the industry is the rule. Chicken houses have sprung up over the past several decades, with chicks delivered and broilers retrieved on schedule for further processing. Over one hundred million broilers are produced in the state annually. Broiler production for 1989 accounted for approximately 93 percent of the total estimated value of poultry production, up from 82 percent in 1985.

Broiler and egg production do not have the same geographical distribution. By virtue of their share of the total, the largest broiler-producing parishes represent the largest poultry-producing parishes, too. Union Parish represents a third of the estimated total poultry production, yet that sum is almost exclusively broilers. Sabine and Lincoln parishes produce another third, again practically exclusively broilers. Twenty-seven other parishes furnish the final third of poultry production. Among them one finds Livingston, Rapides, and Tangipahoa as the top three egg-producing parishes.

Also of importance to the state has been the production of horses. In centuries past the horse provided both personal transportation as well as draft animals. In some southern parishes of antebellum Louisiana, horses outnumbered mules as the draft animal of choice; however, the mule represented the majority of draft animals in most of the state.

Today horse production has largely cut its ties to its former agricultural and transportation roles. Nevertheless, some working animals remain, along with show horses and pets. Indeed, recreation and pleasure are the two reasons most often cited by horse owners for their ownership. This more recent horse production is also tied to the race tracks scattered about the state and also to stud fees. Indeed, income to the state alone from pari-mutuel operations rivals the estimated value of horse production.

In addition to the income from the sale of colts, there also exists income from stud fees. On average the sale of colts accounts for approximately 80 percent of the estimated gross value of horse production. This production is scattered throughout the state; some sixty of Louisiana's sixty-four parishes contribute to horse production.

The three adjacent parishes of Bossier, Webster, and Caddo account for fully a third of the total estimated value of horse production in the state. Perhaps not coincidentally is the presence of the Louisiana Downs racetrack in Bossier City. Another third of the production value comes from eight parishes whose contributions range from 8 percent down to 2 percent. The remaining forty-nine parishes with some production account for the final third, with contributions ranging downward from 2 percent to negligible figures.

Copyright © 1995 by the University of Oklahoma Press

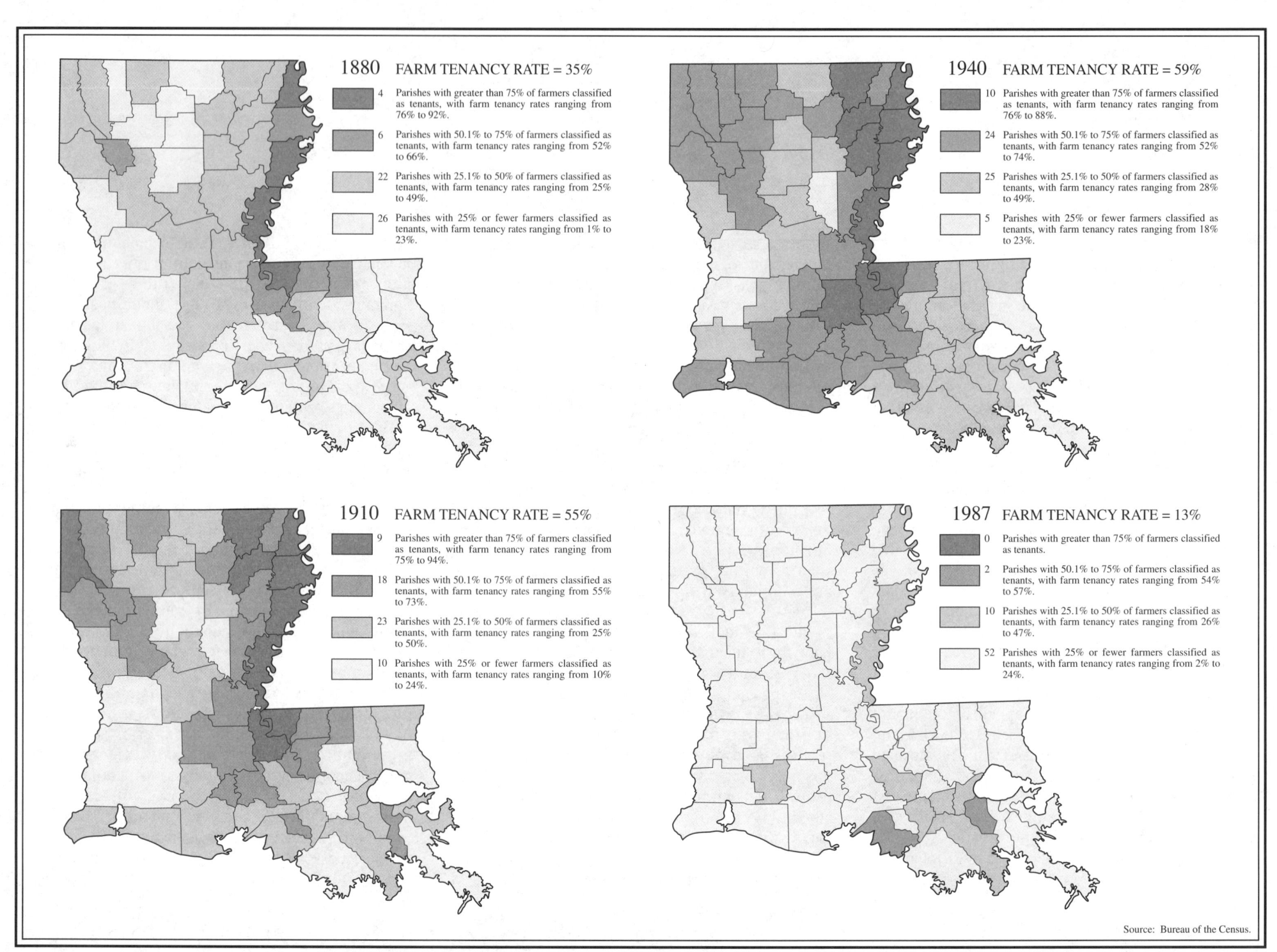

1880 FARM TENANCY RATE = 35%

- 4 Parishes with greater than 75% of farmers classified as tenants, with farm tenancy rates ranging from 76% to 92%.
- 6 Parishes with 50.1% to 75% of farmers classified as tenants, with farm tenancy rates ranging from 52% to 66%.
- 22 Parishes with 25.1% to 50% of farmers classified as tenants, with farm tenancy rates ranging from 25% to 49%.
- 26 Parishes with 25% or fewer farmers classified as tenants, with farm tenancy rates ranging from 1% to 23%.

1940 FARM TENANCY RATE = 59%

- 10 Parishes with greater than 75% of farmers classified as tenants, with farm tenancy rates ranging from 76% to 88%.
- 24 Parishes with 50.1% to 75% of farmers classified as tenants, with farm tenancy rates ranging from 52% to 74%.
- 25 Parishes with 25.1% to 50% of farmers classified as tenants, with farm tenancy rates ranging from 28% to 49%.
- 5 Parishes with 25% or fewer farmers classified as tenants, with farm tenancy rates ranging from 18% to 23%.

1910 FARM TENANCY RATE = 55%

- 9 Parishes with greater than 75% of farmers classified as tenants, with farm tenancy rates ranging from 75% to 94%.
- 18 Parishes with 50.1% to 75% of farmers classified as tenants, with farm tenancy rates ranging from 55% to 73%.
- 23 Parishes with 25.1% to 50% of farmers classified as tenants, with farm tenancy rates ranging from 25% to 50%.
- 10 Parishes with 25% or fewer farmers classified as tenants, with farm tenancy rates ranging from 10% to 24%.

1987 FARM TENANCY RATE = 13%

- 0 Parishes with greater than 75% of farmers classified as tenants.
- 2 Parishes with 50.1% to 75% of farmers classified as tenants, with farm tenancy rates ranging from 54% to 57%.
- 10 Parishes with 25.1% to 50% of farmers classified as tenants, with farm tenancy rates ranging from 26% to 47%.
- 52 Parishes with 25% or fewer farmers classified as tenants, with farm tenancy rates ranging from 2% to 24%.

Source: Bureau of the Census.

Among the other devastations wrought upon the South by the Civil War was the disruption of agriculture. The plantation system especially lay in ruins. Emancipation had expropriated a significant percentage of the planters' capital even as military campaign and blockade destroyed property and crops and disrupted trade. Most of the freed slaves entered their new life lacking any other training than that of field hands. Planters, former slaves, and yeomen farmers alike were plunged into a state of economic flux.

From this disorder arose a new combination of land, labor, and capital. This evolving alliance would swallow up not only most of the rural black population but also many poor whites. The new system was tenancy. Along with its companion, the crop-lien system, tenancy would create a form of debt servitude approaching peonage which lasted into the twentieth century.

Tenancy took many forms. Each involved the landowner's provision of at least land and shelter to the landless cultivators in exchange for their labor and some form of rent. That rent could be cash, a share of the crop produced, or a combination of the two. The amount of the rent was in part based on what else each party brought—tools and implements, seeds, draft animals, and so on. Those who brought the most received the greater return. In such a system the tenant was usually at the disadvantage.

The tenant who brought only his and his family's labor entered the system at its lowest rung—that of a sharecropper. The landlord provided all other supplies. In exchange, the owner received on average half of the crop, which was in most cases cotton.

The lack of ready cash plagued the South, and the crop-lien system rose to fill the gap. Landowner and cultivator alike received food, clothes, and other goods on credit from the local merchant. In return, the proceeds of the cash crop were pledged as collateral. If the landlord also owned the store, more of the crop would flow to him, particularly since such credit advanced was often at rates bordering on, if not surpassing, usury.

The crop-lien web ensnared not only sharecroppers but also yeomen farmers and the occasional land-rich but cash-poor planter. Estimates placed 70 percent of Louisiana's white cotton farmers and nearly all black cotton farmers in such debt near the close of the nineteenth century. One or more bad crop years brought on a state of recurring, seemingly perpetual debt, a condition made even more onerous to sharecroppers when laws were enacted tying them to their creditors until the debt was discharged.

In 1880 more than one-third of all Louisiana farmers were classed by the Census as tenants—14 percent on a cash basis and 21 percent sharecropping or cropping with some cash payments. Most tenants tilled fields of fewer that 50 acres; the average size for all farms was 171 acres. Tenancy rates were highest in the cotton areas of the Mississippi Valley and western Florida Parishes.

The 1910 census showed a tenancy rate which had soared to 55 percent of the state's farms—still 14 percent on a cash basis but now 41 percent croppers or cash-crop combined. Two-thirds of the 66,607 tenants were black; 80 percent of all black farmers were tenants. The average tenant tilled forty acres compared to an average eighty-seven acres for all farms.

In the 1940 census, 59 percent of the state's farmers were tenants, each on average tilling forty-one acres. This figure was more than in 1910 but slightly lower than a 1930 peak, when tenancy encompassed 67 percent of all farms. Thirty-four parishes in 1940 had tenancy rates in excess of 50 percent and ten in excess of 75 percent of their farmers.

After 1940 the tenancy rate continued to fall, to less than half in 1950 and less than one-quarter in 1960. In 1987 only 13.5 percent of the farms were operated by nonowners, usually managers. The rise of mechanized agriculture contributed greatly to the decrease of tenancy, as did expanding economic opportunities. Even the agricultural landscape changed. Fields became larger, tenant shacks and home places disappeared, and crops were grown as far as the eye could see and the tractor could plow. Farming had ceased to be a major way of life for the United States, and with it declined tenancy and its evils.

EMPLOYMENT IN MANUFACTURING
BY
PARISH

Annual Average Percent of Parish Work
Force Covered by Louisiana Employment
Security Law, 1985–1989 *

State Average = 11.6 Percent

14 Parishes with 27% to 41% of work force in this category and accounting for 18.8% of all state workers in this category.

21 Parishes with 12% to 25% of work force in this category and accounting for 37.8% of all state workers in this category.

24 Parishes with 6.3% to 11.3% of work force in this category and accounting for 39.8% of all state workers in this category.

5 Parishes with 3.4% to 5.6% of work force in this category and accounting for 3.6% of all state workers in this category.

* Based on data derived from *Louisiana Employment and Wages*, Research and Statistics Unit, Office of Employment Security, Louisiana Department of Labor, 1985, 1986, 1987, 1988, and 1989.

VALUE ADDED BY MANUFACTURING
BY
PARISH

1987 *

6 Parishes with value added from $1.1 to $1.9 billion and accounting for 55.7% of value added by state manufactures.

17 Parishes with value added from $100 to $900 million and accounting for 30.9% of value added by state manufactures.

30 Parishes with value added less than $100 million and accounting for 5.9% of value added by state manufactures.

11 Parishes whose value added was not revealed and accounting for 7.5% of value added by state manufactures.

* Based on 1987 *Census of Manufactures*, Bureau of the Census, U.S. Department of Commerce.

VALUE ADDED MANUFACTURING FOR SELECTED INDUSTRIAL GROUPS
1972 TO 1987

PRODUCT	1987 ($Million)	% of Total	1982 ($Million)	% of Total	1977 ($Million)	% of Total	1972 ($Million)	% of Total
Food/Kindred	1,381.8	8.40	1,104.8	9.40	777.5	8.3	579.3	13.5
Lumber/Wood	490.6	3.00	268.3	2.30	324.4	3.4	208.9	4.9
Paper/Allied	1,513.3	9.20	NA		692.9	7.4	396.9	9.3
Printing/Publishing	473.1	2.90	351.9	3.00	193.5	2.0	125.3	2.9
Chemical/Allied	6,759.9	41.20	3,098.2	26.40	3,277.8	34.8	1,349.6	31.5
Petroleum/Coal	1,690.6	10.30	2,479.2	21.10	1,857.1	19.7	442.6	10.3
Electronic/Other Electrical	812.9	5.00	NA		316.5	3.4	145.0	3.4
Transportation	1,514.1	9.20	947.0	8.10	551.5	5.9	289.4	6.8
STATE TOTAL	16,425.8	100.00	11,754.6	100.0	9,418.3	100.0	4,282.4	100.0

Bureau of the Census. U.S. Department of Commerce. *Census of Manufactures.*

VALUE ADDED BY MANUFACTURING
TOP TEN PARISHES - 1987

Parish	1987 ($Million)	% of Total
Caddo	1,893.7	11.5
St. Charles	1,697.3	10.3
East Baton Rouge	1,635.5	10.0
Calcasieu	1,425.3	8.7
Ascension	1,367.7	8.3
Orleans	1,133.9	6.9
Iberville	916.3	5.6
Jefferson	791.3	4.8
Ouachita	527.5	3.2
Rapides	425.1	2.6

Bureau of the Census. U.S. Department of Commerce. *Census of Manufactures.*

Manufacturing has a long history in Louisiana but has until the twentieth century largely been linked to the agricultural and timber products of the state. Sugar, cotton, rice, and timber have provided grist for the manufacturing mill on many scales of production. With the discovery and development of the state's oil and gas deposits at the turn of the twentieth century, these new resources began to come to the forefront in employment and value. Particularly after the close of World War II, the "modern" manufacturing state emerged.

The location of manufacturing plants is based on several factors. The availability of raw materials is obviously important. A source of ready labor—sometimes skilled, sometimes merely cheap—is another. Transportation costs are also to be considered, whether for shipping raw materials for processing or finished products for marketing or both. Manufacturing requires other resources—energy, water, and so on—whose proximity may be a factor. Tax breaks may also influence location. Above all, the presence of a market, whether local or remote, is necessary for the production of any goods.

During the 1985–1989 period manufacturing accounted for almost 12 percent of Louisiana's labor force covered by the employment security laws of the state. This represented an average annual work force of 170,133 among the average total of 1,472,532 persons. The total number of workers in the manufacturing sector has declined in recent years, largely as a result of the decline in oil-and-gas-related work, linchpin of the system.

In terms of total numbers employed, the state's parishes most populous with manufacturing workers consist of Orleans (17,912, or 10.5 percent of the total), Caddo (16,946, or 10.0 percent), Jefferson (15,242, or 9.0 percent), East Baton Rouge (13,703, or 8.0 percent), and Calcasieu (10,074, or 5.9 percent). Since these parishes represent the most populous as a whole in the state, one would expect large numbers of manufacturing workers as well. When viewed as a percentage of the total labor force within each parish, however, a different picture emerges. Only Caddo and Calcasieu parishes among this group rank above average in such a measure. Other parishes such as those along the Lower Mississippi Industrial Corridor (below and Map 73) are indicated by this measurement, as well as still other parishes where manufacturing represents a greater than average portion of the total labor force.

A high percentage of manufacturing positions in the labor force, however, does not always translate into a high rank in output. One method of rating the relative output is obtained by calculating the "value added" by manufacturing. This number represents the value of the finished products minus the cost of the raw materials used in their creation. The 1987 Census of Manufacturing found a total value added by manufacturing in Louisiana of $16,425,800,000.

By this measure six parishes contribute more than $1,000,000,000 each to the state's 1987 total. Caddo leads the state with a total value added of $1,893,700,000, fully 11.5 percent of the state's total. St. Charles Parish is second with $1,697,300,000, or 10.3 percent of the total. Following these are East Baton Rouge Parish ($1,635,500,000, or 10.0 percent); Calcasieu ($1,425,300,000, or 8.7 percent); Ascension ($1,367,700,000, or 8.3 percent); and Orleans ($1,133,900,000, or 6.9 percent). Combined, these parishes contribute almost 56 percent.

St. Charles, East Baton Rouge, Ascension, and Orleans parishes account for four of the nine parishes alongside or astride the Mississippi River between Baton Rouge and New Orleans. This corridor contains scores of industrial concerns occupying former plantations. (Kniffen and Hilliard, in *Louisiana: Its Land and People,* provide a detailed map of this corridor and its constituent firms based on data provided by the Louisiana National Bank and the Illinois Central Railroad.) These nine parishes account for more than half of the value added by manufacturing for the whole state.

In the four census years 1972, 1977, 1982, and 1987, the value added by chemical and allied products combined with that of petroleum and coal have contributed from 42 percent to 54 percent of the value added by manufacturing in Louisiana. Food and kindred products, paper and allied products, and, more recently, transportation represent a second, much lower tier, which contributed between 22 percent and 30 percent of the total. A host of other types of products contributes the remainder.

Copyright © 1995 by the University of Oklahoma Press

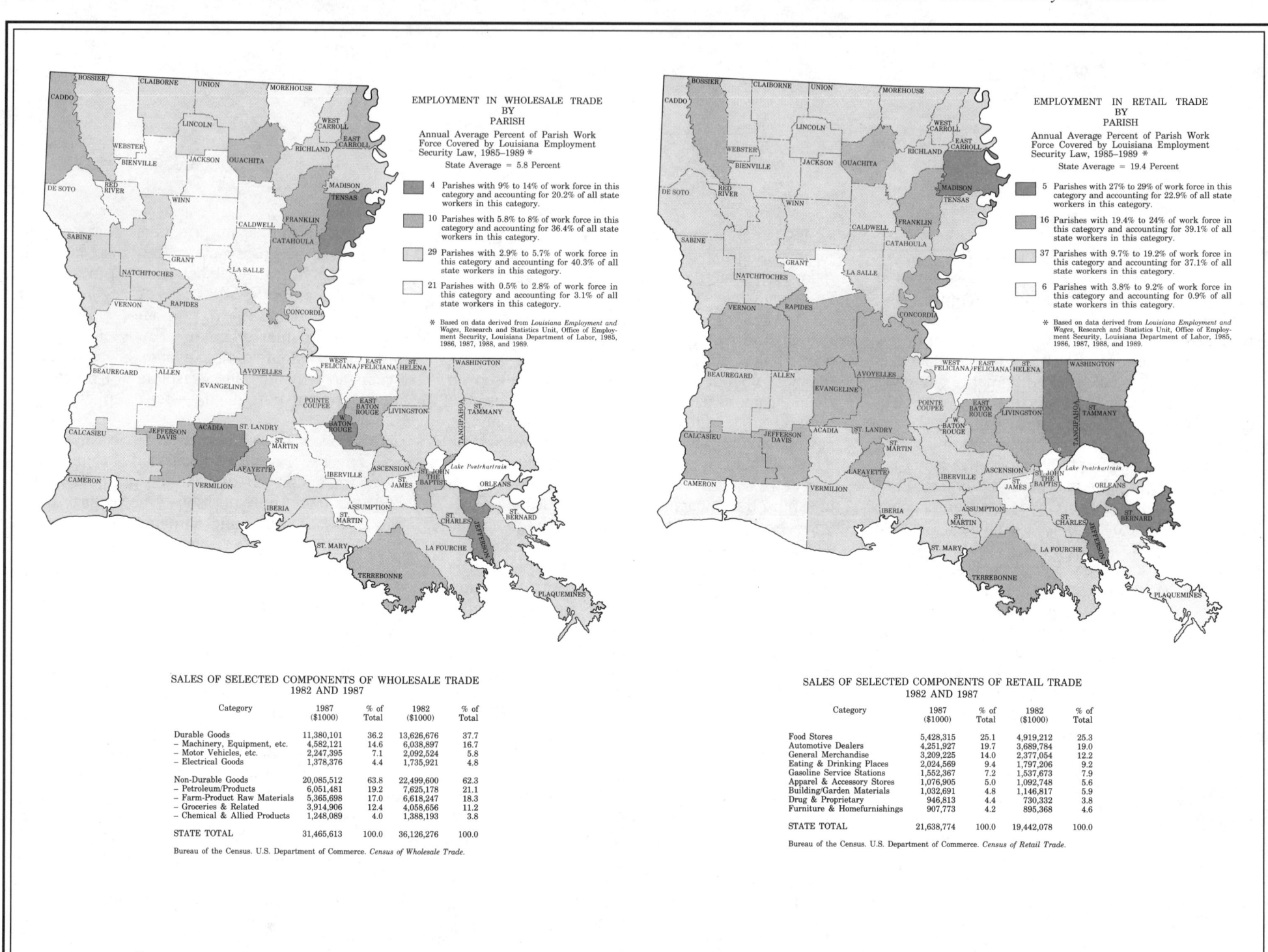

EMPLOYMENT IN WHOLESALE TRADE
BY
PARISH

Annual Average Percent of Parish Work
Force Covered by Louisiana Employment
Security Law, 1985–1989 *

State Average = 5.8 Percent

4 — Parishes with 9% to 14% of work force in this category and accounting for 20.2% of all state workers in this category.

10 — Parishes with 5.8% to 8% of work force in this category and accounting for 36.4% of all state workers in this category.

29 — Parishes with 2.9% to 5.7% of work force in this category and accounting for 40.3% of all state workers in this category.

21 — Parishes with 0.5% to 2.8% of work force in this category and accounting for 3.1% of all state workers in this category.

* Based on data derived from *Louisiana Employment and Wages*, Research and Statistics Unit, Office of Employment Security, Louisiana Department of Labor, 1985, 1986, 1987, 1988, and 1989.

EMPLOYMENT IN RETAIL TRADE
BY
PARISH

Annual Average Percent of Parish Work
Force Covered by Louisiana Employment
Security Law, 1985–1989 *

State Average = 19.4 Percent

5 — Parishes with 27% to 29% of work force in this category and accounting for 22.9% of all state workers in this category.

16 — Parishes with 19.4% to 24% of work force in this category and accounting for 39.1% of all state workers in this category.

37 — Parishes with 9.7% to 19.2% of work force in this category and accounting for 37.1% of all state workers in this category.

6 — Parishes with 3.8% to 9.2% of work force in this category and accounting for 0.9% of all state workers in this category.

* Based on data derived from *Louisiana Employment and Wages*, Research and Statistics Unit, Office of Employment Security, Louisiana Department of Labor, 1985, 1986, 1987, 1988, and 1989.

SALES OF SELECTED COMPONENTS OF WHOLESALE TRADE
1982 AND 1987

Category	1987 ($1000)	% of Total	1982 ($1000)	% of Total
Durable Goods	11,380,101	36.2	13,626,676	37.7
– Machinery, Equipment, etc.	4,582,121	14.6	6,038,897	16.7
– Motor Vehicles, etc.	2,247,395	7.1	2,092,524	5.8
– Electrical Goods	1,378,376	4.4	1,735,921	4.8
Non-Durable Goods	20,085,512	63.8	22,499,600	62.3
– Petroleum/Products	6,051,481	19.2	7,625,178	21.1
– Farm-Product Raw Materials	5,365,698	17.0	6,618,247	18.3
– Groceries & Related	3,914,906	12.4	4,058,656	11.2
– Chemical & Allied Products	1,248,089	4.0	1,388,193	3.8
STATE TOTAL	31,465,613	100.0	36,126,276	100.0

Bureau of the Census. U.S. Department of Commerce. *Census of Wholesale Trade.*

SALES OF SELECTED COMPONENTS OF RETAIL TRADE
1982 AND 1987

Category	1987 ($1000)	% of Total	1982 ($1000)	% of Total
Food Stores	5,428,315	25.1	4,919,212	25.3
Automotive Dealers	4,251,927	19.7	3,689,784	19.0
General Merchandise	3,209,225	14.0	2,377,054	12.2
Eating & Drinking Places	2,024,569	9.4	1,797,206	9.2
Gasoline Service Stations	1,552,367	7.2	1,537,673	7.9
Apparel & Accessory Stores	1,076,905	5.0	1,092,748	5.6
Building/Garden Materials	1,032,691	4.8	1,146,817	5.9
Drug & Proprietary	946,813	4.4	730,332	3.8
Furniture & Homefurnishings	907,773	4.2	895,368	4.6
STATE TOTAL	21,638,774	100.0	19,442,078	100.0

Bureau of the Census. U.S. Department of Commerce. *Census of Retail Trade.*

Wholesalers and retailers move goods from producer to consumer. Wholesale traders act as middlemen, selling merchandise to retailers, to industrial, commercial, institutional and other users, but rarely if at all to the ultimate consumer of that merchandise. Wholesalers serve as temporary warehousers of goods awaiting distribution, often serve as credit suppliers to retailers, and act as "break in bulk" dealers, buying in large quantities then reselling in smaller lots. Retail traders sell that merchandise to the final consumer. Over time the retail trade has moved from a sector based on the single locally owned "mom and pop" store and a recognizable downtown business area to scattered shopping centers and discount houses representing national chains of stores and contributing to economic decline of many small towns. As with other categories of employment in Louisiana, the total number of workers in these two sectors has declined somewhat in recent years. Sales and payroll in the wholesale trade declined, while those measures of retail trade rose.

Wholesale trade goods are divided into durable and nondurable categories. In the 1987 Census of Wholesale Trade, durable goods accounted for 36 percent of total sales, while nondurable goods comprised 64 percent of that total. Forty percent of the durable goods sold fell under the "Machinery, Equipment, and Supplies" classification, supplying items for industrial, farm, transportation, and other users. Among nondurable goods petroleum (30 percent), farm products (27 percent, especially "grains and field [that is, soy] beans"), and groceries (19 percent) accounted for three-quarters of all durable goods; together these three classifications comprised almost half of all wholesale goods sold.

Workers in the wholesale trade averaged 85,855 during the five-year period 1985–1989. This average represented 5.8 percent of the total workers covered by the employment security laws. Louisiana's most populous parishes naturally accounted for the largest numbers of workers in the wholesale trade. As a percentage of total work force in the parish, however, only Jefferson Parish shows up as much above the state average. West Baton Rouge and Acadia parishes represent parishes with high average as well as considerable total employment in this sector of the economy.

In terms of sales Louisiana's wholesalers totaled over $31 billion in the 1987 census year. Only four parishes with known totals accounted individually for 5 percent or more of that total: Orleans (13.3 percent), East Baton Rouge (8.1 percent), Caddo (5.8 percent), and Calcasieu (5.0 percent). Jefferson Parish, with 17 percent of the total establishments engaged in wholesaling, did not have its total sales or other data revealed because of confidentiality considerations.

As with wholesale trade, retail establishments fall into a number of categories. The Census Bureau collects information on nine separate classifications as well as a tenth "miscellaneous" group. When measured by sales, food stores lead all categories, with a quarter of the 1987 Census of Retail Trade total of $21.6 billion. Other major groups were automobile dealers (19.7 percent) and general merchandise stores (14.0 percent). Alone these three classifications comprised almost 60 percent of total sales. They were followed by eating and drinking places, gasoline service stations, apparel and accessory stores, building materials and garden supplies, drug and proprietary stores, and furniture and home furnishings stores.

Eating and drinking places accounted for almost 22 percent of the total number of establishments engaged in retail sales. This category was followed by food stores (16.2 percent), apparel and accessory stores (10.7 percent), and gasoline service stations (8.0 percent). Unlike total sales, which rose from $19.4 billion in 1982 to $21.6 billion in 1987, the total number of establishments engaged in retail trade dropped from 24,814 to 24,307.

The average number of workers in the retail sector during the 1985–1989 period averaged 283,876 or 19.4 percent of the total labor force covered by employment security laws. Again, as with every category of employment, the state's most populous parishes counted the greatest number of retail workers. When measured against the state's average percentage of labor force engaged in retailing, however, only Jefferson Parish emerged as much above average in that group. St. Bernard and St. Tammany parishes in the New Orleans Metropolitan Area showed much higher than average percentages of retail workers in their populations, as did Tangipahoa, also with a sizeable total, and Madison, with relatively fewer.

Copyright © 1995 by the University of Oklahoma Press

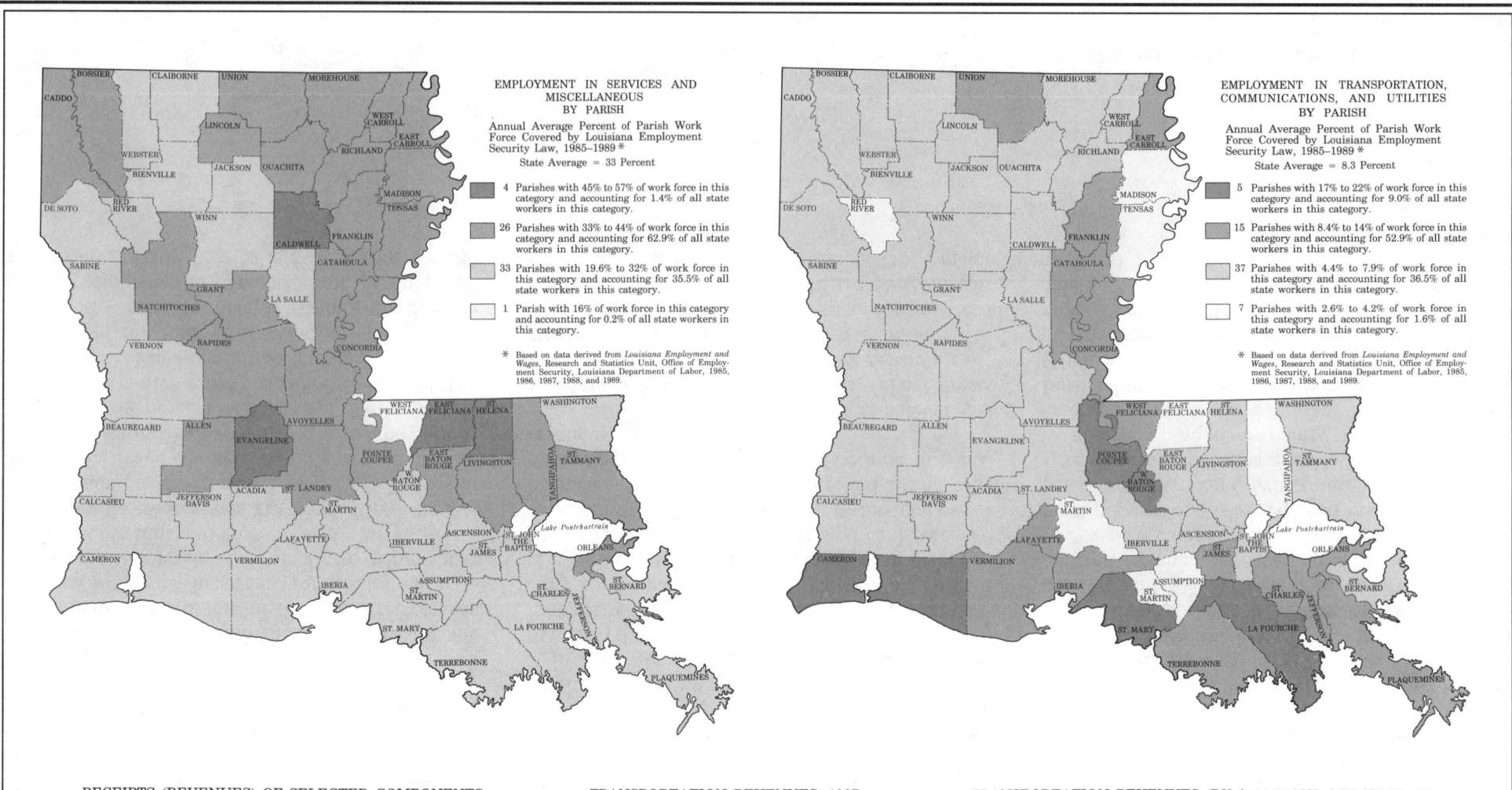

EMPLOYMENT IN SERVICES AND MISCELLANEOUS BY PARISH

Annual Average Percent of Parish Work Force Covered by Louisiana Employment Security Law, 1985–1989 *

State Average = 33 Percent

- 4 Parishes with 45% to 57% of work force in this category and accounting for 1.4% of all state workers in this category.
- 26 Parishes with 33% to 44% of work force in this category and accounting for 62.9% of all state workers in this category.
- 33 Parishes with 19.6% to 32% of work force in this category and accounting for 35.5% of all state workers in this category.
- 1 Parish with 16% of work force in this category and accounting for 0.2% of all state workers in this category.

* Based on data derived from *Louisiana Employment and Wages*, Research and Statistics Unit, Office of Employment Security, Louisiana Department of Labor, 1985, 1986, 1987, 1988, and 1989.

EMPLOYMENT IN TRANSPORTATION, COMMUNICATIONS, AND UTILITIES BY PARISH

Annual Average Percent of Parish Work Force Covered by Louisiana Employment Security Law, 1985–1989 *

State Average = 8.3 Percent

- 5 Parishes with 17% to 22% of work force in this category and accounting for 9.0% of all state workers in this category.
- 15 Parishes with 8.4% to 14% of work force in this category and accounting for 52.9% of all state workers in this category.
- 37 Parishes with 4.4% to 7.9% of work force in this category and accounting for 36.5% of all state workers in this category.
- 7 Parishes with 2.6% to 4.2% of work force in this category and accounting for 1.6% of all state workers in this category.

* Based on data derived from *Louisiana Employment and Wages*, Research and Statistics Unit, Office of Employment Security, Louisiana Department of Labor, 1985, 1986, 1987, 1988, and 1989.

RECEIPTS (REVENUES) OF SELECTED COMPONENTS OF SERVICE INDUSTRIES, 1982 AND 1987

Category	1987 Receipts ($1000)	% of Total	1982 Receipts ($1000)	% of Total
Subject to Federal Income Tax	10,243,284		7,697,708	
—Health Services except Hospitals	3,365,373	32.8	1,614,223	21.0
—Business Services	1,636,509	16.0	2,074,888	27.0
—Legal Services	1,268,188	12.4	722,147	9.4
—Engineering/Architectural/Surveying	1,213,491	11.8	599,640	7.8
—Hotels, Rooming Houses, Camps, etc.	663,128	6.5	564,149	7.3
—Automotive Repair/Services/Parking	557,876	5.4	466,780	6.1
Firms Exempt from Federal Income Tax	3,333,547		495,426	
—Selected Health Services	2,796,153	83.9	54,285	11.0

The data for 1982 and 1987 are not directly comparable due to changes in definitions.
Bureau of the Census. U.S. Department of Commerce. *Census of Service Industries.*

TRANSPORTATION REVENUES, 1987

Category	1987 ($1000)	% of Total
Motor Freight Transportation/Warehousing	1,256,293	37.8
—Trucking and Courier Services	1,120,935	33.7
Water Transportation	1,898,446	57.1
—Water Transportation of Freight	862,435	25.9
—Water Transportation of Passengers	74,343	2.2
—Incidental Services	961,668	28.9
Transportation Services	171,481	5.1
STATE TOTAL	3,326,220	100.0

Bureau of the Census. U.S. Department of Commerce. *Census of Transportation.*

TRANSPORTATION REVENUES (BY $1000) AND PERCENT OF TOTAL FOR SELECTED METROPOLITAN STATISTICAL AREAS, 1987

Category	Baton Rouge	Houma-Thibodaux	Lafayette	New Orleans	Shreveport
Motor Freight Transportation and Warehousing	155,008	13,427	111,417	454,473	155,505
	12.3%	1.1%	8.9%	36.2%	12.4%
Water Transportation	156,383	173,555	21,650	1,208,712	NA
	8.2%	9.1%	1.1%	63.4%	
Transportation Services	13,339	1,552	2,992	127,402	3,707
	7.8%	0.9%	1.8%	74.3%	2.2%

Bureau of the Census. U.S. Department of Commerce. *Census of Transportation.*

Service industries encompass various occupations and represent the largest single employment category in Louisiana. On the other hand, except for retail trade, the average weekly wage for service workers was the lowest in the state. The growth of the service sector of the economy, and the accompanying wage differential, represents a national trend.

The Census of Service Industries divides such establishments into two broad categories based upon whether the "company" was subject to or exempt from federal income taxes. Receipts of tax-exempt services ($3.3 billion) approximate one-third those of taxed businesses ($10.2 billion). Among tax-exempt concerns, the health category—including clinics, hospitals, and the like—accounted for almost 84 percent of total receipts. Other tax-exempt groups included civic, social, and fraternal organizations; museums; child care and family services; and vocational schools.

Firms subject to income taxes in 1987 were divided into eleven specific and one "miscellaneous" category. Health-related establishments ranked first, collecting almost a third of total receipts. Among such establishments, medical doctors' offices and clinics made up half the total. Another quarter came from offices and clinics of dentists. Other such establishments included nursing homes, hospitals, and medical laboratories.

Ranking second to fourth by receipts were business (16 percent), legal (12 percent), and engineering services (12 percent). Business services comprised, among other things, equipment rental, building maintenance, computer programming, pest control, advertising, detective agencies, temporary help, employment agencies, collection agencies, commercial photography, photocopying and duplicating, telephone answering, and interior design. Engineering services included management and public relations as well as engineering, architectural, and surveying establishments. (Legal services had no subdivisions.)

The remaining quarter of receipts came from hotels and other lodging, automotive repair and parking, miscellaneous repair, personal services, amusements, social services, and selected educational services. Personal services included beauty and barber shops, cleaning services, funeral services, photographic studios, and tax preparers. Amusements ranged downward in number from video tape rentals and included motion picture theatres, physical fitness facilities, coin-operated devices, dance studios, commercial sports, racing, and musical groups. Social services establishments were primarily child day-care facilities. Selected educational services included vocational schools and some libraries.

For 1985–1989, employment in service industries averaged 33 percent (485,422) of the state's workers covered by the employment security laws. As in other employment, the most populous parishes ranked first in total numbers. Except for Orleans Parish, however, these parish percentages approximated the state's average or slightly below. Few parishes exhibited much higher than average employment in service industries; even fewer showed much less than the average.

The 1987 Census of Transportation recorded 2,971 establishments within three categories: (1) motor freight transportation and warehousing, (2) water transportation, and (3) transportation services. The first category accounted for fully half the businesses and 38 percent of the total revenues. Within this group, 90 percent of the establishments (and 89 percent of total revenues) were derived from one subdivision—trucking and non–air courier services. This work included general freight carriers, moving companies, garbage and trash collection, dump trucking, and courier services. Nine percent of the businesses fell within the subdivision of public warehousing and storage services.

Water transportation accounts for 32 percent of the establishments and 57 percent of revenues and is subdivided into (1) freight transportation, (2) passenger transportation, and (3) water transportation services. In number of establishments, the services category far exceeds the other two—82 percent to 10 percent for freight and 8 percent for passengers. However, in revenues, services represent only 51 percent of the total, compared to 45 percent for freight transport and 4 percent for passenger transport. The two largest classes of water transport establishments are towing and tugboat services and marine cargo hauling, both within the services subdivision.

Eighteen percent of transportation establishments fall in the category of transportation services. These establishments account for only 5 percent of total revenues. Within this group falls such work as travel agencies, freight shipping services, tour operators, and car rentals.

During the 1985–1989 period an average of 8.3 percent of the state's labor force covered by employment security laws was engaged in economic pursuits tied to transportation—an average of 122,101 annually. Twenty parishes were above the state's average; of these, five were more than twice the state average. Those parishes with higher than average percentages are largely situated along the Gulf Coast and the Mississippi, where maritime occupations are numerous.

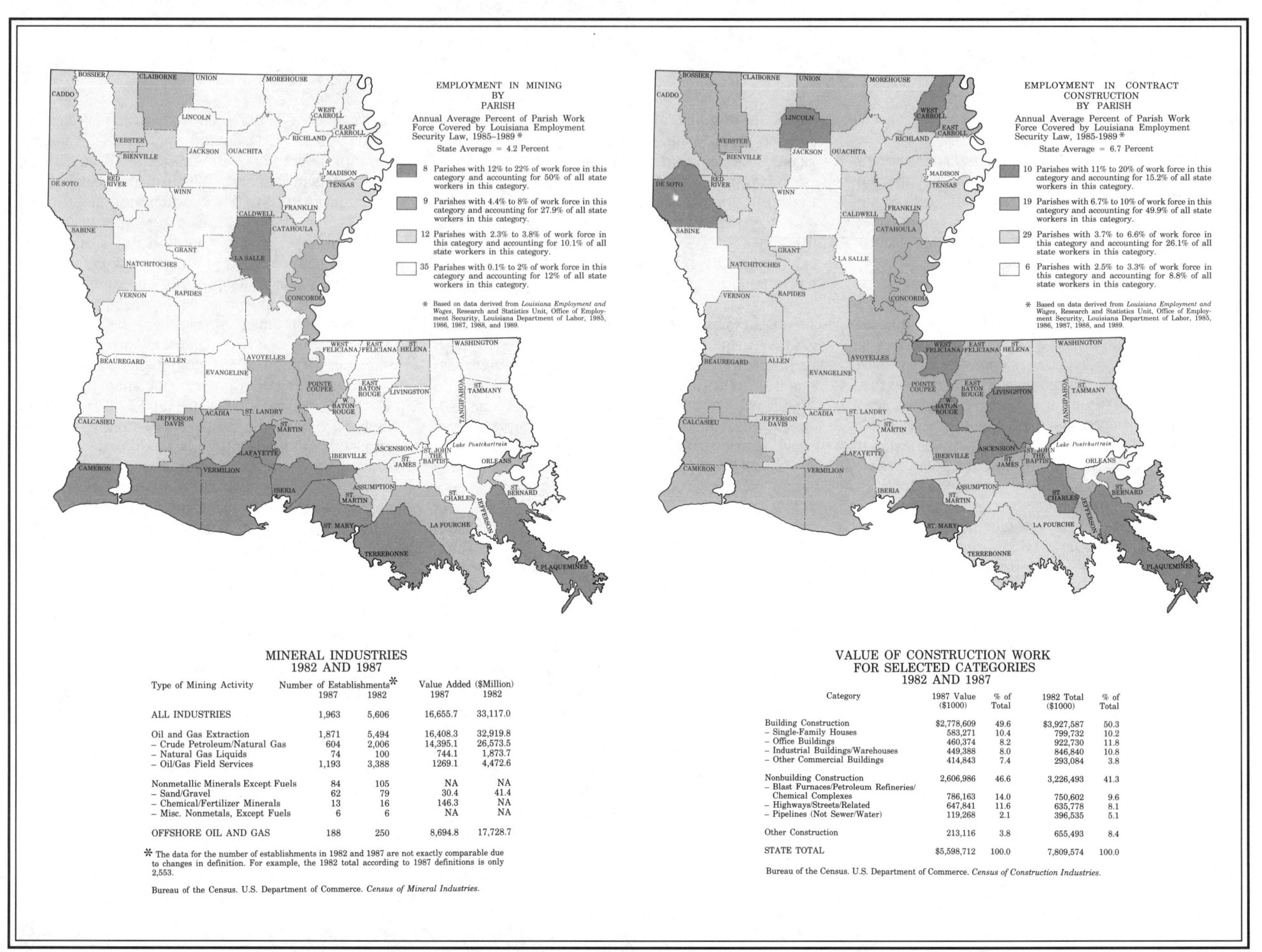

EMPLOYMENT IN MINING
BY
PARISH

Annual Average Percent of Parish Work
Force Covered by Louisiana Employment
Security Law, 1985–1989 *

State Average = 4.2 Percent

8 Parishes with 12% to 22% of work force in this category and accounting for 50% of all state workers in this category.

9 Parishes with 4.4% to 8% of work force in this category and accounting for 27.9% of all state workers in this category.

12 Parishes with 2.3% to 3.8% of work force in this category and accounting for 10.1% of all state workers in this category.

35 Parishes with 0.1% to 2% of work force in this category and accounting for 12% of all state workers in this category.

* Based on data derived from *Louisiana Employment and Wages*, Research and Statistics Unit, Office of Employment Security, Louisiana Department of Labor, 1985, 1986, 1987, 1988, and 1989.

EMPLOYMENT IN CONTRACT
CONSTRUCTION
BY PARISH

Annual Average Percent of Parish Work
Force Covered by Louisiana Employment
Security Law, 1985-1989 *

State Average = 6.7 Percent

10 Parishes with 11% to 20% of work force in this category and accounting for 15.2% of all state workers in this category.

19 Parishes with 6.7% to 10% of work force in this category and accounting for 49.9% of all state workers in this category.

29 Parishes with 3.7% to 6.6% of work force in this category and accounting for 26.1% of all state workers in this category.

6 Parishes with 2.5% to 3.3% of work force in this category and accounting for 8.8% of all state workers in this category.

* Based on data derived from *Louisiana Employment and Wages*, Research and Statistics Unit, Office of Employment Security, Louisiana Department of Labor, 1985, 1986, 1987, 1988, and 1989.

MINERAL INDUSTRIES
1982 AND 1987

Type of Mining Activity	Number of Establishments* 1987	1982	Value Added ($Million) 1987	1982
ALL INDUSTRIES	1,963	5,606	16,655.7	33,117.0
Oil and Gas Extraction	1,871	5,494	16,408.3	32,919.8
– Crude Petroleum/Natural Gas	604	2,006	14,395.1	26,573.5
– Natural Gas Liquids	74	100	744.1	1,873.7
– Oil/Gas Field Services	1,193	3,388	1269.1	4,472.6
Nonmetallic Minerals Except Fuels	84	105	NA	NA
– Sand/Gravel	62	79	30.4	41.4
– Chemical/Fertilizer Minerals	13	16	146.3	NA
– Misc. Nonmetals, Except Fuels	6	6	NA	NA
OFFSHORE OIL AND GAS	188	250	8,694.8	17,728.7

* The data for the number of establishments in 1982 and 1987 are not exactly comparable due to changes in definition. For example, the 1982 total according to 1987 definitions is only 2,553.

Bureau of the Census. U.S. Department of Commerce. *Census of Mineral Industries.*

VALUE OF CONSTRUCTION WORK
FOR SELECTED CATEGORIES
1982 AND 1987

Category	1987 Value ($1000)	% of Total	1982 Total ($1000)	% of Total
Building Construction	$2,778,609	49.6	$3,927,587	50.3
– Single-Family Houses	583,271	10.4	799,732	10.2
– Office Buildings	460,374	8.2	922,730	11.8
– Industrial Buildings/Warehouses	449,388	8.0	846,840	10.8
– Other Commercial Buildings	414,843	7.4	293,084	3.8
Nonbuilding Construction	2,606,986	46.6	3,226,493	41.3
– Blast Furnaces/Petroleum Refineries/ Chemical Complexes	786,163	14.0	750,602	9.6
– Highways/Streets/Related	647,841	11.6	635,778	8.1
– Pipelines (Not Sewer/Water)	119,268	2.1	396,535	5.1
Other Construction	213,116	3.8	655,493	8.4
STATE TOTAL	$5,598,712	100.0	7,809,574	100.0

Bureau of the Census. U.S. Department of Commerce. *Census of Construction Industries.*

The search for gold has been the mainstay for much of Louisiana's history, whether that "gold" represented the metal itself vainly sought by early colonists or the "black gold" which has provided the motive power for the state's economy throughout most of the twentieth century. However, the earliest immigrants to Louisiana—the prehistoric Native American tribes—began the extraction of other minerals. Salt was a valuable commodity for use and trade. Stone and gravel were employed in the production of tools and weaponry. The native earth was shaped into pottery and other products for local use or as trade goods.

The modern mining industry has become associated with the large-scale development of the state's petroleum and natural gas reserves since the late nineteenth century (Map 10). Related salt and sulphur resources have also expanded. The salt trade is of ancient origin but is now largely associated with the Five Islands area of salt domes in southern Louisiana. Sulphur extraction has increased since the invention of the Frasch process in 1941. Superheated water is pumped underground into the sulphur deposits. The melted sulphur is then forced to the surface by the injection of compressed air.

Mining firms employed on average 61,931 workers annually during the 1985–1989 period. This figure represented only 4.2 percent of the labor force covered by the employment security laws. Oil and gas activity, particularly offshore, dominated the distribution of these workers. A string of mainly coastal parishes had labor forces employed in mining that accounted for three to five times the state's average.

The value added by mining according to the 1987 Census of Mining totaled $16,655,700,000— more than $200,000,000 greater than the value added by manufacturing. Of that total, 52.5 percent was derived from offshore oil and gas activity. Of the value added total, 98.5 percent is accounted for by oil and gas activity. Oil and gas also account for 95 percent of all establishments associated with mining.

A comparison with previous censuses reveals the decline of oil and gas activity both in terms of value and workers. Compared with the 1982 value added total of almost thirty-three billion dollars, the 1987 total represents a drop of more than 50 percent. A similar drop in employment also occurred during the five-year period. Still, the total value of oil and gas shipments and receipts in Louisiana, while declining slightly from the 1982 figures, accounted for 16 percent of the nation's total in 1987.

The Commerce Department's *Standard Industrial Classification Manual* lists three construction categories. First is building construction by general contractors or operative builders. Next comes heavy construction, such as highways built by general contractors and selected special trade contractors. Third is construction done by special trade contractors such as electricians, plumbers, and painters. The 1987 Census of Construction Industries includes all three categories, plus the common real-estate categories of "land subdividers and developers, except cemeteries."

The total value for construction worked measured by the 1987 census reached almost $5.6 billion. This represented, however, a 28 percent drop from the 1982 total of $7.8 billion. Construction in the category of blast furnaces, petroleum refineries, and chemical complexes ranked first in value, followed by highways, streets, and so on; single family houses; office buildings; and industrial buildings. These five categories accounted for just over half of the value of the total work. Twenty other categories accounted for the remaining half. These classifications included hospitals, farm buildings, educational buildings, pipelines, oil fields, and marine construction. A particular drop from 1982 was noted in single-family houses, office buildings, industrial buildings, pipelines, and oil fields; this trend followed the decline of the state's economy during that period.

The 1987 census counted 26,981 establishments at work in the state. Of that total, the vast majority (20,642) were nonemployers, and half of those establishments that employed people had fewer than five persons on their payroll. Most of the nonemployer establishments were special trade contractors. Thus, one sees that the total number of establishments represents many self-employed operations.

An average of 97,426 workers per year for the 1985–1989 period was engaged in construction industries. This average represented 6.7 percent of the total state labor force covered by employment security laws. Construction workers were scattered throughout the state. Although the populous parishes held the highest totals of employees, almost as many as not of these parishes showed a less than average percentage of their labor force engaged in construction. Parishes in the lower Mississippi Valley generally showed above-average employment, which is related to the "industrial corridor" along its banks (Maps 73 and 87).

Copyright © 1995 by the University of Oklahoma Press

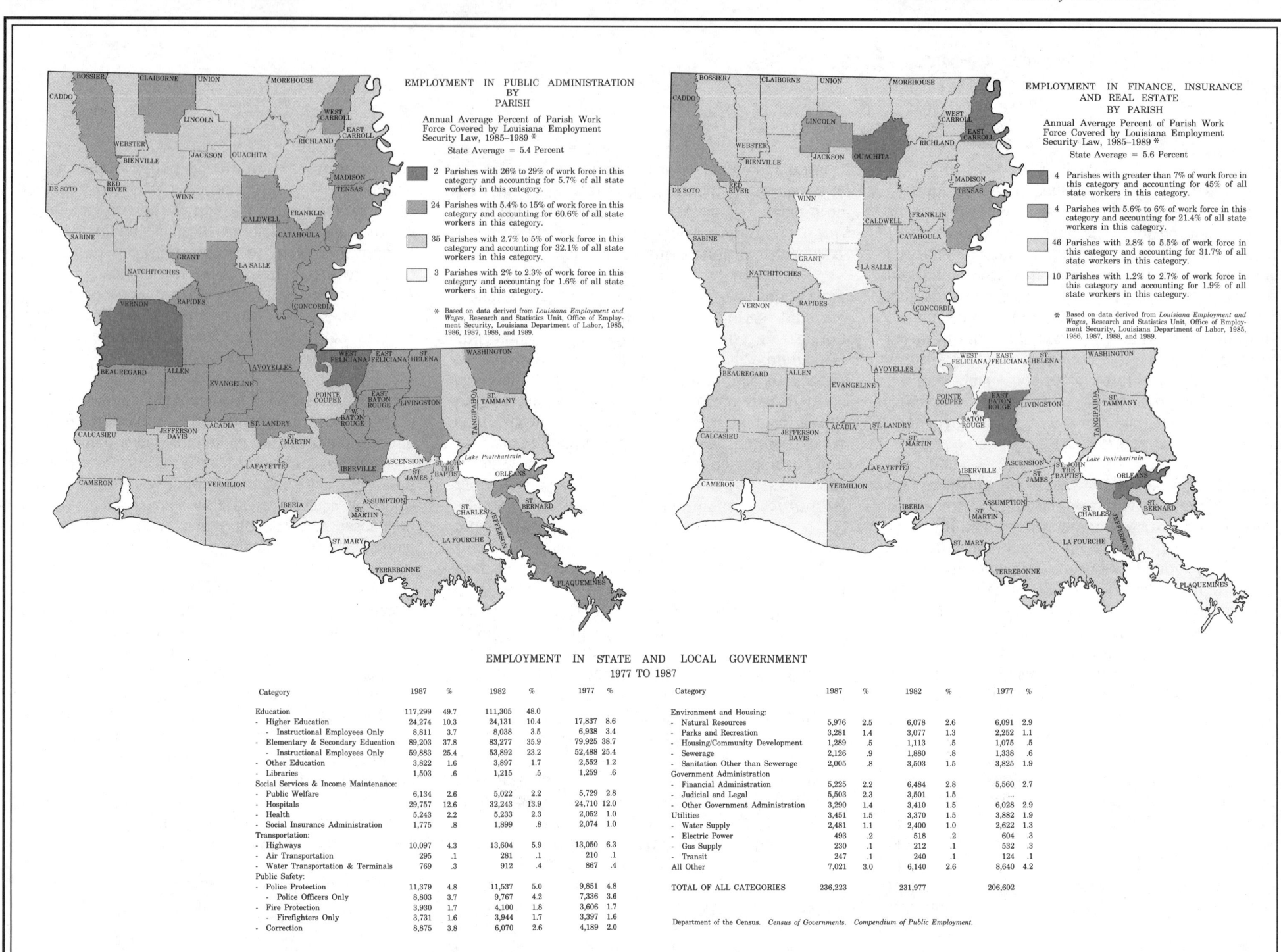

EMPLOYMENT IN PUBLIC ADMINISTRATION BY PARISH

Annual Average Percent of Parish Work Force Covered by Louisiana Employment Security Law, 1985–1989 *

State Average = 5.4 Percent

- 2 Parishes with 26% to 29% of work force in this category and accounting for 5.7% of all state workers in this category.
- 24 Parishes with 5.4% to 15% of work force in this category and accounting for 60.6% of all state workers in this category.
- 35 Parishes with 2.7% to 5% of work force in this category and accounting for 32.1% of all state workers in this category.
- 3 Parishes with 2% to 2.3% of work force in this category and accounting for 1.6% of all state workers in this category.

* Based on data derived from *Louisiana Employment and Wages*, Research and Statistics Unit, Office of Employment Security, Louisiana Department of Labor, 1985, 1986, 1987, 1988, and 1989.

EMPLOYMENT IN FINANCE, INSURANCE AND REAL ESTATE BY PARISH

Annual Average Percent of Parish Work Force Covered by Louisiana Employment Security Law, 1985–1989 *

State Average = 5.6 Percent

- 4 Parishes with greater than 7% of work force in this category and accounting for 45% of all state workers in this category.
- 4 Parishes with 5.6% to 6% of work force in this category and accounting for 21.4% of all state workers in this category.
- 46 Parishes with 2.8% to 5.5% of work force in this category and accounting for 31.7% of all state workers in this category.
- 10 Parishes with 1.2% to 2.7% of work force in this category and accounting for 1.9% of all state workers in this category.

* Based on data derived from *Louisiana Employment and Wages*, Research and Statistics Unit, Office of Employment Security, Louisiana Department of Labor, 1985, 1986, 1987, 1988, and 1989.

EMPLOYMENT IN STATE AND LOCAL GOVERNMENT
1977 TO 1987

Category	1987	%	1982	%	1977	%
Education	117,299	49.7	111,305	48.0		
- Higher Education	24,274	10.3	24,131	10.4	17,837	8.6
- Instructional Employees Only	8,811	3.7	8,038	3.5	6,938	3.4
- Elementary & Secondary Education	89,203	37.8	83,277	35.9	79,925	38.7
- Instructional Employees Only	59,883	25.4	53,892	23.2	52,488	25.4
- Other Education	3,822	1.6	3,897	1.7	2,552	1.2
- Libraries	1,503	.6	1,215	.5	1,259	.6
Social Services & Income Maintenance:						
- Public Welfare	6,134	2.6	5,022	2.2	5,729	2.8
- Hospitals	29,757	12.6	32,243	13.9	24,710	12.0
- Health	5,243	2.2	5,233	2.3	2,052	1.0
- Social Insurance Administration	1,775	.8	1,899	.8	2,074	1.0
Transportation:						
- Highways	10,097	4.3	13,604	5.9	13,050	6.3
- Air Transportation	295	.1	281	.1	210	.1
- Water Transportation & Terminals	769	.3	912	.4	867	.4
Public Safety:						
- Police Protection	11,379	4.8	11,537	5.0	9,851	4.8
- Police Officers Only	8,803	3.7	9,767	4.2	7,336	3.6
- Fire Protection	3,930	1.7	4,100	1.8	3,606	1.7
- Firefighters Only	3,731	1.6	3,944	1.7	3,397	1.6
- Correction	8,875	3.8	6,070	2.6	4,189	2.0

Category	1987	%	1982	%	1977	%
Environment and Housing:						
- Natural Resources	5,976	2.5	6,078	2.6	6,091	2.9
- Parks and Recreation	3,281	1.4	3,077	1.3	2,252	1.1
- Housing/Community Development	1,289	.5	1,113	.5	1,075	.5
- Sewerage	2,126	.9	1,880	.8	1,338	.6
- Sanitation Other than Sewerage	2,005	.8	3,503	1.5	3,825	1.9
Government Administration						
- Financial Administration	5,225	2.2	6,484	2.8	5,560	2.7
- Judicial and Legal	5,503	2.3	3,501	1.5	...	
- Other Government Administration	3,290	1.4	3,410	1.5	6,028	2.9
Utilities	3,451	1.5	3,370	1.5	3,882	1.9
- Water Supply	2,481	1.1	2,400	1.0	2,622	1.3
- Electric Power	493	.2	518	.2	604	.3
- Gas Supply	230	.1	212	.1	532	.3
- Transit	247	.1	240	.1	124	.1
All Other	7,021	3.0	6,140	2.6	8,640	4.2
TOTAL OF ALL CATEGORIES	236,223		231,977		206,602	

Department of the Census. *Census of Governments. Compendium of Public Employment.*

Financial, insurance, and real estate businesses perform a variety of work. Banking institutions represent a large component. Also included are security dealers engaged in the buying and selling of stocks, bonds, and notes. Loan agencies are another subdivision. Insurance carriers and brokers and real estate agents and brokers complete the categories included by the state in this group.

Establishments include independent businesses as well as branches or affiliates of regional or national firms. Employment may range from dozens or hundreds in the largest of the businesses to essentially the self-employed, who may have no other worker on a "company" payroll.

For the period 1985–1989 the annual total of workers within this category averaged 82,809—5.6 percent of the labor force covered by employment security laws. The weekly wage for that same period averaged $389.00—sixth among the nine employment categories. Only eight parishes had average employment greater than the state figure; those significantly higher were metropolitan parishes. This is in part a function of population, with rival agencies vying for business. In part, too, this represents an amassing of money beyond mere population. Regional banks and bank holding companies take over smaller or failed institutions, then move duplicate positions from what now represent branches of the parent firm. That parent corporation resides elsewhere. The smaller place loses positions, with detrimental effects on its overall economic health.

The fact that fifty-six of the state's sixty-four parishes had employment percentages below the state average, and that ten of this group had less than half of the state's average, is a further indica-tion of the trend toward institutional consolidation. Smaller towns and villages may support one or more insurance agencies, but real estate and financial institutions are largely relegated to the more populous centers such as parish seats. The implications for rural parishes as such services, particularly banking, are removed from local control or interest parallel those for other aspects of rural life such as health care.

The public administration category "includes all Federal, State, Local and International government activities, such as the legislative, judicial, and administration functions as well as government owned or operated business enterprises." Of the labor force covered by employment security laws, this group comprised an average annual total of 79,672—5.4 percent of the average for the 1985–1989 period. The average weekly wage for that same period was $372.00—seventh among the nine categories.

A glance through the blue pages of any telephone directory will provide a glimpse of the federal, state, and local government agencies. According to the definitions employed by the 1987 Census of Governments, 452 local governments existed in Louisiana. These included 61 parish governments, 301 municipal governments, 66 school systems, and 24 special district governments. Every parish but East Baton Rouge, Orleans, and Terrebonne has a census-defined parish government. Within those three parishes the government is consolidated within the cities of Baton Rouge, New Orleans, and Houma. Thus, the census considers them municipal instead of parish governments.

Municipal governments exist for cities (munici-palities in excess of 5,000 inhabitants), towns (municipalities with 1,000–5,000 inhabitants), and villages (municipalities with 150–1,000 inhabitants). These include incorporated as well as unincorporated areas. A minimum population of 150 is necessary for incorporation in the parishes of Concordia, La Salle, and Red River; elsewhere a minimum of 300 inhabitants is needed.

Sixty-six school districts exist, one for each parish plus a separate city district for Monroe and for Bogalusa. Other special district governments have been created by the legislature and include water conservation districts, waste disposal districts, regional transit authorities, watershed districts, and several port, harbor, and terminal districts. Still other types of government agencies include drainage districts, fire protection districts, hospital service districts, housing authorities, levee districts, industrial development districts, public trusts, library boards, recreation districts, historic preservation districts, airport authorities, sewerage districts, soil and water conservation districts, and waterworks districts. In addition there exist numerous agencies, boards, commissions, authorities, and so on, created for state, parish, or municipal levels.

The United States has as the basis of its government the concept of representative democracy. Whether within the familiar three branches of our government or the less familiar agencies, numerous opportunities exist for elected or appointed service by citizens. Effective government in large part depends upon civic participation, such participation necessary that, in Abraham Lincoln's words, "government of the people, by the people, and for the people shall not perish from the earth."

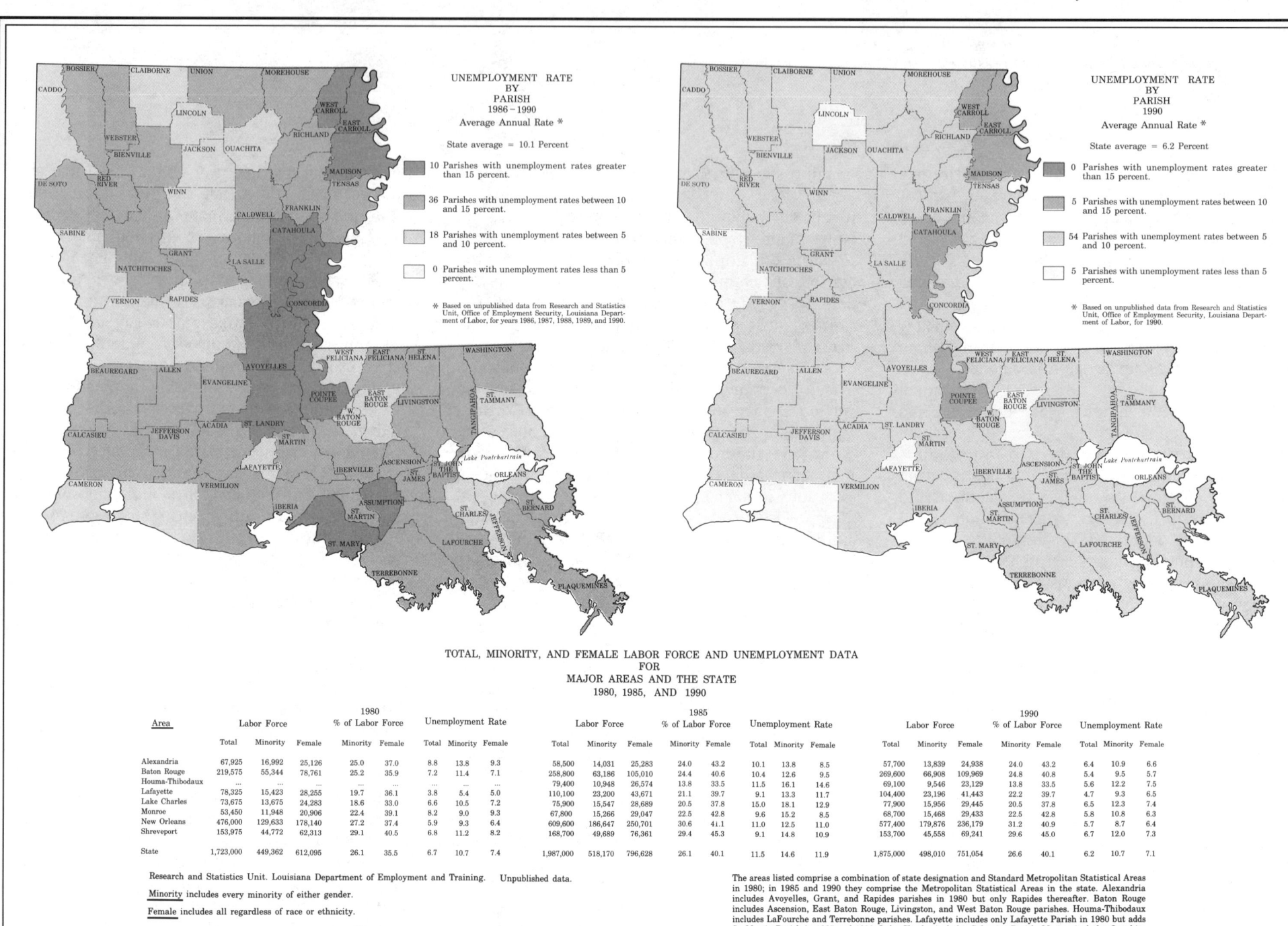

UNEMPLOYMENT RATE
BY
PARISH
1986–1990
Average Annual Rate *

State average = 10.1 Percent

10 Parishes with unemployment rates greater than 15 percent.

36 Parishes with unemployment rates between 10 and 15 percent.

18 Parishes with unemployment rates between 5 and 10 percent.

0 Parishes with unemployment rates less than 5 percent.

* Based on unpublished data from Research and Statistics Unit, Office of Employment Security, Louisiana Department of Labor, for years 1986, 1987, 1988, 1989, and 1990.

UNEMPLOYMENT RATE
BY
PARISH
1990
Average Annual Rate *

State average = 6.2 Percent

0 Parishes with unemployment rates greater than 15 percent.

5 Parishes with unemployment rates between 10 and 15 percent.

54 Parishes with unemployment rates between 5 and 10 percent.

5 Parishes with unemployment rates less than 5 percent.

* Based on unpublished data from Research and Statistics Unit, Office of Employment Security, Louisiana Department of Labor, for 1990.

TOTAL, MINORITY, AND FEMALE LABOR FORCE AND UNEMPLOYMENT DATA
FOR
MAJOR AREAS AND THE STATE
1980, 1985, AND 1990

| | 1980 | | | | | | | | 1985 | | | | | | | | 1990 | | | | | | | |
| | Labor Force | | | % of Labor Force | | Unemployment Rate | | | Labor Force | | | % of Labor Force | | Unemployment Rate | | | Labor Force | | | % of Labor Force | | Unemployment Rate | | |
Area	Total	Minority	Female	Minority	Female	Total	Minority	Female	Total	Minority	Female	Minority	Female	Total	Minority	Female	Total	Minority	Female	Minority	Female	Total	Minority	Female
Alexandria	67,925	16,992	25,126	25.0	37.0	8.8	13.8	9.3	58,500	14,031	25,283	24.0	43.2	10.1	13.8	8.5	57,700	13,839	24,938	24.0	43.2	6.4	10.9	6.6
Baton Rouge	219,575	55,344	78,761	25.2	35.9	7.2	11.4	7.1	258,800	63,186	105,010	24.4	40.6	10.4	12.6	9.5	269,600	66,908	109,969	24.8	40.8	5.4	9.5	5.7
Houma-Thibodaux	...	...	...	...	...	...	...	...	79,400	10,948	26,574	13.8	33.5	5.6	16.1	14.6	69,100	9,546	23,129	13.8	33.5	5.6	12.2	7.5
Lafayette	78,325	15,423	28,255	19.7	36.1	3.8	5.4	5.0	110,100	23,200	43,671	21.1	39.7	9.1	13.3	11.7	104,400	23,196	41,443	22.2	39.7	4.7	9.3	6.5
Lake Charles	73,675	13,675	24,283	18.6	33.0	6.6	10.5	7.2	75,900	15,547	28,689	20.5	37.8	15.0	18.1	12.9	77,900	15,956	29,445	20.5	37.8	6.5	12.3	7.4
Monroe	53,450	11,948	20,906	22.4	39.1	8.2	9.0	9.3	67,800	15,266	29,047	22.5	42.8	9.6	15.2	8.5	68,700	15,468	29,433	22.5	42.8	5.8	10.8	6.3
New Orleans	476,000	129,633	178,140	27.2	37.4	5.9	9.3	6.4	609,600	186,647	250,701	30.6	41.1	11.0	12.5	11.0	577,400	179,876	236,179	31.2	40.9	5.7	8.7	6.4
Shreveport	153,975	44,772	62,313	29.1	40.5	6.8	11.2	8.2	168,700	49,689	76,361	29.4	45.3	9.1	14.8	10.9	153,700	45,558	69,241	29.6	45.0	6.7	12.0	7.3
State	1,723,000	449,362	612,095	26.1	35.5	6.7	10.7	7.4	1,987,000	518,170	796,628	26.1	40.1	11.5	14.6	11.9	1,875,000	498,010	751,054	26.6	40.1	6.2	10.7	7.1

Research and Statistics Unit. Louisiana Department of Employment and Training.   Unpublished data.

Minority includes every minority of either gender.

Female includes all regardless of race or ethnicity.

The areas listed comprise a combination of state designation and Standard Metropolitan Statistical Areas in 1980; in 1985 and 1990 they comprise the Metropolitan Statistical Areas in the state. Alexandria includes Avoyelles, Grant, and Rapides parishes in 1980 but only Rapides thereafter. Baton Rouge includes Ascension, East Baton Rouge, Livingston, and West Baton Rouge parishes. Houma-Thibodaux includes LaFourche and Terrebonne parishes. Lafayette includes only Lafayette Parish in 1980 but adds St. Martin Parish in 1985 and 1990. Lake Charles includes Calcasieu Parish. Monroe includes Ouachita Parish. New Orleans comprises Jefferson, Orleans, St. Bernard, and St. Tammany in 1980 but adds St. Charles and St. John the Baptist in 1985 and 1990. Shreveport includes Bossier, Caddo, and Webster parishes in 1980 but drops Webster thereafter.

The nation's labor force has changed in definition as laws have changed to protect various classes of workers. The Bureau of the Census' 1990 *Statistical Abstract of the United States* defines the civilian labor force as "(a) all civilians, who, during the reference week, did any work for pay or profit (minimum of an hour's work) or worked fifteen hours or more as unpaid workers in a family enterprise, and (b) all civilians who were not working but who had jobs or businesses from which they were temporarily absent for non-economic reasons (illness, weather conditions, vacation, labor-management dispute, etc)." Further, unemployed persons "comprise all civilians who had no employment during the reference week, who made specific efforts to find a job within the previous four weeks (such as applying directly to an employer, or to a public employment service, or checking with friends), and who were available for work during that week, except for temporary illness. Persons on layoff from a job or waiting to report to a new job within thirty days are also classified as unemployed if they are available for work." These two categories form the total labor force. All other civilians sixteen years old or older are classified as "not in the labor force."

People in the labor force may lack work for any number of reasons. Some are laid off; others have voluntarily left jobs to look for new positions. For whatever reason, some of the labor force is without gainful employment; the percentage of unemployed among the total labor force constitutes the unemployment rate.

Various factors at different geographic scales can affect unemployment rates. The opening or closing of a factory, perhaps even a single work shift, can affect local levels. The level of diversification of employment opportunities helps or hinders in the job location. National or regional recessions or boom periods raise or lower unemployment levels, too. The rise and fall of the total labor force can also affect the rate. When people move away for jobs elsewhere, the total labor force declines in number; although the same number of people might remain out of work, the rate, now tied to a lower sum, declines.

With the collapse of oil prices in the 1980s Louisiana's economy was devastated. The oil and gas industry had provided employment for thousands in the state. Moreover, the state itself depended upon severance taxes to fund much of its government and provide basic social services.

A mapping of the 1986–1990 average unemployment rates by parish illustrates the state's economic woes. As a whole the state suffered from an unemployment rate of 10.1 percent while the national rate hovered around 6 percent. Large as this 1986–1990 average was, however, it did represent a decline from the 1984–1988 average of 11.5 percent and the 1985–1989 figure of 11.1 percent. Forty-four of the state's sixty-four parishes had unemployment rates at or higher than the state average. Only twenty parishes had unemployment rates less than that average. The absolute levels ranged from a high of 22.2 percent in West Carroll Parish to a low of 5.1 percent in Lincoln. Many of the "delta" parishes along the Mississippi suffered from the highest unemployment levels.

The preliminary data for 1990 alone show a markedly improved pattern; the unemployment rate had dropped to 6.2 percent. Part of this improvement has been caused by an absolute decline in the size of the labor force, from 1,990,000 in 1986 to 1,875,000 in 1990. Slight improvements in the economy also helped lower unemployment. Whereas ten parishes had unemployment rates above 15 percent for the five-year average, none suffered as high a rate in the single 1990 year. Whereas none held a rate below 5 percent in the 1986–1990 period, five did so in 1990. Absolute variance ranged from 14.4 percent in West Carroll Parish to 3.4 percent in Lincoln.

Employment rates vary among gender and racial groups. Over the decade of the 1980s more women entered the labor force, advancing from 35.5 percent to 40.1 percent of the total. The total minority labor force rose less rapidly, from 26.1 percent of the total in 1980 to 26.6 percent in 1990. However, unemployment rates among all females and among all minorities remained higher than for the labor force as a whole.

During 1986–1990, Louisiana suffered higher unemployment than did any of its immediate neighbors. In fact, the state led the nation or was close to the top in unemployment. Economists agree that several basic changes are needed to prevent a recurring crisis. A greater diversification of employment opportunities away from the reliance on oil and gas is one road; recent inactivity in the "oil patch" may mean that this latest trough in that "boom and bust" industry may be long-term. A better-trained labor force represents another needed improvement; Louisiana, as do most states, faces a crisis in its public education system. For state services and employment, a broader tax base will also be necessary.

Copyright © 1995 by the University of Oklahoma Press

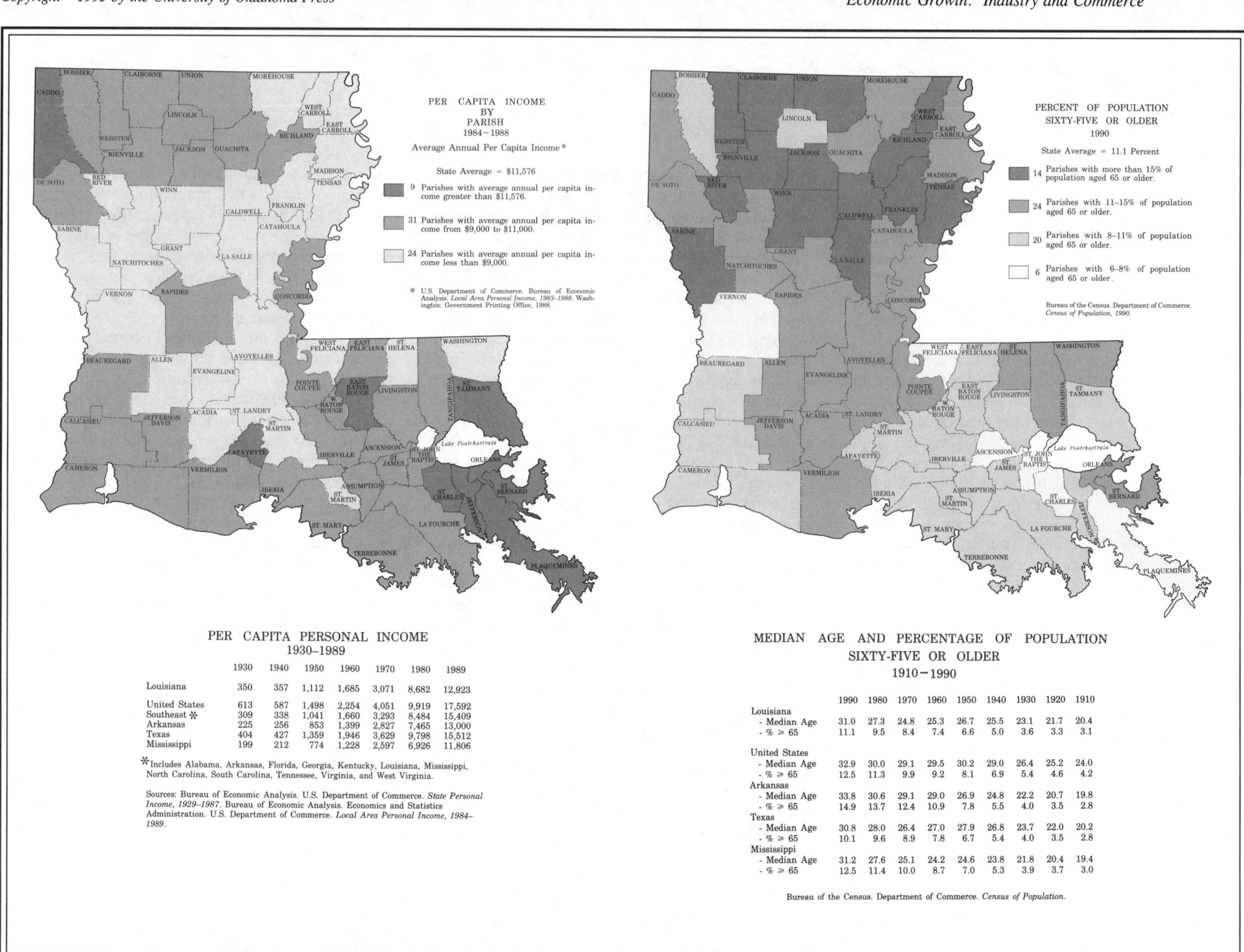

PER CAPITA INCOME
BY
PARISH
1984–1988

Average Annual Per Capita Income *

State Average = $11,576

9 Parishes with average annual per capita income greater than $11,576.

31 Parishes with average annual per capita income from $9,000 to $11,000.

24 Parishes with average annual per capita income less than $9,000.

* U.S. Department of Commerce. Bureau of Economic Analysis. *Local Area Personal Income, 1983–1988*. Washington: Government Printing Office, 1988.

PERCENT OF POPULATION
SIXTY-FIVE OR OLDER
1990

State Average = 11.1 Percent

14 Parishes with more than 15% of population aged 65 or older.

24 Parishes with 11–15% of population aged 65 or older.

20 Parishes with 8–11% of population aged 65 or older.

6 Parishes with 6–8% of population aged 65 or older.

Bureau of the Census. Department of Commerce. *Census of Population, 1990.*

PER CAPITA PERSONAL INCOME
1930–1989

	1930	1940	1950	1960	1970	1980	1989
Louisiana	350	357	1,112	1,685	3,071	8,682	12,923
United States	613	587	1,498	2,254	4,051	9,919	17,592
Southeast ✳	309	338	1,041	1,660	3,293	8,484	15,409
Arkansas	225	256	853	1,399	2,827	7,465	13,000
Texas	404	427	1,359	1,946	3,629	9,798	15,512
Mississippi	199	212	774	1,228	2,597	6,926	11,806

✳Includes Alabama, Arkansas, Florida, Georgia, Kentucky, Louisiana, Mississippi, North Carolina, South Carolina, Tennessee, Virginia, and West Virginia.

Sources: Bureau of Economic Analysis. U.S. Department of Commerce. *State Personal Income, 1929–1987*. Bureau of Economic Analysis. Economics and Statistics Administration. U.S. Department of Commerce. *Local Area Personal Income, 1984–1989.*

MEDIAN AGE AND PERCENTAGE OF POPULATION
SIXTY-FIVE OR OLDER
1910–1990

	1990	1980	1970	1960	1950	1940	1930	1920	1910
Louisiana									
- Median Age	31.0	27.3	24.8	25.3	26.7	25.5	23.1	21.7	20.4
- % ≥ 65	11.1	9.5	8.4	7.4	6.6	5.0	3.6	3.3	3.1
United States									
- Median Age	32.9	30.0	29.1	29.5	30.2	29.0	26.4	25.2	24.0
- % ≥ 65	12.5	11.3	9.9	9.2	8.1	6.9	5.4	4.6	4.2
Arkansas									
- Median Age	33.8	30.6	29.1	29.0	26.9	24.8	22.2	20.7	19.8
- % ≥ 65	14.9	13.7	12.4	10.9	7.8	5.5	4.0	3.5	2.8
Texas									
- Median Age	30.8	28.0	26.4	27.0	27.9	26.8	23.7	22.0	20.2
- % ≥ 65	10.1	9.6	8.9	7.8	6.7	5.4	4.0	3.5	2.8
Mississippi									
- Median Age	31.2	27.6	25.1	24.2	24.6	23.8	21.8	20.4	19.4
- % ≥ 65	12.5	11.4	10.0	8.7	7.0	5.3	3.9	3.7	3.0

Bureau of the Census. Department of Commerce. *Census of Population.*

Louisianians derive income from a variety of sources. Wages and salaries represent by far the largest source of income. Dividends, interest, and rents are a secondary source. The U.S. Department of Commerce totals a variety of classes of income to produce the per capita personal income in its various publications on that subject.

The state's 1989 per capita income averaged $12,923. This figure stood as the second lowest among Louisiana and its three neighbors; only Mississippi had a lower amount. The Louisiana figure approximated only 73 percent of the national average of $17,592 and 84 percent of the southeastern United States average of $15,409.

The 1989 figure depicted in stark terms the aftermath of the economic devastation wrought by the collapse of oil and gas prices in the 1980s. Louisiana's 1980 per capita personal income of $8,682 was lower than the national average; still, it represented a healthier 88 percent of that total. Moreover, the state's income exceeded the southeastern average and was second only to that of Texas among the group of immediate neighbors.

Louisiana had an over-reliance on oil and gas. Its economy was not so diversified that the blow from the loss of that industry could be cushioned. Texas shared a similar fate, but not to such an extent. From a state average that was approximately 98 percent of the national average in 1980, Texas's income fell to 88 percent of the national average in 1989. In Louisiana total personal income in many southern parishes would actually fall as the decade progressed.

On average for the five-year period 1984 through 1988, the state's per capita income totaled $11,576. Only nine parishes exceeded that average. The highest parish average occurred in Lafayette—$14,021. East Baton Rouge, Jefferson, and St. Tammany parishes all had averages in excess of $13,000. St. Charles, Orleans, Caddo, Plaquemines, and St. Bernard all fell below $13,000 but above the state average. Of the parishes in this group of nine, only Caddo was a northern parish.

At the opposite end, Madison Parish's per capita personal income stood at only $6,819, less than half the national average of $14,713. Nine other parishes—Allen, Avoyelles, Catahoula, Franklin, Grant, Sabine, St. Helena, West Carroll, and West Feliciana—had per capita incomes under $8,000. A broad range of parishes made up the group falling under the state average—rural and urban, hill and delta, north and south.

Another measure of Louisiana's population with significance for the future is the percentage of population sixty-five or older. With medical advances and improved dietary patterns, the average life expectancy among Americans has steadily increased. The nation's population has been immunized or medicated in fighting diseases which in former generations decimated the citizenry. Even with the increased occurrence of other diseases, the population is living longer than ever before.

The effects of an aging population are widespread. Retirement age and the actuarial success of the Social Security system were based upon a life expectancy which has now been lengthened. Now retirees may spend a couple of decades or even more in activity with payouts from Social Security far in excess of amounts paid in during their working years. The social services necessary for an aging population have increased; in particular, intensive medical care and nursing homes are on the rise.

For the healthy majority among the older population, opportunities and disposable incomes for wider travel and more services can have an impact on city and parish alike. The trend among regions of the country in actively soliciting retirees is testimony to their increasing numbers and in many cases incomes. An aging population thus can have an effect on which services are needed, which businesses will prosper, and so on.

Persons sixty-five or older made up 11.1 percent of Louisiana's 1990 population. This figure has been part of a steady national and state trend upwards during this century. The figure for Louisiana is less than that for the nation as a whole (12.5 percent) and ranks below Arkansas (14.9 percent) and Mississippi (12.5 percent) among its immediate neighbors.

Those parishes with the largest percent of persons sixty-five or older are in the hill country and some delta parishes in the north. Bienville Parish leads with 18.3 percent of its total in this category. Claiborne with 17.7 percent and Tensas with 16.8 percent were the second and third highest. Hill parishes and agricultural parishes made up a large majority of those thirty- eight parishes with greater than the state average.

The parish with the lowest percentage of those sixty-five or older was Vernon, with only 5.8 percent; second was West Feliciana Parish, with 6.9 percent. Certainly the presence of, respectively, Fort Polk and Angola Prison in those parishes tended to skew the category. Overall, the parishes with the smallest percentages in these categories tended to be southern, metropolitan, and/or industrial.

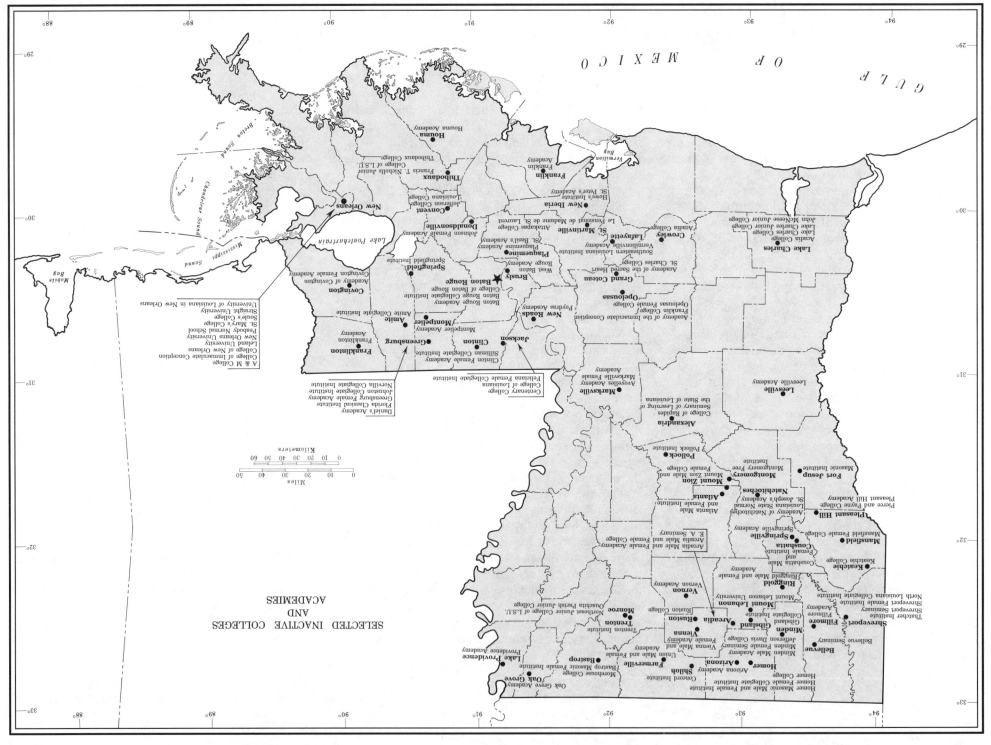

SELECTED INACTIVE COLLEGES
AND
ACADEMIES

Copyright © 1995 by the University of Oklahoma Press

Education, formal or informal, is present in any culture at any period. Before the establishment of any written record, oral tradition perpetuated the history and mythology of the group. At the same time, youths were trained in those practical necessities which would sustain the individual as well as preserve the group. Louisiana has been no different. Even in the present, folk culture often relies on oral rather than written descent to preserve regional or ethnic distinctiveness in an increasingly homogeneous national culture.

Institutional education began during the French colonial era. In 1727 twelve Ursuline Sisters arrived in New Orleans to establish a girls' school. Priests elsewhere taught rudimentary reading and writing. As some planters grew wealthy, they were able to hire private tutors or send their children out of the colony for education. By and large, however, the mass of people reached maturity without the ability to read or write their native tongue.

The Spanish in their efforts to upgrade the colony attempted a measure of public education in New Orleans. This undertaking failed because of public and parochial opposition, including a distaste among the French for being taught in Spanish. Private schools, however, expanded, largely in the cities, while parochial schools and private lessons constituted the majority of educational efforts.

When the American government took over following the Louisiana Purchase in 1803, measures to establish public education continued. These efforts met with the same initial opposition as had those of the Spanish; the citizenry continued to prefer a parochial system, a system which perpetuated their own cultural and religious preferences.

As new settlers arrived, however, particularly those of Protestant denominations who did not favor the Catholic system, an alternative system slowly took shape.

The territorial legislature in 1805 mandated an academy for boys and a library in each county (parish), academies for girls where necessary, and the College of Orleans at New Orleans. This system, controlled by a single board of regents, was modified the following year to provide for county (later parish) control. Financial support proved the undoing of this early system. Indeed, throughout the antebellum period and afterwards the ability to finance public education remained an enduring problem. Before 1845 most support went in the form of grants to existing private schools, with the provision that in return the schools would admit a certain number of students free. The Constitution of 1845 provided for free public schools throughout the state and for an elected state superintendent; by and large the reality remained that state support continued largely in the form of subsidies for private institutions.

The College of Orleans never operated as a true college in the modern sense. State support for that body was withdrawn in 1825 in favor of the College of Louisiana, established that year in Jackson. Twenty years later state support moved from the College of Louisiana to the University of Louisiana in New Orleans. This University of Louisiana grew out of the Medical College of Louisiana (1834) and later became Tulane University. The Louisiana State Seminary of Learning and Military Academy (forerunner to the Louisiana State University) opened near Pineville in 1860 with William Tecumseh Sherman as its first superintendent.

Other colleges received some state support, including the College of Jefferson at Convent (1834) and the College of Franklin at Opelousas (1837). Denominational colleges included the College of St. Charles at Grand Coteau; Centenary College of Louisiana at Jackson and then Shreveport; the College of the Immaculate Conception at New Orleans; and Mount Lebanon University at Mount Lebanon.

Before the Civil War it was illegal to teach a slave to read and write; education for free blacks was scarce as well. During Reconstruction efforts began to educate the newly freed slave population. Denominational groups set up Straight University (1869), the University of New Orleans (1869), and Leland College (1870). In 1879, Southern University was established as a public institution, followed in 1901 by the Colored Industrial and Agricultural School (later Grambling State University) in the northern section of the state.

Many of the "inactive" academies represent nothing more than nineteenth-century preparatory schools. The presence of an academy was considered a mark of culture for the community. Many of these institutions were run by the local pastor and his wife; most of them enjoyed a short lifespan. Other institutions shown on the map represent older names of modern institutions, some from the nineteenth-century and some the twentieth. Many other such academies or institutes or colleges not included led fleeting existences, leaving few records. Still, they comprised much of what "higher education" existed before the twentieth century.

Copyright © 1995 by the University of Oklahoma Press

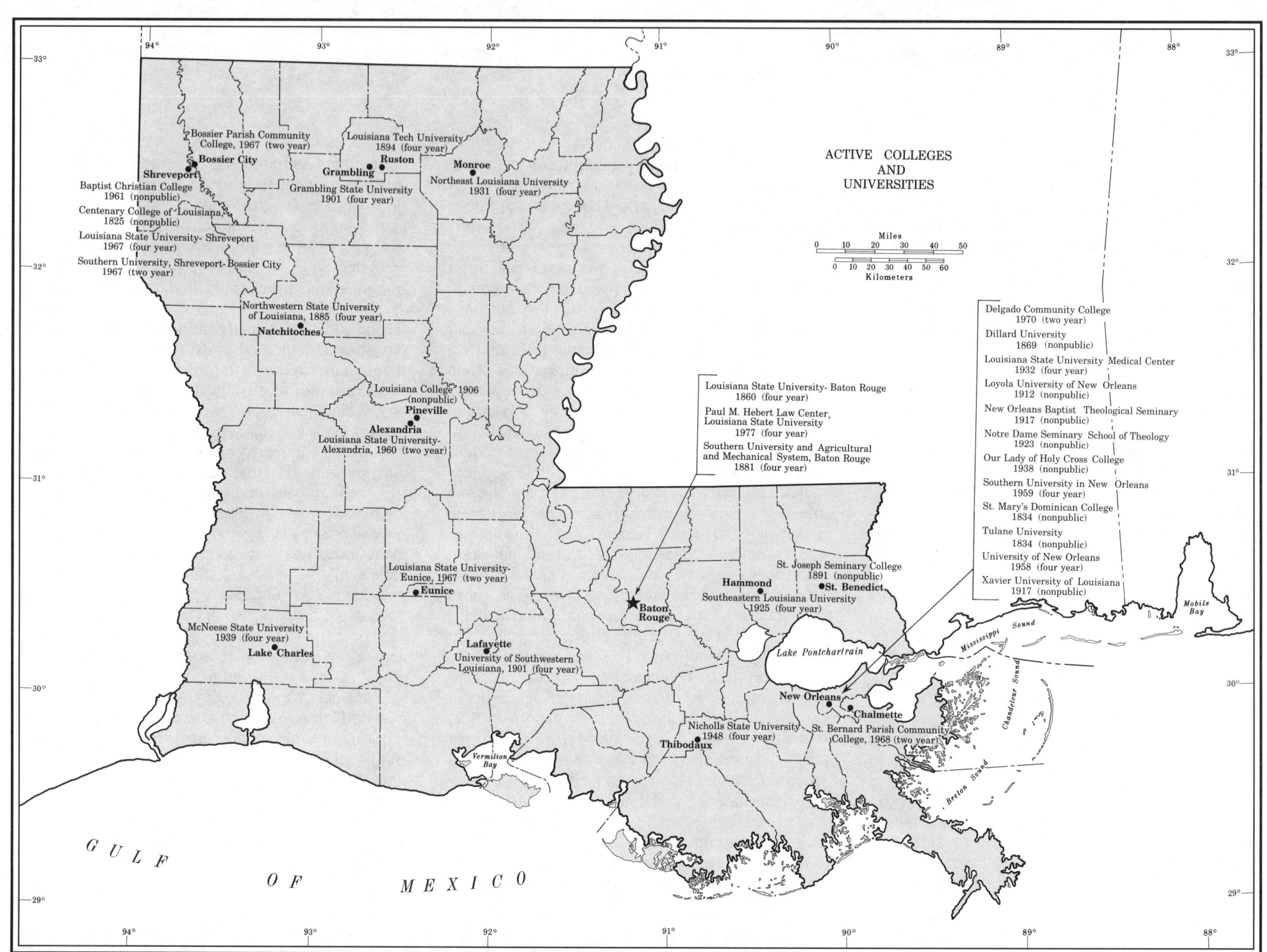

ACTIVE COLLEGES
AND
UNIVERSITIES

Bossier Parish Community
College, 1967 (two year)

Louisiana Tech University
1894 (four year)

Bossier City

Shreveport

Grambling   **Ruston**

Monroe

Baptist Christian College
1961 (nonpublic)

Grambling State University
1901 (four year)

Northeast Louisiana University
1931 (four year)

Centenary College of Louisiana,
1825 (nonpublic)

Louisiana State University- Shreveport
1967 (four year)

Southern University, Shreveport- Bossier City
1967 (two year)

Northwestern State University
of Louisiana, 1885 (four year)

Natchitoches

Louisiana College, 1906
(nonpublic)

Pineville

Alexandria

Louisiana State University-
Alexandria, 1960 (two year)

Louisiana State University- Baton Rouge
1860 (four year)

Paul M. Hebert Law Center,
Louisiana State University
1977 (four year)

Southern University and Agricultural
and Mechanical System, Baton Rouge
1881 (four year)

Delgado Community College
1970 (two year)

Dillard University
1869 (nonpublic)

Louisiana State University Medical Center
1932 (four year)

Loyola University of New Orleans
1912 (nonpublic)

New Orleans Baptist Theological Seminary
1917 (nonpublic)

Notre Dame Seminary School of Theology
1923 (nonpublic)

Our Lady of Holy Cross College
1938 (nonpublic)

Southern University in New Orleans
1959 (four year)

St. Mary's Dominican College
1834 (nonpublic)

Tulane University
1834 (nonpublic)

University of New Orleans
1958 (four year)

Xavier University of Louisiana
1917 (nonpublic)

St. Joseph Seminary College
1891 (nonpublic)

Louisiana State University-
Eunice, 1967 (two year)

Hammond   **St. Benedict**

Southeastern Louisiana University
1925 (four year)

Eunice

**Baton
Rouge**

Lake Pontchartrain

McNeese State University
1939 (four year)

Louisiana State University-
Eunice, 1967 (two year)

Lake Charles

Lafayette

University of Southwestern
Louisiana, 1901 (four year)

New Orleans

Chalmette

Nicholls State University
1948 (four year)

St. Bernard Parish Community
College, 1968 (two year)

Thibodaux

*Vermilion
Bay*

*Mobile
Bay*

Mississippi

Sound

Chandeleur Sound

Breton Sound

G U L F   O F   M E X I C O

Miles
0 10 20 30 40 50

0 10 20 30 40 50 60
Kilometers

Louisiana's colleges and universities crown an educational system of elementary and secondary schools as well as vocational and technical institutions. In 1990–1991 there were 1,460 public and 399 nonpublic elementary and secondary schools in the state, with a total enrollment of 795,609 and 123,898, respectively. Forty-five state-supported vocational and technical schools had a 1991 enrollment of 54,153. In addition there are dozens of proprietary schools—nonpublic institutions offering mostly postsecondary instruction in technical or business trades.

Twentieth-century education has seen many changes. Expanded local, state, and federal appropriations funding both basic and specialized programs testify to the increased importance placed on education. The "baby boom" following World War II multiplied the number of students flowing through the system. In particular, college degrees increased as many parents insisted on their children's earning at least the baccalaureate degree. The state's public education system gradually integrated following the 1954 Supreme Court's *Brown* vs. *Board of Education* decision. At the same time, that process led to the formation of private secondary academies, many of which have over the intervening period faltered.

Twenty-one public and twelve private colleges and universities operate in the state today. Most of them have roots in the late nineteenth or early twentieth century. Many began as "normals" (teacher training) or as industrial institutes. Most began life as two-year institutions, gradually moving to four years and beyond. Most public institutions today enjoy the title "university." In the fall of 1991, 163,848 students were enrolled in the state's public higher education system and 24,270 in the private institutions.

Control of the public institutions rests under various bodies. The Louisiana State University Board of Supervisors oversees the Louisiana State University and Agricultural and Mechanical College, Paul M. Hebert Law Center, Louisiana State University Medical Center, University of New Orleans, and LSU branches at Shreveport, Alexandria, and Eunice. LSU–Baton Rouge is the state's flagship university, offering a comprehensive curriculum. The University of New Orleans, established in 1958 as a branch of LSU, is now free- standing. LSU–Alexandria was established in 1959; the branches at Eunice and Shreveport were authorized in 1964 and opened in 1967. LSU–Shreveport is now a four-year university; the Alexandria and Eunice campuses remain two-year institutions.

Governed by the Board of Trustees for State Colleges and Universities are Grambling State University at Grambling; Louisiana Tech University at Ruston; McNeese State University at Lake Charles; Nicholls State University at Thibodaux; Northeast Louisiana University at Monroe; Northwestern State University of Louisiana at Natchitoches; Southeastern Louisiana University at Hammond; the University of Southwestern Louisiana at Lafayette; and Delgado Community College in New Orleans. The last is a two-year school. Northwestern is the oldest of the group, originating as the Louisiana Normal School in 1885. Louisiana Tech started as the Industrial Institute and College of Louisiana in 1894. Southwestern began as the Southwestern Louisiana Industrial Institute in 1898, and Grambling as the Colored Industrial and Agricultural School in 1901. Hammond Junior College, founded in 1925, later became Southeastern. Ouachita Parish Junior College was founded in 1931 as the forerunner to

Northeast. McNeese began as the Lake Charles Junior College in 1931, and Nicholls as Francis T. Nicholls Junior College in 1948. Delgado Community College opened its doors in 1970.

The Southern University Board of Supervisors controls Southern University and Agricultural and Mechanical College, Scotlandville, and its branches at New Orleans and Shreveport–Bossier City. Southern itself began in 1881, the New Orleans campus in 1959, and Shreveport–Bossier City in 1967. The State Board of Elementary and Secondary Education governs Bossier Parish Community College (1967) in Bossier City and St. Bernard Parish Community College (1968) in Chalmette.

Private institutions operate under various authorities. Centenary College of Louisiana at Shreveport is a United Methodist school founded in 1825, the oldest institution of higher education in the state—indeed, the oldest west of the Mississippi. Tulane University in New Orleans, with roots back to 1834 as the Medical College of Louisiana, became private and was renamed for its benefactor, Paul Tulane. Affiliated with it is the Sophie Newcomb College for Women. Dillard University, New Orleans, was formed in 1935 from the union of the older University of New Orleans and Straight University. Catholic institutions include St. Joseph Seminary College at St. Benedict (1891), Loyola University of New Orleans (1912), Xavier University of Louisiana in New Orleans (1917), and Notre Dame School of Theology in New Orleans (1923). Baptist-affiliated schools are Louisiana College in Pineville (1906), the New Orleans Baptist Theological Seminary (1918), and Baptist Christian College in Shreveport (1961).

SELECTED HISTORICAL AND MILITARY MUSEUMS AND ARCHIVES

SELECTED ARCHIVAL INSTITUTIONS

Alexandria
—LSU–Alexandria, Bolton Library.

Baton Rouge
—Louisiana Department of State. Division of Archives, Manuscripts, and History.
—Louisiana State Library. Louisiana Room.
—Louisiana State University. Louisiana and Lower Mississippi Valley Collections.
—Southern University. Black Heritage Collection.

Hammond
—Southeastern Louisiana University. Archives.

Lafayette
—Catholic Diocese of Lafayette. Archives.
—University of Southwestern Louisiana. Archives and Manuscripts Collection.

Lake Charles
—Catholic Diocese of Lake Charles. Archives.
—McNeese University. Archives.

Natchitoches
—Northwestern State University. Cammie G. Henry Research Center.

New Orleans
—Catholic Archdiocese of New Orleans. Archives.
—Historic New Orleans Collection. Manuscripts Division.
—Louisiana State Museum. Louisiana Historical Center.
—New Orleans Public Library. Louisiana Division.
—Tulane University: Amistad Research Center; Manuscript Section; Newcomb College Center for Research on Women; University Archives; Will Ransom Hogan Jazz Archives.
—University of New Orleans. Department of Archives and Manuscripts.
—Xavier University. Archives.

Monroe
—Northeast Louisiana University. Archives and Special Collections.

Ruston
—Louisiana Tech University. Archives.

Shreveport
—Centenary College of Louisiana. Archives.
—LSU-Shreveport. Archives.

Thibodaux
—Nicholls State University. Archives.

New Orleans

Jackson Barracks
Pharmacy Museum
Confederate Museum
Gallier House Museum
Louisiana State Museum
Bueauregard-Keyes House
Hermann-Grima Historic House
Historic New Orleans Collection
Middle American Research Institute, Tulane
Jean Lafitte National Historical Park, French Quarter Unit

Map labels:

Oil City — Caddo-Pine Island Oil & Historical Society
Homer — Arizona Rural Life Museum, Herbert S. Ford Memorial Museum
Bastrop — Snyder Museum & Creative Arts Center
Epps — Poverty Point
Shreveport — Spring Street Museum, Pioneer Heritage Center, Grindstone Bluff Museum, Louisiana State Exhibit Museum
Ruston — Kidd-Davis House, La. Tech University Museum, Museum of Fashion & Textiles, La. Tech
Grambling — Grambling State University
Monroe — Emy Lou Biedenharn Foundation Center
Alto — Altus Museum
Mansfield — Mansfield State Commemorative Area
Columbia — Louisiana Art & Folk Center & Museum
Natchitoches — Williamson Museum, Fort St. Jean Baptiste
Robeline — Los Adaes
Jena — La Salle Museum
Many — Fort Jesup
Cloutierville — Bayou Folk Museum
Marthaville — Rebel State Commemorative Area
Alexandria
Marksville — Hypolite Bordelon Home
Fort Polk — Fort Polk Military Museum
Jackson — Centenary
Bogalusa — Bogalusa Indian and Pioneer Museums
DeQuincy — Railroad Museum, Dogtrot Museum
Eunice — Eunice Museum
Zachary — Port Hudson
Port Allen — West Baton Rouge Museum
Baton Rouge — Rural Life Museum, LSU, U.S.S. Kidd DD6611, Old Arsenal Museum
Hammond
Slidell — Slidell Museum
Fort Pike
Sulphur — Brimstone Museum
Lake Charles — Imperial Calcasieu Museum
Lafayette — Lafayette Museum
Gonzales — "Tee" Joe Gonzales Museum
New Orleans
Kenner — State Railroad Museum, Kenner Historical Museum
Chalmette — Jean Lafitte National Historical Park, Chalmette Unit
Gretna — State Fire Museum
Thibodaux
Morgan City — Morgan City Museum
Houma — Southdown Plantation Home

MISSISSIPPI RIVER
SABINE RIVER
Sabine Lake
Calcasieu Lake
Vermilion Bay
Lake Maurepas
Lake Pontchartrain
Lake Borgne
PEARL RIVER
Mississippi Sound
Mobile Bay
Chandeleur Sound
Breton Sound

GULF OF MEXICO

Miles
0 10 20 30 40 50
Kilometers
0 10 20 30 40 50 60

Museums, libraries, and archives are the custodians of history and culture. Museums gather in the artifactual handiwork of humankind, whether the projectile point or pottery shard of a previous millennium, an Audubon print, an impressionist painting, a Remington bronze, a Clementine Hunter original, or the patchwork quilt of a hill country parish. Libraries are keepers of the published record, fiction or nonfiction, generated since the developing of printing. Archives largely steward the unpublished record—manuscripts, photographs, and so on—the records of an individual, family, or organization.

Museums exists in various formats. Some collect only art or the art of a various period. Others may be historical in focus, collecting the artifacts of urban or rural life. Still others may specialize in natural history or military matters. Of course Louisiana's numerous museums collect not only items from Louisiana or by Louisianians. The range of human expression across many time periods and different cultures provides myriad reasons and opportunities for collecting. Not only do museums house permanent collections of their own, but they also host traveling exhibitions from other institutions.

Public libraries operate in every parish in the state. In addition many cities sustain library systems of their own. Elementary and secondary schools, as well as colleges and universities, must maintain libraries to support the varied interests or needs of students and faculty. General-purpose libraries serve the public at large usually through their own holdings. Specialized library collections—medical, engineering, state or local history, genealogical, and so on—exist to serve the technical or particular needs of smaller segments of the population. Many larger libraries, especially on college and university campuses, maintain special subject collections within the main library or as branches.

Archives and manuscript collections lie scattered about the state, most often associated with historical societies or colleges and universities. Many of them are public; others are privately operated with varying access to the public at large. Businesses maintain their own corporate archives, and organizational archives exist for fraternal or other societies within the state. Religious archives represent yet another common type. College and university archives, in addition to maintaining the records of their own institution, usually collect on some theme, most often regional in nature. Because archivists deal largely with unique, often fragile materials, such original materials do not circulate outside the repository. With the advent of microfilm, however, many records contained elsewhere have now become available in that format in local institutions.

Historic sites include houses, battlefields, and archaeological and other sites. Such sites are commemorated as relics of a bygone era or as representing some distinctive quality—architecture, a life lived, an event that occurred. Some sites are national in importance, others of a state or local nature. A more recent guide is the National Register of Historic Places, which maintains a list of those places nominated for their contribution to history.

Artifacts, artwork, books, and manuscripts represent opportunities for the individual as well. The family photograph album may contain the records of several generations. A grandparent's diary or correspondence may record the family history of an earlier generation. The individual collector may amass a splendid collection on a subject during one's own lifetime or through generations of careful work. Often public institutions are enriched by the gifts of the private collector.

The past is not always pleasant to remember. Nor is all art of equal appeal to every viewer. Neither is every book suitable to every reader. To commemorate is not to celebrate; neither is the past an era which should be judged by the norms of the present. Yet that which remains hidden represents a story which cannot yet be told. To be proud of one's heritage, race, ethnic origin, region, state, religion, or such is not always to agree with its every aspect. Museums, libraries, and archives collect and preserve not just for the present. They are guardians of the past and present with an eye toward the future. They commemorate the eternal quest of humankind for truth and beauty.

Copyright © 1995 by the University of Oklahoma Press

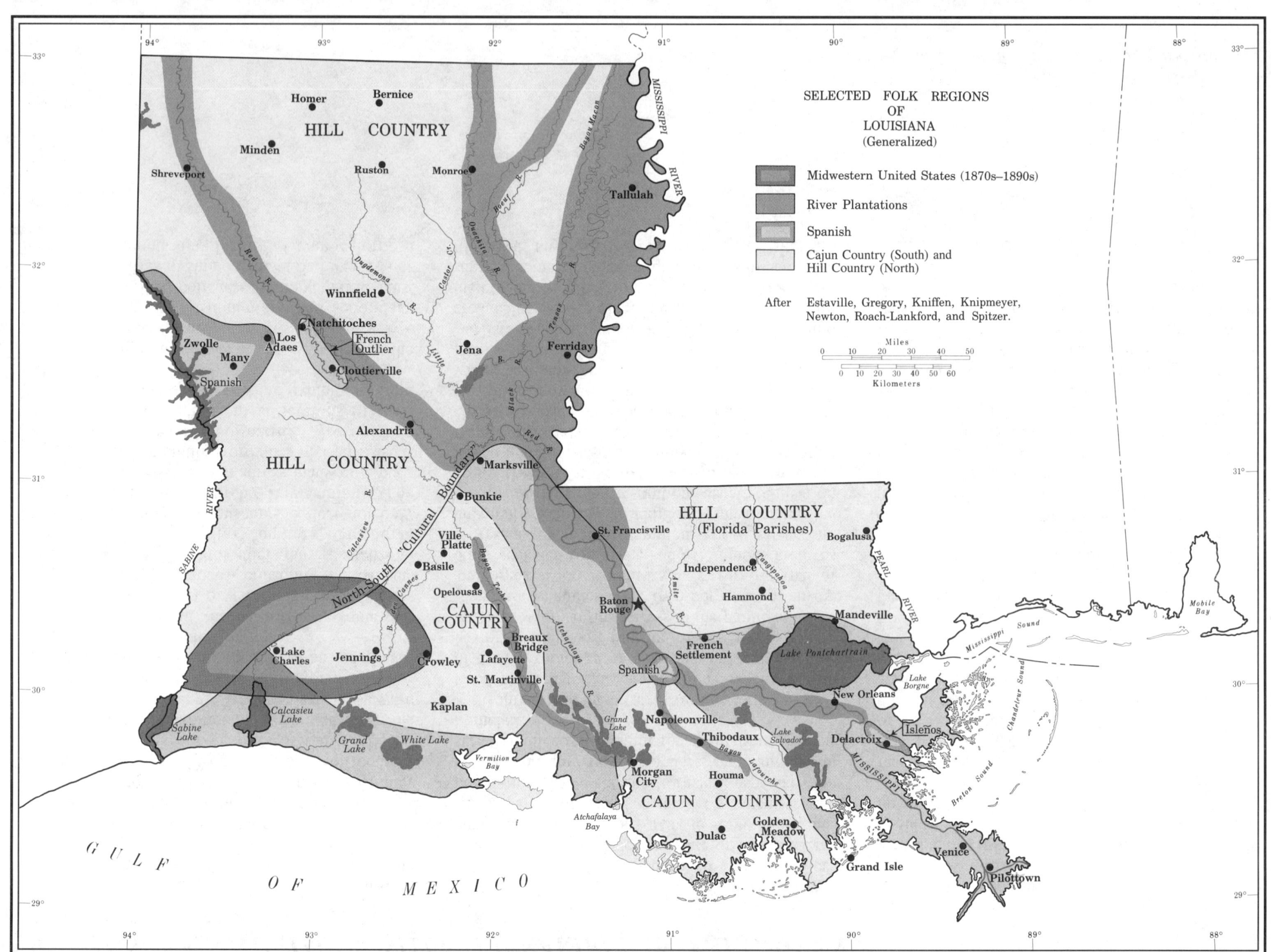

SELECTED FOLK REGIONS
OF
LOUISIANA
(Generalized)

Midwestern United States (1870s–1890s)

River Plantations

Spanish

Cajun Country (South) and
Hill Country (North)

After   Estaville, Gregory, Kniffen, Knipmeyer,
Newton, Roach-Lankford, and Spitzer.

Miles
0   10   20   30   40   50

0   10   20   30   40   50   60
Kilometers

Louisiana has over the past millennia been home to a variety of different peoples. Each of these peoples—individuals, tribes, nationalities—has possessed a culture. As each in turn has come into contact with other cultures, they have exchanged traits, often blurring the distinctions. Minority cultures have often been absorbed into majority cultures. Nevertheless, some have always clung to the old ways. In more modern times, a greater interest has been taken in roots, and insistence upon diversity has come to the fore.

Many traits combine to form a culture. Racial, ethnic, and national origin bring with them language (even regional idiom), religion, foodways, architectural styles, building materials, methods of cultivation, land surveys, forms of government, and other attitudes and practices. Each culture upon entering an area attempts to establish itself according to traditional ways. Yet cultural purity exists only in geographic or temporal isolation. Adaptation may be forced by natural phenomena or rival cultures. Modern mass popular culture can be changed almost instantly by the latest hit television show, movie, or music video.

Louisiana's many Native American cultures are the oldest in the state. Prehistoric tribal populations were decimated by the inadvertent introduction of European diseases by early explorers. Remaining tribes largely allied themselves with one or other imperial power, but some few sought isolation. Remnants of various tribes or groups exist scattered about the state today (Maps 16–22).

The French settlement of Louisiana constituted the region's earliest European immigrants. Throughout the French regime (1699–1763) new French settlers were joined by immigrants from other nations. Of particular significance in the 1720s were settlers from the German states along the Rhine River. The introduction of black slavery by the French brought into the colony other cultures. Settlements were located primarily along the rivers and bayous, where an agricultural economy evolved into the plantation system.

The Spanish regime (1763–1803) introduced another new culture. Yet during this period came still more French; indeed, that group is most often associated with the state. These were the Acadians expelled from French Canada after its seizure by the British. The Acadians would evolve into the modern Cajuns, a culture distinct from the older French families of the state. They would move west of the Mississippi in areas not yet claimed by earlier colonists. Another group entering at this time were Canary Islanders, Spanish yet distinct; in time they would settle south of New Orleans in present-day St. Bernard and Plaquemines parishes.

Anglo-American migration into the bounds of present-day Louisiana also began early. The area of the Florida parishes while under British control (1763–1783) received substantial numbers of settlers. After the Louisiana Purchase of 1803, increased numbers of Americans poured into the territory and then state. Coming as they did from various regions further to the east, they brought with them certain differing patterns which did not make them a truly homogeneous group. Upland South migrants differed from Lowland South. Antebellum plantation owners from the east brought with them different practices from those of the yeomen farmers.

Yet another distinct regional American culture entered the state in the late nineteenth century. In the 1880s and 1890s Midwestern farmers were enticed to settle the southwestern Louisiana prairies when that area was opened by the coming of the railroads. Nineteenth- and twentieth-century foreign immigration has added still more to the state's cultural mix. Italian, Hungarian, Czech, Chinese, Filipino, Vietnamese, and various Hispanic immigrants are among these groups. Beyond national origin is location; rural culture and ways of life differ from urban ones.

Cultures may be identified by examining traits of individual peoples. Beyond these sociological studies is the geographic distribution of such phenomena as place names, house types, religious denominations, folk festivals, and state or national voting patterns. Scholars over time have divided north Louisiana from south Louisiana on such bases as surnames, voting patterns, religious affiliation, and language. Yet any map of cultural regions of the state can be painted only in broad strokes. Many characteristics used to delimit such regions are merely relics upon the landscape. The I-frame houses characteristic of the Midwest help define that region, yet they no longer are built on a widespread basis.

Cultures represent living entities subject to change from within or without. Once the United States was celebrated as a melting pot where different groups shed their old ways to become part of a new, singular American culture. This idea has now been supplanted by the image of a stew. To borrow from one of Louisiana's own cultural groups, the state is more a pot of gumbo from which each spoonful served is different but in which all combine to form a flavor greater than the sum of the individual ingredients.

Copyright © 1995 by the University of Oklahoma Press

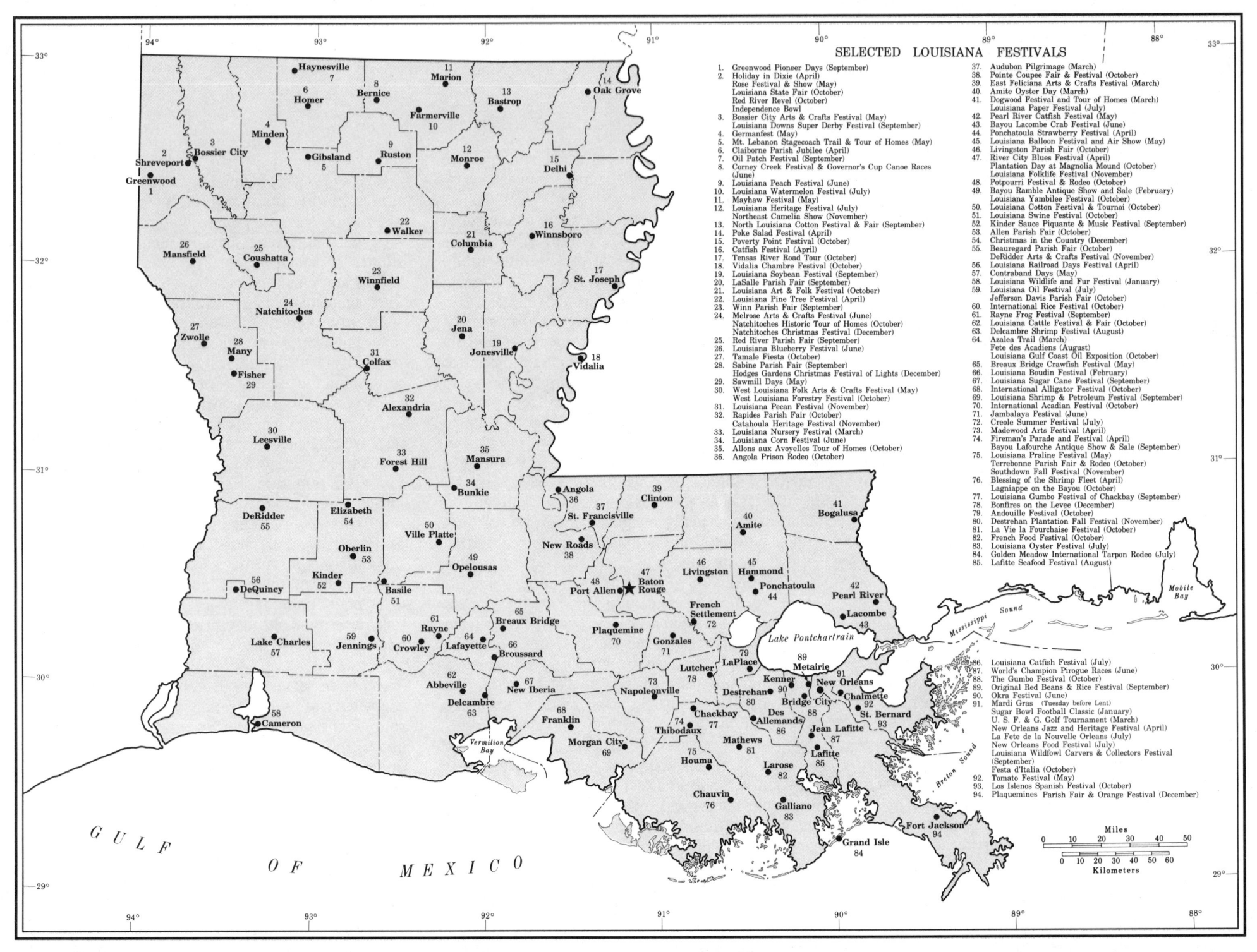

SELECTED LOUISIANA FESTIVALS

Fairs and festivals are of ancient origin; however, in many cases they have metamorphosed in form and function. Early fairs were essentially periodic markets held at longer intervals and on a larger scale than local markets and attracting buyers and sellers from a wider area. Originally many festivals were held to commemorate the planting or harvesting of agricultural products. Others may have had origins in the celebration of religious holy days. In times past such celebrations brought all the townsfolk or neighborfolk together in a break from the usual toil. Today no festival would be complete without inviting everyone from throughout the state or nation to come take part. Celebrations which once were religious in origin have moved from the holy day to the holiday spirit. All these events are also an economic asset to the state.

Louisiana's most famous festival is Mardi Gras (Fat Tuesday). Mardi Gras as a day falls on the Tuesday before Ash Wednesday, the beginning of the Lenten Season in the Christian calendar. Lent itself in the past was a period of fasting, and Fat Tuesday represented the day on which the fat (since it was animal fat) was used up before the start of Lent. Since Lent represents the forty days (excluding Sundays) before Easter Sunday, and since Easter Sunday is essentially the first Sunday after the first full moon after the vernal equinox, the actual date of Mardi Gras varies, but it falls in either February or March.

Mardi Gras as a secular celebration had its origins in early-nineteenth-century Louisiana. The first formal New Orleans parade was held in 1838. Today the period of Mardi Gras stretches from January 6 on to the actual date itself, with much of the celebrations in the final week before Lent. Although it is most often associated with New Orleans, Mardi Gras celebrations are held in other cities and rural areas of the state as well.

Christmas is another Christian holy day about which many festivals and events are arrayed. Parades, festivals of light, and other parties are held and participated in by Christian and non-Christian alike. The Festival of Lights at Natchitoches is a particular attraction of the season. As with Mardi Gras, it is safe to say that the holiday as most often commemorated in these events has ceased to hold much religious significance.

The number of state fairs and festivals has proliferated as more and more towns find a focus for such an event. Louisiana may indeed have more festivals and fairs than any other state in the Union. Part of this proliferation is tied to the tourist trade as cities and towns vie for additional income. Part of the growth is the promotion of a sense of local pride and the celebration and preservation of local culture and customs in a modern setting.

Many aspects of Louisiana culture represent foci for fairs and festivals. Various musical festivals—particularly jazz and bluegrass—are held about the state. Ethnic celebrations occur where those groups are clustered. Natural resources, whether animal or vegetable or mineral, are other reasons for celebration. Annual parish fairs and the state fair at various points are other such events.

These celebrations may have several components. Fairs and festivals are much associated with a parade and perhaps a beauty pageant. Sporting events of various sorts may be held. Craft displays are set up for all to see. Cooking contests feature local talents. Music for various tastes may also be played. Livestock and crop judging may also occur. A traveling sideshow and amusement rides might also be set up. Such events offer areas for folk culture and may serve to validate regional values and tastes.

Festivals also serve educational purposes. The crop or product which serves as the focus may be displayed in all its uses. The beginning fiddler may have the opportunity of practicing with a local elder. Virtuosi may be brought in from out of town to present in living form the habits and knowledge of a past generation. Storytelling contests may bring in local tales and color to regale young and old alike.

As noted above, fairs and festivals serve an economic as well as a commemorate function. The infusion of tourist dollars (Map 99) into the local economy is often a valuable assistance to rural areas and small towns. Total direct and indirect visitor spending in Louisiana was estimated by the U.S. Travel Data Service at $6.95 billion in 1990 alone.

Festivals may also serve as a commemoration. The past that is conjured up is seen alongside the spirit of the present. As flags flutter over many a cemetery on Veterans (formerly Decoration) Day, so, too, do many celebrations offer the opportunity to pay homage to a past that no longer exists. They are part of the mythos of a community, region, or state. They invest a mental image of the state and its regions not only in the minds of its own inhabitants but also in those outside the circle.

Copyright © 1995 by the University of Oklahoma Press

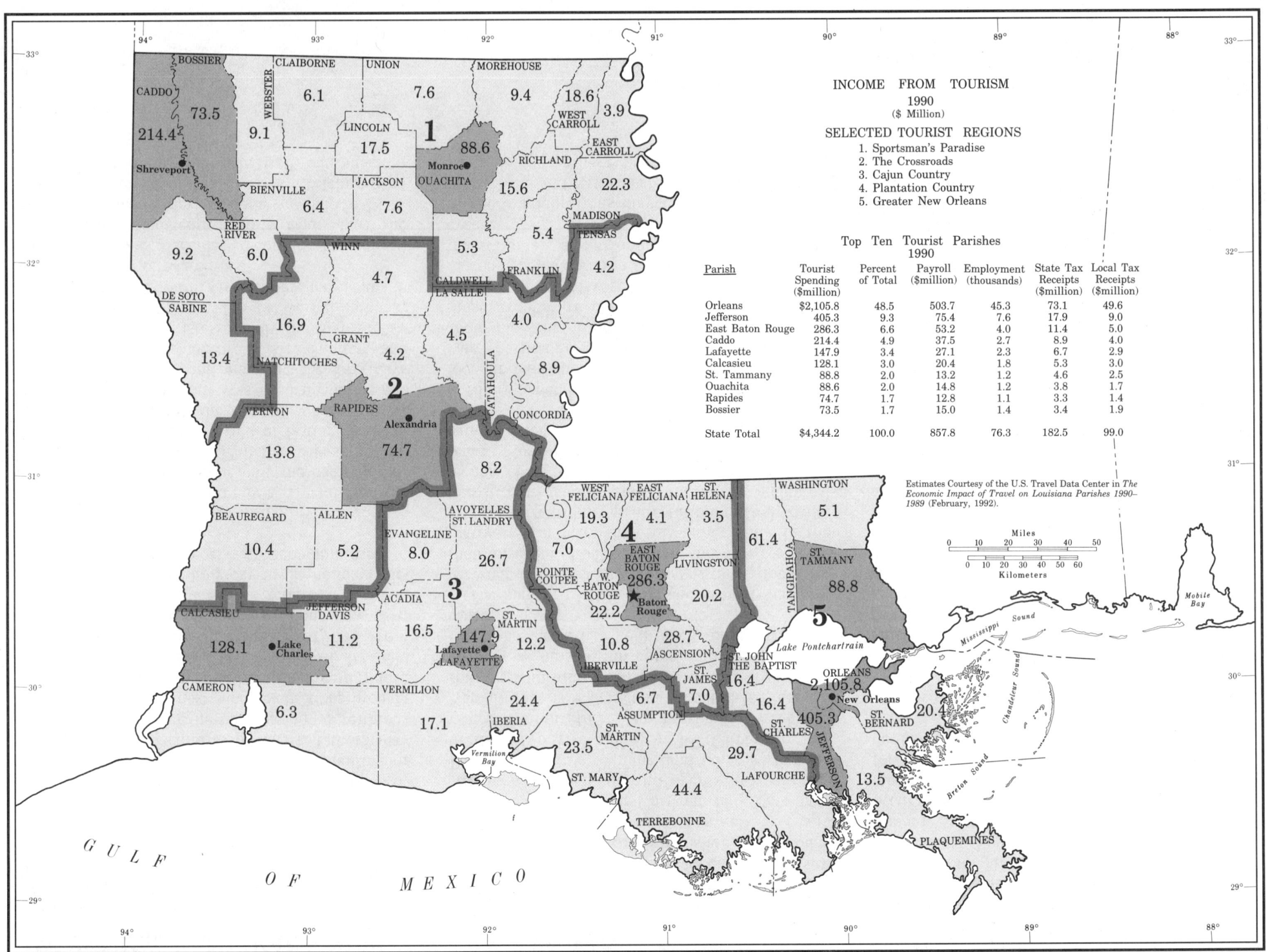

INCOME FROM TOURISM
1990
($ Million)

SELECTED TOURIST REGIONS
1. Sportsman's Paradise
2. The Crossroads
3. Cajun Country
4. Plantation Country
5. Greater New Orleans

Top Ten Tourist Parishes
1990

Parish	Tourist Spending ($million)	Percent of Total	Payroll ($million)	Employment (thousands)	State Tax Receipts ($million)	Local Tax Receipts ($million)
Orleans	$2,105.8	48.5	503.7	45.3	73.1	49.6
Jefferson	405.3	9.3	75.4	7.6	17.9	9.0
East Baton Rouge	286.3	6.6	53.2	4.0	11.4	5.0
Caddo	214.4	4.9	37.5	2.7	8.9	4.0
Lafayette	147.9	3.4	27.1	2.3	6.7	2.9
Calcasieu	128.1	3.0	20.4	1.8	5.3	3.0
St. Tammany	88.8	2.0	13.2	1.2	4.6	2.5
Ouachita	88.6	2.0	14.8	1.2	3.8	1.7
Rapides	74.7	1.7	12.8	1.1	3.3	1.4
Bossier	73.5	1.7	15.0	1.4	3.4	1.9
State Total	$4,344.2	100.0	857.8	76.3	182.5	99.0

Estimates Courtesy of the U.S. Travel Data Center in *The Economic Impact of Travel on Louisiana Parishes 1990–1989* (February, 1992).

Travel is, of course, nothing new on the human scene. From ancient times onward one reads of travels. Itinerant merchants moved from town to town. Military excursions often traversed great distances. Literature and history are full of pilgrims, natural scientists, explorers, or just observers of the land and people. William Bartram, William Darby, and Timothy Flint are just three examples of those whose life and travels brought them into Louisiana and who left accounts of those observations.

The twentieth century has witnessed a veritable explosion in travel and especially tourism, particularly since the end of World War II. The extraordinary expansion of the nation's economy following that conflict led to increased wealth among Americans. Automobiles made personal travel easier in terms of both schedule and destination. Jet aircraft made long-distance travel increasingly swift. People were encouraged to take time off and relax.

Today tourists go to and fro for any of various purposes. The business traveler spends money every day across the state. Entertainment or other forms of recreation are perhaps the primary reason for travel for the majority of the population. An educational experience of historical or artful nature brings people to different places. The contemplation of natural surroundings entices still more. A return to roots or family brings travelers home to Louisiana on many occasions.

Sporting events of various sorts—including the Sugar Bowl and the occasional Super Bowl—bring tourists from far and near. The hundreds of fairs and festivals (Map 98) provide yet another destination for travelers. Cities promote themselves as tourist attractions. New Orleans is the state's premier example, but others do their part. State and national parks and forests, recreation areas, and other such preserves and refuges (Map 8) offer varying levels of comfort and wildernesslike environments to sportsmen, campers, picnickers, or hikers of various sorts. The dozens of museums and historic sites (Map 96) are yet another attraction.

A whole host of services cater to the tourist trade. The motor hotel arose as a competitor to the hotel for the automobile traveler. Restaurants and gasoline stations line the nation's highway routes. State travel bureaus locate centers at state lines along many highways. Travel agents schedule thousands of trips each day. Hawkers of souvenirs, travel guides, and other memorabilia to assist or commemorate a journey ply their trade as well.

An entire industry has grown up at the federal, state, and local levels to promote tourism among citizens of the nation and international travelers as well. Individual companies and chambers of commerce solicit the business or pleasure traveler. Slick publications and photograph-studded travelogues entice the public to visit near or faraway places. Television and radio commercials spout the latest slogan used to engender a positive mental image of the state. As with such offices in other states, Louisiana's Department of Culture, Recreation, and Tourism dates to the period following World War II. From a single person or small group these state agencies have grown to hundreds of employees.

The state has been divided into five tourist regions. Sportsman's Paradise in the north advertises the various opportunities for hunters, fishers, and other people at such places as Poverty Point, Shreveport, and Toledo Bend Reservoir. The Crossroads offers itself as a meeting ground in which Natchitoches is the oldest town in the state and in which other historic sites are located in an area of transition between north and south. Cajun Country focuses on one of the enduring images of Louisiana, a region celebrated in song and word, where crawfish and rice are harvested and swamp, marsh, land, and Gulf meet. Plantation Country outlines the major region of old plantations in the state while extolling the virtues of the state capital and its universities, other historic sites, and the battlefield at Port Hudson. Greater New Orleans is almost self-explanatory to Louisianian and non-Louisianian alike, for the city (with the Vieux Carre, jazz, and varied cuisine) and its hinterland of more rural vistas conjures up even more images than does the name Cajun.

The U.S. Travel Data Service calculated that $6.95 billion was spent directly or indirectly by tourists in Louisiana in 1990. This estimate included $4.7 billion in direct spending. Travel money generated an estimated 84,500 jobs in the state; various taxes raised $197 million dollars, almost 5 percent of all tax collections for that year.

Orleans Parish alone accounts for almost half the direct spending by tourists in the state; however, no parish is untouched. Totals range from the over $2 billion dollars for Orleans to $3.5 million in St. Helena. Symbolized by "Louisiana, a Dream State," "Louisiana, We're Really Cooking Now," "Laissez les Bons Temps Rouler," or whatever slogan, travel and tourism are twin components of a big business in Louisiana.

GAZETTEER

1. PARISH OVERVIEW, 1990

Parish	Parish Seat	Land Area (Square Miles)	Total Population	Density	Total Female	Total Black	Median Age	Per Capita Income	Median Income	Percent in Poverty
Acadia	Crowley	655.3	55,882	32.9	29,286	10,179	30.5	$7,952	$16,022	30.5
Allen	Oberlin	764.6	21,226	10.7	10,494	4,496	32.5	7,394	15,838	29.9
Ascension	Donaldsonville	291.6	58,214	77.1	29,663	13,268	29.4	10,482	27,345	17.7
Assumption	Napoleonville	338.7	22,753	25.9	11,721	7,349	29.7	8,077	20,021	28.2
Avoyelles	Marksville	832.5	39,159	18.2	20,299	10,585	32.7	6,874	13,451	37.1
Beauregard	DeRidder	1160.2	30,083	10.0	14,930	4,489	31.6	10,096	22,442	18.3
Bienville	Arcadia	810.7	15,979	7.6	8,361	6,949	34.6	8,194	16,043	31.2
Bossier	Benton	838.5	86,088	39.6	44,257	17,381	20.6	11,317	26,058	16.2
Caddo	Shreveport	882.1	248,253	108.7	132,319	99,511	32.7	11,604	22,395	24.0
Calcasieu	Lake Charles	1071.2	168,134	60.6	86,494	38,445	31.6	11,233	24,375	18.5
Caldwell	Columbia	529.5	9,810	7.2	5,024	1,760	33.5	8,308	16,069	28.8
Cameron	Cameron	1313.0	9,260	2.7	4,648	503	30.7	10,289	25,164	16.2
Catahoula	Harrisonburg	703.7	11,065	6.1	5,706	2,874	32.3	7,862	14,956	36.8
Claiborne	Homer	754.6	17,405	8.9	8,579	8,041	34.7	8,076	16,073	32.0
Concordia	Vidalia	696.4	20,828	11.5	10,950	7,596	32.3	8,391	17,265	20.6
De Soto	Mansfield	877.3	25,346	11.2	13,332	11,141	32.4	8,330	16,315	29.8
East Baton Rouge	Baton Rouge	455.7	380,105	322.1	197,787	132,328	29.9	13,126	27,224	19.7
East Carroll	Lake Providence	421.5	9,709	8.9	5,142	6,291	28.1	6,059	9,791	56.8
East Feliciana	Clinton	453.4	19,211	16.4	9,207	9,083	31.1	7,746	20,139	25.0
Evangeline	Ville Platte	664.3	33,274	19.3	17,346	8,701	31.1	7,041	13,797	35.1
Franklin	Winnsboro	623.4	22,387	13.9	11,804	7,040	32.4	7,607	15,159	34.5
Grant	Colfax	645.1	17,526	10.5	9,070	2,540	31.9	8,330	17,711	25.5
Iberia	New Iberia	575.2	68,297	45.8	35,356	20,154	29.8	9,466	20,838	25.8
Iberville	Plaquemine	618.7	31,049	19.4	16,007	14,385	30.5	9,449	20,371	28.0
Jackson	Jonesboro	570.0	15,705	10.6	8,211	4,589	34.5	9,960	18,804	23.9
Jefferson	Gretna	305.9	448,306	565.8	232,876	79,042	32.3	12,845	27,916	14.1
Jefferson Davis	Jennings	562.4	30,722	18.2	15,917	5,836	31.5	8,486	18,467	27.3
Lafayette	Lafayette	269.9	164,762	235.7	84,914	36,846	29.8	11,983	24,339	20.2
Lafourche	Thibodaux	1084.8	85,860	30.6	43,889	10,703	29.4	9,250	21,416	22.9
La Salle	Jena	623.9	13,662	8.5	7,188	1,257	34.8	9,015	18,597	21.2
Lincoln	Ruston	471.4	41,745	34.2	21,514	16,590	24.7	9,342	19,254	26.6
Livingston	Livingston	648.1	70,526	42.0	35,595	3,920	30.2	9,946	25,470	14.6
Madison	Tallulah	624.1	12,463	7.7	6,706	7,415	29.9	6,723	12,792	44.6
Morehouse	Bastrop	794.0	31,938	15.5	16,917	13,263	32.0	8,547	17,309	31.0
Natchitoches	Natchitoches	1256.4	36,689	11.3	19,330	13,779	29.2	8,112	15,778	33.9
Orleans	New Orleans	180.6	496,938	1062.1	266,055	307,728	31.6	11,372	18,477	31.6
Ouachita	Monroe	611.0	142,191	89.9	75,131	44,096	30.2	10,593	21,129	24.7
Plaquemines	Pointe a la Hache	844.6	25,575	11.7	12,624	5,944	29.4	9,500	24,076	22.6
Pointe Coupee	New Roads	557.4	22,540	15.6	11,707	9,275	31.6	8,709	18,772	30.3
Rapides	Alexandria	1322.7	131,556	38.4	68,519	36,805	31.4	10,014	20,811	22.6
Red River	Coushatta	388.6	9,387	9.3	4,947	3,589	31.8	7,213	14,831	35.1

Richland	Rayville	558.5	20,629	36.9	10,962	7,539	32.2	7,791	15,298	33.2
Sabine	Many	865.3	22,646	26.2	11,638	3,984	34.5	8,539	16,790	27.1
St. Bernard	Chalmette	465.2	66,631	143.2	34,627	3,111	32.6	10,512	25,482	14.9
St. Charles	Hahnville	283.7	42,437	149.6	21,695	10,253	30.3	11,901	31,777	15.2
St. Helena	Greensburg	408.4	9,874	24.2	5,144	5,127	30.6	7,199	15,475	34.4
St. James	Convent	246.1	20,879	84.8	10,888	10,357	29.4	8,959	23,105	25.5
St. John the Baptist	Edgard	218.9	39,996	182.7	20,419	14,419	28.7	10,454	29,035	18.0
St. Landry	Opelousas	928.7	80,331	86.5	42,089	32,392	30.9	7,671	14,670	36.3
St. Martin	St. Martinville	739.9	43,978	59.4	22,626	14,532	29.2	7,990	19,116	27.3
St. Mary	Franklin	612.9	58,086	94.8	29,715	18,337	29.6	8,777	20,980	27.0
St. Tammany	Covington	854.4	144,508	169.1	73,304	15,917	32.4	13,605	30,656	13.7
Tangipahoa	Amite	790.3	85,709	108.5	44,698	24,527	30.1	8,150	16,849	31.5
Tensas	St. Joseph	602.5	7,103	11.8	3,861	3,785	32.5	7,896	11,931	46.3
Terrebonne	Houma	1255.1	96,982	77.3	49,499	16,032	29.3	9,505	21,765	24.2
Union	Farmerville	877.7	20,690	23.6	10,762	5,767	34.4	8,903	18,083	23.9
Vermilion	Abbeville	1173.9	50,055	42.6	25,801	6,956	31.5	8,752	18,202	26.5
Vernon	Leesville	1328.5	61,961	46.6	27,907	12,867	24.7	8,414	19,147	18.4
Washington	Franklinton	669.6	43,185	64.5	22,344	13,376	33.3	8,292	16,246	31.6
Webster	Minden	595.9	41,989	70.5	22,119	13,277	34.7	9,191	18,716	25.1
West Baton Rouge	Port Allen	191.2	19,419	101.6	9,996	6,993	30.5	10,255	24,852	20.3
West Carroll	Oak Grove	359.4	12,093	33.6	6,313	2,020	34.1	7,611	14,924	27.4
West Feliciana	St. Francisville	406.0	12,915	31.8	4,142	7,149	33.1	6,796	19,402	33.8
Winn	Winnfield	950.6	16,269	17.1	8,216	4,798	33.5	8,728	16,967	27.5
Louisiana	Baton Rouge	43,566.0	4,219,973	96.9	2,118,587	1,299,281	31.0	10,635	21,949	23.6

SOURCE: Bureau of the Census.

2. LOUISIANA OFFICIAL SYMBOLS

State Bird:	Eastern Brown Pelican (*Pelecanus occidentalis*)	State Song:	"Give Me Lousiana"	State Crustacean:	Crawfish
State Flower:	Magnolia	State Insect:	Honeybee	State Reptile:	Alligator
State Tree:	Bald Cypress (*Taxodium distichum*)	State Dog:	Catahoula Leopard Dog	State Gemstone:	Agate

3. POPULATION, 1810–1990

	1990	1980	1970	1960	1950	1940	1930	1920	1910
Total	4,219,973	4,205,900	3,641,306	3,257,022	2,683,516	2,363,880	2,101,593	1,798,509	1,656,388
% change from previous census									
Louisiana	0.3	15.4	11.9	21.4	13.5	12.5	16.9	8.6	19.9
U.S.	9.8	11.4	13.4	18.5	14.5	7.3	16.2	15.0	21.0
Urban	2,871,759	2,887,401	2,422,175	2,060,606	1,471,696	980,439	833,532	628,163	496,516
% Louisiana	68.0	66.5	66.5	63.3	54.8	41.5	39.7	34.9	30.0
% U.S.	75.2	73.7	73.6	69.9	64.0	56.5	56.1	51.2	45.6
Rural	1,348,214	1,318,499	1,219,131	1,196,416	1,211,820	1,383,441	1,268,061	1,170,346	1,159,872
% Louisiana	32.0	31.4	33.5	36.7	45.2	58.5	60.3	65.1	70.0
% U.S.	24.8	26.3	26.4	30.1	36.0	43.5	43.9	48.8	54.4

Continued on next page

ST. JOHN THE BAPTIST PARISH LIBRARY
1334 WEST AIRLINE HIGHWAY
LaPLACE, LOUISIANA 70068

	1990	1980	1970	1960	1950	1940	1930	1920	1910
% change from previous census									
Male	2,031,386	2,039,267	1,771,484	1,592,254	1,319,166	1,172,382	1,047,823	903,335	835,275
Female	2,188,587	2,166,633	1,869,822	1,664,768	1,364,350	1,191,498	1,053,770	895,174	821,113
Median Age									
Louisiana	31.0	27.3	26.2	25.3	26.7	25.5	23.1	21.7	20.4
U.S.	32.9	30.0	28.1	29.5	30.2	29.0	26.5	25.3	24.1
White	2,839,138	2,915,310	2,541,498	2,211,715	1,796,683	1,511,739	1,322,712	1,096,611	941,086
Negro	1,299,281	1,238,472	1,086,832	1,039,207	882,428	849,303	776,326	700,257	713,874
American Indian	18,361	12,841	5,294	3,587	409	1,801	1,536	1,066	780
Eskimo	92	46	—	—	—	—	—	—	—
Aleut	88	45	—	—	—	—	—	—	—
Chinese	5,430	3,091	1,340	731	526	360	422	387	507
Japanese	1,526	1,671	1,123	519	127	46	52	57	31
Filipino	3,731	2,650	1,249	754	—	—	—	—	—
Korean	2,750	2,009	—	—	—	—	—	—	—
Vietnamese	17,598	10,853	—	—	—	—	—	—	—
Asian Indian	5,083	3,036	—	—	—	—	—	—	—
Others	26,604	15,876	3,970	509	3,343	631	545	131	110

	1900	1890	1880	1870	1860	1850	1840	1830	1820	1810
Total	1,381,625	1,118,588	939,946	726,915	708,022	517,762	352,411	215,739	153,407*	76,556
% change from previous census										
Louisiana	23.5	19.0	29.3	2.7	36.7	46.9	63.4	40.6	100.4	—
U.S.	21.0	25.5	30.2	22.6	35.6	35.9	32.7	33.4	33.1	36.4
Urban	366,288	283,845	239,390	202,523	185,026	134,470	105,400	46,082	27,176	17,242
% Louisiana	26.5	25.4	25.5	27.9	26.1	26.0	29.9	21.4	17.7	22.5
% U.S.	21.0	35.1	28.2	25.7	19.8	15.3	10.8	8.8	7.2	7.3
Rural	1,015,337	834,743	700,556	524,392	522,976	383,292	247,011	169,657	126,231	59,314
% Louisiana	73.5	74.6	74.5	72.1	73.9	74.0	70.1	78.6	82.3	77.5
% U.S.	60.4	64.9	71.8	74.3	80.2	84.7	89.2	91.2	92.8	92.7
Male	694,733	559,351	468,754	362,165	369,994	274,596	—	—	—	—
Female	686,892	559,237	471,192	364,750	338,008	243,166	—	—	—	—
Median Age										
Louisiana	19.4	18.6	19.0	—	—	—	—	—	—	—
U.S.	22.9	22.0	20.9	20.2	19.4	18.9	17.8	17.2	16.7	—
White	729,612	941,086	454,954	362,065	357,456	255,491	158,457	89,441	73,383	34,311
Negro	650,804	713,874	483,655	364,210	350,373	262,271	193,954	126,298	79,540	76,556
American Indian	593	628	848	569	173	—	—	—	—	
Chinese	599	333	489	71	—	—	—	—	—	
Japanese	17	39	—	—	—	—	—	—	—	

SOURCE: Bureau of the Census.

* The 1820 total population also included 484 classed as "Other but not Indian."

City	1990	1980	1970	1960	1950	1940	1930	1920	1910	1900	1880	1860	1840	1820	1810
Abbeville	11,187	12,391	10,996	10,414	9,338	6,672	4,356	3,461	2,907	1,536	225	—	—	—	—
Alexandria	49,188	51,565	41,557	40,279	34,913	27,066	23,025	17,510	11,213	5,648	1,800	1,461	—	—	—
Amite	4,236	4,301	3,593	3,316	2,804	2,499	2,536	1,854	1,677	1,547	1,120	—	—	—	—
Arcadia	3,079	3,403	2,970	2,547	2,241	1,601	1,809	1,280	1,079	954	—	—	—	—	—
Baker	13,233	12,865	8,281	4,823	762	150	—	—	—	—	—	—	—	—	—
Bastrop	13,916	15,527	14,713	15,193	12,769	6,626	5,121	1,216	854	787	822	—	—	—	—
Baton Rouge	219,531	219,419	165,963	152,419	125,629	34,719	30,729	21,782	14,897	11,269	7,197	5,428	2,269	—	—
Benton	2,047	1,864	1,493	1,336	741	519	402	—	318	—	—	—	—	—	—
Bernice	1,543	1,956	1,794	1,641	1,524	1,071	965	662	781	—	—	—	—	—	—
Berwick	4,375	4,466	4,168	3,880	2,619	1,906	1,679	1,691	2,183	713	796	—	—	—	—
Bogalusa	14,280	16,976	18,412	21,423	17,798	14,604	14,029	8,245	—	—	—	—	—	—	—
Bossier City	52,721	50,817	41,595	32,776	15,470	5,786	4,003	1,094	775	—	—	—	—	—	—
Breaux Bridge	6,515	5,922	4,942	3,303	2,492	1,668	1,399	1,171	1,339	654	443	—	—	—	—
Bunkie	5,044	5,364	5,395	5,188	4,666	3,575	2,464	1,743	1,765	873	—	—	—	—	—
Cameron	2,041	1,736	—	—	—	—	—	—	—	—	—	—	—	—	—
Carencro	5,429	3,712	2,302	1,519	1,587	914	684	630	609	445	—	—	—	—	—
Church Point	4,677	4,599	3,865	3,606	2,897	1,892	1,037	557	481	—	—	—	—	—	—
Clinton	1,904	1,919	1,884	1,568	1,383	998	702	701	918	960	1,129	—	—	—	—
Colfax	1,696	1,680	1,892	1,934	1,651	1,354	1,141	1,449	1,049	190	—	—	—	—	—
Columbia	386	687	1,000	1,021	920	947	760	434	500	382	219	—	—	—	—
Coushatta	1,845	2,084	1,492	1,663	1,788	1,289	959	962	564	600	488	—	—	—	—
Covington	7,691	7,892	7,170	6,754	5,113	4,123	3,208	2,942	2,601	1,205	567	—	—	—	—
Crowley	13,983	16,036	16,104	15,617	12,784	9,523	7,656	6,108	5,099	4,214	—	—	—	—	—
Denham Springs	8,381	8,563	6,752	5,991	2,053	1,233	1,002	500	—	—	—	—	—	—	—
DeRidder	9,868	11,057	8,030	7,188	5,799	3,750	3,747	3,535	2,100	—	—	—	—	—	—
Donaldsonville	7,949	7,901	7,367	6,082	4,150	3,889	3,788	3,745	4,090	4,105	2,600	—	—	—	—
Eunice	11,162	12,479	11,390	11,326	8,184	5,242	3,597	3,272	1,684	316	—	—	—	—	—
Farmerville	3,334	3,768	3,416	2,727	2,173	1,428	1,137	632	598	458	712	—	—	—	—
Ferriday	4,111	4,472	5,239	4,563	3,847	2,857	2,502	1,044	577	—	—	—	—	—	—
Franklin	9,004	9,584	9,325	8,673	6,144	4,274	3,271	3,504	3,857	2,692	1,702	—	—	—	—
Franklinton	4,007	4,119	3,562	3,141	2,342	1,579	963	964	814	236	—	—	—	—	—
Gonzales	7,003	7,287	4,512	3,252	1,642	857	—	—	—	—	—	—	—	—	—
Grambling	5,484	4,226	4,407	3,144	—	—	—	—	—	—	—	—	—	—	—
Greensburg	585	662	652	512	423	389	262	286	268	315	297	—	—	—	—
Gretna	17,208	20,615	24,875	21,967	13,813	10,879	9,584	7,197	—	—	—	—	—	—	—
Hahnville	2,599	2,947	2,362	1,297	—	—	—	—	—	—	—	—	—	—	—
Hammond	15,871	15,043	12,487	10,563	8,010	6,033	6,072	3,855	2,942	1,511	277	—	—	—	—
Harahan	9,927	11,384	13,037	9,275	3,394	1,082	892	—	—	—	—	—	—	—	—
Harrisonburg	453	610	626	594	544	422	437	399	361	303	243	—	—	—	—
Homer	4,152	4,307	4,483	4,665	4,749	3,497	2,909	3,305	1,855	1,157	718	—	—	—	—
Houma	30,495	32,602	30,922	22,561	11,506	9,052	6,531	5,160	5,024	3,212	1,084	—	—	—	—
Jackson	3,891	3,133	4,697	1,824	6,772	5,384	3,966	2,320	2,146	2,012	880	—	—	—	—
Jeanerette	6,205	6,511	6,322	5,568	4,692	3,362	2,228	2,512	2,206	1,905	698	—	—	—	—
Jena	2,626	4,332	2,431	2,098	1,438	946	1,007	520	680	—	—	—	—	—	—
Jennings	11,305	12,401	11,783	11,887	9,663	7,343	4,036	3,824	3,925	1,539	—	—	—	—	—

Continued on next page

xix. Gazetteer

City	1990	1980	1970	1960	1950	1940	1930	1920	1910	1900	1880	1860	1840	1820	1810
Jonesboro	4,305	5,061	5,072	3,848	3,097	2,639	1,949	837	1,134	—	—	—	—	—	—
Kaplan	4,535	5,016	5,540	5,267	4,562	2,383	1,653	876	315	—	—	—	—	—	—
Kenner	72,033	66,382	29,858	17,037	3,535	2,375	2,440	1,882	—	—	—	—	—	—	—
Lafayette	94,440	81,961	68,908	40,400	33,541	19,210	14,635	7,855	6,392	3,314	—	—	—	—	—
Lake Charles	70,580	75,226	77,998	63,392	41,272	21,207	15,791	13,088	11,449	6,680	838	—	—	—	—
Lake Providence	5,380	6,361	6,183	5,781	4,123	3,711	2,867	1,917	1,568	1,256	—	—	—	—	—
Leesville	7,638	9,054	8,928	4,689	4,670	2,829	3,291	2,518	2,043	1,148	—	—	—	—	—
Livingston	999	1,260	1,398	1,183	—	—	—	—	—	—	—	—	—	—	—
Lutcher	3,907	4,730	3,911	3,274	2,198	2,167	1,481	1,700	—	—	—	—	—	—	—
Mandeville	7,083	6,076	2,571	1,740	1,368	1,326	1,069	1,130	1,166	1,029	753	—	—	—	—
Mansfield	5,389	6,485	6,432	5,839	4,440	4,065	3,837	2,564	1,799	847	770	—	—	—	—
Many	3,112	3,988	3,112	3,164	1,681	1,474	1,239	663	683	354	143	—	—	—	—
Marksville	5,526	5,113	4,519	4,257	3,635	1,811	1,527	1,185	1,076	837	—	—	—	—	—
Minden	13,661	15,084	13,996	12,785	9,787	6,677	5,623	6,105	3,092	1,561	1,113	—	—	—	—
Monroe	54,909	57,597	56,374	52,219	41,272	28,309	26,028	12,675	10,209	5,428	2,070	—	—	—	—
Morgan City	14,531	16,114	16,586	13,540	9,759	6,969	5,985	5,429	5,477	2,332	2,015	—	—	—	—
Napoleonville	802	829	1,008	1,148	1,260	1,301	1,180	1,171	1,201	945	497	—	—	—	—
Natchitoches	16,609	16,664	15,974	13,924	9,914	6,812	4,547	3,388	2,532	2,388	2,785	—	—	—	—
New Iberia	31,828	32,766	30,147	29,062	16,467	13,747	8,003	6,278	7,499	6,815	2,709	—	—	—	—
New Orleans	496,938	557,927	593,471	62,525	570,445	494,537	458,762	387,219	339,075	287,104	216,090	168,675	102,193	46,082	—
New Roads	5,303	3,924	3,945	3,965	2,818	2,255	1,473	1,294	1,352	770	—	—	—	—	—
Oakdale	6,832	7,155	7,301	6,618	5,598	3,933	3,188	4,016	—	—	—	—	—	—	—
Oak Grove	2,126	2,214	1,980	1,796	1,654	1,241	700	398	—	—	—	—	—	—	—
Oberlin	1,808	1,764	1,857	1,794	1,544	962	790	623	232	213	—	—	—	—	—
Opelousas	18,151	18,903	20,387	17,417	11,659	9,980	6,299	4,437	4,623	2,951	1,676	623	—	—	—
Patterson	4,736	4,693	4,409	2,923	1,938	1,800	2,206	2,538	2,998	1,414	—	—	—	—	—
Pineville	12,251	12,034	8,951	8,636	6,423	4,297	3,612	2,188	1,212	617	763	—	—	—	—
Plaquemine	7,186	7,521	7,739	7,689	5,747	5,049	5,124	4,632	4,955	3,590	2,061	1,025	—	—	—
Ponchatoula	5,425	5,469	4,545	4,727	4,090	4,001	2,898	955	1,055	711	293	—	—	—	—
Port Allen	6,277	6,114	5,728	5,026	3,097	1,898	1,524	920	—	—	—	—	—	—	—
Rayne	8,502	9,066	9,510	8,634	6,485	4,974	3,710	2,720	2,247	1,007	—	—	—	—	—
Rayville	4,411	4,610	3,962	4,052	3,138	2,412	2,076	1,499	1,079	366	—	—	—	—	—
Ruston	20,027	20,585	17,365	13,991	10,372	7,107	4,400	3,389	3,377	1,324	—	—	—	—	—
St. Faancisville	1,700	1,471	1,603	1,661	936	821	830	673	966	1,059	721	—	—	—	—
St. Joseph	1,517	1,687	1,864	1,653	1,218	1,096	864	734	740	717	486	—	—	—	—
St. Martinville	7,137	7,695	7,153	6,468	4,614	3,501	2,455	2,465	2,318	1,926	1,606	—	—	—	—
Scott	4,912	2,239	1,334	902	688	407	344	324	239	—	—	—	—	—	—
Shreveport	198,525	205,820	182,064	164,372	127,206	98,167	76,655	43,874	28,015	16,013	8,009	2,190	—	—	—
Slidell	24,124	26,719	16,101	6,356	3,464	2,864	2,807	2,958	2,188	1,129	—	—	—	—	—
Springhill	5,668	6,516	6,496	6,437	3,383	2,822	1,546	748	—	—	—	—	—	—	—
Sulphur	20,125	19,709	15,247	11,429	5,996	3,504	1,888	1,714	—	—	—	—	—	—	—
Tallulah	8,526	11,634	9,643	9,413	7,758	5,712	3,332	1,316	847	—	—	—	—	—	—
Thibodaux	14,035	15,810	15,028	13,403	7,730	5,851	4,442	3,526	3,824	3,253	1,515	1,039	—	—	—
Vidalia	4,953	5,936	5,538	4,313	1,614	1,318	1,141	1,246	1,345	1,022	821	—	—	—	—
Ville Platte	9,037	9,201	9,692	7,512	6,633	3,721	1,722	1,364	603	163	—	—	—	—	—

Vivian	4,156	4,146	4,046	2,624	2,426	2,460	1,646	1,864	826	—	—	—	—	—	—
West Monroe	14,096	14,993	14,868	15,215	10,302	8,560	6,566	2,240	1,127	775	—	—	—	—	—
Westlake	5,007	5,246	4,082	3,311	1,871	—	—	—	—	—	—	—	—	—	—
Westwego	11,218	12,663	11,402	9,815	8,328	4,992	3,987	—	—	—	—	—	—	—	—
Winnfield	6,138	7,311	7,142	7,022	5,629	4,512	3,721	2,975	2,925	—	—	—	—	—	—
Winnsboro	5,755	5,921	5,349	4,437	3,655	2,834	1,965	1,176	821	—	—	—	—	—	—
Zachary	7,297	4,964	3,268	1,542	730	626	524	419	465	—	—	—	—	—	—

SOURCE: Bureau of the Census.

5. POPULATION OF SELECTED LOUISIANA CENSUS-DESIGNATED PLACES

Place	1990	1980	1970	1960	1950
Arabi	8,787	10,248	—	—	—
Avondale	5,813	6,699	—	—	—
Bayou Cane	15,876	15,728	9,077	3,173	2,212
Bayou Vista	4,733	5,805	5,121	—	—
Belle Chasse	8,512	5,412	—	—	—
Brownville-Bawcomville	7,397	7,252	—	—	—
Chalmette	31,860	33,847	—	—	—
Claiborne	8,300	6,278	—	—	—
Cut-Off	5,325	5,049	—	—	—
Destrehan	8,031	2,382	—	—	—
Estelle	14,091	12,724	—	—	—
Galliano	4,294	5,159	—	—	—
Gray	4,260	—	—	—	—
Harvey	21,222	22,709	6,347	—	—
Jefferson	14,521	15,550	16,489	19,353	—
Lacombe	6,523	5,146	—	—	—
Laplace	24,194	16,112	5,953	3,541	2,352
Larose	5,772	5,234	4,267	2,796	1,286
Marrero	36,671	36,548	29,015	—	—
Metairie	149,428	164,160	136,477	—	—
Mimosa Park	4,526	3,737	1,624	—	—
Monticello	4,710	—	—	—	—
Moss Bluff	8,039	7,004	—	—	—
Old Jefferson	4,531	—	—	—	—
Poydras	4,029	5,722	—	—	—
Prien	6,448	6,224	—	—	—
Raceland	5,564	6,302	4,880	3,666	2,025
Reserve	8,847	7,288	6,381	5,297	4,465
River Ridge	14,800	17,146	15,713	—	—
Terrytown	23,787	23,548	13,832	—	—
Timberlane	12,614	11,579	—	—	—
Violet	8,574	11,678	—	—	—
Waggaman	9,405	2,957	—	—	—

6. *PERCENTAGE OF POPULATION TWENTY- FIVE YEARS OLD OR OLDER WHICH HAS COMPLETED HIGH SCHOOL AND COLLEGE, 1940–1990*

Place	1990		1980		1970		1960		1950		1940	
	High School	College	High School	College	High School	College	High School	College	High School	College	High School	College
Louisiana	68.3	16.1	57.7	13.9	24.7	9.1	18.9	6.7	11.4	4.7	9.8	3.5
Mississippi	64.3	14.7	54.8	12.3	23.9	8.1	18.7	5.6	12.3	3.8	8.6	3.0
Arkansas	66.3	13.3	55.5	10.8	25.6	6.7	17.9	4.8	12.9	3.1	8.7	2.2
Texas	72.1	20.3	62.6	16.9	25.1	10.9	21.8	8.1	15.7	6.0	13.2	4.4
United States	75.2	20.3	66.5	16.2	52.3	10.7	24.6	7.7	33.4	6.0	24.1	4.6

SOURCE: Bureau of the Census.

7. *RATES OF ILLITERACY AMONG PERSONS TEN YEARS OF AGE AND OLDER IN DIFFERENT STATES OF THE UNION, 1880–1930*

Place	1930			1920			1910			1900		
	Total	White	Black	Total	White	Black	Total	White	Black	Total	White	Black
Louisiana	13.5	7.7	23.3	21.9	11.1	38.5	29.0	14.2	48.4	38.5	18.4	61.1
Mississippi	13.1	2.7	23.2	17.2	3.7	29.3	22.4	5.3	35.6	32.0	8.0	49.1
Arkansas	6.8	3.5	16.1	9.4	4.5	21.8	12.6	7.0	26.4	20.4	11.5	43.0
Texas	6.8	1.6	13.4	8.3	6.5	17.8	9.9	6.7	24.6	14.5	8.5	38.2
United States	4.3	2.7	16.3	6.0	4.0	22.9	7.7	5.0	30.4	10.7	6.2	44.4

Place	1890			1880			1870*			1860*		
	Total	White	Black	Total	White	Black	Total	White	Black	Total	White	Black
Louisiana	45.8	20.1	72.1	49.1	18.4	79.1	37.9	14.0	61.8	5.1	5.0	6.4
Mississippi	40.0	11.9	60.8	49.5	16.3	75.2	37.8	12.5	59.6	4.4	4.4	14.2
Arkansas	26.6	16.3	53.6	38.0	25.0	75.0	27.5	17.7	56.7	7.3	7.3	16.0
Texas	19.7	10.8	52.5	29.7	15.3	75.4	27.1	12.6	59.4	4.4	4.4	17.5
United States	13.3	7.7	57.1	17.0	9.4	70.0	14.7	8.5	57.2	4.4	4.2	18.8

SOURCE: Bureau of the Census.

*For 1870, "those who cannot write"; for 1860, "cannot read or write" for free persons twenty years of age and older.

8. *PER-PUPIL CURRENT FUND EXPENDITURES FOR PUBLIC ELEMENTARY AND SECONDARY SCHOOLS, 1969–1990, IN CONSTANT 1989–1990 DOLLARS*

	1989–90	1987–88	1985–86	1983–84	1981–82	1979–80	1977–78	1975–76	1973–74	1971–72	1969–70
United States	$4,571	$4,304	$4,060	$3,667	$3,407	$3,416	$3,399	$3,170	$2,998	$2,801	$2,525
South	3,840	3,607	3,439	3,055	2,836	2,806	2,777	2,581	2,370	2,231	1,978
Louisiana	3,390	3,164	3,454	3,041	3,204	2,664	2,742	2,593	2,440	2,448	1,981
% of South	88.3	87.7	100.4	99.5	113.0	94.9	98.7	100.5	103.0	109.7	100.2
% of U.S.	74.2	73.5	85.1	82.9	94.0	78.0	80.7	81.8	81.4	87.4	78.4

SOURCE: John A. Grymes and Irene Baden Harwarth, "Historical Trends," *State Education Facts, 1969–1989* (U.S. Department of Education, 1992).

9. *PER-PUPIL CURRENT FUND EXPENDITURES FOR PUBLIC INSTITUTIONS OF HIGHER EDUCATION, 1969–1988, IN CONSTANT 1989–1990 DOLLARS (based on Full-Time Equivalents)*

	1989–90	1987–88	1985–86	1983–84	1981–82	1979–80	1977–78	1975–76	1973–74	1971–72	1969–70
United States	$7870	$7773	$7522	$6591	$6311	$6640	$6753	$6450	$6779	$6492	$6415
South	8264	8188	7858	6939	6744	6876	6886	6422	6865	6459	6313
Louisiana	7715	7757	7425	7015	7051	7156	6364	5504	6237	5363	6033
% of South	93.4	94.7	94.5	101.1	104.6	104.1	92.4	85.7	90.9	83.0	95.6
% of U.S.	98.0	99.8	98.7	106.4	111.7	107.8	94.2	85.3	92.0	82.6	94.0

SOURCE: John A. Grymes and Irene Baden Harwarth, "Historical Trends," *State Education Facts, 1969–1989* (U.S. Department of Education, 1992).

10. GENERAL NATIVITY OF THE UNITED STATES POPULATION *(Percentage Born in State of Residence)*

	1990	1980	1970	1960	1950	1940	1930	1920	1910	1900	1890	1880	1870	1860*	1850*
Louisiana	80.6	79.7	78.2	81.8	84.7	86.9	86.8	86.9	87.7	88.0	86.3	82.2	75.4	72.6	69.7
Arkansas	67.8	69.2	72.9	77.1	76.8	77.3	72.6	68.3	67.1	64.8	59.2	55.1	48.6	38.7	—
Mississippi	77.9	78.6	81.2	86.7	88.5	90.5	89.1	89.1	87.0	85.9	83.0	76.9	69.1	56.6	—
Texas	71.1	71.1	72.9	75.8	75.6	78.5	74.1	70.9	70.1	66.6	65.8	59.0	51.4	40.5	—
United States	67.1	68.2	68.0	70.3	73.5	77.1	76.2	77.4	78.0	79.1	78.4	77.9	76.7	—	

SOURCE: Bureau of the Census.

*Free Population Only.

11. STATES CONTRIBUTING MOST HEAVILY TO LOUISIANA'S NATIVE-BORN POPULATION FOR VARIOUS CENSUS PERIODS

1950 State	%	1930 State	%	1910 State	%	1890 State	%	1870 State	%	1850** State	%
Mississippi	4.0	Mississippi	4.2	Mississippi	3.5	Mississippi	3.2	Mississippi	4.8	Mississippi	5.3
Texas	2.6	Texas	2.1	Texas	1.6	Alabama	2.0	Virginia*	4.5	Georgia	2.9
Arkansas	1.7	Arkansas	1.6	Alabama	1.4	Virginia*	1.3	Alabama	3.1	Alabama	3.6
Alabama	0.9	Alabama	1.0	Arkansas	1.0	Georgia	1.2	Georgia	2.4	New York	2.7
Missouri	0.4	Georgia	0.4	Georgia	0.7	North Carolina	1.0	South Carolina	1.6	South Carolina	2.2
Tennessee	0.4	Tennessee	0.4	Tennessee	0.4	Texas	0.8	Kentucky	1.2	Tennessee	1.6
Illinois	0.4	Missouri	0.4	Missouri	0.4	South Carolina	0.7	North Carolina	1.1	Virginia	1.6
Georgia	0.4	Illinois	0.3	Virginia	0.3	Kentucky	0.4	Tennessee	1.1	Kentucky	1.4
New York	0.3	Kentucky	0.2	Kentucky	0.3	Arkansas	0.4	Texas	0.7	North Carolina	1.4
Florida	0.3	New York	0.2	Illinois	0.3	Tennessee	0.4	New York	0.6	Pennsylvania	1.2

SOURCE: Bureau of the Census.

*Includes West Virginia.   **Free Population Only.

12. TOP TEN COUNTRIES CONTRIBUTING TO FOREIGN-BORN POPULATION OF LOUISIANA, WITH PERCENTAGE OF TOTAL FOREIGN-BORN, FOR VARIOUS CENSUS PERIODS

1980 Country	%	1940 Country	%	1910 Country	%	1890 Country	%	1870 Country	%	1850** Country	%
Vietnam	10.7	Italy	36.1	Italy	39.1	Germany	29.4	Germany	30.6	Ireland*	35.6
Germany	6.2	Germany	9.4	Germany	17.0	Ireland*	18.6	Ireland*	27.6	Germany	26.2
Cuba	5.6	France	6.7	France	10.2	France	17.0	France	20.0	France	16.9
Great Britain*	4.9	Great Britain*	5.8	Ireland*	7.2	Italy	15.6	Great Britain*	6.1	Great Britain*	7.1
Canada	3.1	Russia	4.4	Great Britain*	5.1	Great Britain*	6.0	Italy	3.1	Spain	2.1
Italy	2.7	Mexico	3.8	Austria	2.7	Canada	1.5	Spain	1.8	Switzerland	1.1
Mexico	2.1	Canada	3.4	Russia	2.6	Spain	1.8	Cuba	1.6	Italy	1.4
Philippines	2.0	Syria	3.0	Canada	2.3	Austria	1.2	Switzerland	1.4	Canada	0.7
India	1.8	Ireland*	2.6	Mexico	1.9	Switzerland	1.0	Canada	1.1	Mexico	0.6
Korea	1.8	Poland	2.1	Poland	1.4	Mexico	0.8	Mexico/Austria	0.7	Sweden/Denmark	0.4

SOURCE: Bureau of the Census. Nations separated by a slash each contributed the same percentage.

* "Ireland" and "Great Britain" refer to the main islands which, until 1921, comprised the United Kingdom. After 1921, "Ireland" refers to both the Republic of Ireland and Northern Ireland, which remained a part of the United Kingdom of Great Britain and Northern Ireland. Great Britain collectively refers to English, Scottish, and Welsh immigrants.

** Free population only.

13. MISCELLANEOUS INFORMATION FOR 1990 (Unless Another Year Is Indicated)

	La	U.S.		La	U.S.		La	U.S.
Approximate mean elevation, (feet)	100	2,000	Personnel per 100,000 civilian population			Per capita state government expenditures	$2,020	$2,047
% of area federally owned, 1989	22.6	29.2	Physicians	188	216	% of general revenues expended for		
% of Non-Federally Owned Land in 1987 in			Dentists	49	59	Education	37.3	36.3
Forest Cover	41.7	20.3	Nurses	430	676	Public welfare	15.7	20.7
Cropland	21.2	21.8	Personnel per 10,000 population, 1988			Highways	8.7	8.7
Pastureland	7.4	6.7	Police (Full-Time Equivalent)	27.4	27.3	Health and hospitals	9.9	8.4
Net power generation as % of total			Corrections (Full-Time Equivalent)	18.0	17.7	Natural resources	2.4	2.0
Nuclear	24.7	20.6	Population per lawyer, 1988	383	340	Women-owned firms as % of total, 1987	27	30
Coal	30.5	55.5	Marriages per 1,000 population	9.4	9.8	Minority-owned businesses, 1987		
Personal income per capita, 1991	$15,153	$19,082	Divorces per 1,000 population	...	4.7	Black	15,331	424,165
Per capita federal income tax, 1989	$1,145	$1,827	% Voting age population registered to vote	70	67	Hispanic	2,697	422,373
% of households on food stamps	16.8	8.7	% Democrat	74	...	American Indian	225	21,380
% of households on AFDP/FSSI*	9.8	6.5	% Republican	18	...	Asian/Pacific Islander	2,583	355,331
Birth rate (per 1,000), 1989	16.6	16.3	Daily-newspaper circulation per capita	0.18	0.25	Foreign direct investment in the United States		
Death rate (per 1,000), 1989	8.6	8.7	% Unemployment, civilian, 1991			Employment as % of all businesses	5.2	4.8
Infant mortality rate, 1988	11.0	10.0	Total	7.1	6.7	Median value/rent of occupied housing unit		
White	9.0	8.5	Male	6.6	7.0	Owner Occupied	$58,500	$79,100
Black	14.3	17.6	Female	7.8	6.3	Renter Occupied	$260	$374
Deaths per 100,000 population, 1989			Government employees per 10,000 population			Crime rates per 100,000—total	6,487	5,802
Diseases of the heart	291.1	295.6	State government	200	154	Violent	898	732
Malignant neoplasms	194.2	199.9	Local Government	368	371	Murder	17.2	9.4
Cerebrovascular disease	56.4	58.6	Per capita state appropriations,			Forcible rape	42	41
Accidents/adverse effects	43.7	38.3	state arts agencies, 1991	0.22	$1.08	Robbery	270	257
Suicides	12.4	12.2	Per capita federal aid to state/local governments	630	533	Aggravated assault	569	424
Homicides/legal intervention	13.2	9.0	Per capita State Government Revenues	$2,115	$2,086	Property	5,588	5,088
Chronic liver disease/cirrhosis	7.4	10.7	% of state general revenues derived from			Burglary	1,438	1,236
HIV	5.6	6.8	Federal government	26.9	22.9	Larceny	3,549	3,195
Chronic obstructive pulmonary disease	25.9	33.7	Local government	0.2	1.5	Motor vehicle theft	602	658
Medicare			Taxes	45.8	58.1	Prisoners sentenced to		
Enrollment (1,000)	531	34,203	Charges and miscellaneous	27.2	17.5	> 1 year per 100,000 population	427	292
Payments ($1,000,000)	1,984	108,707	% of state tax collections generated by					
Medicaid			General sales/gross receipts	30.9	33.2			
Enrollment (1,000)	585	25,255	Motor fuels	9.8	6.4			
Payments ($1,000,000)	1,315	64,859	Alcoholic beverages/tobacco products	2.7	2.9			
Abortions, 1988			Individual incomes	18.0	32.0			
Total (1,000)	17	1,591	Corporations	9.6	7.2			
Rate per 1,000 women 15–44	16.3	27.3	Motor vehicles/operators licenses	2.0	3.6			
Rate per 1,000 live births	241	401						

SOURCE: Statistical Abstract of the United States, 1992.

*Aid to Families with Dependent Children and Federal Supplemental Security Income.

Name	Years in Office	Name	Years in Office	Name	Years in Office
Colonial French		*United States Territorial*		Louis Alfred Wiltz*	1880–1881
Pierre Le Moyne, Sieur d'Iberville	1699	William Charles Cole Claiborne	1803–1812	Samuel Douglas McEnery	1881–1888
Sieur de Sauvole*	1699–1701			Francis Tillou Nicholls	1888–1892
Jean-Baptiste Le Moyne, Sieur de Bienville	1702–1707	*Statehood*		Murphy James Foster	1892–1900
Nicolas Daneaux de Muy	1707–1708	William Charles Cole Claiborne	1812–1816	William Wright Heard	1900–1904
Antoine Laumet, La Mothe Cadillac	1708–1710	Jacques Phillipe Villeré	1816–1820	Newton Crain Blanchard	1904–1908
Jean-Micheîle de l'Epinay	1710–1716	Thomas Bolling Robertson‡	1820–1824	Jared Young Sanders	1908–1912
Jean-Baptiste Le Moyne, Sieur de Bienville	1717–1718	Henry Schuyler Thibodeaux	1824	Luther Egbert Hall	1912–1916
Jean-Baptiste Le Moyne, Sieur de Bienville, and		Henry S. Johnson	1824–1828	Ruffin G. Pleasant	1916–1920
Joseph Le Moyne, Sieur de Serigny (co-govs.)	1718–1724	Pierre Derbigny*	1828–1829	John M. Parker	1920–1924
Pierre Dugue, Sieur de Boisbriant	1724–1726	Armand Beauvais	1829–1830	Henry L. Fuqua*	1924–1926
Étienne de Périer	1726–1732	Jacques Dupré	1830–1831	Oramel Hinkley Simpson	1926–1928
Jean-Baptiste Le Moyne, Sieur de Bienville	1732–1743	André Bienvenu Roman	1831–1835	Huey Pierce Long	1928–1931
Pierre de Rigault, Marquis de Vaudreuil	1743–1752	Edward Douglass White	1835–1839	Alvin O. King	1931–1932
Louis Billouart de Kerlérec	1752–1763	André Bienvenu Roman	1839–1843	Oscar K. Allen*	1932–1936
Jean-Jacques Blaise d'Abbadie	1763–1765	Alexandre Mouton	1843–1846	James A. Noe	1936
Charles Philippe Aubry	1765–1769	Isaac Johnson	1846–1850	Richard Webster Leche‡	1936–1939
		Joseph Marshall Walker	1850–1853	Earl K. Long†	1939–1940
Colonial Spanish		Paul Octave Hébert	1853–1856	Sam Houston Jones	1940–1944
Antonio de Ulloa	1766–1768	Robert Charles Wickliffe	1856–1860	James H. Davis	1944–1948
Alexander O'Reilly	1769–1770	Thomas Overton Moore	1860–1864	Earl K. Long	1948–1952
Luis de Unzaga	1770–1777	Henry Watkins Allen (Confederate)	1864–1865	Robert F. Kennon	1952–1956
Bernardo de Gálvez	1777–1785	Michael Hahn (Federal)	1864–1865	Earl K. Long	1956–1960
Estevan Miró	1785–1791	James Madison Wells	1865–1867	James H. Davis	1960–1964
Francisco Luis Hector, Baron de Carondelet	1791–1797	Benjamin F. Flanders (Military)	1867–1868	John J. McKeithen	1964–1972
Manuel Gayoso de Lemos	1797–1799	Joshua Baker (Military)	1868	Edwin W. Edwards	1972–1980
Francisco Bouligny†	1799	Henry Clay Warmoth	1868–1873	David C. Treen	1980–1984
Sebastián, Marquis de Casa Calvo	1799–1801	P. B. S. Pinchback	1873	Edwin W. Edwards	1984–1988
Juan Manuel de Salcedo	1801–1803	John McEnery	1873	Charles E. Roemer	1988–1992
		William Pitt Kellogg	1873–1877	Edwin W. Edwards	1992– .
Colonial French		Stephen B. Packard	1877		
Pierre Clément Laussat	1803	Francis Tillou Nicholls	1877–1880		

SOURCES: Bennett H. Wall, ed., *Louisiana: A History,* 2d ed. (Arlington Heights, Ill.: Forum Press, 1990), 393–95; Lousiana Legislative Council, *The History and the Government of Lousiana* (Baton Rouge, 1964), 273–74.
*Died in office.
†Acting.
‡Resigned.

REFERENCES

I. Site and Situation

Map 1. Location within the Coterminous United States.
Map 2. Latitude and Longitude

Buchanan, W. C. *Louisiana Geography,* 1–6. Oklahoma City: Harlow Publishing Company, 1957.

Espenshade, Edward B., Jr., ed. *Goode's World Atlas,* xvi, 2–3, 91, 108–109, 125, 126, 128–29. 17th ed. Chicago: Rand, McNally, 1986.

Kniffen, Fred B., and Sam Bowers Hilliard, *Louisiana: Its Land and People,* 11–16, 18–19, 1968. Rev. ed. Baton Rouge: Louisiana State University Press, 1987.

Newton, Milton B., Jr. *Louisiana: A Geographical Portrait,* 1–5. 2d ed. Baton Rouge: Geoforensics, 1987.

II. Physical Setting and Natural Resources

Abington, O. Douglas, Henry W. Bullamore, and David C. Johnson. *Louisiana: A Geography.* 37–70, 117–35. Lafayette: Department of Geography/Urban and Regional Planning, University of Southwestern Louisiana, 1989.

Buchanan. *Louisiana Geography,* 8–20, 31–48.

Kniffen and Hilliard. *Louisiana,* 5–10, 17–85, 166–77, 187–91.

Newton. *Louisiana,* 6–86, 264–68, 275–79.

Map 3. Natural Regions
Map 4. Contour Map
Map 5. Major Landforms

Atwood, Wallace W. *The Physiographic Provinces of North America,* 25–61. Boston: Ginn and Company, 1940.

Calhoun, Milburn, ed. *Louisiana Almanac, 1992–1993,* 254. Gretna: Pelican Publishing Company, 1992.

Fenneman, Nevin M. *Physiography of the Eastern United States,* 65–120. New York: McGraw-Hill Book Company, 1938.

Gannett, Henry. *Dictionary of Altitudes in the United States,* 375–390. 4th ed. U.S. Geological Survey Bulletin 274. Washington, D.C.: Government Printing Office, 1906.

Hunt, Charles B. *Natural Regions of the United States and Canada,* 223–229, 1967. San Francisco: W. H. Freeman and Company, 1974.

Kniffen and Hillard. *Louisiana,* 8–9.

Lockett, Samuel H. *Louisiana as It Is: A Geographical and Topographical Description of the State.* 1873. Edited by Lauren C. Post. Baton Rouge: Louisiana State University Press, 1969.

Newton, Milton B. *Atlas of Louisiana: A Guide for Students,* 45–46. Baton Rouge: School of Geoscience, Louisiana State University, 1972.

Raisz, Erwin. *Landforms of the United States.* 6th ed. 1957.

Rand McNally and Company. *Commercial Atlas and Marketing Guide.* Chicago: Rand McNally, 1991.

Snead, John I., and Richard P. McCulloh, comps. *Geologic Map of Louisiana.* Baton Rouge: Louisiana Geological Survey, 1984.

U.S. Geological Survey. *State of Louisiana. 1968.* Reston, Va.: U.S. Geological Survey, Department of the Interior, 1982.

Map 6. Rivers, Lakes, Waterways, and Floodways

Calhoun. *Louisiana Almanac, 1992–1993.* 271–87.

Carter, Hodding. *Lower Mississippi.* Rivers of America Series. New York: Rinehart, 1942.

Childs, Marquis. *Mighty Mississippi: Biography of a River.* New York: Ticknor and Fields, 1982.

Cry, George W. "Surface Waters of the Lower Mississippi River Region." In *Man and Environment in the Lower Mississippi Valley,* 65–73. Edited by Sam B. Hilliard. Geoscience and Man, Vol. 19. Baton Rouge: School of Geoscience, 1978.

Daniel, Pete. *Deep'n as It Come: The 1927 Mississippi River Flood.* New York: Oxford University Press, 1977.

Davis, Edwin Adams, ed. *The Rivers and Bayous of Louisiana.* Baton Rouge: Louisiana Education Research Association, 1968.

Drago, Harry Sinclair. *Red River Valley: The Mainstream of Frontier History from the Louisiana Bayous to the Texas Panhandle.* New York: C. N. Potter, 1962.

Kane, Harnett T. *The Bayous of Louisiana.* New York: W. W. Morrow and Company, 1944.

Roberts, W. Adolphe. *Lake Pontchartrain.* American Lakes Series. Indianapolis: Bobbs-Merrill Company, 1946.

Saxon, Lyle. *Father Mississippi.* New York: Century Company, 1927.

Tyson, Carl N. *The Red River in Southwestern History.* Norman: University of Oklahoma Press, 1981.

Map 7. Forest Types

Clark, Thomas D. *The Greening of the South: The Recovery of Land and Forest.* Lexington: University Press of Kentucky, 1984.

Louisiana Forestry Commission. *Louisiana Forestry Types.* Baton Rouge: Louisiana Forestry Commission, ca. 1975.

U.S. Forest Service. *The South's Fourth Forest: Alternatives for the Future.* Forest Resource Report 24. Washington, D.C., 1988.

Walker, Laurence C. *The Southern Forest: A Chronicle.* Austin: University of Texas Press, 1991.

Map 8. Parks, Forests, and Wildlife Areas

Clark, *Greening of the South.*

Cowdrey, Albert E. *This Land, This South: An Environmental History.* Lexington: University Press of Kentucky, 1983.

Gulf South Research Unit and Louisiana State Parks and Recreation Commission. *Louisiana State Parks Plan, 1975–1990.* Baton Rouge: Louisiana State Parks and Recreation Commission, ca. 1975.

Louisiana Office of State Parks. Unpublished typescript chronicling development of state park system. Ca. 1990.

Torrey, Raymond H. *State Parks and Recreational Uses of State Forests in the United States,* 117–19. Washington, D.C.: National Conference on State Parks, 1926.

Map 9. Geologic Formations

Bennison, Allan P., comp. *Geological Highway Map of the Southeastern Region: Alabama, Florida, Georgia, Louisiana, Mississippi.* U. S. Geological Highway Map Series, no. 9. Tulsa: American Association of Petroleum Geologists, with the cooperation of the U.S. Geological Survey, 1975.

Calhoun, *Louisiana Almanac, 1992–1993,* 255–67.

Hunt. *Natural Regions,* 223–29.

Murray, Grover E. *Geology of the Atlantic and Gulf Coastal Province of North America.* New York: Harper, 1961.

Snead, John I., and Richard P. McCulloh, comps. *Geologic Map of Louisiana, 1984.* Baton Rouge: Louisiana Geological Survey, 1984

Neil H. Suneson, Staff Geologist, Oklahoma Geological Survey, provided general background for the essay and map.

Map 10. Oil and Gas Production

Franks, Kenny A., and Paul F. Lambert. *Early Louisiana and Arkansas Oil: A Photographic History, 1901–1946.* Montague History of Oil Series, no. 3. College Station: Texas A&M University Press, 1982.

French, T. Michael, and Manuel Lam. *Oil and Gas Producing Industry in Louisiana: A Short History with Long Term Projections.* Baton Rouge: Louisiana Department of Natural Resources, 1986.

Morgan, David Joel. *The Mississippi River Delta: Legal-Geomorphologic Evaluation of Historic Shoreline Changes.* Geoscience and Man, vol. 16. Baton Rouge: School of Geoscience, Louisiana State University, 1977.

Map 11. Floodplain Deposits
Map 12. Mississippi River Delta Systems

Fisk, Harold N. *Geological Investigation of the Alluvial Valley of the Lower Mississippi Valley.* Vicksburg: U.S. Army Corps of Engineers for the Mississippi River Commission, 1944.

Frazier, David E. "Recent Deltaic Deposits of the Mississippi River: Their Development and Chronology." *Transactions, Gulf Coast Association of Geological Societies* 17 (1967): 287–315.

Hunt. *Natural Regions,* 226–30.

Kniffen and Hilliard. *Louisiana,* 54

Kolb, C. R., and J. R. Von Lopik. "Depositional Environments of the Mississippi River Deltaic Plain, Southeastern Louisiana." In *Deltas in Their Geologic Framework,* 17–61. Edited by M. L. Shirley. Houston: Houston Geological Society, 1966.

McCulloh, Richard P., and Rebecca A. Bradley, comps. *Recent Geologic Floodplain Deposits of Louisiana.* Baton Rouge: Louisiana Geological Survey, Department of Natural Resources, 1982.

Morgan. *Mississippi River Delta,* 34–127.

Map 13. Hurricanes

Calhoun. *Louisiana Almanac,* 1992–1993, 129–31.

Dunn, Gordon E., and Banner I. Miller. *Atlantic Hurricanes.* Baton Rouge: Louisiana State University Press, 1960.

Neuman, C. J. *Tropical Cyclones of the North Atlantic Ocean, 1871-1980.* Abbeville, N.C.: National Climatic Data Center, 1981.

Ruffner, James A., and Frank E. Blair. *The Weather Almanac,* 42–79. 2d ed. Detroit: Gale Research Company, 1977.

Simpson, Robert H., and Herbert Riehl. *The Hurricane and Its Impact.* Baton Rouge: Louisiana State University Press, 1981.

Weatherwise Magazine. February issues on hurricanes.

Map 14. Temperature Ranges in January and July
Map 15. Frost Dates, Growing Season, and Precipitation

Climatic data and plots provided by Louisiana Office of State Climatology, John M. Grymes III, State Climatologist; Louisiana Department of Geography and Anthropology, DeWitt H. Braud, Instructor; and LSU CADGIS Research Laboratory, Farrell W. Jones, System Manager.

Cry, George W. *Freeze Probabilities in Louisiana.* Baton Rouge: Louisiana Cooperative Extension Service, 1968.

Fournerat, William M., comp. *Louisiana Climate and Weather, 1951–1980.* Louisiana Map Series, no. 3. Baton Rouge: Department of Geography and Anthropology, n.d.

Muller, R. A., J. D. McLaughlin, and G. J. McCabe. *Probabilities and Climatic Patterns of Precipitation in Louisiana.* Bulletin 799. Baton Rouge: Louisiana Agricultural Experiment Station, 1989.

National Oceanic and Atmospheric Administration. *Climate of Louisiana.* Climatology of the United States, no. 60. Asheville, N.C.: National Climatic Center, Environmental Data Service, 1976.

Owenby, James R., and D.S. Ezell. *Monthly National Normals of Temperature, Precipitation, and Heating and Cooling Degree Days, 1961–90: Louisiana.* Climatology of the United States, no. 81. Asheville, N.C.: National Climatic Data Center, National Oceanic and Atmospheric Administration, U.S. Department of Commerce, 1992.

III. Aboriginal Setting and Native American Tribes

Map 16. **Prehistoric Native American Cultures**
Map 17. **Louisiana Indians ca. 1700**
Map 18. **Indians of Southeastern Louisiana**
Map 19. **Indians of Northeastern Louisiana**
Map 20. **Indians of Northwestern Louisiana**
Map 21. **Indians of Southern Louisiana**
Map 22. **Immigrant Indians**

Coe, Michael, Dean Snow, and Elizabeth Benson. *Atlas of Ancient America,* 36–41, 48–60. New York: Facts on File, 1968.

Ford, James A. *Analysis of Indian Village Site Collections from Louisiana and Mississippi.* Louisiana Geological Survey Anthropological Study 2. New Orleans: Department of Conservation, 1936.

Garrett, Wilbur F., ed. *Historical Atlas of the United States,* 30–35. Washington, D.C.: National Geographical Society, 1988.

Giraud, Marcel. *A History of French Louisiana.* Vol. I, The Reign of Louis XIV, 1698–1715, 62–79. Translated by Joseph C. Lambert. Baton Rouge: Louisiana State University Press, 1974.

Hodge, Frederick Webb, ed. *Handbook of American Indians North of Mexico.* Bureau of American Ethnology, Smithsonian Institution, Bulletin 30. Washington, D.C.: Government Printing Office, 1907.

Indians of Louisiana. Baton Rouge: Governor's Commission on Indian Affairs, n.d.

John, Elizabeth A. H. *Storms Brewed in Other Men's Worlds: The Confrontation of Indians, Spanish, and French in the Southwest, 1540-1795,* 155–225. College Station: Texas A&M University Press, 1975.

Kagan, Hilde Heun, ed. *The American Heritage Pictorial Atlas of United States History,* 22–27. New York: American Heritage Publishing Company, 1966.

Kniffen, Fred B. *The Indians of Louisiana.* 1945. 2d ed. Gretna, La.: Pelican Publishing Company, 1976.

Kniffen, Fred B., Hiram F. Gregory, and George A. Stokes. *The Historic Indian Tribes of Louisiana from 1542 to the Present.* Baton Rouge: Louisiana State University Press, 1987. Kniffen and Hilliard. *Louisiana,* 104-109.

Kunkel, Paul A. "The Indians of Louisiana about 1700: Their Customs and Manner of Living." *Louisiana Historical Quarterly* 34, no. 3 (July 1951): 175–203.

Native Americans of Louisiana. Baton Rouge: Governor's Commission on Indian Affairs, ca. 1988.

Neuman, Robert W. *An Introduction to Louisiana Archaeology.* Baton Rouge: Louisiana State University Press, 1984.

Newman, Robert W., and Nancy W. Hawkins. *Louisiana Prehistory.* 1982. Rev. printing. Louisiana Archaeological Survey and Antiquities Commission, Anthropological Study 6. Baton Rouge: Department of Culture, Recreation, and Tourism, 1987.

Newton. *Atlas of Louisiana,* 50–54.

Swanton, John R. *Early History of the Creek Indians and Their Neighbors.* Bureau of American Ethnology, Smithsonian Institution, Bulletin 73. Washington, D.C.: Government Printing Office, 1922.

——. *Indian Tribes of the Lower Mississippi Valley and Adjoining Coast of the Gulf of Mexico.* Bureau of American Ethnology, Smithsonian Institution, Bulletin 43. Washington, D.C.: Government Printing Office, 1911.

——. *Indian Tribes of North America.* Bureau of American Ethnology, Smithsonian Institution, Bulletin 145. Washington, D.C.: Government Printing Office, 1951.

——. *Indians of the Southeastern United States.* Bureau of American Ethnology, Smithsonian Institution, Bulletin 137. Washington, D.C.:

Government Printing Office, 1946.

——. *Source Material on the History and Ethnology of the Caddo Indians.* Bureau of American Ethnology, Smithsonian Institution, Bulletin 132. Washington, D.C.: Government Printing Office, 1942.

Webb, Clarence H. *The Poverty Point Culture.* 2d ed. Geoscience and Man, vol. 170. Baton Rouge: School of Geoscience, Louisiana State University, 1982.

——, and Hiram F. Gregory. *The Caddo Indians of Louisiana.* 2d ed. Louisiana Archaeological Survey and Antiquities Commission, Anthropological Study 2. Baton Rouge: Louisiana Department of Culture, Recreation, and Tourism, 1986.

IV. European Contact and Settlement

Map 23. Spanish Claims in the United States to 1763
Map 24. Spanish Explorers in Louisiana

Adams, James Truslow, ed. *Atlas of American History,* plates 4–7. New York: Charles Scribner's Sons, 1943.

Bannon, John Francis. *The Spanish Borderlands Frontier, 1513–1821.* 1963. Reprint. Albuquerque: University of New Mexico Press, 1974.

Folmer, Henry. *Franco-Spanish Rivalry in North America, 1524–1763.* Glendale, Calif.: Arthur H. Clark Company, 1953.

Garrett. *Historical Atlas,* 22–25.

Goetzmann, William H., and Glyndwr Williams. *The Atlas of North American Exploration: From the Norse Voyages to the Race to the Pole,* 22–23, 32–35, 138–39. New York: Prentice-Hall, 1992.

Jackson, Jack, Robert S. Weddle, and Winston De Ville. *Mapping Texas and the Gulf Coast: The Contributions of Saint-Denis, Olivan, and Le Maire.* College Station: Texas A&M University Press, 1990.

John. *Storms Brewed,* 221–25.

Kagan. *Pictorial Atlas,* 32–35, 62.

Loomis, Noel M., and Abraham P. Nasatir. *Pedro Vial and the Roads to Santa Fe,* 316–68. American Exploration and Travel Series. Norman: University of Oklahoma Press, 1967.

Meinig, D.W. *The Shaping of America: A Geographical Perspective on 500 Years of History.* Vol. 1, *Atlantic America, 1493–1800,* 4–17. New Haven: Yale University Press, 1986.

Nostrand, Richard L. "The Spanish Borderlands." In *North America: The Historical Geography of a Changing Continent,* 48–64. Edited by Robert D. Mitchell and Paul A. Graves. Totowa, N.J.: Rowman and Littlefield, 1987.

Sauer, Carl Ortwin. *Sixteenth Century North America: The Land and the People as Seen by the Europeans,* 11–46, 107–95, 269–80. Berkeley: University of California Press, 1971.

U.S. De Soto Expedition Commission. *Final Report of the United States De Soto Expedition Commission.* Washington, D.C.: Government Printing Office, 1939.

Map 25. French Claims in the United States to 1763
Map 26. French Explorers in Louisiana
Map 27. Louisiana under French Rule, 1699–1763

Adams. *Atlas,* plates 31, 33, 36–37, 49.

Allain, Mathé. *"Not Worth a Straw": French Colonial Policy and the Early Years of Louisiana.* Lafayette: Center for Louisiana Studies, University of Southwestern Louisiana, 1988.

Belton, William R., Jr., James M. Cumley, and Loretta R. Pedrami, comps. *Louisiana: An Historical Portrait, 1699-1812.* Louisiana Map Series, no. 5. Baton Rouge: Louisiana State University Graphic Services and Printing for the Department of Geography and Anthropology, 1984.

Caruso, John Anthony. *The Mississippi Valley Frontier: The Age of French Exploration and Settlement,* 149–81, 201–204. Indianapolis: Bobbs-Merrill Company, 1966.

Crouse, Nellis M. *Lemoyne d'Iberville: Soldier of New France,* 155–222. Ithaca: Cornell University Press, 1954.

Davis, Edwin Adams. *Louisiana: A Narrative History,* 37–94. 1961. 3d ed. Baton Rouge: Claitor's Publishing Division, 1971.

Eakin, Sue, and Marie Culbertson. *Louisiana: The Land and Its People,* 80–131. Gretna: Pelican Publishing Company, 1986.

Eccles, William J. *France in America,* 1–208. New York: Harper and Row, 1972.

Folmer. *Franco-Spanish Rivalry.*

Garrett. *Historical Atlas,* 24–25, 80–81.

Giraud. *Reign of Louis XIV.*

Goetzmann and Williams. *Atlas,* 62–65, 88–93.

Harris, Cole. "France in North America." In Mitchell and Graves, *North America,* 65–92.

Iberville, Pierre Le Moyne d'. *Iberville's Gulf Journals.* Translated and edited by Richebourg Gaillard McWilliams. University: University of Alabama Press, 1981.

Jackson, Weddle, and DeVille. *Mapping Texas.*

John. *Storms Brewed,* 155–225.

"Journal du Voyage de M. de Bienville des Taensas au Village des Yataches, par les Terres." In *Découvertes et Etablissements des Français dans l'ouest et dans le sud de l'Amérique Septentrionale, 1614–1698,* 4: 432–443. Edited by Pierre Margry. Paris: Maisonneuve, 1888.

Kagan. *Pictorial Atlas,* 32–33, 36–37, 62.

Meinig. *Atlantic America,* 4–8, 24–28, 193–202.

Murphy, Edmund Robert. *Henry de Tonty: Fur Trader of the Mississippi.* Baltimore: Johns Hopkins University Press, 1941.

Newton. *Atlas of Louisiana,* 71.

Sauer, Carl Ortwin. *Seventeenth Century North America,* 137–192. Berkeley: Turtle Island Foundation for the Netzahauleoyotl Historical Society, 1980.

——. *Sixteenth Century North America,* 47–106, 196–212, 269–80.

Surrey, N. M. Miller. *The Commerce of Louisiana during the French Regime, 1699–1763.* Studies in History, Economics, and Public Law, vol. 71, no. 1. New York: Columbia University, 1916.

Taylor, Joe Gray. *Louisiana: A Bicentennial History,* 3–17. New York: W. W. Norton and Company, for the American Association for State and Local History, 1976.

Thiers, Adolphe. *The Mississippi Bubble: A Memoir of John Law.* Translated and edited by Frank S. Fiske. 1859. Reprint. New York: Greenwood Press, Publishers, 1969.

Wall, Bennett H., ed. *Louisiana: A History,* 18–51. 2d ed. Arlington Heights, Ill. Forum Press, 1990.

Weddle, Robert S. *Wilderness Manhunt: The Spanish Search for La Salle,* 15–23. Austin: University of Texas Press, 1973.

Map 28. Spanish and British Claims after 1763

Map 29. Louisiana under Spanish Rule, 1763–1803

Map 30. Louisiana in the American Revolution

Adams. *Atlas,* plates 47, 49–50, 52–53, 60, 82, 88–89.

Bannon. *Spanish Borderlands Frontier,* 190–205.

Belton et al. *Louisiana . . . Portrait.*

Caughey, John Walton. *Bernardo de Gálvez in Louisiana, 1776–1783.* Gretna: Pelican Publishing Company, 1972.

Davis. *Louisiana,* 97–154.

Eakin and Culbertson. *Louisiana,* 132–75.

Eccles. *France in America,* 209–49.

Folmer. *Franco-Spanish Rivalry.*

Garrett. *Historical Atlas,* 84–89.

Johnson, Cecil. *British West Florida, 1763–1783,* 200–219. Yale Historical Publications, Miscellany, vol. 42. New Haven: Yale University Press, 1943.

Kagan. *Pictorial Atlas,* 76–79, 114–15.

Kinnard, Lawrence, ed. "Spain in the Mississippi Valley, 1765–1794. The Revolutionary Period, 1765–1781." *Annual Report of the American Historical Association for the Year 1945,* Vol. 2. Washington, D.C.: Government Printing Office, 1949.

Marshall, Douglas W., and Howard H. Peckham. *Campaigns of the American Revolution: An Atlas of Manuscript Maps,* 100–01, 124–25. Ann Arbor: University of Michigan Press, 1976.

Meinig. *Atlantic America,* 270–88.

Moore, John Preston. *Revolt in Louisiana: The Spanish Occupation, 1766–1770.* Baton Rouge: Louisiana State University Press, 1976.

Nasatir, Abraham P. *Borderland in Retreat: From Spanish Louisiana to the Far Southwest.* Albuquerque: University of New Mexico Press, 1976.

Newton. *Atlas of Louisiana,* 72.

Taylor. *Louisiana,* 18–41.

Wall. *Louisiana,* 52–87.

V. Political Development

Map 31. The Louisiana Purchase and the Adams-Onís Treaty

Davis. *Louisiana,* 157–64.

De Conde, Alexander. *This Affair of Louisiana.* New York: Charles Scribner's Sons, 1976.

Keats, John. *Eminent Domain: The Louisiana Purchase and the Making of America.* New York: Charterhouse, 1973.

Lyon, E. Wilson. *The Man Who Sold Louisiana: The Career of François Barbé-Marbois.* Norman: University of Oklahoma Press, 1942.

Meinig, D. W. *The Shaping of America: A Geographical Perspective on 500 Years of History.* Vol. 2: *Continental America, 1800–1867,* 4–23. New Haven: Yale University Press, 1993.

Sprague, Marshall. *So Vast, So Beautiful a Land: Louisiana and the Purchase.* Boston: Little, Brown and Company, 1974.

Van Zandt, Franklin K. *Boundaries of the United States and the Several States.* U.S. Geological Survey Bulletin 1212. Washington, D.C.: Government Printing Office, 1966.

Whitaker, Arthur Preston. *The Mississippi Question, 1795–1803: A Study in Trade, Politics, and Diplomacy.* New York: D. Appleton-Century Company, for the American Historical Association, 1934.

Map 32. American Explorers in Louisiana

Cox, Isaac J. "The Exploration of the Louisiana

Frontier, 1803–1806." *Annual Report of the American Historical Association for the Year 1904*, 151–74. Washington, D.C.: Government Printing Office, 1905.

Flores, Dan L., ed. *Jefferson and Southwestern Exploration: The Freeman and Custis Accounts of the Red River Expedition of 1806.* Norman: University of Oklahoma Press, 1984.

——. *Journal of an Indian Trader: Anthony Glass and the Texas Trading Frontier, 1790–1810.* College Station: Texas A&M University Press, 1985.

Goetzmann, William H. *Exploration and Empire: The Explorer and the Scientist in the Winning of the American West.* New York: Alfred A. Knopf, 1966.

Goetzmann and Williams. *Atlas,* 140–41.

Harper, Francis, ed. *The Travels of William Bartram,* 265–77. New Haven: Yale Univ-ersity Press, 1958.

Hollon, W. Eugene. *The Lost Pathfinder: Zebulon Montgomery Pike.* Norman: University of Oklahoma Press, 1949.

Jefferson, Thomas. "Message from the President of the United States Communicating Discoveries Made in Exploring the Missouri, Red River, and Washita by Captains Lewis and Clark, Doctor Sibley, and Mr. Dunbar; with a Statistical Account of the Countries Adjacent, February 19, 1806." *Annals of the Congress of the United States.* 9th Cong., 2d sess., 1806–1807, 1076–1146.

Phillips, Paul C. *The Fur Trade,* 2: 505–506. Norman: University of Oklahoma Press 1961.

Map 33. Land Survey Systems
Map 34. Township-and-Range System

Adams. *Atlas,* plate 87.

Garrett. *Historical Atlas,* 98–99.

Hall, John Whitling. "Louisiana Survey Systems: Their Antecedents, Distribution, and Charac-teristics." Ph.D. diss., Louisiana State University, 1970.

——. "Sitios in Northwest Louisiana." *Journal of the North Louisiana Historical Association* 1, no. 3 (Spring 1970): 1–9.

Kniffen and Hilliard. *Louisiana,* 120–35.

Newton. *Louisiana,* 209–27.

Tobin, Edgar. *Edgar Tobin Aerial Surveys,* map AA-5088. 1962.

Map 35. The West Florida Rebellion

Arthur, Stanley Clisby. *The Story of the West Florida Rebellion.* St. Francisville, La.: St. Francisville Democrat, 1935.

Chambers, Henry E. *West Florida and Its Relation to the Historical Cartography of the United States.* Baltimore: Johns Hopkins University Press, 1898.

Cox, Isaac Joslin. *The West Florida Controversy, 1793–1813: A Study in American Diplomacy.* Baltimore: Johns Hopkins University Press, 1918.

Kagan. *Pictorial Atlas,* 144–45.

Map 36. The War of 1812 and the Battle of New Orleans

Davis. *Louisiana,* 177–86.

Kagan. *Pictorial Atlas,* 138–39.

Owsley, Frank Lawrence, Jr. *Struggle for the Gulf Borderlands: The Creek War and the Battle of New Orleans, 1812–1815.* Gainesville: Univ-ersity Presses of Florida, 1981.

Reilly, Robin. *The British at the Gates: The New Orleans Campaign in the War of 1812.* New York: G. P. Putnam's Sons, 1974.

Taylor. *Louisiana,* 52–56.

Wall. *Louisiana,* 111–17.

Map 37. Louisiana in 1861

Davis. *Louisiana,* 189–240.

Hilliard, Sam Bowers. *Atlas of Antebellum Southern Agriculture.* Baton Rouge: Louisiana State University Press, 1984.

——. "Plantations and the Molding of the Southern Landscape." In *The Making of the American Landscape,* 118–21. Edited by Michael P. Conzen. Boston: Unwin Hyman, 1990.

Taylor. *Louisiana,* 57–86.

Wall. *Louisiana,* 117–77.

Map 38. The Civil War in Louisiana, 1861–1862
Map 39. The Civil War in Louisiana, 1863
Map 40. The Civil War in Louisiana, 1864–1865

Davis. *Louisiana,* 243–60.

Hewitt, Lawrence Lee. *Port Hudson: Confederate Bastion on the Mississippi.* Baton Rouge: Louisiana State University Press, 1987.

Kerby, Robert L. *Kirby Smith's Confederacy: The Trans-Mississippi South, 1863–1865.* New York: Columbia University Press, 1972.

McCrary, Peyton. *Abraham Lincoln and Reconstruction: The Louisiana Experiment,* 19–134. Princeton, N.J.: Princeton University Press, 1978.

Miers, Earl Schenck. *The Web of Victory: Grant at Vicksburg.* 1955. Reprint. Baton Rouge: Louisiana State University Press, 1984.

Raphael, Morris. *The Battle in the Bayou Country.* Detroit: Harlo Press, 1975.

Taylor. *Louisiana,* 87–100.

Wall. *Louisiana,* 178–96.

Winters, John D. *The Civil War in Louisiana.* Baton Rouge: Louisiana State University Press, 1963.

——. "Secession and Civil War in North Louisiana." In *North Louisiana: Essays on the Region and Its History.* Vol. 1, To 1865, 159–93. Edited by B. H. Gilley. Ruston: McGinty Trust Fund Publications, 1984.

Map 41. Counties, 1805
Map 42. Parishes and Parish Seats, 1812
Map 43. Parishes and Parish Seats, 1861
Map 44. Parishes and Parish Seats, 1886
Map 45. Parishes and Parish Seats, 1990

Calhoun. *Louisiana Almanac,* 1992–1993, 171–253.

Calhoun, Robert Dabney. "The Origin and Early Development of County-Parish Government in Louisiana (1805–1845)." *Louisiana Historical Quarterly* 18 (1935): 1–105.

Darby, William. *A Map of the State of Louisiana with Part of the Mississippi Territory.* Philadelphia, 1816.

Garrett. *Historical Atlas,* 107.

Historical Records Survey. *County-Parish Boundaries in Louisiana.* New Orleans: Department of Archives, Louisiana State University, 1939.

Kyser, John S. "The Evolution of Louisiana Parishes in Relation to Population Growth and Movements." Ph.D. diss., Louisiana State University, 1938.

La Fon, Bartholomew. *Carte generale de Territoire D'Orleans. Comprenant aussi la Floride Occidentale et une portion du Territoire du Mississipi.* 1805.

League of Women Voters of Louisiana. *A Citizen's Guide to Louisiana Government.* Washington, D.C.: League of Women Voters Education Fund, 1976.

Louisiana Legislative Council. *The History and the Government of Louisiana,* 252–56, 366–68. Research Study 17. Baton Rouge: Louisiana Legislative Council, 1964.

Rowell, June Savoy. "Parish Government." In *Louisiana Politics: Festival in a Labyrinth,* 143–79 Edited by James Bolner. Baton Rouge: Louisiana State University Press, 1982.

Thorndale, William, and William Dollarhide. *Map Guide to the U.S. Federal Censuses, 1790–1920,* 133–41. Baltimore: Genealogical Publishing Company, 1987.

Map 46. U.S. House of Representatives Districts

Constitution of the United States.

Martis, Kenneth C. *The Historical Atlas of Political Parties in the United States Congress, 1789–1989.* New York: Macmillan Publishing Company, 1989.

——. *The Historical Atlas of United States Congressional Districts, 1789–1983.* New York: Free Press, 1982.

——, and Gregory A. Elmes. *The Historical Atlas of State Power in Congress, 1790–1990.* Edison, N.J.: Congressional Quarterly Books, 1993.

Map 47. Louisiana Supreme Court Districts
Map 48. State House of Representatives Districts
Map 49. State Senate Districts

Calhoun. *Louisiana Almanac, 1992–1993,* 349–412, 454–68.

Labbe, Ronald M. "The Judiciary." In Bolner, *Louisiana Politics,* 89–122.

Landry, David M., and Joseph B. Parker. "The Louisiana Political Culture." In Bolner, *Louisiana Politics,* 89–92.

Louisiana Legislative Council. *History and the Government,* 105–23.

O'Connor, Patrick F. "The Legislature." In Bolner, *Louisiana Politics,* 43–74.

Office of the Clerk, Louisiana State House of Representatives. Unpublished regional maps.

Office of the Secretary, Louisiana State Senate. Unpublished district and regional maps.

VI. Population and Urbanization

Map 50. Population of Territory of Orleans, 1810
Map 51. Population of Louisiana, 1860
Map 52. Population of Louisiana, 1900
Map 53. Population of Louisiana, 1940
Map 54. Population of Louisiana, 1990

Davis. *Louisiana,* 201–205, 294–95, 354–55.

Dodd, Donald B., and Wynelle S. Dodd. *Historical Statistics of the South, 1790–1970,* 26–29. University: University of Alabama Press, 1973.

Hilliard. *Antebellum Southern Agriculture,* 20–34.

Maclachlan, John M., and Joe S. Floyd, Jr. *This Changing South.* Gainesville: University of Florida Press, 1956. 28.

Smith, T. Lynn, and Homer L. Hitt. *The People of Louisiana.* Baton Rouge: Louisiana State University Press, 1952.

U.S. Bureau of the Census. *Censuses of 1810–1990.*

U.S. Bureau of the Census. *Statistical Abstract of*

the United States, 1987, p. 8. 107th ed. Washington, D.C.: Government Printing Office, 1986.

Map 55. African American Population, 1810 and 1860

Map 56. African American Population, 1900 and 1940

Map 57. African American Population, 1990

Davis. *Louisiana,* 80, 115, 132–33, 170, 198, 211–13, 294, 304–305.

Dodd and Dodd. *Historical Statistics,* 26–29.

Dorman, James H. "Persistent Specter: Slave Rebellion in Territorial Louisiana." *Louisiana History* 18 (1977): 389–404.

Ezell, John S. *The South since 1865,* 174–97, 453–78. 2d ed. Norman: University of Oklahoma Press, 1978.

Franklin, John Hope, and Alfred A. Moss, Jr. *From Slavery to Freedom: A History of Negro Americans,* 83–180 (especially 85–86, 108–109, 144), 201–494 (especially 217–218, 237). 6th ed. New York: McGraw-Hill Publishing Company, 1988.

Hair, William Ivy. *Bourbonism and Agrarian Protest: Louisiana Politics, 1877–1900,* 83–106. Baton Rouge: Louisiana State University Press, 1969.

Hall, Gwendolyn Midlo. *Africans in Colonial Louisiana: The Development of Afro-Creole Culture in the Eighteenth Century.* Baton Rouge: Louisiana State University Press, 1992.

Hilliard. *Antebellum Southern Agriculture,* 27–38.

Kurtz, Michael L., and Morgan D. Peoples. *Earl K. Long: The Saga of Uncle Earl and Louisiana Politics.* Baton Rouge: Louisiana State University Press, 1990.

Maclachlan and Floyd. *Changing South.* 52, 142–48.

Malone, Ann Patton. *Sweet Chariot: Slave Family and Household Structure in Nineteenth Century Louisiana.* Chapel Hill: University of North Carolina Press, 1992.

Peoples, Morgan. "Negro Migration from the Lower Mississippi Valley to Kansas, 1879–1880." M.A. thesis, Louisiana State University, 1950.

U.S. Bureau of the Census. Censuses of 1810–1990.

Wall. *Louisiana,* 31–32, 164–76, 204–205, 213–18, 241–45, 346.

Map 58. Cities of Northern Louisiana, 1990

Map 59. Cities of Southwestern Louisiana, 1990

Map 60. Cities of Southeastern Louisiana, 1990

Abington, et al. *Louisiana,* 146–77.

Davis. *Louisiana,* 84–85, 142–44, 202–203, 294–95, 354–55.

Gibson, John L. *Poverty Point: A Culture of the Lower Mississippi Valley.* Anthropological Study 7. Baton Rouge: Louisiana Archaeological Survey and Antiquities Commission, Department of Commerce, Recreation, and Tourism, 1983.

Leeper, Clare D'Artois. *Louisiana Places: A Collection of the Columns from the Baton Rouge Sunday Advocate, 1960–1974.* Baton Rouge: Legacy Publishing Company, 1976. Also supplements published in 1976 and 1977.

Millet, Donald J. "Town Development in Southwest Louisiana, 1865–1900." *Louisiana History* 13, no. 2 (Spring 1972): 139–68.

Newton. *Louisiana,* 89–208.

Webb. *Poverty Point.*

Map 61. La Nouvelle Orléans and Nueva Orleans: New Orleans in the Eighteenth Century

Map 62. New Orleans, 1863

Map 63. New Orleans and Environs, 1990

Map 64. The French Quarter (Vieux Carre), 1990

Abington, et al. *Louisiana,* 154–62.

Baughman, James P. "Gateway to the Americas." In *The Past as Prelude: New Orleans, 1718–1968,* 258–87. Edited by Hodding Carter. New Orleans: Pelican Publishing House, 1968.

Bureau of Government Research. *Plan and Program for the Preservation of the Vieux Carre.* New Orleans: Bureau of Government Research, 1968.

Campbell, Edna F. "New Orleans at the Time of the Louisiana Purchase." *Geographical Review,* 9, no. 3 (July 1921). 414–25.

Capers, Gerald M. *Occupied City: New Orleans under the Federals, 1862–1865.* Lexington: University of Kentucky Press, 1965.

Clark, John G. *New Orleans, 1718–1812: An Economic History.* Baton Rouge: Louisiana State University Press, 1970.

Davis. *Louisiana,* 55–57, 99–107, 122–25, 142–44, 165–66, 178–86, 202–203, 224–27, 238–39, 302–306, 315–16, 354–55.

Federal Writers' Project. *New Orleans City Guide.* Boston: Houghton Mifflin Company, 1938.

Hill, Jackson. "Evolution of an Underwater World." *Louisiana Life,* 10, no. 3 (July–August 1990): 24–31.

Lewis, Peirce F. *New Orleans: The Making of an Urban Landscape.* Cambridge, Mass.: Ballinger Publishing Company, 1976.

Sauder, Robert A., and Teresa Wilkinson. "Preservation Planning and Geographic Change in New Orleans' Vieux Carre." *Urban Geography,* 10, 1 (January–February 1989): 41–61.

Saxon, Lyle. *Fabulous New Orleans,* 73-165. New Orleans: Robert L. Crager and Company, 1947.

Map 65. Baton Rouge, ca. 1855
Map 66. Baton Rouge and Environs, 1990

Abington, et al. *Louisiana,* 163–65.

Carleton, Mark T. *River Capital: An Illustrated History of Baton Rouge.* Pictorial research by M. Stone Miller, Jr. Woodland Hills, Calif.: Windsor Publications, 1981.

City-Parish Planning Commission. *Historic Baton Rouge: A Revised Study of Historic Buildings and Sites.* Baton Rouge: City-Parish Planning Commission, 1975.

Davis. *Louisiana,* 52–141, 203, 286, 364.

Meyers, Rose. *A History of Baton Rouge, 1699-1812.* Baton Rouge: Louisiana State University Press, for the Baton Rouge Bicentennial Corporation, 1976.

Map 67. Shreveport, Bosier City, and Environs, 1990

Abington, et al. *Louisiana,* 165–67.

Carruth, Viola. *Caddo 1000: A History of the Shreveport Area from the Time of the Caddo Indians to the 1970s.* Shreveport: Shreveport Magazine, 1970.

Dorsey, Florence L. *Master of the Mississippi: Henry Shreve and the Conquest of the Mississippi.* Boston: Houghton Mifflin, 1941.

Gallant, Kathryn Powell. "Port on the Red," *River Cities* 2, no. 12 (November 1983) through 4,

no. 7 (July 1985).

Henrici, Holice H. *Shreveport: The Beginnings.* Lafayette, La.: Center for Louisiana Studies, University of Southwestern Louisiana, 1985.

Humphreys, Hubert Davis. "The 'Great Raft' of the Red River," In Gilley, *North Louisiana,* 73–91.

McCall, Edith S. *Conquering the River: Henry Miller Shreve and the Navigation of America's Inland Waterways.* Baton Rouge: Louisiana State University Press, 1984.

Thomson, Bailey, and Patricia L. Meador, *Shreveport: A Photographic Remembrance, 1873-1949.* Baton Rouge: Louisiana State University Press, 1987.

VII. Economic Growth: Transportation

Map 68. Railroads to 1880
Map 69. Railroads, 1915
Map 70. Railroads, 1991

Applied Technology Research Corporation, comp. *Louisiana Railroads, 1991.* Baton Rouge: Department of Transportation and Development, 1991.

Bryant, Keith L., Jr., ed. *Railroads in the Age of Regulation, 1900–1980.* New York: Facts on File, 1988.

Clark, Ira G. *Then Came the Railroads: The Century from Steam to Diesel in the Southwest.* Norman: University of Oklahoma Press, 1958.

Estaville, Lawrence E., Jr. *Confederate Neckties: Louisiana's Railroads during the Civil War.* Ruston: McGinty Publications, 1989.

——. "A Small Contribution: Louisiana's Short Rural Railroads in the Civil War." *Louisiana History* 18 (Winter 1977): 87–103.

——. "A Strategic Railroad: The New Orleans,

Jackson and Great Northern in the Civil War." *Louisiana History* 14 (Spring 1973). 117–36.

Interstate Commerce Commission. *Transport Statistics in the United States for the Year Ended December 31.* Washington, D.C.: Government Printing Office, various years.

Legan, Marshall Scott. "Railroad Sentiment in North Louisiana in the 1850's." *Louisiana History* 17, no. 2 (Spring 1976): 125–42.

Martin, Albro. *Railroads Triumphant: The Growth, Rejection, and Rebirth of a Vital American Force.* New York: Oxford University Press, 1992.

Odom, E. Dale. "The Vicksburg, Shreveport, and Texas: The Fortunes of a Scalawag Railroad." *Southwestern Social Science Quarterly,* 44, no. 3 (December 1963): 277–85.

Poor's Manual of Railroads, various years.

Pritchard, Walter, ed. "A Forgotten Louisiana Engineer: G. W. R. Bayley and His 'History of the Railroads of Louisiana.'" *Louisiana Historical Quarterly* 30, no. 4 (October 1947): 1065–1325.

Reed, Merl E. *New Orleans and the Railroads: The Struggle for Commercial Empire, 1830–1860.* Baton Rouge: Louisiana State University Press, for the Louisiana Historical Association, 1966.

Stover, John F. *Railroads of the South, 1865-1900.* Chapel Hill: University of North Carolina Press, 1955.

Map 71. Modern Transportation Systems and Military Installations, 1990

Casey, Powell A. *Encyclopedia of Forts, Posts, Named Camps and Other Military Installations in Louisiana, 1700-1981.* Baton Rouge: Claitor's Publishing Division, 1983.

Federal Aviation Administration. *Statistical Handbook of Aviation, Calendar Year 1989.* Washington, D.C.: Government Printing Office.

Kniffen and Hilliard. *Louisiana,* 143–45, 149–53.

Newton. *Louisiana,* 300–302.

Prophit, Willie. "Louisiana: From Byways to Highways." *Louisiana Contractor,* January 1980, pp. 8–9, 11–12, 14–15, 17, 19–20, 22–23, 25, 27–28, 30–31, 33; February 1980, pp. 10–11, 13, 15–16, 18–19, 21, 23–25, 27; March 1980, pp. 10–11, 13, 15–16, 18–19, 21, 23.

Wall. *Louisiana,* 274–77.

Map 72. Navigable Waterways, 1890.

Map 73. Selected Navigable Waterways, ca. 1990.

Kniffen and Hilliard. *Louisiana,* 62–63, 143–44, 150–51.

Louisiana Department of Transportation and Development. *Louisiana's Water Resources.* Baton Rouge: Department of Transportation and Development, 1978.

McCall. *Conquering the River.*

Meyer, Balthasar Henry. *History of Transportation in the United States before 1860.* Washington, D.C.: Carnegie Institution of Washington, 1917.

Schweitzer, James P. *Waterborne: Louisiana's Ports and Waterways.* Baton Rouge: Louisiana Sea Grant College Program, Louisiana State University Center for Wetland Resources, 1984.

Tanner, H.S. *A New Map of Louisiana with Its Canals, Roads, and Distances from Place to Place along the Stage and Steam Boat Routes.* Washington, D.C.: Government Printing Office, 1833.

U.S. Army, Corps of Engineers, Lower Mississippi Valley Division. *Water Resources Development in Louisiana.* Washington, D.C.: Government Printing Office, 1981.

U.S. Army, Corps of Engineers. *Waterborne Commerce of the United States.* Washington, D.C.: Government Printing Office, 1950, 1960, 1970, 1986.

VIII. Economic Growth: Agriculture

General Sources

Davis. *Louisiana.*

Dodd and Dodd. *Historical Statistics,* 26–29.

Eakin and Culbertson. *Louisiana.*

Fielder, Lonnie L., Jr. *Changes in Louisiana Agriculture, by Parishes and by Type of Farming Areas, with Projections for 1990.* Agricultural Economics and Agribusiness Information Series, no. 51. Baton Rouge: Louisiana Agricultural Experiment Station, 1981.

———; Steve S. Kelly; and Bergen A. Nelson. *Agricultural Statistics and Prices for Louisiana, 1909–1985.* D.A.E. Research Report 659. Baton Rouge: Department of Agricultural Economics and Agribusiness, Louisiana Experiment Station, 1986.

Fite, Gilbert C. *Cotton Fields No More: Southern Agriculture, 1865–1980.* Lexington: University Press of Kentucky, 1984.

Hilliard. *Antebellum Southern Agriculture.*

Kirby, Jack Temple. *Rural Worlds Lost: The American South, 1920–1960.* Baton Rouge: Louisiana State University Press, 1987.

Kniffen and Hilliard. *Louisiana.*

Louisiana Cooperative Extension Service. *Louisiana Summary: Agriculture and Natural Resources.* Baton Rouge: Louisiana State University Agricultural Center, 1985–1989.

———. *Outlook: Louisiana's Agriculture.* Baton Rouge: Louisiana State University Agricultural Center, 1987, 1989, and 1990.

Newton. *Louisiana,* 243–61, 268–75.

U.S. Bureau of the Census. *Census of Agriculture.*

Wall. *Louisiana.*

Zachetmayr, Monika, Quentin Jenkins and Michael McGettigan. *Changing Structure of Agriculture in Louisiana Social Areas, 1940–1978.* Bulletin 743. Baton Rouge: Louisiana Agricultural Experiment Station, 1983.

Map 78. Sugar Production, 1850, 1910, 1985–1989

Becnel, Thomas. *Labor, Church, and the Sugar Establishment: Louisiana, 1887–1976.* Baton Rouge: Louisiana State University Press, 1980.

Heitmann, John Alfred. *The Modernization of the Louisiana Sugar Industry, 1830–1910.* Baton Rouge: Louisiana State University Press, 1987.

Hilliard, Sam B. "Site Characteristics and Spatial Stability of the Louisiana Sugarcane Industry." *Agricultural History* 53, no. 1 (January 1979): 254–69.

Sitterson, J. Carlyle. *Sugar Country: The Cane Sugar Industry in the South, 1753–1950,* 5, 13–16, 23–30, 343–44. Lexington: University of Kentucky Press, 1953.

Map 79. Rice Production, 1850, 1910, 1985–1989

Daniel, Pete. *Breaking the Land: The Transformation of Cotton, Tobacco, and Rice Cultures since 1880.* 1985. 39–61, 134–51, 215–36, 271–89. Urbana: University of Illinois Press.

Dethloff, Henry C. *A History of the American Rice Industry, 1685–1985,* 22, 30, 60–109. College Station: Texas A&M University Press, 1988.

Map 80. Forest Production, 1985–1989

Caldwell, John Michael. "The Forest of the Vintage: A Geography of Industrial Lumbering in North Central Louisiana, 1890–1920." M.A. thesis, University of Oklahoma, 1975.

Clark. *Greening of the South.*

Dawson, Lyndon E., Jr., et al. "The Louisiana Timber Industry: Marketing Channels and Pricing Practices." *Louisiana Economy* 14, no. 4 (May 1981): 5.

Kerr, Ed. "Forestry in Louisiana." *Forests and People* 3 (first quarter 1963; Golden Anniversary Issue): 11–40.

Maki, Wilbur R., Con H. Schallau, Bennett B. Foster, and Clair H. Redmond. *Louisiana's Forest Products Industry: Performance and Contribution to the State's Economy, 1970 to 1980.* Research Paper PNW–RP–371. Washington, D.C.: U.S. Forest Service, 1986.

Williams, Fred E. *Artificial Forest Regeneration in Louisiana: A Comparison with Other Southern States.* Agricultural Economics and Agribusiness, no. 54. Baton Rouge: Louisiana Agricultural Experiment Station, 1985.

Map 81. Cotton Production, 1850, 1910, 1985–1989

Daniel. *Breaking the Land,* 3–22, 91–109, 155–83, 239–55.

Hilliard. "Plantations." In Conzen, *Making of the American Landscape,* 118–20.

Woodman, Harold D. *King Cotton and His Retainers: Financing and Marketing the Cotton Crop of the South, 1800–1925.* Lexington: University of Kentucky Press, 1968.

Map 82. Assorted Feed Grain and Soybean Production, 1985–1989

Fornari, Harry D. "The Big Change: Cotton to Soybeans" *Agricultural History* 53, no. I (January 1979). 245–53.

Hardeman, Nicholas P. *Shucks, Shocks, and Hominy Blocks: Corn as a Way of Life in Pioneer America.* Baton Rouge: Louisiana State University Press, 1981.

Prunty, Merle C., Jr. "Soybeans in the Lower Mississippi Valley." *Economic Geography* 26 (1950): 301–14.

Map 83. Marine and Freshwater Fisheries Production, 1985–1989

U.S. Department of Commerce, National Oceanic and Atmospheric Administration, National Marine Fisheries Service. *Fisheries of the United States.* Washington, D.C.: Government Printing Office, various years.

U.S. Department of Commerce, National Oceanic and Atmospheric Administration, National Marine Fisheries Service. *Fishery Statistics of the United States.* Washington, D.C.: Government Printing Office, various years.

U.S. Department of Commerce, National Oceanic and Atmospheric Administration, National Marine Fisheries Service. Unpublished statistical data.

Zapata, H. O., and L. E. Dellenbarger. "Trends in the Louisiana Seafood Industry." *Louisiana Rural Economis* 51, no. 3 (August 1989): 10–13.

Map 84. Cattle and Calves and Milk Production, 1985–1989

Heagler, Arthur M., and Wayne M. Gauthier. *Twenty-five Years of Changes in the Louisiana Dairy Industry.* Department of Agricultural Economics Research Report 597. Baton Rouge: Department of Agricultural Economics and Agribusiness, Louisiana State University, 1982.

Jordan, Terry G. *Trails to Texas: Southern Roots of Western Cattle Ranching,* 47–49. Lincoln: University of Nebraska Press, 1981.

Map 86. Farm Tenancy, 1880, 1910, 1940, and 1987

Daniel, Pete. *The Shadow of Slavery: Peonage in the South, 1901–1969.* Urbana: University of Illinois Press, 1972.

Hilliard. "Plantations." In Conzen, *Making of the American Landscape,* 122–26.

Schweninger, Loren. "A Vanishing Breed: Black Farm Owners in the South, 1651–1982." *Agricultural History* 61, no. 3 (Summer 1989): 41–60.

Taylor, Joe Gray. *Louisiana Reconstructed, 1863–1877,* 364–406. Baton Rouge: Louisiana State University Press, 1974.

Wall. *Louisiana,* 205–206, 234–36.

Wright, Gavin. *Old South, New South: The Revolutions in the Southern Economy since the Civil War,* 84–115. New York: Basic Books, 1986.

IX. Economic Growth:
Industry and Commerce and Income

General Sources

Abington, et al. *Louisiana*, 106–35.

Ammer, Christine, and Dean S. Ammer. *Dictionary of Business and Economics*. Rev. ed. New York: Free Press, 1984.

Davis. *Louisiana*.

Dellenbarger, Ann Z., and Forrest A. Deseran. *Working in Louisiana: A Profile of the State's Labor Market Areas*. Bulletin 819. Baton Rouge: Louisiana Agricultural Experiment Station, 1989.

Dodd and Dodd. *Historical Statistics*, 26–29.

Hilliard. *Antebellum Southern Agriculture*.

Johnson, David B., and Robert Edwin Sappenfield. "Economies in Change: Employment Shifts among Basic Industries in Louisiana and Neighboring States." *Louisiana Economic Trends*. Baton Rouge: Division of Research and Development, College of Business Administration, Louisiana State University, 1985.

Kniffen and Hilliard. *Louisiana*. 171–77, 186–91.

Louisiana Department of Labor. Research and Statistics Unit. *Louisiana Employment and Wages*. Baton Rouge, various years.

Louisiana State Planning Office, Division of Administration. *The Louisiana Economy: FY 1988 Edition*. Baton Rouge, 1988.

Newton. *Louisiana*, 275–87.

Wall. *Louisiana*, 306–309, 368, 379.

Map 87. Manufacturing, 1985–1989

U.S. Department of Commerce, Bureau of the Census, *Census of Manufactures*. 1977, 1982, and 1987.

Map 88. Wholesale and Retail Trade, 1985–1989

U.S. Department of Commerce, Bureau of the Census, *Census of Wholesale Trade*. 1982 and 1987.

U.S. Department of Commerce, Bureau of the Census, *Census of Retail Trade*. 1982 and 1987.

Map 89. Service and Transportation Industries, 1985–1989

U.S. Department of Commerce, Bureau of the Census, *Census of Service Industries*. 1982 and 1987.

U.S. Department of Commerce, Bureau of the Census, *Census of Transportation*. 1982 and 1987.

Map 90. Mining and Construction Industries, 1985–1989.

U.S. Department of Commerce, Bureau of the Census, *Census of Construction Industries*. 1982 and 1987.

U.S. Department of Commerce, Bureau of the Census, *Census of Mineral Industries*. 1982 and 1987.

Map 91. Finance, Insurance, Real Estate, and Public Administration, 1985–1989

U.S. Department of Commerce, Bureau of the Census, *Census of Governments*. 1977, 1982, and 1987.

Map 92. Unemployment, 1986–1990

Louisiana Department of Labor, Research and Statistics. *Louisiana Labor Force Data*. Baton Rouge, various years.

Maruggi, Vincent, ed. *1990 Statistical Abstract of Louisiana*. 8th ed. New Orleans: Division of Business and Economic Research, College of Business Administration, University of New Orleans, 1990.

Map 93. Per Capital Personal Income and Percentage of Population Sixty–five or Older

U.S. Department of Commerce, Bureau of Economic Analysis. *Local Area Personal Income, 1984–1989*.

U.S. Department of Commerce, Bureau of the Census, *Census of Population and Housing, 1990*.

X. Cultural Growth

Map 94. Selected Inactive Colleges and Academies
Map 95. Active Colleges and Universities

American Council on Education. *American Universities and Colleges*. 13th ed. New York: Walter de Gruyter, 1987.

Calhoun. *Louisiana Almanac, 1992–1993*, 338–49.

Cline, Rodney. *Pioneer Leaders and Early Institutions in Louisiana Education*. Baton Rouge: Claitor's Publishing Division, 1969.

Fay, Edwin Whitfield. *The History of Education in Louisiana*. U.S. Bureau of Education Circular of Information no. 1, 1898. Washington, D.C.: Government Printing Office, 1898.

Fletcher, Joel L. *Louisiana Education Since Colonial Days*. Lafayette: Southwestern Louisiana Institute, n.d.

Louisiana Department of Education. Unpublished data.

Mobley, James William. "The Academy Movement in Louisiana." *Louisiana Historical Quarterly* 30, no. 3 (July 1947).

Riley, Martin Luther. "The Development of Education in Louisiana Prior to Statehood." *Louisiana Historical Quarterly* 19, no. 3 (July 1936): 595–634.

Straughn, Charles T., II, and Barbarasue Lovejoy Straughn. *Lovejoy's College Guide*. 19th ed. New York: Monarch Press, 1989.

Suarez, Raleigh A. "Chronicle of a Failure: Public Education in Antebellum Louisiana." *Louisiana History* 12, no. 2 (Spring 1971). 109–22.

Wall. *Louisiana,* 154–56, 203–204, 269–72, 309–11, 348–50, 376–77, 382–83.

Map 96. Museums, Historic Sites, Libraries, and Archives

Louisiana Association of Museums, et al. *Directory of Louisiana Museums and Historic Sites*. Baton Rouge: Louisiana Association of Museums, 1988.

Stallard, Kathryn E., ed. *Guide to Archival and Manuscript Repositories in the American Southwest*. Society of Southwest Archivists, 1993. Alfred E. Lemmon provided the Louisiana entries.

Map 97. Folk/Culture Regions

Bertrand, Alvin L. *The Many Louisianas: Rural Social Areas and Culture Islands*. Louisiana Agricultural Experiment Station Bulletin 496, 1955.

Del Sesto, S. L., and J. L. Gibson, eds. *The Culture of Acadiana: Tradition and Change in South Louisiana*. Lafayette: University of Southwestern Louisiana, 1975.

Estaville, Lawrence. "The Louisiana French Culture Region: Geographic Morphologies in the Nineteenth Century." Ph.D. diss., University of Oklahoma, 1984.

Kniffen, Fred B. "Folk Housing: Key to Diffusion." *Annals of the Association of American Geographers* 55 (1965): 549–77.

———."Louisiana House Types." *Annals of the Association of American Geographers* 26 (1936): 179–93.

———. "The Physiognomy of Rural Louisiana." *Louisiana History* 4, no. 4 (Fall 1963). 291–

99.

Newton. *Atlas,* 70–95.

———. *Louisiana,* 89–242, passim.

Spitzer, Nicholas R., ed. *Louisiana Folklife: A Guide to the State*. Baton Rouge: Moran Colorgraphic for Louisiana Folklife Program, Office of Cultural Development, Department of Culture, Recreation, and Tourism, 1985.

Map 98. Fairs, Festivals, and Other Events
Map 99. Tourism

Calhoun. *Louisiana Almanac,* 1992–1993. 24–76.

Clark, Thomas D., ed. *Travels in the New South: A Bibliography*. Two vols. Norman: University of Oklahoma Press, 1962.

———. *Travels in the Old South: A Bibliography*. Three vols. Norman: University of Oklahoma Press, 1956.

Feifer, Maxine. *Tourism in History: From Imperial Rome to the Present*. New York: Stein and Day, 1985.

Jakle, John A. *The Tourist: Travel in Twentieth-Century North America*. Lincoln: University of Nebraska Press, 1985.

U.S. Travel Data Center. *The Economic Impact of Travel on Louisiana Parishes, 1990–1989*. 1992.

Numbers in this index refer to maps, not pages. Those in bold indicate that the item will be found on the map.

A&M College (New Orleans), **94**
Abbeville, **37**, **43–45**, **59**, **69**, **70**, **98**
Abita Springs, **60**
Academies, 94, **94**
Acadia College (Crowley), **94**
Acadia College (Lake Charles), **94**
Acadia County, 41, **41**
Acadia Parish, 44, **44**, 45, **45**, **52–54**, **56–57**, **74–76**, 77, **77–78**, 79, **79–81**, 82, **82–87**, 88, **88–93**, **98–99**
Acadian Coast, 41
Acadian Festival, **98**
Acadiana Railway, **70**
Acadians, 29, 50, 97, 99
Acolapissa Indians, 17, **17**, 18, **18**, 20
Adai Indians, 17, **17**, 20, **20**
Adams, John Quincy, 31
Adams-Onís Treaty (1819), 31, **31**
Addis, **60**, **70**
African Americans, 27, 37, 46, 48, 50–55, **55**, 56, **56**, 57, **57**, 78, 80, 86, 94, 97. *See also* Free blacks; Slaves and slavery
Agglomerated settlements, 58–60
Agriculture, 27, 29, 37, 56–57, 74–86, **74–86**, 88
Aguayo, Marqués de San Miguel de, 24, **24**
Air masses, 15
Airline Highway, 66
Airports, 63, 66–67, 71, **71**
Alabama, **1**, 51
Alabama Indians, 22, **22**
Alarcón, Martín de, 24, **24**
Albany, **60**
Alexandria, **2**, 4, 19, **37**, 39, **39**, 40, **40**, **43–45**, 51–54, 59, **59**, 68, **68**,

69, **69**, **70**, 71, **72**, **92**, **94**, 95, **95**, **96**, **98**
Alexandria and Cheneyville Railroad, 68
Alexandria and Western Railroad, **69**
Alfalfa, 77
Algiers, **37**, 51, **62–63**, 68, **68**
Allemands, **60**
Allen, Henry Watkins, 40, 44
Allen, Oscar K., 71
Allen Parish, 44–45, **45**, **53–54**, **56–57**, **74–92**, 93, **93**, **98–99**
Allen Parish Fair, **98**
Alligator Festival, **98**
Allons aux Avoyelles Tour of Homes, **98**
Alluvial processes, 11
Alphenia Landing mound site, **16**
Alsen, **66**
Alto, **96**
Altus Museum, **96**
Alyllon, Lucas Vásquez de, 23
Amelia, **59**
American Rectangular Survey System, 33, **33–34**
American Revolution, 28, 30, **30**
Amistad Research Center, **96**
Amite, **44–45**, **60**, **70**, **94**, **98**
Amite Collegiate Institute, **94**
Amite Oyster Day, **98**
Amite River, 6, **6**, 33
Ammons mound site, **16**
Amtrak, 70, **70**
Anacoco, **59**
Anacoco Lake, **6**
Andouille Festival, **98**
Angie, **60**
Anglo-American Convention (1818), 31
Angola, **98**
Angola Prison Farm, 7
Angola Prison Rodeo, **98**

Animal feed, 73
Apache Indians, 22, **22**
Apalachee Indians, 19, 22, **22**
Apalachicola River, 35
Apportionment, 46–49
Aquaculture, 83
Aquarium of the Americas, 64, **64**
Arabi, **60**, 63
Arcadia, 4, **37**, **45**, **58**, **94**
Arcadia Male and Female Academy/College, **94**
Archeozoic era, 9
Archives and manuscript collections, 96, **96**
Arizona (city), **94**
Arizona Academy, **94**
Arizona Rural Life Museum, **96**
Arkansas, **1**, 50–54, 67, 93, **93**
Arkansas, Louisiana and Gulf Railroad, **69**
Arkansas and Louisiana Missouri Railroad, **70**
Arkansas River, 31
Arkansas Southern Railroad, 69
Arnaudville, **59**, 73
Arpent, 33, **33**
Art and Folk Festival, **98**
Ascension Parish, 18, 42, **42–44**, 45, **45**, **50–53**, 54, **54–57**, 66, **74–86**, 87, **87–93**, **98–99**
Ashland, **58**
Asinai Indians, 26
Assumption Parish, 15, 42, **42–44**, 45, **45**, **50–57**, **74–77**, 78, **78–93**, **98–99**
Atakapa Indians, 17, **17**, 19, **19**, 21, **21**
Atakapan linguistic group, 17, **17**
Atchafalaya Basin, 3, 5, **5**, 11, 39
Atchafalaya Bay, **6**
Atchafalaya River, 6, **6**, 17, **19**, 33, **33**, 39, **72–73**

Atchafalaya Wilderness Center, **8**
Atchison, Topeka and Santa Fe Railroad, **70**
Athens, **37**, **58**
Atlanta, **58**, **94**
Atlanta Male and Female Institute, **94**
Attakapas College, **94**
Attakapas County, 41, **41**
Attakapas Parish, 42
Audubon Pilgrimage, **98**
Audubon State Commemorative Area, **8**
Automobile, 70–71, 99
Avery Island, 10, **70**
Avery Island mound site, **16**
Aviation, 70–71
Avondale, **60**
Avoyel Indians, 17, **17**, 19, **19**
Avoyelles Academy, **94**
Avoyelles Parish, 2, 22, 42, **42–44**, 45, **45**, **50–53**, 54, **54–57**, **74–77**, 78, **78–81**, 82, **82–92**, 93, **93**, **98–99**
Avoyelles settlements, 41
Azalea Trail, **98**

Bailey, Joseph, 40
Bailey's Dam, 40
Baker, **60**, 66
Baker vs. Carr, 46, 48
Baldwin, **59**, **70**
Balize, 72
Balize Delta, 12, **12**
Ball, **59**
Balloon Festival and Air Show, **98**
Banks, Nathaniel P., 38–40, 62
Banks and banking, 91, **91**
Baptist Christian College, 95, **95**
Barataria, **60**
Barataria Basin, **11**
Barataria Bay, **6**, 36
Barataria Bay Waterway, 73

Barbé-Marbois, François, 31
Barksdale Air Force Base, 67, **67**, **71**
Barley, **82**
Barancas Coloradas, 30
Bartram, William, 32, **32**, 99
Base Line, 34, **34**
Basile, **59**, **98**
Basin Street, 61
Baskins, **58**
Bastrop, Felipe Enrique Neri, Baron de, 29
Bastrop, **2**, 4, **37**, **43–45**, **58**, **69–70**, **94**, **96**, **98**
Bastrop Hills, 5, **5**
Bastrop Masonic Female Institute, **94**
Bateaux, 72
Baton Rouge, **2**, 4, 10, 11, **22**, 27, **27**, 29, 30, **30**, 32, **32**, 35, **37**, 38, **38**, **39**, **42–45**, 51–54, 60, 65, **65**, 66, **66**, 68, **68**, 69, **69**, 70, 71, 72, 73, **73**, **92**, **94**, 95, **95**, **96**, **98**
Baton Rouge, Grosse Tete and Opelousas Railroad, 68, **68**
Baton Rouge, Hammond and Eastern Railroad, **69**
Baton Rouge Academy, **94**
Baton Rouge Collegiate Institute, **94**
Battles, 18; Bayou Borbeau, **39**; Bisland (Bethel's Place), 39, **39**; Burnt Corn, 36; Champion's Hill, 39, **39**; Cox's Plantation, 39, **39**; Donaldsonville, 39, **39**; Fordoche, 39, **39**; Grand Coteau, 39; Horseshoe Bend, 36, **36**; Labadieville, 38, **38**; Lafourche Crossing, 39; Lake Borgne, 36, **36**; Mansfield, 40, **40**; Mansura, 40, **40**; Marksville, 40, **40**; Monnett's Ferry, 40, **40**; Nerson's Wood (Irish Bend), 39, **39**; New Orleans, 36, **36**; Norwood's Plantation, 40, **40**; Plains Store,

39, **39**; Pleasant Hill, 40, **40**; Thompson's Hill, 39, **39**; Wilson's Landing, 40, **40**.
Bawcomville, **58**
Bay Marchand Field, 10
Bayou Anacoco, **6**
Bayou Bartholomew, 6, **6, 72**
Bayou Bienvenu, 36
Bayou Blue, **6**
Bayou Boeuf, **6**, 19, 68
Bayou Boeuf settlements, 41
Bayou Cane, **60**
Bayou Castine, 18
Bayou Cocodrie, **6**
Bayou D'Arbonne, 6, **6**, 72, **72**
Bayou de L'Outre, 6, **6**
Bayou Des Cannes, **6, 73**
Bayou Dorcheat, 6, **6**
Bayou Folk Museum, **96**
Bayou Gentilly, **60**
Bayou Goula, **37**, 39, **39**, 68, **68**
Bayou Goula mound site, **16**
Bayou Grosse Tete, 68
Bayou Labranche, 68
Bayou Lacombe, 73
Bayou Lacombe Crab Festival, **98**
Bayou Lafourche, 6, **6**, 16–17, 21, **29**, 33, **33**, 38, **38**, 72, **72–73**
Bayou Lafourche Antique Show and Sale, **98**
Bayou Macon, 6, **6**, 16, **72**
Bayou Manchac, 6, **6**, 26, **26, 27**, 28, 30, 32–33, 65
Bayou Nezpique, **6, 73**
Bayou Pierre, 6, **6**
Bayou Plaquemine, **73**
Bayou Plaquemine Brule, **6**
Bayou Queue de Tortue, **6**
Bayou Ramble Antique Show and Sale, **98**
Bayou Robert settlements, 41
Bayou St. John, 18, 61, **61**
Bayou Sara, 6, **6, 29**, 35, **35, 37**, 68, **68**

Bayou Segnette State Park, **8**
Bayou Taensa, 19
Bayou Tchoupitoulas, **61**
Bayou Teche, 6, **6**, 9, 17, 27, **27**, 29, 33, **33**, 39, **39**, 40, 50, 72, **72–73**
Bayou Teche basin, **11**
Bayou Terrebonne, 72, **72**
Bayou Vermilion, 78
Bayou Vista, **59**
Bayougoula Indians, 17, **17**, 18, **18**, 19, 21
Beans, 74, 77
Beauregard, Pierre G. T., 44
Beauregard–Keyes House, **96**
Beauregard Parish, 44, 45, **45, 53–54, 56–57, 74–79**, 80, **80–93, 98–99**
Beauregard Parish Fair, **98**
Beauregard Town (Baton Rouge), 65, **65**
Beef. See cattle
Belcher, **58**
Belcher Mound site, **16**
Belle Chasse, **60, 63, 70**
Bellevue, **37, 43–44, 94**
Bellevue mound site, **16**
Bellevue Seminary, **94**
Bend, **70**
Benton, **45, 58**
Bernice, **2**, 4, **58**, 69, **69, 98**
Berwick City, **37, 39, 59**
Berwick's Bay, 68
Bethel's Place, 39
Bienville, Jean Baptiste Le Moyne, Sieur de, 20, 26, **26**, 27, 43, 55, 61, 78
Bienville, **58**
Bienville Parish, 4, 5, 9, 43, **43, 44, 44**, 45, **45, 51–57, 74–79**, 80, **80–92**, 93, **93, 98–99**
Big Creek, **6**
Big Cypress State Preservation Area, **8**
Biggs mound site, **16**
Billy Landing mound site, **16**
Biloxi, 27

Biloxi Bay, 26
Biloxi Indians, 22, **22**
Bisland, 39
Black Code, 55
Black Lake, 6, **6**
Black Lake Bayou, 6, **6**
Black River, 6, **6**, 41, 72, **72–73**
Blacks. See African Americans
Blanchard, **58**
Blessing of the Shrimp Fleet, **98**
Blueberries, 77
Blueberry Festival, **98**
Bluestem grass, 7
Blufflands, 3, **3**
Bodcau Lake, 6, **6**
Boeuf River, 6, **6, 72–73**
Bogalusa, **2**, 4, 53, **60, 69–70**, 91, **96, 98**
Bogalusa Indian and Pioneer Museum, **96**
Bogue Chitto River, 6, **6**
Bogue Falaya Park, **8**
Bohemia, **69**
Boll weevil, 81
Bonfires on the Levee, **98**
Bonita, **58**
Bonnet Carre Church, **72**
Bonnet Carre Floodway, 6, **6**
Bonnet Carre Point, **42**
Boothville, **60**
Bordelon, Hypolite, Home, **96**
Bore, Etienne de, 78
Bossier, Pierre Evariste, 43
Bossier City, 54, 58, **58**, 67, **67**, 85, 95, **95, 98**
Bossier City Arts and Crafts Festival, **98**
Bossier Parish, 43, **43–44**, 45, **45, 51–53**, 54, **54–57**, 67, **74–84**, 85, **85–93, 98–99**
Bossier Parish Community College, **67**, 95, **95**
Boudin Festival, **98**
Boundaries, 1, 2, 10, 23, **23**, 25, **25**,

27, 28, **28–30**, 31, **31, 35**, 41, **41**, 42, **42**, 43, **43**, 44, **44–49, 97, 97**
Bourbons, 44, 56
Boutte, **60**
Boyce, 19, **59**
Brashear City (Morgan City), **37**, 38–39, **39**, 68
Breaux Bridge, **37, 59, 98**
Breckenridge, John C., 38
Breton Sound, **6, 11**
Bridge City, **60, 63, 98**
Brimstone Museum, **96**
Broadmoor, **59**
Broussard, **59, 98**
Brown vs. Board of Education, 57, 95
Brownfields, **60**
Brownsville, **58**
Brusly, **60, 66, 94**
Bryceland, **58**
Buffalofish, 83
Bull Bayou Field, 10
Bullfish, **83**
Bullheads, **83**
Bundick Creek, **6**
Bunkie, **59, 98**
Buras, **60, 69**
Burial mounds, 16
Burr's Ferry, 37
Butler, Benjamin, 38

Cabeza de Vaca, Alvar Nuñez, 24, **24**
Cabildo, 29, 64
Cadastral survey, 33
Caddo Field, 10
Caddo Indians, 20, **20**, 43
Caddo Lake, 6, **6**, 20
Caddo Land Cession, **20**
Caddo Parish, 15, 43, **43–44**, 45, **45, 51**, 52, **52**, 53, **53**, 54, **54–56**, 57, **57**, 67, **74–83**, 84, **84**, 85, **85–86**, 87, **87**, 88, **88–92**, 93, **93, 98–99**
Caddo-Pine Island Oil and Historical

Society, **96**
Caddo Treaty (1835), 20
Caddoan Indian culture, 16
Caddoan linguistic group, 17, **17**, 20
Caillou Bay, **6**
Cajuns. See Acadians
Cajun Country, **97, 99**
Calcasieu Lake, 6, **6**
Calcasieu Parish, 43, **43**, 44, **44**, 45, **45, 51–53**, 54, **54–57, 74–83**, 84, **84–86**, 87, **87**, 88, **88–93, 98–99**
Calcasieu River, 5, **5**, 6, **6**, 73, **73**
Calcasieu River basin, **11**
Caldwell, Matthew, 43
Caldwell Parish, 43, **43–44**, 45, **45, 51–57**, 58, **74–93, 98–99**
Calvin, **58**
Camellia Show, **98**
Cameron, Robert Alexander, 44
Cameron, **44–45, 98**
Cameron Parish, 13, 44, **44**, 45, **45**, 52, **52**, 53, **53–54, 56–57**, 59, **74–75**, 76, **76–82**, 83, **83**, 84, **84–93, 98–99**
Camp Moore, **8**, 38
Campti, **37, 58**
Canal Street, 62, 64
Canary Islanders. *See* Isleños
Cane River, **6**
Cankton, **59**
Canton, Miss., 68
Cantrels, **72**
Cape Verde Islands, 23
Carencro, **59**
Carlyss, **59**
Carondelet, Francisco Luis Hector, Baron de, 29, 61
Carroll, Charles, 43
Carroll Parish, 43, **43**, 44, **44**, 51, 55
Carrollton, **37, 43**, 62, **62**, 68
Cartier, Jacques, 25
Carville, **60**
Casa Calvo, Sebastian Calvo de la Puerta y O'Farril, Marquis de, 29

Castor, **58**
Castor Creek, **6**
Catahoula Basin, **11**
Catahoula Heritage Festival, **98**
Catahoula Lake, 6, **6**
Catahoula Parish, 16, 42, **42**, 43, **43**, 44, **44**, 45, **45**, **50–57**, **74–81**, 82, **82–92**, 93, **93**, **98–99**
Catahoula settlements, 41
Catfish, 83, **83**
Catfish Festival, **98**
Catholic Diocesan Archives, **96**
Cattle, 76, 84, **84**
Cattle Festival, **98**
Cecilia, **59**
Cenozoic era, 9, **9**
Census of Agriculture, 74
Census of Construction Industries, 90
Census of Manufacturing, 87
Census of Mining, 90
Census of Retail Trade, 88
Census of Service Industries, 89
Census of Transportation, 89
Census of Wholesale Trade, 88
Census-designated places, 58–60
Centenary College of Louisiana, **67**, 94, **94**, 95, **95**, 96
Centenary State Commemorative Area, **8**, 96
Centerville, 39, **44**
Central Louisiana Gulf Railroad, **70**
Central places, 58–60
Chackbay, **60**, **98**
Chalmette, **45**, 60, **60**, **63**, 95, **95**, 96, **98**
Chalmette Battlefield, 8, 36
Chalmette Plantation, 36
Champion's Hill, 39
Champlain, Samuel de, 25
Chandeleur Islands, 2, 12
Chandeleur Sound, **6**
Charenton, **59**

Chataignier, **59**
Chatham, **58**
Chatot Indians, 22, **22**
Chauvin, **60**, **98**
Chawasha Indians, 17, **17**, 21, **21**
Chemin-a-Haut State Park, **8**
Cheneyville, **37**, **59**, 68
Cheniere Brake, **6**
Cheniere-au-Tigre State Preser-vation Area, **8**
Cheniers, 3, 5, 6, 12
Chicago, Rock Island and Pacific Railroad, 69, **69**, 70
Chicago, St. Louis and New Orleans Railroad, **68–69**
Chickasaw Indians, 19, **19**, 20–21
Chickens. *See* Poultry
Chicot State Park, **8**
Chifoncte District, 35
Chitimacha Indians, 17, **17**, 19, 21, **21**, 22
Chitimachan linguistic group, 17, **17**
Choctaw Indians, 17, 19, **19**, 22, 22
Choctaw language, 65
Choudrant, **58**
Choupique, 83
Christmas, 98, **98**
Church Point, **59**
Churupa Place mound site, **16**
Cities, **2**, 58, **58**, 59, **59**, 60, **60**, 61, **61**, 62, **62**, 63, **63**, 64, **64**, 65, **65**, 66, **66**, 67, **67**, 91
Civil Rights Movement, 57
Civil War, 38, **38**, 39, **39**, 40, **40**, 55, 62, **62**, 66–68, 72
Claiborne, William C. C., 35–36, 43
Claiborne, **42**, 58
Claiborne Group, **9**
Claiborne Parish, 43, **43**, 44, **44**, 45, **45**, **51–57**, **74–92**, 93, **93**, **98–99**
Claiborne Parish Jubilee, **98**
Clarence, **58**

Clark, William, 32
Clarks, **58**
Clayton, **58**
Clear Lake, **6**
Clement VII, 25
Clifton Choctaw, 22
Climate, 2, 14–15
Clinton, 4, 14, **37**, **43–45**, 60, **68–69**, **94**, 98
Clinton Confederate Cemetery, **8**
Clinton Female Academy, **94**
Clinton and Port Hudson Railroad, **37**, 68, **68**
Cloutierville, **37**, 96
Coastal marsh, 3, **3**
Coastal plain, 5
Cochrane, Alexander, 36, **36**
Cocodrie Delta, 12, **12**
Cocodrie Reservoir, 6, **6**
Code Noir. *See* Black Code
Coles Creek Indian Culture, 16, 20
Colfax, **37**, **44–45**, 58, **98**
Colleges, 94, **94**, 95, **95**
Collinston, **58**, **70**
Columbia, 4, **37**, **43–44**, 58, **69–70**, 96, **98**
Columbus, Christopher, 23
Comanche Indians, 32
Commerce, 27, 29, 31, 37, 62–63, 65–66, 71–73
Common law, 47
Company of the Indies, 27, 61
Company of the West, 61
Concord Institute, 69, **94**
Concordia, **29**, 68, **68**
Concordia County, 41, **41**
Concordia Parish, 42, **42**, 43, **43–44**, 45, **45**, **50–54**, 55, **55–57**, **74–81**, 82, **82–90**, 91, **91–93**, **98–99**
Confederate Museum, 96
Confederate States of America, 38–40, 66

Congressional districts, **46**
Constitution of the United States, 46
Constitutions (Louisiana), **43–45**, **47–49**, **56**, **71**, **94**
Construction industries, 90, **90**
Contraband Days, **98**
Convent, **44–45**, **94**, **94**
Converse, **58**
Coochie Brake State Preservation Area, **8**
Cooperative Extension Service, 75–81
Coral Snake mound site, **16**
Corn, 29, 37, 73–74, 77, 82, **82**
Corn Festival, **98**
Corney Creek Festival, **98**
Coronado, Francisco Vásquez de, 23, **23**
Corps of Engineers, 71, 73
Cotile, **37**
Cotile Recreational Area, **8**
Cotton, 27, 37, 39, 55–56, 67, 74, **74**, 77, 81, **81**, 87
Cotton Festival, **98**
Cotton gins, 81
Cotton Valley, **58**
Cottonport, **59**
Counties, 41, **41**, 42, 45
Coureurs de bois, 26, 76
Courts, 47
Coushatta, 4, 20, **44**, **45**, 58, **70**, **94**, **98**
Coushatta Male and Female Institute, **94**
Covington, **37**, **43**, **44**, **45**, 60, **70**, 94
Covington Female Academy, **94**
Crabs, 83, **83**
Crawfish, 83, **83**
Crawfish Festival, **98**
Creek Indians, 36
Creole Summer Festival, **98**
Cretaceous period, **9**
Crooked Creek Recreational Area, **8**

Crooks mound site, **16**
Crop lien system, 74, 81
Cross Lake, 6, **6**, 67
Crossroads, 99
Crowley, **2**, **37**, **44–45**, 52, **59**, **70**, **94**, **98**
Crozat, Antoine, 27
CSX Transportation, **70**
Cuestas, 3, 5
Cullen, **58**
Culture regions, **97**
Custis, Peter, 32, **32**
Cut Off, **60**
Cut-over lands, 7–8, 80
Cypremort Point State Park, **8**
Cypress forests, 7, **7**, 80
Czechs, 97

Dairies, 75–76, 84, **84**
Daniel's Academy, **94**
Darby, William, 99
D'Artaguette Family, 65
Davis, Jefferson, 44
Delcambre, **59**, **98**
Delgado Community College, 95, **95**
Delhi, **37**, **58**, 68, **70**, **98**
Delhi, Baskin and Southwestern Railroad, 69
Delta, **58**, **69–70**
Delta, Mississippi, 11–12, **12**
Delta Queen (Steamboat), **73**
Delta Southern Railroad, **70**
Democratic party, 37, 46, 48
Denham Springs, **60**, 66
De Quincy, **59**, **70**, 96, **98**
De Ridder, **45**, **59**, **69–70**, **98**
De Ridder Arts and Crafts Festival, **98**
De Soto, Hernando de, 21, 23, **23**, 24, **24**
De Soto Parish, 43, **43–44**, 45, **45**, **51–57**, **74–75**, 76, **76–83**, 84, **84–93**, **98–99**

Des Allemands, **98**
Destrehan, **60**, **98**
Destrehan Plantation Fall Festival, **98**
Devall Town (Baton Rouge), 65, **65**
Deville, **59**
Diet, 76, 84
Dillard University, **63**, 95, **95**
District courts, 47
Dixie Inn, **58**
Dodson, **58**
Dogtrot Museum, **96**
Dogwood Festival, **98**
Dolet Hills, 5, **5**
Domestication of plants and animals, 16
Donaldsonville, 6, **29**, **37**, 38, **38**, 39, **39**, **42–45**, 51–52, **60**, **69–70**, 94
Doustioni Indians, 17, **17**, 20, **20**
Doyline, **58**
Drake, Edwin L., 10
Drum, 83, **83**
Dry Prong, **58**
Dubach, **58**
Dubberly, **58**
Dugdemona River, 6
Dulach, **60**
Dunbar, William, 32, **32**
Duncan (Baton Rouge), 65
Duson, **59**

E.A. Seminary, **94**
Eads jetties, 63
Earl K. Long Home, **8**
East Baton Rouge Band (Choctaw Indians), 22
East Baton Rouge Parish, 22, **35**, 42, **42–44**, 45, **45**, **51–52**, 53, **53**, 54, **54–56**, 57, **57**, 66, **74–86**, 87, **87**, 88, **88–90**, 91, **91–92**, 93, **93**, **98–99**
East Camden and Highland Railroad, **70**
East Carroll Parish, 44, **44**, 45, **45**, **52–53**, 54, **54**, 56, 57, **57**, **74–76**,

77, **77–80**, 81, **81**, 82, **82–93**, **98–99**
East Cote Blanche Bay, 6
East Feliciana Parish, 43, **43–44**, 45, **45**, **51–57**, **74–93**, **98–99**
East Feliciana Spring Pilgrimage, **98**
East Hodge, **58**
Eastwood, **58**
Economy, 27, 29, 37, 74–93, **74–93**
Eden Isle, **60**
Edgard, **37**, **43–45**, **60**
Edgefield, **58**
Education, 91, **91**, 94, **94**, 95, **95**, 98
Eggs. *See* Poultry
Elizabeth, **59**, **98**
Elton, **59**
Emancipation Proclamation, 55
Empire, **60**, 73
Employment, **87–92**, **87–92**
Emy Lou Biedenharn Foundation Center, **96**
England Air Force Base, **59**, **71**
England and the English, 23, 25, **27**, 28, **28**, 30, **30**, 31, 33, 35–36, 97
English Turn, 26, **26**, 72
Eocene epoch, 9
Epps, **58**, **96**
Erath, **59**
Eros, 34, **58**
Esplanade, 62, 64
Esso, *See* Exxon
Estelle, **60**
Estherwood, **59**
Eugene Bay Field, 10
Eunice, 34, **59**, **69–70**, 95, **95**, **96**
Eunice Museum, **96**
Evangeline Parish, 44–45, **45**, **53–57**, **74–76**, 77, **77–78**, 79, **79–81**, 82, **82–83**, 84, **84–93**, **98–99**
Evergreen, **59**
Exodusters, 56
Exploration, **23**, 24, **24–25**, 26, **26**, 32, **32**
Exxon, 66

Fairs, 98, **98**
Fairview-Riverside State Park, **8**
False River, 6
Family courts, 47
Farmerville, 34, **37**, **43–45**, 58, 69, **94**, **98**
Farms and farmers. *See* Agriculture
Farragut, David, 38
Faubourgs, 62
Federal Aid Road Act, 71
Federal Barge Line, 73
Feed grains, 77, 82
Feliciana County, 35, 42
Feliciana Female Collegiate Institute, 94
Feliciana Parish, 35, 42, **42**
Fenton, **59**
Ferriday, **58**
Ferries, 66, **71**
Festa d'Italia, **98**
Festival of Lights, **98**
Festivals, 98, **98**
Fete des Acadiens, **98**
Filipinos, 97
Fillmore, **94**
Fillmore Academy, **94**
Financial institutions, 91, **91**
Finfish, 83
Fireman's Parade and Festival, **98**
Fish, 76, 83, **83**
Fish Hatchery mound site, **16**
Fish meal, 83
Fisher, **58**, **98**
Five Islands, 4, 90
Flatwoods, 3, **3**
Flint, Timothy, 99
Flood plain, 11, **11**
Florida, **1**, 24, 28, 30, **30**, 31, 35, **35**, 36, 53
Florida Boulevard, 66
Florida Classical Institute, **94**
Florida Parishes, 4–7, 17–18, 33–34, **34**, 41, 43–44, 50, 65, 97, **97**

Florida Purchase Treaty. *See* Adams-Onís Treaty
Florien, **58**
Flounder, 83
Floyd, **37**, 44
Folk life, 96, 97, **97**
Folklife Festival, **98**
Folsom, **60**
Fontainebleau State Park, **8**
Fordoche, 39, **60**
Forest, **58**
Forest Hill, **59**, **98**
Forest Service, 8
Forestry Festival, **98**
Forests, 3, 7, **7**, 8, **8**, 75, 77, 80, 80
Fort Adams, Miss. Terr., **29**, 32, **32**, 72
Fort Banks, **38–40**
Fort Barrancas (Fla.), 36
Fort Beauregard, 39
Fort Berwick, **38**
Fort Bourbon, 29
Fort Bowyer, Miss. Terr., 36, **36**
Fort Buchanan, **39–40**
Fort Buhlow, 40
Fort Bute, 30, **30**, 65
Fort Butler, 39, **39**, **40**
Fort Butte-a-la-Rose, **38–39**
Fort Charlotte, British West Florida (Mobile), 30, **30**
Fort Chene, **38–39**
Fort Claiborne, Miss. Terr., 36
Fort de la Boulaye, 26, **26**
Fort De Russy, **38–40**
Fort George, British West Florida (Pensacola), 30, **30**
Fort Jackson, **36–37**, 38, **38–40**, 98
Fort Jesup, **37**, **94**
Fort Jesup State Commemorative Area, **8**, **96**
Fort Macomb, **37–40**
Fort Macomb State Park, 8
Fort Maurepas, 26, **26**
Fort Mims, Miss. Terr., 36, **36**

Fort Miro (Monroe), **29**, 32, **32**, 42
Fort New Richmond, 30, **30**, 65, **65**
Fort Panmure, British West Florida (Natchez), 30, **30**
Fort Pike, **37–40**
Fort Pike State Commemorative Area, 8, **8**, **96**
Fort Polk, 59, **59**, **71**, **96**
Fort Polk Military Museum, **96**
Fort Randolph, 40
Fort Rosalie (Natchez, Miss.), **26**
Fort St. Croix, 25
Fort St. Jean Baptiste de Natchitoches, 20, **20**, 27
Fort St. Jean Baptiste State Commemorative Area, **8**, **96**
Fort St. John, **27**, **29**, 36
Fort St. Leon, **27**, 29
Fort St. Marie, **27**, 29
Fort St. Philip, **29**, 36, **36–37**, 38, **38–40**, 72
Fort St. Stephens, Miss. Terr., 36
Fort San Carlos, **29**, 35, **35**, 65, **65**
Fort Shafer, 38
Fort Smith, 40
Fort Stoddert, Miss. Terr., 36
Fort Sumter, S.C., 37
Fort Turnbull, 40
Fort William, Miss. Terr., **36**
France and the French, 23, 25, **25**, 26–27, **27**, 28, 33, **33**, 51, 61, 74, 78, 81, 94, 97, **97**
Francis I, 25
Francis T. Nicholls Junior College of L.S.U., **94**
Franklin, Benjamin, 43
Franklin, **37**, 39, **39**, **42–45**, 52, 59, **94**, **98**
Franklin and Abbeville Railroad, 69
Franklin Academy, **94**
Franklin College, 94, **94**
Franklin Parish, 43, **43**, 44, **44**, 45, **45**, **51–57**, **74–75**, 76, **76**, 77, **77–80**, 81, **81–82**, 83, **83–92**, 93,

93, 98–99
Franklinton, 37, 43–45, 60, 94
Franklinton Academy, 94
Frasch process, 90
Fredericks mound site, 16
Free blacks, 55
Free State of Sabine, 31
Freeman, Thomas, 32, 32
Freezes, 15
French Food Festival, 98
French and Indian War, 23, 25, 28, 35
French Quarter, 8, 61, 61, 62, 62, 63, 63, 64, 64
French Settlement, 60, 98
Freshwater Bayou, 73
Frog Festival, 98
Frontenac, Louis de Buade, Comte de, 26
Fruit, 77
Fur production, 76

Gahagan mound site, 16
Galliano, 60, 98
Gallier House Museum, 96
Gálvez, Bernardo de, 29–30
Galveztown, 29
Gardens, 77
Gardere, 60
Garfish, 83, 83
Gast, Pierre du, Sieur de Monts, 25
General Assembly, 48
Geology, 9, 9
Georgetown, 58, 70
German Coast, 27, 27
German Coast County, 41, 41
German colonists, 27, 50, 97
Germanfest, 98
Germans, 51
Gerrymandering, 46
Gibsland, 58, 70, 94, 98
Gibsland Collegiate Institute, 94
Gilbert, 58, 70

Gilliam, 58
Glass, Anthony, 32, 32
Glendora mound site, 16
Glenmora, 59
Gloster Southern Railroad, 70
Golden Meadow, 60
Golden Meadow International Tarpon Rodeo, 98
Goldonna, 58
Gonzales, 60, 96, 98
Government, 27, 29, 37, 38, 42, 45–49, 57, 60, 66, 91, 91, 92
Governors, 48–49
Grain sorghum, 82
Grains, 77, 82
Grambling, 58, 95, 95, 96
Grambling State University, 94–95, 95, 96
Grammercy, 60, 70
Grand Cane, 58
Grand Canyon of the Mississippi, 11
Grand Coteau, 37, 39, 39, 59, 94, 94
Grand Ecore, 40, 40
Grand Gulf, 39, 39, 72
Grand Gulf group, 9
Grand Isle, 60, 98
Grand Isle East/West State Park, 8
Grand Lake, 6, 6, 19, 21, 39, 39
Grant, Ulysses S., 39–40, 44
Grant Parish, 44, 44, 45, 45, 52–54, 56–57, 58, 74–92, 93, 93, 98–99
Grass Town (Baton Rouge), 65
Grasses, 7
Gray, 60
Grayson, 58
Grayville, 60
Great Britain. See England
Great Depression, 53
Great Raft (Red River), 43, 58, 67, 72, 72
Greensburg, 37, 43, 44, 45, 60, 94
Greensburg Female Academy, 94

Greenwell Springs, 66
Greenwood, 37, 58, 67, 98
Greenwood Pioneer Days, 98
Gretna, 4, 44–45, 60, 62–63, 69–70, 96
Grierson, B. H., 39, 39
Grindstone Bluff Museum, 96
Grosse Tete, 60
Grosse Tete and Baton Rouge Plank Road Company, 68
Growing season, 15
Gueydan, 59
Gulf, Colorado and Santa Fe Railroad, 69
Gulf of Mexico, 68, 83
Gulf and Sabine River Railroad, 69
Gumbo Festival, 98

Hahnville, 18, 44–45, 60
Hall Summit, 58
Hammond, 2, 4, 60, 68–70, 95, 95, 96, 98
Hanna, 70
Hanna mound site, 16
Harahan, 60, 63
Hardtner, Henry, 80
Hardwoods, 7
Harrisonburg, 37, 39, 39, 42–45, 58
Harvey, 60
Haughton, 58
Hay, 77, 82
Haynesville, 37, 58, 98
Haynesville Gas Field, 10
Health care, 89
Heard, William Wright, 69
Heflin, 58
Henderson, 59
Henry, Cammie G., Research Center, 96
Herbert S. Ford Memorial Museum, 96
Herbicides, 81

Heritage Festival, 98
Hermann–Grima Historic House, 96
Hessmer, 59
Heywood, W. Scott, 10
Hickey (Baton Rouge), 65
Highways. See Roads
Highway Commission, 71
Hill country, 97
Hilliard, Sam B., 87
Hills, 3, 3, 5
Hineston, 37
Hispanics, 97
Historic New Orleans Collection, 96
Hodge, 58, 70
Hodges Gardens Christmas Fest-ival, 98
Holiday in Dixie, 98
Holocene epoch, 9, 9
Homer, 4, 37, 43–45, 51, 58, 94, 96, 98
Homer College, 94
Homer Female Collegiate Insti-tute, 94
Homer Masonic Male and Female Institute, 94
Homestead Act of 1872, 80
Hornbeck, 59
Horses, 76, 85, 85
Hosston, 58
Houma, 2, 4, 37, 38, 43–45, 52, 60, 60, 68–70, 73, 92, 94, 96, 98
Houma Academy, 94
Houma Indians, 17, 17, 18, 18, 26, 26
Houma Navigation Canal, 73
House of representatives. See Louisiana House of Represen-tatives and U.S. House of Representatives
Houston River, 6
Houston and Shreveport Railroad, 69, 69
Howe's Institute, 94
Huddleston, 37

Hunter, Clementine, 96
Hunter, George, 32, 32
Hurricanes, 13, 13, 61

Iberia Parish, 44, 44, 45, 45, 52–54, 56–57, 74–75, 76, 76–77, 78, 78–93, 98–99
Iberville, Pierre Le Moyne, Sieur d', 18, 21, 26, 26, 27, 42, 81
Iberville County, 41, 41
Iberville Parish, 42, 42–44, 45, 45, 50–57, 74–93, 98–99
Iberville River. See Bayou Manchac
Iberville and Vermilion Railroad, 69
Ice ages, 5, 9, 11–12
Ida, 58
Illinois Central/Illinois Central Gulf Railroad, 63, 63, 66, 66, 69–70, 70
Illinois Indians, 19
Immaculate Conception, College of, 94, 94
Imperial Calcasieu Museum, 96
Income, 93, 93
Independence, 60
Independence Bowl, 98
Indian Creek Recreational Area, 8
Indian Lake, 21
Indian Mound, 66
Indian Territory (Oklahoma), 19, 22, 26
Indians, 16, 16, 17, 17, 18, 18, 19, 19, 20, 20, 21, 21, 22, 22, 28, 74, 82, 97
Indigo, 27, 29, 74, 81
Industrial lumbering, 7, 80
Industry, 87–91
Inland Waterways Corporation, 73
Inniswold, 60
Insecticides, 81
Insurance industry, 91, 91
Interstate highways, 63, 63, 66–67,

71, **71**
Intracoastal Waterway, 6, **63, 66, 71,** 73, **73**
Iota, **59**
Iowa, **59, 70**
Irazabal, José Calbo de, 30
Irregular survey, 33, **33**
Irrigation, 79
Irvine Light, 6
Isle of Orleans, 6, 25, **27,** 28, **29,** 31, 41
Isleños, 29, 50, 97
Isleños Museum, 8
Isleños Spanish Festival, **98**
Istrouma, 65

Jackson, Andrew, 36, 43
Jackson, **37, 60,** 68, **68,** 94, **94, 96**
Jackson Barracks, **96**
Jackson Confederate State Com-memorative Area, **8**
Jackson group, **9**
Jackson Parish, 43, **43,** 44, **44,** 45, **45,** **51-57, 74-93, 98-99**
Jackson Square, 61, 64
Jambalaya Festival, **98**
Jamestown, **58**
Jax Brewery, 64
Jayhawkers, 39
Jean Lafitte, **60, 98**
Jean Lafitte National Historical Park, 8, **8, 63, 96**
Jeanerette, **59**
Jefferson, Thomas, 31, 32, 43, 62
Jefferson (city), **37,** 51, **60, 62,** 68
Jefferson College, 94, **94**
Jefferson Davis College, **94**
Jefferson Davis Parish, 44-45, **45,** **53-54, 56-57, 74-78,** 79, **79-93,** **98-99**
Jefferson Davis Parish Fair, **98**
Jefferson and Lake Pontchartrain Railroad, **62,** 68
Jefferson Parish, 43, **43-44,** 45, **45,**

51-53, 54, **54-57, 74-75,** 76, **76-81,** 82, **82,** 83, **83-86,** 87, **87,** 88, **88-92,** 93, **93, 98-99**
Jeffersonian Democrat party, 37, 46
Jena, **45,** 58, **96, 98**
Jena Band (Choctaw Indians), 22
Jennings, **2,** 10, **37, 45, 59, 70, 98**
Jennings Field, 10
John McNeese Junior College, **94**
Johnson Female Academy, **94**
Johnston Collegiate Institute, **94**
Joliet, Louis, 25-26
Jonesboro, **45, 58, 69**
Jonesville, 16, **58, 69, 98**
Judicial system, 47
Junction City, **58**
Justices of the peace, 47
Juvenile courts, 47

Kadohadacho Indians, 20
Kansas City Southern Railroad, 63, 66, **67, 69-70**
Kaplan, **59, 70**
Keatchie, **58, 94**
Keatchie College, **94**
Kemper Rebellion, 35
Kenner, 54, 60, **60, 63, 70, 96, 98**
Kenner Historical Museum, **96**
Kent House, **8**
Kentwood, **60, 69**
Kentwood, Greensburg and Southwestern Railroad, **69**
Kentwood and Eastern Railroad, **69**
Kidd-Davis House, **96**
Kilbourne, **58**
Killian, **60**
Kinder, **59, 70, 98**
Kinder Sauce Piquante and Music Festival, **98**
Kisatchie Hills, 4
Kisatchie National Forest, 7-8, **8**
Kisatchie Wold, 5
Knapp, Seaman A., 79
Kniffen, Fred B., 3, 87

Knights of Labor, 78
Know-Nothing party, 37
Koasati Indians, 22, **22**
Koroa Indians, 17, **17,** 19, **19**
Krotz Springs, **59**

La Harpe, Jean Baptiste Bénard de, 21, 26, **26**
La Salle, Robert Cavelier, Sieur de, 18-20, 23, 25, **25,** 26, **26,** 44
La Salle Museum, **96**
La Salle Parish, 22, 44-45, **45,** 53, **53,** 54, **54,** 56-57, **74-90,** 91, **91-93,** **98-99**
La Salle Parish Fair, **98**
La Vie la Fourchaise Festival, **98**
Labadieville, 38, **38, 60**
Labor force, 87-92
Lacombe, **60, 98**
Lafayette, Marquis de, 43
Lafayette, **2,** 4, **44-45,** 52-54, 59, **59,** 69, **70,** 71, **73, 92, 94,** 95, **95, 96,** 98. *See also* Vermil-ionville
Lafayette (New Orleans), 62
Lafayette Museum, **96**
Lafayette Parish, 43, **43-44,** 45, **45,** **51-57, 74-92,** 93, **93, 98-99**
Lafitte, **60, 98**
Lafitte, Jean, 36
Lafourche County, 41, **41**
Lafourche Delta, 12, **12**
Lafourche Parish, 15, 18, 42, **42,** 43, **43-44,** 45, **45,** 50-57, **74-75,** 76, **76-77,** 78, **78-82,** 83, **83,** 84, **84-93, 98-99**
Lagniappe on the Bayou, **98**
Lagoonal lakes, 6
Lake Arthur, **59**
Lake Bistineau, 6
Lake Bistineau State Park, **8**
Lake Borgne, 6, 36, 63, 68
Lake Bruin, 6
Lake Bruin State Park, **8**
Lake Charles, **2,** 4, **37, 43-45,** 52-54,

59, **59, 68-70,** 71, 73, **73, 92, 94,** 95, **95, 96, 98**
Lake Charles College, **94**
Lake Charles Deepwater Canal, **73**
Lake Charles Junior College, **94**
Lake Charles and Northern Railroad, **69**
Lake Charles Railway and Navi-gation Company, **69**
Lake Claiborne, 6
Lake Claiborne State Park, **8**
Lake D'Arbonne, 6
Lake D'Arbonne State Park, **8**
Lake Fausse Pointe State Park, **8**
Lake Larto, 6
Lake Larto State Park, **8**
Lake Maurepas, 6, 28
Lake Pontchartrain, 6, 9, 18, 20, **20,** 26, 28, 32, 68
Lake Pontchartrain Causeway, 62
Lake Prien, 21
Lake Providence, 4, **37,** 39, **39,** **43-45,** 58, **94**
Lake St. Agnes mound site, **16**
Lake St. John, 6
Lake St. John Field, 10
Lake St. Joseph, 18-19, **19**
Lake Tensas, 41
Lakes, 3, 6
Land grants, 84
Land survey systems, 33, **33,** 34, **34**
Landforms, 5, **5, 11-12**
Laplace, **60, 70, 98**
Larose, **60, 98**
Latitude, 2, **2,** 14
Law, John, 27, 61
Lawtell, **59**
Le Pensionat de Madame de St. Laurent, **94**
Lecompte, **59**
Lee, Robert E., 40
Leesville, **2,** 4, **44-45,** 59, **69-70, 94,** **98**
Leesville Academy, **94**

Legislative council, 41, 45
Legislature, 48-49
Leland College, 94, **94**
Lemos, Manuel Gayoso de, 29
León, Ponce de, 23
Leonard Town (Baton Rouge), 65, **65**
Leonville, **59**
Les Allemands, 21, 27, **27**
Lewis, Meriwether, 32
Libraries, 96
Lieutenant governor, 49
Lillie, **58**
Lincoln, Abraham, 44
Lincoln Parish, 44, **44,** 45, **45, 52-54,** **56-57, 74-75,** 76, **76-84,** 85, **85-91,** 92, **92-93, 98-99**
Lindsay, **70**
Lipan Apache Indians, 22, **22**
Lisbon, **58**
Little Chenier mound site, **16**
Little River, 6, **72-73**
Little River basin, **11**
Little Woods mound site, **16**
Livestock, 27, 37, **74-76,** 84
Livingston, Robert, 31, 43
Livingston, **45, 60, 98**
Livingston Parish, 43, **43,** 44, **44,** 45, **45,** 51, **51-53,** 54, **54-57,** 66, **74-84,** 85, **85-93, 98-99**
Livingston Parish Fair, **98**
Livonia, **60,** 68, 70
Lockett, Samuel H., 3
Lockport, **60,** 70
Locust Grove State Commemorative Area, **8**
Logansport, 20, **58**
Lone Star, **60**
Long, Earl K., 57
Long, Huey P., 10, **60, 66,** 71
Long family, 57
Long lots, 33, **33**
Longfellow-Evangeline State Commemorative Area, 8, **8**
Longitude, 2, **2**

Longleaf Pine Hills, **3**
Longstreet, **58**
Loreauville, **59**
Los Adaes, 20, 24, **24**
Los Adaes, San Miguel de los, 24
Los Adaes State Commemorative Area, **8, 96**
Louis XIV, 25–26
Louisiana and Arkansas Railroad, **63, 66, 66, 69–70**
Louisiana Art and Folk Center and Museum, **96**
Louisiana Central Railroad, **69**
Louisiana College, 94, **94,** 95, **95**
Louisiana and Delta Railroad, **70**
Louisiana Downs, **67,** 85
Louisiana Downs Super Derby Festival, **98**
Louisiana House of Representa-tives, 48, **48,** 49
Louisiana and Lower Mississippi Valley Collections, LSU, **96**
Louisiana Meridian, 34, **34**
Louisiana and Northwest Railroad, **69–70**
Louisiana and Pacific Railroad, **69**
Louisiana Petroleum and Coal Oil Company, 10
Louisiana Purchase (1803), 1, 28, **29,** 31, **31,** 35–36, 50, 97
Louisiana Railway and Navigation Company, **69**
Louisiana Southern Railroad, **63, 69–70**
Louisiana State Arboretum, **8**
Louisiana State Archives, **96**
Louisiana State Exhibit Museum, **96**
Louisiana State Fire Museum, **96**
Louisiana State Library, **96**
Louisiana State Museum, **96**
Louisiana State Normal, **94**
Louisiana State Railroad Museum, **96**

Louisiana State Seminary of Learning and Military Acad-emy, 66, 94, **94**
Louisiana State Senate, 48–49, **49**
Louisiana State University and Agricultural and Mechanical College, 66, **66,** 95, **95**
Louisiana State University–Alexandria, 95, **95, 96**
Louisiana State University–Eunice, 95, **95**
Louisiana State University–Shreveport, 67, 95, **95, 96**
Louisiana Supreme Court, 47, **47**
Louisiana Tech University, 95, **95, 96**
Louisiana Tech University Museum, **96**
Louisiana and Western Railroad, 68, **68,** 69, **69,** 79
Louisville and Nashville Railroad, 63, **69**
Lower Mississippi River Industrial Corridor, 87, 90
Loyola University of New Orleans, **63,** 95, **95**
Lucky, **58**
Luling, **60**
Lumber, 27, 37
Lumber industry, 7, 52, 58–60, 69, **87**
Lutcher, **60, 98**
Lydia, **59**

McIlhenny family, **8**
McIntosh mound site, **16**
McLanahan, J., 32, **32**
McNary, **59**
McNeese State University, 95, **95, 96**
Macon Ridge, 5, **5,** 9
Maddox mound site, **16**
Madewood Arts Festival, **98**
Madison, James, 35, 43
Madison Parish, 43, **43–44,** 45, **45,** 51–53, 54, **54–56,** 57, **57,** 74–76,

77, **77–81,** 82, **82–87,** 88, **88–92,** 93, **93,** 98–99
Madisonville, 29, **37,** 60
Magnolia Mound, **98**
Magnolia Town, **65**
Main Pass Field, 10
Maison Rouge, Don Josef, Marquis de, 29
Major, J. P., 39
Mamou, **59**
Mandeville, **37, 60, 70**
Mangham, **58**
Mansfield, 4, 37, 40, **40,** 43–45, **58, 69–70,** 94, **96, 98**
Mansfield Female College, **94**
Mansfield Railway and Transportation Company, **69**
Mansfield State Commemorative Area, **8, 96**
Mansura, 40, **59, 98**
Manufacturing, 27, 29, 37, 87, **87**
Many, **37, 43–45, 58, 70, 96, 98**
Mardi Gras, 98, **98**
Maringouin, **60**
Marion, **58, 98**
Marksville, 2, 4, 19, 29, **29, 37,** 40, **40, 42–45, 59, 70,** 94, **96**
Marksville Female Academy, **94**
Marksville Indian Culture, 16
Marksville mound site, **16**
Marksville Prairie, 19, 22
Marksville State Commemorative Area, **8**
Marquette, Jacques, 25–26
Marrero, 60, **60**
Marsh Island Refuge, **8**
Marshall, 67
Marshes, 3, **3,** 5, 7
Marthaville, **96**
Martin, **58**
Masonic Institute (Ft. Jesup), **94**
Matagorda Bay, 26

Mather (Baton Rouge), 65
Mathews, **60, 98**
Maurice, **59**
Mayhaw Festival, **98**
Meanders, 6
Medical College of Louisiana, 94
Medora mound site, **16**
Melrose Arts and Crafts Festival, **98**
Melville, **59**
Menhaden, 83, **83**
Mer Rouge, **58**
Meraux, **60**
Mermentau, **59**
Mermentau River, 6, 21, **73**
Mermentau River basin, **11**
Merrydale, **60**
Merryville, **59**
Meso–Indians, 16
Mesozoic era, 9, **9**
Metairie, 54, 60, **60, 63, 98**
Metes and bounds, 33, **33**
Metropolitan Statistical Areas, 58, **58,** 59, **59,** 60, **60**
Mexican Gulf Railroad, **37, 62,** 68, **68**
Middle American Research Institute (Tulane), **96**
Midsouth Rail, **70**
Midway, **58**
Midway group, 9
Midwest (U.S.), 79, 97, **97**
Military bases, 71, **71.** *See also* Forts; Presidios
Military towns, 60
Milk, 75–76, 84, **84**
Milliken's Bend, 39
Mimosa Park, **60**
Minden, 2, 14, **37, 44–45,** 51, **58, 69–70,** 94, **98**
Minden Female Seminary, **94**
Minden Male Academy, **94**
Mining industries, 90, **90**
Miocene epoch, **9**

Miró, Estevan, 29
Mission de Nuestra Señora de los Dolores de los Ais (San Augustine, Texas), 24
Mississippi, **1,** 35, **35,** 36, **36,** 42, 50–54, 68, 93, **93**
Mississippi Central Railroad, 68
Mississippi Flood Plain, 3, **3**
Mississippi River, 1, 4, 6, 9, 11, **11, 12,** 16, 17, **19,** 26, **26,** 27, **27,** 28, **28,** 29, **29,** 31, **31,** 32, 33, **33,** 38, **38,** 39, 42, 50–51, 61, **61,** 62, **62,** 63, **63,** 64, **64,** 65, **65,** 66, **66,** 72, **72–73,** 74, 78
Mississippi River basin, **11**
Mississippi River delta, 12, 14, 25
Mississippi River Gulf Outlet, 6, **73**
Mississippi River valley, 7, 36–37
Mississippian Indian Culture, 16
Missouri, Kansas and Texas Rail-road, **69**
Missouri Pacific Railroad, 66, 69
Mobile, 30, **30,** 32, 36, **36**
Mobile Bay, 19, **19,** 26, 30, 36, **36**
Mobile Indians, 22
Mobilian jargon, 17
Monnett's Ferry, 40
Monroe, James, 31
Monroe, 2, 4, **37,** 39, **39,** 43–45, 52–54, 58, **58,** 68, **68–70,** 71, 91, **92,** 94, 95, **95, 96, 98**
Monroe Gas Field, 10
Monroe Uplift, 5
Montegut, **60**
Montgomery, **58, 94**
Montgomery Free Institute, **94**
Monticello, **60**
Montpelier, **37, 42, 60, 94**
Montpelier Academy, **94**
Mooringsport, **58**
Moreauville, **59**
Morehouse, Abraham, 43

Morehouse College, **94**

Morehouse Parish, 43, **43–44**, 45, **45**, **51–57**, **74**, 75, **75–76**, 77, **77–78**, 79, **79–80**, 81, **81–93**, **98–99**

Morgan City, 4, 6, **59**, **68–70**, 96, **98**. *See also* Brashear City

Morgan City Museum, **96**

Morgan's Louisiana and Texas Railroad, 68, **68**, 69, **69**, 79

Morganza, **60**

Morganza Floodway, 6

Morin, Antoine, 78

Morrisonville, **66**

Morse, **59**

Moscoso de Alvarado, Luis de, 21, 24, **24**

Moss Bluff, **59**

Mound, **58**

Mount Driskill, 4, **4**, 5, **5**

Mount Lebanon, **58**, 94, **94**

Mount Lebanon Stagecoach Trail, **98**

Mount Lebanon University, 94, **94**

Mount Zion, **94**

Mount Zion Male and Female College, **94**

Mouton, Alfred, 38

Mugulasha Indians, 17–18, **18**

Mules, 81, 85, **85**

Municipal courts, 47

Museum of Fashions and Textiles, Louisiana Tech, **96**

Museums, 96, **96**

Muskogean linguistic group, 17, **17**, 18

Mutton, 76

Nacogdoches Wold, 5

Napoleon, 31

Napoleonville, **37**, **42–45**, **60**, **98**

Narváez, Pánfilo de, 23–24, **24**

Nassonite Indians, 26

Natalbany, **60**

Natalbany River, **73**

Natchez, **26**, 27, **29**, 30, **30**, 35, 38,

51, **58**, **72**. *See also* Fort Rosalie

Natchez, Urania and Ruston Railroad, **69**

Natchez Indians, 17, **17**, 19, **19**, 21

Natchez Wars, 19, **19**, 21

Natchezan linguistic group, 17, **17**, 19

Natchitoches, **2**, 4, **19**, 20, 24, **24**, **26**, 27, **27**, 29, **29**, 32, **32**, **37**, 39–40, **40**, **42–45**, 58, **58**, **68–70**, **72**, 78, **94**, 95, **95**, **96**, 98, **98**, 99

Natchitoches County, 41, **41**

Natchitoches Indians, 17, **17**, 18, 20, **20**, 26

Natchitoches Parish, 42, **42**, 43, **43**, 44, **44**, 45, **45**, 50–57, **74–75**, 76, **76–79**, 80, **80–81**, 82, **82–93**, **98–99**

National Park Service, 8

National Register of Historic Places, 96

National Republican party, 37

Native Americans. *See* Indians

Natural Gas. *See* Oil and gas

Natural levees, 3, 5

Natural regions, 3, **3**

Naval stores, 80

Neame, Carson and Southern Railroad, **69**

Neo-Indians, 16

New Deal, 60

New France, 25

New Iberia, **2**, 4, **29**, **37**, 39, **39–40**, **44–45**, 52–53, 59, **69**, 70, **94**, **98**

New Iberia and Northern Railroad, **69**

New Orleans, **2**, 4, 8, 18, 21, **21**, **26**, 27, **27**, 29, **29–30**, 31, **32**, 36, **36**, 37, **37**, 38, **38**, 39, **39**, **40**, **42–45**, 47, 50–55, 60, **60**, 61, **61**, 62, **62**, 63, **63**, 64, **64**, 66, 68, **68**, 69, **69**, 70, **70**, 71, 72, **72–73**, 73, 78–79, **92**, 94, **94**, 95, **95**, **96**, 97, 98, **98**, 99

New Orleans (steamboat), 72

New Orleans Baptist Theological

Seminary, **95**

New Orleans and Carrollton Railroad, **62**, 68, **68**

New Orleans Food Festival, **98**

New Orleans, Great Northern Railroad, **69**

New Orleans, Jackson and Great Northern Railroad, **37**, **62**, 68

New Orleans Jazz and Heritage Festival, **98**

New Orleans and Mississippi Valley Railroad, 66

New Orleans and Mobile Railroad, 68, **68**

New Orleans and Nashville Railroad, 68

New Orleans, Natalbany and Natchez Railroad, **69**

New Orleans Naval Air Station, **71**

New Orleans and Northeastern Railroad, **69**

New Orleans, Opelousas and Great Western Railroad, **37**, **62**, 68

New Orleans Pacific Railroad, 68, **68**

New Orleans Public Belt Railroad, **70**

New Orleans Public Library, **96**

New Orleans, Southern and Grand Isle Railroad, **69**

New Orleans Terminal Railroad, **70**

New Orleans, Texas and Mexico Railroad, **69**

New Orleans University, **94**

New Richmond (Baton Rouge), **27**

New Roads, **37**, **43–45**, **60**, **98**

New Sarpy, **60**

New Spain, 26

Newellton, **58**

Newllano, **59**

Nicholls State University, 95, **95**, **96**

Noble, **58**

Norco, 55, **60**

North American Land and Timber Company, 79

North Hodge, **58**

North Louisiana Collegiate Institute, **94**

North Louisiana Cotton Festival and Fair, **98**

North Louisiana and Gulf Railroad, **69–70**

North Louisiana and Texas Railroad, 68

North Toledo Bend State Park, **8**

North Vacherie, **60**

Northeast Junior College of L.S.U., **94**

Northeast Louisiana University, 95, **95**, **96**

Northwest Ordinance of 1785, 33–34

Northwestern State University of Louisiana, 95, **95**, **96**

Norvilla Collegiate Institute, **94**

Norwood, **60**

Notre Dame School of Theology, 95, **95**

Nursery Festival, **98**

Oak Forest, 7, **7**, 80

Oak Grove, **45**, **58**, **94**, **98**

Oak Grove Academy, **94**

Oak Hills Place, **60**

Oak Ridge, **58**

Oakdale, **59**, **69**

Oats, 82, **82**

Oberlin, **45**, **59**, **98**

Oberlin, Hampton and Eastern Railroad, **69**

Ofo Indians, 22

Oil City, **58**, **96**

Oil Exposition/Oil Festival, **98**

Oil and gas, 10, **10**, 58–60, 66–67, 73, 87, **87**, 88, 90, **90**, 92–93

Oil Patch Festival, **98**

Okelousa Indians, 17, **17**, 18, **18**, 21

Okra, 77

Okra Festival, **98**

Old Arsenal Museum, **96**

Old Jefferson, **60**

Old River, 6

Older citizenry, 93, **93**

Oligocene epoch, **9**

Olla, **58**

Olla Field, 10

Oñate, Juan, 23

Onions, 77

Onís, Luis de, 31

Opelousas, **2**, 4, **29**, **37**, 38, **38**, 39, **39**, **40**, **42–45**, 52, **59**, **59**, **69**, 94, **94**, **98**

Opelousas County, 41, **41**

Opelousas Female College, **94**

Opelousas Indians, 17, **17**, 21, **21**

Orange, Texas, 68

O'Reilly, Alejandro, 29

Orleans, College of, 94, **94**

Orleans, Duke of, 61

Orleans, Territory of, 32

Orleans County, 41, **41**

Orleans Parish, 42, **42**, 43, **43–44**, 45, **45**, 50, **50**, 51, **51**, 52, **52**, 53, **53**, 54, **54**, 55, **55–56**, 57, **57**, **74–83**, 84, **84–86**, 87, **87**, 88, **88**, 89, **89–90**, 91, **91–92**, 93, **93**, **98**, 99, **99**

Osage Indians, 32

Osyka, 68

Ouachita County, 41, **41**

Ouachita Indians, 17, **17**, 20, **20**, 26

Ouachita and Northwestern Railroad, **69**

Ouachita Parish, 9, 42, **42**, 43, **43**, 44, **44**, 45, **45**, 50, **50–52**, 53, **53**, 54, **54–57**, **74–93**, **98–99**

Ouachita Parish Junior College, **94**

Ouachita River, 5, **5**, 6–7, 19, **27**, **29**, 32–33, **33**, **72**, **72–73**

Ouachita River basin, **11**

Our Lady of Holy Cross College, **95**

Oxbow lakes, 6

Oxen, **84**

Oyster Festival, **98**

Oysters, 83, **83**

Pacana Indians, 19, 22, **22**
Paincourtville, **60**
Pakenham, Edward, 36, **36**
Paleocene epoch, **9**
Paleo-Indians, 16
Paleozoic era, 9
Palestine, 37
Palmetto Island State Park, **8**
Palmettos, **59**
Paper Festival, **98**
Parish courts, 47
Parish seats, 42–44, 60
Parish State Preservation Area, **8**
Parishes, 41, 42, **42**, 43, **43**, 44–45, **45**
Parishes (ecclesiastical), 41
Parks (city), **59**
Parks (state), 8, **8**
Pascagoula County, 35
Pascagoula Indians, 22, **22**
Pass à Loutre, 12
Passes, 3, 12
Patterson, James, 32
Patterson, **59**
Pattersonville, 39
Pauger, Adrien de, 61
Paul M. Hebert Law Center, 95, **95**
Pawnee Indians, 32
Pea Island, 36
Peabody Normal School, **94**
Peach Festival, **98**
Peaches, 77
Peanuts, 77
Pearl River (city), **60, 98**
Pearl River, 1, 6, 18, 30, **72, 73**
Pearl River basin, **11**
Pease Place mound site, **16**
Pecan Festival, **98**
Pecans, 77
Pemberton, John C., 39
Peñalosa Briceño y Berdugo, Diego Dionisio de, 25

Pensacola, Fla., 26, 30, 35–36, **36**
Pentagon Barracks, 65
Peppers, 77
Per capita income, 93, **93**
Perdido River, 35, **35**, 42
Petroleum. *See* Oil and gas
Pharmacy Museum, **96**
Physiography, 5
Picketts Island mound site, **16**
Pierce and Payne College, **94**
Pierrepart, **60**
Pike, Zebulon Montgomery, 32, **32**
Pine flats, 5, **5**
Pine forests, 7, **7**, 80
Pine Prairie, **59**
Pine Tree Festival, **98**
Pine tree plantations, 74, 80
Piñeda, Alonso Alvarez de, 24, **24**
Pineville, 34, **37, 59**, 94–95, **95**. *See also* Rapides
Pioneer, **58**
Pioneer Heritage Center, **96**
Pipelines, 70, 73
Pirogue Races, **98**
Pirogues, 72
Pischenoa Indians, 18
Pizarro, Francisco, 24
Place d'Armes, 61
Place names, 42, 45
Plain Dealing, 14, **58**
Plains Store, 39
Plank Road, 66
Plantation Country, 99
Plantations, 37, 39, 51, 55, 60, 74, 78, 80–81, 97, **97**
Plants, domestication of, 16
Plaquemine, 21, **37**, 39, **39**, **43–45**, 51, 52, **60, 94, 98**
Plaquemine Academy, **94**
Plaquemine Indian Culture, 16
Plaquemines Delta, 12, **12**
Plaquemines Locks, **8**

Plaquemines Parish, 42, **42–44**, 45, **45**, **50–57**, **74–75**, 76, **76–77**, 78, **78–82**, 83, **83–92**, 93, **93**, 97, **98–99**
Plaquemines Parish Fair/Orange Festival, **98**
Plaucheville, **59**
Pleasant, Ruffin B., 69
Pleasant Hill, 40, **58, 94**
Pleasant Hill Academy, **94**
Pleistocene epoch, 5, 9, **9**
Pliocene epoch, **9**
Pogy, 83
Point à la Hache, **37**, **42–47**
Point mound site, 16
Pointe-Coupee, 18, 27, **27**, **29**, 32, **37**
Pointe Coupée County, 41, **41**
Pointe Coupee Fair and Festival, **98**
Pointe Coupee Parish, 42, **42–44**, 45, **45**, **50–53**, 54, **54–57**, **74–81**, 82, **82–93**, **98–99**
Point Pleasant, **42, 72**
Poke Salad Festival, **98**
Police jury, 43, 45
Poll tax, 56
Pollock, Oliver, 30
Pollock, 34, **58, 94**
Pollock Institute, **94**
Pompano, 83
Pontalba Buildings, 64
Pontchartrain Basin, **11**
Pontchartrain Railroad, **37**, **62**, 68, **68**
Pontchatoula, **37, 60, 98**
Population, 27, 29, 37, 45, 50–57, **50–57**, 58–60, 93, **93**
Pork. *See* Swine
Port Allen, **37**, **42–45**, **60**, 66, **66, 70**, 73, **96, 98**
Port Barre, 6, **59**
Port Gibson, 39, **39**
Port Hudson, **37–38**, 39, **39, 66**, 68, **96**

Port Hudson campaign, 39, **39**
Port Hudson State Commemorative Area, **8**
Port Royal, 25
Port Sulphur, **60**
Port Vincent, **60**
Porter, David, 38–39
Ports, 61, 62–63, 65–66
Poste des Attakapas, 27
Poste des Opelousas, 27
Poste du Rapides, 27
Potpourri Festival and Rodeo, **98**
Poultry, 75–76, 85, **85**
Poverty Point, 8, **8**, 16, **16**, 58, **96**, 99
Poverty Point Culture, 72
Poverty Point Festival, **98**
Powhatan, 58
Poydras, **60**
Poydras Academy, **94**
Prairies, 3, **3**, 5, 37, 59, 79, 84
Praline Festival, **98**
Precipitation, 15
Presbytere, 64
President of the senate, 49
Presidio de Nuestra Señora del Pilar de los Adaes, 20, **20**, 24, **27**
Prien, **59**
Prime meridian, 2
Principal meridian, 34
Privateers, 36
Proclamation Line (1763), 28, 35
Proctorville, 68
Proterozoic era, 9
Provencal, **58**
Providence Academy, **94**
Public administration, 91, **91**
Pulpwood, 80

Quapaw Indians, 19
Quaternary period, 9, **9**
Quebec, 28
Quinapisa Indians, 17, **17**, 18, **18**

Quitman, **70**

Race tracks, 85
Raceland, **60**, 68, **69, 70**
Raft lakes, 3, 6
Railroad Days Festival, **98**
Railroad Museum (DeQuincy), **96**
Railroads, 37, **37**, 52, 62, **62**, 63, **63**, 66, **66**, 67, **67**, 68, **68**, 69, **69**, 70, **70**, 71–73, 76–78, 82, 84–85
Rainfall, 15
Rampart Street, 62, 64
Rapides (Pineville), 27, **27**, 29, **29**, 41
Rapides, College of, 94, **94**
Rapides County, 41, **41**
Rapides Parish, 22, 42, **42–43**, 44, **44**, 45, **45**, 50, 51, **51–52**, 53, **53–57**, **74–75**, 76, **76**, 77, **77**, 78, **78–81**, 82, **82–83**, 84, **84**, 85, **85–93**, **98–99**
Rapides Parish Fair, **98**
Rayne, **59, 98**
Rayville, **44–45**, 58, **70**
Real estate business, 91, **91**
Rebel State Commemorative Area, **8, 96**
Reconstruction, 43, 56
Recreation, 8, 85
Red Beans and Rice Festival, **98**
Red Bones, 22
Red Church, **72**
Red Chute, **58**
Red Cliffs (Pensacola), 30, **30**
Red River, 6, 7, 16, **19–20, 22**, 26, **26–27**, 29, **31**, 32–33, **33**, 39, **40**, 41, 51, 58, 67, **67**, 72, **72–73**, 74, 78
Red River Campaign, 40, **40**
Red River and Gulf Railroad, 69
Red River Parish, 43–44, **44**, 45, **45**, 52–53, 54, **54**, 56–57, **74–83**, 84, **84–90**, 91, **91–93**, **98–99**

Red River Parish Fair, **98**
Red River Railroad, **37, 68**
Red River Revel, **98**
Red River valley, 3, **3**, 5, 7, **11**, 20, 37
Redeemers, 56
Redfish, 83
Reeves, **59**
Religion, 49
Republic of West Florida, 35
Republican party, 46, 48, 56
Reserve, **60**
Resource centers, 60
Retail trade, 88, **88**
Revolt of 1766, 29
Rice, 27, 74, **74**, 77, 79, **79**, 87
Rice Festival, **98**
Richland Parish, 44, **44**, 45, **45**, **52–54, 56–57, 74–76**, 77, **77–80**, 81, **81–93, 98–99**
Richmond, **37, 43**, 58
Richwood, 58
Ridgecrest, **58**
Ridges, 5
Rillieux, Norbert, 78
Ringgold, **37, 58, 94**
Ringgold Male and Female Academy, **94**
Rio del Espiritu Santo, 24
River basins, 11, **11**
River cities, 60
River City Blues Festival, **98**
River Ridge, **60**
Riverfront Expressway, 64
Rivers, **6, 11**, 72, 73
Roads, 29, **29**, 37, **37**, **61–62**, 63, **63–65**, 66, **66–67**, 71, **71**, 90
Robeline, 20, **58, 96**
Rockefeller Refuge, 8
Rodessa, **58**
Roman Catholic Church, 95
Rosedale, **60**
Roseland, **60**
Rosepine, **59**

Rural Life Museum, LSU, **96**
Rural population, 50–54
Russell Sage Refuge, 8
Ruston, **2**, 4, **44–45**, 58, **69–70, 94**, 95, **95, 96, 98**
Ruston College, **94**

Sabine, Free State of, 31
Sabine Bay, 39
Sabine Parish, 22, 43, **43**, 44, **44**, 45, **45, 51–53**, 54, **54–57, 74**, 75, **75**, 76, **76–79**, 80, **80–84**, 85, **85–92**, 93, **93, 98–99**
Sabine Parish Fair, **98**
Sabine River, 1, 6, 17, 31, **31**, 39
Sabine River basin, **11**
Sabine Uplift, 5
St. Basil's Academy, **94**
St. Benedict, 95, **95**
St. Bernard, **37, 42–44, 98**
St. Bernard Delta, 12, **12**
St. Bernard Parish, **42–44**, 45, **45**, 50, **50**, 51, **51**, 52, **52**, 53, **53**, 54, **54–57, 74–75**, 76, **76–87**, 88, **88–92**, 93, **93**, 97, **98–99**
St. Bernard Parish Community College, 95, **95**
St. Bernard State Park, **8**
St. Charles College, **94**
St. Charles Courthouse, **37, 42–43**
St. Charles Parish, **42–44**, 45, **45**, 50–53, 54, **54**, 55, **55–57, 74–76**, 77, **77**, 78, **78–86**, 87, **87–92**, 93, **93, 98–99**
St. Charles River, 25
St. Cosme, Jean-François Buisson de, 21
St. Denis, Louis Juchereau de, 20, 25–26, **26**, 27
St. Francis Courthouse, 42
St. Francisville, 2, **2**, 4, **29**, 35, **35**, **37, 42–45, 60**, 68, **69, 72, 98**
St. Gabriels, 72
St. Genevieve, 32

St. Helena Meridian, 34, **34**
St. Helena Parish, **35**, 42, **42**, 43, **43**, 44, **44**, 45, **45, 51–52**, 53, **53–56**, 57, **57**, 60, **74–83**, 84, **84–92**, 93, **93, 98, 99**
St. James Courthouse, **37, 42–43**
St. James Parish, **42–44**, 45, **45**, 50–54, 55, **55–57, 74–93, 98–99**
St. John the Baptist Parish, **42–44**, 45, **45, 50–53**, 54, **54–57, 74**, 75, **75**, 76, **76–93, 98–99**
St. Joseph, **37, 43–45, 58, 98**
St. Joseph Seminary College, 95, **95**
St. Joseph's Academy, **94**
St. Landry Parish, 6, 42, **42**, 43, **43–44**, 45, **45**, 50, **50–51**, 52, **52**, 53, **53–57, 74–76**, 77, **77–81**, 82, **82–93, 98–99**
St. Lawrence River, 25
St. Louis Cathedral, 64
St. Louis, Iron Mountain and Southern Railroad, 69, **69**
St. Louis Southwestern Railroad, 69, 70
St. Martin Parish, 42, **42**, 43, **43**, 44, **44**, 45, **45**, 50, **50–57, 74–75**, 76, **76–82**, 83, **83–93, 98–99**
St. Martinville, **29, 37, 42–45**, 59, **59**, 94
St. Mary Parish, 15, 42, **42–43**, 44, **44**, 45, **45, 51–57, 74–77**, 78, **78–93, 98–99**
St. Mary's College, **94**
St. Peter's Academy, **94**
St. Reine, 27
St. Rose, **60**
St. Tammany Parish, **35**, 42, **42**, 43, **43**, 44, **44**, 45, **45, 51–53**, 54, **54–57, 74–87**, 88, **88–92**, 93, **93, 98–99**
Salcedo, Juan Manuel de, 29
Salé-Cypremort Delta, 12, **12**
Saline, **58**
Saline Bayou, 6

Salt, 90
Salt domes, 3–5, 10
Sam Houston Jones State Park, **8**
San Augustine (Texas), **24**
San Juan Bautista, 26
San Miguel de Linares, 20
Sanson mound site, **16**
Sarepta, **58**
Sawmill Days, **98**
Sawmills, 7
Schools. *See* Education
Schriever, **60, 70**
Scotlandville, **66, 95**
Scott, **59**
Seafood Festival, **98**
Sections, 34, **34**
Sedimentary rock, 9, 11
Segregation, 95
Senate. *See* Louisiana State Senate and U.S. Senate
Service industries, 89, **89**
Settlement patterns, 33
Seven Years' War, 23, 25, 28, 35
Share-cropping, 56, 81, 86, **86**
Shed Road, 71
Sheep, 76
Sheepshead, 83, **83**
Shellfish, 83
Shenandoah, **60**
Sherman, William T., 39, 94
Shiloh, **37, 69, 94**
Ship Island, 26, **26**, 38
Shongaloo, **58**
Shortleaf pine, 7
Shortleaf Pine Hills, **3**
Shreve, Henry Miller, 67, 72
Shreveport, **2**, 4, **22, 37**, 39, **39**, 40, **40, 43–45**, 51–54, 58, **58**, 66–67, **67, 68, 68**, 69, **69**, 70, 71, **92, 94**, 94, 95, **95, 96, 98**, 99
Shreveport Female Institute, **94**
Shreveport Seminary, **94**
Shrimp, 83, **83**
Shrimp Festival, **98**

Sibley, **58**
Sibley, John, 21, 32, **32**
Sibley, Lake Bistineau and South-ern Railroad, 69
Sibley Reservoir, 6
Sicily Island, 5, **58**
Sikes, **58**
Silliman Collegiate Institute, **94**
Simmesport, 6, **59**
Simpson, **59**
Simsboro, **58**
Sitios, 33, **33**
Slaughter, **60, 70**
Slaves and slavery, 27, 37, 39, 50–51, 55, 94, 97
Slidell, **60, 70, 96**
Smith, Edmund Kirby, 40, 67
Smith, Reuben, 32
Smith Ridge mound site, **16**
Smithfield Place mound site, **16**
Smithport Landing mound site, **16**
Snapper, 83, **83**
Snyder Museum and Creative Arts Center, **96**
Sod, 77
Soil Conservation Service, 82
Sophie Newcomb College for Women, 95, **96**
Sorghum, **82**
Sorrento, **60**
Soto, Hernando de. *See* De Soto, Hernando
Soule's College, **94**
South Mansfield, **58**
South Pass, 12
South Pass Field, 10
South Toledo Bend State Park, **8**
South Vacherie, **60**
Southdown Fall Festival, **98**
Southdown Plantation Home, **96**
Southeastern Louisiana Institute, **94**
Southeastern Louisiana University, 95, **95, 96**
Southern Baptist Convention, 95

Southern Pacific Railroad, 63, **63**, 68–69, **69, 70**, 79
Southern Railroad, 63, **70**
Southern Railway and Navigation Company, **69**
Southern University, 66, **66**, 94–95, **95, 96**
Southern University, New Orleans, 95, **95**
Southern University, Shreveport/ Bossier City, **67**, 95, **95**
Southwest Pass, 12
Soybean Festival, **98**
Soybeans, 73, 77, 82, **82**, 88
Spain and the Spanish, 23, **23**, 24, **24**, 25, 28, **28**, 29, **29**, 30, **30**, 32, 33, **33**, 35, **35**, 61, 74, 76, 84, 94, 97, **97**
Spanish Town (Baton Rouge), 65, **65**
Sparta, **37, 43–44**
Speaker of the house, 48
Spears Store/Spearsville, **37, 58**
Spindletop Field, 10
Sportsman's Paradise, 99
Spring Street Museum, **96**
Springfield, **29, 37, 43, 60, 94**
Springfield Institute, **94**
Springhill, **58**
Springville, **94**
Springville Academy, **94**
Squash, 74
Standard Oil Corporation, 66
Stanley, **58**
State fair, **98**
State surveyor, 43
Steamboats, 37, 62, 72–73
Sterlington, **58**
Straight University, 94, **94**, 95
Strawberries, 77
Strawberry Festival, **98**
Sugar, 27, 29, 37, 55, 74, **74**, 77–78, **78**, 87

Sugar Act, 78
Sugar Bowl Football Classic, **98**
Sugar Cane Festival, **98**
Sulphur (city), **59, 70**
Sulphur, 73, 90, **96**
Sun, **60**
Sunflower, 74
Sunset, **59**
Superdome, 63
Superior Council, 27
Supreme, **60, 70**
Supreme Court of the United States, **10**, 46
Swamps, 3, 5
Swanton, John R., 21
Swartz, **58**
Sweet potatoes, 77
Swine, 76
Swine Festival, **98**

Tabasco, 77
Taensa Indians, 17, **17**, 18–19, **19**, 20–21, 26, **26**, 43
Talleyrand-Périgord, Charles Maurice de, 31
Tallulah, **2**, 4, **44–45, 58**, 68, **69, 70**
Tamale Fiesta, **98**
Tangipahoa, **37, 60**
Tangipahoa Indians, 17, **17**, 18, **18**
Tangipahoa Parish, 44, **44**, 45, **45**, **52–54, 56–57, 74**, 75, **75**, 76, **76–83**, 84, **84**, 85, **85–87**, 88, **88–93, 98–99**
Tangipahoa River, 6, **73**
Tawakoni Indians, 26
Taylor, Richard, 39–40
Tchefuncte Indian Culture, 16
Tchefuncte mound site, **16**
Tchefuncte River, 6, **73**
Teche Delta, 12, **12**
Technical schools, 95
"Tee" Joe Gonzales Museum, **96**

Temperature, 14
Temple mounds, **16**
Tenant farming, 56–57, 74, 81, 86, **86**
Tensas Basin, 3, 5, **11**
Tensas Parish, 43, **43–44**, 45, **45**, **51–53**, 54, **54**, 55, **55–56**, 57, **57**, 58, **74–80**, 81, **81–92**, 93, **93**, **98–99**
Tensas River, **5**, 6, 19, 41, **72**
Tensas River Road Tour, **98**
Terraces, 3, **3**, 5, **9, 12**
Terrebonne Basin, **11**
Terrebonne Parish, 15, 18, 43, **43–44**, 45, **45, 51–57, 74**, 75, **75**, 76, **76–82**, 83, **83–90**, 91, **92–93, 98–99**
Terrebonne Parish Fair/Rodeo, **98**
Territory of Louisiana, 50
Territory of Orleans, 32, 35, **35**, 37, 41, **41**, 45, 50, **50**
Terrytown, **60**, 63
Tertiary period, 9, **9**
Texarkana, 26
Texas, **1**, 27, **27**, 29, 50–54, 67–68, 93, **93**
Texas and Pacific Railroad, 63, 66–67, **67**, 68, **69**
Texas campaign, 39
Thatcher Institute, **94**
Thibodaux, **2**, 4, **37**, 38, **39, 42–45**, 51–52, **60, 68–70, 85, 94**, 95, **95**, **96, 98**
Thibodaux College, **94**
Thibodaux Massacre of 1897, 78
Thomas, Philemon, 35
Thompson's Hill, Miss., 39
Tickfaw, **60**
Tickfaw River, 6, **73**
Tickfaw State Park, **8**
Tidelands, 10, **10**, 90
Timberlane, **60**
Tioga and Southeastern Railroad, **69**

Titusville, Pennsylvania, 11
Tobacco, 27, 29, 74, 77, 81
Toca, **70**
Toledo Bend Reservoir, 6, 99
Tomato Festival, **98**
Tomatoes, 77
Tonti, Henri de, 18–20, 26, **26**
Tornadoes, 13
Touacara Indians, 26
Tour, Pierre le Blond de la, 61
Tourism, 8, 60, 98, 99
Towns, 58–60. *See also* Cities
Township, 34, **34**
Township and range system, 33–34, **34**
Tractors, 81
Trade, 27, 29, 31, 37
Transportation, 27, 29, 37, 60–63, 65–68, **68**, 69, **69**, 70, **70**, 71, **71**, 72, **72**, 73, **73**, 87, **87**, 89, **89**, 91
Transylvania mound site, **16**
Treaty of Fontainebleau (1762), 25, 27–29
Treaty of Fort Jackson (1814), 36
Treaty of Ghent (1814), 36
Treaty of Paris (1763), 19, 22, 24–25, 28
Treaty of Paris (1783), 28, 30, 35
Treaty of San Ildefonso (1800), 31
Treaty of San Lorenzo (1796), 31
Treaty of Tordesillas (1495), 23, 25
Trees, 7
Tremont and Gulf Railroad, **69**
Trenton, **94**
Trenton Institute, **94**
Trinity, **39**
Triumph, **60**
Tropical storms, 13, **13**
Troy Parish, 44
Troyville Indian Culture, 16, **16**, 20
Trucking, 70, 73
Tulane, Paul, 95
Tulane University, **63**, 94–95, **95, 96**

Tullos, 58
Tunica Hills State Preservation Area, **8**
Tunica Indians, 17, **17**, 18–19, **19**, 22
Tunican Linguistic Group, 17, **17**, 19
Tupelo, 7
Turkey Creek, 34, **59**
Turpentine, 80

Ulloa, Antonio de, 29
Unemployment, 92, **92**
Union Male and Female Academy, **94**
Union Pacific Railroad, **63**, 66, **70**
Union Parish, 43, **43**, 44, **44**, 45, **45**, **51–57, 74**, 75, **75**, 76, **76–84**, 85, **85–93, 98–99**
United Methodist Church, 95
U.S. Congress, 46, **46**
U.S.F. & G. Golf Tournament, **98**
U.S. Forest Service, **8**
U.S. House of Representatives, 46, **46**
U.S. Railroad Administration, 73
U.S. Senate, 46
U.S. Travel Data Center, **98**
Universities, 94, **94**, 95, **95**
University of Louisiana, 94, **94**
University of New Orleans, **63**, 95, **95**
University of New Orleans (black), 94, **94**, 95
University of Southwestern Louisiana, 95, **95, 96**
Unzaga y Amezaga, Louis de, 29, 30
Urania, **58**
Urban population, 50–54, 58–60
Ursuline Convent, 64
Ursuline Sisters, 94

Valentine, **70**
Vegetables, 75, 77
Vegetation, 7
Venice, **2, 60**
Vermilion Bayou, 21

Vermilion Field, 10

Vermilion Parish, 43, **43–44**, 45, **45**, 51, **51–57, 74–75**, 76, **76**, 77, **77–78**, 79, **79–83**, 84, **84–93**, **98–99**

Vermilion River, 6, **73**

Vermilionville (Lafayette), **29, 37**, 39, **39, 43**, 68, **68**

Vermilionville Academy, **94**

Vernon, **37, 43, 44, 94**

Vernon Academy, **94**

Vernon Parish, 44, **44**, 45, **52–53**, 54, **54, 56–57, 74–79**, 80, **80–92**, 93, **93, 98–99**

Verrazano, John de, 25

Vial, Pedro, 24, **24**

Vicksburg, Miss., **38, 39**, 68. *See also* Walnut Hills

Vicksburg campaign, 39, **39**

Vicksburg group, **9**

Vicksburg, Shreveport and Pacific Railroad, 37, 68, **68–69**

Vicksburg, Shreveport and Texas Railroad, 68

Victoria, Fisher and Western Railroad, 69

Vidalia, 4, **37**, 39, **39, 42–45, 58**, 68, **69, 98**

Vidalia Chambre Festival, **98**

Vidalia and Western Railroad, 68, **68**

Vienna, **37, 58, 94**

Vienna Male and Female Academy, **94**

Vietnamese, 97

Vieux Carre, 61–64

Vieux Carre Commission, 64

Village St. George, **60**

Villages, 59

Ville Platte, **37**, 39, **45, 59, 98**

Viloxi County, 35

Vinton, **59**

Violet, **60**

Vivian, **58**

Vocational schools, 95

Voting Rights Act of 1975, 57

Waggaman, **60**

Walker, **60, 66, 98**

Walnut Hills, **29, 35–36**, 72

War of 1812, 36, **36**

Warren, **42**

Warren Parish, 42, **42**, 43

Warrenton, 72

Washa Indians, 17, **17, 21, 21**

Washington, George, 43

Washington (city), **37, 59**, 80

Washington Parish, 43, **43**, 44, **44**, 45, **45, 51–57, 74–75**, 76, **76–83**, 84, **84–93, 98–99**

Waterfowl refuges, **8**

Watermelon Festival, **98**

Waterproof, **58**

Waterways, 72–73

Watkins, J. B., 79

Watson, 66

Weather, 14

Webster, Daniel, 44

Webster Parish, 44, **44**, 45, **45**, **52–54, 56–57**, 67, **74–84**, 85, **85–93, 98–99**

Weeks, 70

Weeks Island, 4, **16**

Weitzel, Godfrey, 38

Welsh, 59

West Baton Rouge Academy, **94**

West Baton Rouge Parish, 42, **42–44**, 45, **45, 50–52**, 53, **53–57**, 65, **74–87**, 88, **88–93, 98–99**

West Baton Rouge Parish Museum, **96**

West Cameron Field, 10

West Carroll Parish, 16, 44, **44**, 45, **45**, 52, **52–53**, 54, **54, 56–57**, 58, **74–81**, 82, **82–91**, 92, **92**, 93, **93, 98–99**

West Feliciana Parish, 2, 43, **43–44**, 45, **45, 51–52**, 53, **53–55**, 56, **56**, 57, **57**, 60, **74–92**, 93, **93, 98–99**

West Feliciana Railroad, **37**, 68, **68**

West Ferriday, **58**

West Florida, **27, 29**, 30, **30**, 35, **35, 41, 50**, 65

West Florida Rebellion, 31, 35, **35**, 65

West Indies, 55

West Louisiana Folk Arts and Crafts Festival, **98**

West Pearl River, **73**

Westerfield, 70

Westlake, **59**

Westminster, **60**

Westwego, **60, 63**

Wetlands, **7**

Wheat, 82, **82**

Whig party, 37, 46

White, Edward Douglass, State Commemorative Area, **8**

White Castle, **60**

White Lake, 6

White Sulphur Springs, 37

Whitney, Eli, 81

Wholesale trade, 88, **88**

Wiggins Anticline, 5

Wilcox Group, **9**

Wildfowl Carvers and Collectors Festival, **98**

Wildlife, 75

Wildlife and Fur Festival, **98**

Wildlife management areas/ refuges, 8, **8**

Will Ransom Hogan Jazz Arch-ives, **96**

Williamson Museum, **96**

Williana Terraces, **9**

Willing, James, 30

Wilson's Landing, 40, **40**

Winn, Richard, 43

Winn Parish, 43, **43**, 44, **44**, 45, **45, 51–57, 74–79**, 80, **80–93, 98–99**

Winn Parish Fair, **98**

Winnfield, 4, **37, 43–45, 58**, 69–70, **98**

Winnsboro, 4, **37, 43–45, 58, 98**

Winter Quarters Museum, **8**

Winters, John D., 40

Wisner, **58**

Wolds, 3, 5

Women, **92, 96**

Wood Pump, 63

Woodville, Miss., 68

Woodworth, **59**

Woodworth and Louisiana Central Railroad, 69

Wool, 76

Wright, S. L., 79

Xavier University of Louisiana, 95, **95, 96**

Yambilee Festival, **98**

Yatasi Indians, 17, **17**, 20, **20**, 26

Yazoo Indians, 17, **17**, 19, 21

Yazoo and Mississippi Valley Railroad, 69

Yazoo River, **17**, 19, **19**, 72

Youngsville, 59

Zachary, **60, 66, 96**

Zee, 70

Zwolle, 58, **98**

Zwolle and Eastern Railroad, 69